SHORT STORIES
for Students

Advisors

Jayne M. Burton: Language Arts Teacher, Samuel V. Champion High School, Boerne, Texas. B.A. from Christopher Newport University. Member of National Council of Teachers of English and Sigma Tau Delta International English Honor Society; Chapter President of Delta Kappa Gamma International Society for Key Women Educators.

Kate Hamill: English Teacher, Catonsville High School, Catonsville, Maryland. B.A. from Pomona College; M.A. from University of Virginia; MSEd from University of Maryland.

Mary Beth Maggio: Language Arts Teacher, Schaumburg District No. 54, Schaumburg, Illinois. B.A. from Illinois State University; M.A. from Northern Illinois University.

Thomas Shilts: Youth Librarian, Capital Area District Library, Okemos, Michigan. M.S.L.S.

from Clarion University of Pennsylvania; M.A. from University of North Dakota.

Amy Spade Silverman: Taught at independent schools in California, Michigan, Texas, and New York. B.A. from University of Michigan; M.F.A. from University of Houston. Member of National Council of Teachers of English, Teachers and Writers, and NCTE Opinion Panel. Exam Reader, Advanced Placement Literature and Composition. Poet, published in *North American Review*, *Nimrod*, and *Michigan Quarterly Review*, among other publications.

Mary Turner: English and AP Literature and Composition Teacher. B.S. from East Texas University; MEd from Western Kentucky University.

Laura Jean Waters: Certified School Library Media Specialist, Wilton High School, Wilton, Connecticut. B.A. from Fordham University; M.A. from Fairfield University.

SHORT STORIES
for Students

Presenting Analysis, Context, and Criticism on
Commonly Studied Short Stories

VOLUME 33

Sara Constantakis, Project Editor

Foreword by Thomas E. Barden

GALE
CENGAGE Learning™

Detroit • New York • San Francisco • New Haven, Conn • Waterville, Maine • London

Short Stories for Students, Volume 33

Project Editor: Sara Constantakis

Rights Acquisition and Management:
Margaret Chamberlain-Gaston, Edna Shy

Composition: Evi Abou-El-Seoud

Manufacturing: Rhonda A. Dover

Imaging: John Watkins

Product Design: Pamela A. E. Galbreath,
Jennifer Wahi

Content Conversion: Katrina Coach

Product Manager: Meggin Condino

© 2011 Gale, Cengage Learning

For product information and technology assistance, contact us at
Gale Customer Support, 1-800-877-4253.
For permission to use material from this text or product,
submit all requests online at **www.cengage.com/permissions.**
Further permissions questions can be emailed to
permissionrequest@cengage.com

Gale
27500 Drake Rd.
Farmington Hills, MI, 48331-3535

ISBN-13: 978-1-4144-6697-2
ISBN-10: 1-4144-6697-8

ISSN 1092-7735

This title is also available as an e-book.
ISBN-13: 978-1-4144-7459-5
ISBN-10: 1-4144-7459-8
Contact your Gale, a part of Cengage Learning sales representative for ordering information.

Printed in Mexico
1 2 3 4 5 6 7 15 14 13 12 11

Table of Contents

Why Study Literature At All?

Short Stories for Students is designed to provide readers with information and discussion about a wide range of important contemporary and historical works of short fiction, and it does that job very well. However, I want to use this guest foreword to address a question that it does *not* take up. It is a fundamental question that is often ignored in high school and college English classes as well as research texts, and one that causes frustration among students at all levels, namely why study literature at all? Isn't it enough to read a story, enjoy it, and go about one's business? My answer (to be expected from a literary professional, I suppose) is no. It is not enough. It is a start; but it is not enough. Here's why.

First, literature is the only part of the educational curriculum that deals directly with the actual world of lived experience. The philosopher Edmund Husserl used the apt German term *die Lebenswelt*, "the living world," to denote this realm. All the other content areas of the modern American educational system avoid the subjective, present reality of everyday life. Science (both the natural and the social varieties) objectifies, the fine arts create and/or perform, history reconstructs. Only literary study persists in posing those questions we all asked before our schooling taught us to give up on them. Only literature gives credibility to personal perceptions, feelings, dreams, and the "stream of consciousness" that is our inner voice. Literature wonders about infinity, wonders why God permits evil, wonders

what will happen to us after we die. Literature admits that we get our hearts broken, that people sometimes cheat and get away with it, that the world is a strange and probably incomprehensible place. Literature, in other words, takes on all the big and small issues of what it means to be human. So my first answer is that of the humanist we should read literature and study it and take it seriously because it enriches us as human beings. We develop our moral imagination, our capacity to sympathize with other people, and our ability to understand our existence through the experience of fiction.

My second answer is more practical. By studying literature we can learn how to explore and analyze texts. Fiction may be about *die Lebenswelt*, but it is a construct of words put together in a certain order by an artist using the medium of language. By examining and studying those constructions, we can learn about language as a medium. We can become more sophisticated about word associations and connotations, about the manipulation of symbols, and about style and atmosphere. We can grasp how ambiguous language is and how important context and texture is to meaning. In our first encounter with a work of literature, of course, we are not supposed to catch all of these things. We are spellbound, just as the writer wanted us to be. It is as serious students of the writer's art that we begin to see how the tricks are done.

Seeing the tricks, which is another way of saying "developing analytical and close reading skills," is important above and beyond its intrinsic literary educational value. These skills transfer to other fields and enhance critical thinking of any kind. Understanding how language is used to construct texts is powerful knowledge. It makes engineers better problem solvers, lawyers better advocates and courtroom practitioners, politicians better rhetoricians, marketing and advertising agents better sellers, and citizens more aware consumers as well as better participants in democracy. This last point is especially important, because rhetorical skill works both ways when we learn how language is manipulated in the making of texts the result is that we become less susceptible when language is used to manipulate us.

My third reason is related to the second. When we begin to see literature as created artifacts of language, we become more sensitive to good writing in general. We get a stronger sense of the importance of individual words, even the sounds of words and word combinations. We begin to understand Mark Twain's delicious proverb "The difference between the right word and the almost right word is the difference between lightning and a lightning bug." Getting beyond the "enjoyment only" stage of literature gets us closer to becoming makers of word art ourselves. I am not saying that studying fiction will turn every student into a Faulkner or a Shakespeare. But it will make us more adaptable and effective writers, even if our art form ends up being the office memo or the corporate annual report.

Studying short stories, then, can help students become better readers, better writers, and even better human beings. But I want to close with a

warning. If your study and exploration of the craft, history, context, symbolism, or anything else about a story starts to rob it of the magic you felt when you first read it, it is time to stop. Take a break, study another subject, shoot some hoops, or go for a run. Love of reading is too important to be ruined by school. The early twentieth century writer Willa Cather, in her novel *My Antonia*, has her narrator Jack Burden tell a story that he and Antonia heard from two old Russian immigrants when they were teenagers. These immigrants, Pavel and Peter, told about an incident from their youth back in Russia that the narrator could recall in vivid detail thirty years later. It was a harrowing story of a wedding party starting home in sleds and being chased by starving wolves. Hundreds of wolves attacked the group's sleds one by one as they sped across the snow trying to reach their village. In a horrible revelation, the old Russians revealed that the groom eventually threw his own bride to the wolves to save himself. There was even a hint that one of the old immigrants might have been the groom mentioned in the story. Cather has her narrator conclude with his feelings about the story. "We did not tell Pavel's secret to anyone, but guarded it jealously as if the wolves of the Ukraine had gathered that night long ago, and the wedding party had been sacrificed, just to give us a painful and peculiar pleasure." That feeling, that painful and peculiar pleasure, is the most important thing about literature. Study and research should enhance that feeling and never be allowed to overwhelm it.

Thomas E. Barden
Professor of English and Director of
Graduate English Studies,
The University of Toledo

Introduction

Purpose of the Book

The purpose of *Short Stories for Students* (*SSfS*) is to provide readers with a guide to understanding, enjoying, and studying short stories by giving them easy access to information about the work. Part of Gale's "For Students" Literature line, *SSfS* is specifically designed to meet the curricular needs of high school and undergraduate college students and their teachers, as well as the interests of general readers and researchers considering specific short fiction. While each volume contains entries on "classic" stories frequently studied in classrooms, there are also entries containing hard-to-find information on contemporary stories, including works by multicultural, international, and women writers.

The information covered in each entry includes an introduction to the story and the story's author; a plot summary, to help readers unravel and understand the events in the work; descriptions of important characters, including explanation of a given character's role in the narrative as well as discussion about that character's relationship to other characters in the story; analysis of important themes in the story; and an explanation of important literary techniques and movements as they are demonstrated in the work.

In addition to this material, which helps the readers analyze the story itself, students are also provided with important information on the literary and historical background informing each work. This includes a historical context essay, a box comparing the time or place the story was written to modern Western culture, a critical overview essay, and excerpts from critical essays on the story or author. A unique feature of *SSfS* is a specially commissioned critical essay on each story, targeted toward the student reader.

To further help today's student in studying and enjoying each story, information on audiobooks and other media adaptations is provided (if available), as well as reading suggestions for works of fiction and nonfiction on similar themes and topics. Classroom aids include ideas for research papers and lists of critical and reference sources that provide additional material on the work.

Selection Criteria

The titles for each volume of *SSfS* were selected by surveying numerous sources on teaching literature and analyzing course curricula for various school districts. Some of the sources surveyed include: literature anthologies, *Reading Lists for College-Bound Students: The Books Most Recommended by America's Top Colleges*; *Teaching the Short Story: A Guide to Using Stories from around the World*, by the National Council of Teachers of English (NCTE); and "A Study of High School Literature Anthologies," conducted by Arthur Applebee at the Center for the Learning and Teaching of Literature and sponsored by the National Endowment for the Arts and the Office of Educational Research and Improvement.

Input was also solicited from our advisory board, as well as educators from various areas. From these discussions, it was determined that each volume should have a mix of "classic" stories (those works commonly taught in literature classes) and contemporary stories for which information is often hard to find. Because of the interest in expanding the canon of literature, an emphasis was also placed on including works by international, multicultural, and women authors. Our advisory board members—educational professionals—helped pare down the list for each volume. Works not selected for the present volume were noted as possibilities for future volumes. As always, the editor welcomes suggestions for titles to be included in future volumes.

How Each Entry Is Organized

Each entry, or chapter, in *SSfS* focuses on one story. Each entry heading lists the title of the story, the author's name, and the date of the story's publication. The following elements are contained in each entry:

Introduction: a brief overview of the story which provides information about its first appearance, its literary standing, any controversies surrounding the work, and major conflicts or themes within the work.

Author Biography: this section includes basic facts about the author's life, and focuses on events and times in the author's life that may have inspired the story in question.

Plot Summary: a description of the events in the story. Lengthy summaries are broken down with subheads.

Characters: an alphabetical listing of the characters who appear in the story. Each character name is followed by a brief to an extensive description of the character's role in the story, as well as discussion of the character's actions, relationships, and possible motivation.

Characters are listed alphabetically by last name. If a character is unnamed—for instance, the narrator in "The Eatonville Anthology"—the character is listed as "The Narrator" and alphabetized as "Narrator." If a character's first name is the only one given, the name will appear alphabetically by that name.

Themes: a thorough overview of how the topics, themes, and issues are addressed within the story. Each theme discussed appears in a separate subhead.

Style: this section addresses important style elements of the story, such as setting, point of view, and narration; important literary devices used, such as imagery, foreshadowing, symbolism; and, if applicable, genres to which the work might have belonged, such as Gothicism or Romanticism. Literary terms are explained within the entry, but can also be found in the Glossary.

Historical Context: this section outlines the social, political, and cultural climate in which the author lived and the work was created. This section may include descriptions of related historical events, pertinent aspects of daily life in the culture, and the artistic and literary sensibilities of the time in which the work was written. If the story is historical in nature, information regarding the time in which the story is set is also included. Long sections are broken down with helpful subheads.

Critical Overview: this section provides background on the critical reputation of the author and the story, including bannings or any other public controversies surrounding the work. For older works, this section may include a history of how the story was first received and how perceptions of it may have changed over the years; for more recent works, direct quotes from early reviews may also be included.

Criticism: an essay commissioned by *SSfS* which specifically deals with the story and is written specifically for the student audience, as well as excerpts from previously published criticism on the work (if available).

Sources: an alphabetical list of critical material used in compiling the entry, with bibliographical information.

Further Reading: an alphabetical list of other critical sources which may prove useful for the student. Includes full bibliographical information and a brief annotation.

Suggested Search Terms: a list of search terms and phrases to jumpstart students' further information seeking. Terms include not just titles and author names but also terms and topics related to the historical and literary context of the works.

In addition, each entry contains the following highlighted sections, set apart from the main text as sidebars:

Media Adaptations: if available, a list of audiobooks and important film and television adaptations of the story, including source information. The list also includes stage adaptations, musical adaptations, etc.

Topics for Further Study: a list of potential study questions or research topics dealing with the story. This section includes questions related to other disciplines the student may be studying, such as American history, world history, science, math, government, business, geography, economics, psychology, etc.

Compare and Contrast: an "at-a-glance" comparison of the cultural and historical differences between the author's time and culture and late twentieth century or early twenty-first century Western culture. This box includes pertinent parallels between the major scientific, political, and cultural movements of the time or place the story was written, the time or place the story was set (if a historical work), and modern Western culture. Works written after 1990 may not have this box.

What Do I Read Next?: a list of works that might give a reader points of entry into a classic work (e.g., YA or multicultural titles) and/or complement the featured story or serve as a contrast to it. This includes works by the same author and others, works from various genres, YA works, and works from various cultures and eras.

Other Features

SSfS includes "Why Study Literature At All?," a foreword by Thomas E. Barden, Professor of English and Director of Graduate English Studies at the University of Toledo. This essay provides a number of very fundamental reasons for studying literature and, therefore, reasons why a book such as *SSfS*, designed to facilitate the study of litererture, is useful.

A Cumulative Author/Title Index lists the authors and titles covered in each volume of the *SSfS* series.

A Cumulative Nationality/Ethnicity Index breaks down the authors and titles covered in each volume of the *SSfS* series by nationality and ethnicity.

A Subject/Theme Index, specific to each volume, provides easy reference for users who may be studying a particular subject or theme rather than a single work. Significant subjects from events to broad themes are included.

Each entry may include illustrations, including photo of the author, stills from film adaptations (if available), maps, and/or photos of key historical events.

Citing Short Stories for Students

When writing papers, students who quote directly from any volume of *SSfS* may use the following general forms to document their source. These examples are based on MLA style; teachers may request that students adhere to a different style, thus, the following examples may be adapted as needed.

When citing text from *SSfS* that is not attributed to a particular author (for example, the Themes, Style, Historical Context sections, etc.), the following format may be used:

> "The Celebrated Jumping Frog of Calavaras County." *Short Stories for Students*. Ed. Kathleen Wilson. Vol. 1. Detroit: Gale, 1997. 19–20.

When quoting the specially commissioned essay from *SSfS* (usually the first essay under the Criticism subhead), the following format may be used:

> Korb, Rena. Critical Essay on "Children of the Sea." *Short Stories for Students*. Ed. Kathleen Wilson. Vol. 1. Detroit: Gale, 1997. 39–42.

When quoting a journal or newspaper essay that is reprinted in a volume of *SSfS*, the following form may be used:

> Schmidt, Paul. "The Deadpan on Simon Wheeler." *Southwest Review* 41.3 (Summer, 1956): 270–77. Excerpted and reprinted in *Short Stories for Students*. Vol. 1. Ed. Kathleen Wilson. Detroit: Gale, 1997. 29–31.

When quoting material from a book that is reprinted in a volume of *SSfS*, the following form may be used:

> Bell-Villada, Gene H. "The Master of Short Forms." *García Márquez: The Man and His Work*. University of North Carolina Press, 1990. 119–36. Excerpted and reprinted in *Short Stories for Students*. Vol. 1. Ed. Kathleen Wilson. Detroit: Gale, 1997. 89–90.

We Welcome Your Suggestions

The editorial staff of *Short Stories for Students* welcomes your comments and ideas. Readers who wish to suggest short stories to appear in future volumes, or who have other suggestions, are cordially invited to contact the editor. You may contact the editor via E-mail at: **ForStudents Editors@cengage.com**. Or write to the editor at:

> Editor, *Short Stories for Students*
> Gale
> 27500 Drake Road
> Farmington Hills, MI 48331-3535

Literary Chronology

1825: Mark Twain is born Samuel Clemens on November 30 in Florida, Missouri.

1860: Anton Chekhov is born on January 17 in Taganrog, Russia.

1867: Luigi Pirandello is born on June 28 in Girgenti, Sicily, Italy.

1883: Franz Kafka is born on July 3 in Prague, the capital of the Austro-Hungarian Empire.

1889: Anton Chekhov's "The Bet" is published in *Novoe Vremja* (New Times).

1891: Pär Lagerkvist is born on May 23 in Växjö, Sweden.

1892: Pearl S. Buck is born on June 26 in Hillsboro, West Virginia.

1893: Mark Twain's "The Californian's Tale" is published in *The First Book of the Author's Club: Liber Scriptorum*.

1904: Anton Chekhov dies of tuberculosis in Badenweiler, Germany.

1911: Naguib Mahfouz is born on December 11 in Cairo, Egypt.

1918: Luigi Pirandello's "War" is published. It is published in English in England in 1938 in *A Character in Distress*. It is published in English in the United States in 1939 in *The Medals and Other Stories*.

1919: Franza Kafka's "A Country Doctor" is published in German as "Ein Landarzt." It is published in English in 1945 in *The Country Doctor: A Collection of Fourteen Stories*.

1919: Mark Twain dies of a heart attack on April 21 in Redding, Connecticut.

1920: Isaac Asimov is born on January 2 in Belarus, U.S.S.R.

1924: Franz Kafka dies of tuberculosis of the larynx on June 3 in Klosterneuburg, Austria.

1924: Joan Aiken is born on September 4 in Rye, East Sussex, England.

1924: Pär Lagerkvist's "Father and I" is published in Swedish as "Far och jag." It is published in English in 1954 in *The Marriage Feast*.

1928: William Trevor is born on May 23 in Michelstown, County Cork, Ireland.

1932: Pearl S. Buck receives the Pulitzer Prize for Fiction for *The Good Earth*.

1934: Luigi Pirandello is awarded the Nobel Prize for Literature for his work in drama.

1936: Luigi Pirandello dies on December 10 in Italy.

1937: Bessie Head is born on July 6 in Pietermaritzburg, South Africa.

1937: Patricia Grace is born on August 17 in Wellington, New Zealand.

1938: Pearl S. Buck is awarded the Nobel Prize for Literature.

1949: Mary Robison is born on January 14 in Washington, DC.

1951: Pär Lagerkvist is awarded the Nobel Prize for Literature.

1952: Gary Soto is born on April 12 in Fresno, California.

1953: Pearl S. Buck's "The Good Deed" is published in the *Woman's Home Companion* as "A Husband For Lili."

1961: Isaac Asimov's "The Machine that Won the War" is published in the *Magazine of Fantasy & Science Fiction.*

1973: Pearl S. Buck dies of lung cancer on March 6 in Danby, Vermont.

1974: Pär Lagerkvist dies on July 11 in Stockholm, Sweden.

1975: Patricia Grace's "A Way of Talking" is published in *Waiariki.*

1975: William Trevor's "The Distant Past" is published in *Angels at the Ritz.*

1976: Joan Aiken's "Sonata for Harp and Bicycle" is published.

1980: Bessie Head's "The Lovers" is published in the magazine *Wietie.*

1982: Mary Robison's "Yours" is published in *New Yorker* magazine.

1984: Naguib Mahfouz's "The Norwegian Rat" is published in Arabic. It is published in English in 1991 in *The Time and the Place and Other Stories.*

1986: Bessie Head dies of liver failure on April 17 in Serowe, Botswana.

1988: Naguib Mahfouz is awarded the Nobel Prize for Literature.

1990: Gary Soto's "Broken Chain" is published in *Baseball in April and Other Stories.*

1992: Isaac Asimov dies of AIDS, which he acquired from a blood transfusion, on April 6 in New York, New York.

2004: Joan Aiken dies of natural causes on January 4 in Petworth, West Sussex, England.

2006: Naguib Mahfouz dies after a fall on August 30 in Cairo, Egypt.

Acknowledgements

The editors wish to thank the copyright holders of the excerpted criticism included in this volume and the permissions managers of many book and magazine publishing companies for assisting us in securing reproduction rights. We are also grateful to the staffs of the Detroit Public Library, the Library of Congress, the University of Detroit Mercy Library, Wayne State University Purdy/Kresge Library Complex, and the University of Michigan Libraries for making their resources available to us. Following is a list of the copyright holders who have granted us permission to reproduce material in this volume of *SSfS*. Every effort has been made to trace copyright, but if omissions have been made, please let us know.

COPYRIGHTED EXCERPTS IN *SSfS*, VOLUME 33, WERE REPRODUCED FROM THE FOLLOWING PERIODICALS:

Booklist, v. 99, no. 6, November 15, 2002. Copyright © 2002 by the American Library Association. Reproduced by permission.—*Canadian Slavonic Papers*, v. 35, nos. 3–4, September-December 1993. Copyright © *Canadian Slavonic Papers*, Canada, 1993. Reproduced by permission of the publisher.—*Commonweal*, v. 76, no. 7, May 11, 1962. Copyright © 1962 Commonweal Publishing Co., Inc. Reproduced by permission of Commonweal Foundation.—*Explicator*, vol. 58, no. 2, Winter 2000; vol. 62, no. 1, Fall 2003. Copyright © 2000, 2003 by Helen Dwight Reid Educational Foundation. Reproduced by Heldref Publications, 1319 18th Street, NW, Washington, DC 20036-1802.—*Georgia Review*, v. 49, no. 1, Spring 1995. Copyright © 1995 by the University of Georgia. Reproduced by permission.—*Germanic Review*, vol. 69, no. 1, Winter 1994; vol. 75, no. 2, Spring 2000. Reproduced by permission.—*Hecate*, v. 34, no. 1, May 2008. Copyright © 2008 by *Hecate*. Both reproduced by permission.—*International Fiction Review*, v. 1, no. 1, January 1974. Copyright © 1974 International Fiction Association. Reproduced by permission.—*International Fiction Review*, v. 8, no. 2, Summer 1981. Copyright © 1981 International Fiction Association. Reproduced by permission.—*International Fiction Review*, v. 31, nos. 1–2, January 2004. Copyright © 2004 International Fiction Association. Reproduced by permission.—*Kirkus Reviews*, v. 70, no. 8, September 15, 2002. Copyright © 2002 Kirkus Media. All rights reserved. Reproduced by permission—*London Review of Books*, v. 12, no. 8, September 27, 1990. Copyright © LRB (London) Ltd. 1990. All rights reserved. Appears here by permission of the *London Review of Books*.—*London Times*, August 1, 1998. Copyright © 1998 Times Newspapers Ltd. Reproduced by permission.—*Los Angeles Times Book Review*, June 19, 1988. Reproduced by permission.—*New Republic*, January 23, 1935; v. 141, September 28, 1959; March 24, 1973. Copyright © 1935, 1959, 1973 by The New Republic, Inc. All reproduced by permission of *The New Republic*.—*Publishers Weekly*, v. 249, no. 43, October 28, 2002. Copyright © 2002 by Reed Publishing

USA. Reproduced from *Publishers Weekly*, published by the Bowker Magazine Group of Cahners Publishing Co., a division of Reed Publishing USA, by permission.—*Research in African Literatures*, v. 36, no. 1, Spring 2005. Copyright © 2005 Indiana University Press. Reproduced by permission.—*Revista Chicano-Riquena*, v. 11, no. 2, Summer 1983. Copyright © 1983 Arte Público Press—University of Houston. Reproduced by permission.—*Science Fiction Studies*, v. 15, no. 44, March 1998. Copyright © 1998 by SFS Publications. Reproduced by permission.—*Shenandoah*, v. 51, no. 4, Winter 2001, for "A Voice of Restraint: The Short Fiction of William Trevor," by Ben Howard. Copyright © 2001 by *Shenandoah*. Reproduced by permission of the publisher and the author.—*Studies in Short Fiction*, v. 2, no. 1, Fall 1964; v. 10, no. 3, Summer 1973; v. 15, no. 2, Spring 1978. Copyright 1964 by *Studies in Short Fiction*. Reproduced by permission.—*Style*, v. 39, no. 3, Fall 2005 for "The Poetics of Interruption in Mark Twain's Roughing It," by Jennifer McKellar. Copyright © *Style*, 2005. All rights reserved. Reproduced by permission of the publisher and the author.—*The Washington Post*, December 23, 2001. Copyright © 2001 *The Washington Post*. All rights reserved. Used by permission and protected by the Copyright Laws of the United States. The printing, copying, redistribution, or retransmission of the Material without express written permission is prohibited.—*Times Literary Supplement*, December 1, 1990. Copyright © 1990 by The Times Supplements Limited. Reproduced from *The Times Literary Supplement* by permission.—*World Literature Today*, v. 62, no. 2, Spring 1988. v. 76, nos. 3–4, Summer 2002. Copyright © 1988, 2002 by *World Literature Today*. Reproduced by permission of the publisher.

COPYRIGHTED EXCERPTS IN *SSfS*, VOLUME 33, WERE REPRODUCED FROM THE FOLLOWING BOOKS:

Ahmad Muhammad Atiyya. From *Critical Perspectives on Naguib Mahfouz, Trevor Le Gassick*. Three Continents Press, 1991. Copyright © 1991 by Lynne Rienner Publishers, Inc. All rights reserved Reproduced by permission.—Robert Lynd. From *Old and New Masters*, 1919.

Contributors

Susan K. Andersen: Andersen is a writer with a Ph.D. in literature. Entry on "Sonata for Harp and Bicycle." Original essay on "Sonata for Harp and Bicycle."

Bryan Aubrey: Aubrey holds a Ph.D. in English. Entries on "The Distant Past" and "War." Original essays on "The Distant Past" and "War."

Cynthia Gower Betts: Betts is a playwright, novelist, and freelance writer. Entry on "The Bet." Original essay on "The Bet."

Rita Brown: Brown is an English professor. Entry on "The Machine That Won the War." Original essay on "The Machine That Won the War."

Catherine Dominic: Dominic is a novelist and a freelance writer and editor. Entries on "A Country Doctor," "A Way of Talking," and "Father and I." Original essays on "A Country Doctor," "A Way of Talking," and "Father and I."

Joyce Hart: Hart is a published writer and teacher of creative writing. Entry on "The Lovers." Original essay on "The Lovers."

Michael J. O'Neal: O'Neal holds a Ph.D. in English. Entry on "Broken Chain." Original essay on "Broken Chain."

April Dawn Paris: Paris is a freelance writer with a bachelor's degree in classics and a minor in English. Entry on "The Norwegian Rat." Original essay on "The Norwegian Rat."

Rachel Porter: Porter is a freelance writer and editor who holds a bachelor of arts degree in English literature. Entry on "The Good Deed." Original essay on "The Good Deed."

Bradley A. Skeen: Skeen is a classics professor. Entry on "The Californian's Tale." Original essay on "The Californian's Tale."

Rebecca Valentine: Valentine is a writer with an extensive background in literary theory and analysis. Entry on "Yours." Original essay on "Yours."

The Bet

ANTON CHEKHOV
1889

"The Bet" is a short story written by the prolific Russian writer Anton Pavlovich Chekhov. He wrote it in just seven days in December of 1888 and promised it to his friend and patron, Aleksei Suvori, a newspaper publisher who printed it for the New Year issue (1889) of *Novoe Vremja* (*New Times*). The story was originally titled "Skazka, A Tale." *Skazka* is the Russian word for folk tale or fairy tale. It is "one literary expression of ideological thinking and *'The Bet'* as *skazka* is the best illustration of [Chekhov's] differing artistic idea," says Leslie O'Bell in "Cexov's Skazka: The Intellectual's Fairy Tale." In the late 1890s Chekhov included "The Bet" in a ten-volume collection, *Collected Works*, published by Marx Publishing. Chekhov did not receive worldwide acclaim during his lifetime, and only later, when his short stories were translated into English by Constance Garnett in the thirteen-volume *The Tales of Chekhov*, did he gain widespread scrutiny and tremendous critical acclaim. It was published in New York in 1921 by Macmillan.

"The Bet" is the story of a wager arranged between a banker and a lawyer who are attending a dinner party. It arises from a conversation arguing the merits of capital punishment versus a sentence of life in prison. The men have opposing views on the subject, and a high-stakes wager is set into motion.

In true Chekhovian style, there is no moralistic narrator, no true hero, and no true winner

Anton Chekhov *(The Library of Congress)*

of the bet. He leaves those matters for the reader to sort out, and a solution that is satisfactory or generally agreed upon is not easily reached. On initial observation, this may be unsatisfying, but in the true form of the modern short story, it becomes more and more compelling as the actions and intentions of the men are studied. No pat answers spring forth, and interpretations of the irony in the plot and the powerlessness of the characters require deep introspection. The question of capital punishment is not addressed and becomes secondary to the psychological torture endured by both men. "The Bet" is intriguing and highly compelling not by what is written, but by what is intentionally omitted.

AUTHOR BIOGRAPHY

Chekhov was born on January 17, 1860, in a small southern Russian provincial town called Taganrog. His grandfather had been a serf who purchased his own freedom. His parents were poor; his father kept a small shop in town while his mother tended to six children. He was the third of the six, and he and his two older brothers were abused frequently by his tyrannical father,

Pavel, a religious zealot as well as an alcoholic. Chekhov preferred to think of himself as having no childhood rather than dwelling on the beatings, verbal abuse, and constant religious badgering. It did, however, affect his psyche and view of life, which became evident in the fatalistic themes of his stories and plays. His mother, Yevgeniya was an excellent storyteller, which shaped the ambitions of several of the children, who later became writers.

When Chekhov was sixteen, his father's business failed, and most of the family fled to Moscow to avoid debtor's prison. Anton was left behind to continue his studies and was able to get a room in his own house by tutoring the new owner's son. He was able to join his family two years later in Moscow in their two-room basement apartment. While continuing to study medicine, he wrote frivolous stories and anecdotes in low-brow newspapers called "comedies." His father was no longer able to support the family, and Chekhov bore that burden for the rest of his life. He wrote prolifically, therefore, to provide for the immediate needs of the family even after he gained his medical degree in 1884. Few of his early writings revealed the true genius that would emerge later in his life. Laura Merlin writes in the introduction to *Peasants and Other Stories*, "He often joked that medicine was his lawful wife, and literature his mistress." At that time, his writing was the sole means of support for his family, because he usually did not charge for his services as a physician.

He achieved renown from his newspaper offerings and became a prominent writer. Dimitri Grigorovich saw the potential in his craft and wrote to him, imploring him to try his hand at more serious endeavors. The correspondence moved Chekhov deeply and convinced him that he truly had a gift that he must continue to perfect. Grigorovich introduced him to Aleksei Suvorin, editor of a reputable newspaper, *Novoe Vremya* (*New Times*). Now he could write longer, more serious works that helped him develop his skills as an author. 1886 and 1887 were very prolific years for Chekhov, and he began refining his short, humorous stories into more thoughtful and complex themes while maintaining the austerity in his style. He began to introduce themes of starvation, the plight of the peasants, the tyranny of the government, and the fatality of life. He created life within the minds of his characters through the inclusion of specific details and produced a realism of existence without commentary or preaching.

Just months after obtaining his medical degree, Chekhov contracted tuberculosis from a patient, and he experienced its effects for years. Although the disease would eventually kill him, he spent most of the rest of his life denying that there was anything wrong with him. Taking a short vacation to his hometown in the Ukraine, he was refreshed by boyhood memories. It became the inspiration for "The Steppe" about a Russian boy roaming the vast plains of southern Russia. "The Steppe" was the first of Chekhov's stories to be published by the prestigious journal *Severny vestnik (Northern Journal)* in March 1988. It heralded Chekhov's addition to the ranks of Russia's most renowned writers and marked the emergence of his artistic maturity. Later that year he won the Pushkin Prize for a collection of short stories, *V Sumerkakh (Twilight)*, published the year before.

While his reputation now ranked him on the level of the great Russian novelists Fyodor Dostoyevsky and Leo Tolstoy, Chekhov had little interest in writing novels. He felt it his duty to expose his characters and shine light on them with brief, poignant descriptions and telling behavior without delving into their psyche. He may have taken this stance towards writing as a result of having to make short, succinct entries in weekly publications for so many years, but more likely it fit the philosophy he embraced through the hardships of his life; basically that there are no answers for life, and everyone must work it out for themselves.

Although Tolstoy, the author of *War and Peace* and *Anna Karenina*, had a great impact on Chekhov as a writer, he disliked the religious overtones of these works. He presented his art through the eyes of an agnostic (someone who believes that God is unknown and unknowable) with no commentary on the morality of his characters and their actions. He read widely in French and German and became enthralled with the writings of French short-story master Guy de Maupassant ("The Necklace"), whose stories are not particularly complex, but are filled with the irony of life, and end without a necessarily happy conclusion. Having a *denouement*, or final outcome or resolution of the plot, had been expected, almost necessary to all literature since the classical period. By writing stories without that resolution in the manner of Maupassant, Chekhov distinguished himself from his contemporaries and

influenced many to come, earning him the title "father of the modern short story." He spent his last ten years in the Yalta provinces trying to recover from his now two-decade-long illness. He died of tuberculosis in a spa in Badenweiler, Germany, in 1904, the same year that his first successful play, *The Cherry Blossom*, was produced in Moscow.

PLOT SUMMARY

Part I

The tale told in "The Bet" begins on a dark night in autumn. An old banker is pacing the floor remembering the events of a dinner party he had given fifteen years before on a night much like this one. The party was attended by intelligent acquaintances, and there was a great deal of stimulating conversation. One of the topics discussed was capital punishment, and the majority of the men, especially journalists, agreed in their disapproval of the death penalty. They concurred that it is immoral and barbaric, not suitable as punishment by a government of Christian people.

The banker spoke up to disagree, purporting that although he has experienced neither, he had to insist that the death penalty is far more humane than life imprisonment. In his way of thinking, capital punishment kills swiftly, while life in prison is a slow torture, killing a man continuously over the span of a lifetime. One guest added that he felt both sentences are wholly immoral: he felt that the government should not be allowed to take life from any man in any fashion.

The second protagonist of the story spoke only when he was called upon. He was a twenty-five-year-old lawyer at the time of the party, and he agreed that the two punishments are equally immoral. However, he approached the concept in a more personal fashion, claiming that if he were to choose for himself, he would adamantly choose life imprisonment. He felt he would rather live life any way possible than lose it. A lively discussion began, and the members of the party argued passionately. The banker was fifteen years younger, more impetuous, and got carried away. He struck the table with his fists and shouted at the young lawyer. He challenged the young man by wagering two million rubles that the lawyer could not stay in solitary confinement for five years. The lawyer replied quickly that he would take the bet,

MEDIA ADAPTATIONS

- Barnes & Noble produced a collection of audio CDs titled *The Stories of Anton Chekhov,* by Max Bollinger and Constance Garnetee. It was released by Sovereign in 1999.

- An unabridged version of "The Bet," narrated by William Coon, is available as an MP3 download at Amazon.com. It was released in 2007 by The Greatest Tales.

---

and he incredibly added ten more years to the imprisonment.

The banker jumped at the opportunity and repeated the challenge. The young man repeated his intentions, and the senseless bet was sealed. The banker was ecstatic, as he had many millions to do with as he wished. As the evening continued, he began to laugh and poke fun at the lawyer. He even offered the lawyer an opportunity to change his mind and to think more carefully about what was at stake. The banker taunted him, saying he would surely lose at least three or four years of his youth before he gives up. The banker ended by saying that he felt sorry for his challenger.

The narrative then returns to the present day as the banker, still pacing, obviously disturbed, remembers what happened that autumn night. An older and wiser man now, he asks himself what could have been the point of the bet. He now realizes the frivolity of the whole matter. What is accomplished by a man losing fifteen years of his life and by another throwing away so much money? It certainly does nothing to resolve the issue of capital punishment or life imprisonment, he muses. He confesses that he had been foolish and spoiled and believes that the young lawyer had been senseless and greedy.

The banker remembers the decisions that were made that night. The prisoner was to spend his internment under strict guard in one of the lodges on the banker's property. He was not to leave the lodge or have any human contact for fifteen years. He was not able to even hear a human voice. There was a small window provided for the delivery of food, and he could request wine and tobacco, as well as books, musical instruments, or other diversions. However, if any attempt to leave his confinement was detected, he must forfeit the money.

The first year, the prisoner was lonely and depressed. He played at the piano all day, wrote a bit, but refused wine and did not smoke. He read a little but only light sensational novels and love stories. The second year, he only read the classics. By the fifth year, he began to take wine and was seen lying around on his bed, eating and drinking, and talking to himself in an angry tone. He did not read, tried to write, and spent a good deal of time crying. During the sixth year, he began studying earnestly any volume that could be brought to him. Absorbing himself in philosophy, languages, and history over the course of the next four years, he consumed over six hundred volumes. It was during this time that he wrote a letter to the banker, making an unusual request translated into six of the languages he had studied. He asked that a shot be fired in the garden if his letter was found to be without error in each language so that he would be reassured that his efforts to learn had not been in vain. His request was granted. During the tenth year, he spent almost all of his time reading the gospels of the New Testament, theology, and religious history. For the last two years, the lawyer is not consoled by any of his books, yet he still pores over them looking for answers, only to throw one down and reach for another volume that might soothe his soul.

Part II

The pacing banker is now cursing. The cause of his concerns is now revealed. Over the past fifteen years he has squandered away his millions gambling on the stock exchange and making other ridiculous bets. His darker side emerges. "Why didn't the man die!" he exclaims. It will take all that he has left to pay the lawyer, and he will be left in ruin and disgrace. When the clock strikes three, he opens the door to a safe and retrieves the key that had been left undisturbed for fifteen years. He puts on his overcoat and goes out of the house into the rain. He calls out to the watchman and receives no answer. The banker thinks the guard must surely be inside out of the rain. Further, the banker realizes that suspicion would fall on the watchman, "if I had the pluck to carry out my intention."

Making sure that he is not seen, the banker makes his way to the lodge and opens the door. The locks to the door are closed securely, and he must look through the window to see his prey. The lawyer, sitting at his table, can only be seen from behind: his back, his hands, and the hair on his head are all that is visible. He is motionless, even after the banker taps at the window. The turn of the key in the lock, and the rusty creak of the door create no response. After eight minutes of silence, the banker enters.

The man sitting at the table no longer has the appearance of an ordinary man. His body is like that of a skeleton. Taut yellow skin stretches over hollow cheeks; long curly hair hangs from his head and chin, and his hand is dreadfully thin. On the table there is a sheet of paper on which something is written. At length, the banker realizes the lawyer is asleep. With the lawyer in such poor health, the banker thinks he need only smother him gently with the pillow and the problem will be solved. First, however, the banker decides to see what is written on the page. It is a letter addressed to him. The lawyer has written to the banker that tomorrow he will be free and the terms of the agreement met. Before he leaves, he must reveal what the years in solitude have taught him. He has studied all that men have to offer concerning the good things about the world. He concludes that he despises all that is considered blessed: wisdom, good health, and freedom. Death is the thing common to all men, and he marvels at how the people of the earth try to gain the "worthless, fleeting, illusory" achievements of this life, only to have them obliterated by death.

To prove his disdain for the ways of man and for the money he had once coveted, he announces that he will leave the lodge five hours early and thereby forfeit the bet. When the banker reads this, he kisses the lawyer on the head and runs back to his bedchamber. His tears and relief keep him awake the rest of the night. In the morning the watchmen run to the chamber in disbelief and tell him of the lawyer's early departure. The banker goes to the lodge to confirm their claims and discreetly takes the letter and locks it in his safe.

CHARACTERS

The Banker

The young banker is a prominent man in his community. He likes to give dinner parties to entertain men of intellect and to join in lively controversial conversations. Rather than letting others comment, he is impulsive and gives his opinion first. He is very excitable and ready to take on a verbal challenge, especially if he can fashion the disagreement into a bet. He hastily poses an unthinkable bet, but one he feels he is sure to win. Chekhov describes the banker as "spoilt and frivolous," and he does not pause to think before agreeing to make the bet even more risky. His boisterous and confrontational personality compel him to stand and bang his fist on the table to seal the bet. Later, he begins to ridicule his competitor, although he does offer one last chance to back out. Taunting the lawyer, he assures him there is no way he can win.

As an older man, the banker seems to have more discipline and a more contemplative view of the events of the evening fifteen years prior. He realizes that he had acted out of pride and impulsiveness and that the bet will in no way contribute to resolving the controversial topic of capital punishment. It has taken him fifteen years, during which he squandered the rest of his money on the stock exchange and other frivolous bets, to come to this realization. Only the loss of his millions causes him now to stop and consider the plight of the young lawyer and the bet. The lawyer remained true to his part of the bargain, and now the banker faces total ruin, as it appears the next day he will have to give away his last two million rubles and become penniless. Leslie O'Neil, in "Cexov's Skazka: An Intellectual's Fairy Tale," calls him "the standard-bearer of capitalism." His decision to murder the lawyer reveals that he has not changed and is still willing to take great risks to maintain his way of life. He wants to win the bet, even if he has to cheat.

The Lawyer

The young lawyer is initially represented as a more soft-spoken man among the guests who is not insistent that his opinions be spoken first. Speaking from a more human point of view, he suggests that any kind of life is better that no life at all, but he also is proud and vain in his beliefs as someone who knows little of life and who certainly knows nothing about imprisonment. His disdain for the banker and his soaring pride toward achieving self-perfection paint him in no better light than the banker. He is so idealistic and naive that he ludicrously changes the terms of the bet to make it more perilous for himself, sure that he can withstand the torture put before him in order to prove his beliefs. Over the course of his

TOPICS FOR FURTHER STUDY

- Make a video production of the story. You may use a narrator voice-over or simply change the narration into dialogue. Choose your actors, sound crew, lighting, and set design teams. Make sure the actors memorize their lines and are easily understood. Direct your team of students to make an interesting and thought-provoking work. After viewing the production, lead a class discussion on the merits of the production.

- Write two endings to the story that include what each character might do after twelve o'clock when the bet is over. Make one of the endings what you consider a pleasant resolution to the story. Make the other ending what you consider to be an unpleasant result. You may use a narrator and add bits of dialogue, or you can make it like a movie or play where your writing is all dialogue. Try to include an ironic twist that would fit Chekhov's style of writing.

- Write an essay to answer the question "Who won the bet?" Choose from one of the three options that follow: (1) a version that explains why the banker won the bet; (2) a version from the point of view of the lawyer, explain-

ing what life lessons he may have learned that would be more valuable than money; or (3) a version that explains why neither character won the bet, how the circumstances and the actions of each proved them less than worthy to find happiness.

- Read the young-adult collection *The Surrender Tree: A Collection of Poems about Cuba's Struggle for Freedom* by Margarita Engle. Prepare a dramatic interpretation of one of the poems about freedom, which the lawyer in the "The Bet" so foolishly gave away. Use your acting ability to convince the audience that you truly endure the hardships depicted in the poem you choose.

- Use your video-editing skills to produce a montage of clips and icons that represent greed and materialism. Make the transitions smooth, adding music or voice-over for mood. Work very thoughtfully to produce as professional and artistic a product as you can. It should be at least two minutes in length. Post it to your Web page and invite comments from your classmates on your interpretation.

---

years in confinement, he becomes much more in touch with reality. It is through him that Chekhov illustrates the theme that appears consistently in his work: realism.

Although the young man starts his internment satisfied, playing the piano and reading love stories and resting, as each year goes by, the loss of his independence and contact with human beings turn him into a tortured, emaciated, cynical man, who can no longer find anything of happiness in life or freedom. The lawyer's intentions to give up are not a gesture of acquiescence or spiritual enlightenment concerning the vanity of material things. He is a man in total despair, who cannot find truth or contentment in the beliefs of attaining the personal superiority that

he once held dear. The resolve the young lawyer had in his convictions, which prompted him to arrogantly add ten years to his imprisonment, is now gone. He is a man stripped bare, a mere skeleton, and shell of the man he was before.

THEMES

Greed

Greed is initially one of the driving forces for the lawyer in the story and ironically the impetus for the banker's actions at the end of the story. The young lawyer is willing to throw away the valuable years of his youth for a large sum of

The bet was fifteen years of solitary confinement versus $2 million. (*Brian Goodman | Shutterstock.com*)

money. Later, the impoverished banker is willing to kill the lawyer to keep from having to pay the debt. The lawyer, who spends the time of his imprisonment in self-reflection, the study of philosophy, and the search for happiness, realizes that money is not a source of happiness and that he was foolish to be greedy for money. The banker, however, has solidified his dependence on money even as he loses it, driving him to consider murder.

Imprisonment

The lawyer is tortured by fifteen years of isolation and loneliness because he foolishly gives away his freedom for money. At the start of the bet, he seems totally unaware of how precious and rare a gift freedom is, but after years of imprisonment, he understands how naive he had been in misjudging his need for people, hastily agreeing to solitary confinement, and impetuously volunteering to add ten years to his sentence. The alienation the he feels quickly turns into despair, disillusionment, and finally apathy.

Betrayal

The banker, at the end of the story, is an example of what loss can do to a seemingly harmless person. The loss of his fortune, and finally the two million rubles he will have to pay the lawyer, force him to focus on his pride, his reputation, and the scandal he must endure when it is revealed that he is penniless. His fear of poverty and need for victory in the bet compel him toward murder and the loss of his morality. He is willing to commit murder to keep his money and maintain his standard of life in the community.

Fatalism

Fatalism is a philosophy of life that purports that man is subject to the random events of life, whether good or bad, with no one holding the strings above to plan, protect, or direct him. He is born simply to live a life that is destined to fail. The typical Chekhov hero might have admirable qualities, such as ambition, idealism, and determination to carry out his plans, but he is ultimately always a failure. Alexander Werth, in the *Slavonic Review*, reveals that Chekhov is "a profound fatalist in all his Writings," and quotes Chekhov in a letter to Suvorin: "My Holy of Holies is the human body, health, intelligence, talent, love and the most absolute freedom." To Chekhov, it is the effort of making these things possible in life that make it worth living, not a hope pinned on some eventual success in life or death.

STYLE

Irony
Chekhov strove to depict life's ironies (when the result of a chain of events is not what was expected). In "The Bet," the ironies are tragic for its characters and mirror the life doled out to Chekhov himself. He contracted tuberculosis, a deadly disease that had no cure at the time, only four months after becoming a doctor, something he had spent his tormented youth and young manhood to achieve. His desire to help sick people eventually kills him.

The ironies in "The Bet" are numerous. The arrogant banker is reduced to humility through the loss of his fortune. Once considered an upstanding man of the community, he is reduced to a man who intends to murder his adversary. The lawyer's imprisonment changes him from a man assured of the sanctity of preserving life in any way possible to one who cares nothing for life or freedom. Neither man wins, and neither man is considered morally good or bad, but in the conclusion, irony takes over. The characters' thoughtless last acts serve to free one another. Instead of killing the lawyer, the banker plants a kiss on his head. The prisoner then escapes, freeing the banker from having to pay his debt.

Realism
"The Bet" was offered to the Russian reader as a *skazka*, a peasant's tale in Russia or a fairy tale to a Westerner. However, Chekhov in his ironic, comedic style creates his own very different version of a fairy tale, which has no magic, no flourishes, and no happy conclusion. He approached his stories with staunch realism, pessimism, and foreboding that were as captivating as any fairy tale. He wanted his stories to depict real life, and not many reached a happy conclusion. Werth, in the *Slavonic Review*, quotes Chekhov as he wrote to his editor Suvorin saying, "My business is merely to be talented, *i.e.*, to know how to distinguish important statements from unimportant, to know how to throw light on the characters and

speak their language. Shcheglov-Leontyev blames me for finishing my story with these words, 'There's no making out anything in this world.'" The story is just a slice out of the lives of real people. He does not offer the men in "The Bet" any epiphany of thought, philosophy, or opportunity for redemption. His stories are always about the human condition, bound within the context of his personal attitude towards the meaning of life.

This style of writing had quite a following among some of his contemporaries and many American writers who followed, including Hemingway, Steinbeck, Faulkner, and Updike. Because it was Chekhov's intention to expose emotional reality, he stripped his writing of some of the previous elements necessary for a short story. There was no need for lengthy descriptions, intricate plotlines, or a climax. His short slices of life and sketches were adapted into a genre popular with Western writers who called it modern or realist.

Point of View
"The Bet" is told from the point of view of an objective narrator. In her introduction to *Peasants and Other Stories*, Laura Merlin explains that Chekhov used what T. S. Eliot would later call the "objective correlative," an element that often appears in the modern short story. The narrator's identity is not known, and he offers no embellishments on the story and no prejudices toward the characters and provides no moral for the ending. He relates little commentary on the actions of the characters, except that which is entirely visible to one watching the plot unfold. The narrator gives himself the license to add an exclamation mark when describing how the bet finally was agreed upon, to show the ridiculous nature of it, but he denotes no hero, no winner, and no lesson to be learned from the debacle.

Brevity
Chekhov is brief in telling his stories. He is never long-winded, giving only the necessary details to portray the characters, the events of the story, and any judgments concerning their actions. Because there are no superfluous words added, the reader's interest in what is not written is paramount. Chekhov's strict adherence to this style made him accessible to the peasant and the intelligentsia. What was literally written was appealing to the peasant, and reading between the lines was of greatest import to the intelligentsia. In this style, Chekhov is closely compared with French short-story writer Guy de Maupassant, known for his brief accounts of life stories imbued with irony.

COMPARE & CONTRAST

- **1889:** Russians did not fully appreciate "The Bet," especially because it was depicted as a *skazka*, or fairy tale, but did not contain the elements peasants expected from a folktale.

  Today: Russia is proud of their master of the modern short story. Chekhov revolutionized literature by inventing a new style of story-telling based on realism and not idealism.

- **1889:** The tsarist government of Alexander III is faced with making major reforms as peasants demand change.

- **Today:** Russia's government is a republic, with a president and a parliament. However, there are still elements of autocracy, and Russia is not fully a democracy.

- **1889:** Eighty percent of the Russian people are peasants, many recently freed serfs, and are unable to read. The gentry comprises the other twenty percent.

  Today: Russia has become highly industrialized, the feudal system long banished, and most people are urbanized and educated.

HISTORICAL CONTEXT

Seeds of Russian Revolution

Just prior to the birth of Chekhov in 1860, Russia underwent a widespread uprising to bring about the end of the autocracy of the tsar and the feudal system, setting forth a constitution. In 1861, Alexander II issued an emancipation that freed the serfs and set in motion the first hint of civil rights in Russia. However, the peasants were required to pay for their freedom. The gentry, without their serfs, were unable to maintain their position in society. The law was codified during this time, a process that led to the creation of the legal profession, to which one of the protagonists in "The Bet" belonged. However, even when a constitution was formed, there was still an underlying current of distrust because the tsarist regime failed to relinquish complete control. Richard Hellie, in his essay "The Structure of Russian Imperial History," explains that the emancipation did little to improve the lives of most Russians and merely paved the way for the Russian Revolution in 1917.

During these years, the undercurrents for change began to run swiftly, and the issues of literacy and education came to the forefront. The gentry formed into a group of reformists called Populists, putting forth the idea of a united population that included the peasants. Industrialization brought more workers to Moscow and other cities, and educated men like those in "The Bet" gathered together to discuss sociopolitical ideals. Literature had been highly censored prior to the emancipation, and now writers began to find ways to criticize the current regime and its politics. However, they had to approach it cleverly, because reform was not so complete that open opposition was tolerated. Chekhov managed by simply depicting the inequities of the system without commenting on their moral implications.

Alexander Pushkin, a poet and playwright, helped pave the way for social reform in his writing and is considered the founder of modern Russian literature and the greatest Russian poet. He also wrote historical fiction, and his book *The Captain's Daughter* revealed Russian life under the rule of Catherine the Great. He became a voice for social reformers by 1830 and was sent into exile by the government. While in exile, he continued to write, including his most famous play, *Boris Godunov*, and his novel in poetry *Eugene Onegin*, which were not published until after his release. Leo Tolstoy, a contemporary of Chekhov, wrote two epic novels in his lifetime, *War and Peace* and *Anna Karenina*, which are both considered to be among the best books of all time. He wrote of the hardships of the Russian

For fifteen years, all he could see of the world was through a small window. (d.dz. | Shutterstock.com)

people but was considered too passive by those who sought change in Russia. Even Chekhov, who is not particularly considered a revolutionary, thought Tolstoy too religious and too quick to point to oppression as the will of God.

Fyodor Dostoyevsky's first attempt at writing, *Poor Folk*, was met with great acclaim. However, because he was a member of the Petrashevsky Circle, a literary discussion group of liberal-minded artists who opposed the tsarist autocracy and Russian serfdom, he was arrested and imprisoned in 1849. Serving a sentence of four years at hard labor in Siberia modified his radical political stances. He began to write about themes of humility and submission. He is best known for his novels *Crime and Punishment* and *The Brothers Karamazov* and is considered the greatest Russian philosopher.

Maxim Gorky appeared later on the literary scene, a contemporary of Chekhov. Around 1900, he saw his writing career take off. Using his work as a political voice to speak out against the hardships and deplorable conditions of those at the lowest poverty levels and against the tsarist

government, he was arrested many times. His first book, *Essays and Strategies* (1898), brought him greater acclaim, and he began to associate with the Soviet Nationalist Party. In 1902, Gorky was elected an honorary academician of literature, but Nicholas II had this action reversed. Chekhov left the Academy in protest. Gorky's best play, *Children of the Sun*, was set during an 1862 cholera epidemic but was widely recognized as representative of current political oppression. He is best known for his style of social realism and as a writer for and from the common people.

CRITICAL OVERVIEW

Chekhov's works were not translated into English as readily as they were into French and German. Therefore, he was not well known to English readers until after the Russian Revolution. His great contemporaries, Leo Tolstoy, Alexander Dostoyevsky, Alexander Pushkin, and Nikolai Gogol, had differing opinions about his contributions to Russian literature. Tolstoy and Dostoyevsky were devout Christians who were troubled by the lack of moral presence in Chekhov's prose, but Chekhov was not a religious thinker. Werth, in his essay "Anton Chekhov," describes Chekhov's philosophy of life as "there is no making out anything in this world." Chekhov's decision not to present a moralistic interpretation for his stories and plays was a disappointment to some. However, Tolstoy admired that Chekhov did not judge his characters, even when they were stupid, immoral, or otherwise flawed. Tolstoy served as Chekhov's mentor in striving to learn to uncover human perfection in his characters, but not all of Tolstoy's doctrines were palatable to Chekhov, especially the idea that the human condition was necessarily a spiritual problem. Chekhov also disagreed with his predecessor Nikolai Gogol, a master of Russian realism who had a strict social philosophy that was geared to meet the need for change at that time in Russia. Not being politically motivated, Chekhov agreed with Alexander Pushkin that prose should provoke thought, and more thought, and should stay away from moralizing, sentimentality, and strict philosophies. Although his comrades differed over Chekhov's beliefs, they did finally agree concerning his talent, and he was awarded the Pushkin Prize for Literature in 1888.

Recognition in the West took much longer. The introduction of his stories in Britain brought criticism from E. J. Dillon in 1891, who said that Chekhov was a mere Russian writer fettered by the tyranny and censorship of an oppressive government. Charles Meister, in his essay "Chekhov's Reception in England and America," reveals that "Dillon felt that the effect on the reader of Chekhov's tales was repulsion at the gallery of human waste represented by his fickle, spineless, drifting people." In Joseph Epstein's essay "Chekhov's Lost Souls," he praises the Russian writer by saying that "he has an intense grasp of the souls of ordinary people," but is disappointed by his lack of moral stance, stating that "the point of the story is missed." "Chekhov's stories are not about good and evil; they have no heroes," observes Epstein. He continues, "With only rare exceptions is there anything resembling intrinsic drama." By 1917, with the help of constant comparison with the work of Guy de Maupassant, Chekhov's stories began to garner more acclaim. He was praised for being more compassionate with his characters than Maupassant and was able to more thoughtfully delve into the deepest heart of man, combining his pathos with ironic humor. Virginia Woolf and J. Middleton Murray placed him above James Joyce and Marcel Proust. The writings of Somerset Maugham are heavily influenced by Chekhov. The most notable convert in England was George Bernard Shaw, who declared that he wanted to tear up his plays after reading those of Chekhov. After World War I, the American writers, captivated by his intrinsic talent for truth, began to experiment with his realistic style. He became quickly lauded as the master of the short story and a model to emulate in modern fiction. Among those who were influenced by his talents, many are now American icons: Joseph Conrad, Eugene O'Neill, John Steinbeck, Tennessee Williams, Ernest Hemingway, and William Faulkner.

CRITICISM

Cynthia Gower Betts

Betts is a playwright, novelist, and freelance writer. In the following essay, she proposes that the actions of the clock and the kiss in "The Bet" present clues for a possible denouement for the story and perhaps an insight into Chekhov's theories on the meaning of life.

"The Bet" leaves many questions unanswered. A winner of the bet is not declared. There is a climax when the banker intends to murder the lawyer, but there is no conclusion or epilogue; only an abrupt ending to the story of two men whose lives have been thrown together for fifteen years after a bizarre series of events. Brevity is the hallmark of Chekhov's style. His stories contain no superfluous words. Each sentence is carefully crafted, with what is not included ranking in equal importance with what does appear. Reading his tightly woven prose is like watching a crime drama, where missing an important clue can lead to an erroneous assumption. With Chekhov, however, there is no wrong assumption, and any sense of satisfaction must come from the imagination of the reader because so much is left unexplained. Many readers expect the end of a story to provide some sense of resolution, but Chekhov's spare, realist style often does not plainly provide this kind of gratifying conclusion. Readers are left to find answers for themselves. Two minor events in "The Bet," involving the clock and the kiss, are clues for a possible resolution of the

WHAT DO I READ NEXT?

- "The Gift of the Magi" is a short story written by O. Henry in 1906 that is similar to Chekhov's style of irony and brevity. It is a Christmas story about love and sacrifice with a signature ironic ending.

- "The Necklace" is a short story about greed with a surprise ending written in 1906 by Guy de Maupassant, who greatly influenced Chekhov as a writer.

- Ernest Hemingway's *The Old Man and the Sea* (1952), a book of short-story length, is a product of the modern fiction movement in America. It deals with Chekhov's themes of the perilous human condition, determination, and loss.

- A playwright like Chekhov, Tennessee Williams is often compared to his Russian counterpart. *The Glass Menagerie*, published in 1945, is a story about a young man growing up in the deep south and deals with physical and emotional isolation.

- *Russian Fairy Tales* by Aleksander Afanoev, published in 1945, is a collection of *skazkas* true to the genre that includes the elements of magic and superstition, which Chekhov chose to eliminate in "The Bet."

- *The Year of Impossible Goodbyes* (1991) by Sook Nyui Choi is the story of a young girl from North Korea who survives the Russian and Japanese takeover during the 1940s and escapes to freedom in South Korea.

- *Anastasia: The Lost Princess*, published in 1991 by James Lowell, is the biography of the Romanov family and the last tsar of Russia. Nicholas II, who had tried to make concessions to the peasant uprising, was assassinated along with his wife, Alexandra, and their children in 1918. Anastasia, the famed youngest daughter, is said to have survived the assassination, while others maintain that it is a fable.

- "Peasants" is a short story by Chekhov about the unimaginable hardships of poverty, starvation, dehumanization, and despair endured by the peasants of the Russian villages. Originally published in 1897, it is available in a collection of Chekhov's short stories, *Peasants and Other Stories*, reprinted by Barnes & Noble in 2009.

- "The Rocking Horse Winner" is a compelling short story written by the modern English fiction writer D. H. Lawrence in the 1926 anthology *Ghost Book*. It incorporates the themes of greed and betting.

---

story and, upon further examination, provide insight into Chekhov's theories regarding the meaning of life.

After the story relates the banker's memories of the bet and the lawyer's imprisonment, the clock strikes three. The banker listens, making sure that everyone in the house is asleep. He takes the key to the prison door from his vault and goes out into the wet, blustery night with murder in his heart. If the lawyer remains in the garden cell until the next morning at noon, the banker will lose everything. At the same time, the lawyer has fallen asleep over a document he has written in which he declares his intentions to leave the cell early in order to forfeit the bet and the money. In his fifteen years of study and soul-searching, he has not found that money can bring happiness. This realization provides a release that allows the tortured, emaciated man to sleep, finally, peacefully. So deeply does he sleep that the banker is able to watch him from an outside window for a full five minutes, while he remains totally motionless. The heaviness of his sleep prohibits him from waking when the banker enters the room, takes time to examine his physical deterioration, and then comes up with a plan to smother him with a pillow. Still he slumbers while the banker takes time to read the document on the table. Finally, he does not even stir when the banker kisses him on the head, replaces the paper, and returns to the lodge.

In the document the lawyer has stated that he would leave his room five hours earlier than the stated deadline of twelve o'clock noon. When the clock struck three, the banker devised a murder plan, then unlocked the safe, took the key, and put on his overcoat. Once outside the estate, he realizes that not only is it completely dark, it is also raining, and it will be difficult to make his way to the back of the property where the garden lodges are. The wind is stinging, and unable to see, he must feel his way out to the lodge, over slippery steps and through trees and statues.

To say that this amount of action took place over a span of less than an hour would seem accurate, but it also seems unlikely that a man who has just relieved himself of the anxiety and torture of fifteen years of confinement and has fallen into such a deep sleep would wake in time to leave the lodge early or even on time. It is very possible that it was the immoral banker whose random, gleeful act of kindness in the form of the kiss wakened the lawyer from his trance. This kiss, this seemingly insignificant act of kindness, much like those in fairy tales, or skazkas, was the pivotal moment in the banker's life. By this act, the banker awakened the lawyer, a stand-in for the princess in the fairy tale. In turn, the lawyer's act of self-denial and sacrifice in his plan to run away before the deadline, much like the children's tale of the lion and the mouse (the mouse frees the lion by chewing through the net that traps him, and the lion promises never to eat the mouse), enables him to be free for the first time of the bonds of greed and intellectualism.

Chekhov purported to have no theology, no philosophy, and no interpretation of the meaning of life. It is important to remember, however, that Chekhov is as interested in what is not said as in what is said. Only one generation removed from serfdom, he knew the miseries of poverty. He was abused as a child, working harder in his father's shop than in school. He was then deserted by his family before graduating high school and rented a room in his own house by tutoring the new owner's son. Chekhov would be the sole provider for his family of eight after joining them in Moscow at age eighteen. He wrote stories for local journals to support them while he studied to be a doctor in Moscow and continued to provide for his family for his entire life. Even after becoming a doctor,

He read thousands of books and learned six languages. (*Dmitry Meinikov | Shutterstock.com*)

he refused to ask for payment. During the famine of 1891, he went back to join the poor peasants of the southern provinces, helping to set up soup kitchens and medical care for the starving multitudes. He saved many from death during the cholera epidemic that followed the famine the next year. Traveling to Siberia while very ill himself, he spent time there at the colony of prisoners who were forced to do labor under cruel, harsh conditions. His only novel, *The Island*, chronicled the plight of the prisoners and brought the authorities' attention to the need for prison reform. In his later years in the province of Yalta, he helped build schools, libraries, planted forests, and oversaw charities for the poor. The final, ironic act of sacrifice he achieved in his death. He died of tuberculosis, a disease he had caught just four months after receiving his medical degree from a poor patient from whom he refused to accept payment. In addition to the example of his remarkable life, Chekhov's tales of the plight of the poor and the oppressed lives they led challenge every reader towards charity and sacrifice.

Source: Cynthia Gower Betts, Critical Essay on "The Bet," in *Short Stories for Students*, Gale, Cengage Learning, 2011.

C. J. G. Turner

In the following essay, Turner considers the unique place of "Without a Title" within Chekhov's short-story oeuvre.

The story in question ["Without a Title"] was written at the end of December 1887 and published in *Novoe Vremia* (*New Time*) on 1 January 1888 under the title of "Skazka." This term is often translated "fairy-tale" but, at least in this instance, I should prefer to translate simply "A Tale," since it is not a fairy-tale and "tale" (although often used to translate *povest'*) of itself bears the required connotations of something archaic, perhaps childish, perhaps fantastic. It was, however, removed and replaced by "Bez zaglaviia" ("Without a Title") when the story was republished in a charitable miscellany, *Pomoshch' postradavshim ot neurazhaia* (*Aid for the Victims of the Failed Harvest, Moscow*, 1899).

It covers about four pages of text and its plot may be seen as having four phases plus a coda: first comes a relatively lengthy description of life in a fifth-century monastery; then a townsman arrives, apparently by accident, and, again apparently without forethought, challenges the monks to do something about the sinful life of the nearest town; thirdly, the Abbot of the monastery responds to the challenge by going on a mission to the town; and, fourthly, he returns and reports to the monks on what he had found there. The coda reads: "When he came out of his cell on the following morning there was not a single monk left in the monastery. They had all run off to the town."

If we consider its setting in time and place, what Bakhtin calls the chronotope of the work, then we soon realise that this story is unique in Chekhov's works in being a regular Chekhovian story but set back chronologically to long before Chekhov's lifetime. Few writers have so consistently as Chekhov set their works in their own time and country. Thomas Eekman has called Chekhov "a writer primarily concerned with contemporary and Russian themes [who] never delved into the past." E. A. Polotskaia claims that he wrote only three stories whose action takes place outside Russia or outside his own time: "Without a Title" is set in an Eastern monastery of the fifth century; "Pari" ("The Bet") is set in an unnamed, "obviously European" city (she does not suggest that the title could be a pun!); and "Rasskaz starshego sadovnika" ("The Head Gardener's Story") is a frame-story for an old

THE FABLE AND ITS CHRONOTOPE ARE UNIQUE IN CHEKHOV, BUT THE STYLE, MANNER AND NARRATORIAL STANCE ARE TYPICAL OF HIS EARLY AND ONLY TOO OFTEN HASTILY COMPOSED STORIES."

Swedish legend. And A. P. Chudakov writes that, with the exception of "Greshnik iz Toledo" ("The Sinner from Toledo") and "Without a Title," Chekhov has no works in the genre of historical prose and that "neither of these stylizations can pretend to being historical." Of the other titles offered here, however, "The Bet" may be alien to Chekhov in location ("Gusev" could also have been adduced, set as it is at sea in the Far East; Ariadna and the Anonymous Man too, in their respective stories, spend time in some of the capitals and resorts of Western Europe, like Mme Ranevskaia of *Vishnevyi sad* [*The Cherry Orchard*] and Chekhov himself) but certainly is not alien in time; "The Head Gardener's Story" has an extended contemporary frame such that the legend could almost be called an "inserted narrative" within a contemporary story (nor is it necessarily set back in time by more than a few generations); and "The Sinner from Toledo" is indeed a parodic stylization of another time and place, as is intimated by its subtitle "Translated from the Spanish." But there is no reason for calling "Without a Title" a "stylization": it is merely set in the fifth century, and this fact makes it unique in Chekhov.

There are some surprising features of this story that one is tempted to attribute to Chekhov's haste or negligence (he expended no great time or care on its composition), perhaps sheer ignorance. One surprise is that Polotskaia should set it so positively in an *Eastern* monastery, just as the poet Ia. P. Polonskii should, on its first publication, call it an "Eastern Tale." For the Abbot is said to write Latin verses and, at least in the first edition, it is clear that the monastery is Latin-speaking, although the surrounding populace is Arabic-speaking. Latin-speakers were by no means unknown in Eastern monasteries (witness St. Jerome), but a whole Latin-speaking community would be exceptional. Presumably the claim that it is set in the East is based on the reference to a tiger's having been sighted in the vicinity, since tigers are purely Asiatic and were never found west of Armenia. Strictly speaking the tiger is incompatible with an Arabic-speaking populace in the fifth century, since Arabic was not spoken outside the Arabian peninsula before the spread of Islam in the seventh century. Nevertheless, tigers are clearly depicted in a fine fourth-century mosaic from Algeria, so that one can say at least that they were known further west. Alternatively, it is just possible to suppose that the monk who claimed to have seen one was, through fear or for some other reason, mistaken. If a real locale has to be found for the story, it has also to be on a coast since the monks are said to be able to hear the sea. The first edition mentioned also palms and fig-trees.

A second surprise is the organ that is played by the Abbot. One immediately thinks of large organs in western churches, but that plainly cannot be what Chekhov has in mind if he knows what he is talking about. Both hydraulic and bellows-driven organs had been known since Hellenistic times and were widespread in the later Roman Empire. Nero numbered organ-playing among his skills! But they were used primarily at secular celebrations and never have been used in the Eastern Church. There are, in fact, few written references to them from the fifth century (perhaps as a result of the barbarian invasions), except for some Church Fathers (particularly from the south or east coasts of the Mediterranean) who use the organ as a symbol. It is noticeable, however, that the Abbot plays the organ not in the monastery church (to which there is no reference) but in his cell, which is, of course, remotely possible.

The story is, then, in principle, a highly unusual one for Chekhov with an ill-defined setting; and from this there follow a number of peculiarities. Its opening words tell us that, although set in the fifth century, it is told from a modern point of view ("In the fifth century, *as now*, every morning the sun rose . . ." [emphasis added—C. J. G Turner]). This merely formalizes and makes explicit what, according to A. A. Mendilow, is normal and perhaps inevitable: that the sensibilities of historical fiction should be those of the writer's time. Not only the point of view, but also the lightly ironical tone and the style (with scarcely an archaism in sight) are those of a modern Chekhovian narrator. While this modern narrator allows his imagination to go a little way towards individualizing the characters of the Abbot and the visitor, he is noticeably reticent and vague about the realia of his story: trees, animals, birds, flowers are mentioned, but only once is a tiger specified; and the monastery has cells and gates, but seems devoid of furnishings, and the monks have food and wine for themselves and their visitor, but what they eat we are not told. Chekhov, who knew his trees and birds, as well as monastic fare, normally tells us more; and he was normally careful and accurate about his realia, as D. W. Martin has shown while indicating at the same time that he was not infallible.

The structure of the story is simple. Its opening paragraphs stress repetition, with their imperfective aspects and phrases such as "every day and night went on being just like every preceding day and night" (*vse den' pokhodil na den', noch' na noch'*). This continuum is broken by a one-time (*odnazhdy*) event, the arrival at night of a visitor to the "surprise of the monks." He is an outsider, a foreign body (in the first edition he even spoke only Arabic while "here one can save one's soul only in Latin"), whose visit culminates in a challenging harangue that is reproduced in direct speech. Having completed this task, he is forgotten by the narrator who neglects to tell us anything about his departure. But his challenge has reached home to the Abbot who, in an almost symmetrical action, leaves the monastery for three months, but returns and also makes a speech (rendered, however, in reported speech). The consequence is given cynically in two lines, with "no comment."

It is noticeable that the realia of the story suddenly become more specific in the Abbot's speech. A table is mentioned for the first time, and on the table is a harlot, the first character in the story whose appearance is described. She is wearing silk and brocade. And when the Abbot leaves the brothel he discovers that the town has also "horse-races, bullfights, theatres, and artists' workshops." The impression is given of a Hellenistic or perhaps a North African city in the later Roman Empire. Bullfighting, for instance, was practised in ancient Thessaly, from where it was imported to Rome as an innovation by Julius Caesar. It became especially popular in the Greek cities of the Empire. While gladiatorial contests in which men took part were ended in theory under Constantine and in practice by the early fifth century, the more common *venationes* (in which animals fought against animals—and the more exotic the species the better) continued into the sixth century; artistic representations of them include North African mosaics and a Constantinopolitan ivory from the beginning of the sixth century. Chekhov probably envisaged something more like modern Spanish bullfighting and would have been hard put to it to provide evidence of its existence in the fifth century. The relative richness of concrete detail in the Abbot's account may ultimately be due to the fact that he found it easier to imagine a fifth-century town than a fifth-century monastery, but it does at the same time fulfill a function of inciting the monks' nocturnal imaginations.

There are, however, also a few further incongruities that are more probably attributable to Chekhov's haste than to the deficiencies of the modern narrator. The Abbot is called an "old man" when he is first mentioned but, after "tens of years have passed," he is still the same vigorous old man. The isolation of the monastery is stressed (perhaps in order to justify the extraordinary degree of ignorance and naiveté on the monks' part about city-life) by there being a hundred versts of wilderness between it and the nearest human habitation; yet the wilderness cannot be an absolute desert because the visitor is able to hunt there and because the Abbot, as he crosses it, is encouraged by the babbling brooks and, on his return, he can use the "fresh verdure of spring" for a simile. And whence, incidentally, comes the monastery's supply of food and wine? Either it has more contact with the outside world than we are led to suppose (for years, we are told, the only living souls to show themselves near the monastery were those who were taking refuge from the world) or the desert is indeed blooming.

Although I have rejected "fairy-tale" as an appropriate designation for this story, it is susceptible of the kind of analysis that is reminiscent of Propp's work on fairy-tales: an established and ritual status quo in which a hero-figure is identified in the person of the Abbot is invaded by an intruder from the town who sets the hero a task; the hero goes forth to fulfill the task by doing battle with the dragon of evil; the account of the battle is retarded by seven days before we learn that the prize has eluded the hero, since the princess has remained in the power of the dragon—the town remains unconverted and the harlot has failed to follow in the footsteps of Mary of Egypt or even of Makovkina/Mother

Agnes in Tolstoi's *Otets Sergii* (*Father Sergius*). But in regard to its chronotope the story is further from the genre of the fairy-tale, which typically is totally relocated in space and time, than it is from the kind of romance or *gistoriia* that was popular from Hellenistic times to early-modern Russia and that normally has an ostensible location (perhaps more often in place than in time) but not always one that avoids incompatibilities and inconsistencies.

The story ends with a cynical twist forcibly reminding us of what we had learnt at the start: that it is being told by a modern man. This modern man, unlike his predecessors in folklore and literature, will avoid any implication of a moral beyond the cynical intimations that a cloistered naiveté is dangerous or that the will to convert is hubristic. He is sophisticated enough to laugh at a bunch of fifth-century monks but not sophisticated enough to avoid some incongruities in the telling of his tale. He is, I suggest, a regular Chekhovian narrator, standing apart from his heroes in order to poke gentle fun at their weaknesses but, having once strayed beyond his accustomed milieu, he is just a little out of his depth; and this is what makes it not a stylization, nor a fairy-tale nor a romance, but a regular Chekhovian story. The fable and its chronotope are unique in Chekhov, but the style, manner and narratorial stance are typical of his early and only too often hastily composed stories. But such an anomalous combination was an experiment that he did not repeat, preferring generally to keep his feet firmly on his home turf of late nineteenth-century Russia, which is where even that hallucinatory visitant from a ninth-century Eastern monastery, the Black Monk, makes himself at home.

Source: C. J. G. Turner, "Chekhov's Story without a Title: Chronotope and Genre," in *Canadian Slavonic Papers*, Vol. 35, No. 3–4, September/December 1993, pp. 329–34.

Thomas H. Gullason

In the following excerpt, Gullason uses "Gooseberries" to illuminate the highly flexible qualities of the short-story form and to "counteract the usual [aesthetic] charges leveled against the short story."

What must we do so that the short story can receive the kind of consideration it deserves? We can try to rid the genre of the prejudices that have conspired against it. We can come to it as though it were a fresh discovery. We can settle on one term for the medium, like "short fiction" or

> CHEKHOV SAW THAT LIFE DID NOT
> HAPPEN IN NEAT BEGINNINGS, MIDDLES, AND
> ENDS. HUMAN PROBLEMS ARE NOT SOLVED SO
> NEATLY; THEY GO ON AND ON. CHEKHOV
> CONCEIVED HIS PLOTLESS, EPISODIC STORIES
> TO CAPTURE THIS RHYTHM OF LIFE."

"short story." References to names like "anecdote," "tale," "narrative," "sketch," though convenient, merely add to the confusion and suggest indecision and a possible inferiority complex. Too many names attached to the short story have made it seem almost nameless. Even the provincial attitude of teachers and anthologists has not helped. Most often students are fed on a strict diet of British and American short-story writers. But the short story is not solely a British and American product; it is an international art form, and Continental as well as Oriental, and other authors should be more fully represented in any educational program. As Maurice Beebe reminds us [in *Approaches to the Study of Twentieth-Century Literature*, 1961], "Once translated, Zola, Mann, Proust, Kafka become authors in English and American literature ... ." Once this philosophy is accepted, the short story will automatically increase in vitality and stature.

One way the reader can contribute to a fuller appreciation of an old art is by simply applying the negative criticisms already mentioned— oneness of effect, formulas, and so on—to examples of the modern short story. For an illustration of the older modern story of average length (5000 words), one can go to Chekhov's popular "Gooseberries," written in 1898. Too many readers would probably be so frustrated and so bored by all the talk and the lack of action in this story that they would stop before they really started. A more patient reader would go on trying to understand and appreciate Chekhov's tone before attempting any kind of critical evaluation. For Chekhov tells a story so casually, almost so indifferently, that he himself seems bored. Now on the surface level a Hemingway story, like "The

Killers," moves very rapidly; and we in America are used to quickness. Chekhov insists on putting us into a rocking chair.

On a first study, "Gooseberries" seems to be about Nikolay and the realization of his dreams: of a man once lost as a clerk, who has now found his meaning and validity as a human being, and consequently his freedom. But as Ivan tells the story about his brother Nikolay to Burkin and Alyokhin, the story becomes a study in Nicolay's self-deception and hypocrisy. For as Nikolay achieves what Tolstoy said was all that man needed—six feet of earth—Ivan sees the blindness of both Nikolay and Tolstoy. He says:

> ... six feet is what a corpse needs, not a man .... To retire from the city, from the struggle, from the hubbub, to go off and hide on one's own farm—that's not life, it is selfishness, sloth, it is a kind of monasticism, but monasticism without works. Man needs not six feet of earth, not a farm, but the whole globe, all of Nature, where unhindered he can display all the capacities and peculiarities of his free spirit.

But then the story is also a study of Nikolay as a dead soul, the superfluous man. This is corroborated in many ways. The imagery of fatness clearly reveals Nikolay's dead life; Ivan says:

> I made my way to the house and was met by a fat dog with reddish hair that looked like a pig. It wanted to bark, but was too lazy. The cook, a fat, barelegged woman, who also looked like a pig, came out of the kitchen and said that the master was resting after dinner. I went in to see my brother, and found him sitting up in bed, with a quilt over his knees. He had grown older, stouter, flabby; his cheeks, his nose, his lips jutted out: it looked as though he might grunt into the quilt at any moment.

And yet, though Nikolay is living a life of self-deception and hypocrisy, and though he is a dead soul, he is enjoying every moment of it: to him, his gooseberries are delicious; to his brother Ivan, the realist, they are hard and sour. To Nikolay his illusions are not illusions—they are happy realities. This is only one layer of the several paradoxes relating to illusions and realities in the story.

The story, then, is far too elaborate to be limited merely to Nikolay and his gooseberries. The gooseberries become a focal and radiating symbol, for they also touch the lives of Burkin, Ivan, and Alyokhin specifically, and Russia generally. This story ever expands in meaning and meanings.

For before Ivan tells his story in Alyokhin's house we are told: "It was a large structure of two stories...." Structurally this is a frame story, a story within a story, and gradually the life of Nikolay becomes a first stage in studying a general condition in Russian life. As Ivan tells his brother's story he also tells his own, and reveals, through his constant rationalization, that he too is a dead soul, the superfluous man. He shows the pathos of his whole life, for now an old man, he cries out: "If I were young!" And he has his own deceptions and his own illusions. As he sees Nikolay's failures and his own, he looks to Alyokhin—as a "young" man of forty—to carry the banner of freedom and his idealizations of life. But he can't see—neither can Alyokhin—that Alyokhin is paralleled to Nikolay: both are landowners, one is lost in the work of his farm, the other in his gooseberries. Alyokhin can never realize the ideals mouthed by Ivan; the omniscient author, Chekhov, reflects ironically: "The guests were not talking about groats, or hay, or tar, but about something that had no direct bearing on his [Alyokhin's] life, and he was glad of it and wanted them to go on."

Earlier, Ivan has generalized on Russian life, and, without knowing it, the life of the story. He says:

> Look at life: the insolence and idleness of the strong, the ignorance and brutishness of the weak, horrible poverty everywhere, overcrowding, degeneration, drunkenness, hypocrisy, lying—Yet in all the houses and on all the streets there is peace and quiet; of the fifty thousand people who live in our town there is not one who would cry out, who would vent his indignation aloud.... It is a general hypnosis.

The paralysis of the individual lives and this general hypnosis are sounded in the opening of the story. The atmosphere—the "still" day, "tedious," "gray" and "dull," and later "it was tedious to listen to the story of the poor devil of a clerk who ate gooseberries"—infects everything. By the skillful use of contrast—the "refreshing" rain, the brief entrances and exits of the beautiful and pleasant maid Pelageya, and the ladies and generals in the golden picture frames—Chekhov further ironically studies what becomes the "general hypnosis theme" in Russia. From the choric Burkin at the story's end, we hear that he "could not sleep for a long time, [and he] kept wondering where the unpleasant odor came from." The unpleasant odor refers to the burnt tobacco from Ivan's pipe; this unpleasantness becomes, in a sense, the man with the hammer, mentioned earlier in the story, who is knocking at the reader's mind about happy and unhappy man. The monotony of the day—the rain at the beginning and at the end—and the tediousness of the tale transfers to the reader the paralysis of lives and the hypnosis theme.

The story does not end. Nothing is solved. But the story is like a delayed fuse; it depends on after effects on the reader via the poetic technique of suggestion and implication. We have enough of the parts to complete a significant pattern. This particular, isolated action moves to a more general plane of significance.

We can use "Gooseberries" to counteract the usual charges leveled against the short story. First, let us counteract Poe's legacy of oneness of effect. This story has layer and layer of meanings and plenty of contradictions in these meanings. If there were Poe's oneness here, the reader would not be forced to reread the story. Then we counteract the issue of mechanical formulas. This story seems as artless, as unplanned, as unmechanical as any story can be; it seems to be going nowhere but it is going everywhere. There is no beginning, middle, and end; it is just an episode that dangles. Here Chekhov demonstrates how flexible the form of the short story can be. Further, Mark Schorer's claim that a story means "revelation" and the novel "evolution" does not fit. This story does study change (even on the reader's part), and it also suggests a sense of continuing life, of whole lives; the past, the present, and the future have coalesced to evolve the idea of general hypnosis. Here is the remarkable art of telescoping. The complaint that the story is only a fragment does not fit either; the part comes to represent the whole in "Gooseberries." Even the much criticized episodic structure fits Chekhov's intended rhythm, his manner of viewing life. Chekhov saw that life did not happen in neat beginnings, middles, and ends. Human problems are not solved so neatly; they go on and on. Chekhov conceived his plotless, episodic stories to capture this rhythm of life. And the characters—characters in short stories are usually criticized as "flat" and uncomplicated—work together to create a combination of moods and anxieties that humanize the ambivalences and ambiguities in the Russian soul.

Source: Thomas H. Gullason, "The Short Story: An Underrated Art," in *Studies in Short Fiction*, Vol. 2, No. 1, Fall 1964, pp. 13–31.

N. Bryllion Fagin

In the following excerpt, Fagin argues that Chekhov is essentially a humorist, but his stories show a serious side, with undercurrents of gloom and a stifled groan of pain.

Chekhov is essentially a humorist. His is not the quiet, genial humor of an Addison or a Washington Irving nor the more subtle, often boisterous humor of a Mark Twain. His is rather the cynical chuckle of a grown-up watching a child assume grimaces of deep earnestness and self-importance. In his earlier stories the laughable, and it is a more or less cheerful laugh, with little of the serious behind it, often predominates. But as the stories grow more in volume, the undercurrent of gloom and a stifled groan of pain become more and more audible, until, in the later volumes, his laugh quite eloquently suggests the ominous combination of submission to Fate and Mephistophelian despair.

[In] vain would we look for an exaggeration or an untruthful note in his works. We feel, with that instinctive perception which is higher than knowledge, that it is all too true; that the people he pictures live and act in reality just as they do in his works. For Chekhov as artist is flawless. No detail of any importance ever escapes his knowing eye . . . .

And this verisimilitude is attained not by voluminous description—Chekhov fortunately seems to have been ignorant of the verbose methods of a Wells, for instance—but by a judicious stroke here and there, a word, a short phrase, a mere mention of a peculiar characteristic. Most of his stories are very short—only two or three pages. Yet within these two or three pages a real live man or woman, or both, or a whole group, live through life, each with his peculiar characteristics, environment, dreams, yearning, struggles, sufferings, victories and defeats, always ending with defeat—a logical sequence with Chekhov.

[While] Chekhov quarrels primarily with the representative class—composed of the middle and upper classes—yet he plainly indicates his opinions of the lower class—the peasant, servant, workman—to be no better. In the few stories in which he deals with this lower class, he frankly shows that he is quite remote from his predecessors, as he was also from his successors, the idealistic group of Russian writers, who held up the common people as an ideal. Chekhov's common people are as base and dull as their educated masters. They are cunning and selfish, capable of hypocritical flattery and hideous humbleness to attain their petty ends.

In *The Simulators* the peasants flock to the general's wife whose hobby is homeopathic medicine. They praise and flatter and bless her for the wonderful cure she has effected of all their ills. At the same time they complain of their poverty and receive from her presents of hay, seeds, etc. On leaving her they throw the medicine away, and next week come again to praise and bless her for her magic remedies . . . .

But there is still another side to Chekhov. It is that touch of pity for the wretched people of his stories which is sometimes felt through his flippancy and scorn and contempt in his early works and which becomes the dominant note in his later ones. With age he becomes more serious, and gradually his scathing sarcasm becomes softened and in its place appears a more benevolent tone. After all, these people are helpless. And helpless and cowardly they are merely because life is so hard and every thing in it so deadening! They imbibe it with the air they breathe!

And even man's cruelty and selfishness are not entirely man's fault. It is the grayness, the monotony of life, the defeat of all dreams and aspirations that give him his mold. There is nothing left but to kill that awful creeper—Time—and to forget. Hence, long live vodka!

Of the great masters of realism none perhaps have plumbed the depths of woman's soul—Goethe's *Das ewig Weibliche*—with more perfection of touch than Chekhov. The outstanding feature of all Russian literature is its search for a motive of life. Chekhov's efforts were compensated in his finding but the ancient motive of love as the guiding-star of woman's life, her supreme motive, the highest expression of her soul, the alpha and omega of her being.

And it is in this field of love that Chekhov's women lose their equilibrium. One by one they start out on their quest, cheerfully, hopefully, courageously, and one by one they return, bloodless and lifeless, carrying but burnt embers in their hearts. Some, like Katya in a *Tiresome Story* are killed outright. Others like Sinaida in *The Story of an Unknown Person* still show faint traces of possible life—the last lingering rays of a setting sun . . . .

But after all, what is the difference between Katya and Sinaida? Both have taken their hearts and souls, their very lives, and have thrown them at the altar of love—and have thrown them away.... Both are modern women, daring women, ready to trample on all barriers they might encounter on their way and both have been hurled back cruelly into the abyss of hopelessness never to rise again. And back they come defeated because they live in the enchanted pool of polluted and indifferent waters—in a pale, drab world where nothing, not even love, is worth a pebble; where man is brutally selfish and cannot be trusted; where the stronger woman is destined to become cynical, distrustful and unattractive (*Three Years*). In such a world woman must pay along with man, and often more than man.

And woman does pay—not only in blood and tears and anguish of heart, but in a lowering of ideal values; in degeneration of conception of motive.

Such is the message of this great Russian writer; an endless chain of gray people, passing through a gray life, thinking, building, striving; fighting for the space of a lifetime a battle which they have not chance of winning; then stepping aside to drink of the waters of Lethe.

And yet this message has found fertile soil not only in Russia but wherever modern man dreams and struggles and suffers. Chekhov has come to occupy a place among the world's great writers because, in striking the chords of Russian life, he struck, with that silver touch which is the magic of genius, the elemental chords of universal life ....

[Chekhov's spirit], despite its morbid tone, is virile, beautiful, and rich. What if he did sing but the Tristan and Isolde of life? What if he painted but the gray dusk? There is a charm and a beauty of its own in it, for by the sickly tint of the sun fading in the west we learn to see its glory when it appears in the east on the morrow.

Source: N. Bryllion Fagin, "Anton Chekhov: The Master of the Gray Short-Story," in *Poet Lore*, Vol. 32, Autumn 1921, pp. 416–24.

Robert Lynd

In the following essay, Lynd discusses Chekhov's talent for portraying ordinary people as the basis of a tragic realism.

It is the custom when praising a Russian writer to do so at the expense of all other Russian writers. It is as though most of us were monotheists in our devotion to authors, and could not endure to see any respect paid to the rivals of the

> THUS SYMPATHY AND DISGUST LIVE IN A CURIOUS HARMONY IN TCHEHOV'S STORIES. AND, AS HE SELDOM ALLOWS DISGUST ENTIRELY TO DRIVE OUT SYMPATHY IN HIMSELF, HE SELDOM ALLOWS IT TO DO SO IN HIS READERS EITHER."

god of the moment. And so one year Tolstoy is laid prone as Dagon, and, another year, Turgenev. And, no doubt, the day will come when Dostoevsky will fall from his huge eminence.

Perhaps the luckiest of all the Russian authors in this respect is Tchehov. He is so obviously not a god. He does not deliver messages to us from the mountaintop like Tolstoy, or reveal himself beautifully in sunset and star like Turgenev, or announce himself now in the hurricane and now in the thunderstorm like Dostoevsky. He is a man and a medical doctor. He pays professional visits. We may define his genius more exactly by saying that his is a general practice. There has, I think, never been so wonderful an examination of common people in literature as in the short stories of Tchehov. His world is thronged with the average man and the average woman. Other writers have also put ordinary people into books. They have written plays longer than *Hamlet*, and novels longer than *Don Quixote*, about ordinary people. They have piled such a heap of details on the ordinary man's back as almost to squash him out of existence. In the result the reader as well as the ordinary man has a sense of oppression. He begins to long for the restoration of the big subject to literature.

Henry James complained of the littleness of the subject in *Madame Bovary*. He regarded it as one of the miracles of art that so great a book should have been written about so small a woman. *Tom Jones*, on the other hand, is a portrait of a common man of the size of which few people complain. But then *Tom Jones* is a comedy, and we enjoy the continual relief of laughter. It is the tragic realists for whom the common man is a theme so perilous in its temptations to dullness. At the same time he is a theme that they were bound to treat. He is himself, indeed, the sole source and subject of tragic realism in literature. Were it not for the oppression of his futile and philoprogenitive presence, imaginative writers would be poets and romancers.

The problem of the novelist of contemporary life for whom ordinary people are more intensely real than the few magnificent personalities is how to portray ordinary people in such a way that they will become better company than they are in life. Tchehov, I think, solves the problem better than any of the other novelists. He sees, for one thing, that no man is uninteresting when he is seen as a person stumbling towards some goal, just as no man is uninteresting when his hat is blown off and he has to scuttle after it down the street. There is bound to be a break in the meanest life.

Tchehov will seek out the key situation in the life of a cabman or a charwoman, and make them glow for a brief moment in the tender light of his sympathy. He does not run sympathy as a "stunt" like so many popular novelists. He sympathizes merely in the sense that he understands in his heart as well as in his brain. He has the most unbiased attitude, I think, of any author in the world. Mr. Edward Garnett, in his introduction to Mrs. Garnett's translation of Tchehov's tales, speaks admirably of his "profundity of acceptation." There is no writer who is less inclined to use italics in his record of human life. Perhaps Mr. Garnett goes too far when he says that Tchehov "stands close to all his characters, watching them quietly and registering their circumstances and feelings with such finality that to pass judgment on them appears supererogatory." Tchehov's judgment is at times clear enough—as clear as if it followed a summing-up from the bench. He portrays his characters instead of labelling them; but the portrait itself is the judgment. His humour makes him tolerant, but, though he describes moral and material ugliness with tolerance, he never leaves us in any doubt as to their being ugly. His attitude to a large part of life might be described as one of good-natured disgust.

In one of the newly-translated stories, "Ariadne," he shows us a woman from the point of view of a disgusted lover. It is a sensitive man's picture of a woman who was even more greedy than beautiful. "This thirst for personal success... makes people cold, and Ariadne was cold—to me, to nature, and to music." Tchehov extends

towards her so little charity that he makes her run away to Italy with a bourgeois who had "a neck like goose-skin and a big Adam's apple," and who, as he talked, "breathed hard, breathing straight in my face and smelling of boiled beef." As the more sensitive lover who supplanted the bourgeois looks back, her incessant gluttony is more vivid in his thoughts than her charm:

> She would sleep every day till two or three o'clock; she had her coffee and lunch in bed. At dinner she would eat soup, lobster, fish, meat, asparagus, game, and after she had gone to bed I used to bring up something, for instance, roast beef, and she would eat it with a melancholy, careworn expression, and if she waked in the night she would eat apples or oranges.

The story, it is only fair to say, is given in the words of a lover dissatisfied with lust, and the judgment may therefore be regarded as the lover's rather than as Tchehov's. Tchehov sets down the judgment, however, in a mood of acute perceptiveness of everything that is jarring and vulgar in sexual vanity. Ariadne's desire to please is never permitted to please us as, say, Beatrix Esmond's is. Her will to fascinate does not fascinate when it is refracted in Tchehov's critical mind:

> She waked up every morning with the one thought of "pleasing." It was the aim and object of her life. If I told her that in such a house, in such a street, there lived a man who was not attracted by her, it would have caused her real suffering. She wanted every day to enchant, to captivate, to drive men crazy. The fact that I was in her power and reduced to a complete nonentity before her charms gave her the same sort of satisfaction that victors used to get in tournaments... . She had an extraordinary opinion of her own charms; she imagined that if somewhere, in some great assembly, men could have seen how beautifully she was made and the colour of her skin, she would have vanquished all Italy, the whole world. Her talk of her figure, of her skin, offended me, and observing this, she would, when she was angry, say all sorts of vulgar things taunting me.

A few strokes of cruelty are added to the portrait:

> Even at a good-humoured moment, she could always insult a servant or kill an insect without a pang; she liked bull-fights, liked to read about murders, and was angry when prisoners were acquitted.

As one reads "Ariadne," one feels that those who say the artist is not a judge are in error. What he must avoid becoming is a prosecuting—perhaps even a defending—counsel.

Egoism seems to be the quality which offends Tchehov most. He is no more in love with it when it masquerades as virtue than when it parades as vice. "An Artist's Story"—a beautiful sad story, which might almost have been written by Turgenev—contains a fine critical portrait of a woman absorbed in the egoism of good works. She is always looking after the poor, serving on committees, full of enthusiasm for nursing and education. She lacks only that charity of the heart which loves human beings, not because they are poor, but because they are human beings. She is by nature a "boss." She "bosses" her mother and her younger sister, and when the artist falls in love with the latter, the stronger will of the woman of high principles immediately separates lovers so frivolous that they had never sat on a committee in their lives. When, the evening after the artist confesses his love, he waits for the girl to come to him in the garden of her house, he waits in vain. He goes into the house to look for her, but does not find her. Then through one of the doors he overhears the voice of the lady of the good works:

> "'God...sent...a crow,'" she said in a loud, emphatic voice, probably dictating—"'God sent a crow a piece of cheese.... A crow.... A piece of cheese ...' Who's there?" she called suddenly, hearing my steps.
>
> "It's I."
>
> "Ah! Excuse me, I cannot come out to open this minute; I'm giving Dasha her lesson."
>
> "Is Ekaterina Pavlovna in the garden?"
>
> "No, she went away with my sister this morning to our aunt in the province of Penza. And in the winter they will probably go abroad," she added after a pause. "'God sent...the crow... a piece...of cheese ...' Have you written it?"
>
> I went into the hall and stared vacantly at the pond and the village, and the sound reached me of "A piece of cheese...God sent the crow a piece of cheese."
>
> And I went back by the way I had come here for the first time—first from the yard into the garden past the house, then into the avenue of lime-trees.... At this point I was overtaken by a small boy who gave me a note.
>
> "I told my sister everything and she insisted on my parting from you," I read. "I could not wound her by disobeying. God will give you happiness. Forgive me. If only you knew how bitterly my mother and I are crying!"

The people who cannot wound others—those are the people whose sharp pangs we feel in our breasts as we read the stories of Tchehov. The people who wound—it is they whom he paints (or, rather, as Mr. Garnett suggests, etches) with such felicitous and untiring irony.

But, though he often makes his people beautiful in their sorrow, he more often than not sets their sad figures against a common and ugly background. In "Anyuta," the medical student and his mistress live in a room disgusting in its squalor:

> Crumpled bed-clothes, pillows thrown about, boots, clothes, a big filthy slop-pail filled with soap-suds in which cigarette-ends were swimming, and the litter on the floor—all seemed as though purposely jumbled together in one confusion....

And, if the surroundings are no more beautiful than those in which a great part of the human race lives, neither are the people more beautiful than ordinary people. In "The Trousseau," the poor thin girl who spends her life making a trousseau for a marriage that will never take place becomes ridiculous as she flushes at the entrance of a stranger into her mother's house:

> Her long nose, which was slightly pitted with small-pox, turned red first, and then the flush passed up to her eyes and her forehead.

I do not know if a blush of this sort is possible, but the thought of it is distressing.

The woman in "The Darling," who marries more than once and simply cannot live without some one to love and to be an echo to, is "not half bad" to look at. But she is ludicrous even when most unselfish and adoring—especially when she rubs with eau-de-Cologne her little, thin, yellow-faced, coughing husband with "the curls combed forward on his forehead," and wraps him in her warm shawls to an accompaniment of endearments. "'You're such a sweet pet!' she used to say with perfect sincerity, stroking his hair. 'You're such a pretty dear!'"

Thus sympathy and disgust live in a curious harmony in Tchehov's stories. And, as he seldom allows disgust entirely to drive out sympathy in himself, he seldom allows it to do so in his readers either. His world may be full of unswept rooms and unwashed men and women, but the presiding genius in it is the genius of gentleness and love and laughter. It is a dark world, but Tchehov brings light into it. There is no other author who gives so little offence as he shows us offensive things and people. He is a writer who desires above all things to see what men and women are really like—to extenuate nothing and to set down naught in malice. As a result, he is a pessimist, but a pessimist who is black without being bitter. I know no writer who leaves one with the same vision of men and women as lost sheep.

We are now apparently to have a complete edition of the tales of Tchehov in English from Mrs. Garnett. It will deserve a place, both for the author's and the translator's sake, beside her Turgenev and Dostoevsky. In lifelikeness and graciousness her work as a translator always reaches a high level. Her latest volumes confirm one in the opinion that Tchehov is, for his variety, abundance, tenderness and knowledge of the heart of the "rapacious and unclean animal" called man, the greatest short-story writer who has yet appeared on the planet.

Source: Robert Lynd, "Tchehov: The Perfect Story-Teller," in *Old and New Masters*, 1919, p. 171.

L. S. Woolf

In the following essay, Woolf states that you cannot put down any of Chekhov's short stories without asking a great many questions about the author, about art, and about life.

[Tchehov] more than any other writer challenges one to ask those ultimate questions about Art and his art. For nine out of ten of his stories end for the reader upon several notes of interrogation. You cannot put down the book after reading, say, the story of *The Lady with the Dog* or *A Doctor's Visit* without asking a great many questions about the author, about art, and about life.

His stories raise over and over again that oldest of questions about realism. For Tchehov, as Mrs. [Constance] Garnett and many others have remarked, belongs most obviously to the Maupassant school of "unflinching realists." But that after all does not take us very far, and we may and do legitimately ask about the realist what he is attempting to do with this unflinching realism. The answer is easy in the case of the old photographic and cinematographic realist. Carefully and accurately to convey a piece of bleak and naked life into the covers of a book was to him enough: that *was* the object of his art

and of Art . . . . But if Tchehov is an unflinching realist, his object is most certainly not unflinching realism. It is true that many of his shortest short stories seem at first sight to be the work of a man who has delicately, fastidiously, and ironically picked up with the extreme tips of his fingers a little piece of real life, and then with minute care and skill pinned it by means of words into a book. Thus in *The Head of the Family* he gives us in barely six pages the description of a meal at which the father, a family bully, tortures his wife, his son, and the governess, not physically, but mentally. And having made the reader feel acutely himself the exquisite and sordid torture of the nagging bully, Tchehov leaves him: but he leaves him not as Zola and his school did, or at least obviously intended to do, with a sense of solidity and finality and explanation, but with a sense of incompleteness, of there being surely something on the other side of the page, a feeling of puzzled interrogation. And in many of the other stories this effect is intensified by the fact that the story itself is in the form of an unanswered question.

But this incompleteness, this sense of questioning to which there is no answer, is not in the accidental facts of the stories, it is present because it is part of Tchehov's mind and art. It is present even when the story is rounded off with the completest of finalities, death. Even when the Black Monk appears again to Kovrin and whispers that he is a genius, and Kovrin dies with a "blissful smile upon his face," the reader still feels that for him "the most complicated and difficult part of it is only just beginning."

There is, in fact, in Tchehov's writings a most curious and not immediately obvious contradiction, a contradiction which explains why with all his powers he so often just fails of the highest achievement. At first sight there seems to be a completeness and certainty about his art which only belongs to writers of the very first quality. Dealing with the subtleties of emotions and human relations, he is able with a few words, a single sentence, to place his scenes with all their subtleties vivid and clear-cut before his reader's eyes. Without hesitation or hurry, he picks a word here, a sentence there, and with that contemptuous aloofness which accompanies the certainty of great skill—you can see it at its best in conjurers and billiard players—produces from under the handkerchief a little definite and rounded piece of real life in the form of a short story. That is why so much is made of his "unflinching realism." He has the air of a man who with extreme detachment is going to show you exactly what a little piece of real life is like, and show it to you without comment, without feeling, without any of the tiresome moralisations or bestowal of praise and blame. And yet at the critical moment, when the achievement seems to be most definite, and rounded, and complete, the sensitive reader will, if he be attentive, feel a slight wobble, a tiny tremor of the conjurer's hand. And if he look a little more closely he will see that Tchehov is one of those people who, to change the metaphor, suffer from a bad mental stammer.

The precision of Tchehov's realism masks the mental stammer which afflicted him when he contemplated life. One notable characteristic in all his work is the extraordinary aloofness of the writer. As Mr. [Edward] Garnett has remarked he does not, as Dostoievsky does, identify himself with his characters: he stands by their side, "watching them quietly, and registering their circumstances and feelings with such finality that to pass judgment on them appears supererogatory." Now a method of this sort is extraordinarily effective within a limited range. The subtlest ironies of life and human relations lend themselves peculiarly to its treatment, and over and over again Tchehov turns to that field of human comedy and tragedy. But the "finality" is a distinctly limited finality.... Tchehov's "finality" is the finality of irony, of the man who stands a little aside from life and almost caresses its absurdities. And that is where his mental stammer comes in. His one keen and persistent emotion towards life is bewilderment. He seems to be literally stammering with unanswered questions as to the meaning of these grotesque comedies and tragedies of the human mind, these absurdities and cruelties, passions and pains and exaltations and boredoms of human relationship. And the perpetual and delicious irony, the amazing and refreshing aloofness, the cool precision and the cold realism are the methods by which Tchehov controls his bewilderment and prevents himself overwhelming his reader with a torrent of "Why's" and "What's."

Source: L. S. Woolf, "Miscellany: Tchehov," in *New Statesman*, Vol. 9, No. 227, August 11, 1917, pp. 446–48.

SOURCES

Chekhov, Anton, "The Bet," in *The Tales of Chekhov, Vol. 9; The School Mistress and Other Stories*, Macmillan, 1921, pp. 255–65.

Epstein, Joseph, Review of *Chekhov's Lost Souls*, in *New Criterion*, May 1986, reprinted in "Chekhov's Dilemma," in *Wilson Quarterly*, Vol. 10, No. 4, Autumn 1986, pp. 36–37.

Hellie, Richard, "The Structure of Russian Imperial History," in *History and Theory*, No. 44, December 2005, pp. 97–101.

Meister, Charles W., "Chekhov's Reception in England and America," in *American Slavic and East European Review*, Vol. 12, No. 1, February 1953, pp. 109–21.

Merlin, Laura, Introduction to *Peasants and Other Stories*, by Anton Chekhov, Barnes & Noble, 2009, pp. vii–xii.

O'Bell, Leslie, "Cexov's Skazka: The Intellectual's Fairy Tale," in *Slavic and East European Journal*, Vol. 25, No. 4, Winter 1981, pp. 33–46.

Werth, Alexander, "Anton Chekhov," in *Slavonic Review*, Vol. 3, No. 9, March 1925, pp. 622–41.

FURTHER READING

Chekhov, Anton, *Anton Chekhov's Short Stories*, W. W. Norton, 1979.

The background provided by Chekhov's letters and critical essays inform analyses of the thirty-four stories in this volume, as well as a view on his life and achievements.

———, *How to Write Like Chekhov: Advice and Inspiration, Straight from His Own Letters and Work*, edited by Pierro Brunello and Lena Lencek, Da Capo Press, 2008.

This insightful guide is an excellent tool for understanding the writing style of Chekhov through his letters and excerpts. It is a thorough analysis, broken down by topic, of the writer's spare, realist style.

———, *A Life in Letters*, edited by Rosamund Bartlett, Penguin Classics, 2004.

This new collection offers a selection of correspondence from the writer to his family, editors, and contemporaries and love letters to his wife, Olga. It provides great insight into a man who was generous and charming.

Malcolm, Janet, *Reading Chekhov: A Critical Journey*, Random House Paperbacks, 2002.

This combination biography, travel book, and literary criticism is a wonderful approach to help readers get to know Chekhov. Malcolm describes her travels to Russia, visiting the places he and his characters lived.

Mizner, Arthur, *Modern Short Stories: The Uses of Imagination*, W. W. Norton, 1979.
This excellent compilation of the modern fiction writers who followed Chekhov's literary style include offerings from Joseph Conrad, F. Scott Fitzgerald, Ernest Hemingway, D. H. Lawrence, James Joyce, Virginia Woolf, Eudora Welty, and William Faulkner.

Steinberg, Mark D., and Stephen P. Frank, eds., *Cultures in Flux: Lower-Class Values, Practices, and Resistance in Late Imperial Russia*, Princeton University Press, 1994.
The authors vividly depict the life of lower-class peasantry in the era of late Imperialist Russia into which Anton Chekhov was born. The book provides insight into the cultural lives of the very poor and oppressed, as well

as many of the issues that fill the volumes of his short stories and plays.

SUGGESTED SEARCH TERMS

Anton Chekhov

The Bet

short story

Russian authors

modern fiction

Chekhov AND short story

Chekhov AND modern fiction

Chekhov AND realism

Chekhov AND Russian literature

Broken Chain

GARY SOTO

1990

"Broken Chain," included in Gary Soto's 2000 short-story collection for young adults, *Baseball in April and Other Stories*, tells the story of a seventh-grade boy, Alfonso, who is about to embark on his first date with a girl, Sandra, after he invites her to go bicycle riding with him. The story focuses on Alfonso's emotional ups and downs as he frets about how he looks, how he is dressed, and whether his bicycle will pass muster. Sandra's bike has a flat tire, but Alfonso's brother, Ernie, refuses to loan Alfonso his bike for Sandra to ride. Disaster strikes when the chain on Alfonso's own bike breaks, and he has to walk to make his date with Sandra. Ernie, though, comes to his rescue by appearing with his bike, which he loans to Alfonso. The story ends as Alfonso, with Sandra on the handlebars, rides around the neighborhood on the bike.

"Broken Chain" is similar to the other stories in *Baseball in April* in examining small events and what they can tell the reader about such themes as love, friendship, growing up, and the problems of youth. In this respect they draw on Soto's experiences growing up in the Central Valley of California. His characters are typically Hispanic, but readers recognize that the problems, anxieties, dreams, and desires of his characters transcend particular cultures and are common to everyone.

Gary Soto (AP Images)

AUTHOR BIOGRAPHY

Soto, a Mexican American poet and fiction writer, was born on April 12, 1952, in Fresno, California. When he was just five years old, his father died, and the family struggled to make ends meet. He came from a working-class family, and in his early years he worked on farms in the San Joaquin Valley and in factories in Fresno. Soto was not a particularly good student, but as a youth he came to appreciate the works of such authors as John Steinbeck, Ernest Hemingway, Robert Frost, Thornton Wilder, and Jules Verne.

Soto attended Fresno City College and California State University at Fresno, earning a bachelor's degree in 1974. Two years later, he earned a master of fine arts degree in poetry writing at the University of California at Irvine. As a college student, he was influenced by the novels of Gabriel García Márquez and the poetry of such figures as James Wright, Charles Simic, W. S. Merwin, and Pablo Neruda.

Soto is a prolific author. In addition to poetry, he writes short stories, novels, plays, memoirs, and children's books—most of this work focusing on the daily lives of people in the Hispanic community. Additionally, he taught at the University of California at Berkeley and the University of California at Riverside, where he was a distinguished professor. He also works as the Young People's Ambassador for the United Farm Workers of America. Soto's work has won numerous awards. His first poetry collection, *The Elements of San Joaquin*, won the United States Award of the International Poetry Forum in 1976. His second poetry collection, *The Tale of Sunlight*, was nominated for the Pulitzer Prize. In 1995 his *New and Selected Poems* was a National Book Award finalist.

PLOT SUMMARY

"Broken Chain" is told from the point of view of Alfonso, a seventh-grade boy living in California. At the story's beginning the reader learns that Alfonso is concerned about his looks. He does not like his protruding teeth, which are "like a pile of wrecked cars," and he tries to push them back with his thumb, especially after his mother tells him that the family cannot afford braces. He does sit-ups to chisel his stomach muscles so that he will be attractive to girls and look like he could take a punch. He dreams of being an Aztec warrior such as the one pictured on a calendar above the cash register at La Plaza. He also obsesses about his hair. He wants to look "cool," like the rock star Prince and the bass player from the band Los Lobos (Conrad Lozano). He also dreams about coloring his hair, but he knows that his parents, especially his father, would not approve. Displeased with his appearance, he spends considerable time looking in the mirror, but he takes steps to improve it by using his lawn-mowing money to buy a new shirt.

After having pushed on his teeth for three hours, Alfonso grows bored, so he goes outside to tend to his bike. He encounters his brother, Ernie, who rides up on his bike. Ernie is aggravated, for he and his friend Frostie were to link up with two girls they had met the previous week on Halloween night. The girls, however, did not show up. Alfonso and Ernie sit and contemplate the mysteries of girls.

Alfonso's father drives up in his truck. Alfonso can tell that the softball team for which his father plays lost its game. Knowing that his father will be in a bad mood, Alfonso

MEDIA ADAPTATIONS

- All eleven stories in *Baseball in April and Other Stories* are read by Stephanie Diaz and Miguel Gongora on two audiocassettes produced by Audio Bookshelf in 2000. Running time is about three hours.

leaves. He mounts his bike, and as he is heading to an ice cream store, he encounters a boy and a girl. The boy is hanging upside down from the top of a barbed-wire fence. Alfonso stops and helps extricate the boy, Frankie, who is grateful. Alfonso then talks to Frankie's sister, Sandra, whom he recognizes from school, but the conversation is awkward. Alfonso walks Frankie and Sandra to their home, and when they arrive, Alfonso asks Sandra whether she would like to go bike riding. Sandra indicates that her bike has a flat tire. Alfonso says that he can borrow Ernie's bike for her to ride.

That evening, Alfonso asks to borrow Ernie's bike. Ernie refuses, claiming that he has plans to use it. As the brothers talk about Alfonso's upcoming date, Ernie begins to suspect that Sandra is one of the girls who stood him and Frostie up. Ernie is jealous that Alfonso may have found a girlfriend. The following morning, Sunday, Alfonso and Ernie continue to quarrel about whether Sandra would do something like stand a boy up. Their quarreling continues into Monday as the boys ride their bikes to school.

Alfonso frets about where he is going to get a bike for Sandra to ride. He considers asking his friend, but he knows that his friend will try to charge him money that he does not have. During the school day, Alfonso avoids Sandra because he does not know what to say to her. After school, he returns home and does his chores. Disaster strikes, though, when he goes outside to work on his bike and the chain breaks. He pleads with Ernie to borrow his bike, but Ernie continues to refuse. The bike-riding date is set for 4:30, and Alfonso has no choice but to go on

foot to Sandra's house. He is convinced that Sandra will find him foolish. He is near despair when Ernie appears on his bike and allows Alfonso to use it, to Alfonso's immense relief. As Ernie leaves, Sandra appears at the corner where they had agreed to meet. Sandra is happy to ride on the handlebars, and the two take off on the bike, riding up one street and down another, enjoying their budding romance.

CHARACTERS

Alfonso

Alfonso, a seventh-grader, is the protagonist of "Broken Chain," and the story is told entirely from his point of view. Through Alfonso, the reader enters the world of adolescence, with its hopes, anxieties, awkwardness, and joys. Early on, the reader learns that Alfonso is displeased with his appearance. His front teeth protrude, and because his parents cannot afford braces for him, he tries to push his teeth into place with his thumb. He also does exercises so that he can strengthen his muscles and look attractive to girls. He thinks about his hair and dreams of coloring it or cutting it the way rock stars do, but he knows that his parents would not approve. Although Alfonso would like to have a girlfriend, he does not know very much about girls and is awkward in their presence.

A turning point occurs when Alfonso meets Sandra, a girl from his school, and he earns her gratitude by helping free her younger brother, Frankie, from a barbed-wire fence in which he has become entangled. Alfonso asks her out on a date to ride bicycles, promising her that he will borrow a bike for her to ride. When his brother, Ernie, refuses to loan him the bike, he and Ernie quarrel. As the date approaches, Alfonso accidentally breaks the chain on his own bike and worries that Sandra is going to think him foolish. All ends well when Ernie relents and loans Alfonso his bike. Alfonso, with Sandra riding on the handlebars, rides through the neighborhood, and when Sandra places her hand on Alfonso's, "it felt like love."

Ernie

Ernie is Alfonso's brother. When Alfonso asks to borrow Ernie's bike, Ernie refuses, claiming that he has plans. Ernie and his brother quarrel, for Ernie is convinced that the girl Alfonso has met is one of the girls who had stood up him and his friend. Ernie, though, is in no sense cruel or unfeeling. He feels sorry for his brother and at one point offers him a stick of gum as consolation. Later in the story, as Alfonso is arriving for his date with Sandra, Ernie comes through. He appears with his friend Raymundo and allows Alfonso to borrow his bike. In many ways Ernie is a typical pesky brother, but it is clear that he and Alfonso have a normal relationship.

Father

Alfonso and Ernie's father is described as a *puro Mexicano*, a pure Mexican who would disapprove and think of Alfonso as a "sissy" if he colored his hair. The father plays on a softball team and is elated when the team wins but angry when the team loses.

Frankie

Frankie is Sandra's younger brother. Alfonso encounters Frankie and Sandra when Frankie is entangled in a barbed-wire fence. Frankie is grateful to Alfonso for freeing him.

Frostie

Frostie is one of Ernie's friends. The two boys made a date and were disappointed when the girls failed to show up.

Father Jerry

Father Jerry is the priest who says mass at the church Alfonso and his family attend on Sunday.

Mother

The reader learns little about the mother of Alfonso and Ernie. She does not appear to be a particularly kindly woman. When Alfonso asks her about getting braces for his teeth, she responds not with empathy but by saying that money does not grow on trees. Elsewhere, she tries to end the quarreling between her two sons. The reader is told that she clips coupons from newspapers and magazines and shops at Kmart and J. C. Penney's—details showing that the family is of modest means.

Raymundo

Raymundo is one of Ernie's friends. He and Ernie catch frogs at the canal on the afternoon of Alfonso's date with Sandra. They return in time to allow Ernie to loan his bike to Alfonso.

Sandra

Sandra is Alfonso's love interest. Alfonso recognizes her from school when he encounters her and her brother; the brother is entangled in a barbed-wire fence, and Sandra is grateful when Alfonso helps free him. She is described as cute, with a ponytail, and Ernie wonders whether she is one of the girls who stood him up. Otherwise, the reader learns little about Sandra. She, like Alfonso, feels awkward during their conversations. She is not disappointed that Alfonso was unable to borrow a bike for her, and she enjoys riding with Alfonso on the handlebars of Ernie's bike.

THEMES

Coming of Age

Much of Soto's fiction for young adults can be classified as coming-of-age fiction. This term refers to fiction that examines the anxieties, fears, and hopes of young people who are transitioning from childhood to early adulthood. "Broken Chain" can be viewed as a coming-of-age story about Alfonso. Alfonso is in the seventh grade, which would make him approximately twelve or thirteen years old. He has reached a time in adolescence when he has become concerned about his appearance and his attractiveness to the opposite sex, yet in many respects he is still a boy, imagining himself as a warrior and riding around the neighborhood on his bicycle. He would like to have a girlfriend, but he does not know very much about interacting with girls. A turning point occurs in the story when he meets Sandra and summons up enough courage to ask her out on a date. The two make plans to go bicycle riding together.

Alfonso, however, encounters adversity. The chain on his bike breaks, he is unable to borrow a bike for Sandra to ride. Convinced that he will look foolish, he has to face up to the need to meet Sandra on foot. Fortunately, Alfonso's brother Ernie arrives in time to loan Alfonso his bike, and Alfonso and Sandra are able to take their bicycle ride. They have fun, and much of the awkwardness of their budding relationship disappears. When Sandra puts her hand on Alfonso's, Alfonso experiences the beginnings of young love. His transition from childhood to early adulthood begins.

TOPICS FOR FURTHER STUDY

- The San Joaquin Valley is sometimes referred to as the "nation's salad bowl." Investigate the history, geography, and agricultural development of this region, part of California's Central Valley. Prepare a multimedia presentation in which you describe how the area might have shaped the outlook and experiences of a writer such as Gary Soto.

- Much like any boy his age, Alfonso wants to look cool, like rock stars and other cultural figures. Investigate the popular culture scene of the late 1980s and early 1990s, particularly in the Hispanic community. What trends and styles were popular? Assemble a group of visuals and present them to your class along with explanations of why they were popular.

- "Broken Chain" refers to "a calendar of an Aztec warrior." The reference is very likely to the calendar art of Jesús Helguara, a famous Mexican artist whose calendar paintings for many years hung in many Hispanic homes and businesses. Investigate Helguara's Aztec calendar art in print and online sources. Show your class examples of this art in a digitally-created presentation that explains why the art would have been significant to the Hispanic community.

- Francisco Jimenéz is the author of the young-adult nonfiction book *Breaking Through*, which recounts his experiences as a migrant farm worker in California during his junior-high and high-school years in the 1950s. "Broken Chain" was published later, in a collection published in 1970. In comparing the two works, answer the fundamental question, "What, if anything, has changed in Hispanic culture in California?" Write an essay that compares the two works in reference to that question.

Hispanic American Culture

"Broken Chain" is set in a Hispanic neighborhood and features Hispanic characters. Many of the story's details help to create the texture of the community in which Alfonso is growing up. Some of the characters' names are recognizably Hispanic: Alfonso, Raymundo, and Raul are clear examples, and reference is made to other people named, for example, Yolanda and Orsua. Alfonso dreams of being like an Aztec warrior, a reference to the cultural history of the Hispanic people. The story interlaces Spanish words, including *puro Mexicano* ("pure Mexican"), *Qué pasó?* ("What happened?"), *abuelitas* ("grandmothers"), *pendejos* ("stupid people"), *Chale* ("No way!"), and *menso* ("stupid" or "foolish"). Further, references are made to Mexican foods and Mexican places of business, such as La Plaza. These and other details contribute to the atmosphere of an ethnic neighborhood.

At the same time, the story depicts the blending of Hispanic and Anglo culture, largely through details. For example, Sandra's mother is a teacher's aide at Jefferson Elementary School. Alfonso's mother shops at Kmart and J. C. Penney's, and Alfonso's bike came from Montgomery Ward; these are all chain department stores that can be found in many communities throughout the country. The ice cream store is named Foster's Freeze, and Alfonso thinks of his old school, John Burroughs Elementary. Mention is made of a street named Madison. This intermixing of Hispanic and Anglo details conveys to the reader the blend of cultures in the California neighborhood in which Alfonso lives. It suggests that the surrounding culture, including the popular culture, is transforming the Hispanic community in ways that characters like Alfonso cannot always understand. The story, then, is not a story entirely about Hispanic culture; it invites readers of all cultures into a shared experience.

Family

"Broken Chain" depicts relatively normal family relationships. Alfonso is part of a family that includes his father, his mother, and his brother, Ernie. Little is said about Alfonso's father, but it is clear that as a *puro Mexicano*, he is a first-generation immigrant. He has somewhat stereotypical views of what it means to be a man, for Alfonso believes that if he cut and colored his hair to resemble that of a rock star, his father would think of him as a sissy. Alfonso's mother is somewhat stern; for example, when Alfonso asks whether he can have braces to straighten his teeth, she responds not with sympathy but by indicating that money does not grow on trees.

She also tries to supervise the conflict between Alfonso and Ernie over the bike and Sandra. More at the heart of the story, though, is Alfonso's relationship with Ernie. The two boys have a relationship that is in many ways typical of that between two adolescent brothers. They quarrel, but it is clear that on some level they have affection for each other. Ernie, for example, while refusing to loan Alfonso his bike, feels badly for his brother and offers him a stick of gum as consolation. Later, after Ernie completes his expedition to catch frogs with his friend, he appears on the scene to loan Alfonso his bike—a clear act of kindness and brotherly affection.

Self Image

Much of the early part of "Broken Chain" is taken up with Alfonso's self image, a theme that is common in young-adult coming-of-age fiction. Alfonso spends considerable time looking at himself in the mirror, not because he is vain but because he is troubled by his appearance. Particularly troublesome to him are his protruding front teeth, and he spends hours pressing on his teeth with his thumb, trying to push them back. He thinks about his hairstyle and fantasizes about cutting his hair and perhaps coloring it, so that he can look like a rock star. He also does sit-ups to improve the condition of his muscles so that he can be attractive to girls.

In addition to worrying about his appearance, Alfonso frets about how others will perceive him, particularly girls. After he meets Sandra, he is worried that he will look stupid and foolish to her. He does not know what to say to her, and their conversation is stilted. In his view, his inability to provide Sandra with a bike to ride is a disaster, for he thinks that this will make him seem foolish to her. The story, though, ends happily, for Sandra does not appear to care about whether Alfonso can provide her with a bike, and the two enjoy a bike ride through the neighborhood with Sandra on the handlebars.

Disappointment

Much of the story arc of "Broken Chain" has to do with disappointment and the ability to overcome it. Early in the story the reader learns that Alfonso is disappointed with his looks, in particular his protruding front teeth. He is disappointed when his brother, Ernie, refuses to loan him his bike so that Sandra will have a bike to ride. He is immensely disappointed when he breaks the chain of his own bike so that he has

Alfonso's bicycle chain broke into several pieces.
(Jan Vancura | Shutterstock.com)

to appear for his bike-riding date with no bike. The story, though, demonstrates that disappointment can be overcome. One way of doing so is through family. Although Ernie resists loaning Alfonso his bike, in the end he comes through and gives Alfonso the bike at the crucial moment. Another way of overcoming disappointment is by simply bearing down and doing what needs to be done. It would have been easy for Alfonso cancel his date with Sandra. Rather than doing so, though, he gathers his courage and goes to meet her on foot. This ability to confront and overcome disappointment is part of the coming-of-age theme of the story. Alfonso is able to reconcile himself to the situation as it is, showing that he is on his way to growing up.

Romantic Love

In its essence, "Broken Chain" is a love story. It depicts the beginnings of a romance between Alfonso and Sandra. Alfonso works up courage to ask Sandra for a bike-riding date, and she accepts. Alfonso goes through the normal emotions of an adolescent boy as he frets about his upcoming date and how he will look to Sandra.

The story depicts the awkwardness of the two as they get to know each other. The story ends on an optimistic note as Alfonso and Sandra ride on Ernie's bike through the neighborhood, and the reader is told that "it felt like love." Of course, the reader has no idea what the future will hold for Alfonso and Sandra; the characters exist only within the boundaries of the story. However, most readers—both young adults and adults—will recognize the first stirrings of romantic love that they felt during this period of their lives. The love story is quiet; it is not a tortured romance such as that depicted in Shakespeare's *Romeo and Juliet*. It is a story of detail, of minor incidents that add up to a larger truth: that love comes in many forms, and feelings for another person are an important part of growing up.

STYLE

Point of View
"Broken Chain" is told entirely from the point of view of Alfonso. The story is narrated in the third person, meaning that the story is told not *by* Alfonso but *about* him, and he is referred to as "he" and "him." This point of view allows Soto to portray the thoughts and emotions of Alfonso, and those thoughts and emotions are the focus of the story. The third-person narrator, though, never comments on the action. The details of the story and Alfonso's experiences are allowed to speak for themselves. Further, the narrator never enters the minds of other characters. The reader sees those characters from the outside, as Alfonso perceives them.

Setting
The setting of "Broken Chain" is a mixed Hispanic-Anglo neighborhood in California. Reference is made to Santa Cruz, suggesting that the community is located relatively near that city. The precise location of the setting is not as important as Soto's ability to recreate the texture and day-to-day life of the people who live there. Although the story is brief, the reader feels immersed in the community, with references to La Plaza, the Mayfair Canal, Foster's Freeze, the various schools, Rudy's Speedy Repair, Color Tile, and other places that would be part of the ordinary life of a boy living in that place at that time. Soto's treatment of setting also suggests the transformation that is taking place in the Hispanic community of California.

Alfonso and his family are Hispanic, and many of the boys' friends are Hispanic as well, yet the surrounding culture is working a change in life in Alfonso's community, one to which Alfonso will have to adapt.

Dialogue
In one sense, the dialogue of "Broken Chain" is not very interesting. Alfonso and his brother talk briefly about the usual things adolescent brothers might talk about, and they argue about whether Sandra is one of the girls who stood up Ernie and his friend. When Alfonso and Sandra converse, they have little to say that is interesting. This mundane dialogue is, in a paradoxical way, interesting to the reader because it is indicative of the kind of conversation that adolescents might actually have. Dialogue is not used so extensively that it would bore the reader; it is used just enough to create character.

HISTORICAL CONTEXT

Popular Culture
"Broken Chain" makes no reference to any historical events, and the story does not take place with any particular events as a backdrop. The story does, however, embody some cultural trends that were becoming apparent in the late 1980s, when it was presumably written. ("Broken Chain" appeared in a collection published in 1990.) One was the growing popularity of Hispanic popular culture. Reference is made to Los Lobos ("The Wolves"), a popular, Grammy Award-winning rock band that had gotten its start in the late 1970s. By the late 1980s, Los Lobos was one of the more popular bands in America. Other Hispanic musicians were popular, including Carlos Santana, Ruben Blades, Celia Cruz, Gloria Estefan, Jerry Garcia, Selena, and Paula Abdul. Additionally, during the 1980s major motion-picture studios released more work by Hispanic producers and directors. Some of these films include *La Bamba*, *El Norte*, *Crossover Dreams*, *Born in East L.A.*, and *Stand and Deliver*. Prominent Hispanic actors included Edward James Olmos, Lupe Ontiveros, Elpidia Carrillo, Andy Garcia, Raul Julia, Mercedes Ruehl, and Maria Conchita Alonso. Hispanic art and culture was breaking stereotypes, entering the mainstream, and achieving a wide audience among Hispanics and non-Hispanics alike.

COMPARE & CONTRAST

- **1990:** The Hispanic population of California is about 7.6 million.

  Today: The Hispanic population of California is estimated to be just over twelve million.

- **1990:** The Immigration Act of 1990 increases the limits on legal immigration to the United States.

  Today: Immigration is a contentious issue in the United States. Many people are concerned about illegal immigration from Mexico and Central America. In 2010 Arizona passes SB1070, a controversial law enacted to enforce federal immigration law in that state.

- **1990:** A youth in California is able to ride a bicycle without wearing a helmet.

  Today: As of 1994, Californians under the age of eighteen are required to wear a helmet while riding a bike on the streets.

- **1990:** Many consumers purchase bicycles from the Montgomery Ward department store.

  Today: Montgomery Ward goes out of business in 2001; in 2004 the company becomes an online retailer called Wards; it does not sell bicycles.

Immigration

Although "Broken Chain" does not deal with the issue of immigration, immigration forms part of the backdrop of virtually any work by a Hispanic American author. During the 1980s, the United States experienced the largest wave of immigrants in its history. The first major wave occurred from about 1840 to 1880, when five million people, most of them from northern and western Europe, arrived in the United States. The second major wave occurred in the early years of the twentieth century, when about nine million people arrived; large numbers of these immigrants were from southern and eastern Europe. Immigration slowed between the two world wars, but after World War II, the pace picked up, and during the 1980s about ten million immigrants found a home in the United States. A significant proportion of these immigrants were from Mexico and Central and South America (as well as Asia). Most of these Hispanic immigrants were concentrated in border states, including California. This wave of immigration created a critical mass of people that enabled Hispanic art and culture to flourish. This popularity of Hispanic culture continued throughout the 1990s and into the new century, with numerous artists and musicians gaining widespread acclaim.

CRITICAL OVERVIEW

At the time he published *Baseball in April*, Soto was known primarily as an award-winning poet. Thus, his fiction did not attract perhaps quite as much attention as it might otherwise have. Numerous publications, though, took some notice of the collection's publication, and critics were nearly unanimous in their reaction to it. Writing in the *School Library Journal*, Janice C. Hayes calls the collection "insightful" and concludes that "young readers should easily identify with the situations, emotions, and outcomes presented in these fine short stories." A contributor to *Booklist* calls the stories in the collection "funny and touching friendship stories, great for reading aloud." Writing for *English Journal*, Alleen Pace Nilsen and Ken Donelson note that the stories "tell about Latino youngsters who seem tough on the outside—or at least they hope they look that way—but are terribly vulnerable a quarter of a centimeter in." The reviewers conclude by referring to the stories as "uncontrived and simple." One of the fullest reviews of *Baseball in April* was written by Roberto González Echevarria for the *New York Times Book Review*. He refers to the stories as "sensitive and economical." The overall theme of the collection, in Echevarria's

He was distraught over how to tell Sandra about his broken bike. *(Monkey Business Images / Shutterstock.com)*

view, is "individual and social change being provoked by strong outside forces." He concludes that the collection is a "bittersweet account of reconciliation to the givens of self and life while growing up." Finally, Diane Roback, writing for *Publishers Weekly*, praises "Soto's ability to crystallize a moment" and calls the stories in the collection "honest and moving."

CRITICISM

Michael J. O'Neal

O'Neal holds a Ph.D. in English. In the following essay, he examines "Broken Chain" as an example of "slice-of-life" fiction.

Any survey of fiction, including novels and short stories, reveals that authors use widely varying tactics when it comes to the selection of a topic. Some authors, by preference or temperament, select topics with wide historical significance; an example might be Boris Pasternak's *Doctor Zhivago*, which is set within the grand sweep of events surrounding the Russian Revolution. Still other

authors are more interested in detailed character development and psychological portraiture. Examples include Gustav Flaubert's *Madame Bovary* and Leo Tolstoy's *Anna Karenina*. Other authors are more interested in external action. Many novels and short stories with military, nautical, or Western themes (that is, books about the American West) emphasize events rather than the psychology of characters. The Western and military novels and stories of Louis L'Amour are good examples of works in which the emphasis is on rollicking good action, with little interest in the deeper motivations of characters.

Gary Soto's fiction, though, does not fit into any of these categories. "Broken Chain" does not touch on historical events; the basic events in the story could have taken place anywhere, at any time, and although the story, like most of Soto's fiction, is Hispanic-themed, it does not examine the sociology of the Hispanic community, nor does it place a great deal of emphasis on external action. The characters do things, but the actions they perform are not particularly significant, other than to themselves. The story does

WHAT DO I READ NEXT?

- Victor Martinez's 1996 novel *Parrot in the Oven: Mi Vida: A Novel* is, like "Broken Chain," a coming-of-age story of a Hispanic youth.

- Gary Soto's 1993 short-story collection for young adults *Local News* chronicles the everyday lives of adolescents growing up in a Chicano neighborhood in California.

- Sandra Cisneros is the author of a short-story collection, *The House on Mango Street*, published in 1983. The stories in the collection chronicle the life of Esperanza Cordero in the Hispanic quarter of Chicago.

- Sonya Sones's 2001 verse novel *What My Girlfriend Doesn't Know* tells the story of a high school freshman who is an outsider and the butt of jokes. His status improves when a popular girl becomes his girlfriend.

- The classic novel of a boy, his adventures, and his relationship with a girl is Mark Twain's *Tom Sawyer*, published in 1876. Tom is about the same age as Alfonso in "Broken Chain" and, like Soto's character, is caught between childhood and adolescence. His relationship with Becky Thatcher is an important element of the novel.

- For a look at high school life and the process of coming-of-age in 1960s Japan, read Ryu Murakami's *Sixty-Nine*, published in 2006.

- *Gary Soto* by Tamra Orr (2005) provides insight into Soto's life and work. In particular, it focuses on his journey from being a poorly educated day laborer to an award-winning author.

---

place some emphasis on the psychology of Alfonso, particularly the issue of his self image, but again, Soto does not engage in an in-depth psychological portrait. Rather, the reader gets to know Alfonso primarily through the author's depiction of the details of Alfonso's life during a brief span of time.

This type of fiction is often referred to as "slice-of-life" fiction, and the short story, with its limited scope, is well suited to this approach. In this type of story, the author carves out a moment in time in a character's life. The moment might be an hour, a day, or a week, but the "moment" is a defined, limited period during which the reader witnesses the character in his or her day-to-day life. Little or no reference is made to larger events; the reader learns little or nothing about the character's life before and after the moment in time. Rather, the author uses detail to develop the texture of the character's life during that period of time. By emphasizing small details, the minutiae of the person's life, the author hopes to create sparks of recognition in the reader. The details are likely to be similar to what readers have experienced in their own lives. Thus, as the reader proceeds through the work, he or she has moments of recognition. The primary reader response might be something such as, "Yes, I remember doing that, or thinking that, or having an experience like that. Yes, I remember quarreling with my brother, or asking my parents for something they couldn't give me, or having that first awkward conversation with a person of the opposite sex."

"Broken Chain" presents a slice of Alfonso's life, a period of about three days shortly after Halloween, from the time just before he meets Sandra on a Saturday until the following Monday afternoon when he has his bike-riding date with her. Early on, the reader learns some details about Alfonso that set the stage for the action of the story. In particular, the reader learns that he is an adolescent boy who is concerned about his appearance. The story also sketches in details that help the reader form a picture of Alfonso's life: his relationship with his parents, his family's socioeconomic status (suggested by his own lack of money and his mother's need to clip coupons from newspapers), and his relationship with his brother, Ernie.

At that point, the story turns to the principal action, as Alfonso encounters Sandra and her brother, makes a date with her, tries to borrow his brother's bike for the date, and fails. Along the way the reader is given a feel for the texture of Alfonso's community: La Plaza, the ice cream store, the schools, Rudy's Speedy Repair, and his father's Datsun truck. The reader suspects that Alfonso lives on the periphery of his brother's group of friends, including Frostie and Raymundo. Alfonso rides a bike, but not just any bike. The bike he rides is from Montgomery Ward, so it is not a fancy titanium bike (although it is a ten-speed), just an ordinary middle-class bike. Sandra's mother is a teacher's aide, not just at any school, but at Jefferson Elementary. Alfonso's father plays on a softball team that had a game, not just against another unspecified team but against the team from Color Tile (a retail chain that sells floor and bathroom tile). Ernie has an outing not just to go "someplace" to do "something" with Raymundo but to go catch frogs at the Mayfair canal. Gradually, by the accumulation of these kinds of details, the reader forms a picture of the life that Alfonso leads and the community in which he leads it.

The crisis of the story again is more in the nature of a detail. No one dies. No one is arrested and jailed. No critical historical event takes place. The story contains no gangs, no guns, no drug use, no crime or racial discrimination, no conflict with the non-Hispanic community. Rather, the chain on a bicycle breaks. In the larger scheme of things, a broken bike chain would be of virtually no importance, but it is important to Alfonso, just as similar minor catastrophes might be important to any boy in his situation, and again, the reader will have a moment of recognition thinking about similar minor events that took on major importance in his or her own life. It is crucial to note that Soto never comments on these details. The reader is never "told" by an intrusive narrative voice what the details mean. Rather, Soto allows the details to slowly accumulate, one after another, until the reader responds in an appropriate way. Most readers would recognize Alfonso's reaction as he approaches the meeting place with Sandra, minus his bike:

> He waited at the corner a few minutes, hiding behind a hedge for what seemed like forever. Just as he was starting to think about going home, he heard footsteps and knew it was too late. His hands, moist from worry, hung at his sides, and a thread of sweat raced down his armpit.

Just as the story picks up with Alfonso's life on a day sometime after Halloween, it ends abruptly with the ride he and Sandra take on Ernie's bike. They hit potholes, and Sandra "screamed with delight." Most importantly, "when it looked like they were going to crash, she placed her hand over his, and it felt like love." Virtually every reader can recognize this first blossoming of love for another. In the real world, it is likely that Alfonso and Sandra will eventually go their different ways, perhaps

Thanks to his brother's change of heart, they were able to ride the bike together. (*Liv fris-larsen /*
Shutterstock.com)

remaining friends, perhaps not. However, this slice of Alfonso's life is critical for him, for it represents an early step into a more adult, more mature perspective on life, one in which he recognizes human interaction as more important than appearances.

Source: Michael J. O'Neal, Critical Essay on "Broken Chain," in *Short Stories for Students*, Gale, Cengage Learning, 2011.

Patricia de la Fuentes

In the following essay, de la Fuentes explores Soto's use of ambiguity as a poetic device.

Although Aristotle was "inclined to consider all ambiguity as a perversion or failing of language instead of its natural and valuable quality," by the Seventeenth Century, the Spanish theorist and critic Baltasar Gracián firmly established, in his famous treatise "Agudeza y Arte del Ingenio," the fundamental importance of ambiguity as a poetic device. More recently, the English critic

> IT IS INTERESTING TO NOTE THAT
> ALTHOUGH THE CHRISTIAN BACKDROP IS NOT
> CONSPICUOUSLY NEGATED IN SOTO'S POETRY, IT
> DOES NOT OCCUPY A PROMINENT PLACE IN HIS
> PHILOSOPHICAL VISION."

William Empson further clarified the status of this device by stating that "an ambiguity...is not satisfying in itself, nor is it, considered as a device on its own, a thing to be attempted; it must in each case arise from, and be justified by, the peculiar requirements of the situation." In spite of Aristotelean disapproval, however, ambiguity not only became accepted as "a natural, subtle, and effective instrument for poetry and dramatic purposes" in Greek literature, but is still considered a valuable rhetorical technique by modern writers.

If we understand Empson correctly, ambiguity should be something more than rhetorical ornamentation and a convenient vehicle for creative exuberance. Besides these superficial qualities, which also have their place in the creative process, ambiguity should be intrinsically functional in the sense of contributing to the internal tension of a poem; i.e., it should form part of the organic structure of the work and create, through a series of ironies, subtle contradictions and dislocations, multiple ramifications and levels of meaning, which give technical brilliance and, above all, intellectual and emotional significance to the poem.

Ambiguity acquires validity, Empson seems to suggest, in direct proportion to its function of sustaining the subtlety, delicacy and compression of poetic thought and adding suggestive, profound and complex nuances to the narrative structure of the poem. In effect, the value of ambiguity as a poetic device may be measured in terms of its organic function, manifest in unexpected or ironic repercussions, resonances or ramifications of language which, by their very dissonance, add surprising perspectives to the poetic design.

On the other hand, if such dissonant perspectives introduced through an ambiguity should distort too violently or frivolously the organic unity of the poem, such a device would lose its valid function and become an obstacle to rather than a vehicle for poetic expression. By posing a serious threat to the unity of the poem, a non-organic ambiguity not only clouds the meaning but also reveals a lack of artistic maturity.

It would seem, therefore, that the effective use of ambiguity as a poetic device requires a highly developed sensitivity to linguistic subtleties; and it is not surprising that in Chicano literature, in its newly acquired status as a legitimate branch of American Letters, no great number of poets have yet emerged as masters of the art of poetic ambiguity. Among those who have achieved this distinction, however, the Californian poet Gary Soto deserves special consideration for his exceptionally high level of linguistic sophistication.

One of the principal characteristics of Soto's poetry is the apocalyptic vision it reflects of the universe. Recurring images of loss, disintegration, decadence, demolition, solitude, terror and death create a desolate landscape in which the voice of the narrator is that of a passive, impotent observer, helplessly caught up in the inexorable destruction of human ties. Within this seemingly hopeless, profoundly grey world of Soto's poems, however, occasional affirmative images introduce muted, contrapuntual notes of something akin to hope.

In his first collection, *The Elements of San Joaquin*, for example, the presence of dust, both from the fields and from the mortal remains of the men who work them, and the action of the wind that sweeps everything before it and reduces all things to dust, are two of the most persistent images. Both dust and wind are elements of an environment that is both hostile and indifferent to human solitude and suffering. Soto often juxtaposes these two images in the same poem to suggest apocalyptic forces:

> The wind strokes
> The skulls and spines of cattle
> To white dust, to nothing.
> ("*Wind*")

At first glance, this image appears to be totally negative since it depicts the slow, irreversible disintegration of the cattle skulls, and by extension those of mankind as well, into dust and then into nothingness. Faced with the terrifying indifference of the wind, which destroys everything—mountains, cattle, or the footprints of beetles, each individual existence becomes inconsequential, ephemeral, all traces of its presence obliterated as if it had never been. Upon closer examination, however, we discover an image that functions on multiple levels in this passage, one which is simultaneously harmonious and discordant. On one hand, the image "strokes" accentuates the terror and aggression implicit in the action of the wind because it denotes hitting or striking a blow which wounds or destroys, an attack; the image conjures up visions of axes, swords, fists and whips, all instruments of aggression or death. On the other hand, "strokes" also carries a denotation which is at odds with the implacable violence of the wind since it represents the diametrically opposite action of caressing, flattering, soothing. On another level, "strokes" also means the sound of a bell or clock ringing the hour, an image which inevitably recalls the passing of time, an action which brings with it the natural disintegration and wearing away of things, a universal law to which man has yet to discover an alternative.

It is clear, therefore, that the implicit ambiguities of the word "strokes" add psychological and emotional dimensions to an image that would be notably diminished had the poet chosen a word with less resonances and dissonances like "reduces" or "pulverizes." But the question still remains as to whether the inclusion of this ambiguity, which undoubtedly adds complex nuances to the narrative structure of the poem, is justified by what Empson calls "the peculiar requirements of the situation." Can we affirm, for example, that this device transcends its metaphorical function within the passage to contribute more profoundly to the organic structure by acquiring a more pervasive significance in relation to the rest of the poem? If we listen carefully, we hear the resonances of this stroking caress which the poet subtly introduces in the process of physical disintegration, and which is none other than the process of death itself, echoing in the following stanzas where they modify the image of the wind as it exercises its annihilative action on the narrator:

> Evenings, when I am in the yard weeding,
> The wind picks up the breath of my armpits
> Like dust ...

Here, in a less obvious manner, the wind already initiates its action of reducing man to the white dust of his own bones, of reintegrating him into the elements, in a cycle which returns the human body to its beginnings in the dust, an image clearly infused with biblical echoes.

Within this apocalyptic framework, however, the same affirmative note from the previous stanza is clearly heard. In this case, what the wind carries off is the "breath" of the narrator's armpits, that is to say the sweat of a man who works his yard. On a negative level, this exhalation of sweat certainly suggests the physical disintegration of the body, a loss of vital essences which the narrator can never recuperate, a prefiguration of death, in other words. Simultaneously, on a second, affirmative level, the same action is an irrefutable sign of life, since by sweating the narrator reaffirms his existence. On the metaphorical level, this ambiguity creates a tension between life and death since the exhalation of sweat experienced by the narrator is a prefiguration of the exhalation of the spirit in the moment of death which can lead either to the defeat of total annihilation, or to the triumphant beginning of a new life. Another alternative, as the poem suggests, is an harmonic resolution between these two seemingly contradictory states.

This fundamental ambiguity of the poem, which begins as a poetic device in the style of Gracián's "agudeza simple" or simple conceit, introduced by the poet to create uncertainty regarding the precise function of the destructive wind, acquires increasingly significant dimensions and resonances as it is gradually revealed as a unifying force within the poem. By reducing all the creation to dust: the mountains, reduced grain by grain to loose earth; the cattle, whose bones become white dust; the insects, birds and plants, whose tracks are obliterated by its action, and finally man, whose exhalations are dissipated in the air, the wind acquires the personification of an anti-generative, anti-mythic force. Parallel to this negative vision, however, a regenerative force coexists within the poem which mitigates the negative indifference of the wind. Without being diverted from its destructive course, the wind pushes beyond physical disintegration, beyond chaos, beyond nothingness, to initiate a new creative cycle of existence, within which, ironically, the same demolishing wind becomes a generative force:

> The wind picks up the breath of my armpits
> Like dust, swirls it
> Miles away
> And drops it
> On the ear of a rabid dog.
> And I take on another life.
> ("*Wind*")

At this point it becomes evident that the ambiguity between the contradictory functions of the wind is far more profound than a simple rhetorical conceit and that, on the contrary, it constitutes the axis upon which the poem itself hinges since it establishes a dramatic tension between the disintegrative and regenerative forces operant within the poem.

The importance of this device of ambiguity in Soto's poetry becomes apparent in the consistency with which it is used to create precisely this impression of dramatic tension within the apocalyptic framework so characteristic of his artistic expression. Repeatedly one encounters similar images of disintegration and death mitigated by an ironically positive twist:

> The pores of my throat and elbows
> Have taken in a seed of dirt of their own.
> ("Field," *ESJ*)

> ... Angela beaten and naked in the vineyard
> Her white legs glowing.
> ("Telephoning God," *ESJ*)

> And a sewer line tied off
> Like an umbilical cord
> ("Braly Street," *ESJ*)

> Roots cradling the skull's smile
> ("Blanco," *TS*)

> A harmonica grinning with rust
> ("Song for the Pockets," *TS*)

Although these rhetorical ambiguities reflect the ironic vision so characteristic of this poet, Soto achieves his highest artistic brilliance and aesthetic subtlety in those poems, of which "Wind" is an excellent example, in which ambiguity becomes an expansive force not only by multiplying metaphorical and linguistic levels of meaning, but also by dilating the philosophical and dramatic dimensions of the fundamental theme of human existence. Such existence is revealed in Soto's poetry as a long and painful *via crucis*, a spiritual pilgrimage into a past peopled by spectres of privation, loneliness and death. Nevertheless, subtly but unequivocally, Soto manages to counterbalance this inhospitable existence by incorporating ambiguities that not only reduce the power of death to subjugate man definitively, but also substantially reduce the terror and finality of annihilation by implying a capacity in man to survive and overcome the limitations of his destiny.

This creative ability to dislocate, divert, counteract or even invert the significance of one poetic level with that of another, less obvious, though perhaps more representative of the philosophical vision implicit in the poem, is especially apparent in poems which examine different facets of death, such as "The Starlings" (*TS*), "The Wound" (*TS*), "The Morning They

Shot Tony Lopez" (*ESJ*) and "Avocado Lake" (*ESJ*). This latter poem is a notable example of the artistic control Soto exercises over the different levels of a poem through judicious use of ambiguity.

It is interesting to note that although the Christian backdrop is not conspicuously negated in Soto's poetry, it does not occupy a prominent place in his philosophical vision. Therefore, when the poet speaks of death, he usually does so in worldly, physical terms related to individual existences that have been truncated or worn down by indifferent forces. His narrative control and lack of sentimentality in treating this subject confer on this narrator a rather cold, omniscient perspective. The emotional involvement of the poet himself, which gives Soto's poems their human depth and warmth, finds expression only indirectly on the metaphorical level in the ambiguities the poet introduces to offset the cold objectivity of the narrator.

In "Avocado Lake," for example, this counterbalance between the narrative or literal and the metaphorical levels creates a significant dramatic tension between the action of death, that irreversible fact of a man drowned in the lake, and the reaction of the narrator, who recreates the life of the dead friend and conceptualizes his death from another perspective. On the narrative level, death undoubtedly has the upper hand, since the body floats under the water before being removed and subjected to the useless attempts at artificial revival.

On the metaphorical level, however, the scene is subtly slanted towards another reality where the power of death is subverted. Here the rigidity of the dead friend is softened, his "body moves under the dark lake," his hands "Are those of a child reaching for his mother." The very power of death is diminished by images of revival and reawakening: "The grey film peeled like tape from the eyes," and "The curled finger rubbed and kissed." The following day, at dawn, life is unequivocally reaffirmed in the presence of a young girl who plays by the same shore, skimming "pebbles across the lake, / Over what remains of him—"

The significance of this passage is that death has not been able to take everything; something of the man has remained to reintegrate itself into the elements, to initiate another cycle of existence in the physical world: "His phlegm drifts beneath the surface, / As his life did." This is another version of the dust swirled away by the wind and dropped "On the ear of a rabid dog... to take on another life" (*ESJ*). In this latter example, however, the combination of dry wind and human heat translates into the choleric humour of the mad dog. In the case of the drowned man, his introduction into the cold humidity of the lake is no less than an extension of his own phlegmatic, sluggish, existence. Rudderless and drifting with the currents during his lifetime, the drowned man finds within the lake an existence entirely compatible with his vital essences. By suggesting this conclusion, the narrator achieves, through an astute handling of dialectic ambiguity, a reconciliation with the reality of death without sacrificing the philosophical ideal of a continued or regenerated existence.

Undoubtedly, such linguistic and metaphorical subtleties do not occur fortuitously but only as the deliberate result of a series of creative efforts and impulses. Without going into the genesis of the creative process, we can nevertheless conclude that when a poet like Gary Soto exhibits such clear control over the organic nuances of a central ambiguity in his work, he demonstrates an advanced degree of creative development and a deliberate, intelligent attempt to refine the quality of his art.

Source: Patricia de la Fuentes, "Ambiguity in the Poetry of Gary Soto," in *Revista Chicano-Riqueña*, Vol. 11, No. 2, Summer 1983, pp. 34–39.

SOURCES

Diner, Hasia, "Immigration and U.S. History," in *America.gov*, http://www.america.gov/st/peopleplace-english/2008/February/20080307112004ebyessedo0.171 6272.html (accessed September 23, 2010).

Echevarria, Roberto González, Review of *Baseball in April and Other Stories*, in *New York Times Book Review*, May 20, 1990, p. 45.

"Gary Soto," in *Booklist*, October 1, 1993, p. 335.

"Gary Soto," in *Encyclopedia of World Biography*, http://www.notablebiographies.com/news/Sh-Z/Soto-Gary.html (accessed September 23, 2010).

Hayes, Janice C., Review of *Baseball in April and Other Stories*, in *School Library Journal*, June 1990, p. 126.

Nilsen, Alleen Pace, and Ken Donelson, Review of *Baseball in April and Other Stories*, in *English Journal*, December 1991, p. 86.

Passell, Jeffrey, "Recent Trends in Immigration," in *Pew Hispanic Center*, http://migration.ucdavis.edu/cf/files/2009-may/Passel.pdf (accessed September 23, 2010).

Roback, Diane, Review of *Baseball in April and Other Stories*, in *Publishers Weekly*, March 30, 1990.

Rodríguez, David, *Latino National Political Coalitions: Struggles and Challenges*, Taylor & Francis, 2002.

Soto, Gary, "Broken Chain," in *Baseball in April and Other Stories*, Houghton Mifflin Harcourt, 2000, pp. 1–12.

FURTHER READING

Augenbraum, Harold, and Ilan Stavans, *Growing Up Latino: Memoirs and Stories*, Houghton Mifflin, 1993.
This collection of stories and memoirs deals widely with Hispanic culture and experience. It includes classic and contemporary writing that articulates the joys and struggles of Hispanic life in a variety of settings.

———, and Margarite Fernández Olmos, *The Latino Reader: An American Literary Tradition from 1542 to the Present*, Houghton Mifflin Harcourt, 1997.
This anthology presents a complete history of the Latino American literary tradition, from the mid-sixteenth century to the present day. It includes history, memoirs, letters, essays, fiction, poetry, and drama. Some of the selections are from rare and little-known texts translated into English for the first time.

"California Cultures: Hispanic Americans," in *Calisphere*, 2010, http://www.calisphere.universityofcalifornia.edu/calcultures/ethnic_groups/ethnic3.html (accessed September 14, 2010).
This Web site is a comprehensive look at the lives and culture of Hispanic Americans living in California. Links take the reader to a wide variety of topics such as "Cultural Traditions and the People," "Everyday Life," and "Politics, Culture, and Art."

Kanellos, Nicolás, *Short Fiction by Hispanic Writers of the United States*, Arte Publico Press, 1993.
This volume is a collection of short stories by many celebrated Cuban American, Mexican American, Puerto Rican, and other Hispanic authors of the United States and is sometimes used as a textbook in high-school English classes. The volume contains introductory essays that place each of the works in its historical and social context.

SUGGESTED SEARCH TERMS

Gary Soto

Soto AND Hispanic fiction

Soto AND bildungsroman

Broken Chain

Baseball in April

coming of age fiction

Hispanic fiction

Latino fiction

Chicano fiction

San Joaquin Valley

Hispanic immigration

Soto AND Broken Chain

The Californian's Tale

MARK TWAIN

1893

Mark Twain is commonly regarded as the greatest American writer. Herman Melville might have written more profound works, but Twain has the advantage of being more thoroughly, more archetypically American in his character. Twain's stories often take place in colorful local American settings with the presentation of accurately, even lovingly, observed dialectical speech. "The Californian's Tale" is not among Twain's better-known stories, though it originates in the gold fields of California where Twain worked as a reporter during the Civil War, the same setting as "The Celebrated Jumping Frog of Calaveras County" (1865), the story that launched Twain to national prominence as a writer. "The Californian's Tale," however, remained a brief sketch in Twain's notebook from that time until 1892. It indulges in a sentimentality of the kind Twain so often satirizes in his other works. Recently the story has become a centerpiece in the reevaluation of Twain's attitudes about race.

"The Californian's Tale" was first published in 1893 in *The First Book of the Author's Club: Liber Scriptorum*, an experimental volume that might have become the first work in a subscription series (one of many money-making schemes Twain attempted at this time) if it had proved more successful. The story is better known from its republication in Twain's 1906 anthology *The $30,000 Bequest and Other Stories*.

Mark Twain (© *Pictorial Press Ltd.* | *Alamy*)

AUTHOR BIOGRAPHY

Samuel Langhorne Clemens (who wrote as Mark Twain) was born on November 30, 1835, in Florida, Missouri. He grew up in Hannibal, Missouri, on the Mississippi River, where his father was a judge. After the death of his father when Twain was eleven years old, he worked a variety of jobs, including typesetting, and wrote for the newspaper in Hannibal, which was edited by his brother, Orion Clemens. Twain educated himself during this period of his life by reading in public lending libraries. Twain's first great ambition in life was to work as a steamboat pilot on the Mississippi. He achieved this goal and later found inspiration from it for his pen name, Mark Twain. A crewman on a riverboat would measure the river's depth with a rope marked in fathoms (lengths of six feet) and call back the information to the pilot. Mark Twain meant two fathoms, the depth necessary for navigation.

Twain's career as a pilot was cut short in 1861 when the Civil War curtailed commercial navigation on the Mississippi. Perhaps because of an early manifestation of a pacifism that became pronounced later in Twain's life, he went with his brother Orion to the Nevada territory, where he eventually tried and failed to make a career as a miner. This period of his life is the subject of his semiautobiographical novel *Roughing It* (1872), and provided material for his so-called California stories, including "The Celebrated Jumping Frog of Calaveras County" and "The Californian's Tale." Twain was working as a journalist in San Francisco in 1865 when the former story made him a national success. For the rest of his life, Twain made his living writing and lecturing. In 1884 he published *The Adventures of Huckleberry Finn*, acknowledged as one of the greatest American novels. It is perhaps the most effective satire against racism ever written.

Twain enjoyed unprecedented success as a writer and proved as popular in England as in America. After extensive travels through the Pacific and Europe, Twain settled in Connecticut and married in 1870. His humorous style, biting satire and skepticism, and above all, his ear for the American language, helped to create the very structure of modern American literature. He used his celebrity to champion the progressive causes of women's suffrage, racial equality, and pacifism, and to criticize imperialism.

Twain valued inventiveness as a cornerstone of the American character and reveled in living in an age of scientific advancement. He became a close friend of Nikola Tesla, the greatest inventor of his age. Twain obtained many patents for inventions of his own, but none ever proved profitable. He invested much of his large income in a newly invented typesetting machine that eventually proved unworkable, leaving him bankrupt in 1894. At a time when he might have been peacefully retired, in the 1890s Twain had to work more furiously than ever before, writing and lecturing, first to prop up his faltering business scheme, then to pay his creditors. "The Californian's Tale" belongs to this flurry of activity. After the first decade of the twentieth century saw the death of his wife, Olivia, and two of his daughters, Twain mused wistfully that the return of Halley's Comet, which had passed through the sky at his birth, would see him leave this life, and indeed he died of a heart attack in Redding, Connecticut, on April 21, 1910, the day after the comet brushed close to the earth.

PLOT SUMMARY

An unnamed narrator begins "The Californian's Tale" with a description of himself as a prospector thirty-five years before. He then turns to a description of the land he was working. The story takes place in the valley of the Stanislaus River, which rises in the Sierra Nevada mountains on the border between Nevada and California and flows into the San Joaquin River in the central valley of California. Still high in the mountains, the narrator says of the locale: "It was a lovely region, woodsy balmy, delicious." The area is now deserted, but it had once been thick with miners. This would have been in 1849 when large numbers of prospectors and miners first came to California during the gold rush. They stayed only as long as there was abundant gold to be found on the surface, and by the time of the story, the area is completely deserted. Some areas where there were once towns have completely returned to a state of nature, and the narrator knows they existed only from his memory of them, while others are overgrown ruins. The many homes that were simply abandoned (since they could not be sold) are signs that their inhabitants were "defeated and disappointed families." This, combined with the lyric description of the mountain landscape, evokes a rather sad, idyllic mood. The last inhabitants of the country are also the first, the original miners, or those few of them who actually struck it rich but then lost their fortunes (perhaps through claim-jumping, gambling, or some other human folly), and remained because they were ashamed to go back to civilization where they would have to admit not their bad luck but their failure. They were men "grizzled and old at forty, whose secret thoughts were made all of regrets and longings."

As he wanders through this "lonesome land" the narrator is pleased to finally meet another human being, a man about forty-five years old who is living in one of the few cottages built in the place's heyday that had not been abandoned to become overgrown. In fact, it was kept in the best order and even had a garden. His name is later revealed to be Henry. The narrator is invited in and is even asked to stay, since in this nearly uninhabited region everyone depends on and extends hospitality. He had previously stayed in many of the old miners' shacks and is happy to stay in the cozy cottage. The house is well kept and well provisioned and is even decorated, with "war pictures from the Eastern illustrated papers tacked to the walls."

The narrator admires the careful decoration of the home of his host and sees in it "the score of little unclassifiable tricks and touches that a woman's hand distributes about a home." Indeed, his host is eager to tell him that all of the decorations are the result of his wife's work. He goes through a strange ritual of making minor adjustments to a piece of fabric and quickly says he can do that only because he has seen his wife fix it so often. He has a whole philosophy to offer on the topic. Only women, he says, know how to arrange decorative details. Men can learn how to do so by rote, as he did from watching his wife, but can never understand the science of it. This is a build-up that intensifies the surprise to come at the end of the story, but it is also starts to develop the maniacal character of Henry's veneration of his wife.

The story starts on a Wednesday, and the narrator expects to leave the next day. But Henry leads the narrator, via a little game, to the discovery of a daguerreotype (early photograph) of his wife. The woman in the picture is indeed beautiful and quite young. Henry tells the narrator that his wife is nineteen years old and that the picture was taken on their wedding day. Even though Henry is about forty-five, the difference in ages between him and his wife would have been less odd in the nineteenth century, even if things were as they so far seem. Henry reveals to the narrator that his wife is away visiting her relatives for two weeks and ought to back late Saturday night. She would be disappointed not to meet a man as obviously cultivated as the narrator. When the narrator is reluctant to impose on Henry's hospitality for so long, his host fetches his wife's photograph and challenges him to refuse the invitation of her face. The narrator can't bring himself to do that and so agrees to stay.

On Thursday evening, Tom, one of the stranded miners who lives nearby, comes to visit. He asks if there is any news about Henry's wife. Henry admits that he has recently had a letter, which he reads, with the exception of some lines that pertain only to himself. He reads the letter and the narrator describes it as beautifully written, but does not actually report to the reader any of the text of it. It ends however, with messages of affection for Tom, Joe, Charley, and other neighbors. Reading letters aloud was a quite common practice in the nineteenth century, since they were the only possible form of communication over a distance. Compare it to the modern practice of forwarding e-mails or perhaps passing a phone around a group of brothers and sisters so they can all have a turn talking to their grandmother. The letter is read aloud, rather than passed around, not only to preserve Henry's privacy, but also because literacy was comparatively rare.

Tom cries when he hears the letter, which is so out of place that Henry comments on it. Tom responds somewhat feebly that it is because he is getting old, and then seems confused over the date she is supposed to come back. Of course he is merely humoring Henry and playing along with anything he suggests. He cries over the depths of the tragedy the narrator as yet knows nothing about.

On Friday the same scene is played out, but with another miner named Joe. When he hears the letter read, he cannot help but cry out, "Lord, we miss her so!"—a completely inappropriate response to the supposed circumstances and one that also betrays or foreshadows the truth.

On Saturday both the narrator and Henry seem to become increasingly anxious throughout the day, although Henry's wife is not expected to arrive until nine o'clock that night. They bicker, and Henry cowers before his guest. As evening approaches, Charley, the third miner, arrives and hears the ritual reading of the letter. He makes a special point of reassuring Henry rather too forcefully that nothing could possibly have happened to his wife, despite the fact that as far as appearances go, there is no reason to think that anything had happened to her. Once the other two miners arrive, all three join in with Henry's house-decorating mania, adorning the house with cut flowers. Each one has brought an instrument and, as nine o'clock approaches, they begin to play, anticipating the arrival of everyone else in the vicinity for a regular party to celebrate Henry's wife's return. But, of course, no one else lives in the district any more. They are recalling the ghosts of nineteen years ago when she had been expected to return, and there had been a party, but the tragic news came in her place. This goes on, with a considerable amount of drinking until the miners evidently give Henry a sleeping potion (they have to warn the narrator against taking that glass). As he passes out, they tell him that the hoof beats he hears are Jimmy Parrish coming to say that Henry's wife's horse has gone lame but that she will be back soon.

After Henry has passed out, Joe tells the narrator that nineteen years ago, under the circumstances they have tried to recreate that night, Henry's wife was abducted by Indians within five miles of home. Henry mentally collapsed. Since then he has "lost his mind" and rebuilt his

existence around denying the truth of what happened. This ritual is performed once a year on the anniversary of the abduction. The rest of the time Henry imagines his wife is living with him and only recalls her trip away from him as the date nears. Nineteen years ago there was a party with twenty-seven men and many women as well, but now there are only the three of them left.

CHARACTERS

Charley

Charley is one of the three miners who, out of pity for Henry, play along with his delusion. He makes an even greater show of play-acting his part than the others do, fervently reassuring Henry that nothing could have happened to his wife.

Henry

Although the narrator has more lines than Henry and in many ways looms larger, Henry is the most important character in the story, since it is wholly about his peculiarities and ultimately about his unendurable loss. While the point is debatable (the ambiguity supplies part of its interest), it is most likely that Henry is the Californian of the story's title. While the narrator is the Californian who tells the tale, Henry is the Californian it is about. He is introduced into the story when the narrator happens to walk by his house and is invited in to be his guest and then to stay until Henry's wife returns, when there will a party attended by all the locals. Henry begins to talk at length about his wife as though she is still alive. In particular he rearranges every little detail of the house's decoration—redistributing the folds of draped fabric hanging over picture frames, for instance. He claims he has learned precisely how to imitate his wife in every detail of such arrangements, even if he could never understand how to make them on his own. These precise imitations have almost the character of a religious ritual, in the same way that the Eucharist is celebrated in remembrance of the Last Supper, but at the same time they are a neurotic displacement of his grief. It is doing these little things that *she* did that lets him push away from his conscious mind the fact of her loss. He acts so that he does not have to think. The narrator picks up the almost religious quality of his host's mania when he thinks of using the towels that are too perfectly arranged and too perfectly white as a kind of "profanation." He senses, without quite realizing it consciously, that he is in a shrine.

As is revealed by the end of the story, Henry's wife was abducted many years ago by Indians, and everything that happens through the story is an elaborate ritual that allows Henry to deny the truth to himself. The three neighboring miners play along with him out of pity. The truth is revealed only at the end of the story; the reader can then understand many earlier events of the narrative in a different light as foreshadowing that conclusion. One effort to foreshadow Henry's breakdown involves the photograph of his wife taken on their wedding day (evidently the only one he has of her). At one point, when the narrator is reluctant to stay until she returns, Henry shows the picture to him and challenges him, "There now, tell her to her face you could have stayed to see her, and you wouldn't." This is somewhat odd, even knowing only what has been revealed so far, but in the full context of the story it seems that Twain is trying here to define Henry's madness. Once the end is reached, it will seem clear to the reader that a symptom of Henry's madness is an inability to tell his wife and her photograph apart at some level, that he is forced to accept this image as the reality. From the point of view of the plot, it is details like this that will make the ending so satisfying. The reader will recall all of these details and conclude for himself that Henry is insane. In this way the reader is being shown the plot device far more effectively than it could be bluntly told.

Twain provides some insight into Henry's interior condition when on the day of his wife's expected arrival he becomes increasingly agitated and says, "I know she's not due till about nine o'clock, and yet something seems to be trying to warn me that something's happened." In retrospect it clear that on some level Henry is aware of the truth and is actively ignoring or repressing it so that it does not overwhelm him. Henry's compulsive repetition of his wife's feminine touches around the house, his confusion about her identity with her photograph, his foreboding, and above all his denial that she is dead, all seem to conform to psychoanalytical ideas about repression: Henry denies the traumatic truth of the central fact of his life and the anxiety that the repression attempts to deny works itself out in neurotic symptoms of compulsive repetition, so that he reenacts the trauma again and

again in many different ways until he finally he succumbs to a narcotic when the truth can no longer be kept at bay. Of course, Sigmund Freud's psychological work was all in the future in 1892 and Twain could have had no inkling of it. Perhaps this is an instance of what Freud meant by his claim that literary artists had often anticipated him. Above all, it would seem at first that the narrator meant his description of the inhabitants of the Stanislaus valley as men, "whose secret thoughts were made all of regrets and longings," to apply to the ruined miners, but by the end it seems that Twain more clearly meant it to apply to Henry himself.

Henry's Wife

Henry's wife does not appear in the story, though she lies at its heart. She was abducted by Indians many years ago, within six months of her marriage. One of the miners who knew her speculates that she is "[dead] or worse." She is never named but is referred to as *she* or *her*. It is as though her name is too sacred to speak aloud. The narrator describes her photograph, taken on her wedding day, as beautiful. Everything else the reader learns of her is mediated through Henry's obsessive memorialization of her and is not likely to come very close to the reality of her character. But he presents her as incredibly meticulous in the arrangements of the house's ornaments, even living as they were on the frontier. This is on the one hand a stereotype applied to women of the period, but on the other hand, it seems far more characteristic of Henry's veneration of her memory. Similarly, the most obvious way the reader might learn about her character is from her letter that is read by Henry. But not a single word of it is directly quoted. It is as if she is now completely irrelevant because it is only her memory that is kept alive in Henry's madness. The other thing Henry says about her is that she is interested in talking to educated people and had accumulated vast knowledge on her own through reading. Here, perhaps, is a reflection of Twain's own self-education.

Joe

Joe is another of the miners who have known Henry since before the loss of his wife and who come to visit him every year to help him with the reenactment of the tragedy that allows him to deny the terrible truth. It is clear that his affection for Henry and his wife is genuine and he is moved to help his friend as best he can out of pity, however bizarre a form that pity must take. He is the one who tells the narrator the truth about what happened after Henry passes out.

Narrator

"The Californian's Tale" is told by a first-person narrator who is never named in the context of the story. Unlike many of Twain's most famous characters, he speaks in perfectly standard English. While this might seem unusual compared to a stereotypical expectation that a prospector would be uneducated, it must be remembered that Twain spent several years as a prospector himself and that, in 1882, prospectors of precisely the same type as the narrator were eager to hear the aestheticist poet Oscar Wilde give a lecture in Leadville, Colorado, during his tour of the United States. While "The Californian's Tale" relies in many respects on Twain's experience as a prospector, the narrator cannot, as is so often the case in Twain's writing, be taken as a fictionalized version of the author himself. He says that the events he described happened thirty-five years ago (circa 1857), whereas Twain's own prospecting days began at most thirty years before the time when the story was written. So the narrator is instead meant to be an old hand of the kind Twain encountered in the mining camps of Nevada and California. But the narrator nevertheless has many points of similarity to Twain. Henry recognizes the narrator as being among the kind of people his wife likes to meet: "people who know things, and can talk— people like you." This must have been a reaction Twain often heard himself in the mining camps he frequented in the early 1860s, though we are in fact never shown any evidence of the narrator's particular cultivation. As the story progresses, the narrator becomes more and more passive and an instrument for telling Henry's story, so his character is not much further developed.

Tom

Tom is the first of the local miners to visit Henry, as early as Thursday evening before the Saturday night reception. Although the narrator eventually dwells on how beloved Henry's wife is among the locals, and how much they look forward to her return, Twain describes him as "clothed in grave and sober speech." In other words, he not acting like someone expecting a celebration, but like someone who is mourning.

This is a foreshadowing of the truth that will be revealed at the end. Tom's weeping when he hears the ritual rereading of the letter that he must have memorized by now, as well as his participation in the whole charade that he considers comforting to Henry, speaks of the deep affection he must have had for the couple in happier times.

THEMES

Sentimentality

Sentiment is genuine feeling. The sentimental is feeling carried to excess. Sentimental literature often exaggerates the emotional intensity of characters and passages to evoke emotions in its readers. To a subtle reader, such exaggeration rings false and becomes ridiculous. There would be nothing humorous in crying over one's dead wife, but when Henry and all of the miners cry over Henry's dead wife, a figure that is presented more as an angel than a woman, it starts to verge on comedy. When they engage in almost fetishistic flower arranging in honor of her memory, the narrative veers towards the absurd. These are exactly the kinds of exaggerated details that Twain, as a rule, delights in satirizing when they are used by other writers. For instance, he satirizes tear-jerker scenes of excessive or inappropriate grief in *The Adventures of Huckleberry Finn* through the death of a girl who is eulogized by rereading the good poetry that she wrote based on obituaries she read in the newspapers:

> Despised love struck not with woe
> That head of curly knots,
> Nor stomach troubles laid him low,
> Young Stephen Dowling Bots.

But in "The Californian's Tale," the excessive sentimentality is presented in its own terms, just as in the authors Twain usually mocked. Twain was a realist who used irony to take the wind out of the sails of everything false and pretentious, particularly if the false and pretentious were also popular. But in the early 1890s Twain, obsessed with worries over his economic plight and the health of his own family members, called a truce in his realist war on sentimentality and wrote a number of stories that indulged in rather than lampooned popular sentimental excesses, including "The Californian's Tale."

TOPICS FOR FURTHER STUDY

- Many resources exist online for the study of Native American history and culture, for example, the bibliographies maintained by the Smithsonian Institution or the electronic library of primary and secondary sources maintained by the University of Washington. Use these and other online and print resources to learn about Native American culture and then write a short story in which the main character is a Native American woman whose husband was killed many years before by American soldiers.

- Rewrite one scene from "The Californian's Tale" in an ironic voice, treating it in the same manner in which Twain usually treated sentimental literature.

- During his time spent as a journalist in the West, Twain could easily have written the human interest story on which "The Californian's Tale" is based. How would the journalistic approach differ from that of the short story? Many libraries and schools have online access to the *San Francisco Chronicle* historical database, beginning in 1865. If

your institution can give you access, read a few relevant articles to pick up the writing style, and then write an article based on the events that inspired Twain.

- Laura Ingalls Wilder's *Little House on the Prairie* books are beloved young-adult classics. Write a short story in which one the characters from those novels is kidnapped by Indians.

- The Library of Congress maintains a large collection of scans of daguerreotypes online. After researching the style of such images, recreate the portrait of Henry's wife in a photograph, drawing, or painting.

- Bret Harte was a friend of Twain's and a fellow reporter on various San Francisco papers in the 1850s and 1860s. He also became a prolific novelist, setting much of his work in Gold Rush–era California, such as his 1860 novel *The Work of Red Mountain*. Read some of Harte's fiction, as well as more of Twain's California stories, and write a paper comparing the two authors.

Femininity

When the first nugget that set off the California Gold Rush was found, no one in the logging camp around Sutter's Mill knew for sure if it was gold or not, so Elizabeth Wimmer, the camp cook, let it boil in a pot of lye overnight. When it emerged unscathed, none doubted it was gold. Although most of the prospectors who would come to California were men, a woman stood at the heart of the first discovery of the gold, and many women flooded into the state with the gold rush. Some were wives and daughters of the new prospectors, but others came for quite other purposes. Most of the men came from the northern United States, which helped to make the position of women who did not come as wives and mothers difficult, as Nancy J. Taniguchi argues in her article in the Summer 2000 issue of *California History*:

Most had been reared with the typical American conventions of the day by good, God-fearing mothers. Their slice of society was preoccupied with the notion of the "separate spheres" in which men went out and swung the ax, killed Indians, engaged in sordid politics, pursued grasping commerce, and gambled for gain, while women, pure vessels of societal morality, stayed home to nurture havens for embattled males when they should be able to return.

Women who fell outside this nurturing role in the home were considered "bad." This applied not only to prostitutes, of which there were many working in the gold fields, but to women who wished to set up as entrepreneurs in other fields of work, although the unsettled conditions of the frontier allowed a space for such women to flourish briefly. The idea of women prospecting

The cottage was cared for with a garden of flowers in front. *(great_photos / Shutterstock.com)*

and mining for themselves was unthinkable and did not materialize. Women who fit themselves into the role of creating an otherworldly beauty and virtue within the household, however, were praised without limit. The type was celebrated by Eliza Farnham in *California, In-doors and Out*, a call for women of the desired type to come to California to help build up the frontier:

> There is no inviolate fireside in California that is not an altar; no honorable woman but is a missionary of virtue, morality, happiness, and peace, to a circle of careworn, troubled, and often, alas, demoralized men.

Henry's wife in "The Californian's Tale" was in every sense the realization of this ideal. That is, in every sense save for being real. By the time the story takes place, nineteen years after her death, she exists as a figment of the miners' imaginations as she does in that of her husband, erected as an ideal saint in contact only with this idealized version of reality. Her memory has been reshaped to fit this ideal, regardless of what she may actually have been like in life.

STYLE

Pseudo-Memoir

Twain's writing is exceptionally hard to characterize with respect to genre. Many of his works, for example, *A Connecticut Yankee in King Arthur's Court*, are clearly novels. But other works, like *Innocents Abroad*, are almost impossible to classify. A large body of his work consists of travel narrative, in which he was ostensibly reporting on his journeys for one or another American newspaper, and the narratives seem to have some relationship to the actual journeys, but much of the material he presents consists of literary satires and moral fables. It is often difficult to disentangle a report that might be called the truth from fiction. Similarly, works he labeled autobiographical contain much that is obviously fiction. Twain was clearly not concerned about the distinction, and it is difficult for his readers to disagree. "The Californian's Tale" presents itself as a memoir of a narrator who never gives his name. Is it Twain? He certainly had experiences similar to those described. Yet it is impossible to reconcile the details of the narrative with Twain's life. On the other hand, the story is possibly based on a real event Twain recorded in his journal in February 1865: "Baden, crazy, asking after his wife who had been dead 13 years—first knowledge of his being deranged." But this is an experience he had in the mining camps of a later gold rush in Nevada. Like many short stories and novels, "The Californian's Tale" presents itself as a memoir in order to heighten the reader's sense of the realism of the events. In this case that seems to be all that Twain is doing. Many works of fiction are reinterpretations of real events or memories.

Lyricism

Twain often makes fun of the florid language that dominated the gothic romances that were the most popular literature of his day. But in "The Californian's Tale," he shows his ear for a beautiful lyric style that is elevated through its simplicity, whose elegance the gothic writers never approached. A sentence like

> In the country neighborhood thereabouts, along the dusty roads, one found at intervals the prettiest little cottage homes, snug and cosey, and so cobwebbed with vines snowed thick with roses that the doors and windows were wholly hidden from sight—sign that these were deserted homes, forsaken years ago by defeated and disappointed families who could neither sell them nor give them away.

evokes a melancholy beauty worthy of Greek literature. The landscape of ruins is described as beautiful. This sets an entirely different tone for the story than if Twain had chosen to describe the same landscape as squalid and ugly. Characterizing the landscape in this way conditions the reader's reaction to the characters who live in it and disposes the reader to be sympathetic to characters who might otherwise seem petty and unlikable.

HISTORICAL CONTEXT

The California Gold Rush

On January 24, 1848, James Marshall, a workman at John Sutter's saw mill on the American River in the Sierra Nevada Mountains of California discovered a large gold nugget. A huge store of surface gold was discovered, and the news rapidly spread around the world, carried by new communications miracles such as the telegraph, the steamship, and the daily newspaper. As a result, people flocked from all over the world to prospect for gold; over 300,000 people came within a few years. They became known as Argonauts, after the Greek heroes who sought the Golden Fleece, or Forty-niners after the year most arrived in the gold fields. There had never been a mass migration like this in history, of men (and only very few women) moving into a territory that was lawless (California had just been acquired from Mexico by the United States and was not even organized as a territory, so there was no controlling legal structure), for the purpose not of acquiring new land to live on, but of pursuing a fantasy of limitless wealth by "striking it rich" in the gold fields. The result was a chaotic jumble of greed, honor, and racism, and became the foundation of a new region—the West—of the United States. But all of this lies in the past of "The Californian's Tale." Twain's story takes place quite literally among the ruins, architectural as well as human, of the gold rush.

Racism

However much progressive Americans fought to change it, and however much it was responsible for the cataclysm of the Civil War, until the Emancipation Proclamation in 1863 and the postwar civil rights amendments, white supremacy was very much enshrined in the U.S. Constitution and in the laws of the United States. Feelings of racial superiority had much to do with the Mexican-American War of 1846–1848, which brought California into the United States, setting the stage for the gold rush. Indians who lived on the public land where the gold fields lay felt they had a right to go on living there as their ancestors had for decades or centuries. But white Californians, anxious to monopolize the new resource, simply brushed them aside. One of the first acts of the new California state legislature was to make it legally possible to enslave Indians (a situation unique among the states), and to begin a policy of concentrating Indians on reservations, with the result that the American Indian population of California dropped by three quarters within ten years of the gold rush. Large numbers of Chinese immigrants came to California because of the gold, but they were legally proscribed from enjoying the same rights as white prospectors. Many Chinese women were kept as prostitutes. Unlike the case of American Indian women, this was illegal, but nevertheless real. Twain himself witnessed racial violence carried out against the Chinese when he worked as a

COMPARE & CONTRAST

- **1850s:** The primary means of communication between friends and family members separated by distance is the exchange of letters, which might be shared or read aloud by the recipient to a larger group of interested parties.

  Today: Communication is generally carried out through e-mail, by telephone, or through social networks online, making it much easier for one person to directly communicate with all of the members of a group.

- **1850s:** Literacy is comparatively rare and any form of advanced education rarer.

- **Today:** Literacy is nearly universal (though the United States has the lowest literacy rate of any developed nation), and many Americans attend college.

- **1850s:** There is little or no effective treatment for mental illness, and few or no public health services are available for the mentally ill.

  Today: Mental health issues can be treated by a wide variety of modalities, and such services are widely available and often covered by medical insurance.

---

reporter in San Francisco. He saw a Chinese man stoned by a gang of white men while a police officer calmly looked on. His editor forbade him to write the story since any criticism of white racism against the Chinese would have had an adverse effect on newspaper sales. The idea of Indian abduction that Twain introduces in "The Californian's Tale" is a white racist fantasy of the kind Twain loved to skewer with his razor-sharp irony, but in this case he uncharacteristically presents it as a sentimental trope.

CRITICAL OVERVIEW

Twain's "The Californian's Tale" is unremarkable enough and received very little notice in contemporary reviews. Modern critics have been struck by its sentimentality. James D. Wilson argues in *A Reader's Guide to the Short Stories of Mark Twain* that the unwonted sentimentality of "The Californian's Tale" is conditioned by Twain's real-life relationship with his wife. The chronology cannot be definitely established, but she may have received a fatal medical diagnosis immediately prior to Twain's writing the story. Everett Emerson, in *The Authentic Mark Twain*, as well as in *Mark Twain: A Literary Life*, argues

rather that the sentimentality in "The Californian's Tale" and many other of Twain's works of the same period, is able to overcome Twain's marked preference for realism because the author was oppressed by age, financial concerns, fatigue, depression, and many other factors and simply found it easier to embrace the sentimentality his sardonic wit had always lampooned.

"The Californian's Tale" has also been used as evidence in the discussion of Twain's racial attitude toward Native Americans. For James C. McNutt, writing in the *American Indian Quarterly* in 978, the story is a signpost on the evolution of Twain's views on Indians from the conventional to the enlightened. But for Helen L. Harris in *American Literature*, "The Californian's Tale" is part of a portfolio of evidence convicting Twain of lifelong racism.

CRITICISM

Bradley Skeen

Skeen is a classics professor. In the following essay, he examines "The Californian's Tale" in the context of those critics who have used the story as evidence of Twain's attitudes toward race.

He always expected to make a rich strike but he never did. (Lee Torrens / Shutterstock.com)

The United States begins, historically, legally, and in every other vital sense, with the words, "We hold these truths to be self-evident, that all men are created equal," which stand at the head of the Declaration of Independence. But the man who wrote that, Thomas Jefferson, owned slaves, and the economy of at least half of the United States at that time was based on the exploitation of Americans of African descent as slaves. That dichotomy, between what was professed to be true, and what really was true has been the main fault line within America ever since. The nation was shaken to its foundations over the issue of race in the Civil War and the civil rights movement. Even after the election of the first African American President in 2008, some Americans refuse to admit that Barack Obama is a U.S. citizen. While America has consistently moved toward its original stated goal of a society in which differences like race are irrelevant to civic life, racism has always been, and still is, a great problem for America, limiting the country's true potential.

Mark Twain purposefully made himself a controversial figure, out of sheer contrarianism.

Twain had a sharp eye for hypocrisy and recognized it in American attitudes toward race. His greatest novel, *The Adventures of Huckleberry Finn*, is also one of the greatest indictments of racism ever written. The story, set before the Civil War, concerns a homeless teen-aged boy, Huck, who befriends the slave Nigger Jim and sets out to help him escape from slavery to the northern free states and then to Canada. The critical strategy that Twain follows is to have Huck believe that he ought to follow the existing white supremacist laws of the United States, while every inner impulse he has tells him that it is right to help his friend attain his natural human dignity as a free man. Ironically, Huck concludes that all of the better angels of his nature that tell him to serve the cause of freedom are evil because they want him to break the law. Huck is too immature to draw the obvious conclusion from this circumstance, but the reader cannot help but realize that, in fact, it is the laws limiting freedom that are evil. Twain could not have written the novel any other way, because no American publisher in the 1880s would have touched a novel that openly celebrated the

WHAT DO I READ NEXT?

- Delilah Beasley's *The Negro Trailblazers of California* (1919) collects historical material, including primary sources and photographs, and documents the African American experience in California in the gold-rush period, providing a different cultural perspective. The book is available in a digitized version at Google Books.

- The 2003 *Oxford Companion to Mark Twain*, edited by Greg Camfield, offers a variety of introductory essays on the study of Twain's work.

- Although Twain always wrote for an adult audience, *The Adventures of Tom Sawyer* (reissued in a facsimile edition by Oxford University Press in 1996 along with Twain's complete works), has always been a special favorite of young-adult readers.

- Jo Ann Levy's *They Saw the Elephant: Women in the California Gold Rush* (1990) gives an overview of women's experiences en route to and in early California.

- *The Destruction of California Indians*, written by Robert F. Heizer in 1974, deals with relations between the native population and the new settlers who came with the gold rush.

- Kevin Starr's 1973 *Americans and the California Dream: 1850–1915* discusses the place of California in the American imagination in the aftermath of the gold rush.

- *A Young Australian Pioneer: Henry Mundy*, a 2004 publication by Les Hughes, is a narrative account of one man's experience with the Ballarat Gold Rush in Australia.

- History books often recount the experience of Chinese immigrants building the transcontinental railroad, but in fact, many Chinese immigrated to America because of the gold strike in California. Christopher Corbett's *The Poker Bride: The First Chinese in the Wild West* (2010) is a novel that wraps the story around the history of the time period.

> TWAIN HAD A SHARP EYE FOR HYPOCRISY AND RECOGNIZED IT IN AMERICAN ATTITUDES TOWARD RACE."

equality in dignity between blacks and whites at a time when American culture was already producing and countenancing the Jim Crow segregation laws in a vain attempt to heal from the Civil War by ignoring the problem of racism. Constrained by the censorship of its day, *Huckleberry Finn* is one of the most frequently censored books today. Its opponents, entirely missing the point of the novel, mistakenly accuse the book of racism because it uses the word "nigger," as though any other word could have been used in the language of its time and place.

Despite Twain's obvious and pronounced opposition to racism, some scholars in the 1970s wished to indict Twain for racism against American Indians, using "The Californian's Tale" as their chief evidence. The more standard version of this view, Followed, for instance, by James McNutt in "Mark Twain and the American Indian," maintains that Twain's views evolved from an early embrace of commonly held racist views of Indians to a more benign paternalism in his old age. Helen L. Harris, in "Mark Twain's Response to the Native American," adopts a harsher view: "Mark Twain has been called the 'champion of the oppressed,' but when he wrote of the Native American he was unfailingly hostile." It seems possible that these evaluations of Twain were arrived at through a failure to understand his ironic tone. Harris, for instance, quotes a passage from *Innocents Abroad* to the effect that the "vile, uncomplaining impoliteness" of Indians made "a white man so nervous and uncomfortable and savage that he want[ed] to exterminate the whole tribe." For Harris, this reflects Twain's own views. But it also seems possible, since at that time white men were swiftly exterminating the Indian tribes, that Twain is commenting on that fact to suggest that that course of action is irrational. Isn't the point of the passage that it is the white men who are acting savagely, for they all hypocritically call Indians savages? Twain makes the same point a bit more plainly in his

Autobiography. He says that while Americans claim that the national motto is "In God We Trust," it is really "When the Anglo Saxon wants a thing *he just takes it.*" Twain leaves no doubt that he is criticizing white robberies of the freedoms of other races when he adds that the call to brotherhood *e pluribus unum* ought to be replaced with the humiliating orders given to an inferior: "Come, *step lively!*" Twain is mocking American imperialism and racism, not joining it.

The perceived problem with "The Californian's Tale" concerns its presentation of white stereotypes about Indians. The fate of Henry's wife, the character who is so pointedly missing from the story, is viewed as a racist slur by critics like McNutt and Harris. At the end of the story, the miners reveal to the narrator that Henry's wife is dead. When he asks in amazement for confirmation of the startling news, "Dead?" he is told "That or worse... [T]he Indians captured her within five miles of this place, and she's never been heard of since." There is no doubt that Twain is here evoking popular myths about Indians from white American culture. Every reader of "The Californian's Tale" knew that the "or worse" expressed the fear that Henry's wife had been raped. In melodrama and gothic novels rape was euphemistically called 'a fate worse than death.' A raped woman would be seen as morally unclean, however unjustly, and forced to live as a social outcast. The social body is secure enough in its own sense of rightness that it considers exclusion from itself to be worse than death. McNutt points out that the literature of the time was filled with lurid sexual fantasies projected onto Indians. He offers two popular books by Richard Irving Dodge, *The Plains of the Great West and Their Inhabitants* (1877) and *Our Wild Indians* (1883), as supplying the details that Twain left unspoken. Harris, with more bluntness and less evidentiary support, asserts of "The Californian's Tale," "Twain did not have to mention massacre or rape: the nation knew that Indians held a monopoly on these crimes." Many stories that purported to contain true accounts of abduction by Indians were in fact wholly or partially fictional. The market for such stories was very large and invited writers to fabricate, especially in an age when fact-checking was rare and difficult. But what are the realities behind these popular conceptions?

The myth of abduction is a very old one in the British Isles. From the Middle Ages there are many reports of women being abducted by faeries, as Thomas Keightley reports in *The Fairy Mythology* (an early compendium of fairy lore): "They are fond of carrying off women whom they make wives of." As with folk beliefs about witches, these traditions were carried to America and fitted into the new landscape by reimagining the abducting others as Indians. Today the same kind of stories are told about alien abduction. Whatever these stories are about—perhaps group definition or a desire for release through transgression, depending on who tells them— they follow a pattern that is disconnected from reality. This alone might make them subject to Twain's irony. And, as McNutt discusses at some length, Twain made an attempt to satirize tales of Indian abduction in the short-story draft "Huck and Tom among the Indians," in which Huck Finn and Tom Sawyer set out to rescue a woman kidnapped by Indians. The presence of Tom Sawyer in a Twain story almost always means that some romantic literary convention is being ridiculed. But Twain never finished the story, perhaps because he realized a satirical story about rape would be too awkward to approach successfully.

This is not to say that Americans of European descent, including women, were not kidnapped by Indians. As the frontier moved across America, small- and large-scale raiding by both sides made such abductions inevitable. But the lure of free land or even the chance of making a fortune as a miner invited white Americans to live on land Indians claimed as their own without much protection from American military forces. But the legitimate accounts of Indian abduction make it clear that the usual motive for such kidnapping was ransom; in that case the hostage would be released relatively unharmed in a few weeks or months. Certainly rapes did occur, but only in a minority of cases; it could not be automatically assumed as the fictional literature of the period would have it. In other cases, a woman might be taken by an Indian warrior to replace a dead wife, or even another dead relative such as a daughter or sister, who had been killed in a conflict with whites. In many Indian cultures that was a just transaction. Women might live voluntarily in such a situation and even refuse to return to white society when the chance came. Mary Jemison is an example of a white woman who was captured by the Seneca during the War of 1812 and adopted into the tribe to compensate for women killed by the Americans. She then

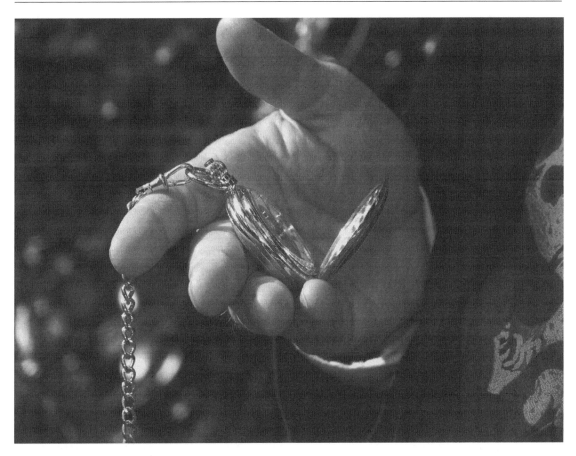

As the time grew closer, he checked his watch often. (Anita Patterson Peppers | Shutterstock.com)

voluntarily married a Seneca man, and took a second Indian husband when the first died. She dictated her story to a journalist, but made no effort to go back to her old life. Indeed, as the Seneca nation disintegrated under pressure from the United States, she made a new life for herself as a private landowner, disdaining the conventions of the white society that would surely have rejected her if she had tried to rejoin it. American women, after all, were beginning to struggle for their freedom within white society in the 1850s.

Far more frequently, however, Indian women were abducted and raped by whites. California during the 1850s was one of the few times and places in American history where Indian slavery was legal (not that it was not practiced illegally before the Civil War), and many Indian women in California were forced to work in slave brothels. Even Indian women who had married white men were on occasion kidnapped out of their homes by the U.S. Army and deported to reservations.

The hypocrisy, sensationalism, and cognitive dissonance surrounding the theme of Indian abduction provides ample scope for Twain's irony to dismantle. Does Twain satirically attack white violence against Indians in "The Californian's Tale" as he did so effectively elsewhere, and does he expose the evils of white mistreatment of Indians as he did white treatment of blacks? The answer must be no. There is no trace of ironic attack against the establishment in "The Californian's Tale." In fact, in the first description of the Stanislaus valley it seems that he is beginning to make an ironic point when he says it "had once been populous, long years before, but now the people had vanished." Surely he means the Indians who had been exterminated or driven out by the whites? But no, he means the miners who had come in 1849 and had long since departed. The Indians might never have existed, until they are called in from offstage at the end of the story to carry out their conventional crime of abduction and rape. But this does not mean that Twain is betraying his lifelong opposition to racism, which he denounced in many works before and after "The Californian's Tale." Rather it seems that for the same reasons—whatever they may have been—Twain surrendered in this story to popular sentimentality, he surrendered also to convention. His mastery of American dialectical speech also vanishes in this story where it could have added a great deal. Twain's realist barriers against sentimentality and convention were overwhelmed by moral fatigue and produced a work that would be simply popular.

Source: Bradley Skeen, Critical Essay on "The Californian's Tale," in *Short Stories for Students*, Gale, Cengage Learning, 2011.

Jennifer McKellar

In the following essay, McKellar examines a wide range of Twain's techniques of interruption, breaking them down into several categories.

When read as a book, as an entity that is a sustained, connected, and reasonably consistent unit of prose, Mark Twain's *Roughing It* presents its narrative—and the author himself identifies the book as "a personal narrative"—in a rather disorderly and rambling form. Throughout the text, Twain employs various sorts of interpolative techniques that interrupt the narrative to differing degrees and effects; his use of interruption is worth examination not only because it is so extensive but also because it shapes the style that is so characteristically his own.

As Lee Clark Mitchell, in his article "Verbally Roughing It: The West of Words," notes, "the structural incoherence of *Roughing It* has convinced most readers to leave it alone, except insofar as it anticipates aspects of Twain's later style" (68). The few critics who have considered the book worthy of sustained discussion in and of itself have generally remarked upon one or another of Twain's uses of interruption; indeed it would be difficult not to do so, considering the extent to which they pervade the text. The notice that has been given to the book's interruptions, however, has been contained and manipulated toward furthering particular readings of the text, rather than explored as a fundamental principle of the text. Mitchell argues that the book is primarily constructed upon an analysis, a landscape as it were, of words and how they are used, concluding that the West that Twain portrays is ultimately characterized by language rather than topography; while in the course of his argument,

> WHILE TWAIN DOES FREQUENTLY RELY ON DASHES AND PARENTHESES AS PRINCIPAL STRUCTURES OF INTERRUPTION, HE ALSO APPROPRIATES THE MOST FAMILIAR OF GRAMMATICAL STRUCTURES—THE SENTENCE OR THE PERIOD. IT IS PERHAPS HIS MOST STRIKING USE OF FORM BECAUSE IT IS SIMPLE AND YET EFFECTIVE."

Mitchell makes passing note of some of Twain's interruptions, he refers to them only insofar as they relate to Twain's manipulation of language into the subject of the novel and he does not perceive them to be connected to an overall structure of interpolation. Harold H. Kolb, Jr., in "Mark Twain and the Myth of the West," delineates four different attitudes toward the American West that "collectively, make up the myth of the West" (120), claiming that in *Roughing It* Twain continually assumes and then discards these various attitudes in order to stand "astride a complex mythology he helped to create" (120). Kolb observes that "the narrative thread of *Roughing It* is continually broken by references to events that puncture the place and time of the story" in order to diminish the exoticizing of the West (130). However, like Mitchell, who construes Twain's handling of language as a dismissal of "conventional narrative logic" (Mitchell 69), he does not suggest that Twain substitutes an alternative logic or structure; both simply presume that the novel adopts a "looser attitude" toward structure (Mitchell 70).

This paper will examine a wide range of Twain's techniques of interruption and will propose that these techniques constitute a pervasive formal structure to which the text consistently adheres, a structure that does not merely interfere with the construction of a narrative structure but rather supplants such a structure altogether. To depict the variety of areas to which Twain extends the principle of interruption, I will attempt to categorize his uses of it according to the following distinctions: the interpolative structuring of chapters; textual interruptions (items that interfere with the main text of the book); narrative interruptions (stories not directly related to the account of Twain's journey); factual interruptions (passages that [presumably] present "facts" or information, usually about the West); and syntactical interruptions (employment of established grammatical structures to interfere with the flow and meaning of clauses). Yet these categories often intersect—certain passages may be relevant to more than one category, others may demonstrate forms of interruption that do not fit neatly into any one category, passages in one category may have purposes similar to some in another category—all of which merely reinforces the suggestion that the principle of interruption functions as the central element of structure within the book.

1. THE INTERPOLATIVE STRUCTURING OF CHAPTERS

Roughing It is unquestionably episodic, wandering from one topic to another, interlacing stories, information, opinion, and moralizing. It does utilize a loose narrative structure (the story of Twain's adventures in the West), as Mitchell notes; what is curious about it, however, is that Twain does not use this narrative framework to tie the book neatly together. By choosing not to divide his experiences and miscellaneous comments into tidy chapters, he seems to revel in using the narrative as a point of departure for his commentary, rather than a border for purposes of containment.

At times, he sets up scenes and topics only to stray from them, such as in chapter 60, which begins with a long (more or less) narrative paragraph about the narrator's removal to a mining camp in Tuolumne but proceeds to dwell "at some length upon this matter of pocket mining"—not because it pertains to the narrative but simply "because it is a subject that is seldom referred to in print" (857). Another such drifting occurs in the very next chapter, where Twain introduces Dick Baker and recounts his story of his cat Tom Quartz—a chapter that would be a neatly contained unit, a story within a story, but for the final two paragraphs, the first of which presents the narrator musing to the reader about whether or not he should continue to relate his wanderings (a minor, perhaps tolerable, digression) and the second of which gives an extended, and rather dry, series of definitions of mining terms (a rather obtrusive detour that is notably not encapsulated

in a footnote). At other points, he introduces topics only to leave them hanging, lingering: chapter 11 unapologetically ends his account of the infamous desperado Slade with an abrupt call for investigation. Chapters such as these reveal Twain's construction of his narrative framework to be a contrivance, a mischievous hoax upon the reader: he develops it in the beginning chapters only to call attention to his later dismantling of it.

Still other chapters confirm this proposition, for Twain comments frequently upon his own processes of writing, denoting his awareness of structure and flaunting his disregard for a sustained narrative. A passage more than halfway through chapter 48, which hitherto has focused primarily on the topic of juries, unexpectedly announces, "My idea, when I began this chapter, was to say something about desperadoism"—and so the chapter immediately averts its focus. In chapter 58, Twain inserts a story that could easily have been its own chapter, his first experience of an earthquake (he even notes that he could have fleshed out his brief account), into a chapter cluttered with other random bits and pieces; furthermore, he makes no attempt to gently transition from the earthquake into his next subject but merely announces that he "will diverge from the subject." Similarly, in chapter 50, he embarks upon the story of Capt. Ned Blakely, another chapter with the potential to be an orderly installment; but again, Twain denies that potential, flaunting the fact that the story is a "digression" and that he "digress[es] constantly" throughout the book. Even the final chapter does not end with the termination of Twain's journey; a "MORAL" supplants the natural ending of this travelogue, a moral that has little to do with the book and nothing at all to do with the West in particular.

All of these instances suggest an adherence to abrupt change (as opposed to coherence or unity) as an aesthetic principle, a principle that Twain himself asserts when discussing criteria for beauty in landscape; accordingly, he substitutes interpolation for cohesion and narrative structure as the basis for his organizational scheme. The overall structure of *Roughing It* thus parallels that of Jim Blaine's story concerning his grandfather's ram: it wanders incessantly and is not a story at all really but simply a piling on of ruminations and musings, accompanied by a quality of thinking aloud (of thinking through and about the writing process) on the part of the storyteller.

2. TEXTUAL INTERRUPTIONS

Supplementing the book's structure is a handful of common features that Twain employs so as to further the disruption of the text. In many of his works, Twain utilized paratextual elements such as prefaces, appendices, footnotes, and illustrations, which, largely insignificant in themselves, constitute disturbances or interruptions not only due to their status as accompanying materials that modify the main text and shift the reader's attention away from it, but also in *Roughing It* owing to his particular treatment of them. In the preface, for example, Twain significantly identifies the text as a narrative, a classification that he deflates throughout the book. However, his more unusual work occurs in the other supplementary materials.

The original illustrations in *Roughing It* were an important feature of the book since it was first conceived and published as a subscription book, a "'coffee-table' book of the nineteenth century [that was] filled with illustrations" (David 1). As with any illustrations, they interact with the text in several ways. They offer commentary upon the text that may affect the reader's interpretation of it. For instance, a picture of a Chinese merchant carrying a long pole strung with mice accompanies chapter 54 of the book, in which Twain (via an excerpt from one of his newspaper articles) relates the story of his interaction with a Chinese merchant who offered him "small, neat sausages" which he refuses because he "suspected that each link contained the corpse of a mouse"; the "ethnic joke handled so subtly in print but with less discrimination in the picture" (David 3) caricatures the printed scene, exaggerating its effect. The illustrations also highlight the particular scenes that they depict, potentially disturbing the prominence that the text might give to or refuse certain scenes through length and vividness of description. These aspects of the illustrations were not within the author's control, as he was on a lecture tour at the time of the compilation of most of the illustrations (David 2). However, Twain did harness the potential of illustrations to interact with his text in a more robust sense. In three places, he incorporates (or anticipates, since the illustrations were added after the text was completed) the illustrations as subjects within the text: in chapter 44, the narrator comments that his revenge on Mr. Stewart "will be found in the accompanying portrait"; in chapter 54, the narrator refers the reader to a Chinese laundry bill that is illustrated "below"; and in chapter 70, a handwritten note and its various translations becomes an extended subject. (2) In these instances, the illustrations cease to be merely supplementary materials that the reader may choose to ignore but become necessary parts of the book that cause or demand the reader to pause. They very literally interrupt the process of reading in a rather pointed way.

In contrast to the illustrations, the three appendices to the book do not derive their primary significance from their status as interrupting agents. They stand out as curiosities not, as their status as appendants might suggest, because they diverge from the main text in terms of subject, genre, or general relevance, but because they seem continuous with it. In no way is it clear on what basis they were relegated to this secondary status; certainly, they do not directly connect to Twain's individual experience, but neither does much of the rest of the text. Indeed, if the author had allocated every section of *Roughing It* that was of such peripheral significance into appendices, there would be little left of the main text. Furthermore, Twain approaches the appendices in virtually the same way that he does his chapters, with excerpts from existing sources, with wry quips from the narrator (in discussing Brigham Young, he notes that "there was but one dignity higher which he could aspire to, and he reached out modestly and took that—he proclaimed himself a God!"), even with footnotes. Why he relegates the history of Mormonism and not that of the Sandwich Islands, or the story of Conrad Wiegand and not that of Slade (for he claims to have met both of them personally), to the position of appendix is an utter mystery.

The footnotes that Twain frequently attaches to the text in *Roughing It* seem to be every bit as unnecessary as the appendices. They tend to include two sorts of material, information and opinion or commentary from the narrator; the ones that offer commentary tend to be signed ("M. T."), while the informational ones are not. Yet he does not hesitate to liberally sprinkle both information and commentary into the body of the main text; the information and comments in the footnotes might just as easily have been inserted via dashes or parenthesis, devices which he freely uses. While in one sense, the footnotes (like the appendices) form another type of interruption within the text, their true significance lies in what they expose about the rest of the text. The coherence of the appendices and the footnotes with the rest of the book reveals the nature of the whole to consist largely of vaguely relevant details that are but flimsily attached to one another; the majority of the text might be properly described as auxiliary material. The footnotes and the appendices, then, accentuate the structure of the entire book as predominantly nonnarrative, as appendicular, as interpolative.

3. NARRATIVE INTERRUPTIONS

The digressions and wanderings strewn throughout the book constitute one of the more conspicuous aspects of interruption. Although the narrative of *Roughing It* centers upon Twain's adventures on the western frontier, he finds occasion, and not merely once, to enter into accounts of incidents that occurred during his travels around the Mediterranean. In the midst of a discussion on sage brush (which is itself a factual interruption), he diverts to telling a story of how "a camel took charge of [his] overcoat" in Syria; when discussing stage coaches, many of which were "in the hands of Mr. Ben Holliday," he is reminded of "an incident of Palestine travel which is pertinent here" and proceeds to tell a story that begins with a reference to Mr. Holliday but is followed by the admission, only a few lines later, that the story "is not about Ben Holliday, but about a young New York boy by the name of Jack." In the first instance, Twain admits being "diverted from my subject," and in the second, he unambiguously discounts the link between his story about Jack and his previous discussion on stage-coaches by his dismissal of Holliday as the subject.

The objective of such digressions is clearly humorous; what is not quite as transparent is that such excursions away from the topic at hand do not simply provide humor of their own accord, but actually produce humor by their method of interruption, or, at least, this is what Twain himself claims. In his essay "How to Tell a Story," he describes a humorous story as being "rambling and disjointed" and states that "to string incongruities and absurdities together in a wandering and sometimes purposeless way. . . is the basis of the American art [of humor]"; a humorous story "depends for its effect upon the manner of the telling." And indeed, it is the manner of the telling that shapes the humor of the digressions in *Roughing It*. For the humor of his story about the camel eating his overcoat comes not simply from its own rambling nature

but also from its emergence from a discussion of sagebrush and its eventual return to this same discussion; the contrast between the two lends absurdity to both his story and his delayed statement (which takes on an exaggerated importance) concerning the average height of sagebrush.

Narrative interruptions in the form of tall tales, such as the legend of Slade, also disrupt the narrative of the book. The mythical account of Slade (who was a real person) displaces the stagecoach ride as the subject at hand, including an excerpt concerning the infamous desperado from a real book by a Prof. Thos. J. Dimsdale (Smith 587–88). Throughout Twain's complex portrait of Slade, romantic and realistic elements war with each other to define Slade. The romanticized image of the desperado that he presents throughout chapters 10 and 11 is subverted at the end of each chapter: in chapter 10, the narrator encounters Slade with romantic expectations ("Here was romance, and I sitting face to face with it!") only to discover a mild-mannered gentleman with compassion for a stranger weary with traveling; in chapter 11, the narrator emphasizes Slade's "tears, prayers and lamentations" at the time of his death. A real person intrudes upon the romantic legend that Twain outlines; Charles Kemnitz explains that Twain "produces tension between the expected romantic image [of the West] and his realistic description" (21) in order to combat the primary danger of romanticizing: innocence (22).

Yet Twain refuses the simplistic approach of progressing from the romantic to the realistic, from innocence to experience. Nowhere is this more apparent than toward the end of the book when he recounts his experiences in the Sandwich Islands. He inserts large portions (enough to constitute several chapters) that he claims are from his diary; actually, these passages are revised versions of a letter that was published in the *Sacramento Union* (Smith 709). By constructing these passages as diary entries, Twain replaces his tone of reflective contemplation, of recounting an experience already completed, with one of immediacy. He recognizes romantic ideology as a legitimate factor in human experience, one that cannot be culled and extracted, one that constantly reasserts itself despite any amount of realistic experience. And so, to construct a genuine tension between the romantic and the realistic in *Roughing It*, Twain uses stories to interrupt and displace other stories, other accounts, as demonstrated by his accounts of Slade; tall tales intrude upon the narrator's journey, and his adventures and experiences in turn infringe upon legend. As a result, *Roughing It* cannot be accurately characterized as possessing one narrative strain, or thread, from which it sometimes deviates, for it does not present one account but a series of accounts that play off of each other for their effect.

In addition to displaying the book's lack of a single narrative strain, the narrative interruptions in *Roughing It* also showcase the peripheral nature of the book's approach to its subject (the West). Perhaps the most notable series of narrative interruptions, Jim Blaine's story (or lack thereof) of his grandfather's old ram illustrates this deftly. Throughout his story, Blaine whisks the listener from one character to the next but never returns to the subject of the ram. Twain remarks that the story of the ram remains "a dark mystery." So, likewise, does his own story of the West: he circles about the topic, from one story to the next, but never seems to arrive at it directly. He approaches, but never reaches, "the West" itself. But perhaps this is precisely his point, as other interpolated narratives confirm. After relating an incident concerning a drunken man while on a stagecoach heading East, the narrator notes that "one drunken man necessarily reminds one of another," and proceeds to relate an unrelated story concerning another drunken man. What occurs here conveys an attitude of similarity, one which Kolb lists as one essential in the mythogizing of the West, an attitude that suggests that the West is not an entity separate from the rest of the world but one that coheres with it; one drunken man in California is like any other drunken man and perhaps has more connection to him than to the West. This again suggests that the distinguishing nature of a subject like that of the West is never actually broached but merely approached without ever arriving; the stories that Twain tells happen to be situated in the West, but they do not necessarily disclose the nature of that place.

Thus the disruptive stories that *Roughing It* boasts serve to destabilize both its chosen narrative and subject, while never completely erasing them as issues of concern in the text (which would abolish the status of these stories as interruptions). The West and the story of Twain's adventures there are dubious entities within the text, having a presence that is uncertain, being persistently questioned and probed, though never permanently tossed aside as irrelevant, always taken up again.

4. FACTUAL INTERRUPTIONS

Also undermining any narrative structure the book might claim are the recurring insertions of "facts" and information—on such topics as sagebrush, coyotes, jackass rabbits, silver mining, pocket mining, the process of jury selection, Mormonism, the customs of Hawaiian natives, and desperadoism—information that "appears to stew out of" the author throughout the book. This information begins to emerge from Twain in the very "Prefatory," in which he states that the book "is merely a personal narrative," but which hastily embarks upon a description of the amount and sort of information that is in *Roughing It*, followed by an offering of regret for the information and a facetious explanation of its presence; however, just as the main topic of the preface suggests that the stated purpose of the book may differ from its actual one, the introduction and presentation of information in the book serves as merely a pretext for more important work, for judgments and analyses of various sorts.

Despite his hearty apology in the preface, Twain often parades his factual and informational sections before the reader. He announces at one point that "this is a good time to drop in a paragraph of information"; at another, he interrupts the narrative at hand to insist that "these are actual facts." Much of the information that he includes has a similar tag of some kind, drawing the reader's attention to its status and thereby encouraging readers to engage with the text as they would with other information, to read it with a rational and possibly critical eye, to examine it rather than passively consuming it as a "resting reader whil[ing] away an idle hour." Furthermore, the repeated assertions of the text's factual nature have a propensity to challenge their very claim, to promote a questioning attitude on the part of the reader; as Kolb notes, these asides concerning the truth of incidents or facts examine the location of authority, with no unambiguous answer being proposed (133–34). For example, when introducing a historical account about Kamehameha I, a Hawaiian ruler (an account that could be classified as a narrative interruption as well as a factual one), Twain appeals to the story's source as being from a book (and thus, presumably, more well-founded than the oral accounts of the natives, who "can only conjecture"); but then he immediately challenges the validity of the source by casually remarking, "I do not know where the narrator got it." Kolb claims (discussing the passages on the coyote and the jackass rabbit specifically) that Twain shifts interest from the content of the text to its rhetoric (130); accordingly, certain of these factual interludes actually function less as informational passages (since the information presented is regarded as uncertain) and more as metatextual elements, inquiring into the processes (or lack thereof) by which we attribute factuality and accuracy to texts.

Other factual interruptions in *Roughing It* provide Twain with opportunities to integrate other sorts of analyses. In some cases, his narrator assumes the position as a giver of information in order to embark upon moralistic explorations. While ostensibly describing "the meagre remains of an ancient heathen temple" in the Sandwich Islands, the narrator gradually slips into a sardonic moralistic pondering about ancient natives who died and "never knew there was a hell!" In other cases, information-giving functions as a way for the narrator to guide the reader in a less objective sense. In chapter 39, the narrator relates a joke, a comment made by an Indian ("Dam stove heap gone") after his stove blew up in a rather fantastic manner, and then offers the following "fact": "I will explain, that 'heap' is 'Injun-English' for 'very much.' The reader will perceive the exhaustive expressiveness of it in the present instance." This, presumably, functions as an explanatory aside to the reader; really, however, it is directive: it tells the reader not only how to interpret the word "heap" but how to interpret the joke. It comments on why the Indian's statement is funny (i.e., for its "exhaustive expressiveness") in a way that is humorous in its own right. Walter Blair's description of Mark Twain's humor neatly explains what is occurring in this passage; he describes his humor as being twofold: it involves both the story and its teller, the "funny monologue" and the "funny monologist." The informational fact that Twain offers operates primarily as a pretext for the narrator, the funny monologist, to emerge in order to manipulate and augment the reader's response.

There are still other indications as well that hint that Twain's inclusion of information is not quite as straightforward a project as one might imagine. He commences chapter 52 by announcing its topic as instruction on the silver mines and stating that "the reader may take this fair warning and skip, if he chooses." Later in the chapter, he refers the reader back to previous chapters for aforementioned information, in case the reader has forgotten it, but follows this referral with a qualifier: "you can go back and find it again . . . if so disposed" (my emphasis). This qualifying comment suggests that this chapter is not ultimately "about" or dependent upon the factual information and that the reader may continue without the relevant information apparently without any significant consequence. Another passage suggests this as well. In chapter 50, Twain states, in regard to a "scrap of history" about a certain Capt. Ned Blakely, that "the information I am about to offer is apology enough in itself," despite his apology in the preface for the profusion of information, implying that there is something inherently redeeming about the information itself. My suggestion is that this something is its power as a story, its power to invoke the imagination (of both the narrator and the reader), and that this capacity forms the basis for most, if not all, of the information passages in *Roughing It*. Thus the chapter about silver mines can (and should) be read as constructing an experience of being near to (and consequently subject to its inclusion as a part of daily life) and inside of a silver mine rather than as a dry informational interlude. This also explains why Twain proceeds to relate information after challenging its authenticity or soundness. Kemnitz argues a similar point—that "memory and imagination make experience from observed data" (21); this interpretation of the factual interruptions in *Roughing It* also links them to the narrative ones, for they both illustrate Twain's manipulation of various types of data to construct a collage of experiences of the West, which, ultimately, must substitute for the thing itself.

5. SYNTACTICAL INTERRUPTIONS

Often the more noticeable digressions in *Roughing It*, which encompass both factual and narrative interruption, are driven or supplemented by certain grammatical features that designate a set of smaller interruptions that are more or less contained within a given topic or situation. The most noteworthy of these are dashes and parentheses (or the square brackets known as crotchets that Twain tends to use), which might be expected, these being prominent grammatical structures of interruption. Dashes are used frequently for several purposes. They signal an often unanticipated reversal of some kind, such as in his description of a desperado: "when he shouldered his way to a bar, the shouldered parties wheeled indignantly, recognized him, and—apologized." Akin to this are dashes used to indicate occasions where the narrator inflicts a treacherous act of equivocation upon the reader during which he begins (or appears to begin) to mitigate a claim and then promptly proceeds to embellish it all the more; for example, after commenting on how few of the murderers in Nevada had been punished, he states, "I do not desire to be extravagant—it may have been less." Also, Twain employs the dash to tamper a meditation just at the point of absurdity, so that the absurdity is posited and yet denied full expression; when pondering the sentimental charm that distance lends to California scenery, he applies this idea with increasing expansiveness, from the forests and meadows, to the climate and weather conditions, to the architecture, until finally he states: "Even the playful earthquake is better contemplated at a dis—However there are varying opinions about that." All of these uses of dashes, while their purposes vary according to their context, nonetheless exemplify Twain's tendency to disrupt what he just said, to turn it about and manipulate the situation in a pointed fashion.

Whereas the dashes in Twain's text signal some sort of crux or turning point, his parentheses often allow an interjection by the narrator. These interjections usually comment reflexively on the writing process and its curiosities; they also tend to suspend the narrative time and place and allow the narrator to address the reader more directly. At one point, the narrator even actively engages the reader in regard to diction: "Eureka! [I never did know what Eureka meant, but it seems to be as good as proper a word to heave in as any when no other that sounds pretty offers]." To some extent, Twain's use of parentheses mirrors his larger topical interruptions; when temporarily abandoning a discussion about the funeral of Buck Fanshaw in order to embark upon a discussion of slang, he refers to his shift as occurring "in parenthesis." But while such interruptions by the narrator do turn away from the topic at hand, they do not turn outward toward another similar topic so much as they turn inward toward the author fumbling, groping, with his own writing.

While Twain does frequently rely on dashes and parentheses as principal structures of interruption, he also appropriates the most familiar of grammatical structures—the sentence or the period. It is perhaps his most striking use of form because it is simple and yet effective. He uses the period mark to create artificial pauses that build expectation and allow the following sentence to capitalize on this momentum. For this reason, he often begins sentences with and, thereby increasing the reader's anticipation for what is to follow, while intimating a turning of some kind similar to that of the dash. But by commencing sentences with conjunctions, he shows that these pauses are artificial and contrived, that they are deliberately elongated by a period, since a comma would have sufficed for purely grammatical purposes. For example, after declaring that four months of sunshine will lead a person to wish for any change whatsoever, Twain asserts: "you will take an earthquake, if you cannot do better. And the chances are that you'll get it, too." Such pauses are instrumental in creating Twain's peculiar humor. In "How to Tell a Story," Twain proclaims the pause to be "an exceedingly important feature in any kind of story," and especially important in a humorous one. By delivering the nubs of his stories or musings in short, pointed sentences, Twain is able to fashion the pause that he values in oral storytelling into a forceful written format.

By adapting the techniques that he used in the lecture hall into a model for writing, Twain crafts an interpolative style that is almost instantly recognizable and that functions as an efficient vehicle for both his humor and his serious commentary (which, at their best, cannot always be clearly separated). *Roughing It*, in its adherence to Twain's characteristic structure, perhaps transcends his other, more traditional works as being, in some sense, the most distinctive and original of them all. The interruptions which he generates not only enhance his art but are perhaps the very foundation of it, upon which his success or failure depends. That he was intensely and clearly aware of this, as evidenced by his incisive analysis of his own art in "How to Tell a Story," suggests that ingrained with the humor for which he is most famous is an earnestness, a sincerity, about his work that should not be quickly dismissed or easily forgotten and which might ultimately situate his work in a place not so far removed from some of his more somber Victorian contemporaries.

Source: Jennifer McKellar, "The Poetics of Interruption in Mark Twain's *Roughing It*," in *Style*, Vol. 39, No. 3, Fall 2005, pp. 336–49.

Michael Tritt

In the following review, Tritt describes "The Man That Corrupted Hadleyburg" as Twain's cynical view of the individual and society portrayed in Stowe's story.

When he describes Jack Halliday as "the typical 'Sam Lawson' of the town" in "The Man that Corrupted Hadleyburg," Mark Twain artfully invokes not only the character of Sam Lawson from Harriet Beecher Stowe's *Oldtown Folks* but also the community of Oldtown. To date, critics have given only the slightest attention to the reference to Lawson and no attention at all to the communal resonance. Yet Stowe's dewy-eyed portrayal of Lawson and of village life is layered within—and significantly contributes to—Twain's cynical view of the individual and of the society portrayed in his story.

Stowe's novel, published in 1869, traces the fortunes of three orphans who find refuge in Oldtown, a small village in postrevolutionary New England. There, they experience what one of the characters describes as "the simplest, purest, and least objectionable state of society that the world ever saw" (Stowe). Notably, it is a community thoroughly imbued with integrity: "the one thing that was held above all things sacred and inviolate in a child's education in those old Puritan days was to form habits of truth" (Stowe).

Twain's village, initially characterized as quaint, neighborly, and, above all, honest, appears to resemble Oldtown. The narrator describes Hadleyburg as a "[...] most honest and upright town [... which] began to teach the principles of honest dealing to its babies in the cradle, and made the like teachings the staple of their culture." Yet, as the story develops, the corruptibility of the villagers is revealed, as is their un-Christian lack of charity. Early in the story, Mary Richards suggests that the inhabitants "cared not a rap for strangers" and that the town was "narrow, self-righteous and stingy." Twain pointedly evokes the issue of charity at home—and abroad—when he depicts Mary Richards reading the *Missionary Herald* as the stranger arrives with the sack of gold. Stowe makes specific mention of the popularity of the *Herald* among the New England folk as well; by contrast, however, it is entirely in keeping with

the charitable nature (at home and abroad) of that community characterized by its "ethic of care" and its "extended network of friendship and kin [...]" (Stowe).

Such striking echoes and yet ironic contrasts between the communities are easy to enumerate. In Oldtown, so honest are the inhabitants that "[...] one could go to sleep at all hours of the day or night with the house door wide open, without bolt or bar, yet without apprehension of any to molest or make afraid" (Stowe). The Richards do not lock the door of their house either, yet when gold is introduced into their home, Mary "flew to [the door] all in a tremble and locked it, then pulled down the window shades and stood frightened, worried and wondering if there was anything else she could do toward making herself and the money more safe." In Oldtown, the "fundamental principle of life in those days" was a "grand contempt for personal happiness when weighed with things greater and more valuable [...]" (Stowe); in Hadleyburg, self-interest seems to obliterate just about everything else as, one by one, the nineteeners succumb to dreams of personal advancement. Stowe's New England village is a simple, neighborly place, with its meetinghouse, schoolhouse, tavern, and town store. Inhabitants typically spend a "leisure moment in discussing politics or theology from the top of codfish or mackerel barrels, while their wives and daughters were shopping among the dress goods and ribbons [...]" (Stowe). Such neighborly chitchat, and even the dialogue between husband and wife, effectively end in Hadleyburg with the temptation of gold: the streets were "empty and desolate," "lifelong habit[s]" were "dead and gone and forgotten, [...] nobody talked now, nobody read, nobody visited—the whole village sat at home, sighing, worrying, silent [...]."

Twain's allusion to Sam Lawson forces a specific comparison with Jack Halliday. Yet the similarity is limited to each being considered "the village do-nothing" in his respective community. The kindness of the first and the meanness of the second are consistent with the tenor of the villages in which they live. Although Halliday is described as "[...] the loafing, good-natured, no-account, irreverent fisherman, hunter, boy's friend, stray-dog's friend [...]," there is no such good nature evident. Rather, he takes great pleasure in the misery of his fellows. This is manifest in his comments, for example, which "grew daily more and more sparklingly disagreeable [. . .]," and in his derisive behavior, as he "laugh[s] at the town, individually and en masse." Lawson, on the other hand, is compassionate and humble to a fault. A comment he makes to the narrator reveals his nature: "There's all sorts of folks that go to make up a world, and Lord massy, we mustn't be hard on nobody; can't spect everybody to be right all around" (Stowe). Not only does Lawson believe that "money ain't everything in this world," but he is "ready to come down at any moment to do any of the odd turns which sickness in a family makes necessary [. . .]" (Stowe).

Although "The Man that Corrupted Hadleyburg" has been described as "self-indulgent, crowded with incident and anecdotal digression [. . .]" (Seelye 151), the allusion to Sam Lawson, and by extension to the New England community in *Oldtown Folks*, integrally connected to the author's ironic and scathing portrayal of small-town America, belies such criticism. At the same time, it illustrates the extent to which "every syllable, every word, every utterance set to paper reflects amalgamation and repetition of countless types, stereotypes and precedents" (Plotel and Charney xv).

Source: Michael Tritt, "Twain's 'The Man That Corrupted Hadleyburg' and Stowe's *Oldtown Folks*," in *Explicator*, Vol. 62, No. 1, Fall 2003, pp. 19–21.

Gary Sloan

In the following review, Sloan applauds a critic who called "The Man That Corrupted Hadleyburg" an ironic parable.

In a compelling analysis, tainted only by one curious omission, Earl Briden reads Mark Twain's short story "The Man That Corrupted Hadleyburg" as an ironic parable on the Fortunate Fall, with the character Howard L. Stephenson, the titular "Man," as a guise for Satan in his conventional role as tempter and master of guile. Henry Rule had already laid some of the groundwork by adducing copious textual evidence of the Stephenson-Satan nexus; Stanley Brodwin, Mary Rucker, Gerald Marshall, Susan Harris, and others had adumbrated the ironic dimension.

Hadleyburg's fall from grace, the scandalous disclosure that its vaunted honesty is all pretense, fails, Briden shows, to precipitate any collective moral redemption. The fall is fortunate only in a crass, mercenary sense. In Briden's words, "[T]he town learns only a 'commercial' lesson from its experience: it adds cleverness, prudence, a cagey circumspection to its 'virtues,' and thus reveals a superego still infantile in its concern to sidestep apprehension and enable the community to hold on to its new good name" (133). In their moral enslavement to the communal mind, the Richardses are representative. Edward Richards's deathbed confession that he is no better than the other Nineteeners is prompted by fear of exposure, not moral transformation (131–32). Unexplained by Briden and the others is the thematic import of Stephenson-Satan's lasting ignorance of Richards's guilt. Unaware that Mr. Burgess has suppressed Richards's self-incriminating note, Satan (as Stephenson will hereinafter be called) gives Richards forty thousand dollars, the proceeds from the sale of the gilded lead. In a note to Richards, Satan explains the gift:

> "I am a disappointed man. Your honesty is beyond the reach of temptation. I had a different idea about it, but I wronged you in that, and I beg pardon, and do it sincerely. I honor you—and that is sincere too. This town is not worthy to kiss the hem of your garment. Dear sir, I made a square bet with myself that there were nineteen debauchable men in your self-righteous community. I have lost. Take the whole pot, you are entitled to it." (Twain, *Short Stories*)

After the note, Satan vanishes from the story. Since Satan is conventionally the Prince of Lies, one might at first suspect that the note is sardonic and the intent malevolent. Perhaps Satan knows Richards is guilty and aims to prick his conscience. Were that Satan's design, it is speedily balked: "Within twenty-four hours after the Richardses had received their checks their consciences were quieting down, discouraged; the old couple were learning to reconcile themselves to the sin which they had committed." True, the Richardses are soon sucked into a maelstrom of inward torment—not, however, from penitent conscience, but from fear of being "found out." Twain drops no narrative hints that Satan's note might be disingenuous. Throughout the story, the narrator candidly delineates characters' motives, thoughts, and intentions. All textual evidence points to a reliable narrator. Twain, then, must have wanted Satan to be duped, to think Richards is honest and upright. Why? Just for the frivolous irony of depicting the Archdeceiver deceived? Irony of a deeper sort may be afoot.

Twain had a lifelong empathy for Satan, with whom he came to identify. He was on the side of the devil and knew it. He thought that Christians unfairly stigmatized and suppressed Satan, not letting him tell his story. Twain considered Lucifer-Satan morally superior to Jehovah and Jesus Christ. As Twain grew older, he became thoroughly disillusioned with the "damned human race." For himself, he abandoned all hope of any secular salvation predicated on belief in human goodness. His brooding anguish [was] intermitted only when he was writing.

In "The Man That Corrupted Hadleyburg," Twain may have hit on a way to save himself vicariously. He could do so by saving his alter ego, Satan, and at the same time, he would right a long-standing wrong to the fallen cherub. To be eligible for redemption, Satan must believe in the little lump of goodness that leavens the whole loaf; he must believe that unalloyed virtue is not all a dream. In short, the Prince of Lies must be lied to. Hence, Twain grants Satan the illusion that Richards is a paragon of virtue. To safeguard the illusion, Twain must remove Satan from the story before Richards makes his public confession. Viewed in this way, the story might be subtitled: "The Corrupt Town that Saved Satan."

Source: Gary Sloan, "Twain's 'The Man That Corrupted Hadleyburg,'" in *Explicator*, Vol. 58, No. 2, Winter 2000, p. 83.

SOURCES

Derounian-Stodola, Kathryn Zabelle, ed., *Women's Indian Captivity Narratives*, Penguin Books, 1998.

Emerson, Everett, *The Authentic Mark Twain: A Literary Biography of Samuel L. Clemens*, University of Pennsylvania Press, 1984.

———, *Mark Twain: A Literary Life*, University of Pennsylvania Press, 2000.

Farnham, Eliza W., *California, In-doors and Out*, Dix, Edwards, 1856, http://books.google.com/books?id=MfJl95dANcUC&source=gbs_navlinks_s (accessed August 31, 2010).

Fishkin, Shelley Fisher, ed., *A Historical Guide to Mark Twain*, Oxford University Press, 2002.

Harris, Helen L., "Mark Twain's Response to the Native American," in *American Literature*, Vol. 46, No. 4, 1975, pp. 495–505.

Hurtado, Albert L., *Indian Survival on the California Frontier*, Yale University Press, 1988.

Keightley, Thomas, *The Fairy Mythology*, George Bell, 1905, p. 259, http://books.google.com/books?id=LUU KAAAAIAAJ&source=gbs_navlinks_s (accessed August 31, 2010).

McNutt, James C., "Mark Twain and the American Indian: Earthly Realism and Heavenly Idealism," in *American Indian Quarterly*, Vol. 4, No. 3, 1978, pp. 223–42.

Taniguchi, Nancy J., "Weaving a Different World: Women and the California Gold Rush," in *California History*, Vol. 79, No. 2, 2000, pp. 141–68.

Twain, Mark, *The Adventures of Huckleberry Finn*, in *Mississippi Writings*, Library of America, 1982, pp. 617–912.

———, *The Autobiography of Mark Twain*, edited by Charles Neider, Harper & Brothers, 1959.

———, "The Californian's Tale," in *The $30,000 Bequest and Other Stories*, Oxford University Press, 1996, pp. 103–14.

———, *Mark Twain's Notebook*, edited by Albert Bigelow, Harper & Brothers, 1935, pp. 1–8.

Wilson, James D., *A Reader's Guide to the Short Stories of Mark Twain*, G. K. Hall, 1987, p. 12.

FURTHER READING

Carrigan, Henry L., ed., *Boundless Faith: Early American Women's Captivity Narratives*, Paraclete, 2003.

Carrigan's collection of narratives explores the often important role that private religious faith played in the personal experience of American women held captive by Indians.

Grunwald, Lisa, and Stephen J. Adler, eds., *Women's Letters: America from the Revolutionary War to the Present*, Dial, 2005.

This anthology provides a sample of American women's letters, highlighting the very literary form that Twain suppresses in "The Californian's Tale."

Operé, Fernando, *Indian Captivity in Spanish America*, translated by Gustavo Pellón, University of Virginia Press, 2008.

Operé presents the historical reality and literary pattern of Indian abduction in the Hispanic world, presenting a contrasting view to the American experience, but one which nevertheless has relevance to California of the 1850s.

Seaver, James E., *A Narrative of the Life of Mrs. Mary Jemison*, edited by June Namias, University of Oklahoma Press, 1995.

> This edition of Jemison's captivity narrative has been edited and annotated with the young-adult audience in mind.

Tinnemeyer, Andrea, *Identity Politics of the Captivity after 1848*, University of Nebraska Press, 2006.

> Tinnemeyer address a variation of the captivity theme in popular literature, in which Mexican women are kidnapped and married to white American settlers, in which case the abduction is viewed as liberation. She deals with the political and cultural use to which such narratives were put.

Twain, Mark, *Roughing It*, American, 1872.

> *Roughing It* is Twain's semi-autobiographical novel that deals in part with his experiences in the mining camps of Nevada and California in the 1860s.

SUGGESTED SEARCH TERMS

Mark Twain

The Californian's Tale

captivity narrative

sentimentality AND literature

California Gold Rush

Native American AND California

Mark Twain AND San Francisco

women AND gold rush

Mark Twain AND Native Americans

gold prospecting history

A Country Doctor

FRANZ KAFKA

1919

A German-speaking author born in what is now the Czech Republic, Franz Kafka became known for stories that possessed eerie dreamlike qualities and hidden meanings. His short story "A Country Doctor" is no exception to this characterization. "A Country Doctor" is ostensibly a story about a rural physician who is called away during a snowstorm to attend to a dying child. Yet the story features elements of the bizarre and the unreal. A mysterious groom procures a team of horses for the doctor, when moments before there were no horses to be found. The groom, having bitten the doctor's servant, Rose, informs the doctor that he will not accompany him, but will be staying with Rose instead. As the groom sends the doctor away, he chases Rose into the house. The confused doctor knows he must help a patient, though he fears for Rose's safety. In addition to the impossible speed of the horses, and the presence of the violent, unknown groom, other strange elements appear in the story. The doctor's patient, a child, possesses an unexplained deep, rose-colored wound festering with strange little worms. For no apparent reason, the child's family, as well as a group of village elders who have appeared, strip the clothes from the doctor and carry him to the boy's bed, laying him down next to the wound. Unable to help the boy, the doctor seeks to escape. Yet the horses, which had earlier galloped at unearthly speeds, now trudge home slowly, with the naked doctor freezing in the carriage. The strange story has generated Freudian

Franz Kafka (AP Images)

and biographical interpretations, yet critics admit that such analyses are speculative. The meaning of the story, which offers no sense of resolution or redemption, continues to generate critical debate.

Originally published in German in 1919 in the short-story collection *Ein Landarzt: Kleine Erzählungen*, "A Country Doctor" was translated into English and published in the collection *The Country Doctor: A Collection of Fourteen Stories* in 1945. Vera Leslie translated the collection, which was published by Counterpoint. The story is available in a variety of collections, including *Franz Kafka: The Complete Stories*, published by Schocken Books in 1971.

AUTHOR BIOGRAPHY

Kafka was born on July 3, 1883, in the city of Prague, which at the time was the capital of the Austro-Hungarian Empire. The region was occupied by both Czechs and Germans. Kafka's father, Hermann Kafka, was of German Jewish descent, and the young Kafka was raised speaking Czech at home and German at school. Kafka's mother, Julie Löwy Kafka, came from an old Prague family. Kafka's parents owned and operated a haberdashery business in Prague. Kafka, and the three sisters who were born after him, were often cared for by Czech-speaking servants while their parents were busy with the day-to-day operations of their business. Enrolled in school at the age of six, Kafka began to speak primarily German. At ten, he entered the Alstädter Deutsches Gymnasium, a German preparatory school. In 1901, Kafka enrolled at the German Karl-Ferdinand University in Prague, where he studied law. In 1907, after receiving his doctorate in law, Kafka immediately found employment with Assicurazioni Generali, an Italian insurance office in Prague.

The following year, Kafka began publishing fiction; his first short works appeared in the Munich literary magazine *Hyperion*. Kafka took advantage of a better job opportunity in 1908 and secured a position with the Workers' Accident Insurance Institute, a semigovernmental agency. He still worked in Prague but had the opportunity to travel. Kafka continued to work and write during this time. In 1912, he met Felice Bauer, a woman with whom he would have a turbulent, on-again, off-again relationship. He published the first portion of a longer novel in 1913. The published section was *Der Heizer*, and it represented only the opening chapter of a much longer work, *Der Verschollene* (*He Who Was Lost without a Trace*), which Kafka never completed but which was assembled and published by his friend Max Brod and published after Kafka's death as *Amerika* (1927). Over the next year, Kafka courted Bauer, who lived in Berlin, through correspondence. He visited her several times, and they became engaged for a short time in 1914. World War I broke out that same year, but between his position with the semigovernmental agency and being diagnosed with bronchitis (a condition later more accurately identified as tuberculosis), Kafka did not serve in combat. He published one of his best-known works, *Die Verwandlung* (translated and published as *The Metamorphosis*, 1937), in 1915.

In 1917, Kafka and Bauer agreed to marry when the war was over, but after he was diagnosed with tuberculosis, Kafka called off the engagement once again. On medical leave from his job, Kafka moved to Bohemia to live with his sister and her husband. He continued to write but contracted influenza during the 1918 pandemic and was confined to his bed for weeks. While he was recovering,

Kafka met and became engaged to Julie Wohry-zek, but he called off this engagement as well. In 1919, Kafka published *Ein Landarzt: Kleine Erzäh-lungen* (translated and published as *The Country Doctor: A Collection of Fourteen Short Stories* in 1945). Kafka's health continued to worsen, and after 1920 he was forced to take frequent and extensive sick leaves. He wrote extensively during these prolonged absences from work. After 1922, Kafka's sick leaves were no longer renewed, and he retired. He traveled to the Baltic coast with his sister and her family in 1923 and met Dora Diamant, with whom he became romantically involved. He lived with Diamant in Berlin until 1924, when she accompanied him to a sanatorium near Vienna, Austria, where he died on June 3, 1924, of tuberculosis of the larynx.

PLOT SUMMARY

"A Country Doctor" opens with a note of urgency. The doctor is attempting to find trans-port to a young patient who is waiting in another village, some ten miles away. The doctor possess a gig, or a light carriage, but his own horse had died during the night. The doctor has sent his servant girl to try and procure a horse from another villager. The girl returns empty-handed, and in frustration, the doctor kicks in the door of his long-empty rundown pigsty. The pigsty, however, is no longer empty. A lit lantern hangs from a rope, and a man crouches inside the low-ceilinged structure. As the door flaps in the wind, the doctor smells the scent of horses. When the mysterious man asks if he should yoke up the horses, the doctor and the girl laugh in surprise. Through a strange bit of maneuvering, the horses squeeze through the small door and exit the pigsty, revealing their immense presence. Ordered by the doctor to help the groom harness the horses, the girl is alarmed when the groom grabs her and presses his face against hers. As she steps away, the doctor notices teeth marks on her face. The enraged doctor scolds the groom, suddenly beginning to wonder who he is and where he has come from. The groom finishes his preparations with the horses and orders the doctor to get into the gig. After the doctor offers to drive, as the groom does not know the way, the groom informs the doctor that he will be traveling on his own, as he, the groom, intends to stay with Rose. Although it is not revealed

how the man knew the serving girl's name, she runs in fear for her safety, indeed, her life, into the house and locks the door behind her. The doctor, fearful as well for Rose, insists that the groom accompany him, but the groom claps his hands and sends the horses on their way.

As the doctor rides off, he can hear the sound of the door splitting as the groom bursts into his house in pursuit of Rose. Before the doctor can even think of turning back, he discovers that he has already arrived at his patient's farmyard; the trip had been instantaneous. The blizzard has ceased, and the patient's family rushes the doctor into the house.

As the doctor examines the child, noting that he is without a fever, but is neither warm nor cold, the boy throws his arms about the doctor's neck and entreats him to let him die. The doctor examines his instruments, thinking that "the gods" have interceded by sending the horse and groom. He now remembers Rose and contemplates how he can possibly save her from the groom. At this moment, the horses put their heads through the window, as if watching him, "summoning" him to return to Rose. The child's family try to make him comfortable, helping him with his coat and pouring him a glass of rum. Putting his head to the boy's chest, he surmises "that the boy was quite sound." Feeling as though he has been called without cause, the doctor becomes frustrated with the frequency with which such summons occur, and now, Rose, who had lived with him for years almost unnoticed by him, he realizes, is in mor-tal danger. Surveying the worried family once more, the doctor hesitates, wondering if in fact the boy really might be ill. With the horses whinnying urgently, the doctor approaches the boy again, discovering at the child's hip a large open wound, "rose-red" in color and festering with long, thick rose-red, blood-speckled worms "with small white heads and many little legs." Now the doctor is certain that the boy cannot be cured. Yet the family is pleased to realize that the doctor has identified the source of the child's illness. The boy now whis-pers once again to the doctor, asking if he will save him.

At this point, family members along with village elders strip the clothes off the doctor. A school choir led by a teacher sings a strange song, chanting, "Strip his clothes off, then he'll heal us, / If he doesn't, kill him dead." Naked, the doctor is placed in bed next to the boy, along-side the open wound. Everyone leaves the room. The doctor hears a voice in his ear, presumably the child's, chastising him. The boy whispers that not only can the doctor not help him, now he's crowding him on his own deathbed. In response, the doctor wonders aloud, "What am I to do?" The child is not consoled. After assuring the child that his wound "is not so bad," the doctor begins once again to think of escaping. Gathering his clothes, coat, and bag, he throws them out of the window and into the gig, and clambers out the window, still naked. Instead of galloping, the horses now plod slowly home through the snow. The doctor laments that he will never make it home in time to save Rose, and he expresses his feelings of betrayal at having been called out on a "false alarm" yet again.

CHARACTERS

The Boy

Like most of the characters in Kafka's "A Country Doctor," the boy in the story is unnamed. He is the patient to whose aid the doctor has been summoned during the blizzard. The boy's condition seems to confuse the doctor initially. Although the doctor determines that the boy does not have a fever, he is "gaunt," his eyes are "vacant," and he seems to be neither warm nor cold. The boy pleads to the doctor to let him die. Soon, the doctor comes to the conclusion that the boy is quite well. Upon closer examination, though, the boy's true condition is revealed. The boy has a large open wound on his hip. In it, a profusion of white worms wriggled from deep inside the wound toward the exterior. The doctor describes the worms as "thick and long as my little finger." The child now asks the doctor if he will save him. After the doctor is placed in bed next to the boy, the child whispers to the doctor, telling him he has "very little confidence" in him. Somehow, the child knows about the doctor's supernatural transportation, the horses who brought the doctor to the boy in an instant. He dismisses the doctor in this way, for he didn't even arrive on his own. Rather, as the boy points out, the doctor was "blown in" to the boy's home. After complaining that the doctor is crowding him, he states, "What I'd like best is to scratch your eyes out." As the conversation continues, the doctor reassures the boy that his wound is not really that bad. The boy then quiets and lies

still, at which point the doctor escapes. As the doctor is unable to help the boy, the boy and his wound are sometimes regarded as a symbol of the doctor's powerlessness. This is underscored by the fact that the wound is repeatedly described in terms of its rose color, prompting an association with the servant girl Rose, whom the doctor is also unable to protect from violation by the groom.

The Boy's Family

The boy's family members do not have speaking roles within the story. In fact, the doctor seems unable to understand them at all. As he steps from his gig, he describes their speech as "confused ejaculations," which he cannot make sense of. They are only briefly identified individually. The sister of the patient takes his coat, the father offers him rum, the mother encourages the doctor to drink it. Thinking that the boy is well, the doctor closes his bag and reaches for his coat. In response, the father, confused, sniffs at the glass of rum, while the mother bites her lip, and the sister holds a blood-soaked towel. They stand mute instead of directing the doctor's attention to the boy's wound, which he finds after reluctantly taking another look at the child. After the doctor has examined the wound, the family seems "pleased" that the doctor has at last made this discovery. They allow guests into the room, including extended family, village elders, and a school choir. Inexplicably, the family and the village elders strip the doctor of his clothing, carry him to the boy's bed, and place him naked next to the child, on the side with the wound. The fact that they do not speak to the doctor, that they allow this strange collection of other people into their child's sickroom, and that they strip the doctor naked and put him in bed with their child all lend to the story its bizarre, dreamlike quality.

The Choir

The choir is a school choir led by a teacher, invited by the family into the boy's room where the doctor is examining the boy. As the family and the village elders are stripping the doctor, the choir sings a strange tune in which they refer to stripping the doctor as a precursor to being healed. They then chant that if he fails to cure them, he should be killed. The refrain "only a doctor" is repeated by the doctor himself at various points in the story, when he laments the gap between what is expected of him, and what he can actually do. Later, as the doctor escapes, he can hear the children singing again a "new but faulty song," in which patients are extolled to be joyful because "the doctor's laid in bed beside you!" Like a chorus in an ancient Greek tragedy, Kafka's choir comments on the events transpiring. The presence in the story of this element is another surreal, dreamlike aspect.

The Doctor

The doctor is the protagonist, or main character, of "A Country Doctor." As a first-person narrator, he refers to himself as "I" and provides the sole perspective available in the story. Throughout the story, the doctor is shown to have grave doubts about his abilities. At the same time, he seems perpetually frustrated by false alarms, that is, by being called out to a patient's home only to discover that the patient is fine. He describes being badly paid but is still "generous and helpful to the poor." As the strange events of the story unfold, the doctor is occasionally surprised, but never as alarmed as one might expect. When he sees a strange man crouching in his pigsty, asking if he should yoke up the horses, the doctor does not know what to say, but simply crouches down "to see what else was in the sty." The servant girl Rose jokes, "You never know what you are going to find in your own house," and she and the doctor laugh. Neither seems surprised to see two enormous horses emerge from the small, low pigsty. The doctor is shocked, however, when the groom attacks Rose, and he fears for her after the groom's clap sends the horses on their way. His attention is repeatedly drawn back to Rose throughout the course of the story. The doctor admits that while Rose has lived with him for years, he has scarcely noticed her, but now, to yield her to the groom, "that sacrifice was too much to ask." That he expresses his concern for Rose in these terms suggests that his feelings have blossomed from the those of an employer to those of a lover, even though he had not noticed her for many years. The doctor's understanding of the groom's horrid intentions for Rose have perhaps forced him to admit his true feelings. When he realizes that he will never make it home in time to save Rose, the doctor laments "in my house the disgusting groom is raging; Rose is his victim; I do not want to think about it anymore." His own vulnerability—he is pulled by "unearthly" horses, naked, in the winter—is emphasized, which serves the purpose as well of highlighting his similarity to Rose, who is most likely vulnerable, exposed, and suffering at the same moment.

The Groom

The groom is a mysterious figure who appears out of nowhere to create havoc and pursue his horrid aims. In his strange and sudden appearance, with his mastery of horses with supernatural speed and his evil desire for Rose, the groom seems like a character out of a nightmare. He provides the doctor with the means to attend to a patient in need, but appears to do so only to have the opportunity to attack Rose without the doctor's interference. It has been suggested that the groom represents the doctor's own sexual desire for Rose. Before the horses have taken the doctor out of earshot, the doctor hears the groom forcibly breaking into his house, splitting the door open.

Rose

Rose is the doctor's servant. She is sent to try and find a horse for him in the village, and then is ordered by the doctor to help the groom harness the horses he has provided for the doctor. She jokes with the doctor in a good-natured manner, but is soon bitten by the groom, who has pressed her to him as if he was going to kiss her. When the groom tells the doctor that he will be staying at the doctor's house with Rose while the doctor is away, the horrified Rose shrieks in terror and runs into the house. The doctor hears her locking the door and extinguishing the lights in all the rooms "to keep herself from being discovered." It is not revealed what Rose suffers at the hands of the groom, but the doctor seems certain she will be raped and possibly murdered.

The Village Elders

The village elders are ushered into the boy's room by the family members. With the boy's family, they disrobe the doctor and carry him off to place him in the boy's bed. Their peculiar presence and behavior contribute to the bizarre, dreamlike nature of the story.

THEMES

Futility

In "A Country Doctor," Kafka explores the related themes of futility and powerlessness. The doctor repeatedly draws attention to his feelings of helplessness and the overall uselessness of his efforts. He is unable to save Rose, and unable to heal the boy, and his thoughts return to this sense of powerlessness with great frequency. As the story opens,

TOPICS FOR FURTHER STUDY

- Kafka is known for stories that incorporate elements of the absurd or bizarre. One of his best-known is the novella *The Metamorphosis*. Read this work and consider its irrational, unrealistic, or absurd elements. How does Kafka incorporate these elements into his story? Are these strange features explained in any way? Does Kafka suggest that the story is meant to be taken as a dream? Analyze the story's structural elements, such as plot, characterization, and language. How do these features complement the elements of the bizarre or surreal? Write an essay in which you detail your analysis of the story.

- S. E. Hinton's 1975 young-adult novel *Rumble Fish* deals with themes of nihilism, self-destruction, and the perceived emptiness of life. With a small group, read Hinton's novel, reprinted by Laurel Leaf in 1989, and consider the way Hinton treats the issue of life's meaninglessness, or the relativist nature of morality and ethics. After you have read the novel, watch the 1983 film adaptation of the novel. Do Hinton's philosophical themes translate to film? Or are the deeper issues lost? Does the time frame of the novel or the film affect the way the themes are conveyed to a twenty-first-century young-adult audience? As a group, create an online blog in which you discuss these issues and share your opinions.

- Japanese author Inagaki Taruho wrote a number of prose pieces during the 1920s, around the same time Kafka was writing. The collection *One Thousand and One-Second Stories* gathers many of these short pieces in one volume. The work in this collection has been described as surrealist fiction that often resembles poetry. Read several of the pieces in this volume, published in 2000 by Sun & Moon Press, and consider the ways in which the stories are similar to Kafka's fiction. Do they use imagery and narrative techniques that seem unrealistic or bizarre? How are they different from Kafka's work in tone and theme? Prepare an essay or an oral report in which you share your comparison with the class.

- Using works such as the 1993 *Realism, Rationalism, Surrealism: Art between the Wars,* by Briony Fer, David Batchelor, and Paul Wood, explore the art movements that inspired modernist transformations in literature. Select a style of art (such as cubism or surrealism) or a particular artist and create a Web-based report in which you summarize the history and distinguishing features of the style or the artist's work; create links to images of significant works by the artist or images that exemplify the style. Alternatively, create your own artistic work in the style you have selected or that emulates the work of your chosen artist. Be prepared to discuss the particular characteristics that mark your piece as an example of a particular style or as similar to the work of the artist you have selected.

- Sigmund Freud's work influenced many modernist writers, including Kafka. Using print and electronic sources, research Freud's life and write a biographical essay on Freud. Be sure to discuss his major published works and cite all of your sources.

the doctor is already frozen with his sense of hopelessness. He "stood there forlornly" as the snow gathers on him and is "unable to move." Compelled into action by the mysterious groom who has made ready the gig and horses, the doctor is driven off while the groom makes clear his violent intentions toward Rose. Thinking his patient is not seriously ill, the doctor vows to return home to try and save Rose, all the while cursing those who call him out without cause during the night. As the doctor prepares to leave, he sees the confused family and reluctantly re-examines the boy. The doctor

The doctor grabbed his bag and waited for the maid to come back with a horse. *(James Steidl | Shutterstock.com)*

here demonstrates his inability to commit to a course of action. Thus far he has done little with the child except listen to his breathing; his thoughts are focused on Rose. Yet he pauses to take another look at the child, and in doing so finds the child's wound. He believes that the child is "past helping." His actions are misinterpreted by the family as an effort to try and save the child, and consequently the family and the village elders take matters into their own hands by disrobing the doctor and placing him in bed with the boy. The doctor is acted upon by the family; he does not act in order to save the child. Rather, the doctor has already written the boy off as past saving. Nor does the doctor act to save Rose. Although the doctor claims, despite being naked, to feel "altogether composed and equal to the situation," he realizes that there is nothing to do for the child except lie to him and make his escape. Having delayed his departure for so long already, the doctor finally leaves the boy's home, but admits, once the horses' plodding pace becomes evident, that Rose is already lost to him. The doctor has the sense that he has "wander[ed] astray." Feeling betrayed by the circumstances, the doctor characterizes his futile visit to the boy

as another "false alarm," and one that cannot be made right.

Absurdity

"A Country Doctor" contains a number of elements that are outside the realm of the realistic framework of his story, elements considered absurd or bizarre. These elements combine to underscore Kafka's twin theme of futility, suggesting the relationship between life's ultimate meaninglessness and an individual's perception of powerlessness. In the story, the doctor and Rose fall prey to the groom's evil manipulations. The groom is an absurd figure himself, given his sudden, unexplained appearance crouched in the doctor's pigsty. His horses are described as "unearthly," and they clearly have unnatural characteristics, such as their ability to transfigure their form to fit in a pigsty and their ability to cover a distance of ten miles in a heartbeat. The boy's family members also behave in a bizarre fashion, never speaking to the doctor or pointing out the boy's wound. Furthermore, they allow the village elders and the school choir to enter their child's sickroom. As the family and the elders disrobe the doctor, the children in the school choir sing about killing him. All of these elements go unexplained; they seem like the odd and inexplicable parts of a dream. Combined with the doctor's lack of power and agency, these strange features of the story support the notion that the world is an absurd place, and that it is futile to attempt to find meaning and value in it.

STYLE

First-Person Narration

"A Country Doctor" is narrated in the first person by the doctor. He refers to himself as "I," and the story is told entirely from his perspective. When authors choose this style of narration, they sacrifice the ability to depict the thoughts and feelings of other characters, but gain unlimited access to the mind of the narrating character. Because everything in the story is processed through the filter of the narrating character's thoughts and perceptions, the reader must consider how reliable the narrating character is. Given the strange things that happen in the course of the story, the doctor's reliability may legitimately be called into question. The story reads like a bizarre dream, and the reader may wonder if, in fact, the doctor is dreaming, or is in some way perceiving events that are not really happening. At the same time, the author is presenting a particular view of reality, and the doctor may be as reliable a narrator as can exist in such a world. Despite his indecision and ineffectual nature, he is nevertheless depicted as calm and rational throughout much of the story, even feeling "composed" after he has been stripped naked. Kafka's use of a first-person narrator, who appears to be one of the few realistic characters in an otherwise bizarre world, supports his themes of futility and absurdity.

Surrealism

Surrealism is a style of literature that gives more weight to the reality of the subconscious mind than to external realities. Although surrealism as an artistic and literary movement did not fully take shape until the 1920s, critics note that elements of Kafka's work prefigure the movement in many ways. Surrealism is linked with the work of Freud, who posited the notion that dreams are the realm of the subconscious, that they reveal hidden fears and desires. In "A Country Doctor," the surrealist elements are those that lend the work the feel of a dream. The ways in which aspects of the story do not correspond with the laws of nature emphasize the dreamlike quality of the work. The horses, for example, are clearly too large to be stabled in the pigsty, yet they emerge from it as if they are being birthed, or "squeezed out" from the small entryway. As they exit, they unfold themselves to stand tall, "their bodies steaming thickly." They also transport the doctor ten miles, literally in an instant. One moment he is at his home, the next he is at his patient's farmhouse. Despite the impossibility of this speed, they cannot return the doctor home as quickly, and they plod unbelievably slowly. Other bizarre elements and events in the story also serve to underscore its dreamlike nature. The doctor is stripped naked and placed in bed next to the boy. The boy's wound and its infection are portrayed in grotesque and unbelievable detail. The worms are described as the length and thickness of the doctor's finger, and the wound itself is said to be the size of his palm. Yet when the movement of the worms is described, the wound itself seems as though it would have to be much larger and quite deep to accommodate a number of many-legged worms crawling from the "interior of the wound toward the light." The presence of the choir, chanting that the doctor must either heal his patient or be killed, is another surreal element that is interjected into the narrative. Such elements stand in stark contrast to the realistic premise of a country doctor being summoned in the middle of the night to attend to a dying patient.

HISTORICAL CONTEXT

Artistic and Literary Modernism

In the years leading up to and immediately following World War I, a number of European writers began to approach literature in a new way, rejecting the narrative modes of the past, and seeking innovative new modes of expression. Such transformations became known as modernism, a term used to define an array of elements in both art and literature. The literary branch of the movement was inspired in part by a similar evolution in the world of the visual arts, where realistic representations were

COMPARE & CONTRAST

- **1919:** In postwar Europe, the influence of Sigmund Freud becomes increasingly widespread, as his views on hysterical illness and psychoanalysis are employed in the treatment of individuals suffering from the traumatic war-related events.

  Today: Despite criticisms of Freud's theories by modern professionals in the fields of psychiatry, his contributions to the field and to the understanding of the mind continue to be re-evaluated and revalued, as evidenced by works such as Dr. Donald Carveth's 2006 lecture "Sigmund Freud Today: What Are His Enduring Contributions?"

- **1919:** European literature is characterized by modernist themes, such as alienation and despair, and modernist styles, in which stream-of-consciousness narration is employed, as in James Joyce's *Ulysses*, published in serial form between 1918 and 1920, and in book form in 1922, or Marcel Proust's *Remembrance of Things Past*, published in parts between 1913 and 1927. Other modernist writers, such as Franz Kafka and the Russian Andrei Bely, incor-

porate the use of absurd, dreamlike elements or symbols in their modernist writings.

  Today: Many works of modern European literature reflect a world conflicted and scarred by late-twentieth-century wars (particularly those in Eastern Europe, such as the 1992–1995 Bosnian War) and a collective psyche that reacts to such horror with despair and nihilism. Writers in this vein include Vera Rudan, Michal Ajvaz, and Zafer Senocak.

- **1919:** At the close of World War I, the Austro-Hungarian Empire is dissolved. Czechoslovakia is one of the newly established nations, along with Austria, Hungary, and the Kingdom of Serbs, Croats, and Slovenes, which later becomes Yugoslavia. Prague, the former capital of the empire and Kafka's birthplace, becomes the capital of Czechoslovakia.

  Today: After a turbulent period of Communist rule, Czechoslovakia splits to became the Czech Republic and Slovakia in 1993. The president of the Czech Republic in 2010 is Vaclav Klaus and the prime minister is Petr Necas. In Prague, Kafka's former haunts are now the destinations of literary-minded tourists.

---

eschewed in favor of art that focused on individual perceptions rather than external reality.

In art, abstract painting was explored, emphasizing such elements as lines, colors, or shapes rather than direct representation. Such experimentation can be seen in the works of Henri Matisse, Pablo Picasso, and Georges Braque. In literature, writers experimented with stream-of-consciousness narration, attempting to capture the flow of thoughts and impressions rather than adhering to traditional principles of narration. In both art and literature, the writings of Sigmund Freud shaped the course of modernist approaches to expression, as he revealed the significance and prevalence of the workings of the unconscious mind. As John

Turner points out in the 2003 *Encyclopedia of Literary Modernism*, Freud's theories regarding the mind and the benefits of psychoanalysis, although published in the early years of the twentieth century, became prevalent during and immediately following World War I.

Not only were the writings disseminated among a wider audience, but Freud's approach to analysis was employed with individuals suffering from traumatic war experiences. Kafka's interest in Freud is well documented. As the authors of the 2005 *Franz Kafka Encyclopedia* point out, Kafka references Freud's work numerous times in his letters and journals. While modernism in many ways centered on an approach to literature that emphasized the unconscious mind, the significance of the individual, and the rejection of traditional modes of expression, thematically, modernist works increasingly focused on such topics as alienation, anxiety, and despair following the tragedy of World War I.

Writers such as Marcel Proust, James Joyce, T. S. Eliot, Ezra Pound, and Franz Kafka have all been associated with the literary modernist movement. The surrealist movement, which the works of Kafka anticipate in many ways, is often seen as an outgrowth of modernism. As a movement, surrealism was outlined by the 1924 publication of French writer André Breton's *Manifesto of Surrealism*.

Post–World War I Eastern Europe

The Austro-Hungarian Empire witnessed the genesis of World War I when the heir to the Austro-Hungarian throne, Archduke Franz Ferdinand, and his wife, Sophie, were assassinated in June 1914 in an effort by Serbian terrorists to destroy the empire's hold on the southern Slavic region. The war began, essentially, as a revolution in this region, and owing to a web of European alliances, the conflict rapidly spread across Europe.

Following the war, the Austro-Hungarian Empire dissolved, leading to the formation of a number of nations, including Austria, Hungary, Czechoslovakia, and a region that would later combine its various components to form Yugoslavia. The radical reorganizations of so many boundaries and economies resulted in widespread and long-term economic depression during the years between World War I and World War II for countries in this region.

Looming to the east was a new socialist Russia, the republic that emerged in the aftermath of World War I. The conclusion of the war spawned a socialist revolution that ended czarist rule in Russia. As a political philosophy that had transformed Russia, socialism spread to many of the Russian Soviet Republic's Eastern European neighbors in the wake of the economy-destroying years of war and the painfully slow recovery. Czechoslovakia fared better than other Eastern European nations in terms of its postwar economy. It had inherited much of the former empire's industry and was characterized by a relatively stable government in which cooperation from a number of disparate political parties was maintained.

The horses pushed open the bedroom window.
(kotomiti | Shutterstock.com)

CRITICAL OVERVIEW

Kafka's "A Country Doctor," has been analyzed from a variety of approaches, although the work's abstract nature limits the possibilities of definitive readings of the texts. It has been studied in Freudian terms, in terms of its relation to Kafka's life, and for its bizarre, surrealist elements. As Richard H. Lawson observes in a 1989 essay for the *Dictionary of Literary Biography*, Freudian interpretations focus on Rose and the boy's rose-colored and -shaped wound to emphasize the impotence of the doctor, whereas the groom symbolizes the "doctor's long-suppressed id." (In psychoanalysis, the id is a term that refers to the part of the mind in which reside instinctive impulses and desires.) Lawson cautions, however, that "exhaustive Freudian explication is apt to become mere reductivism."

According to Winifried Menninghaus in *Disgust: The Theory and History of a Strong*

Sensation (2003), other critics of "A Country Doctor" have attempted to link the story with Kafka's own life by suggesting that the child's wound represents "Kafka's own lung infection," or alternatively, that it may be compared to "Felice as the 'sore' in his life." (Felice was Kafka's lover and sometime fiancée.) Menninghaus goes on to study the story from a different angle, finding that "the story thus appears as the discovery and acknowledgment of the desire to possess Rose" but that the doctor is engaged in the process of "the censuring of this desire" throughout the course of the story. Menninghaus additionally mentions the Christian significance some critics associate with the boy's wound. The wound is a focal point in other critical analyses as well.

Lawrence Rothfield, in *Vital Signs: Medical Realism in Nineteenth-Century Fiction* (1992), explores the ways in which Kafka uses the wound as an opportunity to contort the realistic elements of the story, further underscoring the abnormal bent of the tale. "Kafkaesque modernism," Rothfield states, "challenges realism on the issue of the opposition between truth and pathology." Furthermore, Rothfield emphasizes the symbolic nature of the boy's wound as a register for the doctor's fear and longing. The wound, states Rothfield, reflects the doctor's "complicated sexual feelings."

Another critical avenue toward extracting meaning from Kafka's work examines the dreamlike qualities of "A Country Doctor." Jerrold Levinson, in his 1996 *The Pleasures of Aesthetics: Philosophical Essays*, suggests, in fact, that Kafka's story could be taken as "a stylized dream report." In his 2002 *The Myth of Power and the Self*, Walter H. Sokel ties together the biographical approach to the work and the focus on its dreamlike qualities, maintaining that the work "presents in the hieroglyphic language of dreams a clear and exact presentation of Kafka's inspirational process and the problems it posed in his life." Sokel regards the work as exemplifying the conflict in Kafka's life between his art and his personal fulfillment.

CRITICISM

Catherine Dominic

Dominic is a novelist and a freelance writer and editor. In the following essay, she maintains that

> THE WORLD KAFKA DEPICTS IN 'A COUNTRY DOCTOR' IS ONE PLAGUED BY EVIL, FUTILITY, AND FAILURE; IT IS DEVOID OF ANYTHING OBVIOUSLY GOOD OR MEANINGFUL."

in "A Country Doctor" Kafka uses the doctor, the groom, and the boy's family as means of exploring the philosophical notions of nihilism and ethical nihilism.

In Franz Kafka's "A Country Doctor," the eponymous character finds himself compelled along a course of action in which he is unable to save his servant girl from being raped, and in which he is unable to cure the boy with the infected wound. His experiences reveal the presence of evil, which he is unable to combat. The self-righteous doctor sees evil around him, but not within himself, and yet Kafka suggests that the doctor's own actions are not motivated by good intentions either. The world Kafka depicts in "A Country Doctor" is one plagued by evil, futility, and failure; it is devoid of anything obviously good or meaningful. In portraying this absence of moral goodness, Kafka explores the philosophical notion of moral or ethical nihilism.

Moral or ethical nihilism is a philosophical school of thought in which it is posited that no moral or ethical values exist. The more general concept of nihilism suggests the utter meaninglessness of life. In "A Country Doctor," Kafka touches on this notion as well, specifically in regard to the boy's family. In terms of the story's ethical nihilism, the absence of moral values is revealed in the relation of both the groom and the doctor to the servant girl, Rose. Kafka depicts the girl only in terms of her usefulness to the doctor, and as an object of desire for both the doctor and the groom. Initially, the groom's intentions toward Rose are clear; he grabs her as if to kiss her, and then bites her. While the doctor scolds the groom, he nevertheless considers the fact that the strange man is helping him by providing conveyance to his patient. Whatever qualms the doctor may have about the groom, the doctor does not bother thinking about the

WHAT DO I READ NEXT?

- Kafka's *The Trial* was not finished or published during his lifetime and he had in fact instructed his friend and literary executor Max Brod to burn all of his incomplete, unpublished manuscripts, including the manuscript for *The Trial*. Brod had the book, which focuses on the theme of alienation, published in 1925. A modern edition in English was published by Schocken in 1998.

- *The Diaries of Franz Kafka: 1910–1923* reveal much about Kafka's life, relationships, and literary and philosophical influences. Edited by Max Brod and first published in English by Schocken in 1948, the work was reprinted in 1988.

- Sigmund Freud's influential work *The Interpretation of Dreams* was originally published in 1899. It is available in a modern English edition published by Basic Books in 2010.

- *Friedrich Nietzsche*, edited by prominent literary critic and scholar Harold Bloom, is a work geared toward young adults. In it, Nietzsche's writings and his analysis of the philosophy of nihilism are explored and critiqued by a number of critics. This collection of essays was published in 1987 by Chelsea House.

- *The Golden Age*, published in 2001, and translated into English and published in 2010 by Dalkey Archive Press, is by Czech author Michal Ajvaz. The novel combines surrealist elements into its narrative, exploring the borders between external and perceived realities.

- Mexican American author Gary Soto's young-adult novel *Buried Onions*, originally published in 1997 and reissued by Graphia in 2006, explores themes of despair, cynicism, hopelessness, and ethical relativism.

matter further. It is significant that the doctor climbs into the gig *after* the groom has bitten

Rose. Once in, he is powerless to stop the horses from fleeing at their master's command. Yet a small window of time existed between the groom's biting of Rose and the doctor's climbing into the gig. Had the doctor considered it ethically necessary to protect Rose, he had, during this window, both cause and opportunity to do so.

Once in the family's home, the doctor's thoughts return repeatedly to Rose. He states his desire to rescue her, to "pull her away from under that groom." But moments later, it is clear that his intentions are selfish. His thoughts are not of protecting her from harm or keeping her safe. Rather, when he thinks of harm coming to Rose, it is characterized as an injustice that *he* personally will suffer. Thinking of her prettiness, and how he has failed to notice Rose for years, the doctor now pouts, "that I should have to sacrifice Rose this time as well," in addition to all the nights he has had to give up in tending to villagers who called him "needlessly," would be "too much to ask." It is as though the thought of the groom having his way with Rose sparks in the doctor a reminder of what he has been missing. He seems to now want Rose for himself. His comments suggest that he does not possess a noble desire to protect Rose, but that he has, instead, developed a physical urge, similar to the groom's, to possess her. The doctor wishes to escape the boy and his family in order not to save Rose, but to "restore Rose *to me*" [emphasis added]. Although the doctor perceives the groom's intentions to be evil, his own intentions are virtually the same, despite his self-righteous characterization of them.

In his role as healer to the villagers, the doctor similarly reveals the difference between the way he views himself and what his thoughts and actions make plain. Although claiming to be "generous and helpful to the poor," he seems wholeheartedly annoyed with the villagers he treats, stating that "the whole district made my life a torment," by calling him out repeatedly during the night. He initially dismisses the boy as "sound and best turned out of bed with one shove." After a closer examination, he deems there is nothing he can do to save the child he now deems to be fatally ill. In fact, the only thing the doctor does in terms of the boy's treatment is make a show out of removing a pair of tweezers from his bag, and listening to the boy's heartbeat. Having been disrobed and made to lie next to the boy in bed, the doctor tells the child, who

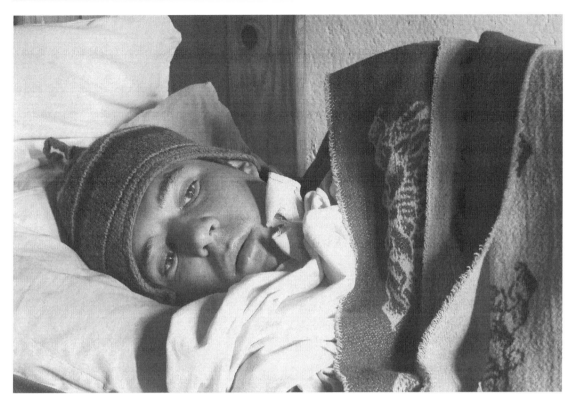

The young man begged the doctor to let him die. *(Ljupco Smokovski / Shutterstock.com)*

complains of the doctor's inadequacies, and of the fact that the doctor is crowding him, "Believe me, it is not too easy for me either." He then lies to the child and tells him the wound is not as bad as it seems. Perplexingly, the doctor goes on to say, "Done in a tight corner with two strokes of the ax. Many a one proffers his side and can hardly hear the ax in the forest." He seems to be suggesting amputation as a treatment for the boy's festering wound. The doctor proceeds to escape through the window. The doctor, then, seems to have no moral compulsion to do anything to relieve the boy's pain, makes no effort to attend to the wound in any way, nor does he confer with the family in any kind of sympathetic fashion.

Once he escapes, the doctor realizes he will never save Rose. "My successor," he states, "is robbing me, but in vain, for he cannot take my place; in my house the disgusting groom is raging; Rose is his victim." The successor is the groom, who is taking what the doctor views as his, that is Rose. The doctor asserts that this theft is in vain, that his place (with Rose) cannot be taken, for, in fact, the doctor has never

indulged in his desire, he has never possessed Rose in this way. Yet his thoughts have revealed his own selfish, low intentions. Furthermore, his actions as a doctor have underscored his lack of ethics in this role as well. The world of "A Country Doctor" is one devoid of moral values.

In Kafka's depiction of the boy's family, he underscores the futility of communication and the valuelessness of sacred traditions. As Alan Pratt states in his 2001 essay on nihilism for the *Internet Encyclopedia of Philosophy*, nihilism incorporates the belief that "nothing can be known or communicated." Throughout the story, the family repeatedly fails to communicate in any meaningful way with the doctor. He first hears them when he arrives at their home, but can discern nothing "from their confused ejaculations." Although the doctor and the boy converse, none of the family members ever speak to the doctor directly, nor does he speak to them. As he turns to go, after only a cursory examination of the boy, the sister misinterprets the doctor's actions, and she moves to take his coat. The father pours the doctor a drink, while the mother beckons wordlessly to the doctor to consume the beverage. When the doctor attempts to leave, each family member seems perplexed, but they ask the doctor no questions, nor does he offer any diagnosis. After the doctor has examined the wound more closely, the family members seem to read in the doctor's actions a desire to stay and be of further service. The doctor contemplates for a moment the way the villagers seem to have "lost their ancient beliefs" and expect too much from doctors. He allows them to "misuse" him for their "sacred ends" and does not object when they undress him and put him in bed with the child. No words are exchanged, and the efforts of the family and the village elders are just as futile and meaningless in terms of their ability to cure the boy as is the doctor's inaction.

Kafka portrays a world without moral value, without goodness, without meaning in terms of communication or action. All well-intentioned efforts in the story are futile; there are no positive results. The boy is not saved, nor is Rose. The bizarre elements in the story, such as the appearance of the stranger and his horses in the pigsty, the "unearthly" abilities of the horses in terms of their speed and in the way they urge the doctor to return to Rose, the strange qualities of the wound, and the inexplicable nakedness of the doctor all serve to emphasize this sense of futility and meaninglessness. When these factors are also considered, the world Kafka presents to the reader is one in which there is a basic absence of sense, of reason.

Source: Catherine Dominic, Critical Essay on "A Country Doctor," in *Short Stories for Students*, Gale, Cengage Learning, 2011.

Rochelle Tobias

In the following excerpt, Tobias addresses the question of what ends the doctor serves when he is called to his patient's sickbed.

Of all the accusations made against the country doctor in Kafka's tale by the same name, none seems more harsh than the one the patient whispers as the doctor is laid next to him in bed: "[Du] kommst nicht auf eigenen Fu[Beta]en." While this observation would scarcely seem to compare with the usual charges made against the doctor—he has been accused, for example, of selfishness, passivity, and inconsiderateness—it nonetheless is more condemning, because it is based on the simple fact that the doctor does not arrive at the sickbed by his own means. Rather, he is transported there by "unearthly horses" which materialize out of thin air; they at least appear unexpectedly on his

> INSOFAR AS THE DOCTOR CANNOT LEAVE HIS HOUSE HE FAILS TO LIVE UP TO HIS DETERMINATION. ALTHOUGH HE IS TRAPPED IN THE PROPER—NAMELY HIS PROPERTY—HE CANNOT RISE TO THE CALLING THAT SUPPOSEDLY DEFINES HIM."

property from a pigsty that he had not used in years. The gift of the horses enables the doctor to travel to his patient. But his trip no longer takes the form of a late-night house call once he grabs hold of the reins of the horses, which appear "durch die Kraft der Wendungen ihres Rumples," through a turn of their rumps which suggests a "Redewendung" or turn of phrase as well. Once the doctor latches on to these mythical horses, he is drawn into a mythical realm where he is forced to make a sacrifice in order to accomplish what he calls sardonically holy aims, "heilige Zwecke."

These holy aims might simply be the achievement of peace or rest. In a diary entry written in 1922, when Kafka's tuberculosis had advanced to a critical state, Kafka recalls the story "Ein Landarzt" which he completed in 1917. In a somewhat paradoxical formulation he argues that rest cannot be neglected but must be attained through the mobilization of new forces which exceed the forces that one has available. He then cites the appearance of the horses in "Ein Landarzt" as one of those rare occasions where help was granted to one who had reached the limit of his resources: "Hier allerdings gibt es Oberraschungen, das mu[Beta] der trostloseste Mensch zugeben, es kann erfahrungsgema[Beta] aus Nichts etwas kommen, aus dem verfallenen Schweinestall der Kutscher mit den Pferden kriechen." Kafka's characterization of the horses as a stroke of good fortune would seem to run counter to his tale—a tale in which the doctor is not only undressed and laid in bed with the sick but finally sentenced to perpetual wandering when his horses refuse to take him home or bring him back to his own bed. But his insistence that this gift alone is what enables the "most despondent of men" to rest calls into question what it is that the doctor is supposed to accomplish in this work.

His visit to his patient would at first seem to be in the service of "heilige Zwecke," holy aims, since nothing is more holy than the aim of the medical profession: to cure the ill, to save them from death. To achieve that, however, the doctor must himself be in possession of health; that is, he must be able to travel to the sickbed on his own two feet to restore another to health. The doctor's health is the condition for the realization of his aim, since his calling is what he incarnates each time he rescues another from death. He becomes what he calls in a scarcely veiled allusion to Christ "ein Weltverbesserer" each time he helps another escape the threat of death. In this tale, however, there is no "Weltverbesserer." The doctor introduces the term only to explain, "Ich bin kein weltverbesserer."

What ends the doctor then serves will be the focus of this paper. To whose sickbed is he called? And what, finally, can he do as one who must rely on figurative feet and metaphoric horses to travel to the ill and infirm? The doctor's means of transport are by no means incidental in this work, since if the doctor is a figure for the writer, as so many critics have suggested, it is these very means (tropes, turns, and figures) that link them in their nighttime labors.

Three times in this short work, the doctor asks what it is that he does. The question fast arises as he thinks of Rosa, his loyal servant, whom he left behind in the hands of a predatory horse groom: "Was tue ich, wie rette ich sie?," it comes up again as he establishes that his patient is healthy and his visit unnecessary: "Was tue ich hier in diesem endlosen Winter!"; it arises one final time as the doctor is laid next to the patient in bed who, it ends up, is suffering from a fatal wound to the hip: "Was soll ich tun?" The question is striking given the doctor's initial certainty that he has important business to do which cannot be delayed. Delayed, of course, it is, from his opening statement: "Ich war in gro [Beta]er Verlegenheit: eine dringende Reise stand mir bevor; ein Schwerkranker wartete auf mich in einem zehn Meilen entfemten Dorfe; v... aber das Pferd fehlte, das Pferd." What detains the doctor, according to this statement, is the absence of a means to take him toward his end, a patient in a distant village. His horse, he tells us, died the night before "as a result of overexertion." Without a second horse, he cannot travel to his patient; he is caught in a terrible dilemma.

This is at least the doctor's predicament, as he understands it. He is prepared in every respect to travel, with the exception of a horse, a vehicle. Nonetheless, insofar as this one circumstance prevents him from answering the call he has received, it calls into question his ability to be a country doctor, the one name we have for him. As such a doctor, he is required to answer requests for help, although on this occasion he cannot despite his best intentions. This occasion, consequently, represents both a starting and a stopping point, a point at which he may renew his title as doctor, and one at which he may lose it if he cannot attend to his patient tonight. Both possibilities are written into the doctor's posture; he stands, as he puts it, "reisefertig schon auf dem Hofe," ready to embark on a journey and finished with journeying, done with his work as a country doctor.

If the doctor is, as I suspect, finished with his work, it is because of an injury he sustains, one which is represented in this text through the death of his horse but which extends beyond this one circumstance. For a horse alone can be replaced; the doctor himself admits as much when he later claims, "waren es nicht zufallig Pferde, mu[Beta]te ich mit Sauen fahren." What is irreplaceable is the mobility the doctor loses, the fitness to exercise his trade which is represented through the vehicle of his horse, but which finally has the doctor's health or well-being as its tenor. For this reason, the consequences of this loss are so grave for the doctor's person. If he cannot attend to his patient, if he cannot venture from his yard, he cannot be a country doctor. He is stripped of his raison d'etre: "Immer mehr vom Schnee tiberhauft, immer unbeweglicher werdend, stand ich zwecklos da."

The doctor's admission that he stands "zwecklos" in his own courtyard would at first glance seem to refer to the mere fact that he does nothing; he does not even help his servant Rosa find out if a neighbor might lend him a horse. But the admission refers to his peculiar standstill as well which prevents him from making the movement necessary to reaffirm his purpose or "Zweck." This movement is dialectical, requiring a means through which the doctor can return to the aims or ends ("Zwecke") defining him. These ends take the form of the doctor's calling or trade; he must attend to the patient who has called him to renew his calling as his own, as that which he embodies. From the outset, he stands deficient vis-a-vis this end, since only he has received this call; "[es] war nur fur ihn bestimmt," as the gatekeeper in "Before the Law" might say. This demand pertains only to him, for only he has elected for himself the task of curing the ill, of saving them from death. It is this purpose which in fact awakens him at night, calling him to a distant village to rescue someone. The doctor would not feel motivated—or mobilized—to answer this request if he did not already define himself as someone who serves this end. But in choosing this end as his exclusive measure, he also condemns himself to falling short of his determination in his immobility. Without a horse, without means, the doctor cannot reach the end he has set for himself as a human being. To this extent, then, he stands "zwecklos" in his courtyard. Once he can no longer move toward his end, what remains of him is what cannot be put to work, what serves no purpose.

Insofar as the doctor cannot leave his house he fails to live up to his determination. Although he is trapped in the proper—namely his property—he cannot rise to the calling that supposedly defines him. Something hinders him in progressing toward the end that is not only his livelihood, but life itself. In one of the few readings attentive to the religious dynamics in this work, Bluma Goldstein contends that the doctor must be a medium for a spiritual life to rescue others from sickness and death. As a model for such a process, she points to the rabbis of Hasidic legend, in particular the Zaddikim who, because of their extreme piety, were endowed with the gift of performing miracles. Goldstein argues that several aspects of Kafka's story parallel the legends of the Zaddikim recorded in Alexander Eliasberg's *Sagen polnischer Juden*, a popular anthology of Hasidic folklore that Kafka is known to have possessed. However compelling these examples may be, they are nonetheless of secondary importance in her reading. Her primary concern is to show that the Zaddik represents the ideal, against which the country doctor is measured. The Zaddik heals, she points out, in drawing out the divine sparks in the individual. These sparks stem from the act of creation, when the vessels containing divine light burst and were dispersed throughout the world. The sparks nonetheless represent a unity: the unity of divine light or even divine substance. In releasing the sparks in others as well as in himself, the Zaddik brings

forth a spiritual life that inheres in both and which transcends their mere physical existence.

The country doctor may, as Goldstein contends, fail to be a Zaddik, but only because he cannot be a Christ, who heals the ill and raises the dead in a manner surprisingly similar to her account of the Zaddik. Indeed, what Goldstein argues is the unequivocally Jewish strain in this work bears a striking resemblance to the figure of Christ, as Kafka understood it. In an earlier version of his now famous aphorism, "Der Messias wird erst kommen, wenn er nicht mehr notig sein wird." Kafka addresses the Christian notion of the redeemer directly:

> Der Messias wird kommen, bis der zugelloseste Individualismus des Glaubens moglich ist, niemand diese Moglichkeit vernichtet, niemand die Vernichtung duldet, also die Graber sich offnen. Das ist vielleicht auch die christliche Lehre, sowohl in der tatsachlichen Aufzeigung des Beispieles dem nachgefolgt werden soll, eines individualistischen Beispieles, als auch in der symbolischen Aufzeigung der Auferstenhung des Mittlers im einzelnen Menschen.

The first sentence of this aphorism requires some explanation. Kafka uses the term "bis" in lieu of "wenn," as was apparently customary in Austro-Hungarian dialect; in one diary entry, he even notes that he was prone to confuse the two terms. This aphorism, then, like the later one, is primarily concerned with the condition for the coming of the Messiah, the prerequisite for his advent. Christian doctrine, according to Kafka, illuminates this condition in two respects: First, it offers an example of someone who rose from the grave; and secondly it offers a symbol of the resurrection that can occur in each individual.

It is in this latter function that Christian doctrine bears on the healing process. Christ as "ein einzelner Mensch," a single human being, is subject to death. What enables him to transcend his finite existence is the "Mittler," the intermediary of a spiritual life resurrected in him. Although Christ is often identified as this intermediary, Kafka refrains from doing so here in order to distinguish between Christ the individual and Christ the supposed savior; in other words, he distinguishes between Christ as an example of someone who was saved and Christ as the symbol of the intermediary who can save every human being. As such a symbol, Christ is in fact compelled to save, for only in saving others does he simultaneously save himself, that is, he can demonstrate that he is a vehicle for a life victorious over death only if he repeatedly delivers others to this life, which is also the consummate state of health. For this reason, the priests who follow in his image are sometimes referred to as well as "doctors of the soul," particularly in their pastoral mission. In administering the sacraments, they elevate the souls of their parishioners to a spiritual life which they incarnate, at least for the moment of the ritual.

"Ein Landarzt" invokes this model of healing on more than one occasion. The doctor even invites the comparison with priests when he complains that the people in his region are always asking the impossible of him. They demand that he heal them ("heilen"), which in German has the added, connotation of redeeming or saving, as indicated by the number of words based on this root, including sacred ("heilig"), salvation ("Heil"), and savior ("Heiland"). They turn to the doctor, as he puts it, because they have "lost the old faith." For this reason, the local priest sits at home unraveling his vestments, whereas he is summoned to the deathbed, as if to administer the last rites, which mark not only the end of life on earth, but also the beginning of an everlasting life in heaven. Several critics have argued that Kafka understood the task of the writer in a similar vein, in part because of one diary entry where he states that although work such as "Ein Landarzt" brings him occasional satisfaction, he will only find happiness if he can transform the world "ins Reine, Wahre, Unveranderliche." But it is precisely this end which the doctor fails to attain, since he himself has been touched by sickness, or even death, inasmuch as he cannot rise to his own designation. In other words, he is wounded, perhaps in the rump or hip, because he cannot incarnate the calling that supposedly sustains him.

His one means of sustenance in his predicament is, in fact, his sickness, which reveals to him more than he knew he had in his house, the metonymy for his wounded body or infirm person. Confined to his courtyard, the doctor starts pacing around its perimeter and in a moment of distraction and frustration ("zerstreut, gequalt" kicks the door of a pigsty he had not used in years. To his astonishment, he discovers there both the smell of horses and an individual who offers to bring him to his patient: "'Soll ich anspannen?' fragte er auf allen Vieren hervorkriechend." The offer is ambivalent, inasmuch as it is unclear who or what should be yoked up, either the still-invisible horses, suspected of being there

only because of the smell, or the man who, crouched on all fours, could be said to be volunteering himself as a horse for the purposes of the trip; that is, a man whose "Bestimmung" or "Zweck" would be being a horse, a means toward an end. The doctor's and Rosa's response to this man would only underscore his degradation to the extent that they identify him as a thing found by chance on the property: "'Man wei[Beta] nicht, was fur Dinge man im eigenen Hause vorratig hat,' sagte es [das Dienstmadchen], und wir beide lachten." Laugh the two may, for in the heart of the proper (das "eigene Haus") they discover what they had not known and what they cannot appropriate. Although these "things" are found on the doctor's property, they do not belong entirely to him; he does not recognize them as his own, as part of his own person. For this reason, perhaps, Kafka referred to the horses and horse groom in the story as the appearance of "something out of nothing," which suggests as well the appearance of what till now had been a lack, a deficit hindering the doctor's realization. This deficit, however, now becomes the doctor's means. It opens a space for him to figure what he would need to make the dialectical movement toward his own completion. All this in a figure . . . .

The horses emerge through the door as if they were being born into the world; indeed, the way in which they enter the courtyard— head first, rear last, limbs packed close to the chest—all suggests birth. This birth, however, has an element of the uncanny as well, since the horses that come to be rapidly outsize the pigsty in which they had been held; that is, they inflate in passing through the door into almost mythical creatures, creatures whose strength and size recall "homerische Gestalten," the term Kafka coined to describe the horses he saw in the country in 1917. They acquire this stature, however, only by virtue of a series of "turns" which push them from inside to outside and set them in the world. These turns are not visible to the eye; indeed, the horses they eject through the door effectively conceal them. They are nonetheless the condition for the visibility of the animals, as they are first and foremost "Redewendungen." What the text describes as the repetitive turnings of the horses' buttocks are in fact the turns of phrase, which the text deploys at this very moment to create the means the doctor lacks. In other words, the text refers, "durch die Kraft der Wendungen," to the work it does, turning out phrases that turn nothing into something; in short, storytelling. What makes this coincidence significant—a coincidence in which the text speaks of what it does—is that it simultaneously catapults the story, which had reached an impasse in the doctor's stasis. It brings or pulls the story from the doctor's yard to the bedside of his patient in a village ten miles off. This space, however, cannot be seen as a continuation of the former one, as what renders it accessible is a "Redewendung" that creates something out of nothing.

Source: Rochelle Tobias, "A Doctor's Odyssey: Sickness and Health in Kafka's 'Ein Landarzt,'" in *Germanic Review*, Vol. 75, No. 2, Spring 2000, p. 120.

Ursula Maria Mandel

In the following essay, Mandel agrees with a study of Kafka's short fiction by Allen Thiher that emphasizes its allegorical nature and immensely complex narrative.

Allen Thiher's sophisticated study of Kafka's short fiction is a welcome addition to the critical canon. A thoughtful, challenging, and immensely readable examination of both the short fiction Kafka published during his lifetime and the posthumously published texts, the work is to be commended, first of all, for meeting its publisher's objective: "To provide in-depth critical introductions to major modern and contemporary writers," to give "a comprehensive overview of the artist's short fiction including detailed analysis of every significant story . . . ," to provide "biographical materials" and "a representative selection of critical responses." The author accomplishes a considerable task for an introductory volume, given the wealth of the material to be covered and the vast interpretive dimensions of a single Kafka text and its nearly insurmountable analytical complexity.

Thiher meets the objectives by unifying and limiting the interpretive scope of the texts to such themes and motifs as the notions of closure and rhetorical self-referentiality, the crossing of communicative space and, therefore, the necessary examinations into motion and immobility. Also examined are the impossibility of knowing and certainty for reasons of metaphoric dissemination, language and its fall into history, the dynamics governing the rhetoric of dreams, and lastly, the artist and his at once dynamic and fraudulent pursuits. The seasoned scholar will find these discussions fascinating and challenging reading; those new to Kafka's linguistic mysteries

> THE *MEDITATIONS* TEXTS ARE VIEWED AS LESS ALLEGORICAL THAN LATER KAFKA TEXTS BUT INSTRUMENTAL IN THE DEVELOPMENT OF KAFKA'S DISTINCTIVE STYLE AND NARRATIVE TECHNIQUE AND SYMPTOMATIC OF POSTMODERN SENTIMENTS."

and to the intricacies of literary criticism may feel a bit lost. Given the introductory nature of the Twayne Series, the new scholar will have to bring a broad knowledge of contemporary philosophical, literary, and linguistic theory and their application in order to be able to ponder intelligently, at times, such basic thoughts that a Kafka word, taken literally, creates an insoluble paradox, and a Kafka text, taken allegorically, is about interpretation and the lack of apodictic meaning, both linguistically and metaphysically.

Part I of the volume examines the short fiction, and Thiher, investigating the Nachlass first, emphasizes the allegorical nature of Kafka's fiction, establishing his primary motif; self-referentiality, by way of the immensely complex narrative, "Description of a Struggle." Elucidating the text's troublesome passages, Thiher notes that the narrator uses "the power of language to confer being" (p. 5) on his thoughts and desires, views the narrative divisions of the tale as constituting "allegories about the story's own functioning," (p. 7) and the text as a whole as the "enactment of a struggle to narrate a closed text" (p. 4). Observing that moving through space suggests the textural and metaphorical, but futile, struggle toward meaningful closure, the author finds the purely linguistic creature in "A Crossbread" particularly suggestive of the failure to effectively cross communicative space, a dynamic that the free play and randomness of the linguistic sign raises to the level of self-referential paradox in such texts as "The Bridge," "The Great Wall of China," "The Advocates," and "Wedding Preparations in the Country."

The *Meditations* texts are viewed as less allegorical than later Kafka texts but instrumental in the development of Kafka's distinctive style and narrative technique and symptomatic of postmodern sentiments. Emphasizing once again closure, self-referentiality, and motion as primary objects of investigation, Thiher calls attention to the Derridean observation that such texts as "Before the Law," "Conversation With a Supplicant," and "The Stoker," published separately, yield interpretations other than they acquire contextually. (Here it would have been helpful to give the distinguishing characteristics of these dichotomous interpretations.) "Supplicant," in particular, "illustrates one of the central directions taken in Kafka's work: the world is an infinitely expanding realm of signs that promise that everything has a meaning even as the continued expansion assures that we shall never know what it is" (p. 21).

Three of the *Meditation* texts are singled out for their specific subject matter, women. "Clothes," "Rejection," and "Unhappiness" emphasize the well-worn thematics of the erotic, sensual, ensnaring nature of women that, ghost-like, haunts [as the Jungian anima?] the heroes of Kafka's tales. But no further illumination on the status of women in Kafka is offered, except that they, as embodied Eros, keep the [male] characters from "the [anguished] desire to move on and stay in motion" (p. 28).

The best known of Kafka's short fiction, "The Judgment," "The Metamorphosis," "In the Penal Colony," "A Country Doctor," and "The Hungerartist" are investigated in terms of the motifs found in "On Parables," which sets up, according to Thiher, "a form of self-referential metalanguage" (p. 33), its paradoxes and pitfalls, based on the premise that a Kafka text "stops the reader from making reference to a transcendent discourse" and "becomes a self-referential interrogation about the text's relation to any other realm" (pp. 36/35). Valid as these observations are, closure and self-referentiality limit the interpretive scope of the narratives, and the lack of comparative methodologies from the scholarship—omitted in the work in general—is here most apparent, as the analyses appear incomplete and less convincing. Georg's drowning in "The Judgment" is viewed as "perhaps the fall of discourse finally into silence" (p. 40). That it falls for the sake of Georg's misrepresentations does not seem satisfactory in the light of the author's own motifs of closure, motion, and self-referential paradox.

The fall of language and the deceptiveness of memory together with the notions of closure, both linguistically and meta-physically, are also pursued in "The Metamorphosis." Both Gregor's preference for garbage presented on a newspaper and the father's newspaper reading—discourse once again tied to father and son—are considered indicative of language and the writing of history as fallen and inadequate discourse, a motif that is also pursued in the "The Penal Colony." Establishing the writing of history, of which the machine is symbolic, as a progressive falling away of language from its original oneness with the Law, both guardian and machine become part of a memory beyond recall. This does not adequately explain, however, the tremendous power of myth (here particularly the myth of salvation), its perpetuation, its fanatic advocates, and its tragic victims - all inseparable from language as a vehicle of myth . . . .

Thiher considers texts contained in "A Country Doctor" in terms of their explain, however, the tremendous power of myth (here particularly the myth of salvation), its perpetuation, its fanatic advocates, and its tragic victims—all inseparable from language as a vehicle of myth.

Thiher considers texts contained in "A Country Doctor" in terms of their "expressionistic dream rhetoric," which "unfold while paying no attention to the laws of logic" (pp. 68/69). The doctor, as "an interpreter of signs, quite literally a semiologist" enables Thiher to draw a parallel to the term Odradek in "The Cares of a Family Man" as a philological term that draws attention to itself and once again reminds the reader of the self-referential qualities in the Kafka text. Thiher's exegeses end with the collection in *The Hungerartist*, and the author's investigations poignantly express Kafka's ambiguous feelings toward his own art as at once inferior and superior, as transfiguration and as substitution.

The excerpts of Kafka's autobiographical writings (Part II) are well chosen for their contextual insight into some of the short fiction and into Kafka, the writer. The invaluable staples of primary and critical bibliographies, chronologies, and indices (following Part III of the volume) serve this function as well.

The collection of critical essays (Part III), selected for their diverse theoretical approaches to the Kafka texts, are also fascinating reading. Stanley Corngold investigates authorial intentionality versus the deliberate or unintentional incongruencies of the texts. Ruth Gross examines the perceptual and emotional ambiguities of the narrator toward Josephine, the singer, as a creature simultaneously exalted and scorned, giving the reading the interesting perpective that the burden of proof of Kafka's women characters lies with the perceiver. Doreen Fowler interprets "The Penal Colony" in terms of Judeo-Christian myths and doctrine, whereas William Dodd, using the same text, applies the Freudian principles of Id, Ego, and Superego. "From Marx to Myth: The Structure and Function of Self-Alienation in Kafka's 'Metamorphosis.'"

The strengths of the present volume are its organization, its thorough analysis of troublesome Kafka passages, and the definition of theoretical terminology and/or restatement of complex ideas in a comprehensible manner. Less fortunate is the methodology's presentation as definitive or exclusive without intratextual, comparative criteria taken from the immensely vast and diverse scholarship, although the collection of critical essays and bibliographical entries seeks, in part, to serve this function. I recognize the tremendous work involved in putting this critical volume together, however; such exegetical exclusiveness does not over-shadow the comprehensibility of the work, its challenges, its overall presentation of a difficult subject, its capacity to provoke thought and to add to the reader's knowledge of the enigma that is a Kafka text.

Source: Ursula Maria Mandel, Review of *Franz Kafka: A Study of the Short Fiction*, in *Germanic Review*, Vol. 69, No. 1, Winter 1994, pp. 38–40.

John J. Brancato

In the following review, Brancato interprets the literary views in "A Country Doctor," especially the use of a country doctor as a metaphor in the story.

Kafka's "A Country Doctor" is a surrealistic tale about the powerlessness of scientific man in confrontation with the brute force of nature. Although Kafka suggests the cyclical and interdependent aspects of all life, he makes it very clear that *only* man has the capacity to feel ultimately betrayed by life. This short story captures a profound sense of futility through its nightmarish quality. Coming to the end of "A Country Doctor" has the same effect as waking from a bad dream—the incubus has been lifted and we are relieved, but we also know that our anxieties, crystallized by the dream, are still very much with us.

Kafka uses a country doctor's experience, real or imagined, as a metaphor for the failure

> KAFKA HAS CRYSTALIZED HERE THE
> DILEMMA OF THE MODERN SCIENTIST: HE CAN BE
> HONEST OR HE CAN OFFER PLACEBOS."

of scientific man to assuage the pain of dying. The doctor answers his alarm bell, which warns him of the death of one of his patients, but the alarm turns out to be a "false alarm," since he can do nothing to save his patient or himself from death. Equating the consciousness of the doctor with scientific knowledge, Kafka suggests that although modern man has tried to make science replace his ancient beliefs, it is unable to perform well in this sacred capacity. Modern man has worshipped science, and scientists have assumed the role of gods. Because of this apotheosis, when scientists find themselves impotent in the face of death, their self-condemnation is as great as the condemnation that they are subjected to by the general populace. In this story the country doctor becomes as helpless as the patients he is trying to cure. (An archaic meaning of the word "patient," by the way, is "to be acted upon rather than acting.")

Throughout the story we see evidence of the doctor's helplessness. When we first meet him he is in "great perplexity." He has answered his night bell but is "forlorn," "distressed," and "confused" about how to get to his "seriously ill patient." Although nature is working against him (the blizzard, the death of his own horse), he is willing to accept his role as country doctor if he can find a means of getting to the patient. When his servant Rose returns from seeking assistance, she confirms what he already knows—that no one has volunteered to help him. We see the doctor, however thwarted, accepting his role despite human selfishness and indifference. Up to this point in the story the reader can identify with the setting and the situation on a realistic level. It is then that the nightmarish quality of the plot begins.

In the dreamlike incidents that follow, Kafka gives us further objectification of the doctor's sense of futility and betrayal. There is a proliferation of those uncontrollable forces of nature that so often determine what we can and cannot do in life. On his own property the doctor discovers two horses and a groom in an abandoned pigsty. As he looks into the open door of the sty, he discovers, crouched on his hams, a groom who offers to yoke up two horses. The doctor and Rose laugh at what they unexpectedly find in their own backyard. In language that suggests the process of defecation (a basic, natural process), the doctor describes the emergence of the horses from the sty—horses who "by sheer strength of buttocking squeezed out through the door hole," and whose bodies "steam thickly." The doctor's momentary relief at finding a way to get to his patient is negated when the groom bites Rose's face. The doctor calls the groom a "brute" but at the same moment feels he cannot condemn one who is offering help when no one else has. Sensing this acceptance, the groom does not even respond to the doctor's threat. ("Do you want a whipping?") The entire sequence suggests man's dilemma in confrontation with the inexplicable forces of nature. From out of his "yearlong uninhabited pigsty" (his farm is effete) comes an opportunity to get where he wants to go. The condition is that he will have to lose Rose, his only human contact on the farm and a person whom he has taken for granted. Nature, benign or malignant, has offered help, but not without exacting a toll. The scientist must often abandon his own comforts and humane concerns if he wants to have any effect at all. He laments the loss of his Rose, but he justifies his complicity with the groom by telling himself that he is doing his official duty.

The groom may represent natural man—or the devil. (One meaning of the word groom—"a forked stick used by thatchers"—is reminiscent of representations of the devil.) The doctor's involvement with the groom is another source of his growing sense of powerlessness. The groom not only prepares the way for the doctor to fulfill his official business but also becomes Rose's "bridegroom." Although the doctor feebly protests, he can do nothing to keep the groom from this unwilling and frightened "bride." The scientist has lost control of himself, and in a "storming rush" that buffets all his senses, he arrives at his patient's house, which turns out to be uncannily close (suggesting a growing human bond). The implication is that the scientific man may submerge his own basic sexual impulses in order to answer a more altruistic call. His willingness to accept help that requires the sacrifice of Rose, however, may

make him seem in league with the devil rather than God. Expediency, Kafka seems to be saying, is the rule for the modern scientist.

The veneration of his patient's family only makes the doctor feel greater powerlessness. After he is "almost lifted" out of his gig by the parents and sister, he finds himself in the "unbreathable" air of the sickroom. He wants to open a window, but duty calls him directly to his patient. The boy entreats the doctor to let him die (as though he could control life and death), while the doctor thinks "blasphemously" about the helpful gods who got him to his patient. He is reminded at this point that he cannot return to save Rose because the horses cannot be controlled. The horses, just at this moment, do what the doctor himself didn't do—they maneuver the windows open with their heads, and the parents, afraid of such unbridled forces, cry out. The horses, Brother and Sister, suggest the incubus and succubus that the family fear will take the boy's life.

Although the doctor would like to return home, he allows himself to be "cajoled" closer to the bed and "yields" to examine the boy. One of the horses whinnies loudly as the doctor puts his head to the boy's breast. (The succubus does not want the doctor to help the boy.) Oddly, the doctor finds nothing wrong with his patient. He has done his duty however, and he rationalizes his failure to find anything wrong by saying "the boy might have his way, and I wanted to die too." The doctor admits defeat: "to write prescriptions is easy," he says, "but to come to an understanding with people is hard."

Kafka has crystalized here the dilemma of the modern scientist: he can be honest or he can offer placebos. The country doctor would like to avoid the dilemma entirely, but the evidence of the "blood-soaked towel" finally gets him to admit "conditionally" that the boy is as seriously ill as he has told us at the beginning of the narrative. The horses' whinnying together at this point may be doing so not, as the doctor thinks, because the sound is "ordained in heaven" to assist his examination, but to protest his interference with the death process.

The doctor admits to the true enormity of the force he is fighting when he gives a "low whistle of surprise at the rose-red wound containing worms" that "wriggle toward the light." Here the doctor suddenly uses the past tense, as if in an afterlife, to tell the boy he was past helping. The wound itself suggests cyclic regeneration. (The worms are feeding on the wound that is killing the boy.) The doctor calls the wound the "blossom" in the boy's side. Out of destruction, the scientist knows, new life will emerge.

Again the doctor is powerless—he cannot communicate what he has seen and what he knows to be the bitter truth. The boy's family won't let him. The doctor is forced to act the role of God. They are pleased that the doctor has acted by busying himself with the boy, but the doctor knows his service is futile. "They misuse me for 'sacred services'" he thinks, while the parson, who once might have offered the consolation they need, uselessly "unravels his vestments." The doctor knows he is not omnipotent, but the mystical choir is being taught nevertheless to sing "Only a doctor, only a doctor." Even after he is stripped and placed in bed with the boy, he must suffer the accusations of the dying patient. He tries to comfort the boy by telling him that his wound is not as bad as some—he even gives the boy the "word of honor of an official doctor" on this point. Here again we see the physician forced into a situation that he tries to make the best of. The doctor's being placed at the right side of the boy's wound does not position the boy at the right hand of God but on the left hand of Science, a false god. After the doctor has shared the deathbed with the boy for a little while and has attempted to mitigate his fears, he decides it is time to go home. He leaves without bothering to put on his clothes, since he hopes to be home as quickly as he came. This is not the case, and, still stripped of his clothes, recognizing a "new but faulty" song of the children that goes "O be joyful, all you patients, The doctor's laid in bed beside you!" he mounts a horse. The horses are no longer Brother and Sister but old men crawling through the "snowy wastes."

He will not reach home, for he is being led to his death by the "unearthly horses." His impotence is once again underlined when he cannot reach the fur coat hanging from a hook on the back of the gig. He knows and we know that "it [dying] cannot be made good, not ever." The inscrutable forces of nature move on, and although no one can ever take the doctor's place, his irreplaceability is no comfort to him. He is alone and alienated. No one will lift a finger to help him in the end. The alarm has indeed been false, for there is nothing he can do to keep the end from being hard. Once man tries

to act by answering the night bell, he loses his innocence and feels disappointed when his presumptions about having power turn out to be incorrect. This age, for Kafka, seems the "most unhappy of ages," for science is no better than religion in assuaging pain—the pain of knowing that we must all die. "Betrayed! Betrayed!" is the country doctor's cry, and we know the reason.

Source: John J. Brancato, "Kafka's 'A Country Doctor': A Tale for Our Time," in *Studies in Short Fiction*, Vol. 15, No. 2, Spring 1978, pp. 173–76.

SOURCES

Carveth, Donald L., "Sigmund Freud Today: What Are His Enduring Contributions?," in *York University Web site*, 2006, http://www.yorku.ca/dcarveth/freudtoday (accessed September 22, 2010).

"A Country Study: Czechoslovakia (Former)," in *Library of Congress Country Studies*, http://memory.loc.gov/frd/cs/cstoc.html (accessed September 22, 2010).

"Czech Republic," in *CIA: World Factbook*, https://www.cia.gov/library/publications/the-world-factbook/geos/ez.html (accessed September 22, 2010).

Gray, Richard T., Ruth V. Gross, Rolf J. Goebel, and Clayton Koelb, "Freud, Sigmund," in *Franz Kafka Encyclopedia*, Greenwood Press, 2005, pp. 99–100.

Kafka, Franz, "A Country Doctor," in *Franz Kafka: The Complete Stories*, edited by Nahum N. Glazter, Schocken Books, 1971, pp. 220–25.

Krockel, Karl, "Germany," in *Encyclopedia of Literary Modernism*, edited by Paul Poplawski, Greenwood Press, 2003, pp. 158–60.

Lawson, Richard H., "Franz Kafka," in *Dictionary of Literary Biography*, Vol. 81, *Austrian Fiction Writers, 1875–1913*, edited by James Hardin, Gale Research, 1989, pp. 133–68.

Levinson, Jerrold, "Intention and Interpretation in Literature," in *The Pleasures of Aesthetics: Philosophical Essays*, Cornell University Press, 1996, pp. 175–213.

Menninghaus, Winifried, "The Wound in the Text and the Text as Wound: The Story 'A Country Doctor,'" in *Disgust: Theory and History of a Strong Sensation*, translated by Howard Eiland and Joel Golb, State University of New York Press, 2003, pp. 318–31.

Pratt, Alan, "Nihilism," in *The Internet Encyclopedia of Philosophy: A Peer Reviewed Academic Resource*, 2001, http://www.iep.utm.edu/nihilism/ (accessed September 22, 2010).

Rothfield, Lawrence, "The Pathological Perspective: Clinical Realism's Decline and the Emergence of Modernist Counter-Discourse," in *Vital Signs: Medical Realism in Nineteenth-Century Fiction*, Princeton University Press, 1992, pp. 148–74.

Sokel, Walter H., "Franz Kafka," in *The Myth of Power and the Self: Essays on Franz Kafka*, Wayne State University Press, 2002, pp. 35–64.

Turner, John, "Psychoanalysis," in *Encyclopedia of Literary Modernism*, edited by Paul Poplawski, Greenwood Press, 2003, pp. 330–41.

FURTHER READING

Church, Margaret, *Time and Reality: Studies in Contemporary Fiction*, University of North Carolina Press, 1949.
    Church explores the treatment of time and reality in modernist fiction, focusing in particular on the work of such writers as Marcel Proust, James Joyce, Thomas Mann, Virginia Woolf, William Faulkner, and in the postmodern writings of Jean-Paul Sartre. Church's work provides students of Kafka with a means of comparing his work with that of his contemporaries.

Greenburg, Martin, *The Terror of Art: Kafka and Modern Literature*, Basic Books, 1968.
    Greenburg offers a detailed thematic analysis of Kafka's work.

Mitchell, Stephen A., and Margaret J. Black, *Freud and Beyond: A History of Modern Psychoanalytic Thought*, Basic Books, 1996.
    The authors provide a study of Freud's work and discuss his contribution to and influence in the field of psychiatry and psychoanalysis.

Murray, Nicholas, *Kafka: A Biography*, Yale University Press, 2004.
    Murray's acclaimed biography explores Kafka's brief life and his works, portraying him as something more than the tormented soul that he has often been reduced to in analyses of him and his work.

Quackenbush, Craig, ed., *Falling from the Sky*, Another Sky Press, 2007.
    Quackenbush's collection is an array of experimental and surreal short fiction by numerous modern authors from around the world.

SUGGESTED SEARCH TERMS

Kafka AND Country Doctor

Kafka AND German literature

Kafka AND Czechoslovakia

Kafka AND modernism

Kafka AND surrealism

Kafka AND Freud

Kafka AND modernism

Kafka AND Metamorphosis

Kafka AND psychoanalysis

Kafka AND short stories

The Distant Past

WILLIAM TREVOR

1975

"The Distant Past" is a story by the renowned Irish writer William Trevor. It was first published in Trevor's short-story collection *Angels at the Ritz* in 1975, and it has been reprinted in a number of Trevor's later collections, including *The Collected Stories* (1992) and *Ireland: Selected Stories* (1995). The story is set in Ireland over a period of about fifty years, from about 1920 to the early 1970s, and deals with the conflicts in that country between the British and the Irish, and between Protestants and Catholics. The protagonists are an unmarried brother and sister, Mr. and Miss Middleton, who are Irish Protestants living near a town that is about sixty miles from the border between the Republic of Ireland and Northern Ireland. They have lived there all their lives and remain loyal to Britain. Until sectarian conflict breaks out in Northern Ireland in the late 1960s, they get on well with the local people, who are Catholics, and it seems that old antagonisms have long faded away. But that proves not to be the case, and as the violence in Northern Ireland grows, the Middletons face ostracism from the people they formerly counted as friends. It turns out that the past casts a long shadow over the present. The story is interesting not only as an example of the work of one of the best short-story writers in the world but also because it shows how the twentieth-century conflict in Ireland affected ordinary people there over a long period of time.

William Trevor (Getty Images)

From the 1960s and continuing into the twenty-first century, Trevor produced a steady stream of novels and short-story collections and won many prestigious awards. His first collection of short stories was *The Day We Got Drunk on Cake and Other Stories* (1967), followed by *The Ballroom of Romance and Other Stories* (1972) and *Angels at the Ritz and Other Stories* (1975), which contains "The Distant Past" and received the Royal Society of Literature award. Later short-story collections included *Family Sins and Other Stories* (1990), *The Collected Stories* (1993), *After Rain* (1996), *The Hill Bachelors* (2000), which won the *Irish Times* Literary Prize, *A Bit on the Side* (2004), and *Cheating at Canasta* (2007). His novels include *Mrs. Eckdorf in O'Neill's Hotel* (1969), which was shortlisted for the Booker Prize, and *The Children of Dynmouth* (1976), which won the Whitbread Novel Award, as did *Fools of Fortune* (1983). Later novels include *Nights at the Alexandra* (1987), *The Silence in the Garden* (1988), *Felicia's Journey* (1993), which was named Whitbread Book of the Year, *Death in Summer* (1998), *The Story of Lucy Gault* (2002), which was shortlisted for the Booker Prize, and *Love and Summer* (2009). In 2008, Trevor received the Bob Hughes Lifetime Achievement Award in Irish Literature.

AUTHOR BIOGRAPHY

Trevor was born on May 24, 1928, in Michelstown, County Cork, Ireland, into a middle-class Protestant family. His father was a bank official. Trevor was educated in Dublin, and he received a B.A. in history from Trinity College, Dublin, in 1950. For several years he worked as a teacher in Armagh, Northern Ireland, and he married Jane Ryan in 1952. They later had two sons.

In 1953, Trevor and his wife moved to England, where he pursued a career as a sculptor. Although he had some success in that field, he decided to turn to writing instead. His first novel, *A Standard of Behaviour*, was published in 1958. From 1960 to 1964, Trevor worked as an advertising copywriter in London, but the success of his novel *The Old Boys* (1964), which won the Hawthornden Prize in 1965, encouraged him to pursue writing as a full-time career. He moved with his family to Devon, in southwest England, where, as of 2010, he still lives.

PLOT SUMMARY

"The Distant Past" is set in the Republic of Ireland and tells the story of a brother and sister, Mr. and Miss Middleton, who are all that is left of a Protestant Irish family living in a predominantly Catholic country. The family used to be prosperous, living in a large house called Carraveagh, three miles out of town. But the family wealth was squandered by the siblings' father, who spent too much money on a Catholic woman from Dublin. When he died in 1924, the siblings found their inheritance much reduced from what they had expected. The siblings blamed not only the Catholic woman but also the new Irish government. Ireland had just gained its independence from Britain, but as Protestants, Mr. and Miss Middleton remained loyal to England. However, they got along well enough with the Catholic townspeople. They would drive into town to sell their eggs and socialize. Indeed, their relationships with these folks have flourished in spite of their political and religious differences. They have even learned to laugh together about former incidents that had divided them, in particular a potentially violent incident involving the Middletons, Fat Cranley the town butcher, and two other farmers. This had happened a long time ago, when the Middletons were children. The Irish were fighting for their independence, and British troops were in the land. Fat Cranley and the two other men had stood in the hall of Carraveagh, the Middletons' home, with shotguns, awaiting the arrival of British troops. The children, along with their parents and aunt, had been locked in an upstairs room. However, the troops never appeared, so violence was averted.

As the years go by, the Middletons retain their loyalty to the British crown. They protest when prayers for the monarchy are no longer said in St. Patrick's Cathedral, and in 1953, they display a small British flag in their car on the day of the coronation of Queen Elizabeth II. The local people find this amusing and joke about it to the Middletons.

During the 1950s and 1960s, the town flourishes, benefiting greatly from tourism, including people from England and the United States. In contrast, however, the fortunes of the Middletons decline. The brother and sister are now in their mid-sixties, and they cannot afford to repair the leaking roof on their formerly splendid house. They look forward to their weekly trips into town and the socializing they do there. They remain loyal to Britain but no one in the town seems to mind, and the Middletons are respected. Visitors think it remarkable that old hostilities could so completely be laid aside.

In 1968, there is a violent incident in Belfast, in which Irish nationalists blow up some post offices. Belfast is the capital of Northern Ireland, which remains under British rule. The townsfolk and the Middletons are shocked by the bombings and condemn them.

Civil unrest continues in Belfast and Derry, another city in Northern Ireland. At first the townspeople the Middletons know say the violence has nothing to do with the South. But then British troops are sent to Northern Ireland to quell the violence, and the situation appears to get worse, with violence spreading to towns on the border between Northern Ireland and the Republic of Ireland.

The unrest discourages tourists from visiting Ireland, and the town's prosperity declines. It is sixty miles from the border. The residents become angry about the decline in business, and old memories of civil conflict return. They start to treat the Middletons differently, remembering how the Middletons remained loyal to the British. Now there is silence when they appear, and some people turn their heads away when they see the Middletons coming. The townspeople no longer view the Middletons' old beliefs as relics from the past that should be ignored. Instead, they become hostile to the Middletons. The Middletons are left to regret these changes in their circumstances. After so many years of mutual tolerance, during which they had formed good relationships with the people in the town, the old days of hostility have returned, and they can see no end to them this time. As they look to their impoverished future, they decide they must sell their four Herefords (beef cattle) and their hens. They have nothing to look forward to as they continue to live in their old ruined house, isolated by the hostility of the townsfolk. They realize that because of the strife that has engulfed Ireland and the old wounds it has reopened, they will die without friends.

CHARACTERS

Reverend Bradshaw

Reverend Bradshaw succeeds Reverend Packham as the pastor of St. Patrick's Protestant Church. He regards the Middletons as anachronisms, relics from a bygone era.

Breen

Breen was a farmer who waited along with Maguire and Cranley in the hall at Carraveagh to attack the British troops.

Canon Cotter

Canon Cotter is a clergyman in the town during the times of prosperity. He at first wonders whether having so many tourists come will lead to a decline in morals, but he discovers that this does not happen. He thinks highly of the Middletons, and when Miss Middleton is ill, in 1958, he drives out to Carraveagh with pullets and ducks for her to eat. However, he rejects them after the violence breaks out more than a decade later.

Fat Cranley

Fat Cranley owns a butcher's store in the town. Back in the days before Irish independence, he was a supporter of the Irish nationalist cause. On one occasion, he stood in the hall of Carraveagh, the Middletons' home, with a shotgun, waiting to shoot at British troops who were said to be on the way. The troops never arrived, however. As memories of that incident faded over the years, Cranley became friends with the Middletons. He even joked about it with them, and it appeared that there were no hard feelings. He would even slip into their order a free piece of mince for the Middletons' dog, pretending that otherwise it would be thrown away. By the late 1960s he is sixty-six years old and overdue to retire from his butcher's business, but he finds it hard to get around to the business of selling it. When the violence spreads in Northern Ireland, Cranley withdraws his friendship from the Middletons and wants people to forget that he was ever kind to them.

Mrs. Duggan

Mrs. Duggan is a woman from the town who used to chat with the Middletons, but after the violence begins in Northern Ireland she refuses even to reply when they speak to her.

Mrs. Gerrity

Mrs. Gerrity owns a grocery store in the town. She is friends with the Middletons, who regularly sell their eggs to the store. They all share a drink afterward.

Mr. Heely

Mr. Heely owns a hotel in the town. He is a leader in the local business community. When the town starts to prosper, he renames and then expands his successful hotel and also organizes an annual Salmon Festival to boost tourism. He and the Middletons are friends.

Maguire

Maguire was one of the three men who waited in the hall at Carraveagh to attack the British troops.

Mr. Middleton

Mr. Middleton is a bachelor who lives with his sister, Miss Middleton. They come from a long-established Anglo-Irish Protestant family that used to be affluent, until Mr. Middleton's father squandered the family wealth. Mr. Middleton and his sister then grew up in more dire circumstances, although they still occupied the large family house, Carraveagh, which was built in the eighteenth century. They are very attached to their house, even though they do not have the money to keep it in good repair and wonder why they never sold it. Mr. Middleton and his sister are both loyal to the British crown even though they live in an independent Ireland.

They are both of thin build and do not speak much to each other. At one point Mr. Middleton's sister observes that she can never tell what her brother is thinking, and they do not speak to each other about painful or difficult topics. This is in spite of the fact that they seem to spend most of their waking hours together and share the same political and religious views. The narrator usually refers to them both at once as "they," as if they are one person. They have lived together for so long and lead such quiet, undramatic lives that it seems as if they do not possess individual personalities. When they are shunned by the people in the town who were formerly their friends, Mr. Middleton tells his sister there will be no end to the bad situation, and she agrees with him, but they do not discuss it further. He realizes that they will both face this silent hostility for the rest of their lives, and there is nothing they can do about it.

Miss Middleton

Miss Middleton is the sister of Mr. Middleton. There is a physical resemblance between them; both have "a bony countenance, with pale blue eyes and a sharp, well-shaped nose and high cheekbones." Near the end of the story, Miss Middleton is sixty-six years old. She is very similar to her brother, and they share the same views. Miss Middleton enjoys good relations with the townspeople until the violence begins north of the border. She is shown with her brother on two occasions sharing a smile and a laugh with Fat Cranley over the long-ago incident in which Cranley was prepared to shoot British soldiers. When relations with the townspeople break down she is resigned to living out the rest of her life with her brother as a social outcast.

Reverend Packham

Reverend Packham was the pastor of St. Patrick's Protestant Church in the town during the 1920s. He died soon after World War II.

THEMES

Past

The main theme in "The Distant Past" is how the past still affects the present, even fifty years later, even though for many of the intervening years the past events appeared to be laid to rest. After most of Ireland gains independence from Britain in 1921, old conflicts in the town fade away. The Middletons, an Anglo-Irish family who remain loyal to Britain, are able to get along fine with the Catholic people in the town whose loyalties are to Ireland, not Britain. Old animosities are forgotten. This even includes the incident in which Fat Conroy and two other men stood in the hall of the Middletons' house, ready to shoot British soldiers, while the Middletons, who were children at the time, were locked in an upstairs room. Many years later, the participants in that incident are able to laugh with each other about it. It seems as if old wounds have healed. When violence breaks out again in the late 1960s, this time between Protestants and Catholics in Northern Ireland, it seems at first that it will cause no harm to relations in the town. The Catholic townspeople and the Protestant Middletons speak about the outbreak of violence with a common voice, condemning the violence. But when British troops are sent to Northern Ireland and tourism to the town plummets because people fear that Ireland is no longer a safe place to visit, attitudes change. People are angry about the drop in trade and seek someone to blame. As a result, the friendships that have for years crossed political, religious, and cultural barriers quickly snap. The changing tides of history serve to revive tribal feelings within the citizens of the town, who reject the Middletons because the two represent the wrong group, even though they remain the same people who had for years chatted happily with the locals in stores and bars. The change shows that the "distant past" has a power over the present that no one in the prosperous 1950s and early 1960s would have suspected. It is not so much that the people themselves have changed. They are simply reacting to the larger forces of history that are shaping Ireland at this particular time, and over which they have no control. In this sense people are the playthings of history; a sudden turn in events somewhere relatively far away can have drastic repercussions on ordinary folk who thought that the trouble of the past was safely in the past. The sudden reawakening of issues from the distant past unfortunately reveals the townspeople at their worst; they fall prey to

TOPICS FOR FURTHER STUDY

- Use Internet and print sources to research the wars in the Balkans in the 1990s that resulted from the breakup of Yugoslavia. In what ways did the ethnic violence in a country such as Bosnia resemble the conflict in Northern Ireland from the late 1960s to the 1990s? For reference you can consult *Ireland*, by Edward Patrick Hogan (Chelsea House, 2003), and *Bosnia: Fractured Region*, by Eric Black (Lerner Publishing, 1998), both of which are books for young adults. Present the results of your research to the class as a multimedia presentation.

- Read another story by Trevor that deals either directly or indirectly with the Troubles in Northern Ireland. Some examples are "Lost Ground" (in *After Rain* and *Ireland: Selected Stories*), "Another Christmas" or "Attracta" (in *Lovers of Their Time*), and "Autumn Sunshine" or "Beyond the Pale" (both in *Beyond the Pale*). Write an essay in which you compare and contrast one of these stories with "The Distant Past."

- Go to Google maps (http://maps.google.com/help/maps/mymaps/create.html). Create a map of Ireland. Identify six places on the map and add text that explains why they are important places in Irish history. What happened in those places? When? Publish the map on your Web log to share it with your friends.

- Using Internet research, create an interactive timeline for the Troubles in Northern Ireland. Pay particular attention to how the Troubles were resolved. Give a class presentation in which you present the key issues and events in the Troubles. Comment also on the situation in Northern Ireland today. Are the Troubles entirely in the past, or do some issues linger on? Search Google news for the latest reports about Northern Ireland to link to your presentation.

The Middletons were accompanied over the years by a series of red setters. *(Reddogs | Shutterstock.com)*

pettiness and mean behavior toward two people who bear no responsibility for the current events.

Ostracism

Not long after the violence breaks out again in Northern Ireland, the Middletons became outcasts in their own community, rejected by the people with whom they have lived in close proximity their entire lives. This could also be called ostracizing, an act by which a community or society expresses its scorn and rejection of people it does not approve of yet cannot physically remove. The townspeople cannot force the Middletons to move—even the Middletons cannot bring themselves to leave their old family home—but they are able to make them feel extremely unwelcome. They do this by refusing to speak to them, turning away when they see them approaching, even refusing to reply when one of the Middletons speaks to them directly. The townspeople choose to remember certain things and forget others. Fat Cranley the butcher, for example, no longer wants anyone to know that he used to slip into the Middletons' order free pieces of meat for their dog. Such an act

of kindness is a thing of the past. Cranley prefers that people remember, from the distant past that now seems not so distant, how he stood in Carraveagh, the Middletons' home, ready to shoot British soldiers.

In making outcasts of the Middletons, the townspeople behave in a very cruel manner. A kind of unspoken collective decision has been made about the brother and sister, and no one has sufficient independence of thought, or bravery, to point out the obvious: the people they are ostracizing have not done anything to deserve it; they are the same people they were when everyone was getting along well. They are simply being used as scapegoats by a community that is angry because its prosperity has been threatened by the reduction in tourism.

STYLE

Point of View

The story is told by a limited third-person narrator from the point of view of the Middletons. This means that the narrator knows everything about the Middletons—their personal history, their thoughts, and their feelings. The narrator does not have this insight into the other characters, who are revealed only through what they do or say and by what the Middletons think of them. The focus of the story is thus on how the Middletons experience their world, and how that experience changes over time.

Symbolism

The Middletons' house, called Carraveagh, is used as a symbol of British rule and power in Ireland. The house contains various images that represent British history and tradition. A portrait of the Middletons' father, who served in the Irish Guards (loyal to Britain) and had once talked with Queen Victoria, hangs on the wall, as does the Cross of St. George, the patron saint of England. There is a Union Jack (the British flag) propped in a vase on the mantelpiece. British power over Ireland is on the wane, however, and this is symbolized by the disrepair into which the house falls. This takes place while the nearby town, symbolizing in this case Ireland, becomes more prosperous. After the conflict breaks out in Northern Ireland and the Middletons are ostracized, the brother and sister remove from Carraveagh all those signs of British tradition, suggesting that British influence is finally on the way out.

COMPARE
&
CONTRAST

- **1920s:** Following the signing of the Anglo-Irish treaty in 1921, Ireland is partitioned into Northern Ireland and the Irish Free State. From 1922 to 1923 there is civil war in the Irish Free State between those who accept the partition of the country and the republicans, led by Eamon de Valera, who want to continue to fight for a united Ireland.

  1970s: In January 1972, British troops fire on civil rights demonstrators in Londonderry, Northern Ireland. Thirteen people are killed. The incident becomes known as "Bloody Sunday" and arouses fierce resentment among the Catholic population.

  Today: In 2010, Britain completes an official inquiry into Bloody Sunday. The report states that the killings were unjustified because the demonstrators were peaceful and offered no provocation. British prime minister David Cameron apologizes for the incident.

- **1920s:** In Northern Ireland, the Protestant majority solidifies its hold on power. The police force is overwhelmingly Protestant, and state funds go to predominantly Protestant schools. Protestants gerrymander electoral districts and abolish proportional representation.

  1970s: Northern Ireland is marked by continuing sectarian violence. The Irish Republican Army (IRA) attempts by terrorism to force Britain to withdraw from Northern Ireland. The British government makes some attempts to reduce discrimination against the Catholic minority and to promote power-sharing agreements between Northern Ireland and the Republic of Ireland. However, these measures are largely unsuccessful.

  Today: Northern Ireland remains a part of the United Kingdom, and the sectarian violence has largely ended. Northern Ireland has its own 108-member Northern Ireland Assembly, and power is shared between Protestants and Catholics. Elections are held on the basis of proportional representation.

- **1920s:** The Irish Free State is a mostly agrarian economy, and economic policy is aimed at improving efficiency in agriculture. In the mid-1920s agriculture provides 35 percent of gross domestic product (GDP) and over half of all employment. However, during this decade prices for Ireland's agricultural products fall, and there is little economic growth. Because of a lack of economic opportunity, emigration is high.

  1970s: The Republic of Ireland enters the European Economic Community in 1973. However, a combination of factors, including the Troubles in Northern Ireland and labor disputes, inhibit economic growth.

  Today: Ireland's economy is dominated by industry and services rather than agriculture. Following a twelve-year period of steady economic growth, Ireland enters a recession in 2008. GDP falls nearly 8 percent in 2009. The Irish government attempts to bring down the budget deficit by making drastic cuts in spending.

HISTORICAL CONTEXT

Irish History

"A Distant Past" was first published in 1975, seven years after the Troubles (as the conflict was known) broke out in Northern Ireland. However, strife in Ireland goes back hundreds of years, and the modern conflict cannot be understood without some knowledge of that past.

From the sixteenth century, Ireland had been dominated by England. England believed it had to maintain control over Ireland because it did not want Ireland to become a base from which an enemy could launch an attack. England conquered much of Ireland by military force and sent settlers over to rule it, especially in the northern province of Ulster. The settlers were Protestants, but the Irish were Catholics. This sowed the seed for future conflict, since the Irish Protestants of the twentieth century were for the most part descended from those early English settlers and remained loyal to the British crown.

As the population of Ireland increased during the nineteenth century, so did its poverty, which culminated in the famine of 1845 to 1849, which resulted from the failures of the potato crop. During this century also, Irish nationalism began to rise, and a movement for Irish self-government emerged in the last quarter of the century. This was supported by the British prime minister, William Ewert Gladstone, but his efforts to pass a home rule bill in the British parliament failed in 1886 and 1893. The British parliament finally passed the Third Home Rule Act in 1914, but implementation of the act, which provided self-government for Ireland within the United Kingdom, was postponed until after World War I (1914–1918).

The 1910s and early 1920s were violent times in Ireland. In Dublin in 1916, the Easter Rising of Irish nationalists in Dublin was quickly suppressed by the British, who took severe reprisals against the rebels. In 1919, the Irish parliament, rejecting any dealings with Britain, declared Ireland to be an independent republic. This led quickly to a war between the British and the Irish nationalists, in the form of the Irish Republican Army (IRA). The British relied mainly on the Royal Ulster Constabulary but sent auxiliary forces, whose khaki uniforms led them to be known as the Black and Tans. The Black and Tans became notorious for their brutality. (This is the period in the story when Fat Conroy is ready to shoot British troops.)

In 1921, Irish leaders signed a treaty with Britain that created the Irish Free State, in which the vast majority of people were Catholics. However, the new state did not include the six northern counties in Ireland that made up Ulster: Antrim, Armagh, Down, Fermanagh, Londonderry, and Tyrone. In these counties the Protestants were in the majority, and they continued to be part of the United Kingdom, although they were granted self-rule. Ireland was thus partitioned into two: the twenty-six southern counties that made up the Irish Free State and the six northern counties that constituted Northern Ireland.

They drove to town with a small Union Jack displayed on their car. (Dariush M. | Shutterstock.com)

The Troubles

The modern Troubles in Ireland began in late 1968, when Catholics in Northern Ireland began demonstrating for civil rights. Northern Ireland at the time was dominated by the Protestants, who comprised about two-thirds of the population and discriminated against Catholics. The demonstrations led to violent clashes between Catholics and Protestants, and in 1969 British troops were sent to Ulster to keep the peace. However, as "The Distant Past" reveals, the violence only got worse. The IRA, in support of the Catholic population, mounted a campaign of terrorism designed to expel the British from Northern Ireland and create a united Ireland. The IRA was opposed by the Protestant Unionists, who formed their own militant groups and carried out attacks of their own. In 1971, as mentioned in the story, the British government introduced a policy of internment (detainment without trial) of IRA members. From then until 1975, when internment was abolished, over two thousand men were imprisoned. In 1972, the British government prorogued (or suspended) the Northern Ireland parliament and began direct rule of the province from London. The cost in human life during this period was heavy. In one twenty-one-month period in 1971 and 1972, 589 people died in Northern Ireland as a result of the Troubles, and 8,223 people were injured.

CRITICAL OVERVIEW

Trevor has long been acknowledged as one of the greatest living writers of the short story. When his *Collected Stories, Volumes 1-2* was published in 2009, Andrew McKie, reviewing the book for the *Spectator*, acknowledged the appropriateness of this description. Picking out two stories from the collection, he comments that they express some of Trevor's main themes. Those themes, which might well also be applied to "The Distant Past," are a sense of possibilities that have passed the protagonists by, and which will not come again; their impulse to examine their position, but a reluctance to act to change it; a pervasive sense of regret allied with an acceptance of their character and the necessity of continuing to endure their circumstances.

A number of scholars have commented on the story. For Mary Fitzgerald-Hoyt, writing in *William Trevor: Re-imagining Ireland*, the Middletons in the story end up suffering because they willfully remain ignorant of or insensitive to Irish history and how it still influences the present: "Nurtured as they are in the imperialist values of their late father, raised to think of themselves as superior, the Middletons, poor and elderly, are now rendered powerless." Geoffrey A. Schirmer, in *William Trevor: A Study of His Fiction*, notes that although the story is less complex in theme and characterization than many of Trevor's stories, it does contain some of his typical themes. These include, for example, the notion that "the past cannot be discounted, that history almost always makes itself felt in the present, often, in Ireland at least, in tragic ways." He also observes that the story shows "individual values as threatened by history, and by ideological commitments."

CRITICISM

Bryan Aubrey

Aubrey holds a Ph.D. in English. In the following essay, he examines "The Distant Past" in terms of three hundred years of Irish history.

> TOO OLD TO MOVE AWAY, AND POWERLESS TO AFFECT THE TIDE OF HISTORICAL EVENTS THAT IS SWEEPING BACK TO ENGULF THEM, THEY ARE LEFT TO CONTEMPLATE THEIR ISOLATION, WHICH THEY KNOW WILL NOT END UNTIL THEIR DEATHS."

In "The Distant Past," William Trevor's sad tale of two elderly siblings in Ireland whose best times have past, so much lies just below the surface: the long, dismal, fractious relations between England and Ireland and between Protestants and Catholics. The exact location of the town in Ireland where the story takes place is not stated, but it is within sixty miles of the border between the overwhelmingly Catholic Republic of Ireland and British-ruled Northern Ireland, where the Protestants have a two-to-one majority.

The story of the Middletons is one of changing times and shifting fortunes. The Middleton family has been living in Ireland since the eighteenth century. The large family house called Carraveagh was built during the reign of Britain's King George II, who ruled from 1727 to 1760, and for over a century and a half the Middleton family, known originally rather grandly as the Middletons of Carraveagh, was part of the Anglo-Irish Protestant aristocracy. The eighteenth century was a period of Protestant ascendancy in Ireland, a continuation of a situation that had been established a century earlier. According to Alan Dures in his book *Modern Ireland*, "By 1665 Protestants owned just under four-fifths of the land but were only a third of the population." The growth in landownership among Protestants had been part of the policy of the English government toward Ireland. England wanted to prevent the establishment of a Catholic Ireland because that would make England vulnerable to powerful Catholic nations like France and Spain. In the seventeenth century, then, the English government freely granted land in Ireland to those it favored, dispossessing Catholic landowners in the process. The situation of the Catholics further deteriorated in the eighteenth century. As a result of an act of the British parliament, Catholics were not allowed to be members of the Irish parliament,

WHAT DO I READ NEXT?

- *A Bit on the Side* (2004) is one of Trevor's most recent short-story collections. It contains twelve stories and has been hailed by reviewers as one of his best collections. Once more Trevor shows his insight into and empathy for characters whose lives have not turned out the way they envisioned but who carry on as best they can.

- *After Rain* (1996) is another collection of Trevor's short stories. The twelve stories are set mostly in England and Ireland, and all of them display Trevor's uncanny gift for examining ordinary lives and relationships. One story, "Last Ground," is set in Northern Ireland during the Troubles. A Protestant boy meets a woman in an orchard who says she is Saint Rosa, a Catholic saint. When the boy speaks in public about the saint, the Protestant community is angry with him, with tragic consequences.

- *The Oxford Book of Irish Short Stories*, edited by William Trevor (reissue edition, 2010), is a collection of forty-six stories by Irish writers, ranging from anonymous early folktales to stories from the modern era. Writers represented include Trevor, Oliver Goldsmith, Maria Edgeworth, Oscar Wilde, James Joyce, Liam O'Flaherty, Joyce Cary, Elizabeth Bowen, Bernard Mac Laverty, Mary Lavin, Edna O'Brien, John Montague, and Desmond Hogan.

- *A Boy from Ireland: A Novel*, by Marie Raphael (2007), is a coming-of-age historical novel set in 1901 and aimed at young-adult readers. Fourteen-year-old Liam, whose missing father is English, is sent to live in rural Ireland with his uncle, who is fiercely anti-English. In Ireland, Liam gets bullied at school because of his English connections. When his uncle goes to New York to raise money for the Irish nationalist cause, he takes Liam with him. In New York, Liam finds more conflict between the English and the Irish, and also racial conflict between black and white people. He is also pursued by a bully. However, through friendship and his love for a horse, he finds a way to move beyond the past.

- *Sudden Fiction Latino: Short-Short Stories from the United States and Latin America* (2010) edited by Robert Shepard, James Thomas, and Ray Gonzales, is a collection of sixty-five stories, none of which exceeds 1,500 words. Established writers such as Sandra Cisneros and Junot Diaz are presented alongside some of the greats, such as Gabriel Garcia Marquez, Isabel Allende, and Jorge Luis Borges. There are many new writers included as well.

- *A Short History of Modern Ireland* (2003), by Richard Killeen, is a concise history of Ireland since the 1790s. Killeen clearly explains the course of the troubled relations between Ireland and Britain and how Irish independence occurred. He also explains how Irish Protestants in Ulster resisted the drive to an independent, united, republican Ireland. The book also deals with topics such as industrialization, urban growth, and the decline of the Irish language.

---

which was therefore dominated by Protestants. Restrictions were placed on Catholic landownership, and Catholics were banned from educating their children in the Catholic faith.

Poverty in this period was widespread amongst the largely Catholic Irish peasantry. During years of famine, such as between 1726 and 1729—in the early years of George II's reign, when the Middletons were building Carraveagh—thousands of peasants died of starvation. The country failed to prosper in part because Irish industry and agriculture were held back by restrictive trade laws passed by the British parliament. Tariffs on Irish exports such as woolens were imposed to protect English markets. The Protestant Irish were also affected by these anti-Irish measures, and not all of them were sympathetic to England, the mother country. However, the landed Protestant gentry still had every reason to be pleased with their lot as part of what was known as the Protestant ascendancy. As Robert Kee notes of the Protestants in his book *Ireland: A History*:

> [T]he term is apt because not only were they *above* the majority but also they had soaring aspirations on their own account, as can be seen from the magnificent country houses they built for themselves all over Ireland... and the splendour and taste with which they adorned [them].

The Middletons' Carraveagh was one of these houses, adorned with the trappings of wealth, privilege, and tradition, the latter stemming not from Ireland but from Britain. For over a century and a half it appears that the Middletons enjoyed this privileged position in their community and remained loyal to the British crown. The father of the Mr. and Miss Middleton in "The Distant Past" served in the Irish Guards, a regiment of the British Army, and, so his children remembered, used to say that "God and Empire and Queen formed a trinity unique in any worthy soldier's heart." Their father even met and talked with Queen Victoria, thus linking the Middletons to the pinnacle of power in the British Empire.

It is not difficult to imagine the dismay and anger the Middletons in the story must have felt in the early 1920s, when they were young. They had been raised in a family that had long been accustomed to privilege and wealth. People in that kind of situation do not usually like to face change, and for the young Middletons, there were two major changes at the time. Their father died in 1924, and they immediately discovered that he had squandered the family fortune by showering a Catholic woman in Dublin with expensive gifts. Now they would live in much diminished circumstances. Not only this, they had witnessed the coming of Irish independence in 1921 and would now be living in a country that no longer paid allegiance to the King of England.

The Middletons react to these events by blaming the new government, as well as the Catholic woman, and by refusing to accept the magnitude of the change that has taken place in Ireland. Their remark to the Reverend Packham, a Protestant clergyman in the town, that the new Irish government "would not last" and that there was no point in "green-painted pillar boxes and a language that nobody understood" shows that they see only the superficialities of the situation. It does not occur to them, perhaps because they are so close to the situation, that they are witnessing the inevitable march of history—the push for Irish independence had been growing stronger and stronger for several generations—nor do they see the justice in a people's desire to rule themselves rather than being subservient to the government of what they regard as a foreign land. In dismissing the Irish language, they fail to see how important language is to Irish identity. In the mid-eighteenth century, the majority of Irish people spoke Irish, and by the mid-nineteenth century about half the population spoke that language. After that it went into decline, with English becoming the dominant language. Irish nationalists, however, regarded English as the language of the conqueror, and they tried to revive the use of Irish. It is arguable, according to the authors of *The Oxford Companion to Irish History*, that "the loss of the Irish language is the decisive event in Irish history, since it altered radically the self-understanding of the Irish and destroyed the continuity between their present and their past." The Middletons, deeply attached to their own past, cannot recognize the importance of the past for their Catholic neighbors.

However, in spite of the fact that political events do not unfold the way the Middletons would like, as a minority in a newly independent Ireland they do not fare badly. The family fortunes do not revive, but the Middletons, even with their attachment to Britain, are accepted by the townsfolk, who seem willing to forget old scores, including the time when three local men occupied Carraveagh and were ready for a confrontation with British soldiers. Time heals old wounds, it would appear. An old symbol such as the Union Jack (the British flag), which had formerly aroused so much passion, by the 1950s stirs only amusement and jocular remarks from the locals as the Middletons display it in the back window of their car at the time of the coronation of Britain's Queen Elizabeth I. The flag they display is pointedly described as "small" and is "propped up" in the car's rear window. The symbol of the once mighty empire has been reduced to a cheap trinket that a tourist might buy. The Middletons are regarded as harmless eccentrics even by other Protestants, such as the Reverend Bradshaw of St. Patrick's Protestant Church, who unlike them has no interest in reviving the lapsed practice of offering prayers for the British Royal Family.

All in all, it seems as if the Middletons will live out their days in peace. The simple ties of affection that they build with the townsfolk over the passage of years seem far more important than old ideologies. By the 1950s and 1960s, when prosperity comes to the town (even as the Middletons sink further into genteel poverty), it seems unthinkable that there could ever be a return to the animosities of the past. Indeed, when the first signs of sectarian conflict appear in Belfast in 1968, Miss Middleton cannot imagine that the trouble north of the border will pose a serious problem for them. It seems unreal to her. What is real, she thinks, are the personal concerns of individuals, such as "the afflictions and problems of the old butcher [Fat Cranley] himself, his rheumatism and his reluctance to retire." Miss Middleton feels an affinity with the butcher because they are the same age, neither has children, and Cranley is reluctant to sell his business, just as the Middletons have been reluctant to sell Carraveagh.

Nevertheless, this story emphasizes that the past only appears to have vanished. In fact, it remains alive, like a sleeping beast, ready to reawaken. Everything remains fine until the local people find that their own welfare is affected by the outbreak of violence in Northern Ireland. The town's prosperity evaporates as tourists no longer come. It turns out that Christian attitudes of tolerance are all very well but do not survive long when people find themselves threatened by economic insecurity. They need a scapegoat for their unhappiness, and as old memories revive, the Middletons make a convenient target. Former kindnesses are now denied. Canon Cotter, for example, once went out of his way to help Miss Middleton when she was ill, driving out to Carraveagh twice a week with fresh food supplies. But now he turns his head away when he sees the Middletons' car approaching. Such are the cruelties that the past can wreak upon the present, and the Middletons become victims of it. Too old to move away, and powerless to affect the tide of historical events that is sweeping back to engulf them, they are left to contemplate their isolation, which they know will not end until their deaths. It is worse, they realize in the forceful last line of the story, "than being murdered in their beds."

A NUMBER OF TREVOR'S STORIES, MOST NOTABLY 'THE DISTANT PAST' AND 'LOW SUNDAY, 1950,' DEAL WITH THE TRAUMA OF THE ANGLO-IRISH WAR (1919–21), ESPECIALLY ITS IMPACT ON THE PROTESTANT COMMUNITY."

Source: Bryan Aubrey, Critical Essay on "The Distant Past," in *Short Stories for Students*, Gale, Cengage Learning, 2011.

Ben Howard
In the following excerpt, Howard provides examples of stylistic economy in Trevor's stories.

... In an interview for the *Paris Review* (1989), Trevor remarked that the short story is "an art of the glimpse," whose "strength lies in what it leaves out." And in Trevor's story "Mr. Tennyson," an English teacher by that name makes a similar remark on style. "It's very good," he tells his pupil, "[b]ut you're getting too fond of using three little dots at the end of the sentence. The sentence should imply the dots."

Mr. Tennyson's advice has unwittingly romantic overtones, offered as it is to a schoolgirl who is in love with him. But strictly as a principle of style, his advice might speak for William Trevor, whose sentences—and stories—often "imply the dots." And to turn from Trevor's regulation of tone to his disposition of narrative detail is to see how the same restraint that governs his modulations of tone also controls his deployment of exposition, description and contextual information. "Omissions are not accidents," wrote Marianne Moore; and the principle of stringent economy that led her to omit, in her *Complete Poems* (1967), all but the first three lines of her poem "Poetry," operates in Trevor's stories as well. Present in even his earliest stories, it is most prominent in his most recent.

At the purely stylistic level, Trevor's economy of statement shapes his thumbnail sketches, especially those which introduce minor characters. In "Kinkies," for example, a married man who is attempting to seduce a young designer describes his wife as a woman who "once dropped, deliberately, a seven-pound weight on his foot." Nothing more is said—or needs to be. And in

"Bodily Secrets," we glimpse Mr. Sweetman, a miserly surveyor with the county council, who "if he gave you a lift in his car...had a way of mentioning the high price of petrol." Trevor has likened the short story to an Impressionist painting, and in their dense evocations of places and landscapes, his stories sometimes resemble Impressionist art. But in his swift, incisive sketches of minor characters, he brings Asian painting to mind. One thinks of the seventeenth-century painter-swordsman Niten (Miyamoto Musashi), who could render a leaf or stem in a single brushstroke.

Beyond Trevor's stylistic economies, his artistry reveals itself in his gradual and partial revelation of contextual detail. Though sometimes established at the outset, the circumstances of a story more often emerge by increments, as though a picture were developing in a photographer's tray. In a few instances, such as "A Day" and "Gilbert's Mother," the facts remain uncertain, and the reader is left to wonder whether an alcoholic's husband is really having an affair or a mother's son is really a serial killer. In other stories, such as "The Bedroom Eyes of Mrs. Vansittart," reality rebukes appearance, and a woman widely perceived as promiscuous turns out to be virtuous and long-suffering. Most often, however, the stories fully disclose their social contexts but do so gradually, allowing the reader an active role in the process. In "The Mourning," for example, a naïve young navvy named Liam Pat Brogan leaves his Irish parish and finds work in London, where he hopes to better himself. Slowly it dawns on the reader and Liam Pat alike that he is being used by the IRA, whose operatives exploit his insecurities for their own political ends. Similarly, in "Good News," it gradually becomes apparent that the nine-year-old Bea, who wins a part in a made-for-television movie, is the victim of a broken home, who vainly hopes that her "good news" will bring her parents back together.

If Trevor's artistic tact is evident in his disclosures of circumstantial detail, it is even more conspicuous in his treatment of violence, whether the violence be physical, verbal or emotional. Violence is not infrequent in Trevor's stories, but it rumbles off stage or seethes beneath a placid surface. With few exceptions, its effects are presented indirectly, if at all. A number of Trevor's stories, most notably "The Distant Past" and "Low Sunday, 1950," deal with the trauma of the Anglo-Irish War (1919–21),

especially its impact on the Protestant community. Others address the "Troubles"—the sectarian violence of Northern Ireland, renewed in 1969 and continuing to the present day. Of the stories in the latter category, the best known is "Beyond the Pale," which brings the reality of political violence into the lives of leisured British escapists vacationing in Northern Ireland. But the most horrifying is "Lost Ground," which depicts a political fratricide.

The victim in this story is Milton, a Protestant adolescent in County Armagh, who claims to have experienced multiple visitations from a "Papist saint." Bewildered by his encounters with a spectral woman who calls herself St. Rosa, Milton consults with a Protestant minister, whom he alarms, and later with a Catholic priest, whom he offends. Not long afterward, Milton becomes a self-ordained soapbox minister, preaching a gospel of forgiveness to his fearful, unforgiving neighbors. At first an embarrassment to his family and tribe, Milton is later judged a traitor, and his own brother Garfield, a butcher's assistant in Belfast, is appointed executioner. Locked in his bedroom, unaware of the gravity of his offense, Milton works on a jigsaw puzzle:

> He found another piece of the elephant's gray bulk. In the distance he could hear the sound of a car.... He watched while a door opened and a man he had never seen before stepped out from the driver's seat. The engine was switched off. The man stretched himself. Then Garfield stepped out too.

Although this scene is as suspenseful as its counterpart in the film *Harry's Game*, Trevor's treatment is far less sensational. With a degree of tact rare in contemporary writing, the cold-blooded murder of a sixteen-year-old boy is left to the reader's imagination.

Trevor's withholding of violent detail, like his withholding of descriptive and contextual information, is in part an aesthetic matter. Like the trumpeter Miles Davis, who is said to have had an instinct for the telling note, Trevor has an instinct for the telling detail—and the wisdom to leave the others out. But Trevor's withholding of information, especially when it concerns a character's inner life, is more than a technical matter. In the larger context of Trevor's art, it reflects an ambivalence with respect to personal privacy, be it that of a virgin or a serial killer. In both his novels and his stories Trevor exposes the secrets and examines the surreptitious activities of his characters. In two instances, the novel *Death in*

Summer and the story "The News from Ireland," he has created voyeuristic, unscrupulous butlers, who read their employers' mail and otherwise pry into their intimate lives. But Trevor, as narrator, has also shown a reluctance to violate the privacy or pluck the mystery of a human life. Although such inquiry is the storyteller's right, Trevor has shown remarkable restraint in exercising his authorial privilege.

Trevor's ambivalence with respect to privacy permeates his memoirs as well as his fiction, and the former provides a useful perspective on the latter. "The Warden's Wife," one of the most revealing vignettes in *Excursions in the Real World*, depicts a "bent figure in her forties," an intelligent woman educated at Oxford and Cambridge, who lived in the shadow of her pompous, obtuse husband, occupying "a twilight of her own." Rumored to have been beautiful in her youth but shackled to a "declared enemy of the sensual life in all its aspects," Mary Savery was viewed with fascination and respect by the schoolboys at St. Columba's, a boarding school in the Dublin mountains. Like the other boys, Trevor was permitted only glimpses of the Warden's wife, as she weeded flowerbeds in her garden. But on one occasion, Trevor spoke to her in private. They discussed a boy who had been experimenting with fasting. "Is there a noticeable difference in him?" asked the Warden's wife. "His breath is bad," Trevor replied.

> She nodded. It would be so, she agreed, only adding as she returned to her roses that some of the saints who starved themselves must have developed unpleasant breath; their cells or caves could not have been agreeable places to visit. I went away, feeling I shared a secret with her, for I was certain that the conversation we had would not be confided to her husband.

Forty-three years later, when Trevor reads Mary Savery's obituary in the *Old Columban*, a secret of another order comes to light. During her years at St. Columba's, it turns out, Mary Savery had made herself an expert "in matters of the turf, regularly attending race-meetings." A woman "who on the face of it had been smudged away to nothing, dwelt profitably on form among the callous prefects at High Table lunches, while her husband held forth about potatoes or recalled the day he met de Valera." Charmed by this revelation of a private life that "mocked the paucity of our invention," Trevor wonders whether Mary went alone, "even secretly, to race-meetings," and whether "she laughed silently" at her pretentious social environment. Reclusive in her lifetime, she

remains a mystery after death, despite the discovery of her private obsession.

The spirit of Mary Savery lingers in Trevor's stories, which contain a rich bounty of secrets and private obsessions, not all as benign as Mary's. "Are you good at secrets?" asks Ralph de Courcy, a frail young man in "Virgins," addressing one of two schoolgirls who are in love with him. After one of his admirers returns to her home in England, de Courcy writes identical love letters to both girls, a bit of perfidy disclosed only after his early death and only to one of the girls, who keeps the secret to herself. In "Bodily Secrets," a handsome dowager and her second husband conceal two secrets: that beneath her folds of clothing her body is no longer attractive and that her husband prefers the company of men. And in "Three People," Vera Schele guards a darker secret, namely that she murdered her invalid sister.

A fascination with secrets and, more broadly, with what the poet E. L. Mayo called "the bright privacies of the inner life," is of course not unique to Trevor. As Frank O'Connor remarks in *The Lonely Voice*, it is the province of the short-story writer to deal with the private lives of the "submerged" populations. And as V. S. Pritchett, paraphrasing O'Connor, notes, the short story is an art "fundamentally drawn to startling dramatic insights and the inner riot that may possess the lonely man or woman at some unwary moment in the hours of their day" (*Collected Essays*). What is distinctive in Trevor's fiction is the degree to which the privacies of the inner life and the secrets of the heart are addressed in a spirit of humility and restraint, as mysteries to be honored rather than problems to be solved. "There is this cave /," wrote the poet James Wright, "In the air behind my body / That nobody is going to touch." And with few exceptions Trevor's stories respect that untouchable place, even as they probe the mystery of human motive.

Nowhere is Trevor's respect more apparent than in "The Hill Bachelors," the story of a young man who returns to his parents' farm after his father's death. As the only unmarried son, Paulie is expected to return and to assume his father's responsibilities. And despite his growing recognition that by accepting the traditional role he is reducing the likelihood of finding a wife and having a family, Paulie elects to take his place among

Ireland's rural bachelors. As for his motives, Trevor has this to say:

> Guilt was misplaced, goodness hardly came into it. Her widowing and the mood of a capricious time were not of consequence, no more than a flicker in a scheme of things that had always been there. Enduring, unchanging, the hills had waited for him, claiming one of their own.

Despite its grave and choric tone, this passage propounds more questions than it answers. Dismissing the obvious, psychological motives for Paulie's decision—guilt, altruism, sympathy, convention—the narrator posits a mysterious, archetypal force at work in the human psyche. Resorting to an anthropomorphic metaphor—the hills claiming one of their own—Trevor offers a lyrical but partial explanation, leaving the mystery intact.

Source: Ben Howard, "A Voice of Restraint: The Short Fiction of William Trevor," in *Shenandoah*, Vol. 51, No. 4, Winter 2001, pp. 164–86.

SOURCES

Connolly, S. J., ed., *The Oxford Companion to Irish History*, Oxford University Press, 1998, pp. 261, 302.

Donald, Robert Bruce, "The Irish Free State in the First Half of the Inter-War Period: Policy and Economic Reality," in *Associated Content*, February 12, 2007, http://www.associatedcontent.com/article/147121/the_irish_free_state_in_the_first_half_pg8.htm l?cat=37 (accessed August 4, 2010).

Dures, Alan, *Modern Ireland*, Wayland, 1973, p. 11.

Fitzgerald-Hoyt, Mary, *William Trevor: Re-imagining Ireland*, Liffey Press, 2003, p. 59.

"Ireland," in *CIA: World Factbook*, https://www.cia.gov/library/publications/the-world-factbook/geos/ei.html (accessed August 4, 2010).

Jarrett, Derek, *Britain: 1688–1815*, Longman, 1970, pp. 76–79.

Kee, Robert, *Ireland: A History*, Little, Brown, 1982, p. 56.

McKie, Andrew, "Strictness and Susceptibility," in *Spectator*, January 23, 2010, p. 32.

Schirmer, Geoffrey A., *William Trevor: A Study of His Fiction*, Routledge, 1990, p. 138.

Trevor, William, "The Distant Past," in *Ireland: Selected Stories*, Penguin, 1998, pp. 22–30.

FURTHER READING

Foster, R. F., ed., *The Oxford Illustrated History of Ireland*, Oxford University Press, 1989.

> This book examines Irish history from the earliest times up to the late 1980s. There are over two hundred illustrations and twenty-four full-color plates, as well as a detailed chronology.

MacKenna, Dolores, *William Trevor: The Writer and His Work*, New Island Books, 1999.

> MacKenna analyzes how the circumstances of Trevor's life shaped his work, and presents a view of how his creativity evolved over a period of forty years. She also includes an interview with Trevor.

Morrison, Kristen, *William Trevor*, Twayne's English Authors Series, No. 501, Twayne Publishers, 1993.

> This is a survey of Trevor's work. It includes a chronology and an annotated bibliography. One topic Morrison examines is whether Trevor's work offers any resolution to the problem of evil that his work often explores.

Trevor, William, *Excursions in the Real World: Memoirs*, Penguin, 1995.

> Trevor's memoir consists of twenty-nine short essays in which he recalls, with the same sure touch that he shows as a short-story writer, many people and incidents from all phases of his life in Ireland and England.

SUGGESTED SEARCH TERMS

William Trevor

William Trevor AND The Distant Past

history of Ireland

Troubles AND Northern Ireland

internment

Protestant Ascendancy

Bloody Sunday AND Northern Ireland

Irish Republican Army

Republic of Ireland

Partition of Ireland

Battle of the Boyne

IRA Hunger Strike

Father and I

PÄR LAGERKVIST

1924

Swedish author Pär (Peter) Lagerkvist earned a reputation as one of the preeminent Swedish writers of the twentieth century, having written prolifically in a variety of genres, including short stories, novels, and poetry. His short story "Father and I" was originally published in 1924 in Swedish as "Far och jag." It was translated into English by Alan Blair and published in the 1954 collection of Lagerkvist's short stories *The Marriage Feast*. The work exemplifies Lagerkvist's simple, precise style. Centered on a walk through the woods shared between father and son, the story, which is told from the nine-year-old child's point of view, begins on a Sunday afternoon and is initially light and carefree in tone. As the sun sets and the sky begins to darken, so does the story's tone. The child begins to grow fearful, and he is terrified to discover that he is not reassured by his father's attempt to comfort him. The father places his trust in God, yet the son finds only a heightened sense of panic when considering God's omnipresence. Lagerkvist offers no resolution at the story's conclusion; the work ends with the child fearing a lifetime of darkness and uncertainty. While the father-son relationship is at the heart of the story, the reference to God infuses the story with religious significance, and the child's fear and distrust take on deeper meaning than if he had simply questioned his father and his beliefs. Light and darkness also take on symbolic import when regarded within the context of the story's spiritual themes.

Pär Lagerkvist (© *Bettmann* / *Corbis*)

AUTHOR BIOGRAPHY

Born on May 23, 1891, in the town of Väjö in Sweden, Lagerkvist (whose surname was originally spelled Lagerqvist) was the youngest of the seven children of Anders Johan Lagerqvist and Johanna Blad. His father was a railway foreman. Having themselves been raised in the rural country of the province of Småland, in which the town of Väjö is located, Lagerkvist's parents retained many of the customs of the countryside and bonds with the farming communities of the region. The Lutheran religion of Lagerkvist's parents was juxtaposed with his exposure to the thinking of Charles Darwin at Väjö Secondary Grammar School, where Lagerkvist was further influenced by socialist philosophy. In his final year at school, Lagerkvist became a member of an anarchist group. In 1909, Lagerkvist helped organize a group known as Röda Ringen, or the Red Ring, dedicated to exploring and debating philosophical, political, and religious issues. He graduated from grammar school in 1910, enrolling a year later at the University of Uppsala with the aim of becoming a writer.

After studying literature and art history for a short time, Lagerkvist left school in order to pursue his literary ambitions. In 1912, he published his first work of prose, *Mäniskor* (People). With his brother's income as a schoolteacher helping to support him, Lagerkvist continued to write and seek publication. He traveled to Paris in 1913 with the financial backing of several of his siblings. He published a literary manifesto, along with collections of poetry and fiction. After serving time in the military during World War I, he traveled extensively. The year 1916 found Lagerkvist in Copenhagen, Denmark. There he met Karen Sörensen. He continued to write extensively and publish, though he remained quite poor. Though in poverty, he married Sörensen in 1918, and the couple soon had a baby girl. Lagerkvist's poetry and plays at this time were influenced by modern art movements such as expressionism and as well as developments in philosophy, such as existentialism.

After abandoning his wife and daughter, Lagerkvist traveled for several years. He published *Onda sagor* (Evil Tales) in 1924, a collection containing "Father and I." He divorced his wife in 1925 but eventually gained custody of his daughter. Lagerkvist then married Elaine Halberg Sandels, with whom he had twin sons. Years of travel and writing followed, though the family settled for some time in Stockholm. Lagerkvist was awarded the Nobel Prize for Literature in 1951. Focusing heavily on the novel form in this next phase of his career, Lagerkvist continued to explore philosophical and religious issues. His last published novel was *Mariamne*, in 1967. He died on July 11, 1974.

PLOT SUMMARY

As "Father and I" begins, the first-person narrator recalls a Sunday afternoon when he is nearly ten years old, and he and his father decide to go for a walk in the woods. They are going to listen to the birds, although the narrator insists that there is no significance to this fact, that there is nothing "extra special or wonderful" about the event. His father simply has some free time. Having the privilege of walking along the railroad, because the father works on the railway, the pair enters the wood quickly. The narrator describes the songs of various birds, and other sights and sounds of the forest as well. Still close to the railway, father and son move down to an embankment as a train passes. The child watches as his father and the driver greet one another with casual salutes. The walk continues along the railroad, past an oat field, over a bridge. After a brief stop for a glass of milk at the plate layer's cottage, the father and son travel on toward the river. They arrive at the location upstream where the father had lived as a boy. Near the next station, this is also where a semaphore (a system for sending messages to drivers along the railway) is situated, and the father checks to make sure it is working properly. They spend a considerable amount of time along the river, throwing stones into the water. The narrator recounts briefly the stories his father tells him about being a boy and fishing on that river. A pleasant afternoon having been spent, the two turn toward home.

The decision to return home corresponds with the setting of the sun. As the sky begins to darken, the pleasant mood of the story changes as well. First, the boy thinks of how his mother would be growing worried. He then begins to notice things about his surroundings, and his observations reveal the way a young child's imagination transforms his reality. The child notes that the trees "stood listening to every step we took, as if they didn't know who we were." While the woods had up until moments ago been viewed as a pleasant place to be, now the child perceives that he and his father are out of place, and perhaps unwelcome. He notes a glow-worm "staring at us." His sense of unease at thus being watched is amplified by the walk across the bridge where the stream below roars as though it wants to devour them. As they go on, the child notes how calm his father appears, and he is mystified by this, since he himself has become terrified. He fears breathing too deeply, feeling that it is dangerous to inhale the darkness, because then it would get inside of him and kill him. Everything seems unreal and dangerous to the boy.

Huddling close to his father, he asks him why everything is so "horrible when it's dark." His father contradicts him, assuring him by holding his hand and stating that it is not horrible at all. When the boy disagrees, the father insists, "No, my child, you musn't think that. Not when we know there is a God." Yet the boy continues to be consumed by fear. He now additionally feels an enormous gap open

between his father and him. Realizing that there is nothing his father can offer that can comfort him, the boy reveals that God seems "horrible" to him, in that God is everywhere, unseen but present in the darkness. Without warning, an unscheduled train comes hurtling through the darkness, and father and son leap to the safety of the embankment. The boy observes that the train is shrouded in darkness; the only light visible is that given off by the coal fire powering the engine. He notices as well that, oddly, his father does not recognize the driver, who stares ahead into the darkness and does not turn to hail his father as the driver of the earlier train had done. Filled with dread and breathing heavily with fear, the boy, along with his father, hurry toward their home. Offhandedly the father comments how strange the train was, and that he did not recognize its driver. Despite his father's nonchalance, the boy imbues the mysterious train with symbolic meaning, stating that it was a foreshadowing of "the anguish that was to come." To the child, the train represents all of life's unknowns, and all the things from which his father will be unable to shield him. The boy is suddenly certain that his life will be consumed by such darkness, that it will be very different from his father's life, "where everything was secure and certain." The story ends with the child's contemplation of impenetrable and eternal darkness.

CHARACTERS

The Father

In "Father and I," the Father is depicted as a kind, loving parent. As the story is told from the child's point of view, all the reader knows of the father is filtered through the son's recollection. The father takes his son for a long walk because he is free from work that Sunday afternoon. The father, apparently a friendly man, hails an engine driver, a man he knows through his work on the railroad. He also, with his son, pays a visit to the plate layer and his family, enjoys their hospitality, and admires pig, hens, and fruit trees. The child comments that it is their habit on walks such as these to visit the place where his father lived as a child. The father also talks about fishing with the son, showing him good places to drop a line, and talking about fishing in the same river as a boy. He takes turns with his son throwing pebbles into the river, seeming to enjoy the relaxing afternoon with his child. As they walk back, the father is calm and quiet in the dark, and he responds reassuringly to his child's fears about the darkness. Not only does he assure him that there is nothing horrible about the dark, he takes his son's hand in a further effort to comfort him. The boy persists, and the father insists that there is nothing to fear, not since they have the knowledge that there is a God. The father feels reassured and comforted by his faith, and he expects his son to feel the same way. The son does not speak of the matter again, and consequently, neither does the father. The train that frightens the child is regarded as a curiosity by the father. He simply comments on the strangeness of it coming by at that particular hour, and that he did not know the driver. Unlike his son, he reads nothing further into the dark train; he simply shrugs it off. The fact that the father is remembered by the narrator—the son, years later—as a loving, affectionate, and faithful man intensifies, through contrast, the fearful, anxious, doubtful nature of the son.

The Mother

The child's mother does not appear in the story, but she is referred to several times by her son, who narrates "Father and I." He observes that she is unable accompany his father and him on their walk because she must stay home to prepare the evening meal. As it begins to grow dark, the boy thinks of his mother at home with supper waiting, worrying about them. The child states that his mother "was always afraid something was going to happen." At the time he expresses this thought, he feels that this notion is silly, as nothing had happened; it had been a lovely day, and he and his father were quite happy. By the end of the story, though, the boy's fears of darkness and the unknown, and his corresponding sense of hopelessness, seem to mirror his perception of his mother's ever-present sense of anxiety.

The Son

The child in the story is nearly ten years old. The story is narrated from the youth's point of view, but the narrator's perspective is one in which he is looking back at this childhood incident from a point in time many years later. Although the father never calls his son by name, the reader knows the child is male, because the father refers to him as "my boy." As the story opens, the boy is shown to be observant and eager. His feelings toward his father are affectionate, warm, and

proud. The boy likens himself to his father, and he enjoys this sense of connection, as when he declares that "we were sound, sensible people, Father and I." As the father checks on the semaphore, the child notes, "he thought of everything." Admiring his father so, the child is reluctant to let him down, so when his father does not carry him over the bridge in the dark as he would have liked, he says nothing, for he supposes his father wants him to be unafraid, like him. While marveling at his father's sense of calm, the boy himself grows increasingly fearful in the dark. The things he imagines are reflective of his young age; everything seems more frightening in the dark. Yet when he seeks his father's reassurance, his father indicates that his own trust is placed in God. The little boy takes no comfort in this statement, and his disappointment that he and his father are so dissimilar regarding this point is severe. Even once the two make it home safely, the boy is shaken and terrified. His fears of the dark have been inflated to incorporate a larger terror of the unknown, of a bleak future where no certainty can be found.

THEMES

Father-Child Relationships

In Lagerkvist's "Father and I," the narrator reveals much about his relationship with his father. Some critics, such as Csanád Siklós, in a 2007 essay on Lagerkvist for the *Dictionary of Literary Biography*, have regarded this story as semiautobiographical in nature, and have viewed the narrator's relationship with his father within this context. Regardless of this perspective, the boy's relationship with his father provides the framework of the story and is treated primarily in positive terms. Throughout much of the story, the child has nothing but praise and admiration for his father. He enjoys identifying the ways in which he and his father are similar, noting for example that "we were sound, sensible people, Father and I." Watching his father in his professional capacity—greeting railway drivers, checking equipment—the boy is aglow with pride. Although there is little dialogue in the story, the boy informs the reader of the stories his father shares with him, recollections of his own youth. The father is not taciturn with his son but communicates freely about topics of interest to the boy, like fishing. Together they

TOPICS FOR FURTHER STUDY

- Lagerkvist's story "Father and I" is set in rural Sweden and was published in 1924, several years after World War I. Using print and electronic sources, research either the geography and culture of Sweden, or the history of Sweden, beginning with its status in Europe at the onset of World War I in 1914. Consider incorporating images such as photographs or maps to help explain various aspects of your report. Either write a written report or create a Web page accessible by your classmates. Include links to related sources.

- Some of Lagerkvist's fiction is said to be somewhat autobiographical in nature. Research Lagerkvist's life and write a biographical essay about him. Include discussions of his best-known works, and investigate the relationship between his fiction and his life. Consider the way his family's religion and his exposure to art and philosophy during his travels shaped his views and his writings. Provide dates for significant events in his life, such as his birth, his marriages, and his death. Be sure to cite all of your sources.

- Lagerkvist is associated with the modernist movement. In particular, his poetry is regarded as the most modernist of the genres in which he wrote. Research the characteristics of one of the schools of modernist poetry (expressionism or imagism, for example), and write your own modernist poem. Be sure to identify, whether you present your material in oral or print form, the particular mode of modernist poetry you studied and emulated.

- Lagerkvist's "Father and I" deals in part with a young boy's sense of alienation. Similarly, the protagonist of Matt de la Peña's young-adult novel *Mexican White Boy* feels isolated, from both his family and from his larger community. With a book group, read de la Peña's novel. As you discuss the book, consider the sources of Danny Lopez's feelings of loneliness, betrayal, and isolation. In what ways does the author attempt to mirror Danny's isolation for the reader? Does the author use symbols, imagery, and metaphors to underscore his themes? Post your discussion online as a blog, or write a summary of the group's analysis of the novel and share it with the class. *Mexican White Boy* was published in 2008 by Delacorte Books for Young Readers.

- In many of his writings, Lagerkvist reveals a sense of anguish focused on the void of meaning he perceives in the world. As a result, Lagerkvist has been associated with the philosophical school of thought known as existentialism. Using print and electronic sources research existentialism. Search for the origins of this movement and discuss the variations in meaning put forth by the main philosophers associated with the movement. Create a Web page that contains your findings, and invite classmates to post comments or questions about the philosophy, which you moderate.

---

throw stones into the river, enjoying themselves together, and growing tired together. As they walk home, the father, sensing his son's fear, comforts his child as best he can, holding his hand and telling him he has nothing to be afraid of. Like any father, he seeks to erase his child's worry. From the father's perspective, nothing changes in terms of his relationship with his son during the course of the story. While the story ends on a dark note, with the child resisting the comfort his father has offered and being overcome with his fears, the narrator nevertheless has taken pains to depict the father in a nearly faultless light. Despite the panic of the child, the father's relationship with him offers a promise that while the child's fears may not always be understood, the boy will be loved and cared for. Yet for the child, the father's inability to offer him true comfort from his fears and doubts proves to be a turning point in their relationship.

Faith

In "Father and I," Lagerkvist explores two distinctly different attitudes about faith, viewpoints exemplified by the father and the son. When the son grows fearful about the dark, almost in a panic as he imagines the woods as a sentient entity watching him, he seeks reassurance from his father. The father, clearly calm and comfortable in the darkness, states that their knowledge of God's existence offers protection from fear and doubt. The father, at peace with his world, is consoled and unintimidated by anything that might seem "horrible" because the mere fact of God's existence serves as a source of comfort to him. Upon hearing his father's statement about God, the boy describes feeling "lonely, forsaken." His sense of loss is twofold. Not only does he realize that the notion of God does not comfort him, but his understanding that he and his father "didn't think the same" on this issue is a stunning blow. He has lost the sense of connection he had previously shared with his father, a connection portrayed in the first half of the story. The boy is stunned that his father was unable to ease his fear. In contemplating the notion of God's existence being a comfort, the child states that the very thought of God was "horrible." He explains, "It was horrible that he was everywhere here in the darkness ... And yet you could never see him." With the passing of the unscheduled train in the dark, the boy's terror increases. His horror is juxtaposed with his father's casual response to the incident. He comments that it was strange that the driver was unknown to him, and he walks on, unruffled. For the child, this incident underscores his fearfulness and "the anguish that was to come." He looks ahead to his future, to all that is not yet known, to everything that his father "knew nothing about" and would not be able to protect him from. For his father, the boy has come to realize, things were "secure and certain." He was protected from terror of the unknown by his faith. The boy envisions his own future as starkly different from that of his father. His own life was not "real," but just an existence of careening through unending darkness. The boy's conversation with his father about God suggests that

He and his father went for a walk one Sunday afternoon. (Merrill Dyck / Shutterstock.com)

the father regards God as benevolent and protective. His existence is conflated with his goodness for the father, since the very idea of God's presence is a comfort. The child does not seem to doubt the existence of God. He senses the presence of God everywhere in the darkness. Yet this notion of God's presence is unsettling for the child, indicating that the boy either questions God's power, God's goodness, or both.

STYLE

First-Person Narration

Lagerkvist employs first-person narration in "Father and I." In this narrative style, the narrator refers to himself as "I," and the work takes place entirely from this narrator's point of view. Occasionally, in this style, the narrator is a minor figure in the story. More commonly, as is the case with "Father and I," the first-person narrator is the protagonist (main character) of the story. By utilizing a first-person narrator, the author is able to convey all of that character's thoughts and feelings. Yet this style of narration is often viewed as limiting, as it prohibits the author's access to the thoughts and feelings of other characters. All the reader knows is filtered through the narrator. The reader must therefore question whether or not the narrator is a reliable one. In Lagerkvist's story, the narrator is of an undisclosed age, looking back and recalling an earlier time, when he was not yet ten years old.

Past-Tense Narration

By combining a first-person narrator with the use of the past tense, Lagerkvist presents the reader with an interesting perspective. While the boy in the story is almost ten years old, the narrator is clearly older; the story reflects his remembrances of a time long past. This is revealed in the opening sentence of the story, when the narrator states, "When I was getting on toward ten, I remember, Father took me by the hand one Sunday afternoon." As the story progresses, the reader becomes involved in the story from the child's point of view. At the same time, the reader must remember that the events are being sifted through the filter of age and experience. Only in the story's opening and closing is the reader reminded that time has past since the event. The narration from the youthful perspective is steadfastly childlike. Yet at the story's conclusion, although the narrator does not draw attention to the fact that the story is a recollection, as he does in the opening, he refers to his future, speaking of what his life would be like as a person for whom faith has offered no comfort. He speaks of "the anguish that was to come" as if he already has knowledge of it, has experienced it. This serves as a reminder to the reader that he has, in fact, already experienced it. In this final paragraph, Lagerkvist conflates his boyhood fears with the actual "anguish" he has experienced as the adult who looks back and relates the story.

HISTORICAL CONTEXT

Post–World War I Europe

After the end of World War I, Europe was a region in transition. Nations were shifting from wartime economies to peacetime economies, and the transition was rife with difficulties. Millions of veterans were required, out of economic necessity, to secure employment upon their return to their families. Many of the industries for which large numbers of veterans had worked prior to the war had shifted their production to war materials. Now those industries were seeking to regain sustainability in a postwar economy in which military demands had become drastically lower than in wartime. Often, veterans had no jobs to return to, or due to injuries sustained during the war, they were no longer able to return to their previously held positions. Additionally, shifts in European political boundaries that occurred after the war changed the trade agreements that had previously been in place. As Raymond F. Betts summarizes in *Europe in Retrospect: A Brief History of the Past Two Hundred Years*, "While European production recovered and exceeded postwar records, the percentage of the growing world market held by Europe declined. Relatively speaking, therefore, European economic vitality had slipped." On a less measurable scale, the mood of European countries had dramatically transformed as the horrors of warfare and the enormous casualties so many countries suffered were etched into the collective consciousness. European postwar culture was pervaded by a sense of hopelessness and persistent anxiety.

European Literary Modernism

Changes in cultural attitudes in post–World War I Europe are inevitably reflected in the artistic and literary works of the time period. The trauma of the war leads to the erosion of ideals and belief systems. Belief in science and in God are disrupted in the aftermath of the war. Even in the years leading up to the war, observes Susan Brantly in *A History of Swedish Literature*, "Rapid developments in technology result in the dehumanization of large portions of society and the increased aggressiveness that culminates in World War I. Science becomes a tool of the powerful, not a guarantor of order." Brantly describes the impact of these changes on people's faith, explaining that a "loss of divine order and meaning" leads to a world "perceived as inherently absurd, chaotic, and meaningless." In this void, the modernist movement begins to take shape. In the visual arts, modernist movements include dadaism, in which everything is regarded as absurd and meaningless, and the subsequent surrealist movement, in which the subconscious mind is the source of inspiration while reason is rejected. Such developments in the visual arts influence similar transformations in European literature. As Brantly points out, poetry is a

COMPARE
&
CONTRAST

- **1924:** Although Sweden remained neutral during World War I, in the aftermath the nation faces the same economic struggles as other European countries, experiencing an economic depression and frequent changes in governmental leadership.

  Today: Having maintained its neutrality through World War II, Sweden remains a neutral nation. It is not a member of NATO, the North Atlantic Treaty Organization, a military alliance of the governments of several nations. Sweden supports many of the United Nations' peacekeeping efforts by supplying humanitarian aid where needed and is also a member of NATO's "Partnership for Peace" program. It additionally trains armed forces to serve in peacekeeping capacities for UN, NATO, or EU (European Union) missions.

- **1924:** In the wake of the 1900 publication of Sigmund Freud's *Interpretation of Dreams*, in which Freud offers a psychoanalytic analysis of Shakespeare's character Hamlet, Freud's notions regarding the prominence of the subconscious mind influence many modernist writers in the 1920s. As noted in the 2003 *Encyclopedia of Literary Modernism*, edited by Paul Poplawski, modernist writers, including D. H. Lawrence, Ezra Pound, and T. S. Eliot, reveal in their work an attempt to explore the subconscious mind, a notion that prior to Freud's work was largely unknown.

  Today: Many works of literary fiction explore psychological connections between an adult's existence and his or her child-

hood. Several prominent works, in both film and literature, focus on the mind's ability to construct its own reality. Works such as Yann Martell's 2002 *Life of Pi*, Chuck Palahniuk's 1998 *Fight Club*, adapted for the screen in 1999, and the 1999 film *The Matrix* explore philosophical notions of existence, reality, and knowing, and the role of the subconscious mind in constructing such notions.

- **1924:** European art movements such as expressionism, cubism, surrealism, imagism, and Fauvism reject traditional forms of realistic representation and focus on more abstract forms of expression. Artists representing these movements explore the subconscious mind, the fractured nature of identity, or alternative ways of viewing reality. The disillusionment and despair generated by World War I contributes to the development of these ideas.

  Today: Following World War II, modernism yields to the notion of postmodernism in the world of artistic expression. While modernism rejects many of the traditions that had preceded it, it nevertheless sought new methods of exploring and expressing reality, and it found new meaning in the subconscious, for example. Postmodernism is alternately seen as a rejection of, or a revision of, modernist methods, and encompasses a wide variety of art forms, including conceptual and performance art, both of which produce work that often, by design, cannot be put in a museum and subsequently question the boundaries of what is regarded as art.

"favored genre of modernists," as elements of visual art movements are easily adapted to imagistic poems. Lagerkvist, for example, in his poetry, was heavily influenced by visual expressionism, in particular cubism. Expressionism focuses on subjective interpretation and representation of what the artist sees. In cubist works,

the artist depicts his vision from a variety of angles, underscoring the fragmented nature of consciousness. In addition to the influence of visual art movements on literary modernism, the thought and writings of individuals such as Sigmund Freud and Friedrich Nietzsche influence the works of many modernist writers.

It suddenly got dark and the boy was afraid. *(puchan | Shutterstock.com)*

Freud founded the psychoanalytic school of psychology and explored the depths of the subconscious mind and its influence on behavior. Nietzsche, a German philosopher, is associated with nihilism—the view that the universe is utterly devoid of meaning—and existentialism—the notion that an individual's free will, in a world devoid of universal truths, is the only means by which choices can be made. In addition to Lagerkvist, other modernist writers include T. S. Eliot, author of the expressionist poem *The Waste Land* (1922), and Marcel Proust, who wrote the multivolume stream-of-consciousness novel *Remembrance of Things Past*, published in 1922.

CRITICAL OVERVIEW

Lagerkvist's work is often reviewed within the context of his modernism. Many critics observe that Lagerkvist's expressionist poetry marked

him as a modernist as early as 1916, when his poetry collection *Ångest* (Anguish) was published. Lagerkvist is commonly regarded as ahead of his time in this respect, and his modernist status is contrasted with Swedish modernism, which, as Brantly has observed in *A History of Swedish Literature*, was not really fully underway until the 1940s. Brantly further comments on Lagerkvist's "Father and I," stating that in the story, "a mysterious train serves as a symbol for the existential anguish that separates a young boy from the secure, religious world of his father." Lagerkvist's alignment with the existentialist philosophical school of thought that Brantly explores is also underscored by other critics, who emphasize the writer's sense of pain and estrangement from the worlds of both faith and reason. Arnold L. Weinstein, for example, in *Northern Arts: The Breakthrough of Scandinavian Literature and Art from Ibsen to Bergman*, notes that in "Father and I" and in other similarly autobiographical works, Lagerkvist's "trademark emotions are anguish, pain, and the certainty of being outside the calm order of reason, by dint of a sensibility that can never find peace." Similarly, John Shea, in *Stories of God: An Unauthorized Biography*, describes what he terms "Mystery" as an "abyss" in which "No protective symbols are available, no interpretive culture buffers its impact on the human soul." He asserts, "For many in the twentieth century it is this chaotic face of Mystery which has revealed itself. Par Lagerkvist in 'My Father and I' has seen it."

> LADEN WITH TELLING IMAGERY AND SYMBOLISM, 'FATHER AND I' REVEALS A PERSPECTIVE THAT, WHILE STARK, IS FULL OF COMPLEXITY. THE STORY SHOULD NOT SIMPLY BE NOTICED IN PASSING AS AN EXAMPLE OF LAGERKVIST'S EXISTENTIAL ANGST."

CRITICISM

Catherine Dominic

Dominic is a novelist and a freelance writer and editor. In the following essay, she explores the imagery, symbolism, and narratorial voice employed by Lagerkvist in his short story "Father and I," maintaining that Lagerkvist's use of nature imagery, the symbolism of light and darkness, and the narrator's duality result in a story that explores the complexities of fear in the narrator's faithless existence.

"Father and I" has received less critical attention than either Lagerkvist's poetry or his novels. Typically, critics comment on the existential anxiety the story's ending reveals; alternatively, they consider the work's autobiographical nature. Yet the short work of prose is a fine example of Lagerkvist's skill as a storyteller, and it is rich with philosophical meaning. Laden with telling imagery and symbolism, "Father and I" reveals a perspective that, while stark, is full of complexity. The story should not simply be noticed in passing as an example of Lagerkvist's existential angst. Rather, an examination of the story's nature imagery, its symbolism, and its narratorial voice yields a deeper understanding of the emotional turmoil emphasized by the story's ending.

As "Father and I" opens, the narrator reveals his dual nature. Recalling a time when he was a child, he tells the story from a later point in time, presumably after he has reached adulthood. Lagerkvist happens to have been thirty-three years old when the story was published. The narrator's perspective is such that he reveals the thoughts and feelings he experienced as a young boy, but these are expressed as remembrances and therefore filtered by the passage of time. For most of the story, though, the narrator's perspective is centered in that almost-ten-year-old mind. The observations, as well as his way of expressing himself, underscore the narrator's youth. Only in the opening sentence and at the story's end does the narrator, through direct statement or through his manner of expression, convey the sense that his adult self is now the main narrating voice.

In the beginning of the story, the narrator comments that he and his father had been "brought up with nature and used to it." He insists that taking a walk and listening to the birds was not something planned or fussed over. Rather, "It was just that it was Sunday afternoon and Father was free." Soon, despite his stated nonchalance, the child notices precise details concerning the birds and their songs, as well as other details about the trees, flowers, insects, and the very earth itself. All of his observations paint a vivid picture of energy, vitality, and cheerfulness. As a train approaches, the child and his father move off the tracks. The boy observes the way his father offers a friendly salute to the driver of the train. The familiarity represented by the train and its driver is noted by the boy but not dwelt upon. Later, this notion of the familiar will become more important to the child. Even the railroad tracks are described in terms suggestive of the narrator's optimism. The sun shines on the rails, and the greasy smell of the sleepers, or railroad ties, is intermingled with scent of wildflowers. The whole world seems friendly; the telegraph poles "sang as you passed them." The idyllic tone of the scene continues; father and son hold hands as they cross a rail bridge over a stream by stepping from sleeper to sleeper. They have milk with neighbors, they toss stones in the river and speak of the father's own childhood. The natural imagery in this section of the story—the sun, the

WHAT DO I READ NEXT?

- Lagerkvist's novel *The Dwarf* was originally published in Swedish as *Dvärgen* in 1944. The English translation by Alexandra Dick was first published in 1945 and then reprinted by Hill & Wang in 1958. In this psychological, philosophical, and allegorical novel, Lagerkvist explores the nature of evil and of personal identity, and the role of the individual within society. It is one of the few of Lagerkvist's many works that is still available in English translation.

- Edith Södergran was, like Lagerkvist, a Swedish modernist poet, and is considered to be among the most influential poets in this category. A number of her poems have been collected in the volume *Love and Solitude: Selected Poems from 1916 through 1923*. This volume was translated by Stina Katchadourian and published in a bilingual (Swedish and English) edition by Fjord Press in 1981 and again in 1992.

- T. S. Eliot, a British and American citizen of American birth, wrote during the same time as Lagerkvist and was also considered a modernist in terms of his expressionist poetry. Many of his writings published during the years between the two world wars, including his long poem *The Waste Land*, published in 1922 and his play, *The Family Reunion*, published in 1939, contain existentialist themes and modernist sensibilities. Both are available in *T. S. Eliot: Complete Poems and Plays, 1909-1950*, published by Houghton Mifflin Harcourt in 1952.

- David Cottington's *Cubism in the Shadow of War: The Avante-garde and Politics in Paris, 1905-1914* explores the development of the artistic movement of cubism in Paris in the years leading up to World War I. Lagerkvist was in Paris in 1913, and it was at this time that he was exposed to cubism and other art movements, which would later influence his poetry. Cottington's work was published in 1998 by Yale University Press.

- *Existence in Black: An Anthology of Black Existential Philosophy*, edited by Lewis Gordon, is a collection of writings concerned with existentialism from an African perspective. The contributors to the volume represent a wide range of cultural, ethnic, and racial backgrounds. The collection was published by Routledge in 1996.

- *Sophie's World: A Novel about the History of Philosophy*, by Jostein Gaarder, is a young-adult novel in which the protagonist, a young girl named Sophie, explores a number of philosophical issues in a series of letters exchanged with a philosopher. Gaarder is a Norwegian philosophy professor. His work was translated by Paulette Moeller and was originally published by Harcourt Brace in 1970. The work has since been reprinted a number of times, most recently by Farrar, Straus & Giroux in 2007.

---

chirping, fluttering birds, the carpet of flowers, the fresh shoots on the trees—underscores the boy's happiness and peacefulness. In this portion of the story, the light is reflective of everything perceived by the boy to be good, not only in the world around him but in his state of mind and in his relationship with his father.

At this point in the story, father and son decide to turn home. The tone and the imagery of the story shift. All that is associated with the day, with the light, begins to turn dark. There are two paragraphs of transition, where Lagerkvist takes advantage of the gradual transition of day to twilight and then to night to build the story's emotional tension. The boy notes how the woods are changing during twilight. He thinks of his mother's anxiety, how she would worry about her son and husband. The boy is noticing the shift from day to night, but he arrests his own sense of disquiet by thinking of his mother's fears rather than his own. He reminds himself that "it had been a lovely day, nothing had happened that shouldn't. We were content with everything." In the next paragraph, the boy finds it more difficult to keep his fear at bay. Everything he had found to be cheerful in the sunlight is transforming before his eyes. In the dark, the trees are now anthropomorphized. The boy observes, "The trees were so funny. They stood listening to every step we took, as if they didn't know who we were." The child suddenly regards himself as the unfamiliar element in the woods; he feels unrecognized, unwelcome, out of place. The boy's sense of estrangement increases as the nighttime walk continues. When he and his father walk over the train bridge as they had done earlier in the story, the boy is surprised to find that his father does not carry him across. Instead, they hold hands, just as they had done earlier. The boy realizes that his father, whether or not he has perceived his son's fear, "probably wanted me to be like him and think nothing of it." The child, however, now has a strong sense that he is not like his father.

The boy's sense of isolation and estrangement escalates further as the walk home continues. Watching his father, the boy wonders how he is managing to remain calm. The boy's panic grows. He looks around, seeing "Nothing but darkness everywhere. I hardly dared take a deep breath, for then you got so much darkness inside you, and that was dangerous." He believes that to breathe in the darkness means that one will die soon. Significantly, the narrator chooses this moment to remind the reader, "I remember quite well that's what I thought then." The narrator's status as an adult looking back to his youth is reiterated at this particular moment in order to emphasize the importance of this sentiment. The darkness begins to take on an increasingly symbolic meaning for the boy, as it is associated with danger and death. As the story continues, it becomes clear that for the narrator, darkness also serves as a symbol for alienation and unbearable uncertainty.

Seeking some comfort, the boy asks his father, "why is it so horrible when it's dark?" The way the narrator frames the question suggests the complexity of its meaning. The pronoun "it" in this sentence does not refer back to anything in particular. He may mean the woods, life, their walk. His indefinite usage overlays a universal quality to his question. Darkness itself, to the narrator, is horrible in its all-encompassing nature. As the conversation with the father progresses, the reader continues to learn what darkness means to the narrator. His father expresses that belief in God eliminates the need for fear. This assertion serves as another turning point in the story. Just as the onset of twilight shifts the tone of the story from light to increasing darkness, the father's proclamation of faith generates a further escalation in the narrator's sense of trepidation and isolation. After proclaiming to the reader his sense of abandonment, the boy states, "It was so strange that only I was afraid, not Father." Not only can his father not comfort him, but he has marked himself as different from his son by virtue of his faith. The boy finds the notion of a God existing "everywhere here in the darkness" to be a terrifying one. The telegraph poles, which previously the boy thought of as singing, now "rumbled" with the presence of God. The boy feels his heart constricting, as if the darkness itself was crushing it.

As the boy descends into emotional and spiritual despair, an unexpected train thunders through the darkness, forcing father and son off the rails and onto the embankment. The boy is shocked to see that his father does not recognize the driver of the train. While the father thinks it odd that the train was unscheduled and the driver unfamiliar, the boy is consumed with "dread." Whereas the appearance of the scheduled train during the daylight hours, a train piloted by a man the father recognized, reassured the boy with a sense of familiarity, regularity, and predictability, the unscheduled train in the darkness represents all that is dark, unknown, and horrific. He states that he "sensed what it meant." This time, it is clear that the boy's "it" refers to the dark train. He goes on, "it was the anguish that was to come, the unknown, all that Father knew nothing about, that he wouldn't be able to protect me against." All of the imagery associated with the darkness, all it implies, culminates in this symbol. The child feels utterly alone, vulnerable, threatened. Furthermore, he projects himself into the future, stating with certainty, "That was how this world, this life, would be for me; not like Father's, where everything was secure and certain." As an adult, the narrator knows this statement to be true; as a child he could only imagine the anguish to come. The child's father, the child is certain, is insulated from these terrors by his faith. In the absence of a faith in the goodness of God, in the

They headed home, guided by the dark tracks. *(Donald R. Swartz / Shutterstock.com)*

ability of God, or the in the power of his own human father to protect the him, the child is certain that he will be tormented by "the darkness that had no end." The pain and anguish of the eternal darkness into which the narrator plunges at the end of the story is felt more deeply by the reader as it stands in contrast to the hope, optimism, and peace conveyed in the first half of the story. The narrator, so dramatically altered by his experience, explores the gradations of happiness in the first half of the story, only to erase, shade by shade, that joy in the second half of the story. Next, the emptiness that remains is filled first with gentle worry, then fear, then panic, and finally absolute terror and emotional and spiritual agony. In only several pages of prose, Lagerkvist leads his reader skillfully through a lifetime's worth of emotion and philosophical realization, ending the story with a sense of the eternal nature of the darkness that must be endured.

Source: Catherine Dominic, Critical Essay on "Father and I," in *Short Stories for Students*, Gale, Cengage Learning, 2011.

Adèle Bloch

In the following essay, Bloch investigates the role of the mythical female in Lagerkvist's fictional works.

Lagerkvist may be viewed from many angles. Labelled an "existentialist" by some critics, he can be compared to his hero Ahasuerus, the Wandering Jew who revolts against the injustice of fate, the opacity of the world, the silence of nature and of the divine. For him the Schopenhauer-Freudian concept is valid: man is the author of his own fate, since whatever happens to the individual comes from within. Yet man needs a sense of purpose. Even if there is no real proof of the existence of an external God or Ideal Love or of any ultimate truth, man will create a pattern, or reinterpret his life according to a superior order, for he cannot tolerate the utter nihilism of the arbitrary absurdity inherent in his condition. Existence may precede essence, but Lagerkvist's heroes unconsciously live their lives according to some mythological image or archetype. They all pattern their personalities and follow the paths indicated to them by buried biblical or heathen traditions. Some are more aware than others. They come to understand these mythical forces at maturity. Others garner this understanding only on the verge of death. Others yet, such as Barabbas, die in the maternal darkness of the unconscious.

> WOMAN IS A SYMBOL OR PRODUCT OF
> THE MALE'S ASPIRATIONS, FEARS OR IDEALS. HE
> KEEPS PROJECTING THESE QUALITIES UPON THE
> FEMALE RATHER THAN TRULY RELATING TO A
> HUMAN BEING."

Lagerkvist uses the theory of mythological archetype projection very much in the manner of Thomas Mann whose heroes fashion their natures and destinies according to certain legendary prototypes. Fuller recognition of identification with mythical figures is slowly attained by certain individuals, as the generations move towards more civilized levels of conscience. In the case of Lagerkvist's fictional characters, complete self-realization can be gained only after a lifetime of guilt, struggles and reenactment of some original sins. His heroes descend into hell several times and undergo several partial epiphanies while groping for final answers which cannot be definitely stated. They also change identities along the way. One thing, however, remains a leitmotiv: their pilgrimage is always placed under the aegis of the Magna Mater. She may assume many masks: the sea of oblivion, the hounding witch, the virgin saint of Christianity, the pagan huntress, to name but a few, but she is the feminine dark side of the earth, as conceived by the male spirit. Her modifications are due to the state of mind of man, who projects his own emotions and symbolism upon the female, according to his age, his upbringing and his times. She is present in all of Lagerkvist's works and completely engulfs his later novels.

Lagerkvist's heroes, females as well as males, spend their lives in the search for a God or Ideal which would give them a sense of purpose, of peace and of value. In their peregrinations, they must confront their shadow side, namely the Great Mother, upon which they project their own desires, fears and guilt. Basically, the Mythical Mother is neither absolutely good nor absolutely bad. In the circle of life, vice and virtue, moral criteria, are relative. The unconscious may well assume a threatening face, especially to the uninitiated: "Lagerkvist is a very

dwelling place of dualisms, of contending opposites, darkness and light, good and evil, the cosmic and the familiar, life and death, comfort and despair."

In order to experience a rebirth, it is necessary that these characters come in contact with the divine under its manifold guises. Such a spiritual epiphany requires one or many descents into hell, often expressed as the mines, the bowels of the ship, or the Delphic wombpit. It entails one or several attempts to realize the presence of a soul or "anima," as translated by a variety of symbols.

It is a matter of scant importance whether Lagerkvist is actually a literary exponent of Freudian or Jungian theories. Both interpretations are equally valid in his case. From a Freudian angle, his heroes, when they refer to their childhood at all, were often brought up under abnormal conditions. The Dwarf and Barabbas were warped by parental rejection; Giovanni, the Pilgrim at Sea, was brought up in an atmosphere of hypocrisy by a puritanical mother within the confines of a "stifling, narrow little home." This mother is a typical castrating woman, and her son is overly attached to her. He later becomes a priest to suit her possessive schemes, but falls subsequently into the clutches of an exploiting older mistress, and is finally destroyed by both women. Barabbas, scarred by his father, unwanted by his mother, finds his father in Oedipal fashion and kills him without recognizing his identity, thus enacting an age-old myth, redolent also of the ritual father sacrifice of Chronos by his sons. The Dwarf, less titanic in proportions, has been stunted by maternal rejection: "Thus did my mother sell me, turning from me in disgust when she saw what she had borne and not understanding that I was of an ancient race. She was paid twenty scudi for me and with them she bought three cubits of cloth and a watchdog for her sheep." The Sybil, although brought up by loving parents, grows up without siblings and day-dreams her adolescence away, rejecting the joys of normal life, only to crave them later in almost hysterical fashion, like so many of Thomas Mann's heroes and heroines.

But although formative trauma may explain some of these characters whose dreams also elicit a strongly sexual content, they are too deeply rooted on common ground and extra-individual symbolism to account for mere infantile repression and adult compensation. The archetypes after which they pattern themselves transcend their own Vita, have resonances in the outside world and in the consciousness of their whole species. Actually Freud himself postulated in *Totem and Taboo*, written in 1913, the existence of a collective mind, while acknowledging his debt to the sociologist Wundt and to C. J. Jung with whom he did not yet disagree. Lagerkvist's fictional heroes are seldom personal; often they are so archetypal in nature as to remain nameless or designated by such vague mythological appellations as "the woman he called Diana," "the Sybil," "the Babe." They represent a whole race or group of kindred men. Some are reprobates such as the Dwarf, Barabbas or King Herod, who belong to the ancient red-haired progeny of Cain, Esau and Judas, sinners and sinned against, firebrands endowed with Promethean traits. On the other hand there is a constant reappearance of minor Cabiric characters, lavatory keepers, pagan temple servants or Christian lay brothers who lead the weary soul to rest, thus mirroring the role of Hermes Psychopompos. It is significant that Tom-Thumb chthonic deities have the soles of their feet black, while their heads are bathed in radiance. All are shrouded in hermetic ambiguity which stems from their dual role: service of Apollo, the paternal god of light, and yet devotion to the dark goddess of the underworld.

Lagerkvist rarely elaborates, he suggests in streamlined fashion. Yet every word is pregnant with symbolic meaning. He usually avoids dating the stage on which he places his works, so as to endow them with a cyclical sweep. Some of the locales are loosely set in early Christianity (although he never refers to Christ by name, but by circumlocution so as to emphasize the archetypal nature of the Messianic prototype), others are placed in Apocalyptic days. Still others take place in a prehistorical setting with futuristic overtones. Lagerkvist will not pinpoint his tales in a given span. He presents us with the wheel of time, the returning aeons, blending the ancient with the modern, while the subterranean roots push their ramifications far into the archaic matriarchal antiquity. The past resonates in the present, as the circle revolves from cradle to grave. Meanwhile the locket, which for him symbolizes life and the womb, typical aspects of the Great Mother, gets handed from one person to the next. Characters fade and reappear from one work to the next.

One feature, though, remains constant, despite its many guises: that is the Anima Figure of feminine visage of the collective mind. It provides not only a poetic pattern, a meaning which has to be discovered by the writer, his heroes and his readers, to gain more insight into an opaque and seemingly senseless universe, but it lends cohesion to the entire work.

The Magna Mater may not even appear in womanly guise in some novels, as she may be expressed by a more abstract natural symbol such as the sea. *Pilgrim at Sea* is the saga of a man "named Giovanni, after the disciple *He* loved best," and who seeks solace in the embrace of the maternal sea of oblivion, after having been hounded by a castrating mother and a similar mistress. He is tied with a John the Baptist role, and his element is the water which cleanses past sins and washes away painful memories. He surrenders to "the sea—the great and endless sea which in its indifference forgives all things. Primeval, irresponsible, inhuman." Giovanni turns blind as he sinks in the fluid grip. Until his end, he never relinquishes the empty locket snatched from his lover. He neither comes to realize the symbolic meaning of his escape into the primitive waters of the Flood, nor is he capable of reaching an adult stage of maturity.

Barabbas, who would scorn women, confronts the Magna Mater in the form of unrelieved darkness, the night of ignorance. For him, she means utter nothingness, death which he welcomes after a life of tribulations. She finally delivers him from his fetters and from the burden of an existence barren of human companionship.

The Magna Mater personifies nature for most heroes. In the *Sybil*, she is Gaia, the Pagan Earth Goddess. She is also the underground side of Apollo the Sun-god, worshipped at Delphi in his sacred grove and shrine. The virgin Pythia who spends her life in the devotion of the paternal god of light is nevertheless overcome by dionysian forces which create a terrifying split in her. While she places herself under the protection of the chaste father-spirit, her descent into the hell of the oracular pit grows more orgiastic. Finally a Pan-like goat overpowers her amidst the snakes of the cleft. Subsequently, she bears an imbecilic son whose enigmatic smile reflects the animal side of the archaic matriarchal goddess who had been worshipped at Delphi before being supplanted by the male deity, Apollo. The forces of conscious light and of maenad-like possession constantly vie in her, until old age, when she comes to realize that the divine may display a variety of attributes, some bestial, others harmonious. Here the Great Mother represents an undifferentiated, preconscious stage of adaptation. Her main symbols are rivers and wells, trees, vegetals, and finally animals such as the serpent, fraught with ritual and sexual overtones, the black goat, the sheep and the lame black mare of Scandinavian mythology, which heralds the approach of death at midnight. Lagerkvist, in common with Thomas Mann, likes to mingle all mythologies, mixing the Mediterranean with the Norse and with the Oriental in order to emphasize the common ground from which all myths have sprung.

The Magna Mater often represents a face of the moon. She can be typified as a horrid dark moon witch, connected with Hecate. As such, she relives in the form of the malicious old hags which reappear in most of his novels. She takes the shape of a vindictive old woman who ruins her children or her wards. More often she is revealed in a pleasanter phase, that of Diana, the Huntress. Tobias, one of the principal heroes, meets his love at the well, under the boughs of the sacred oak tree. "She was like a virgin whom no one could utterly possess." She is savage, accompanied by hunting dogs, free of a human past, relations, or cares other than roaming the forests in a wild, unwomanly fashion. To the man, Diana means chastity which he must ravish in an act fraught with classical symbolism. But the magical aura of the lunar goddess is destroyed as soon as the rape is consummated. Diana becomes a woman, stripped of daemonic forces. No longer can she be confused with a mythological figure lurking in her lover's consciousness, and so he abandons her.

Parallel but contrasting with this pagan lunar incarnation, we find noble silvery Mariamne in an eschatological setting which foreshadows the coming of Christianity. Depraved King Herod meets the Maccabeean princess, precursor in appearance and in nature of the Virgin Mary "on the road to Damascus, only a little way beyond the Gate of the City, amidst flowers." Like Paul, the Apostle, he is smitten with blindness at the miraculous vision. The tyrant experiences a partial rebirth which temporarily mitigates his fierceness and causes his bride to be considered as a savior by the people for whom she intercedes. The metamorphosis, however, does not last and Herod degrades and kills her in a scene fraught with Othello-like overtones.

Diana and other heroines of Lagerkvist then conform to the next stage of the Magna Mater's earthly appearances, that of the Scarlet Woman of Babylon. To men she is a scorned harlot, the butt of every degradation which, however, makes her more desirable as a sexual object. The woman herself is not so depraved as the male imagination would picture her, but she loses her youth and innocence in the course of a career foisted upon her by the vagaries of life. The Great Mother is now embodied in a figure which abounds in Lagerkvist's novels: that of the middle-aged woman, ready to seduce a younger boy. She is greatly feared by her prey, who yet feels drawn to her, as she plays the part of Potiphar's wife. Finally she causes the downfall of her youthful victim whom she swallows in a murky situation, yet fraught with the delights of the incest taboo. Actually, she appears more dangerous to the uninitiated male than she is in reality.

The Magdalen phase is the sequel to that of the Sinner. There we see the fallen woman regenerated by love and sacrifice for man, her Savior Image. Diana as well as other heroines voluntarily die for their own and their lover's regeneration. This aspect of the redeemed and redeeming Margaret figure leads next to the Beatrice-like guiding spirit which is more abstract and unsullied by past stains. This is the pure "anima" symbol which leads the hero to his salvation.

To the older man, the Great Mother appears in the travesty of Mary, the Mater Dolorosa. She wears the blue cloak of the Madonna and guides the weary traveller to full awareness, amnesty for the sins of existence, and finally ushers in death, eternal sleep and absolution. She bears the serene expression of the Mother of God.

Her image may linger in a man's consciousness even beyond the grave. In the short story, "The Wave of Osiris," a deceased king is about to be led into the courts of Osiris, the god of the dead, when a golden statuette of Isis elicits a vivid interest in him. Although the idol crumbles into dust, the feminine figure has provided the man with his last mediating link between being and nothingness, terrestrial and nether-worldly existence.

Despite the fact that Magna Mater has transformed herself in the image of many earthly women, her unity is never in doubt. Her voice and gait betray her oneness. To one single hero she might appear under the likeness of several females: his own carnal mother, his virgin bride, sacred harlot, patron saint, and guide to the beyond. She might even adopt an anima shape such as the vulture, the serpent, the bitch or the sow. Yet these are but some facets of the Great Mother. Tobias, the dying hero, realizes that she is but One: his own experience of the Eternal Feminine. At least he is free to die in peace as the splits between darkness and light, nature and religion fade away. After he draws his last breath, she repossesses her locket or chain of life. The cycle which is ended for one man shall go on for others, as tomb and womb are interchangeable.

The Magna Mater has very little to do with the true nature of the women who confront Lagerkvist's heroes: the Dwarf sees the Princess as a loathsome Temptress, Bernardo, alias Leonardo da Vinci recognizes an angelic quality in her Mona-Lisa-like smile, her lover celebrates her beauty in Petrarchan verse whereas her husband considers her as a commonplace elderly wife. Woman is a symbol or product of the male's aspirations, fears or ideals. He keeps projecting these qualities upon the female rather than truly relating to a human being. Misunderstanding and alienation are the basis of the relationship, as in the typical case of Herod who seeks a love with whom he can never communicate: "She was new to him and his very opposite; and from this arose also his inability to understand her, or to enter into her alien, cool, emotional world." On the other hand, Lagerkvist's women (except for the exalted somewhat masculine Sybil) are much closer to nature and more pragmatic than the men.

It is noticeable that in all of his fiction, love can only thrive on sex, stealth, violence and prohibition. This allows the mind of the subject to endow his object with mythological traits. Never does he depict a permanent relationship, one in which personalities and basic needs are understood and respected. Men insist on forcing their partners to re-enact archetypal patterns, thus excluding insight of true feminine psychology and of the real flesh and blood woman, who naturally suffers from such a basic misunderstanding.

Both men and women adopt various mythological roles in their search for the divine. Whether they follow a course decided upon by free existential choice or unconsciously, according to biblical or pagan stereotypes, is immaterial. They all try to find a certain harmony between their aspirations and the enigmatic natural world. They all seek to decode the irony of their fates, in order to render life meaningful. Some succeed in finding an answer and die surrounded by bright light, others return to the embrace of darkness. In the end, ambiguity may still reign. Lagerkvist does not ultimately solve the question. Yet this very ambiguity may be yet another face of the Magna Mater, that of the eternal silence of nature.

Source: Adèle Bloch, Essay in *International Fiction Review*, Vol. 1, No. 1, January 1974, pp. 48–53.

Adèle Bloch

In the following essay, Bloch finds similarities between the main influence on and themes found in the work of Lagerkvist, Thomas Mann, Nikos Kazantsakis, and Jacques Roumain.

In the nineteen forties and fifties while the world was still in the throes of war and social upheaval, four novelists wrote fictional works with similar archetypal themes. Thomas Mann is the senior author as his *Joseph Cycle* most directly influenced the work of his younger colleagues. The Scandinavian Pär Lagerkvist so closely followed in his footsteps that similar characters and structures can be found throughout his entire opus, from the popular *Barabbas* through the *Sybil* and the *Holy Land*. The fictional works of the Greek poet Nikos Kazantsakis such as the *Greek Passion* and the *Last Temptation of Christ* also display the same mythological images and patterns. Finally, repercussions of almost identical archetypal figures impress the reader of the novels of Jacques Roumain, a Haitian poet and writer of fictional works, such as *Gouverneurs de la Rosée* ("Governors of the Dew") which won him worldwide acclaim just prior to his untimely death in 1944.

It is significant that these four novelists came under the influence of Nietzsche, that all four view life as myth, and that all studied mythology. All had read Wundt's sociological studies, and all were impressed by Freud's *Totem and Taboo*, where he postulates the existence of a "Collective Unconscious." It must be emphasized that this work dates back to 1913, a period when Freud still collaborated with the philosopher C. G. Jung, with whom he was to feud later on. Finally, all four, including the Haitian who had studied anthropology in Zurich, were directly influenced by the Jungian Archetype Projection theories and openly acknowledged their debt to the Swiss psychologist.

"

TO ALL THESE WRITERS, THIS TYPE
EPITOMIZES COLLECTIVE INTERCHANGEABLE
WOMANHOOD THAT GOES THROUGH SIMILAR
PHASES: VIRGIN GIRLHOOD, WIFEHOOD,
HARLOTRY, KINDLY BUT DEMANDING
MOTHERHOOD, AND ULTIMATELY SAINTHOOD."

A study of the backgrounds of these four authors reveals certain similar patterns. Thomas Mann was born into a stolid mercantile family in Hamburg, but he did have a Brazilian mother who instilled a note of spontaneity and musicianship into the formal household. During his entire life, Thomas Mann felt the split between conventional paternal milieu and the lure of more artistic and Bohemian life style. His own desire for the joys of normalcy and of mediocre domesticity, sharply conflicted with latent homosexual and anarchistic tendencies, such as one sees reflected in his protagonists as well.

Lagerkvist was born into a stifling Puritanical background. His father was a pastor, and his mother a cold, censorious hypocrite, who was to poison his entire life with feelings of guilt and resentment. His long quest for meaning in life, whether on a religious or on an existential plane, never ceased and was reflected throughout his opus.

Kazantsakis was born in a Greek Orthodox family of peasants on the Isle of Crete, at the crossroads between European, Asian, and African cultures. While he revered his saintly mother, he was torn by feelings of ambivalence towards his father, whose coarse machismo he would emulate in vain. Even during his childhood he felt the split between two antagonists: Greece and Turkey, active virility and artistic sensitivity, a clash between the procreative traditions of his ancestors, and his own fear of women. Later in his life, he became an active Leninist and he died a guest of Mao in China, in 1957.

Jacques Roumain was born into a well-to-do family of Port-au-Prince mulattoes. After studying in Europe and in the U.S.A., he rejected the privileges of his bourgeois family. He revolted against several repressive regimes in his island, and founded the Communist Party there. After repeated incarcerations, as well as torture, he died in 1944 at the age of thirty-seven, under suspicious circumstances.

A reader of the works of these writers is struck by the recurrence of parallel themes. In some cases, the fictional types seem to mirror each other. The first, and most pervasive, is the prototype of the "hero." For Thomas Mann this figure is incorporated in the pseudo-biblical character of Joseph, whom he endows with typical heroic traits, such as a charismatic physique, early separation from a virginal mother, and a life fraught with trials and tribulations. This particular Joseph wills himself into some of the roles which he assumes, and which vary according to the stages of his development and to the locales in which he is cast. Not fate alone, but also his own subconscious manipulations determine his path. So, for instance, he plays the part of a Baal sorcerer while in Canaan, the role of Tammuz-Attis-Adonis Corn-gods while in Syria, and later on, while in Egypt, he comes to successively impersonate dismembered Osiris, Anubis the jackal-god, and the sacred Apis bull. Throughout, he identifies with the playful Graeco-Roman god Hermes-Mercury.

Lagerkvist's "hero" prototypes are often anti-heroes, as is the case for the "Dwarf" and for "Barabbas." In their case, the epiphanies are ambivalent or aborted, and in the final outcome, they submit to unremitting darkness or existential despair.

The divine hero, such as conceived by Kazantsakis and by Roumain, is more Christlike. True to messianic tradition, the hero chooses to suffer immolation so that his ultimate sacrifice may redeem the community. The Greek Christ impersonator is a shepherd named Manolios, while his Caribbean counterpart is a peasant whose name, significantly, is "Manuel." Both these characters are very human, but their mission grows on them so that their people come to accept them as saviors.

Another constant theme which dominates the works of all four of these writers, is that of the "magna mater" or "great mother." If the Jungian jargon of "anima projection" or "archetype" is to be avoided, this recurrent image can be referred to as the "eternal feminine," as Goethe called it, or the "female face of the earth," to use Kazantsakis's own terminology. This "great mother" is associated with animals such as the snake, which is omnipresent in all the works, the vulture, the goat, and the black mare of Scandinavian mythology. She is not only symbolized in these animate forms, but is also associated with water symbols (such as the sea of oblivion and the well of purity), plant symbols (such as flowers and trees), and astral bodies (such as the morning star and the moon). To sum up, she comes to represent all of nature in its benevolent and nurturing aspects as well as in its destructive ones.

This mythical female, who in most cases impedes the progress of the hero, represents yin, or the dark forces of nature. She operates on a much broader scope than the hero's carnal mother. In any case, the umbilical cord must be severed if individuation is to be achieved: "Siehe, man musz sie durchschneiden, die Nabelschnur, dasz sich das Kalb von der Mutterkuh löse und werde zum Stiere des Lichtes" (*Joseph*, p. 866). The female element represents an archaic matriarchal order which the hero must supersede.

Woman represents a threat to Mann's, to Kazantsakis's, and to Lagerkvist's heroes: she means sloth and natural conservatism geared to a procreative purpose: "But man with God v would have been obliterated by hunger, fear and cold; and if he survived these, he would have crawled like a slug midway between lions and lice; and if with incessant struggle he managed to stand on his hind legs, he would never have been able to escape the tight warm embrace of his mother the monkey"...(*Last Temptation of Christ*, p. 281). To a man who is dedicated to his Apollonian mission, she is a mere distraction. (Of course this is only true in the case of the outstanding man endowed with an artistic or prophetic vocation.) However, for even this type of man, it is not easy to renounce what Thomas Mann ironically designates as "Die Wonnen der Gewöhnlichkeit," the common joys of everyday living. The Promethean hero, however, is constantly warned that he cannot stagnate in trivial existence, lest he be caught in the spokes of the wheel of time. And so he must break loose from the grip of the Mother, the family, the tribe, and even from the nation. Often this "magna mater" appears quite unreal as she is a figment of man's imagination or a projection of his atavistic superstition. Part of growth and maturity depends on the demystification of this myth. Ultimately, the female element can become a Beatrice-like benign guiding spirit who helps the dying hero to find peace.

For Thomas Mann, Mut, wife of Potiphar, the Eunuch, embodies all these traits. Her very name suggests the Mother. She is represented as a frustrated middle-aged temptress who plays the role of Babylonian Astarte-Ishtar, the goddess who seduces her son Gilgamesh, the Asian Earth Goddess Cybele who emasculates her son Attis, and "Eset als Geierweibchen" (*Joseph*, p. 968), Egyptian Isis who is the consort as well as the mother of dismembered Osiris. Her utterances are reminiscent of Hellenic Phaedra, Medea, Dido, the Maenads, and witches engaged in black magic under the spell of Hecate's dark moon. Thomas Mann, in his letters and his essays, declares that he purposely mixed all his mythologies so as to point to the ground common to all humans and to exorcise the Nazi myth of racial superiority. It is by no means accidental that he thus fuses biblical, Assyrian, Egyptian, and African prototypes, "Denn das Typische ist ja das Mythische schon, insofern es Ur-Norm und Ur-Form des Lebens ist, Zeitloses Schema und von je gegebene Formel, in die das Leben eingeht, in dem es aus dem Unbewuszten seine Zuge reproduziert" (*Joseph*, p. 162).

Lagerkvist features a nameless temptress who is an almost exact replica of Mut. She, too, is over thirty, married in a loveless arrangement, and eager to seduce a naive youth in an atmosphere of social sham and secrecy, so as to denounce him later on. Like her Egyptian counterpart, she displays a thin aristocratic face which contrasts with a voluptuous body. Both heroines end their careers by filling life's void with religious practices.

Kazantsakis depicts similar types such as the Magdalenes and the widows who never relent in their pursuit of younger men: "I must look at you, because woman is issued from the body of man and still cannot detach her body from his ... Allow me to look at you, therefore, my child" (*Last Temptation of Christ*, p. 329). These predatory females coax, mother, and smother the chaste young hero in a fruitless attempt to attain one single goal, common to all: namely motherhood. Jacques Roumain's Haitian heroines are less hysterical and more natural in their maternal parts. But they too risk death and social disgrace in order to fulfill their sexual mission. Like several similar heroines in Kazantsakis's and in Lagerkvist's work, Grace, a character in *La*

Montagne ensorcelée, an early novel by the Caribbean author, is stoned by the superstitious populace.

To all these writers, this type epitomizes collective interchangeable womanhood that goes through similar phases: Virgin girlhood, wifehood, harlotry, kindly but demanding motherhood, and ultimately sainthood. Sometimes she is pure, sometimes ribald, at times castrating and malevolent, but at all times she represents the earth with its lures as well as its bondage to eternal cycles. The old adage "from womb to tomb" is valid in all cases, as the Apollonian Sun-hero must escape from her clutches if he will attain light and freedom.

Two of these authors, Thomas Mann and Kazantsakis were open misogynists, the other two display more sympathy for the plight of the female. All of them, however, equate signs of ascent with pure light, the sword, the flame, and the flight of the Phoenix, which are yang or male symbols, whereas the yin is typified by backwardness, sex, and the sow, emblematic of the female world.

Throughout their work, these writers conspicuously mix their myths. Mann deliberately injects pagan elements into the biblical. He borrowed some traits from Frazer's *Golden Bough*, several from Frobenius's African studies, others yet from Dacqué's Chaldean studies, and amalgamated the entire opus with Egyptological and Classical lore. Lagerkvist introduces elements from Norse mythology into early Christian settings. In his case, the milieus are so stylized that the reader may wonder whether he depicts an apocalyptical time, the present, or some future epoch. Lagerkvist points to the syncretism of myths by leaving his characters so vague as to render them universal. Kazantsakis illustrates his own theory of mythological accretions when he associates the Crucified Jesus with a supernatural black child and dying Odysseus with a "Little Negro Fisher Boy." In the case of Jacques Roumain, his hero Manuel is placed in Haiti which is at the crossroads, like Kazantsakis's Crete. Here too, European Christianism is mixed with the pagan Voodoo cult, which has supplanted earlier Dahomean traditions. His is a transplanted culture, resulting from upheaval and forced amalgam. Although he is a modern Marxist, Manuel bears attributes which derive from the ancestral African cults, as well as from the Catholic religion. Significantly, he resembles

> ALL HIS FICTION IS FREIGHTED WITH PHILOSOPHY, BUT IN THE BEST OF IT NARRATIVE STRUCTURE AND SCENE FINELY SUPPORT THE BURDEN."

the immolated god Ogoun, whose effigy is often confused with the images of suffering Jesus. Likewise, Erzilee, the goddess of love and of the springs, is compared not only to an African deity, but to the Sirens, Mélusine, Fata Morgana, and the Lorelei: "A minuit, elle sort de la source et chante et peigne sa longue chevelure ruisselante que ça fait une musique plus douce que les violons. C'est un chant de perdition pour celui que l'entend ..." (*Gouverneurs*, p. 166).

This desire to inject deliberate anachronisms in their novels, to suspend historical and spatial conventions, should come as no surprise since all four writers were interested in the works of anthropologists, ethnologists, and mythologists such as Franz Boas, Mircéa Eliade, and Claude Lévi-Strauss, who were concerned with the universality of the myths. So, in their own fictional opus, they wanted to illustrate the primeval community of mankind by depicting the similarities in their heroes' fate and actions. Mythological syncretism is therefore presented in almost identical fashion by all four.

Source: Adèle Bloch, Essay in *International Fiction Review 8*, Vol. 8, No. 2, Summer 1981, pp. 114–18.

Richard M. Ohmann

In the following excerpt, Ohmann explains Lagerkvist's short fiction as a search for the meaning of life.

It is over forty years now since the appearance of Paer Lagerkvist's first piece of extended fiction, *The Eternal Smile*. In that tale the dead sit talking desultorily of their lives and their sufferings, until, stirred by one of their number to hatred of "life's insult to man," they decide to seek out God, to "call him to account for everything." After wandering for thousands of years through desolation and darkness, they come on God, a tired old man sawing wood, who answers their outraged "Why?" by quietly repeating "I have done the best I could."

Their anguish erupts: "But what did you mean by it all then? You must have meant something. What did you intend by this that you set going, by all this unimaginable life? We must demand a complete understanding of everything, and also the confusion which is in everything.... We must demand coherence in everything, peace for our thought, for our tormented struggling heart, and also we must demand that there shall be no coherence, no rest, no peace. We must demand everything."

In humility, God replies, "I am a simple man. I have worked untiringly. I have stood by my work day after day for as long as I know. I have demanded nothing. Neither joy nor sorrow, neither faith nor doubt, nothing. I only intended that you need never be content with nothing." Somehow this dark riddle soothes the millions; they trek back to where they came from, content with a quotidian "life" which is "the one thing conceivable among all that is inconceivable."

If a writer *begins* with the stark metaphysical encounter with God and nothingness, where does he end after forty years and eight novellas (his plays and verse are not my concern here)? Lagerkvist's new book, *The Death of Ahasuerus* published in Sweden in 1960, leaves us in pretty much the same place, or rather the same no place. God's name is spelled with a small letter now, and he never appears in person; he dropped from sight after *The Eternal Smile*, as Lagerkvist moved still farther away from religious certainty. But the central pattern is still the same: an endless quest for meaning, represented by a physical journey; confrontation with suffering; a defiant approach to God; a paradoxical revelation of God's finiteness; and a final reconciliation to death, which is at the same time a reconciliation to life.

Ahasuerus, the Wandering Jew, is of course the archetypal wayfarer, and as such, a natural symbol for Lagerkvist, who used him before in *The Sibyl*. Now we meet him near the end of life, with centuries of drifting behind him, at an inn for pilgrims to the Holy Land. His eyes are desolate; he stares into darkness. For all his experience he has learned nothing, except that he is incomprehensibly and endlessly persecuted by God. He falls in with one of the pilgrims, a hardened ex-soldier named Tobias, who never kneels, except once, involuntarily, in the presence of a dead woman who bears the stigmata. Under the strange compulsion of this vision Tobias is

making a pilgrimage he does not understand; he too, as Ahasuerus would have it, is *chosen* by God: in God's power. With him is a woman, once a virgin huntress, whom he raped and turned into a harlot.

This nondescript party of outcasts lags behind the rest of the pilgrims and is further delayed by a mountain snowstorm. A mysterious arrow, apparently aimed at Tobias, is intercepted by the woman, and she dies. The two men reach the port of embarkation just after the pilgrims have sailed. Tobias, wild with disappointment, gives all his money to three scoundrelly-looking men who claim they are sailing for the Holy Land in their battered yawl. He embarks on his dubious voyage, perhaps to be destroyed in a tempest, perhaps to be killed by the sailors, perhaps to arrive at his goal; we do not know which. Ahasuerus languishes and dies in a monastery at the port.

That's all that happens. As often in Lagerkvist's fiction, the burden rests not on narrative, but on spare, iconographic scenes (the shriveled woman with the stigmata, the arrow in the mountain pass), on the emotions of the characters and, preeminently, on metaphysical speculation. For Lagerkvist is a relentlessly philosophical writer, and his theme is always the same: man's suffering and its relation to a greater power than himself. The entire story of this book seems merely a scaffolding erected to hold the deathbed of Ahasuerus, and his final thrust at understanding. To what insight is he raised? That all mankind, not Christ alone, is crucified: "I understand this; I discovered it at last: man lies forsaken on his bed of torment in a desolate world, sacrificed and forsaken, stretched out upon a little straw, marked by the same wounds as yourself... though only you are called the Crucified."

Christ, who cursed the Wandering Jew, was actually his brother in pain. A crucifixion requires a crucifier, and that role Ahasuerus assigns to God: "He sacrifices men! He demands continual sacrifice—human sacrifice, crucifixions!" The hateful revelation is, paradoxically, a release for Ahasuerus, a release from the power of God. By his own strength he has "vanquished god"; the discovery of divine wickedness lifts the centuries-old curse of ignorance, solves the onerous riddle, and writes a coda to the endless wanderings. At last Ahasuerus can die.

But there is a final twist to the argument. Though the pilgrim's quest is futile, his intuition must be valid. "Beyond the gods, beyond all that

falsifies and coarsens the world of holiness…
there must be something stupendous which is
inaccessible to us." It is that holy thing, hidden
from men by God, which Ahasuerus embraces in
dying, in passing into mystery. He dies happily in
a miraculous burst of light, which he values no
less for the knowledge that it is simple diurnal
sunlight.

An imprecation that is a triumph and an
affirmation, an understanding that is no understanding, a commonplace miracle: the paradoxes
suit Lagerkvist's agnostic temperament, and they
are strongly felt. But the reader may wonder if
the strange affirmation which ends this book
is adequately contained by the main action,
whether the metaphysical position has in the
story itself what T. S. Eliot calls an "objective
correlative," a hard-won concreteness that stands
for and evokes the abstract feeling or thought.
And he may wonder, too, whether cosmic affirmation, even of this ambiguous cast, is a possible
consequence of Lagerkvist's tormented search.

The two points are related. All his fiction is
freighted with philosophy, but in the best of it
narrative structure and scene finely support the
burden. And in the best of his fiction that burden
is overwhelmingly one of doubt and brooding
evil, not of reassurance. Uncertainty and suffering are woven into the very fabric of experience
as Lagerkvist most powerfully feels it; affirmation in his world is like a candle in the outer
darkness.

In the autobiographical *Guest of Reality*
(1925) the boy Anders is besieged by reminders
of death. His family lives above a railway station
restaurant, where the casual guests and the
passing trains speak of transiency and imperma-
nence. The beer garden, festive at night, is desolate and frightening during the day.

At play, Anders digs a hole in the sand, and
a well-intentioned man tells him that when children dig holes someone in the house is going to
die. The boy has a nightmare of the living and
the dead, all in one huge grave, with a mighty but
incomprehensible voice speaking overhead. In
the yard is an ice house, cold and windowless,
which terrifies Anders, but curiously attracts
him too. He goes in, and stands shivering but
immobilized by fear of death. A dismal old
woodcutter, a thunderstorm, his grandfather's
wrinkles, these too threaten the perilous security
of family and home.

Yet around the humble labor of the father,
the graceful domesticity of mother and sister,
there is an aura of almost unbearable beauty
(like that in *Our Town*, or Agee's *A Death in the
Family*) unbearable because so fragile. Anders
prays in the woods: "let none of them die, for
certain, not one. Let Father live, let Mother, let
his brother and sisters… Let not one possibly
die. Let everything be as it was. Let nothing be
changed!" But the equilibrium *is* shattered; his
grandmother does die, and even before, while
she wastes away, Anders thinks of her as dead.
To live is to be dying; to be dying is to be dead;
this is the one certainty.

After this tale Lagerkvist never again dwells
so forcefully on the poignance of ordinary existence, but the certainty of death is with him for
good and the uncertainty of nearly everything
else. For above all, Lagerkvist is the apostle of
uncertainty and ignorance. A "religious atheist,"
he has called himself: one who is temperamen-
tally religious, but who finds nothing to pin his
faith on. That man should yearn for comprehension, yet be sunk in a world of suffering which is
incomprehensible: that condition rankles as an
outrage in the hearts of Paer Lagerkvist's compelling anti-heroes….

[The universe is incomprehensible to the
heroes of Lagerkvist's best fiction, including]
The Hangman (1933), *Barabbas* (1950), and *The
Sibyl* (1956). The hangman confronts God with
an indictment and a question, but for an answer
there is only God's stony gaze and "the icy wind
of eternity…. There was nothing to be done. No
one to speak to. Nothing." Barabbas asks himself, at last, if there has been any meaning in his
life, and can find none: "But this was something
he knew nothing about." And the Sibyl, though
she has been possessed a hundred times by the
divine spirit, can only say "I know nothing."

In the chaos of life, God should be a pole of
certainty, of order; thus the dead who seek God
in *The Eternal Smile* are seeking "what is always
true." But they find only the enigmatic old
wood-cutter. Similar figures are the silent,
stone-faced God whose stare mocks the hangman's query, and the silent, smiling, idiotic son
whom the Sibyl has borne to God…. Behind
God's inscrutability is his multiformity, the very
reverse of system and order. For the Sibyl, her
god is "both evil and good, both light and darkness, both meaningless and full of a meaning
which we can never perceive, yet never cease to

puzzle over." This jumble of opposites she can neither hate nor love.

Others in Lagerkvist's books, however, are not content with a riddle, particularly one that implicates human beings in senseless pain. Hence Ahasuerus' conviction (in *The Sibyl*) that God is evil, heartless, malignant, and his final defiance of God in the new book. Hence the dwarf's nausea at talk of divine harmony. And hence Barabbas' hate for Christ, the sacrificer of men.

These figures, along with the hangman, radiate an extraordinary malignance. They hate man, too, for his cruelty, for his arrogance, or for his ignorance. The Christian message, "love one another," falls with extreme oddity on their ears. Who can understand such words, within the human landscape of these books the torture, thievery, rape, battle, and slavery that fill Lagerkvist's pages? And his heroes, through whose eyes and whose words we see the world (since Lagerkvist rarely intrudes an authorial point of view), have been especially ill-treated by itv .

[The] hangman, with his blood-red clothes and his symbolic responsibility for human cruelty; Barabbas, whose mother hated him at his birth, and who must move through incredible scenes of Roman inhumanity toward his eventual crucifixion, strangely drawn to those very Christians who most despise him; the Sibyl, wrenched from a simple life to be the uncomprehending mouthpiece of the god, who jealously kills her lover and impregnates her with an idiot son; Ahasuerus, alone denied the blessing of death, because of what seems to him a random and trivial act: all are outcasts, set off from other men, hated by them, persecuted by God, and deprived even of knowledge. Their lives are moved by forces they do not understand, or, worse, by no force at all, by chance (Barabbas lives, Christ dies: "it just turned out that way"; Barabbas' crucifixion, too, "just turned out like that"). Isolation and hate are the air they breathe.

In these, the strongest of Lagerkvist's tales, there are to be sure some traces of beauty, but a beauty that reaches us gravely qualified by the rancor or skepticism through which it sifts. There is the Sibyl's passionate love idyll—but we hear it from the lips of a ruined old woman who knows what a jealous god can do. There is the simple nobility of the early Christians—clouded over by the blank skepticism of Barabbas . . . . The only nobility that survives, finally, is that of the tormented heroes themselves. It issues in uncertainty and rebellion, at best.

But uncertainty and rebellion are not dishonorable conditions. In any case, the world as Lagerkvist sees it offers no other terms: take it or leave it, take it or die. In his best work—and it ranks with the best in contemporary Europe—there is no compromise with them. Reassurance and peace, as in *The Death of Ahasuerus*, are not materials he is at home with.

Source: Richard M. Ohmann, "Apostle of Uncertainty," in *Commonweal*, Vol. 76, No. 7, May 11, 1962, pp. 170–72.

SOURCES

Betts, Raymond F., "Disorder: Europe in the 1920s," in *Europe in Retrospect: A Brief History of the Past Two Hundred Years*, D. C. Heath, 1979, pp. 125–36.

Brantly, Susan, "Into the Twentieth Century: 1890-1950," in *A History of Swedish Literature*, edited by Lars G. Warme, University of Nebraska Press, 1996, pp. 273–380.

Jannson, Matt, "Swedish Modernism," in *Modernism*, Vol. 2, edited by Astradur Eysteinsson and Vivian Liska, John Benjamins, 2007, pp. 837–46.

Lagerkvist, Pär, "Father and I," in *The Marriage Feast*, Hill & Wang, 1954, pp. 30–34.

"Psychoanalysis," in *Encyclopedia of Literary Modernism*, edited by Paul Poplawski, Greenwood Press, 2003, pp. 330–41.

Shea, John, "Exceeding Darkness and Undeserved Light," in *Stories of God: An Unauthorized Biography*, Thomas More Press, 1978, pp. 11–40.

Siklós, Csanád, "Pär Lagerkvist," in *Dictionary of Literary Biography*, Vol. 331, *Nobel Prize Laureates in Literature, Part 3: Lagerkvist-Pontoppidan*, Thomson Gale, 2007, pp. 3–26.

"Sweden and the United Nations," in *Regeringskansliet: Government Offices of Sweden*, http://www.sweden.gov.se/sb/d/11728 (accessed September 1, 2010).

"Sweden: History," in *Encyclopedia of the Nations*, http://www.nationsencyclopedia.com/Europe/Sweden-HISTORY.html (accessed September 1, 2010).

"Swedish Armed Forces International Centre," in *Swedish Armed Forces*, http://forsvarsmakten.se/en/Organisation/Centres/Swedish-Armed-Forces-International-Centre/ (accessed September 1, 2010).

Weinstein, Arnold L., "Speaking God: Kierkegaard and Lagerkvist," in *Northern Arts: The Breakthrough of Scandinavian Literature and Art, from Ibsen to Bergman*, Princeton University Press, 2008, pp. 10–40.

Witcombe, Christopher L. C. E., "Art & Artists: Modernism and Postmodernism," in *What Is Art . . . ? . . . What Is an Artist?*, http://www.arthistory.sbc.edu/artartists/modpostmod.html (accessed September 1, 2010).

FURTHER READING

Harrison, Charles, *Modernism*, Cambridge University Press, 1997.
> Harrison offers a concise overview of the modernist art movement and provides photographs of the works of many of the artists discussed. The work is divided into chapters based on the type of artistic representation being analyzed.

Sherry, Vincent, *The Great War and the Language of Modernism*, Oxford University Press, 2003.
> Sherry provides a detailed analysis of the writers associated with the literary modernist movement. He studies the influence of the war on the writers of this time period, exploring the way history and politics shaped the literature of the modernists.

Sjöberg, Leif, *Pär Lagerkvist*, "Columbia Essays on Modern Writers" Series, No. 74, Columbia University Press, 1976.
> In this fifty-two-page essay, printed as a single book in Columbia's series of essays, Sjöberg offers a brief critical biography of Lagerkvist.

Wartenberg, Thomas E., *Existentialism: A Beginner's Guide*, Oneworld Publications, 2008.
> Wartenberg introduces the philosophical concept of existentialism in layman's terms, drawing references to contemporary culture in order to illustrate various concepts.

SUGGESTED SEARCH TERMS

Lagerkvist AND Father and I

Lagerkvist AND modernism

Lagerkvist AND cubism

Lagerkvist AND Swedish literature

Lagerkvist AND existentialism

Lagerkvist AND The Marriage Feast

Lagerkvist AND "Nobel Prize"

Lagerkvist AND autobiography

Lagerkvist AND short story

The Good Deed

PEARL S. BUCK

1953

"The Good Deed" by Pearl S. Buck was first published in 1953 in *Woman's Home Companion* magazine under the title "A Husband for Lili." It was subsequently published as "The Good Deed" in *The Good Deed: and Other Stories of Asia, Past and Present*, a collection of ten of Buck's stories that range in time from World War II to the date of publication in 1969. The story involves a clash of traditional and progressive ideologies, centering around the theme of old versus new, and includes ruminations on marriage and on Chinese culture. Buck, a lifelong proponent of cultural exchange and understanding, promotes it in most of her fiction, including "The Good Deed."

AUTHOR BIOGRAPHY

Buck was born Pearl Comfort Sydenstricker to Absalom and Caroline Sydenstricker on June 26, 1892, in Hillsboro, West Virginia. Both of her parents were Southern Presbyterian missionaries stationed in China. She was born while her parents were on a leave of absence in the United States, and the family moved back to China when she was just three months old. Aside from trips to the United States, Buck spent her entire childhood in China. Buck was educated primarily by her mother and spoke both English and Chinese. In 1910, Buck left China to enroll in Randolph-Macon Woman's College in

Pearl S. Buck

Lynchburg, Virginia. She returned to China shortly after her graduation in 1914, when she received information that her mother was extremely ill. In 1915 she met her future husband, John Lossing Buck, an agricultural economist and missionary, in China. They were married on May 13, 1917, and soon moved to Suzhou, a town in the Anhui province. It was this economically impoverished town that served as the inspiration for Buck's most famous work, *The Good Earth*.

The Bucks had a troubled and unhappy marriage almost from the beginning. From 1920 to 1933, Buck and her husband primarily lived in Nanking on the campus of Nanking University, where they both had teaching positions. Buck taught English literature. In 1921 they had their first daughter, Carol, who was tragically afflicted with phenylketonuria (PKU) and was severely mentally retarded. That same year, Buck's mother died and her father moved into Buck's home. In 1924 the couple left China for John's sabbatical year, during which time Buck worked on her master's degree at Cornell University. While in America, in 1925 the couple adopted their daughter Janice. Buck received her degree from Cornell in 1926 and

immediately returned to China with her family. Several westerners who lived in the Bucks' town were murdered during the Nanking Incident of 1927. After spending some time in hiding, the family fled to Shanghai and then Japan. They eventually moved back to Nanking despite persistently uncertain conditions.

Although the 1920s were particularly tumultuous for Buck, it was during this period that she wrote productively. Her essays and stories were published in journals such as the *Nation*, the *Chinese Recorder*, and *Atlantic Monthly*. Her first novel, *East Wind, West Wind*, was published in 1930 by the John Day Company. In 1931, John Day published Buck's best-selling and most widely read novel, *The Good Earth*, which won the Pulitzer Prize for the Novel in 1932.

In the early 1930s, Buck's marriage became increasingly troubled. She and John divorced in 1935. Buck then married Richard Walsh, a John Day publisher. Because of increasingly dangerous conditions in China, and to be closer to her daughter Carol, who was living in an institution in New Jersey, Walsh and Buck moved back to the United States and settled in Pennsylvania. She and Walsh adopted six more children over the next several years. In 1938, Buck was honored with the Nobel Prize in Literature. She was the first American woman to receive the prize. She continued to write and publish prolifically, often on matters concerning Chinese and American cultural relations. She was a longtime activist dedicated to cultural understanding and exchange between Asia and the Western world; she and her husband founded the East West Association, which is dedicated to this cause. In 1953, "The Good Deed," which is very much in keeping with the theme of East-West relations, was first published in *Woman's Home Companion* under the title "A Husband for Lili."

On March 6, 1973, at the age of eighty, Buck died of lung cancer at her home in Danby, Vermont. She designed her own gravestone, which is inscribed with the Chinese characters for Pearl Sydenstricker. Her impact on American literature, as well as on East-West cultural exchange, is undeniable.

PLOT SUMMARY

At the beginning of "The Good Deed," set in New York City's Chinatown in 1953, the omniscient narrator reveals that Mr. Pan is preoccupied with his mother, old Mrs. Pan. Mr. Pan made many sacrifices to finance his mother's move from her politically tumultuous and unsafe village in Szechuan, China, to his family home in New York City so that he would have peace of mind and know that she was safe. Unfortunately for Mr. Pan, old Mrs. Pan's move was involuntary, and he soon observes that she is miserable in her new home. As Mr. Pan and his wife, young Mrs. Pan, become increasingly worried about the elderly woman, they try different tactics to make her happy, to no avail. For example, when they prepare her favorite foods, she claims that they do not taste the same because they were not made with the water from her village.

Old Mrs. Pan is also very old fashioned, does not understand American customs, and has a difficult time relating to the other members of her new household. The four Pan children as well as young Mrs. Pan speak Chinese very poorly, and, because old Mrs. Pan does not speak English, they cannot communicate. Old Mrs. Pan also finds the children disrespectful and unruly, and is confused by the fact that they would rather watch television (an appliance completely foreign to old Mrs. Pan) than have Chinese lessons or listen to their grandmother's stories. She likes her son's American-born wife although she does not understand how she can be considered a Chinese woman, having never set foot in China. Because old Mrs. Pan is unable to help with the housework (the appliances confuse her) and unable to speak Chinese with anyone except her son, who is at work for most of the day, old Mrs. Pan grows increasingly lonely and feels useless. She just sits all day, doing nothing, loses her appetite, and becomes increasingly thin. Her son and his wife become more and more worried about her, and one day, Mr. Pan asks his wife if she can find someone to come and speak Chinese with the old woman during the day to cheer her up. Young Mrs. Pan immediately remembers her old schoolmate, Lili Yang, who is now a social worker for Chinese families and is fluent in the language.

The next day, young Mrs. Pan calls Lili and explains her plight. Lili agrees to come and speak to the woman, and within a few days she shows up at the apartment. As old Mrs. Pan and Lili talk, Lili delights and flatters her by asking her about her village back in China and her old life there. Old Mrs. Pan is thrilled to have someone

to speak to in Chinese, and also impressed that Lili seems to be familiar with old Chinese customs. When the conversation turns and old Mrs. Pan begins questioning Lili about her personal life, she quickly discovers, to her horror, that the twenty-seven-year-old woman is unmarried with no marriage prospects. Old Mrs. Pan, a staunch believer in arranged marriage, immediately asks, "'How is this? . . . "are your parents dead?'" Lili informs the woman that her parents are dead, but that it is inconsequential because in America parents do not arrange marriages for their children. Lili explains that in America, young people choose their own partners, or rather, the men choose their partners while the women sit around and wait to be chosen. Old Mrs. Pan is shocked and horrified by this news. "'Do you tell me that there is no person who arranges such matters when it is necessary? . . . And they allow their women to remain unmarried?'" she asks. Old Mrs. Pan finds this entirely unacceptable. She studies Lili's face, observing that she is not a pretty girl, and worries that despite her kind and caring personality, she will never find a husband unless one is arranged for her. Unbeknownst to her, this is a worry that Lili shares; she badly craves a husband and a family, but is afraid that no man will ever want to marry her. After some consideration of this unfortunate situation, old Mrs. Pan decides that she will take it upon herself to arrange Lili's marriage. She believes that if she can find a husband for Lili, it will count as a good deed that will help get her into heaven. Lili is moved and comforted by this promise, although she does not believe that old Mrs. Pan, who cannot even speak English, can find a husband for her.

When Mr. Pan arrives home from work later that day, he immediately notices a change in his mother. She pulls him away from dinner preparations to tell him about her plan to arrange Lili Yang's marriage. Mr. Pan gives old Mrs. Pan the same speech Lili did, explaining that in America marriages are not arranged. Old Mrs. Pan declares it "barbarous" and asks her son why a good, marriageable woman should remain single simply because of her looks. She commands her son to find a suitable bachelor among his coworkers and introduce him to her so that she can orchestrate a meeting between the young man and Lili, with herself standing in as Lili's mother. Mr. Pan emphatically argues that he cannot help her in this plan, and tells her that the men at work would laugh at him if he were to propose such a thing. However, old Mrs. Pan insists, and eventually her son agrees to help. When Mr. Pan explains his mother's crazy plan to his wife over dinner, she says, to his surprise, that she thinks the plan is a good idea. When Mr. Pan criticizes arranged marriage, pointing out that back in China young couples are unhappily matched quite frequently, his wife argues that things are just the same in America and points out the high divorce rate. She adds that the American way of marriage puts women at a vast disadvantage, since the men get to do the choosing.

Meanwhile, in her bedroom old Mrs. Pan sits by her window watching the young Chinese men on the street, considering which one might be a good match for Lili. She does this the next day and the next, and soon staring out the window in search of potential suitors becomes one of her favorite pastimes. One day, a young man from the street looks up and smiles at the old woman, a gesture she returns with a wave. Every day after this the young man smiles at Mrs. Pan, so she begins to watch him closely. She discerns that he works at the china shop across the street, and decides that he is surely unmarried as she has never seen him with a young woman.

Later that evening, she asks her son about the man. Somewhat amused with her thinly veiled scheming, he informs her that the young man is James Lim, the son of Mr. Lim, the owner of the china shop and also the richest man on the block. Mr. Pan tells his mother that there is no way that James Lim would submit to an arranged marriage, as he is a handsome college graduate, only spending his summer at home to help his father, and that he will want to chose his own wife. After further discussion, old Mrs. Pan becomes frustrated that she and her son do not see eye to eye. She decides that she must establish contact with the young man on her own, without the help of her son or his wife, who would laugh at her.

The next Saturday, when her son is at his office and young Mrs. Pan is at the market, old Mrs. Pan enlists the help of her eldest grandson, Johnnie, to make it across the street to the china shop. Once there, James Lim beckons her, to her great excitement, in perfect Chinese, to come and sit down. Pretending to be a customer, she casually inquires about his heritage and background as he helps her shop, and she eventually brings their conversation around to the subject of Lili Yang by offhandedly dropping her name. When

James Lim asks who Lili Yang is, Mrs. Pan answers him indirectly by giving a speech about how beauty is not an indicator of a young woman's worth. James Lim listens with amusement, for he instantly understands that the old woman is hoping to set him up with Lili Yang, but he is nevertheless charmed with Mrs. Pan. After the two finish talking and the old woman purchases two bowls, James Lim insists on helping her back across the street.

Later that evening when she reveals the events of the day to her son and his wife, young Mrs. Pan is astonished, but Mr. Pan cheerfully tells her not to interfere, believing that his mother's project is good for her morale. Mr. Pan is so delighted with his mother's change in attitude that he even decides to aid her without her knowledge. He calls Lili Yang, and asks that she come by the house again to talk with old Mrs. Pan. When old Mrs. Pan hears that Lili is coming back, she is secretly thrilled. When Lili arrives a few days later, Mrs. Pan asks her to help her across the street so that she can buy a gift for young Mrs. Pan at the china shop. Lili happily acquiesces, not knowing what she is getting herself into. When the two women arrive at the shop, old Mr. Lim, James Lim's father, recognizes the old woman and asks her and Lili to come into the back of the store for tea. When James comes into the back to serve them, he introduces himself to Lili Yang in English. Lili is surprised that James knows who she is, so James explains that she has come up in a prior conversation of his with Mrs. Pan, a fact that embarrasses Lili. However, Lili and James seem to hit it off quickly and begin conversing in English while old Mr. Lim and old Mrs. Pan speak in Chinese. The old couple exchange information about their young counterparts, while the young chat enthusiastically about their own lives. When Lili asks James to tell her more about his decision to become a doctor, James proposes that they finish their discussion on a riverboat ride on Sunday. Lili, who is finding James quite charming, is ecstatic about this prospect.

After the date is arranged, James excuses himself to help the waiting customers, and old Mrs. Pan shoos Lili away to wrap the dishes she is purchasing. With both of the young people out of the way, Mr. Lim and Mrs. Pan speak in hushed voices about arranging a match, with Mrs. Pan standing in for Lili's mother. The two of them, quite pleased with themselves and the good deed they are going to do, decide on

Sunday for a meeting between the young couple, completely unaware that James and Lili have already arranged a date.

CHARACTERS

James Lim

James Lim is a twenty-eight-year-old college graduate who is studying to be a doctor and is spending the summer at home to help his father run his china shop, which is located directly across the street from the Pans' apartment. Old Mrs. Pan notices that he is handsome and has a strong set of white teeth that are set off by two gold ones. He and his father are originally from the Chinese province of Shantung. Old Mrs. Pan first encounters James Lim when he smiles at her from the street as she sits at her window. She returns the gesture with a wave, and every day after that the two exchange these pleasantries. He is polite, respectful, and familiar with the old Chinese customs that old Mrs. Pan idealizes.

Mr. Lim

Mr. Lim is James Lim's father and also the owner of the shop across the street. He is known to be the richest man on the block. He is friendly, polite, and respectful to old Mrs. Pan. The two share a similar mindset and a belief in traditional Chinese customs.

Billy Pan

See Mr. Pan

Johnnie Pan

Johnnie Pan is the Pans' eldest son and old Mrs. Pan's grandson. He was born in the United States and has no knowledge of Chinese customs and cannot speak Chinese. Old Mrs. Pan is somewhat frightened of the Pan children. She feels that they are loud, disruptive, and disobedient, and because they cannot speak Chinese, she is unable to communicate with them.

Mr. Pan

Mr. Pan is old Mrs. Pan's son and a strong patriarch who works hard to support his family. Although he was born in China, he is fully adapted to American culture and customs. His marriage with young Mrs. Pan was arranged by friends of his parents living in New York City; however, he fell in love with young Mrs. Pan

before they were married in New York. He saved up a great deal of money and took risks to be able to bring his mother to America, where he believed she would be safer, and he becomes upset and worried when Mrs. Pan exhibits signs of depression after being transplanted from her home. He and his wife try desperately to make his mother happy and comfortable in her new home. He tries to explain American customs to his mother, but he eventually resigns himself to the fact that she will probably never understand their new way of life. Mr. Pan is quite amused by his mother's plot to find a husband for Lili, but because he understands that her project is making her happy, he does not interfere.

Old Mrs. Pan

Old Mrs. Pan is the stubborn, scheming, and caring elderly mother of Mr. Pan and the widow of a wealthy landowner in China (Mr. Pan's father). Mrs. Pan desperately misses her home in Szechuan, China, and is unappreciative of her son's efforts to move her to New York City. She believes in old Chinese customs such as arranged marriage and is completely bewildered and disgusted by American culture. She particularly does not understand what she perceives as Americans' disrespect for their elders and their ancestors. She becomes quite depressed in her new home in Chinatown. She feels bored and vulnerable because she cannot speak English and therefore cannot communicate with anyone except her son, so she spends most of her time staring woefully out her bedroom window. However, when she meets Lili Yang, she regains a sense of purpose and immediately livens up. She firmly believes that Lili would be an excellent wife for a man who could look past her appearance, so she cleverly crafts a plot to arrange a marriage for her. She believes that finding a husband for Lili and arranging her marriage will count as a good deed, and serve as a credit to help her get into heaven.

Sophia Pan

See Young Mrs. Pan

Young Mrs. Pan

Young Mrs. Pan is Mr. Pan's wife, the mother of their four children, and a homemaker. She was born in America and has never set foot in China, leading old Mrs. Pan to be confused as to how she could actually be Chinese. Young Mrs. Pan believes in American customs, although she sympathizes with old Mrs. Pan's point of view, and also believes that women, particularly unattractive ones, are disadvantaged by the American way of life. She is excited and supportive of old Mrs. Pan's plan to find a husband for Lili, as she has often felt sorry for Lili in the past because she hasn't had luck finding a husband.

Lili Yang

Lili Yang is a generous, caring, yet unattractive young woman who comes to visit old Mrs. Pan and speak Chinese with her at the request of young Mrs. Pan, who is a close friend and old schoolmate of hers. Despite being born and raised in America, she speaks Chinese very well and possesses a thorough understanding of Chinese culture, which makes old Mrs. Pan take an immediate liking to her. She is twenty-seven years old and unmarried at the beginning of the story, and through her discussion with old Mrs. Pan it is revealed that she greatly laments that fact. Lili is a social worker and the head of the Children's Bureau in Chinatown, New York City. Old Mrs. Pan believes Lili has great potential to be a good wife, but thinks she has been overlooked because she is not particularly pretty. When old Mrs. Pan reveals her plan to find a husband for Lili, Lili is secretly relieved because although she very much wants to be married, she does not believe she can find a husband on her own.

THEMES

Cultural Conflict

The contrast between old and new cultures, tradition and progress, and East and West, are dominant themes throughout Buck's entire body of work and are certainly dominant in "The Good Deed." Old Mrs. Pan, who is literally old in the sense of advanced age, is also traditional and old fashioned. She is set in the beliefs and behaviors she carried over with her from China and finds certain aspects of American life, particularly the American way of marriage, completely appalling. Meanwhile, her son, Mr. Pan, has adapted to American customs despite being born and raised in China. Unlike his mother, he believes that marriages should be based on love, not arranged by one's parents. However, throughout the story it seems increasingly as if old Mrs. Pan's traditional stance, and Mr. Pan's progressive stance, may not be so different after all. His wife, young Mrs. Pan, can see merit in

both approaches, and points out that plenty of unhappy marriages result no matter what method is involved. Additionally, both Mr. and Mrs. Pan's marriage and Lili and James's date are simultaneously based on arrangement and genuine interest. Buck blurs the lines between the two positions to demonstrate the merit in each perspective.

Marriage

In "The Good Deed," the theme of marriage is the primary vehicle through which Buck contrasts old and new, but the preoccupation with marriage throughout the work is also indicative of its time and place. In 1950s America, the ideal of the perfect housewife became the visible and prominent role for many American women to aspire to. Lili Yang, whatever her motives may be, certainly craves a husband and a family, and her lack of these things is a source of grief and embarrassment for her. Though Lili and old Mrs. Pan probably believe in the importance of marriage for different reasons, they both acknowledge the necessity of marriage for women. Marriage is a theme that is woven throughout the story and ties together many other elements.

Chinese Culture

Family relationships are incredibly important in traditional Chinese culture, and also in many of Buck's works, including "The Good Deed." Almost all of the action and the conflict take place within the Pan family unit and are based on the tension between old Mrs. Pan's traditional Chinese culture and the Pan couple's progressive Chinese American perspective. Through the lens of old Mrs. Pan, many aspects of Chinese culture are revealed. For example, she does not understand why her grandchildren are so disobedient, even though her son explains to her that parents in America have a different attitude toward raising children. Mr. Pan also touches upon the difficulty of maintaining one's original heritage and culture in a new environment when he says to his mother, "They are always with Americans . . . it is difficult to teach them." Old Mrs. Pan also believes that Americans and Chinese are entirely different beings and should remain segregated even while living in the same city. Throughout the story, all of old Mrs. Pan's actions and reactions are indicative of her culture, from her inability to operate the faucet at the kitchen sink, to her shock at the scantily clad women in her daughter-in-law's American magazines.

TOPICS FOR FURTHER STUDY

- Buck often stated that in her early work she aimed to emulate the style of traditional Chinese stories, which are straightforward narratives in which the author demonstrates who a character is by what they say and do, rather than telling the reader directly. Research the structure and style of the traditional stories or folk tales of your own heritage, or a heritage you are interested in, and write a short story in which you try to mimic that style.

- As is explained by Miss Lili Yang, young Mrs. Pan, and old Mrs. Pan in "The Good Deed," many American women were disadvantaged by the social structures of the 1950s. Go online and research how the situation of American women has changed since then. Do you think it has significantly improved? Are there any ways in which you think it has remained stagnant? How are the social expectations of women different from those of men today? Using a computer, create a chart compiling your findings.

- Much of the conflict in "The Good Deed" stems from a disagreement between old Mrs. Pan and her son about what is the best method of marriage. Old Mrs. Pan believes in the superiority of traditional Chinese arranged marriages, while her son, Mr. Pan, believes people should marry for love, the way most people do in America. Expectations of family structure, including marriage, vary widely from culture to culture. Pick a culture different from your own, and research the most prominent qualities of family structure within that culture. Create a PowerPoint presentation comparing and contrasting a typical family in the culture you have researched with your own family.

- Read *American Eyes: New Asian-American Short Stories for Young Adults*, edited by Lori Carlson. The stories in this collection depict young Asian Americans who sometimes experience a clash of cultures between the culture they have grown up knowing and their Asian roots. Do you think old Mrs. Pan could relate to the struggles of the young characters in any of these stories? How so? Write an essay explaining how old Mrs. Pan's difficulties in "The Good Deed" compare to those of one of the young protagonists of this collection.

STYLE

Structural Simplicity

"The Good Deed" is a straightforward chronological story told without any gimmicks or complicated devices by a third-person omniscient narrator. Buck's characteristic elegant and simple storytelling style is quite purposeful; she said many times in interviews and speeches that she aimed to mirror stylistic techniques of traditional Chinese narratives in her writing. In such stories, the narrator is omniscient, or all-knowing, and the characters reveal their personality through dialogue and action rather than through the narrator's exposition. Although "The Good Deed" does contain slightly more exposition than Buck's earlier work, it is still in keeping with these stylistic tenets.

Situational Irony

In Paul A. Doyle's analysis of Buck's work, "Pearl S. Buck's Short Stories: A Survey," he notes that many of her stories end with an "ironic bite." This is very much the case in "The Good Deed," which ends with situational irony. Situational irony occurs when the reader or audience is privy to information that one or more of the characters does not possess. Situational irony can be humorous, or it can add a deeper layer of interest to a story. At the end of the story, old Mrs. Pan tricks Lili Yang into being introduced to the handsome James Lim at the china shop across the street. Unbeknown to Lili, old Mrs. Pan does not simply wish to buy some bowls for her daughter-in-law, but rather, is hoping to arrange a match between Lili and

Mrs. Pan sadly remembered the large home she shared with her husband in China. *(leungchopan / Shutterstock.com)*

James. However, once Lili and James begin talking, it is evident that they are interested in one another and do not need their elders to arrange a match for them. While the young couple enthusiastically chats in English, old Mrs. Pan and James's father, Mr. Lim, speak in Chinese.... "What do you say? Shall we arrange a match?" the old woman asks Mr. Lim. Mr. Lim agrees and the two agree to set the young couple up on the coming Sunday. Humorously, however, old Mrs. Pan does not realize that while she was talking to Mr. Lim, James had already asked Lili to join him on a riverboat ride on Sunday.

HISTORICAL CONTEXT

Repeal of the Chinese Exclusion Act and the Second Wave of Chinese Immigration

In the 1930s and 1940s, Buck's fictional depictions of life in China, such as *The Good Earth*, were best sellers in America. Her 1953 story "The Good Deed" is a depiction of a Chinese American immigrant family. Until 1943, it was extremely difficult for Chinese citizens to gain entry to the United States as a result of the Chinese Exclusion Act. The act, passed May 6, 1882, was the first significant law limiting immigration to the United States. It enforced a ten-year moratorium on Chinese labor immigration (which had increased dramatically as Chinese labor was used to build the transcontinental railroad) and required Chinese citizens hoping to enter to gain the approval of the Chinese government. Moreover, it placed strict laws on Chinese immigrants already living in the United States, and required them to gain certification to reenter. It also prevented anyone of Chinese origin from becoming a naturalized United States citizen. The law was set to expire in 1892 but was extended for another ten years and then became permanent in 1902. The passage of the act was the result of widespread anti-Chinese sentiments that can be traced back to the California Gold Rush of the mid-nineteenth century. The gold rush coincided with a period of poverty in China, so the thousands of Chinese who immigrated to California in search of wealth and opportunity had little to lose. However, this rapid flow of immigration led to increased competition for jobs and wealth in the United States and quickly led to prejudice and

COMPARE & CONTRAST

- **1950s:** The Chinese Exclusion Act is recently repealed, and 0.2 percent of Americans counted in the 1950 census claim Asian origin.

  Today: There are no immigration restrictions targeted at a specific racial group, and 4.4 percent of Americans in 2008 claim Asian origin.

- **1950s:** The median age for a woman to marry is twenty years old.

  Today: The median age for a woman to marry is twenty-six years old.

- **1950s:** The Korean War, part of the larger cold war, makes the United States and China political opponents.

  Today: The United States is China's largest economic investor, and the two countries are the most powerful forces in the global economy.

racism against new Asian Americans. In addition to further spreading bias and racism against the Chinese, the act also led to the first great wave of commercial human smuggling. After World War I, the Immigration Act of 1924 further limited Chinese immigration and extended the restrictions to people from many other countries as well.

The Chinese Exclusion Act was repealed by the Magnuson Act in 1943, just ten years before "The Good Deed" was published. The act, passed during World War II when China became an ally of the United States, allowed Chinese citizens already living in the United States to become American citizens, and also granted 105 visas to Chinese immigrants per year. However, in California it was still illegal for a Chinese person to marry an American until 1948. Chinese immigration restrictions were not loosened again until the passage of the Immigration and Nationality Act of 1965.

Evolving Gender Roles

Considering the social pressures women faced in the 1950s to be ideal wives and mothers, it is unsurprising that Lili Yang feels ashamed and grievous about her single status in "The Good Deed." Media depictions of wholesome families and homemaker mothers in the 1950s were largely propagated by television programs, which shaped the social expectations of women. The women who had gone to work during World War II because of a surplus of jobs left empty by young soldiers were pressured back into the home at the end of the war. However, the resistance of some women to give up their new, higher-paying jobs, and in consequence their newfound independence, incited business and government propaganda campaigns that spread the message that it was patriotic for women to return to their positions as wives and mothers. This was aided by the glorification of the 1950s housewife, as depicted on television programs such as *Leave it to Beaver* and *Father Knows Best*. This media trend continued well into the 1960s.

CRITICAL OVERVIEW

By and large, Buck's critics have focused on her novels rather than her short fiction. One notable exception is Paul A. Doyle's essay "Pearl S. Buck's Short Stories: A Survey," published in the *English Journal*. Although Doyle does not discuss "The Good Deed" explicitly in his essay, he addresses other stories of Buck's that are thematically similar and that were published in the same general time period. In his essay, Doyle asserts that many of Buck's stories concern "'Old and New,' treating the clash between the old, traditional ways and customs of China and the new Western influences." Doyle also notes that in Buck's short stories she aimed to emulate traditional Chinese tales: "The love

She confided in her son about her promise to find a husband for Lili. *(wong sze yuen | Shutterstock.com)*

story, the working out of a plot, and the external portrayal of character—these are the principal qualities which Mrs. Buck seeks to emulate," writes Doyle. Doyle further points out that Buck's short stories, for the most part, are not modern for their time, but rather, "of the old-fashioned spellbinding school of fiction." In regard to this fact, he claims that most of her stories leave the reader with an "ironic bite" at the end.

In Xiongya Gao's chapter "Buck's Critics" in her book *Pearl S. Buck's Chinese Women Characters*, Gao notes that most of the criticism concerning Buck's work is focused on how, in it, "various aspects of the Chinese life are faithfully and realistically portrayed." Gao explains that while the majority of American critics preferred her novels set in China, many Chinese scholars and critics have been quite harsh concerning Buck's depictions of the country. According to Gao, many Chinese critics have claimed that Buck's descriptions of China are unrealistic,

though Gao attributes this criticism to the distance between Chinese scholars and peasants. Gao remarks, "The Chinese critics' attacks have done considerable damage to Buck's reputation."

Doyle, Gao, and Phyllis Bentley in her essay "The Art of Pearl S. Buck," published in the *English Journal*, all make note of the characteristic simplicity of Buck's style. As Bentley phrases it, "The grave, quiet, biblical speech, full of dignity, in which Mrs. Buck, without ever 'raising her voice,' is able to render both the deepest and lightest emotions... is a fine example of an instrument perfectly adapted to its task." Bentley also praises Buck's talent for characterization, and, like Doyle, notes ways in which her work, through its structure, emphasizes what is important in Chinese family life. Some critics have claimed that Buck's earlier work is stronger than her later work, but regardless, her impact on American fiction and particularly the literature of Chinese Americans is undeniable.

CRITICISM

Rachel Porter

Porter is a freelance writer and editor who holds a bachelor of arts in English literature. In the following essay, she offers a deconstructive analysis of the two competing ideologies in "The Good Deed."

Buck's "The Good Deed" is a work that clearly centers around two competing ideologies: old Mrs. Pan's faith in arranged marriage and her son's belief in the American tradition of choosing one's own spouse. These opposite ideologies are vocalized by their respective proponents and are intertwined throughout the story, but they are fully illustrated when old Mrs. Pan explains, to her son's dismay, that she plans to arrange a marriage for Lili Yang. Mr. Pan has to hold back his laughter during this conversation and deems his mother's plan "absurd." Yet when old Mrs. Pan puts her scheme into action, and the two belief systems are, in a sense, "tested" by the events of the story, surprisingly neither one prevails. It seems that it would be easy for American readers who do not have any experience with arranged marriage to naturally side with Mr. Pan. To many Americans the idea of an arranged marriage is antiquated, a practice of the past. In 1953 when "The Good Deed" was first published (and as is true today), the custom of arranged marriage had died out in most of the world and was still being widely practiced only in Asia. The commonly held viewpoint in America, and many other parts of the world, is that both people involved in a marriage will be happier in the long term if the marriage is based on love.

In the story, Mrs. Pan's dated viewpoint seems to be aligned with her character as a whole; she is nothing if not old-fashioned, and in fact, this characteristic is sometimes exaggerated to the point of (seeming) silliness. She cannot perform simple tasks around the house because she doesn't understand how to work the faucet, she is confused by the moving picture box that is the television, and the other characters around her, particularly her son, are often amused by her old-fashioned beliefs and naïveté. None of the characters, Lili herself included, have any faith that old Mrs. Pan will actually be able to arrange a marriage. In her initial argument for arranged marriage, she points out the fact that her son's marriage was arranged, although it is

revealed to the reader than her son and his wife fell in love on their own, and only pretended to allow their elders to arrange their marriage out of respect, and to appease them. Her son's unwillingness to tell her the truth has the effect of making her appear foolish to the reader, as she is essentially arguing with false proof. Moreover, this situation is humorously repeated at the end, when she and the elderly Mr. Lim decide to arrange a marriage between Lili and James, entirely unaware that James had already asked Lili out on a date. The final scene gives the impression that, not only is the American way of marriage superior, but also that the joke is on the old folks, who think they're doing their young counterparts a favor, when in actuality, Lili and James will probably allow themselves to be "set up" so as not to spoil the elderly people's fun. Thus, the ending of the story seems to reinforce the notion that old Mrs. Pan is a tiresome, old-fashioned, and somewhat superfluous ancient woman, while her preferred method of marriage is similarly old-fashioned and ineffective. Yet, upon closer speculation, the reader will realize that the balance between the Eastern belief in arranged marriage, and the Western position against it, is much more complicated, and in fact the story does not offer reinforcement of the notion that one way is superior to the other.

The first indicator of complexity, or rather, indeterminacy, in the story is young Mrs. Pan's tentative defense of arranged marriage. When Mr. Pan goes to inform his wife of his mother's "absurd" plan, his wife's response surprises him, "'I can see some good in it myself,'" she states. She then explains that when she was young she frequently worried about finding a husband, and knowing that someone else would find one for her would have relieved her of a great deal of anxiety. She further insists that just as many unhappy marriages occur in the United States as in China, yet when a marriage fails in the United States it is much worse for the woman because she has to leave the family, while back in China it is the man who leaves, to which Mr. Pan had no response. Furthermore, the illusion that old Mrs. Pan's scheming to set Lili up with James was unnecessary immediately collapses as the reader realizes that although Lili and James took a liking to each other right away, they probably would have never met in the first place were it not for old Mrs. Pan's secret matchmaking. What emerges at the end of the story between Lili and James is not necessarily a

WHAT DO I READ NEXT?

- *The Joy Luck Club*, published in 1989, is a best-selling novel by Amy Tan. The novel centers around four Chinese American families, particularly the mothers and daughters of those families, living in San Francisco, California. The four mothers meet frequently to eat Chinese foods such as dim sum, play the Chinese game mahjong, and talk. They call themselves the Joy Luck Club. The mothers, who were all born in China, and the daughters, who were all born in America, suffer from both generational and cultural gaps in understanding. Throughout the novel, the mothers tell of the hardships they experienced in China, while the daughters try to communicate the challenges they have faced growing up in America.

- *American Born Chinese*, by comics artist Gene Luen Yang, is a young-adult graphic novel that was published in 2006. The book has won several awards and was listed as a National Book Awards finalist. The story follows Jin Wang, a lonely middle schooler of Taiwanese parents, the Chinese cultural icon Monkey King, and an all-American teenager named Danny who is horribly ashamed of his Chinese cousin Chin-Kee, who is the embodiment of every negative Chinese stereotype. These three plot lines are interwoven throughout the book and eventually converge at the end.

- *The Good Earth*, published in 1931 and available in many modern editions, is Buck's most famous work of fiction and the one for which she was awarded the Pulitzer Prize for the Novel in 1932. The long-time best-selling novel is the story of a Chinese family living in China prior to the 1949 revolution. It chronicles the hard-working Wang Lung, and his wife O-Lan's progress from poverty to financial security.

- *Chinatown New York: Portraits, Recipes, and Memories* is a nonfiction work published in 2007 by Ann Volkwein. The book provides an intimate portrait of life and culture in New York City's Chinatown.

- *Arranged Marriage: Stories* is a 1994 collection of short stories by Chitra Banerjee Divakaruni. Each of the eleven stories follows a female Indian protagonist, living either in India or America, and somehow involved with an arranged marriage, including an immigrant bride in California, and a woman in India with an abusive husband.

- *Bread Givers* is a novel by Anzia Yezierska that was first published in 1925 and is available in a 2003 third edition. It is the story of the Jewish American Smolinsky family, scraping by in New York's Lower East Side. Sara Smolinsky, the narrator, is the only one of her sisters who has the courage to step outside traditional women's stereotypes and challenge her overbearing Jewish fundamentalist father, who believes that women are worthless unless they have a man. As Sara gains independence and becomes more acquainted with American culture, her life begins to change for the better.

---

match based on pure arrangement or infatuation, but rather, something of a hybrid. Lili and James would never have met had it not been for old Mrs. Pan's determination to get them together; yet, as young, progressive Americans it is probable that they would not have stood for any further arrangement between the two of them if they did not genuinely like each other.

Ingeniously, Buck's ending renders the ideological struggle between Mr. Pan and his mother completely irrelevant. Based on her ending, it doesn't matter which method is superior, because for Lili and James, the two methods are perhaps not mutually exclusive. However, there is no way to determine if this is the case, as the reader is not privy to what the outcome

---

Her grandchildren preferred to look at moving pictures in the box that stood on the table. (*Péter Gudella / Shutterstock.com*)

will be. What is obvious is that old Mrs. Pan's scheming does not turn out to be in vain, as her son assumed it would, and her old-fashioned methods are surely not as useless as they originally appeared. During Lili's initial conversation with old Mrs. Pan, she appeared hopeless, destitute, and perhaps even pathetic. By the end of the story, thanks to her elderly friend she apparently no longer feels condemned to live her life alone. Therefore, the ending of "The Good Deed" does not prove that either ideological viewpoint is better than the other, but offers a fluid melding of the two that causes the meaning of the story to be ambiguous. Furthermore, the story is cut short. It ends before the reader can learn whether or not old Mrs. Pan actually succeed in arranging a marriage. The reader is only given a hint that things might in fact work out between Lili and James, but no answer is provided as to whether or not they will actually marry, which further contributes to the ambiguity of the ending. However, the story's conclusion is perhaps not so surprising considering Buck's lifelong campaign for cultural exchange and mutual understanding, particularly between the United States and China.

Source: Rachel Porter, Critical Essay on "The Good Deed," in *Short Stories For Students*, Gale, Cengage Learning, 2011.

Helen F. Snow

In the following essay, Snow discusses why the Chinese resented Buck's writing, and subsequently asked her to leave China.

No one was more astonished by the fantastic popularity of *The Good Earth* than its author, Pearl S. Buck, then a university teacher in Nanking, where her husband, J. Lossing Buck, also taught. I arrived in China a few weeks after it appeared, in 1931. Neither the foreigners nor the Chinese liked it. The missionaries felt it lost them "face"; so did the nationalist Chinese, chiefly because of its "pornography." Yet for 40 years, the picture of China that was imprinted on the Western mind was the one Mrs. Buck had drawn. She must have got hold of a piece of the truth somewhere, I thought, if not about China then about humankind in a primitive setting.

After 1931, Pearl Buck was no longer welcome in China (she left permanently in 1934), except for a brief hiatus after 1949 when the Peking regime invited her back along with a few other foreigners (she did not accept). In 1972, when she tried to get a visa she was turned down because, said the Communists, her writing had "for a long time taken an attitude of distortion, smear and vilification toward the people of China and their leaders." Visiting Nanking, earlier this year, I wanted to photograph the house where *The Good Earth* had been written, but couldn't find it. The youthful Nanking information department had never heard of her or her book. I walked among the grey, shabby faculty houses at the University of Nanking realizing that whoever lived in Pearl Buck's historic house did not know it, or care.

Why do the Chinese resent her writing? The reason, I think, is one seldom stated: she violated some basic taboos, ancient and modern, about sex and childbirth. It was this, also, which helped make her a best seller in the West where she was among the first popular novelists to describe in detail childbirth and menstruation. To the Chinese she did not get at the essence of their civilization, the delicacy of human relations expressed in certain social taboos, especially in speech and writing. For example even today, one does not take a photograph of man and wife touching each other. (I tried it.) The Chinese feel Mrs. Buck degraded the dignity of Chinese women, which is ironic, since the chief appeal of her books in the West is to women. She was a maternal woman writing for women about the problems of women.

The Chinese Communists do not try to hide their poverty or the struggle against nature (locust invasions, famines) or the tragedy of peasant life under the "old society," and when Pearl Buck "speaks bitterness," they like it. It is Mao Tse-tung, after all, who insists that the intellectuals go down among the peasants to learn the truth about them, *from* them. What the Chinese Communists *don't* like is Mrs. Buck's glorification of the worst features of the old society, especially that of the upper classes—concubinage, for instance, and the whole pattern of the old Confucian family system, the very things the Communists are trying to uproot forever. Her strongest theme—the "yearning for sons"—is what is still making it difficult to control overpopulation in China. It was Mrs. Buck who "yearned," not Chinese women.

The wellspring of her writing was that she never had a normal child and was afraid she could not have one, though she did have one retarded child in 1921 and adopted nine more. (She told me that J. Lossing Buck did not tell her for years that his family had a history of retarded children.)

In *The Good Earth* Wang Lung finds some treasure, becomes prosperous, takes a second wife. But he had no class consciousness, the Communists say. They look upon this as a puerile plot (which it is, of course—the poor-boy-makes-good American story, without reality for the Chinese peasant). The real Chinese peasant was often in rebellion. And in fact he did bring about the revolution in China from 1927 to 1949. He was not, the Communists say, a lump of the good earth, but a "heroic" fighter in the "class struggle."

"But," I said to my Chinese hosts, "you have to remember that Pearl Buck made more friends for the Chinese than any other influence."

"But what kind of Chinese—and what use is that if it's all based on untruth? If she had told the truth, the books would not have been popular," was the rejoinder.

The Good Earth was written chiefly for money to support Mrs. Buck's child. Behind it was a very sophisticated editor who encouraged her in the new "naturalism" and who knew how to tailor books on China, including those of Lin Yutang. This was Richard J. Walsh, whom Pearl Buck married in 1935. It was one of the happiest and most successful literary teams of all time. They had first come to call on my husband (Edgar Snow) and me in Peking in 1934, during their extended courtship. They were both partners in several of my pioneer researches on China. They also supported the Gung Ho industrial cooperatives.

Pearl Buck had everything she wanted—except a normal child. And she wanted everything, as she used to say. She was an island, offshore to any land. She was also an island in time far ahead of herself and yet isolated in a never-never past that had gone even when she lived in China.

Source: Helen F. Snow, "An Island in Time," in *New Republic*, March 24, 1973, pp. 28–29.

Malcolm Cowley

In the following excerpt, Cowley compares Buck's portrayal of China in The Good Earth *with works by two other non-Chinese authors.*

[It] would have seemed a great deal better if [*A House Divided*] had appeared ... before the publication of *Man's Fate* and *A Chinese Testament*. This doesn't mean that [Mrs. Buck] has been even slightly influenced by Malraux or Tretiakov. On the contrary, she has completed her trilogy of Chinese life exactly as she must have planned it from the first, taking what she regards as the three most vigorous Chinese types—the farmer, the war lord, the student—and treating them in three long novels that together summarize fifty years in the life of a family and a nation. It happens, however, that the student-hero of her new novel strongly resembles the student-hero of *A Chinese Testament*—not for any reason of literary derivation, but simply because the type is widely prevalent in China and because both Tretiakov and Mrs. Buck have portrayed it honestly. It also happens that the first section of *A House Divided* deals with the same period of the Chinese revolution that was more fully treated in *Man's Fate*. The two comparisons force themselves on the reader. Mrs. Buck suffers in both cases, for the other books, in their different ways, are better as literature, more vivid, more compelling.

I would not say that they are truer to Chinese life. Mrs. Buck has spent so many years in the country, has studied the language so well, has lived on such terms of friendship with the people, that she makes Tretiakov and Malraux seem like tourists dropping ashore from a round-the-world cruise. She has a truly extraordinary gift for presenting the Chinese, not as quaint and illogical, yellow-skinned, exotic devil-dolls, but as human beings merely, animated by motives we can always understand even when the background is strange and topsy-turvy. The Chinese themselves are in general eager to praise her work; many of them say that no native writer has painted a more accurate picture of their country.... She seems to know China so well that she no longer judges it even from the standpoint of "the native Chinese"—whoever he may be—but rather from the standpoint of a particular class, the one that includes the liberal, three-quarters Westernized scholars who deplore the graft and cruelty of the present government but nevertheless keep their heads on their shoulders and hold their noses, and support General Chiang Kai-shek because they are afraid of what would happen if he were overthrown.

The hero of *A House Divided* belongs to this class. Mrs. Buck presents him with deep sympathy, but she does not succeed in making his character seem admirable or even likable....

In the classical age of Corneille and Racine there was a rule that only kings or queens could be the subject of tragedies. The rule, I think, was not entirely nonsense, for it meant that tragedies enacted themselves on a high stage built, as it were, of human conflicts and aspirations. Translated into modern terms, it would mean that novels and dramas should deal preferably with men and women who are in a high degree conscious of themselves, of the parts they play in the world, of the social conditions by which they are molded (and which in turn they help to mold). They should deal, in other words, not with the typical or average but with the *representative*. Particularly in a novel that describes a revolutionary crisis, it is a mistake, I think, to present a hero who sees only the blank underside of events and cannot even choose the side he wants to fight for. The real dramas take place among the planners, the agitators, the new leaders thrown up violently by the masses like rocks from a volcano—and, on the other hand, among the capitalists and generals who are organizing their counterplots and trying to buy or bully a mass support for themselves. This is the sound principle that André Malraux followed in writing *Man's Fate*, and it is one of the reasons why the climax of the novel has the power of a great tragedy.

His revolutionists are in a prison yard waiting to be burned alive—but they have all known the cause they were fighting for, they have calculated the risks they were running, and now, at the moment of death, they find a bitter and exalted reward in their feeling of nearness to one another.... It happens that Mrs. Buck describes a similar scene in *A House Divided*. Scores of Chinese students are arrested for having revolutionary literature; they are kept moaning in a cell overnight and then, in the morning, they are driven out to be killed. It is pathetic and strong enough, but it is also rather futile, for the victims have no very clear idea of the cause for which they are dying. The cutting short of all their lives seems less a tragedy than a regrettable and essentially meaningless accidentv....

Source: Malcolm Cowley, "The Good Earthling," in *New Republic*, January 23, 1935.

SOURCES

Bentley, Phyllis, "The Art of Pearl S. Buck," in *English Journal*, Vol. 24, No. 10, December 1935, pp. 791–800.

Buck, Pearl S., "The Good Deed," in *The Good Deed: And Other Stories of Asia Past and Present*, John Day, 1969, pp. 227–54.

"Chinese Exclusion Act (1882)," in *OurDocuments.gov*, http://www.ourdocuments.gov/doc.php?flash = old&doc = 47 (accessed August 20, 2010).

Doyle, Paul A., "Pearl S. Buck's Short Stories: A Survey," in *English Journal*, Vol. 55, No. 1, January 1966, pp. 62–68.

"Families and Living Arrangements," in *U.S. Census Bureau*, http://www.census.gov/population/www/socd emo/hh-fam.html (accessed August 20, 2010).

Frenz, Horst, "The Nobel Prize in Literature 1938," in *NobelPrize.org*, http://nobelprize.org/nobel_prizes/litera ture/laureates/1938/buck-bio.html (accessed August 20, 2010).

Gao, Xiongya, "Buck's Critics," in *Pearl S. Buck's Chinese Women Characters*, Associated University Presses, 2000, pp. 16–22.

Gibson, Campbell, and Kay Jung, "Historical Census Statistics on Population Totals by Race," in *U.S. Census Bureau*, September 2002, http://www.census.gov/popula tion/www/documentation/twps0056/twps0056.html (accessed August 20, 2010).

Hunt, Michael H., "Pearl Buck: Popular Expert on China, 1931–1949," in *Modern China*, Vol. 3, No. 1, January 1977, pp. 33–64.

Magagnini, Stephen, "Chinese Transformed 'Gold Mountain,'" in *Gold Rush*, http://www.calgoldrush.com/part3/ 03asians.html (accessed August 20, 2010).

Millard, Rosie, "One Day as a Perfect 1950s Wife," in *Sunday Times* (London, England), http://women.time sonline.co.uk/tol/life_and_style/women/families/article 3510810.ece (accessed November 4, 2010).

"Pearl Sydenstricker Buck, 1892–1973," in *University of Pennsylvania Department of English Web site*, http:// www.english.upenn.edu/Projects/Buck/biography.html (accessed August 20, 2010).

reader to fully understand how momentous her accomplishments were.

Kwong, Peter, and Dusanka Miscevic, *Chinese Americans: The Immigrant Experience*, Universe, 2000.
Despite being one of the earliest immigrant groups to enter the United States, Chinese immigrants were frequently the target of exclusion laws and prejudice. Kwong and Miscevic's book examines the unique struggles of Chinese immigrant families, such as the Pans, to make lives for themselves in America.

Leong, Karen J., *The China Mystique: Pearl S. Buck, Anna May Wong, Mayling Soong, and the Transformation of American Orientalism*, University of California Press, 2005.
Leong's book focuses on American Orientalism in the 1930s and 1940s, as well as three women (including Buck) who were commonly associated with China. Long explores both how perceptions of China affected the identities of these women, and also how these women's public association with China lead to the gendering or feminization of the country, from an American perspective.

Min, Anchee, *Pearl of China: A Novel*, Bloomsbury, 2010.
Min's fictionalization of Buck's life is told through the voice of her imagined Chinese best friend, Willow Yee. This biographical novel gives readers a unique perspective on Buck's life.

Spurling, Hilary, *Pearl Buck in China: Journey to the Good Earth*, Simon & Schuster, 2010.
Spurling enriches her in-depth biography of Buck with information on Chinese history and literature. Incorporating ample primary source material, as well as a fair amount of historical background, Spurling provides a realistic depiction of Buck within her time and place.

FURTHER READING

Conn, Peter J., *Pearl S. Buck: A Cultural Biography*, Cambridge University Press, 1996.
Conn's biography of Buck chronicles her life-long commitment to cultural understanding and her literary accomplishments. This revisionist account seeks to provide a holistic portrait of the author, not only as a storyteller, but as an outspoken activist, feminist, advocate, and fund-raiser. Conn places Buck's activities and achievements in her time and place for the

SUGGESTED SEARCH TERMS

Pearl S. Buck

Pearl S. Buck AND The Good Deed

Pearl S. Buck AND short stories

Pearl S. Buck AND Nobel Prize

Pearl S. Buck AND activism

Pearl S. Buck AND Asian women

Pearl S. Buck AND Chinese culture

Pearl S. Buck AND Chinese literature

The Lovers

BESSIE HEAD
1980

Bessie Head's short story "The Lovers" is the author's version of an old Botswana folktale, one that warns of dire circumstances should anyone act contrary to old tribal traditions. In this story, a young girl falls in love with a village boy, an act that was forbidden in their time. Girls were not even allowed to look at boys, let alone talk to them, make friends with them, and consummate their relationship. Marriages were arranged for the benefit of the entire village not for the whimsical emotional needs of the couple. Therefore when Tselane, the female protagonist, becomes pregnant and asks her parents' permission to wed, the members of the tribal village become embroiled in angry arguments. Fear for the safety of the village hurls the young lovers away from their kin and their home and leads to a sad ending. As in many folktales, there is a lesson to be learned.

Head's short story was first published in a somewhat radical magazine called *Wietie* in 1980. The publication was produced in South Africa and much of its subject matter was written in protest against the apartheid political system. The magazine was subsequently closed down by the South African censors. "The Lovers" was later acquired by Penguin Books and republished in a collection of short stories called *Book of Southern African Stories* in 1985. Though Head's story was not directly in

She sought shelter in the cave and was surprised to find that she was not alone. (*Tyler Olson | Shutterstock.com*)

opposition to apartheid, it did question traditional values as well as the lack of freedom that many black South African women experienced in Head's time.

AUTHOR BIOGRAPHY

Head led a very difficult life that started and ended in tragic circumstances. Head's mother, Toby Emery, was white and was living in South Africa. When she became pregnant with her daughter, she was sent to an asylum because she had an illicit relationship with a black man. Head was born on July 6, 1937, in the asylum, Fort Napier Mental Hospital, in Pietermaritzburg, South Africa. She would never know her father because her mother never identified him. She would barely even know her mother, who remained in the hospital until she committed suicide when Head was only six years old.

As a newborn, Head was adopted by a white couple, who shortly afterward gave the baby back when they discovered that she was "colored," the term used to identify mixed-race individuals. Later, Nellie and George Heathcote, a mixed-race couple, took Head in. For a long time Head believed them to be her real parents. It was not until she was fourteen years old and living in a boarding school that Head found out the truth about her heritage. A school official broke the news to her that Nellie Heathcote was not her real mother. The news devastated Head.

At eighteen, Head finished school, earning a certificate that allowed her to teach, a profession that, after two years, she decided she did not like. Just before she turned twenty-one, she quit teaching and became a journalist. She said good-bye to her adopted parents and headed for Cape Town, where she wrote for a local paper, the *Golden City Post*. In Cape Town, she was shunned by the blacks in the community because she did not speak the local language, Afrikaans. When she turned to the local mixed-race population, she found that they considered her too black. The following year she moved to Johannesburg, hoping to find a more accepting social environment.

In Johannesburg, Head was hired by the magazine *Home Post*, where she met professional writers who helped improve her writing skills, but troubled times were still ahead of her. She joined the Pan-Africanist Congress, a group of people intent on ending racial discrimination in South Africa. She was later arrested for her political activities. Around this same time period, she was sexually assaulted by a man she thought of as a friend. These tensions in her life proved too much for her, and she attempted to commit suicide.

When Head regained her mental health, she returned to Cape Town and began her own newspaper called the *Citizen*, in which Head expressed her feelings against apartheid. It was during this time that she met Harold Head, whom she would marry in September 1961. Their son, Howard, was born the following year. In the next few years, Head recognized that her marriage was deteriorating and longed to move away from the oppression she felt under apartheid. She was becoming more interested in writing fiction and thought that living in another country might inspire her. Not until 1964 would Head realize her dream. She was granted a one-way exit permit to Botswana, which meant that once she left South Africa she would never be able to return.

Life was not easy for her in Botswana. She took various jobs as she traveled around the country. She wrote at night and finally made a breakthrough with her first novel *When Rain Clouds Gather* (1968). Head produced several more books, including *Maru* (1971), *A Question of Power* (1974), *Looking for a Rain God* (1977), and *A Bewitched Crossroad* (1984). However, problems also followed her, including several mental breakdowns. She also began to drink and to hallucinate, and her health failed. On April 17, 1986, Head died of liver failure in Serowe, Botswana.

PLOT SUMMARY

Beginning

"The Lovers" begins with the mention of a love affair that blossoms one summer in a time when love affairs are strictly forbidden. It is also a summer of very frequent rain. The rain usually is preceded by the warning of clouds in the later afternoon, giving the village women who are out in the field plenty of time to hurry back to their huts.

On this particular day, one of the young women working in the field fails to notice a large thorn, and in her haste to beat the rain home, she steps on the thorn and cries out in pain. She tells the younger girl with her to hurry home and that she will come as soon as she removes the thorn from her heel. However, the thorn proves to be more difficult to extract than she had imagined. In addition, the rain begins to beat on her head, so she finds a cave in some nearby rocks and takes shelter.

No sooner does she enter the cave than she realizes she is not alone. There is a young man in the cave with her. She finds that his face and his tone of voice make her feel safe, and she relaxes. The rain, in the meantime, pours down so hard and with so much noise that the two of them cannot hear the thunder.

As it turns out, the young man is a cattle herder and spends his free time making clothes and other leather goods. To do this work, he carries a set of sharp tools. When he sees that the girl has a thorn in her foot, he offers to take it out. She allows him to help. She is surprised by how comfortable she feels in his presence, as men and women traditionally live separately from one another, especially those who are still unmarried. Even married couples have only rare occasions when they come together. That is why the young girl is caught off guard by the ease that she feels and that the young man exhibits in the close quarters of the cave. As a matter of fact, the young man is so comfortable that, instead of looking away, he "stared her directly in the eyes." She looks at him as well, finding him "very pleasing to look at."

After he finishes extracting the thorn from her foot, she asks him if he is "the son of Rra-Keaja." The young man confirms this, telling her that he is the first-born in his family. She replies, telling him that she is also the first-born in her family and that her name is Tselane, "the daughter of Mma-Tselane."

Keaja then tells her about his family. His father has three wives. Each wife has first-born sons. As he talks, Tselane realizes from the tone of his speech that Keaja is more serious and more complex than she is. Whereas Tselane is light-hearted and chatty, Keaja has "an immense range of expression and feeling at his command." He is extremely serious one moment and at another "his eyes lit up with humour [sic]." He shocks her with his straightforwardness as well as the simplicity of his words. "I don't like my mother," he says, explaining that both he and his father like to do what they want, but Keaja's mother insists on trying to control them.

Keaja shocks Tselane further when he declares that he disapproves of arranged marriage, the traditional custom of their village. His father has suffered through an arranged marriage with his mother. It did not work out well. Keaja also confesses that his mother abused him when he was a boy—scratching him and throwing stones at him. As soon as he could, he, like his father, learned to avoid the woman. Keaja spends most of his life away from home. He lives out in the fields with his family's cattle. When he does come home, he bears gifts, such as milk and blankets, in an attempt to appease his mother.

Tselane, at first, does not know how to decipher the details of Keaja's life as he reveals them to her. She has only known the strictest traditions of her tribe, in which children are controlled by their parents and no one ever questions the rules they live by. It is even taboo, or forbidden, to talk about their elders as Keaja does. His discussion about his family has "abruptly jolted [her] into completely new ways of thought."

When the rain slows down, Tselane stands and the two of them walk together in the dark to their village. Tselane lives on the far western side of the village, whereas Keaja lives on the far eastern side.

Middle

Tselane's father has recently taken a second wife, Mma-Monosi. Her father had seemed discontented with Tselane's mother and is seldom home, but when Tselane arrives home that evening, Mma-Monosi is there along with Mma-Tselane. Tselane loves her mother and Mma-Monosi equally, but the two women have very different personalities. Mma-Tselane acts like a queen but takes only a vague interest in the women around her. Mma-Tselane is a staunch supporter of village traditions.

Mma-Monosi, once she became Tselane's father's second wife, took over all the housekeeping chores, which freed Mma-Tselane to take on the role of entertaining local women by listening to their stories of child rearing and other domestic woes. Although the two adult women in Tselane's life are similar in many ways, they also differ. Whereas Mma-Tselane, despite her poor health, remains emotionally stable, Mma-Monosi's temperament wavers with the emotional environment around her. If things are going well, Mma-Monosi is strong, but if emotional turbulence influences their lives, Mma-Monosi's mental state deteriorates, especially whenever anyone criticizes her or reprimands her. Most of the time, Tselane finds a comfortable balance between the two mother figures in her life.

After her mother goes to bed on the day that Tselane first encounters Keaja, Tselane goes to Mma-Monosi's side and tells her she has a question to ask. She brings up the subject of arranged marriages and asks Mma-Monosi if she approves of them. This question is so unexpected that Mma-Monosi loses her breath. She warns Tselane that if anyone but her had heard this question, Tselane would be in trouble. "Such things are never discussed here!" Mma-Monosi says. Tselane is a little confused. She thought that all young people questioned life as they grew up. Mma-Monosi makes it clear to Tselane that is something no one should ever do. Questioning life upsets a delicate balance, and life should always be in order. Mma-Monosi then confesses that she knew of someone who had questioned life and horrible things happened, but when Tselane questions her further, Mma-Monosi does not provide any more answers. She merely says, "It is too terrible to mention."

On the other side of the village, after Keaja arrives at home, he offers the women of his family the cow's milk he had carried home. All the mothers who are there inquire about their sons who live and work with Keaja at the cattle post. Keaja tells them that all is well and that he plans to return to the post early the next day. His mother has nothing to say to him. In contrast, when Keaja joins his father, Rra-Keaja, who is eating in a separate hut, the young man is greeted joyfully. Keaja's father loves his son and dotes on him. While they eat, his father announces that he has begun negotiations for a bride for Keaja. At this news, Keaja is struck with fear. He asks the name of the woman that his father is considering. His father, however, tells him that he cannot discuss that information. The negotiations are at a critical point. Keaja then wants to know how far the negotiations have gone. "Have you committed yourself in this matter, father?" Keaja asks. His father answers in the affirmative, telling his son that he has given his word. They will not know for possibly another six months whether the other family accepts the offer.

At this news, Keaja suggests that he find his own wife. Surprised by his son's words. Rra-Keaja says that he must have a terrible weakness if his son is able to talk to him in this way. Though Rra-Keaja often talks to his son about matters that other parents never indulge in, he thinks maybe he has gone too far. However, Rra-Keaja lets Keaja's comments go without any reprimand. The previous year, Keaja went through an initiation process that all young men of marriageable age go through. During this time he learned about sexual relationships between men and women. He also learned what was acceptable and what was not. If any of the rules of the village about sex were broken, great punishment would befall the entire family. This catastrophe could also extend to the entire village, depending on the seriousness of the infraction.

Tselane has also experienced an initiation process for women. The rules for women were much more complex than those for the young men, because of the women's menstrual cycle and pregnancy. The people of the village believe that a woman, more so than a man, could completely destroy a village if she acted inappropriately in terms of sexual relationships. All women have to follow rules as to how to act during menstruation, child birth, and miscarriages. If she does not, the village could lose all their animals and crops. There is no room for passion. Sexual relationships are based on rational, practical concepts and must take rule over the emotions. No one is allowed to question these beliefs, otherwise the village would lose its harmony.

None of these rules stop Tselane and Keaja's relationship. They meet in secret, and as time passes, their passions grow. They often discuss their predicament. Keaja tells Tselane about his father's planning a marriage for him. He wants to avoid this but he can think of no way to do so without causing trouble. Also he tells Tselane that if he could choose, he would select her as his wife. She tells him she is afraid of nothing, but she needs time to sort through her thoughts.

Over time, Tselane becomes distraught, caught between her emotions and her duty toward her family and village. Her mind is so cluttered with mixed feelings that she becomes physically ill and is confined to bed for several days. When she is finally

strong enough to meet Keaja again, they share such intimate feelings that they feel as if they had willed themselves to already be married.

End

As the crops in the field reach their full growth, Tselane realizes she is pregnant. Her secret love affair with Keaja can no longer be kept a secret, so Tselane and Keaja come up with alternative plans for what they might do. First they consider an emergency escape from the village should it become necessary. They know the news about the pregnancy will not be easily accepted by their parents or by the villagers. Their love affair has broken many rules, and now they have to pay the consequences. Their choices are narrowed down to leaving the village without informing anyone about the pregnancy or telling their parents and waiting to see how everyone reacts. They decide to inform their parents of their love and to ask for permission to marry.

Tselane's mother is at first in shock as the results of her daughter's pregnancy would surely, at the least, destroy her standing in the village. When Tselane's father is told, he reacts with an angry outburst. Tselane, in the meantime, is sent into her family's hut and is told not to go anywhere without Mma-Monosi.

Keaja's father is quick to go visit Rra-Tselane after his son tells him of his wishes to marry Tselane. Rra-Keaja tells Rra-Tselane that he is willing to have his son marry Tselane if Rra-Tselane agrees. However, Rra-Tselane does not believe a marriage at this point would do any good. On hearing this, Mma-Monosi runs after Rra-Keaja, who leaves the Tselane compound feeling dejected. Mma-Monosi urges Rra-Keaja to go the tribal chief and beg for his son's life. When Mma-Monosi returns home, she tells Tselane the terrible story from the past that she had refused to tell earlier. There once was a young man who refused to marry the woman his family had chosen. Instead, he asked to marry a woman whom he loved. The tribal council ruled against the young man and killed him in punishment. They also killed the young girl he loved. Mma-Monosi says that in this case, the young couple had no physical contact, implying the complexities of Tselane's case were much worse. Mma-Monosi pledges her life to Tselane, telling her that she would do everything in her power to save her. "No one will injure you while I am alive," Mma-Monosi says.

The village council cannot make a decision because the villagers are in such an uproar. Some of the people ask for forgiveness, while others ask for death. In the end, the council orders the young couple to leave the village for a few days so tempers can die down. Keaja and Tselane choose a route and travel up a hill that was near the village.

When the day approaches for the young couple to return, tempers begin to rise again, but the couple does not come back. The village people wait several days, and still Keaja and Tselane do not appear. A search party is formed and sent out in the direction that the young couple took. They come back with no clues as to where the couple is or suggestions as to where they might have gone. At this news, Mma-Monosi's collapses. As if in a daze, Mma-Monosi walks toward the hill. As she approaches, she imagines she sees Tselane and Keaja. They are standing on top of the hill. Then, the rocks part, creating a wide gap in the earth. The young lovers scream as the earth swallows them. A few minutes later, Mma-Monosi sees the spirits of Tselane and Keaja rise from the hole.

Mma-Monosi makes her way back to the village and tells everyone what she had seen. In grief, Mma-Tselane also makes the journey up the hill and also sees the same vision. Weakened by what she saw, Mma-Tselane returns home and dies.

The village takes all of this as a bad omen and decides it is not safe to live there. The villagers pack up everything they own and move away. Many years later, another tribe who did not know about the tragedy moves into the area. Without ever having heard this tale, they too eventually see the tragedy play out on top of the hill. Even to this day, the author recounts, the legend remains. The hill where Tselane and Keaja disappeared is still called The Hill of the Lovers.

CHARACTERS

Keaja

Keaja is the young man who falls in love with Tselane. He is a fearless young man, unafraid of speaking his thoughts. He is also unusual. He has met no other peer who is as determined as he is to go against the accepted traditions of his tribe. Even before he met Tselane, he opposed arranged marriages. Her willingness to consider some of his ideas about freedom probably help

Keaja fall in love with Tselane. Once he gains her commitment to be together with him, Keaja very rationally plans their options.

Although others in his village suffer through marriages that have little or no positive emotional effects on their lives, Keaja believes that the expression of his feelings, especially in the matter of love and marriage, is crucial to his mental health. He has seen how others, in particular his mother and father, live their lives either in numbness or in misery. They accept the traditional rules without regard to their own health and happiness. Then they suffer through the long years of matrimony, often ending up not even being able to converse with one another.

Keaja is also courageous. He is not afraid to take a path that no one else has followed or, worse yet, that has led others to their deaths. He would rather die than to live contrary to what he believes.

Tselane is impressed by Keaja because he speaks so straightforwardly. He does not censor his thoughts for any reason. He looks at her intently, which no other boy in her village is strong enough to do. Keaja's thoughts, as he expresses them to Tselane, are both expressive of his emotions as well as clearheaded and to the point. His words make her look at the world in a completely different way.

Mma-Keaja

Never referred to by name in the story, Mma-Keaja is Keaja's mother and the first of Rra-Keaja's three wives. Keaja is her only child. Keaja does not have a good relationship with his mother. Mma-Keaja is a woman who thrives on controlling those around her. Both Keaja and his father are very much opposed to being controlled, so they keep their distance from her. When Keaja comes home for brief moments, his mother is shown as not wanting to have any conversation with him. Keaja speaks to his father's other wives and leaves gifts for all the women, including his mother. This is done for his mother not out of love but rather as an appeasement. He wants to put her in a good mood so she will leave him alone.

Mma-Monosi

Mma-Monosi is the second wife of Tselane's father. Though Tselane states that she loves both her mother and Mma-Monosi in equal amounts, it is to Mma-Monosi that Tselane turns when she wants to express her thoughts. Mma-Monosi is more physically and emotionally expressive to Tselane than Mma-Tselane.

Possibly because of her openness, Mma-Monosi is less stable than Mma-Tselane. Tselane relates that as long as the situation that surrounds the family is stable, Mma-Monosi remains calm. She is able to control her emotions and act rationally. However, if the environment is emotionally charged, Mma-Monosi tends to panic and to react irrationally. For example, when Tselane breaks the news to her family that she is pregnant, Mma-Monosi becomes very agitated and fearful for Tselane's life. Though there is reason to be afraid, because Tselane has committed a very serious crime against the tribal laws, the author suggests that Mma-Monosi's reactions may be a bit hysterical. This may be what influences Mma-Monosi, when she climbs to the top of the hill where Tselane and Keaja disappeared, to see a vision of their death. What is interesting, though, is that it is Tselane's mother who cannot handle the emotional impact of Tselane's pregnancy and death. Mma-Tselane dies shortly after Tselane and Keaja disappear, whereas Mma-Monosi survives in spite of her so-called emotional instability.

Mma-Tselane

Mma Tselane is Tselane's mother and Rra-Tselane's first wife. Tselane thinks of her mother as queen-like in the way that she carries herself and treats the people around her. Mma-Tselane appears to enjoy having people come to her to tell her their stories, but she does not become overly involved in their lives. She remains emotionally separated from those around her. She gives orders to Tselane and directs her life, but they do not share their feelings with one another. Tselane never considers going to her mother while she is dealing with all her new emotions that are roused by Keaja. When Keaja suggests that one of the options for them is to secretly leave the village and start a life somewhere else, Tselane declines to do this because of the effect it would have on her parents. Tselane, although she turns to Mma-Monosi for emotional support, nonetheless loves her mother.

Tselane believes that her father had grown tired of her mother and that is why he took a second wife. Mma-Tselane, from Tselane's point of view, enjoys her somewhat solitary life. Mma-Tselane is not a solitary figure: she does not keep to herself. However, even though she is often surrounded by women, she remains emotionally aloof. When Tselane confesses that she is pregnant, Mma-Tselane's first concern is her own loss of esteem in the village, not the mortal danger that her daughter is facing. She appears to be a self-contained personality who enjoys her position in the village and would do anything to retain it.

Rra-Keaja

Rra-Keaja is Keaja's father. Keaja's mother is Rra-Keaja's first wife. According to Keaja, his father took on other wives because he was forced to marry Mma-Keaja against his will and could not stand her. This is one of the main reasons that Keaja does not want to take part in an arranged marriage. He does not want to suffer the same fate as his father.

Rra-Keaja is a soft-spoken man who fears he may have spoiled his son by doting on him. He often takes time to talk to his son, sharing his thoughts about life. Other fathers often ignore their children and never explain anything to them. They make plans for their children without consulting with them. Rra-Keaja blames himself for Keaja's rebellion against the tribal traditions. He worries that he may have been too soft on Keaja and thus encouraged the boy to consider breaking the taboos. He therefore is anxious to fix the problem by quickly marrying Keaja and Tselane. He appeals to Tselane's father to go along with this plan, but Tselane's father does not see how this would solve any problem. This demonstrates that Rra-Keaja may be more forward thinking than Tselane's father. Like his son, Rra-Keaja may also be more willing to express his emotions than Rra-Tselane is.

Rra-Tselane

Rra-Tselane is Tselane's father and Mma-Tselane's and Mma-Monosi's husband. He has a high position in the village, working directly with the chief as well as being the owner of vast herds of cattle that are taken care of by other men. He has little presence in Tselane's life other than as an authoritative figure. It is possibly because of his high position that he refuses to go along with Keaja's father's plan to have their children quickly married. Rra-Tselane states that the union between Keaja and Tselane would do little for either family. He does not consider what his refusal might do to his daughter. Whereas Keaja's father is more empathetic to the children, Rra-Tselane is rigidly in favor of following tradition.

Tselane

Tselane is the female protagonist of this story. She is the only daughter of Rra-Tselane and Mma-Tselane. During a thunderstorm, when she seeks shelter in a nearby cave, Tselane meets Keaja. She is quickly thrown off balance by Keaja because he introduces her to thoughts and feelings that she never imagined existed. He is nothing like anyone she has ever spoken to. It does not take long for Tselane to fall in love with Keaja, but in allowing her emotions to flow, Tselane becomes physically ill. Some of Keaja's thoughts are entirely against the traditions of the tribe, and this makes Tselane feel like the ground under her feet has become unstable. When she tries to express what is happening to her, her father's second wife, Mma-Monosi, warns Tselane not to further explore her thoughts. Mma-Monosi warns Tselane that terrible things could happen not only to her but to the entire village.

However, Tselane cannot help herself once Keaja stirs her thoughts. She questions the traditions that she has always looked upon as strict laws that cannot be changed. When her love for Keaja deepens, she gives herself entirely over to the young man, believing that they have, in effect, become married by their acts of lovemaking.

Tselane, though very naive in the beginning of the story, quickly develops the courage to think for herself. She takes Keaja's ideas and makes them her own. She does not accept Keaja's thoughts blindly, however. She takes her time, thinks them through, and comes to her own conclusions. It is Tselane who suggests that she and Keaja ask their parents' permission to marry rather than running away without telling them that she is pregnant. Although what she has done may eventually hurt her family, she does not want to act as a coward. She wants to own up to what she has done and is ready to suffer the consequences.

THEMES

Freedom

Freedom to love and to think one's own thoughts is a major theme in "The Lovers." The young protagonists believe in their right to have freedom, but in the closed society that they inhabit in Head's story, they are told that to think on one's own is to create havoc and chaos for themselves and their society.

Because there is fear that freedom of choice might cause disorder and problems, their society demands that everyone follow the rules that were established sometime in the distant past. In this society, rules are never to be questioned or challenged. No one is to think about them, discuss their feelings about them, or in any way hint that it is time to change them. No one in this story has an inherent right to freedom. However, it is freedom that the two young lovers fight for.

There are no aspects of freedom that are positive, according to most of the story's characters. As a matter of fact, even the thought of freedom scares most of them. Many would rather lean on the beliefs of their ancestors even if they do not like the results. When Tselane and Keaja, the protagonists in this story, try to experience freedom, they literally disappear from the face of the earth. Their attempts to be free are so detrimental to the tribe that the whole community must eventually leave their tribal grounds. The desire for freedom from the restrictions of their society, the story might imply, is what causes the young lovers' deaths.

Love

There is little room for love in the society that is portrayed in this story. The villagers might learn to love what has been demanded of them, but it is believed that no one should encourage their emotions, especially the emotion of love. The consequences of love within this society are obvious. The protagonists in this story have the audacity and naivety to think they can fall in love. They have a choice, but it is not whether or not to love one another. Their emotions naturally lead them into a love affair. Their choice is whether or not to acknowledge that love and accept the consequences that await them. One of the lessons of the story seems to be that it is easiest if everyone ignores love. It is not that love is wrong but that love upsets the order that has been set by ancestral elders, and the leaders of the village believe those elders knew what was best. Love is perceived as a selfish need and not necessarily the best thing for the survival of the society. When Keaja's father expresses his love for his son, he worries that his love is a sign of weakness. He also is concerned that his love has led his son astray. The lesson appears to be that it is better to follow one's head than to follow one's heart.

TOPICS FOR FURTHER STUDY

- Create a map of Africa in any medium of your choice. You might draw it, paint it, make a three-dimensional model, or produce an image online. Label all the countries and their capitals. Include the dates, if applicable, when each country was colonized, by which country, and when it won its independence. In South Africa, locate the cities in which Head lived. Do the same for Botswana. Then share your project with your class.

- Find a folktale about lovers from Native American lore. Try collections such as *The Girl Who Helped Thunder and Other Native American Folktales* (2008) by James Bruchac, *Native American Folktales* (2008) by Thomas A. Green, *Native American Myths* (1994) by Robert Gish, or another publication. How do the themes compare with those in Head's story? Does the story you found end tragically? Is the conflict that of tradition versus the individual? Write a paper about the similarities and the differences in the stories.

- Lead a discussion on teen dating in your class. Create an outline to direct the discussion, and be prepared to stimulate the discussion should your classmates run out of topics. Topics might include some of the taboos that your parents have placed on you in terms of dating. You might also want to discuss how the social rules have changed over the generations from your grandparents' time to current times. Discuss what girls might want that boys do not in terms of dating and vice versa. How important are emotions in a dating relationship? End the discussion about ten minutes before the end of class to allow a wrap-up of all the ideas that were expressed.

- Research the statistics on teenage pregnancies over the years. Make a chart that demonstrates the rise or fall of teen pregnancies for the past fifty years. What are experts saying causes the rise or fall? Present your findings to your class in a PowerPoint or other multimedia format.

- Write a short story in the form of a folktale. Have the story revolve around a societal issue, such as teen drinking, dropping out of school, food disorders, or divorce. Make sure that your story conveys a lesson you want your audience to learn concerning your topic.

- Research cultures in which planned marriages are still the norm. Focus your search on Asian, Indian, or Middle-Eastern cultures. How strict are these social practices? In which countries do they still exist? Are there penalties if the young people involved do not go along with their parents' wishes? Create a Web site at which you can post all your findings. Invite a discussion from students in these countries. How do they feel about the practice? Provide links to some of the sites where you found information for your project. Then show your results to your class.

Tradition

Tradition is an inherited thought pattern or course of action. Traditions are set sometime in the past by the ancestors of a community. Although those ancestors might have had the good of the community in mind when the traditions were set, time may have eroded the tradition's value. This is when modern thinking and tradition clash.

In "The Lovers," the protagonists challenge the traditional ways of their village. They evaluate some of the traditional laws, witness some of the misery that is caused by those traditional laws, and think it is time to change them. One might argue that the young lovers are not mature enough or experienced enough to understand the full consequences that their proposed changes

Rain-filled clouds suddenly filled the skies. *(tarczas | Shutterstock.com)*

might cause. Marriage for love, for example, might undermine the established tribal hierarchy that is needed to keep the community functioning at its best. Others, in more progressive communities, might find the traditional ways stifling, especially in communities where individual rights are prevalent. Tradition might also impede creativity, subduing new thought.

However, tradition has its place. Tradition sets patterns that are easy to follow without demanding rethinking. Tradition also offers a strong link to the past, helping to connect a society by offering mutual memories. The question of tradition versus individual creative thought is not answered in Head's story. The author merely posits the debate.

STYLE

Folktale/Parable

"The Lovers" is often described as a folktale or a parable. Folktale is a general term that covers a range of storytelling styles. Most definitions

include elements of the oral tradition of storytelling, stories that were memorized and recited rather than being written and read. Another classification that many scholars agree on is that folktales were stories of the common people, therefore the prefix "folk." Some definitions of the folktale include legends that are based on true events but then embellished as time goes by.

Whereas "The Lovers" fits this description, some literary scholars refer to Head's story as a parable. A parable could be included in a subset of the folktale, but it has a specific intention. A parable, at its heart, is a story that attempts to teach a lesson and can be used as a guideline for behavior. There are many parables in the New Testament of the Bible. Jesus, according to the Bible, taught his lessons through parables, such as the story of the "Prodigal Son." Other belief systems, including Judaism, Sufism, and Buddhism, also use parables. Head's short story tells what will happen if two young lovers go against the moral code and traditions of their village.

Time and Place

Head lived in South Africa and Botswana. Though the exact location of "The Lovers" is never mentioned, readers can assume that the setting of this story is somewhere in Africa. Whereas setting is often an important element in a story (so much so that sometimes the setting is referred to as one the characters of a story), in "The Lovers," the specific physical setting really does not affect the story. The social conditions of setting are, however, very significant for this story: it must take place in a close-knit community or village that has a long history of traditional rules that, if broken, could lead to the punishment of death. In many modern countries, such as those in Europe, the setting would have to be a place that existed a long time ago, but there are still some countries that exist in the twenty-first century in which the practice of arranged marriages still exists, and going against this practice could include severe punishment.

HISTORICAL CONTEXT

Botswana

Botswana is located in southern Africa between Zimbabwe and Namibia and bordered on the south by South Africa. Although once a British protectorate, Botswana won its independence in 1966 and has since thrived because of its dynamic economy, one of the strongest in Africa. Botswana's economy is based on diamond mining and on tourism, which is proving to be a good money-maker as the country creates huge nature preserves that attract visitors.

Almost two million people live in Botswana, with the median age being twenty-two years of age. During the apartheid years in South Africa, Botswana experienced a high rate of immigration from that county. Today, Zimbabweans top the list of immigrants entering Botswana because of the very poor economy and unstable government in Zimbabwe. At least 60 percent of the population of Botswana now lives in urban areas, such as the capital city of Gaborone.

One major challenge in modern-day Botswana is AIDS. The Botswana government has invested in an aggressive medical program to curtail the epidemic, which is one of the worst in all of the African countries. The Botswana government is also being pressured by an organization of the San people (some of Botswana's indigenous people who are also sometimes referred to as Bushmen), called the First People of the Kalahari. Somewhat similar to the treatment of Native Americans in the United States, the Botswana government removed the tribes of Bushmen from their ancestral land and placed them on reservations. The San people want to return to their land so they can practice their traditional way of tribal life. The Botswana government, at this point, is not allowing this. The San people claim their people are suffering from mental and physical illnesses due to their inability to live in their traditional manner.

South Africa

The Khoisan people are the indigenous tribes of what is now called South Africa. The Khoisan people have lived in the area for thousands of years. Members of the Khoisan are believed to be made of two different tribes, the Khoe and the San (also sometimes called Bushmen).

The Dutch were the first white settlers on the southern tip of Africa and were the first Europeans to set up a settlement, Cape Town, which was established in 1652 as a stopover for their ships. When the British came later in 1802, the Dutch (referred to as Boers and later as Afrikaners) moved farther north. The discovery of diamonds and gold about sixty years later brought huge waves of immigration as well as the subjugation of the local, tribal people, who were enticed to work in the mines for little pay.

In 1910, the Dutch and the British living in South Africa came together to establish a whites-only government called the Union of South Africa. By 1948, the apartheid system was put into place and established the separation of races, favoring the white minority over the black majority. Apartheid harshly punished blacks and many black leaders, especially those who were members of the African National Congress (ANC), including Nelson Mandela and Stephen Biko. In 1962, Mandela was arrested and convicted of sabotage, for which he was sentenced to life in prison. Biko was imprisoned and was killed while serving his sentence in 1977.

Eventually international boycotts of South Africa as well as internal protests led to the demise of apartheid and the formation of a majority rule government in 1994. Mandela's sentence was commuted after he served twenty-seven years in jail. While in prison, Mandela had become a national hero and was elected the first

COMPARE
&
CONTRAST

- **1980s:** South African Defense Force soldiers invade Gaborone and kill several African National Congress (ANC) activists living in Botswana. This action is condemned by the United Nations Security Council.

  Today: Jacob Zuma, a leading member of the ANC party, is president of South Africa. The first president after the fall of apartheid, Nelson Mandela, was also a member of the ANC.

- **1980s:** As the apartheid system strengthens, South African authors write to promote protest against the system. Popular South African black authors include poet Mzwakhe Mbuli, novelist Menan du Plessis, rapper Lesego Rampolokeng, and Miriam Tlali, the first black woman to publish a novel in South Africa.

  Today: Topics of a more personal nature are emerging in South African literature. Many novelists write about AIDS, crime, exiles returning to the country, and the rise of a black middle class. Popular authors of the twenty-first century include Phaswane Mpe, K. Sello Duiker, and Zakes Mda.

- **1980s:** The Botswana economy grows through its mining of diamonds and the raising of food exported mostly to South Africa. Botswana is one of the most politically and economically stable countries in Africa.

  Today: Although the Botswana economy continues to expand, the stability of Botswana could falter due to the AIDS epidemic. An aggressive program to eradicate AIDS from its population has been established, but Botswana remains a country with one of the highest numbers of people infected in the world, even higher than South Africa.

---

black president of South Africa in the first election where all citizens, regardless of race, were allowed to vote.

There are approximately forty-nine million people living in South Africa today, with 61 percent of the people living in urban areas such as Johannesburg, South Africa's largest city. Black Africans make up 79 percent of the population, with almost equal numbers of whites and mixed-race people making up the rest. Eleven languages are recognized as official in South Africa, and include Zulu, Xhosa, Afrikaans, English, and Sesotho.

CRITICAL OVERVIEW

Head is often referred to as one of the best African writers. Jane Starfield, for instance, in her critique of Head's work in the *Journal of Southern African Studies*, makes note of Head's "literary eminence." Starfield finds Head's work "rich with life" and her writing intense. Head's "writings beat paths through many areas of human experience," Starfield writes. In the end, Starfield concludes, Head's writing, as a whole, became, for the author, "a formal and powerful antidote to oppression."

In his *African Studies Review* critique of the book *Critical Essays on Bessie Head*, Robert Cancel describes Head as being "critically hailed as one of the brightest voices in African literature at the time of her death." Since that time, Cancel continues, Head's work has "remained the subject of ongoing scholarly discussion." Head not only was "a fine writer," Cancel writes, the timing of her writing was also significant. "She came to literary prominence at a time and place of great significance." Cancel is referring to Head's own life, her mixed race in a country controlled by an apartheid government, as

He had collected a bundle of wood for her to take home. *(Theo Malings / Shutterstock.com)*

giving her topics for her material. It was through the author's "perseverance, single-minded vision and creativity" that she was able to produce a "professional identity within a shifting and often hostile environment."

Writing for *Choice*, F. Alaya states that Head was "a woman whose genius transcended private suffering" and, who as a writer, was committed "to decency and justice," not only for herself but also for "her embattled South Africa homeland." Meanwhile, in an article written for the *Washington Post*, Charles Larson describes Head's writing as an "honorific" achievement. At the end of her life, Head was, according to Larson, "black Africa's preeminent female writer of fiction." Larson also describes Head's 1973 novel *A Question of Power* as the author's "masterpiece."

Focusing on Head's short stories, Michael Thorpe, writing in *World Literature Today*, finds that Head's shorter works "lend themselves especially well to an understanding of Head's aims as a writer." She had a "kinship with the village storyteller of oral tradition." As with the typical material that was used by the traditional

storyteller, Head's stories are "intended to entertain and enlighten." Sonita Sarker, in *Feminist Writers*, also touches on what she found to be Head's aim in writing. Sarker begins her article by calling Head "one of Southern Africa's most powerful voices of the 1970s and 1980s." Sarker concludes that "in combining grotesque evil with profound beauty" in her stories, Head "fulfills" the "main function" of being a writer, which as Head had often claimed was that of "infusing life with magic and conveying its wonder."

CRITICISM

Joyce Hart

Joyce Hart is a published writer of more than thirty nonfiction books for students and a teacher of creative writing. In the following essay, she examines the characters in "The Lovers" and their relation to the concept of self versus society.

"The Lovers" offers a view of what can go wrong in a confrontation between an individual's

WHAT DO I READ NEXT?

- Head's first novel was *When Rain Clouds Gather* (1968). The male protagonist of this story, who is based on Head's husband, leaves South Africa illegally and begins a new life in Botswana in a village of traditional people and a mix of refugees. The theme of traditional values versus modern ideas dominates much of the story.

- In 1974, Head wrote *A Question of Power*, an autobiographical novel about her mental breakdown. The protagonist, Elizabeth, is of mixed races and leaves South Africa with her son to find a new home in Botswana. After tremendous social pressures placed on Elizabeth in her new country, she begins to suffer from nightmares and hallucinations. Eventually, it is her love of and responsibility for her son that pull her back to health.

- For more short stories similar to "The Lovers," read Head's *The Collector of Treasures and Other Botswana Village Tales* (1977). Two of the main themes in this collection are the position of women in the tribal community and the breakdown of the traditional family.

- Some of Head's short stories, along with those of fellow African authors Can Themba and Alex Laguma, have been collected in *Deep Cuts: Graphic Adaptations of Stories*

by Can Themba, Alex Laguma, and Bessie Head (1993). The stories are illustrated with drawings that make the worlds of the stories come alive for young-adult readers.

- J. M. Coetzee is a white South African who has often written about the racial discrimination in his home country. Coetzee has won many literary awards in his lifetime, including the famed Booker Prize, which he was awarded twice, as well as the 2003 Nobel Prize in literature. *Life and Times of Michael K* (1983), which won the Booker Prize, is one of his most popular novels. The story involves a young man caught in the middle of war-ridden South Africa during the height of apartheid.

- James Welch's *The Death of Jim Loney* (2008) follows the life of a man of mixed heritage: Native American and white. Jim Loney lives in a small Montana town and feels lost because he cannot fit in. Neither the Native American nor the white community is willing to accept him as one of their own. The author demonstrates the challenges of modern-day Native Americans in telling this story, as readers witness the trials that Jim Loney must endure.

---

pursuit of his or her personal desires versus the needs of the community. Head establishes the characters in this story to represent one side or the other of this debate. Some characters are totally supportive of the rules of society being strictly observed, which, in turn, shapes their personalities and their actions. Other characters want to completely abolish society's rules and start down the path toward individual rights and freedoms, whereas a third group of characters is caught somewhere in between. The story ends without coming to a precise conclusion as to which belief works best.

At the far right of the debate is Rra-Tselane, father of the female protagonist of this story. Rra-Tselane represents the ruling system of the tribal society of this tale. He is not the head of the tribe, but he is one of the chief's assistants. Rra-Tselane is portrayed as a well-to-do man of high standing, a benefactor of the hierarchy that rules his tribe. He is one of the tribal leaders to whom people look for guidance. He owns large herds of cattle and has enough wealth to afford to have other men look after them. Rra-Tselane is a rational man who leads by example and always follows tribal law. When he is approached

> THERE IS THE POSSIBILITY THAT
> TSELANE AND KEAJA MADE THEIR WAY TO
> ANOTHER VILLAGE AND LIVED HAPPILY EVER
> AFTER. HOWEVER, THIS IS A PARABLE, AND THAT
> IS NOT THE LESSON THAT THE STORYTELLER
> WANTED TO TELL. OR WAS IT?"

by Keaja's father, who proposes that Keaja and Tselane (the male and female protagonists) marry, Rra-Tselane does not consider his daughter's welfare nor that of Keaja when he responds to the offer. Rra-Tselane considers only his community. He suggests that the marriage of his daughter and Keaja would benefit neither the families nor the community and refuses to allow the marriage.

If there is any affection between Rra-Tselane and his daughter, this story does not expose it. Tselane never mentions that her father expresses his emotions, and Rra-Tselane never acts in an emotional way in anything he does. There is no discussion of his love for any member of his family. His role in this story is to represent an unemotional approach, which includes favoring the good of the society over that of the individual.

Tselane's mother also appears to follow this line of thought, but with a twist. Like her husband, Mma-Tselane exhibits a lack of emotional connection to those around her, especially to her daughter. However, it is not made clear if she does this for the betterment of her society or if she is motivated by personal preference. Mma-Tselane reacts to her daughter in a somewhat cold, rational way, and readers do not know whether this is because she believes an unemotional approach to relationships is proper or whether she merely does not like people, including her own daughter.

Tselane describes her mother as being queen-like in the way that she relates to the other villagers. Mma-Tselane gives the other women her time as an authority figure, but she does not demonstrate any emotions as she listens to the village women's stories. She does not exhibit empathy

for them. Instead she comes across as a woman who enjoys her stature, being the first wife of one of the village leaders. She appreciates that the women come to her. Their actions show the respect that they have for her, but what aspect of Mma-Tselane's personality does this attention satisfy? Perhaps she is pleased to accept their respect for the good of the community, or maybe the respect of the village women satisfies a more personal need for Mma-Tselane.

Mma-Tselane's reaction to her daughter's illicit pregnancy encourages the latter interpretation. When Mma-Tselane discovers that her daughter has broken the village taboos and has become pregnant, she reacts only with concern for her own welfare. It seems that Mma-Tselane dies because she is so distraught about what she stands to lose in terms of her stature in the village. Therefore, in Mma-Tselane's case, though she may seem to conform to the rules for the village's benefit, she could easily have personal motives for all her actions. Therefore, her character is caught somewhere in the middle of the debate regarding the value of personal needs versus the needs of society.

Keaja, the young male protagonist in Head's story, is the character who is farthest to the left of the debate of individual versus society. Most of Keaja's thoughts are in favor of individual freedom. He does not want to go through with the upcoming marriage that his father is planning for him. He wants a wife of his own choosing. He does not want to tell anyone, except for Tselane, about his determination to win his freedom. He is willing to leave his village without telling anyone where he is going. There is little about the village life that attracts him. He wants to think for himself and is brave enough to face the hardships of his decisions. Keaja knows he might have to leave home and strike out on his own into a completely unknown world. The fact that it could be difficult does not worry him. However, he does not express any thoughts about how his decision to leave and do as he pleases will affect his family or his village. All he knows is that he does not agree with the age-old traditions of tribal law and sees little benefit in sacrificing his own needs for those of the village.

Rra-Keaja is less extreme in his views than his son. He appears to have respect for the tribal laws, at least philosophically, but he admits to breaking some of the more subtle rules, such as inviting his son into a discussion of the boy's future. Most fathers in this society do not talk to their children as he has done with his son. Rra-Keaja identifies this as a weakness inside of him, a weakness he might have handed down to his son. By being weak and making his son weak in the process, Rra-Keaja fears he might also have weakened the village.

Rra-Keaja dotes on his son. He is not afraid of showing affection for his child. Rra-Keaja is also very willing to amend his son's infraction against tribal law. He immediately goes to Rra-Tselane and proposes what he believes is a solution for the situation. He suggests that the two families agree to the marriage of Keaja and Tselane in order to cover the impending birth of their child. There is no mention of Rra-Keaja's standing in the community. Nor is there a statement about his financial status. However, by the fact that Rra-Tselane quickly rejects the idea of the marriage, stating that the union would not be good for the families, one could conclude that Rra-Tselane feels that Keaja is not worthy of Tselane, or at least not worthy of her family's standing. Keaja's father, though, seems not to be concerned with this. Being more open to his emotions, he appears to be mainly concerned for the survival and happiness of his son. Though he means well and tries to live within the tribal system, Rra-Keaja represents someone who is somewhat tempted by the expression of emotions and personal freedom, but his basic loyalties lie with what is best for the community.

Mma-Monosi, Tselane's father's second wife, is more difficult to place in this debate. Tselane describes Mma-Monosi as extremely unbalanced in terms of her emotions, but Mma-Monosi is also very aware of (as well as afraid of) the tribal laws that favor the society over the individual. Readers are not told whether it is merely her fear of the laws or her respect for them that makes Mma-Monosi implore Tselane not to break any of the tribal taboos. There is a sense that Mma-Monosi understands the needs of the individual but lacks the courage to express them as succinctly as Keaja. For these reasons, Mma-Monosi appears to live with a secret longing for personal freedom, but because of her fear, she goes along with the village rules.

Finally there is one character who seems to be right in the middle of the debate: the female protagonist, Tselane. Here is a young girl whose whole world is turned on its head when she meets and listens to Keaja and his progressive ideas.

Tselane had never thought of the topics that Keaja discusses with her. When she hears his talk of individual freedoms, she is literally blown off her feet. She becomes so ill, she cannot walk.

After considering what Keaja suggests, Tselane falls in love with the young man but decides that it is not right to run away without telling her parents. This demonstrates Tselane's connection to her community. She takes pleasure in considering personal freedom, but she also wants her parents' consent or at least wants them to know what her thoughts are, and she does not want to run away without letting them know that she still cares about them. Unlike Keaja, who is more deeply entrenched in the liberation of his emotions and the freedom to think for himself, and unlike her father, who decides everything only through his rational thoughts, Tselane views life with both emotions and logic. She is willing to go against the village rules to benefit herself, but she seems to wish she could have it both ways. She wants her freedom to chose the man she loves and to expand her mind with new thoughts, but she also wants the more conservative and traditional people in her life to understand her needs and not abandon her.

The story ends with Mma-Monosi's image of Tselane's and Keaja's death. This vision could embrace a hard lesson: that conforming to tradition and considering the greater good of the community are always more important than any chance for individual freedom and personal happiness. However, the vision could also be just a figment of an unbalanced woman's imagination. Mma-Monosi, as Tselane described her, is a wreck when emotions are running high. When there is trouble, Mma-Monosi cannot be counted on. She becomes unstable. Therefore, the vision could merely reflect her fears. Perhaps the rest of the villagers also believe that Mma-Monosi's vision shows the true fate of the young lovers, but no one knows for sure what happened to them. All they know is that they disappeared and never came back to the village. There is the possibility that Tselane and Keaja made their way to another village and lived happily ever after. However, this is a parable, and that is not the lesson that the storyteller wanted to tell. Or was it? Head might have left the ending of this story ambiguous so that readers could come to their own conclusions.

Source: Joyce Hart, Critical Essay on "The Lovers," in *Short Stories for Students*, Gale, Cengage Learning, 2011.

They met secretly as lovers and friends. (*Sebastian Tomus | Shutterstock.com*)

Femi Ojo-Ade

In the following excerpt, Ojo-Ade reviews several studies that explore the variety of themes in the complex corpus of Head's works.

Maxme Sample and her fellow critics have put together an impressive collection of essays on Bessie Head, a writer whose tortured life and the works derived from it provide excellent material for forays into the mysteries of the human heart and soul. The critics explore a wide variety of themes from the complex Headian corpus: life under apartheid, and in exile; place and space; the revolution of language; definitions and implications of madness; and being a woman, or issues of feminism.

What the text basically contributes to the growing number of studies on the late South African writer is the scope of methodologies and ideologies brought to bear on the subject. Frantz Fanon, Edward Relph, Yi-Fu Tuan, Lacan, Kirby Farrell, Dori Laub—such are the theoreticians and ideologues used to dissect Head's life and works. Among the most compelling chapters of the book are Maureen Fielding's "Agriculture and Healing" (ch. 2); Maxine Sample's "Space: an Experiential Perspective" (ch. 3); Colette Guildmann's "Bessie Head's Maru: Writing after the End of Romance" (ch. 4), and Helen Kapstein's "A Peculiar Shuttling Movement" (ch. 5).

Fielding uses the novel *When Rain Clouds Gather* to show how Bessie Head, instead of breaking down under the weight of trauma and oppression, wrote to liberate and to heal herself and her sick society. The objection that one would have to this interesting analysis is in regard to Fielding's efforts to restrict Head's experience to her condition as a woman. She is not the only one desirous of such feminist exclusivism. Indeed, the whole book has an underpinning of Western feminism that would make one wonder about the much vaunted objectivity of those trying to deconstruct African ethos and tradition. The tendency to emphasize individualism is seen in several of the critics' failure to recognize the importance of community in Head's work. In the conclusion of her chapter, Fielding mentions the necessity of "various components of agriculture [coming] together to create a sustainable future" (24). Yet she desists from using the word community, which would certainly describe the process being described. That word would also apply to Guildmann's comments on *Maru* (63). That fourth chapter is a good example of how feminist critics force their ideology upon the African text. Perhaps is a recurrent word in Guildmann's analysis, as she makes every effort to particularize events to suit her purpose.

Kapstein's valiant effort in breaking down the theme of madness in Head's work is definitely food for thought. It raises several questions, especially as one realizes that madness, while being potentially subversive, does not erase the marginalization and the diminished status of the mad person. In other words, what real, positive possibilities does the state of madness hold for the individual, and for the society? What is the cause of madness? Another point regarding this chapter is the use of language. Kapstein quotes Fanon's seminal work, *Les damnés de la terre*, in translation (*The Wretched of the Earth*), using the word native for Fanon's original, *le colonisé*. This is through no fault of the critic's; nonetheless, that very word is a subtle affirmation and confirmation of the history of Africa and African literature in the hands of Western experts. Thus, the native literature is seen through the superior eyes of the masters and mistresses from abroad. While one cannot complain that Head's work has aroused the interest of critics from near and far, one would have liked to see some inside knowledge of African culture and esthetics put into play in the book under discussion. Finally, the fact that all the critics are women may be a statement of its own.

Source: Femi Ojo-Ade, "Critical Essays on Bessie Head," in *Research in African Literatures*, Vol. 36, No. 1, Spring 2005, p. 127.

Alan Ramon Ward

In the following essay, Ward discusses Head's treatment of racism in Maru.

Bessie Head's commentary in *Maru* (1971) is delivered at the personal level, though it purports a solution to the racism suffered by the Masarwa people. The novel traces the symbolic

> **IF EVERYBODY UNITED HEAD WITH HEART AS MOLEKA DOES, RACISM WOULD DISSOLVE AS THE PEOPLE WHO BELIEVE IN IT WOULD STOP BELIEVING. RACISM WOULD SIMPLY CEASE."**

change of Dilepe village (Botswana) and, by extension, that of Africa, effected by a single Masarwa woman who can read and write. The young Margaret Cadmore enters the scene with the expectation of "one day" helping her "people." She is shy. She has an awkward manner. She is not personable. This has led some critics to misunderstand Head's vision and call it a failed one. Huma Ibrahim, for instance, believes "that Margaret Cadmore remains the perfect victim of racism and sexism throughout th[e] novel." For Ibrahim, Margaret is only the passive recipient of good will: "surely the nexus of Masarwa struggle is not to accept charity but to enter consciously into the new definition of a nation." It is true that Margaret never enters the national discourse of racism as a political leader or even makes her purpose known. But Head has the unassuming Margaret single-handedly change the course of that community's history.

Head realizes that racism, no matter what its origin, is perpetuated by individuals, and individuals can decide to reject any measure that runs counter to what they consider right. There is many a travesty, after all, to which the human race could subscribe for its economic viability (feeding our bad students to the better ones, for instance) but that our humanity prevents us from considering. In Dilepe village, where wealth is hoarded and resources distributed inefficiently, racism has created a subordinate caste, the Masarwa, to carry the burden of this inefficiency. But this is not humane. Head seems to suggest in *Maru* that human beings are capable of racism because over time their hearts have come to live separately from themselves. Just as Moleka, a main character, has "taken his heart out of his body and hidden it in some secret place," these people, without hearts to guide them, can believe ideas without considering their inhuman implications. If one could reunite head with heart in these people, perhaps promoting racism would seem as unreasonable as eating students. *Maru* is the story of racism being overcome in this way, at an individual level, related symbolically by a quartet of characters: the men, Moleka and Maru, and the women, Margaret and Dikeledi.

I shall show that before Margaret appears in Dilepe, Moleka and Maru represent two parts of a single individual. Moleka represents the self without the heart and Maru represents the missing heart. Through a well-developed metaphor in the text, we come to think of Moleka as a sun, powerful on its own, and as a thunderstorm, but one that needs a cloud from which to draw rain. The cloud is Maru, who represents the heart that Moleka lacks. If Moleka had a cloud, a heart, of his own, he would be complete—he could combine sunshine with rainfall and produce a rainbow.

Early in the story, during Moleka's first interaction with Margaret, Moleka gains a heart for the first time by falling in love with her. Maru, noticing himself displaced in Moleka's life, acts as a jealous lover and does all he can to ruin Moleka's new connection to Margaret. But as Maru finds out, Margaret has not replaced Maru as Moleka's heart, but given Moleka a heart of his own. Finding himself tragically useless, Maru begins to dream of escaping from the society for which he has always felt contempt. He recognizes Margaret, who despite falling in love with Moleka keeps herself away from him, as a soul mate. Margaret and Maru, not in love but both suffering because of their love for Moleka, escape together, to a setting rife with imagery alluding to Moleka. Moleka's love for Margaret is, in the end, transferred to Dikeledi, or at least the text gives us every hope that it will be: after he marries Dikeledi, and after Maru marries and disappears with Margaret, Moleka "laughed and laughed. Everything else went smoothly for Dikeledi." Moleka and Dikeledi become the unprejudiced chiefs of the Dilepe Tribal Administration. Institutionalized racism will no longer be tolerated.

The situation of the Masarwa is improved, and it is Margaret who becomes the impetus for change in two decisive ways: first, by symbolically reuniting Moleka with his heart; second, by withholding herself from him so that he can unite with the efficient, unprejudiced, and leader-bound Dikeledi. That Margaret is not forceful in her methods, even that she is unaware of them, does not diminish the symbolism of her being the catalyst for change. That she is unconscious of her role perhaps even speaks to the inevitability of the effected change. By her efforts, "the wind of freedom" enters the space of the Masarwa tribe, the "dark airless room in which their souls had been shut for a long time."

Before going any further, Maru's representation as cloud must be considered as it relates to the possibility that Maru and Moleka represent two parts of the same character before Margaret's appearance: Maru representing the heart, Moleka representing the self without the heart.

By associating Maru with the cloud that needs a force to produce water, and Moleka with the force that needs a substance, the cloud, a relationship of dependence is emphasized between the two characters. V. S. Menager-Everson notes that "in Setswana maru means 'cloud,'" and that in the story, Maru is "indeed that banking of clouds" that is unable to "release its beneficial downpour." Johnson also sees Maru as a cloud, and that "a comparison is implied between the cloud that fails to produce rain and the chief who fails to relieve the distress of his people," namely, Maru. Moleka is representative of water from torrential rains. According to Johnson, Moleka is explicitly linked with the vitality of a thunderstorm. When Moleka spoke, "his voice had such projection and power that the room vibrated." Moleka's vitality is also suggested in a strong association with the sun. "Comparisons of Moleka with the sun are explicit," says Johnson, and Menager-Everson agrees that "Moleka is 'sun.'" Head's narrator tells us explicitly about Moleka's "body that felt like a living pulsating sun"; that "Moleka was a sun around which spun a billion satellites"; that his eyes were "two yellow orbs of light"; that he "felt the sun in his own heart." But Moleka is incomplete. From the first page, "bright cloudless skies hold no promise," notes Joyce Johnson, and it is a "soft steady rain" that people long for. Moleka has the ability to draw it as from a well, but the source of water lies with the cloud. Maru is the source with whom Moleka must negotiate to combine his sun with water.

Other aspects of the text confirm that, before Margaret arrives, Moleka is incomplete without Maru. Moleka is "split in two" and "only half the statement of his kingdom." He has grown "accustomed to having a shadow next to him." This "shadow" is introduced as another part of him that keeps "shyly" silent while Moleka maneuvers his way into a woman's bed. It is only upon hearing Moleka address this shadow that we learn what he calls this part of himself: "of course Maru."

Before Margaret appears, Maru's and Moleka's relations with women follow divergent patterns. Moleka's behavior is consistent with him having no heart. He is interested in the physical only. He intellectualizes sex, knows everything "about the female anatomy," and needs to find more and more "horrible sensations" in order to keep his affairs interesting. He uses women, gives them no love, ruins them emotionally, and dumps them, all the while remaining "unhurt, smiling." Juxtaposed with this behavior is Maru's love life. He gives too much love, so much so that "the weakest" of his women "went insane, and walked about the village muttering to themselves." This love is described as a "nameless terror," indicating that Moleka and Maru belong to "opposing kingdoms." Maru "always fell in love." He loves all his women and is himself broken by each one, "taking to bed" with a "deep sorrow."

While Moleka is "a living dynamo," future king "of the African continent," this way of being is unfathomable to Maru, "as though shut behind a heavy iron door." Maru is shy and quiet and has only five friends, that is, two "shadows," one spy, a sister, and Moleka, "in a village of over fifty thousand people." Maru is "not the kind of personality to rule the masses" but one whose sole purpose is to "love," and be loved intensely, like a heart. Yet Maru is the greatest manipulator in the novel acting rashly, selfishly, and even cruelly. How does one explain this paradox in Head's description?

To understand Maru's character, I think, we must understand the novel's symbolism. The pivotal moment in the novel's symbolic movement, the unification of self and heart in Moleka, comes directly after Moleka and Margaret meet for the first time, at the old library where Moleka has arranged for Margaret to stay.

"It was a long single room" which was "covered in layers of dust and cobwebs": the place they are entering has remained unused for some time. We notice an immediate change in the rhythm of the narrative as they enter the library, from the preceding scene of "goats and people" jumping and vans swooping up hills to Moleka's strange brooding. Margaret does not understand what he is doing, all of a sudden "deep in thought," and decides he must be "retrieving his breath," though he has not exerted himself. He is "slowly" pacing "up and down," his movement paralleled by "a big black scorpion" which scuttles "across the room." Moleka's "head [is] bent" toward the ground and the scorpion, as though he were in consultation with the animal. The scorpion seems to be placed as a metaphor for the unwitting Maru, who is being replaced as the heart of Moleka. The scorpion is "disturbed at their entry."

In this part of the scene, Margaret wants Moleka to leave the table where it is, and Maru as the scorpion shows us by angry reactions that he wants Moleka to do the opposite, that is, to remove the table. We later see this chain of events repeated when Maru wants Moleka to retrieve a bed lent to Margaret, and Margaret, of course, wants to keep the bed to sleep on.

Moleka's body language leads us to believe that he converses symbolically with the scorpion upon first entering the room. Whatever is exchanged between them, Head states that the scorpion becomes "angry," a strange description for a small creature ostensibly interested in self-protection, and threatening, "his tail alertly poised to strike." The scorpion wants Moleka to remove the table similar to Maru, who later wants him to remove the bed. Moleka moves to raise the table "as though to fold its supports and remove it." Margaret "hear[s]" him and "bursts out nervously: 'please don't remove the table.'"

He keeps "his hands touching the table," but refrains from lifting it. He stops to absorb the moment, using the table to steady himself. At that moment, Moleka feels compelled to do as Margaret asks, against Maru's wishes. "Why?," he asks, but his tone, "deepened in a strange way," like "something sweet," like "a note of music," reveals that he already feels the answer. Something has changed his voice so dramatically that from one moment to the next, Margaret can "hardly recognize" it; something has changed him so dramatically that she suspects "magic" is at play. "A moment ago he had been a hateful, arrogant man. Now, he had another face which made him seem the most beautiful person on earth."

As mentioned earlier, Maru is associated with both cloud and heart, neither of which Moleka possesses before the scene in the library. Margaret is the first to notice the "cloud" around Moleka's eyes, as well as his sun, which "lit up" the faces of people who looked at him. When

Moleka chooses not to remove the table, Margaret sees this sun produce its first rainfall. What results is a "rainbow of dazzling light." He no longer needs Maru's cloud to be complete. She overhears him thinking aloud: "first there was one of you. Now there are two of you." She seems to think he is referring to being in love with her. But the statement could also refer to his realization of the change Margaret has effected in him: first there was only one, Maru, providing him with a heart. Now there are two, both Margaret and Maru. But unlike Maru, Margaret is not completing Moleka but giving Moleka his own heart. Moleka no longer needs Maru as his shadow. "The scorpion crossed his path and he quietly crushed it with his foot." "Oh," she says, and indicates what has changed in him by raising "her hand towards her heart."

Moleka is in love for the first time, with Margaret, and Margaret is in love with him. Moleka changes his disposition toward everyone, and everyone notices Moleka's changed state of mind. He is the talk of the town when he invites Seth, the prejudiced education supervisor, to dinner and feeds a Masarwa "with the same fork" with which he feeds himself. Even Ranko notes that "Moleka is a changed man." Usually Moleka says: "hey, Ranko, you damn fool, come here." But later, it is: "Ranko, please fetch me a packet of cigarettes out of the shop." Indeed, from his experience with Margaret, Moleka gains not just love but the ability to love at various levels.

But as the story would have it, Margaret, the Masarwa, does not marry Moleka, soon to be chief of the Batswana. Moleka marries the princess of the tribe, Dikeledi, while Margaret marries Maru, a social hermit, albeit one of royal descent, who disappears with her so that rumors of his death start up immediately.

Why does Maru marry Margaret? From the time Maru first hears of Margaret, his language when speaking of her is the language of possession. She is "gold" and he will "steal" it because he has "grown tired of the straw." She is the prize to a contest for which he is ready to cheat in order to win: "report the minute she mentions the name of anyone who has taken her fancy and I shall mess everything up." His plan is not to fall in love with her or even to convince her to fall in love with him. instead he intends to threaten her: "if you do not agree to marry me, you will stare at the moon for the rest of your days." When Maru first expresses interest in Margaret, he is not curious about who she is. There is no description of his being conflicted or impassioned as he is for Moleka. Never once do we see a personal connection between him and Margaret. He sets up her pictures not for what they are of her but for what they are of him: when a painting is sent to him to which he cannot relate, he sends it back: "you keep it. I don't like it." Others he hangs up like mirrors about his room. Even when Maru says he loves Margaret, the context reduces his professed love to covetousness: "what will I do if she does not love me as much as I love her? . . . Kill her."

Maru wants Margaret out of jealousy over Moleka. Before seeing Margaret for the first time, "something was violently agitating his heart" when Ranko tells him how changed Moleka is by Margaret. Immediately Maru feels the ramifications of Moleka's new love: "I am so lonely." "Moleka . . . has a heart of gold," Maru remembers, his heart growing "cold with fear." He confronts Moleka, starting an argument smacking of a lovers' quarrel.

As the novel progresses, we see a change in Maru's relationship to Margaret. Symbolically, seeing that he has been replaced as the heart of Moleka, he begins to notice the connection he has with Margaret. Like Maru, Margaret has been an outcast. Maru is often described as a "God" and Margaret has made Moleka into a god: "who else made a god overnight but a goddess?," Maru reasons. Furthermore, they have both given to Moleka and are no longer needed: Maru, as the heart that has been replaced; Margaret, as the lover who will never be the wife. Because they both love Moleka, yet cannot be with him, they both have the same need and only each other to fill the void. Together they are more whole than they would be apart. Margaret warms to Maru's "torrential expressions of love," a description reminiscent of Moleka, who has become the "thundercloud" that carries with it the rain. They situate themselves where they can find comfort from the "low horizon where the storm brooded," symbolic of Moleka as sun and thundercloud. They surround their house with "yellow daisies," flowers of the sun and translated directly from Maru's dreams. We are told that Maru nurtures them so carefully because they "resembled the face of his wife and the sun of his love," Moleka.

According to Menager-Everson, characters are "moisture deficient" when sad and absorb "fluid" as they grow happier. Without Moleka, Maru lives in perpetual drought. "Didn't I tell you not to break up the clods?" he yells at Ranko, "they are for conserving moisture." The "white grass" around the house is "parched." Maru can produce no moisture himself. The rains have not come, it is a "hot, dry summer," and Maru, like "those black storm clouds," must live "in thick folds of brooding darkness." He is in darkness because he has lost his sun, Moleka. He is dry because he has lost his thundershower, Moleka. In many ways the story is beautiful for its tragedy: Maru the heart sacrificed to the sun, the sun united with Maru's sister.

The dynamic of this last relationship between Moleka and Dikeledi unfolds as follows. In the scene in which Maru sees Margaret for the first time, Moleka sees her for the last time. From then on, the novel tells the story of Moleka privately understanding his new awareness of love, and the story of Maru maneuvering to steal away with Margaret. Maru, through Ranko, leads Moleka directly into Dikeledi's arms. Moleka, though in love with Margaret up to the end, and though understanding that "a pre-arranged trap had been set for him," begins to feel love for Dikeledi. In Moleka's own words, "one woman set his heart aflame and he had turned around and put all that fire into another woman's keeping." Dikeledi is a "living dynamo," among the natural "queens of the African continent." Once Moleka understands that he is no longer the old Moleka since meeting Margaret, but "Moleka, with something added," as he puts it, he is able to put this "something," his heart, to use. As chief of the Tribal Administration, and with Dikeledi, he will change Dilepe and better the conditions of the Masarwa.

Head's response to the problem of institutionalized racism is not a battle call for the self-emancipation of the Masarwa. But it would be wrong to dismiss Head without understanding that, in effect, she is calling for the self-emancipation of humanity, which includes Masarwa emancipation. If everybody united head with heart as Moleka does, racism would dissolve as the people who believe in it would stop believing. Racism would simply cease. Although this vision is unrealistic, it is beautiful nonetheless. Individuals, together, would lead Africa out of its dark place and into the swelling sunlight, where temperate rains fall, and there are rainbows.

Source: Alan Ramon Ward, "Using the Heart: The Symbolism of Individual Change in Bessie Head's *Maru*," in *International Fiction Review*, Vol. 31, Nos. 1–2, January 2004, pp. 19–26.

Maya Jaggi

In the following excerpt, Jaggi provides a favorable assessment of Tales of Tenderness and Power.

The monthly magazine *Drum* (which began life in Cape Town in 1951 as *The African Drum*) was one of the first major outlets for black South African writing. Selected from 1950s editions of the magazine, the stories in *The Drum Decade* range from short fiction by Ezekiel Mphahlele, Alex La Guma, Richard Rive, Bloke Modisane and James Matthews to reportage and testimony (borrowing from story-telling conventions) by Can Themba, Nat Nakasa, Henry Nxumalo and Casey Motsisi. Set in the townships of the 1950s, they evoke in particular the vanished ethos of Sophiatown, Johannesburg's vibrant, cosmopolitan free-hold community which the regime bulldozed in 1962 to make way for the white suburb of Triomf.

In the often tough, cynical prose that became a hallmark of *Drum*'s style, its writers both mirrored and mythologized shebeen life, the violent criminal underworld of the *tsotsi* or gangster, and the pervasively Americanized culture of B-movies at the "bioscope," jazz and street patois or *tsotsitaal*. Some of these stories seem unable to penetrate beyond the putative glamour of the streetwise *tsotsi*, relying on improbable melodramatic intrigue and cardboard characterization. (The latter is most dismally evident in the deadly temptresses, exploitative shebeen queens and other female stereotypes who haunt these pages.)

But the prevailing note is one of protest. *Drum* affirmed a black urban identity at a time when the Nationalist government (in power since 1948) was attempting to "retribalize" Africans, relegating them to a pool of cheap, menial labour without a permanent presence in the supposedly white cities. Striving to articulate the "black experience" at the onset of apartheid, *Drum* writers documented and dramatized the violence and tension exacerbated by racial reclassifications, forced removals and segregated resettlement. They protested against the police raids and constant harassment that accompanied the pass laws and prohibition. (It was until 1962 illegal to sell European alcohol to "non-whites.") . . .

Bessie Head was among writers of the *Drum* generation (she wrote for a sister publication, *Golden City Post*) who fled into exile in the 1960s. She died in 1986, at the age of forty-nine, in her adopted homeland of Botswana, the acclaimed author of four novels, a collection of short stories and a social history of Serowe, the village she made her home and refuge for twenty years. According to the autobiographical writings published posthumously as *A Woman Alone*, Head consciously eschewed explicit political allegiances in her fiction, preferring to probe what she saw as the deeper truths concerning human good and evil, and the misuse of power. These truths found their most powerful expression in the novels, *Maru* (1971), which explores the enigma of racial prejudice through the treatment of a virtual slave-caste of "Bushmen" in Botswana, and *A Question of Power* (1974), a fictional account of her own protracted mental breakdown.

Brief, fragmentary and sometimes repetitive, *A Woman Alone* builds a surprisingly coherent portrait of a sensitive, compassionate and talented writer transcending an onerous legacy. (The illegitimate child of a white woman who died incarcerated in a mental asylum and a black stable-hand, Head learnt of her origins at thirteen, through the almost casual cruelty of a mission teacher.) These notes and sketches yield valuable insights into Head's views on politics, literature and feminism. They also confirm the solace she eventually found in rural Botswana: suffering from a lack of family or roots, and, like most South Africans, from "a very broken sense of history," she describes the healing sense of continuity and belonging she derived from "the old tribal way of life and its slow courtesies."

Head's passage from the bruising realities of South Africa's townships to the humble idyll of Serowe is reflected in *Tales of Tenderness and Power*, posthumously collected stories which date from the early 1960s to the 1980s and testify to Head's subtlety, versatility and prowess as a story-teller. While some resemble the "tough tales" of the *Drum* school, others celebrate village life, history and mythology in Botswana. All are enriched by Head's distinctive vision, whether in their scornful exposure of corruption and abuses of power, or their epiphanic moments of generosity and tenderness.

Source: Maya Jaggi, "In the Shadow of Apartheid," in *Times Literary Supplement* (London, England), December 1, 1990, p. 1326.

SOURCES

Alaya, F., Review of *Bessie Head: The Road of Peace of Mind: A Critical Appreciation*, in *Choice*, Vol. 46, No. 5, January 2009, p. 896.

"Botswana," in *CIA: World Factbook*, at https://www.cia.gov/library/publications/the-world-factbook/geos/bc.html (accessed August 25, 2010).

"A Brief Sketch of the Life of Bessie Head," in *Bessie Head Heritage Trust*, http://www.bessiehead.org (accessed August 21, 2010).

Cancel, Robert, Review of *Critical Essays on Bessie Head*, in *African Studies Review*, Vol. 48, No. 1, April 2005, pp. 195–96.

Head, Bessie, "The Lovers," in *Global Cultures*, edited by Elisabeth Young-Brueh, Wesleyan University Press, 1994, pp. 300–13.

Larson, Charles, "Bessie Head, Storyteller in Exile," in *Washington Post*, February 17, 1991, p. X4.

"The San People," in *Kalahari Peoples*, http://www.kalaharipeoples.org/san_people.html (accessed August 28, 2010).

Sarker, Sonita, "Bessie Head: Overview," in *Feminist Writers*, St. James Press, 1996, pp. 227–28.

"South Africa," in *CIA: World Factbook*, https://www.cia.gov/library/publications/the-world-factbook/geos/bc.html (accessed August 25, 2010).

Starfield, Jane, "The Return of Bessie Head," in *Journal of Southern African Studies*, Vol. 23, No. 4, December 1997, pp. 655–64.

Thorpe, Michael, "Treasures of the Heart: The Short Stories of Bessie Head," in *World Literature Today*, Vol. 57, No. 3, Summer 1983, p. 414.

FURTHER READING

Abrahams, Cecil, ed., *The Tragic Life: Bessie Head and Literature in Southern Africa*, Africa World Press, 1990.
    This is a collection of essays about Head's life and her work. Topics include feminist viewpoints of Head's writing, the political influence on her work, as well as an examination of the imagery that Head used to create her stories.

Ayo, Yvonne, *Eyewitness: Africa*, DK Children, 2000.
    This young-adult survey of the continent of Africa explores the many countries and cultures that exist there. Included is an overview of the geography of the land, the history, as well as the many wild herds of animals that wander the open lands.

Clark, Nancy L., and William H. Worger, *South Africa: The Rise and Fall of Apartheid*, Longman, 2004.
    This accessible book offers the reader an

overview of the history of the political system of apartheid that ruled South Africa for almost fifty years. The authors look at the early signs of racism that began with the South African nationalist period, as well as the political protests that gained power and eventually helped to topple apartheid.

Joyce, Peter, *This Is Botswana*, New Holland, 2005.
This book offers readers a quick but thorough look at the African country of Botswana through words and photographs. Readers will enjoy viewing the massive Kalahari Desert that makes up most of the country, as well as the waterways of the Okavango delta. The author provides insights into the people of the land as well as a report on the wildlife that lives there.

Main, Michael, *Botswana—Culture Smart! A Quick Guide to Customs and Etiquette*, Kuperard, 2007.
This book is intended as a guide for people who plan to visit Botswana. However, the information included in this book also allows readers who have no intention of visiting the country to better understand the people who live in Botswana. Included are details about the traditions, the history, religions, and politics. Also included are the types of food peo-ple eat, the social taboos, and the spoken and unspoken languages.

Mathabane, Mark, *Kaffir Boy: An Autobiography—The True Story of a Black Youth's Coming of Age in Apartheid South Africa*, Free Press, 1998.
Mathabane grew up in South Africa during apartheid and experienced the horrors of racial discrimination at its worst.

SUGGESTED SEARCH TERMS

Bessie Head

Bessie Head AND apartheid

Bessie Head bibliography

Bessie Head AND African writers

The Lovers AND Book of Southern African Stories

Bessie Head AND The Lovers

Bessie Head AND Botswana

apartheid AND African literature

The Machine That Won the War

Isaac Asimov, along with Robert Heinlein and Arthur C. Clarke, is often considered one of the founding figures of modern science fiction. Asimov's "Robot" and "Foundations" series have had a profound impact on the perception of science fiction in popular culture. Some of his works were filmed for television in the 1950s and 1960s, and his ideas provided much of the source material for films and television shows such as *Star Wars* and *Star Trek*. His short-story "The Machine That Won the War" grapples with the thorniest questions of the cold war, when human civilization hung in the balance between war and peace, and deals with the difference between perception and reality in the public understanding of computer science at the beginning of the information age. Asimov's terse prose style exemplifies the ideals of simplicity and clarity that are often valued in science fiction, in a story that is very much representative of this period of science fiction. Asimov's story can be compared with other cold war science fiction, including Ray Bradbury's "There Will Come Soft Rains" and Stanley Kubrick's film *Dr. Strangelove, or: How I Learned to Stop Worrying and Love the Bomb*, as they all deal in their different ways with the theme of the extinction of our species through war. "The Machine That Won the War" was published in the 1969 collection *Nightfall and Other Stories*. It is also available in *Isaac Asimov: The Complete Stories: Vol. 1*, published by Broadway in 1990.

ISAAC ASIMOV

1961

Isaac Asimov (Getty Images)

AUTHOR BIOGRAPHY

Asimov was born on January 2, 1920, in a rural village in Belarus (then the Soviet Union). Three years later his family immigrated to the United States. He began reading science fiction in the pulp magazines sold in his family's candy store in Brooklyn, New York. He was an active science fiction fan throughout his teenage years, and he attended the first World Science Fiction Convention in 1939. Shortly thereafter, he began publishing science fiction in the pulp magazine *Astounding Science Fiction* under the tutelage of editor John W. Campbell. Asimov was unusual among early science fiction authors in gaining a prominent place within the scientific establishment. After working as an engineer in aircraft research during World War II, he earned a doctorate in biochemistry from Columbia University in 1948 and taught at Boston University until 1958. He published all of his best-known science fiction works in the 1940s and 1950s, including *I, Robot*, the "Foundation" trilogy,

and the short story "Nightfall." Asimov's stories tended to be rooted in scientific reality as "hard" science fiction, though he did popularize ideas such as hyperspace, a plot device to allow human beings to quickly travel between stars, glossing over the physical realities that would be involved in such a voyage.

Asimov was appalled in 1958 when the Soviet Union beat the United States in the first round of the space race by launching the satellite *Sputnik*, and like many Americans, he decided that educational reform was the answer to winning the competition with the Soviet Union. Since he was already in a position to give up his teaching position and support himself as a writer, he did so, and he transformed his writing career so that he mainly produced works popularizing science, such as *The Intelligent Man's Guide to Science* (1960), reaching a far larger audience than he could have as a teacher. For the next ten years, Asimov wrote little science fiction, although he considered it his first love. "The Machine That Won the War," written in 1961, was the first science fiction story he had produced in several years, and it was written simply to keep his hand in the genre. In the 1970s and 1980s, Asimov returned to science fiction, writing more "Robot" and "Foundation" novels, and eventually combining those two series and most of his other works in one grand setting, called a future history in science fiction terms. Asimov wrote more than five hundred books of all types, making him one of the most prolific authors in history. He won both the Hugo and Nebula awards, the most prestigious prizes in the science fiction genre, several times.

In 1983, Asimov underwent heart bypass surgery and was infected with HIV from a blood transfusion (at that time, the blood supply was not screened for HIV). He died of AIDS in New York City on April 6, 1992.

PLOT SUMMARY

Asimov credited the great science fiction editor John W. Campbell with teaching him to begin a story no nearer its beginning than necessary, and "The Machine That Won the War" begins after the war in question is over, some decades or centuries in the reader's future. Lamar Swift, the executive director of Earth and its colonies, is in an underground facility that houses Multivac, a supercomputer whose calculating abilities are popularly credited with having won the ten-year-long war against the Denebians. Swift is meeting with John Henderson, Multivac's chief programmer, and Max Jablonsky, its chief interpreter. Multivac itself has been temporarily shut down after the victory, but it will no doubt soon begin performing calculations for peacetime work. The situation recalls the real-life ENIAC, one of the first computers built, which prepared reference tables for artillery fire during World War II and then took over various civilian tasks after the war. The Multivac facility had been crowded with workers during the ten years of the war, but it now is deserted except for the three men who "had instinctively sought out... the one peaceful corner of a metropolis gone mad" with jubilant celebration after the war. This is patterned after the wild celebrations on Victory over Japan (VJ) Day in New York at the end of World War II.

The three men share a sense of relief at the end of the war and its anxiety, expressed in Henderson's excited cry, "They're destroyed! They're destroyed!" He is referring to humanity's defeated enemy, the inhabitants of the planetary system around the star Deneb. Nothing further is said about the Denebians throughout the course of the story, except to mention that they had no computer similar to Multivac. It is mentioned that the human military disposed of a weapon that could warp space so as to destroy whole planets. The reader is left to speculate whether that is what was done to the inhabited planets around Deneb.

Jablonsky says that the celebrating populace believes that Multivac was "the machine that won the war." The official story that was told to the public was that every action of the Denebians was calculated on the basis of probability by Multivac, allowing the human (Solar) forces to thwart them, and that everything the Solar military did was also on the recommendation of the computer, resulting in final victory. The military and the government actually believed that this was so, but they were also aware that there had been lapses in the system, such as a time when, according to Henderson, "after our Spywarp was blasted out of hyperspace we lacked any reliable Denebian data to feed Multivac and we didn't dare make *that* public."

However, each of the three men in this room know more profound ways in which Multivac failed, or rather ways in which Multivac could

not have hoped to succeed because of human error. They had kept these failures secret during the war, but they now reveal them to each other. Henderson reminds the other two that Multivac is "just a big machine. No better than the data fed it." He explains that he realized that all of the statistics he was being given about industrial and military matters to program into Multivac were being systematically falsified by human error: "Group leaders, both civilian and military, were intent on projecting their own improved image... so they obscured the bad and magnified the good.... [They] had their own skins to think of and competitors to stab." Once he had realized this truth, Henderson could not reveal it because public morale depended on belief in the infallibility of Multivac. He decided, therefore, not even to report this to his superior Jablonsky, but to use his own initiative to fix the figures used in programing Multivac based on "intuition." He simply "juggled [the numbers] till they looked right." At the same time, though, Henderson claims to have written programs to compensate for the bias, so the situation remains unclear.

Jablonsky reassures Henderson that it didn't make any difference what he had done. Jablonsky himself had come to believe that during the later part of the war, Multivac was physically unreliable. His technicians who maintained the hardware of Multivac had been shifted to other parts of the war effort (even though Multivac was acknowledged as the most important part of the war effort), and replaced with poorly trained workers who were either too young or too old for military service. He suspected the same was true of the factories supplying spare parts for Multivac. Accordingly, Jablonsky had no confidence in the figures being produced by Multivac, so in the analyses that he passed on to Swift for action he "introduced the bugger factor." (This term, more commonly known as a computer bug, also refers to the real-life ENIAC. This computer had 18,000 circuits, controlled by vacuum tubes. Insects would sometimes get into the works and cause a short circuit, requiring a technician to actually go inside the computer to remove the insect, or debug the computer. By 1961, the term "bug," which would eventually give rise to related terms such as "computer virus," meant any hardware failure.) Jablonsky means that he changed the figures Multivac produced to compensate for the mechanical faults. So he, too, relied on "intuition" to alter the figures in the reports he generated for Swift. Director Swift is not at all dismayed to hear that Multivac had failed in the information it provided him and that he supposedly relied on. He experienced tremendous anxiety at the thought of following the orders of a computer, so he was uncertain about doing so:

> Multivac might seem to say, Strike here, not there; do this, not that; wait, don't act. But I could never be certain that what Multivac seemed to say, it really did say; or what it really said, it really meant. I could never be certain.

Swift did not feel himself bound to follow the recommendations in Jablonsky's reports interpreting Multivac's findings, based in turn on the data provided by Henderson. The other two are anxious to learn how Swift made his decisions instead. Swift likes old-fashioned things and carries a pocket full of coins around with him, in an age when financial transactions are made electronically. Swift demonstrates how he made his decisions by flipping a coin. Any machine used in making a decision, he points out, is technically a computer, so that coin flip is the real "machine" that won the war.

CHARACTERS

The Denebians

In "The Machine That Won the War," a coalition that consists of a politically united Earth and its colonies on other planets and moons in the solar system has just won a war against Deneb. The Solar Federation has been at war with Deneb for the last ten years and has spent every moment anxiously expecting a sudden attack. Now, as Henderson says, "we're alive and it's the Denebians who are shattered and destroyed." The humans were able to win the war, at least supposedly, because they possessed the Multivac computer, which was able to reliably predict and suggest the means of countering every Denebian action in the war. "The Denebians had nothing like it." Exactly how the Denebians were defeated is never stated, but there is mention of "interstellar warps that could swallow up a planet clean, if aimed correctly." It is possible that this weapon was used on the Denebian home world and any militarily significant colonies it possessed. "Shattered and destroyed," then, is a euphemism for killed.

The most significant information about the Denebians in the story, the fact that every one of them (or almost every one them—surely it would have meant billions of deaths if the Denebians had done the same thing to Earth) is dead. That the author does not mention this directly is significant. After their victory, the three characters of the story are in a triumphant mood and do not wish to spoil it by any considerations that might call their actions into question, so they ignore what must be the unimaginable civilian casualties that they inflicted on the enemy. The Denebians are conceived of by the characters in the story strictly as a threat to their own safety that has been eliminated, as if they had diverted the course of a meteor to prevent it from hitting the Earth. It is often the case in war that the enemy is dehumanized, presented as a *them* that all of *us* can join together in opposing. Asimov goes further here: the Denebians are denied any character at all, so there can be no possibility of feeling compassion or regret. Neither the characters nor the reader is distracted from the plot of the story by even a moment's consideration of the Denebians' character.

A few more facts can be deduced about the Denebians. Deneb is a star about 1,500 light-years from our sun. (A light-year is the distance light can travel in one Earth year: almost six trillion miles.) It is one of the brightest stars in our sky. The name of the star is Arabic and means "the tail," referring to its location in the constellation Cygnus (the swan). It is 200 or 300 times more massive than our sun, twenty times larger, and 60,000 times brighter; the solar wind it ejects is 100,000 times as intense as the sun's. It is, moreover, rapidly expanding in size and will soon (in astronomical terms) become a supernova. This history of recent expansion would suggest that any inhabited planets that might once have existed around Deneb would have been long ago destroyed by the star itself. For the same reason, it is inconceivable that there could be a Earth-like world where human beings could live in orbit around Deneb. It is relatively young, much younger than the several-billion-year history of evolution of life on Earth that produced humanity. This star is an extremely poor candidate as a home for intelligent aliens. Why, then, did Asimov choose it? The consideration in its favor is that the name Deneb is relatively familiar to anyone in his audience who had any experience with astronomy. The sound of the name is itself suggestive and somewhat unpleasant; especially in the adjectival form *Denebian*. The writers of *Star Trek* seem to have reached the same conclusion, as the term "Denebian slime devil" is used as an insult on that show. It is also interesting that in this story, human beings are said to have colonies on the Moon, Mars, and Titan (a moon of Saturn). These are not merely research stations but real colonies with industrial facilities and large main-frame computers. This is somewhat odd, since it is a premise of the story that human beings have mastered some means of travel between star systems in a length of time no longer than months or a few years. Why do the people of Earth not have colonies in other solar systems? Asimov carefully controls and limits the information available, leaving the reader free to speculate on these matters. Precisely because the Denebians are not described as aliens, it is possible that Deneb is just a convenient name that Asimov took from an astronomy textbook without thinking too much about the character of the star itself (a very common practice in science fiction). The Denebians themselves may even be human colonists in revolt against the human central government. That is certainly the simplest explanation in several respects. It conforms with everything else that can be deduced about Asimov's preferred writing habits, does not require that something as startling as an advanced alien civilization be introduced into the story with comment or description from the author, and plays upon the human history of genocide against other human beings.

John Henderson

Henderson had been the chief programmer of Multivac during the war with Deneb. He realized that the raw data concerning war production and other vital factors that he had to program into Multivac which he was given by civilian and military leaders was biased because of the personal vanities and rivalries of his informants. Accordingly, he altered the data based on what his best guess about the objective figures might be.

Now that the war is over, Henderson expresses a tremendous sense of relief that Denebian civilization has been "shattered and destroyed" and the anxiety of the Denebians' long-standing threat against Earth has been removed, probably a commonly held emotion.

One of the first writers of science fiction in the sense of treating a new idea's impact on

society was H. G. Wells. He was famously criticized by his friend the novelist Henry James that in his writing, Wells put the traditional aesthetic concerns of literature second to the new idea, so his work lacked typical literary features such as realistic and detailed characterization. Wells defended himself on the grounds that characterization was irrelevant in a world where the accelerating pace of change brought about by technology and industrialization had destabilized every conventional frame of reference. The science fiction author and theorist Philip K. Dick took this subordination of character as a formal criterion of science fiction. For him, the new idea that makes the story science fiction (as opposed to some more traditional genre) replaces character as the most important part of the story. For Dick this is especially true in short stories, where the idea is liable to drive out character altogether, though the sheer length of novels requires that carefully drawn characters play their part in sustaining the reader's interest in the text. No writer of science fiction has ever exemplified this rule in practice as Asimov does. David N. Samuelson, in a review, "The Legendary Dr. Asimov," put it very plainly when he said that an analysis of character in Asimov's writing must be "an attempt to defend the indefensible—Asimov's characterizations." This is nowhere more true than in "The Machine That Won the War," where the characters are reduced to the simplest sketches, to the degree that the casual reader would probably be hard pressed identify much memorable difference between them.

Max Jablonsky

Jablonsky is the chief interpreter (analyst might be a more modern term) of the data produced by Multivac. His importance is reflected in the fact that he was the only person allowed to smoke cigarettes in the Multivac complex. During the war, he reasoned that the mechanical aspects of Multivac were faulty, and so he introduced his own corrections in the reports he sent to Swift.

Lamar Swift

Swift is the executive director of the Solar Federation; he is the head of government for a united Earth and Earth's off-world colonies (including, at least, the Moon, Mars, and Titan). During the war he rarely left "the Mansion," presumably an official residence similar to the White House. Throughout the story, he is wearing a military uniform. It is possible for a civilian head of state to wear a military uniform (for example Winston Churchill, the British Prime Minster during World War II, was entitled to wear a Royal Navy uniform and frequently did so). It is also possible that the social and political stress of interplanetary war resulted in a military dictatorship.

Swift is distrustful of modern technology, and he did not feel entirely comfortable basing his conduct of the war on the advice of a computer. This also manifested itself in his discomfort in using the "credit system tied to a computer-complex" (something similar to today's debit card transactions or Internet banking); he still carries old-fashioned coins around with him. Like Jablonsky, he smokes cigarettes. He reveals that during the war, he made all of his military decisions by flipping a coin.

THEMES

Technology and Civilization
In the Middle Ages, most Christians believed that history was a straight line leading uphill from the fall from the Garden of Eden in Genesis to the final redemption of humans and their acceptance into the new paradise on Earth promised by the book of Revelation. In the nineteenth century, the industrial revolution created unprecedented wealth and prosperity in Western Europe and the United States. Christian belief was adapted to the idea of progress: that science, technology, and industrialization would lead ever upward to higher and higher standards of living, discovery, and achievement. This was also true of Communism, which, in its original formulation by Karl Marx, taught that a succession of crises in industrial society would eventually result in what he called the worker's paradise. Capitalism, likewise, imagined that life and learning would continue to improve forever, like a line on a graph leading forever upward. In the later part of the twentieth century this view was abandoned as simplistic. It was realized that industrial civilization was self-limiting, since it polluted the environment and used up irreplaceable resources. While technology undeniably improves the lives of those it benefits, it is also directly responsible for making warfare more and more destructive, resulting in the terrible loss of life in the two world wars. The invention of nuclear weapons made it possible

for warfare to exterminate all life on Earth. During the period from the 1950s to the 1980s, the two nuclear superpowers of the United States and the Soviet Union seemed poised to do just that, diverting a large proportion of their economy to the creation of weapons that could serve no other purpose. Moreover, while the conflict between the two countries was at its root political, it was often couched in ideological terms, as if the pretext for such unlimited destruction was differences of opinion about how progress ought to proceed.

Science fiction, especially the sort that dominated until the 1960s, tightly embraced the myth of progress. It was an article of faith in science fiction that human existence was leading toward the single goal of spaceflight and the colonization of first the solar system and then other star systems. Technology was the means by which this would be accomplished. "The Machine That Won the War" is a typical example of science fiction's worship of progress. The colonization of the galaxy by human beings proceeds, until it meets the obstacle of the Denebians. However, technology provides the answer to the problem in the form of a new, unimaginably destructive weapon that evidently can destroy whole planets or star systems, along with all their inhabitants, in an instant. Because it furthers progress, this is viewed in the story as purely a good thing, and ethical implications are not considered. Also in line with the belief in progress, the war is conducted by a computer. It is only in this context that the ending of the story, where the technological system is revealed to have failed because of human limitations, can be seen as the irony that Asimov clearly intended it be.

War
War stands in the background as the main theme of "The Machine That Won the War." It is treated as a McGuffin (a literary device named by the film director Alfred Hitchcock who frequently used it in his own work), that is, the war being engaged in is of intense interest to the characters of the story, but the war is never brought to the forefront to become the focus of the reader's attention. Asimov treats the war in this way because he does not want the reader to consider the full implications of the war. It appears through Asimov's indirect references that the Terran victory in the war is achieved by completely exterminating every member of the alien race that lived in the Deneb star system.

TOPICS FOR FURTHER STUDY

- The plot of "The Machine That Won the War" encompasses the destruction of an entire alien species and their culture (the Denebians) without describing either in any way. Write your own story from the viewpoint of the Denebians, paying special attention to developing their alien culture. You can address questions such as how Deneb and Earth came into conflict or why their conflict could apparently be resolved only by the complete destruction of one or the other.

- If "The Machine That Won the War" is read as a cold war allegory, the alien culture of Deneb stands for the Soviet bloc. While Asimov tells the reader nothing about the culture of Deneb, or what contact with an alien has meant for the people of Earth, the real-life Communist culture of the 1960s produced its own fictions of how human culture might interact with aliens. Watch the Soviet film *Solaris* (1972) and the Czech film *Fantastic Planet* (1973). How do they compare in the presentation of human interaction with an alien culture with Asimov's story? Write a brief paper exploring this topic.

- Harlan Ellison's script for a film based on Asimov's *I, Robot*, published in 2004 under the tile *I, Robot: The Illustrated Screenplay*, is frequently called the best science fiction screenplay ever written. (This script, written in the late 1970s, is unrelated to the movie that was released in 2004.) The episodic character of the script has many structural similarities to "The Machine That Won the War." Read the screenplay and use it as a model for adapting a scene from "The Machine That Won the War" as part of a screenplay. Enlist other students as actors, record your scene, and edit it using iMovie or another video editing program. Play it for

your class or post it to YouTube, and invite comments on it from your classmates.

- In "The Machine That Won the War," Solar military forces use hyperspace. This is a science fiction concept that is often invoked to allow interstellar (that is, between different stars) communication or travel that would not be possible according to the ordinary laws of physics. The concept is widespread in science fiction, but it first became widely known from Asimov's works and was possibly invented by his mentor John W. Campbell (though the word itself existed previously). The word also has other meanings and uses in other contexts. Use the Internet to research the term *hyperspace* and its various meanings as it changed over time and from context to context. This could be done in several ways. For example, use Google Books or Google Scholar to search for *hyperspace* in works written before 1900, and then again in works written between 1920 and 1970; how do the results change? Search for *hyperspace* with different limiting keywords, such as *mathematics*, *science fiction*, or *spiritualism*. Search for video clips that mention hyperspace. Organize the findings of your research in a PowerPoint presentation and present it to your class.

- Sophisticated computers possessing artificial intelligence are often present in science fiction stories. Sometimes they are benign, as in *Star Trek*, but sometimes their intelligence is seen as presenting a threat to their human inventors, as in Frank Herbert's *Dune* or D. F. Jones's *Colossus*. Write a paper placing "The Machine That Won the War" on this continuum from helpful to hostile computers.

This is a reflection on the fact that the nature of war was profoundly changed by the invention of nuclear weapons and the threat of mutually assured destruction that led to the cold war standoff between the united States and the Soviet Union. For Asimov, the threat of war

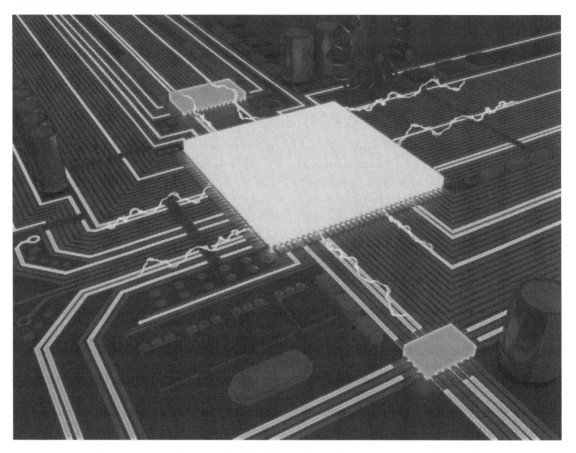

Jablonsky said he introduced the bugger factor to adjust the machines according to his intuition.
(immrchris | Shutterstock.com)

was too terrible to contemplate. Though he brings the war in the story to its final genocidal end, he looks away from that unpleasant truth and indulges the reader instead in a Luddite fantasy where modern science and technology fail in the face of simple human luck.

STYLE

Science Fiction

Asimov became a fan of science fiction in the 1930s. At the time, this was a different experience than would have been possible in any other sort of literature. Fans read a fairly narrow body of literature, the short stories and novels published in science fiction magazines such as *Amazing Stories* (edited by Hugo Gernsback) and *Astounding Stories* (edited by John W. Campbell). Fans corresponded and met with each

other, and with the editors and writers, to discuss their preferred literature, and even met in national conventions (the first was held in New York in 1939). This phenomenon has become more familiar in recent years as other genres of literature (such as comic books) have developed their fandoms following the science fiction model. Meanwhile, science fiction fandom has become larger and begun to play a role in determining taste in mass-market film and television shows, since the "fanboy" is seen as a guaranteed market for producers. A functional definition of science fiction, therefore, is literature and other media accepted by the fan community *as* science fiction. This includes material that in some ways has very little claim to be science fiction, such as *Star Wars*, but excludes work that incorporates the very kind of ideas most associated with science fiction but do not interest the fans, such as Margaret Atwood's *Oryx and Crake* or P. D. James's *The Children of Men*. Although they often do not explicitly acknowledge it, critics and publishers divide literature on precisely this criterion of fan appeal. Asimov's work is undoubtedly science fiction in this sense; even his nongeneric and nonfiction works primarily found their readership in the fan community. Asimov also emerged from within the fan community, beginning to write short stories while he was in high school and eventually publishing them in the science fiction pulp magazines. In fact, his first dozen or so stories were all published by Campbell, who helped to foster many writers through the transition from fan to professional.

Of course, it is also possible to define science fiction on thematic grounds. One of the most sophisticated thinkers about the nature of science fiction was the science fiction author Philip K. Dick, who belongs to the generation that followed Asimov's. In a private letter later prefaced to the first volume of his *Collected Stories*, Dick begins to define science fiction in distinction to "space adventure." By space adventure he means a book or film like *Star Wars*, which is a conventional adventure story that uses the appearance of sophisticated technology (but with very little thought about how such technology might work, or its implications) as window dressing, in the same way another adventure story might use magic or the costumes of some historical period. A great deal of science fiction falls into this category, including, for instance, John W. Campbell's own writings. For Dick, true science fiction is a story about the world as it is, changed by the introduction of a new idea. The idea "must be truly new (or a new variation of an old one) and it must be intellectually stimulating to the reader; it must invade his mind and wake it up to the possibility of something he had not up to then thought of." Science fiction differs from other literature, according to Dick, in that "the true protagonist...is an idea and not a person." The new idea is frequently a new piece of technology, or it may simply be a new way of looking at the world. The story that unfolds from the new idea examines how the world that is familiar to the reader will or might be changed as a result. The writings of authors such as H. G. Wells and Jules Verne are science fiction in this sense, though they can only be considered as ancestral to science fiction as a fannish phenomenon. "The Machine That Won the War" qualifies as science fiction in Dick's generic sense, since it explores the impact of computer technology on human existence, albeit satirically, so

that it turns out that human nature prevents it having any impact at all.

Allegory

An allegory is a type of story in which things represent other things or ideas, telling two stories at once. Sometimes, readers may find in a story a meaning that was never intentionally put there, as when a Christian allegory of salvation and restoration to heaven is found in the (pre-Christian) story of the *Odyssey*. However, it can also be a useful technique for satirical or political purposes. For instance, Jean Anouilh's 1943 play *Antigone* is in most respects not very different from Sophocles' ancient Greek play *Antigone*, but in its context in Nazi-occupied France, it is clear that Creon's tyranny in the play is meant to be a caricature of Nazi tyranny. If the playwright had openly written against the Nazis, he would have been arrested and executed, but the allegorical presentation allowed the audience to understand his coded message.

Asimov famously rejected techniques such as allegory: "I made up my mind long ago to follow one cardinal rule in all my writing—to be *clear*. I have given up all thought of poetically or symbolically or experimentally, or in any of the other modes that might (if I were good enough) get me a Pulitzer prize." Nevertheless, "The Machine That Won the War" is a perfectly transparent allegory. In the story, the people of Earth are at war with the inhabitants of the Deneb star system. Although human beings have evidently colonized planets around several different stars, the inhabitants of Deneb threaten to eradicate the entire human race. But as the war develops, it is the inhabitants of Deneb that are exterminated. The story was written in 1961, at the height of cold war tensions between the United States and the Soviet Union. It is clear that the risk of absolute destruction faced by both sides in Asimov's fictional war stands for the absolute destruction with which each side threatened the other in the cold war. Why did Asimov treat his subject allegorically? He certainly faced no concerns over censorship. It may be that the anxieties generated by the real-life risk of nuclear war were too uncomfortable to be treated openly as mere background material for the one-line joke made at the end that is the purpose of the story. If the story took place within a contemporary, realistic setting, the extermination of the Denebians, which the reader is supposed to take in stride to set up the story's ending, would translate to the deaths of three hundred million Eastern Bloc civilians, a thing not to be taken in stride.

Impersonal Narrator

"The Machine That Won the War" uses an impersonal narrator who tells the story from an omniscient viewpoint, quoting and describing the story elements (like reported speech) that the author considers important and ignoring others. In this case, such a technique allows Asimov to forego describing details such as character and setting that would have been of importance to any of the characters in the story if one of them had told it from his own particular viewpoint.

HISTORICAL CONTEXT

Computer Science

In his autobiography, *In Joy Still Felt*, Asimov describes the genesis of "The Machine That Won the War." On May 22, 1961, he had dinner with John R. Peirce and J. J. Coupling, two of the leading computer scientists of that era, and was inspired by their conversation to write the story the next day. They must have reminded him that computers did not have to have all the then well-known trappings of punch cards and tape memories, but that the term computer referred to any device that aided calculation. In the story Asimov wrote, the vital decision is made not by the supercomputer Multivac but by the simplest possible device for speaking in the binary language of computers, yes or no: the flipping of a coin.

Although the origins of computing go back into classical antiquity, modern computers developed from devices used by the military in World War II, such as the Enigma machine that broke the German military codes and the fire control computers on American battleships. Through the 1950s, computers remained enormous machines, larger than a house, containing thousands of vacuum tubes and programmed by feeding into them thousands of punch cards. The first computer to combine programmability with electronic computing was ENIAC (Electronic Numerical Integrator and Computer), which became operational at Harvard in 1945. It filled several rooms but was less powerful than a modern pocket calculator. It was used to solve problems in weapons targeting (suggestive of Multivac's role in Asimov's story).

The first commercial computer was UNIVAC (Universal Automatic Computer) in 1951. The general public became impressed with the future potential of computers through films, such as the 1957 *Desk Set*, in which the computer EMERAC was presented as a sort of oracle that, after merely examining a few punch cards, could instantly provide the answer to any question, in English. Asimov's Multivac is a computer of the same kind, a symbol of progress and the power of technology to solve all of mankind's problems. Multivac is a coinage like EMERAC, based on the famous computers of the day. Such made-up computer names were commonplace; a rather clever one was coined by the science fiction writer Kurt Vonnegut, who called his fictional computer in *Player Piano* EPICAC (a play on "ipecac," a medicine used to induce vomiting).

The Cold War

During World War II, the United States and the Soviet Union had fought as allies against the Axis nations. They emerged from that war as the predominant military powers and as opponents on political and ideological grounds. The United States already possessed nuclear weapons technology, and by 1949 the Soviet Union had developed it too. Open conflict between the two superpowers could have resulted in a nuclear war, possibly ending all life on Earth. Therefore, no general war broke out between the two, but there developed instead what was called a cold war, with conflicts on the political level and open fighting being conducted only with each other's stand-ins, as in Korea, Vietnam, and Afghanistan. The mechanism that kept this relative peace was mutually assured destruction (MAD). This doctrine held that if either superpower attacked the other, it could be sure of being completely destroyed itself by the retaliatory attack. To make sure that its deterrent was effective, each nation took measures to ensure that a surprise attack by the enemy would not destroy its own ability to respond. To this end, fleets of nuclear-armed bombers were kept in the air at all times, and nuclear missiles were kept ready to be launched from submarines. Commanders of these second-strike forces had some authority to launch a retaliatory attack, in case the first strike interrupted the chain of command. This meant that a full exchange of nuclear weapons from both sides could be completed within as little as fifteen minutes and could possibly result from misinterpretation or a mistake. The acronym MAD

COMPARE
&
CONTRAST

- **1960s:** The world is at the height of the cold war between the two superpowers, the United States and the Soviet Union. A full-scale nuclear war that might wipe out civilization or even all life on Earth seems to be a real possibility.

  Today: The Soviet Union collapsed as a superpower in the late 1980s, and tensions between the Russian successor state and the United States are comparatively eased. Nuclear terrorism, in which a radical group might destroy a single city with a nuclear weapon, or a nuclear exchange between regional powers, such as Pakistan and India, is a more pressing concern than the possibility of a general war.

- **1960s:** Computers exist only as large mainframes owned by the government, businesses, or universities and are outside the experience of most people.

  Today: Most Americans regularly use a personal computer and services such as the Internet that had little public profile even as ideas in the 1960s. Large mainframe computers have little place in popular consciousness.

- **1960s:** Despite a few television shows like *The Twilight Zone*, science fiction is viewed as the province of a small, mostly adolescent market.

  Today: Science fiction is among the most popular mass-market genres.

was given new meaning by critics, who pointed out the madness of the idea that the very procedures that were supposed to prevent nuclear war in fact made it possible and even likely.

In "The Machine That Won the War," the real-life cold war is analogous to the stalemate that existed between Earth and Deneb that kept everyone on Earth in constant anxiety for years, fearful that they could be killed at any moment by a Denebian attack. In Asimov's story, the situation is resolved by Earth developing an overwhelming first-strike capability, allowing Earth to attack without fear of retaliation. As a result, they destroy the entire Denebian civilization. This is analogous to a situation in which the United States developed a first-strike capability that guaranteed they could attack the Soviet Union without fear of reprisal. If such an attack were to be carried out, it would mean killing two or three hundred million people in the Soviet Union and its Warsaw Pact allies. Could mass murder on such a scale have been justified to end the risk of even greater destruction? It is hard to think that there could have been justification, since there never was a full nuclear exchange

and it does not appear likely now that there will be in the foreseeable future. In Asimov's story, the decision to make a first strike attack (euphemistically called winning the war) is assigned to a computer. However, the stand-in for the American president in Asimov's story feels that he cannot leave such a decision to a computer: "The horror of the responsibility of such decisions was unbearable and not even Multivac was sufficient to remove the weight." Asimov treats the matter surprisingly lightly and sets it up as a joke. The punch line reveals that the decision was made by flipping a coin.

CRITICAL OVERVIEW

By the author's own admission, "The Machine That Won the War" is a minor work. Asimov published it in the October 1961 issue of *Fantasy and Science Fiction*, largely to keep his hand in at science fiction. That genre was his first love, but he neglected it for years in favor of nonfiction works promoting science. Accordingly,

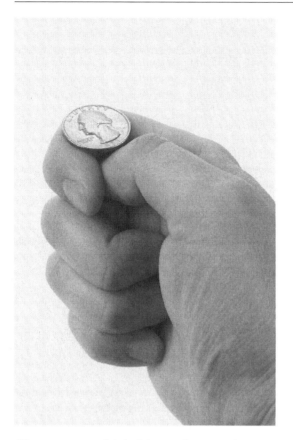

The most powerful decision-maker won the war.
(Feng Yu | Shutterstock.com)

publication of *Isaac Asimov*, edited by Joseph D. Olander and Martin Harry Greenberg in the "Writers of the 21st Century" series. As the editors point out in their introduction, the purpose of the series was to bridge fannish culture and the academic criticism of literature, worlds that until then had been largely separate. The project was possible because of individual scholars who had emerged from science fiction fandom who generally wrote about more conventional literature but were ready to take up the criticism of their first avocation. This established Asimov's work as part of the canon of science fiction meant to be taken seriously by academics. This body of work also included that of Robert Heinlein and Arthur C. Clarke, as well as younger figures such as Philip K. Dick and Ursula K. Le Guin. Perhaps Asimov's most enduring contribution to science fiction, in the estimation of his biographer Michael White, was to anchor the interplanetary romances of the preceding generation of science fiction in something like scientific reality. This is the basis of the claim that Asimov is the father, if not of science fiction as a whole, then of hard science fiction.

CRITICISM

Rita M. Brown

Brown is an English professor. In the following essay, she analyzes "The Machine That Won the War" as an example of cold war science fiction.

this story has received relatively little criticism. Most critics, like James Gunn in his magisterial *Isaac Asimov: The Foundations of Science Fiction*, limit themselves to summarizing the stories, or merely point out that the description of Multivac in "The Machine That Won the War" is inconsistent with the description of other computers Asimov gives the same name in a number of different stories (a notable discrepancy, given Asimov's mania for creating consistency between stories that another author might have left separate). Gunn also makes the observation that in general Asimov prefers to have characters discuss the events of the story, rather than experience them, so they can analyze what happened, as they do in "The Machine That Won the War." Marjorie Mithoff Miller, in "The Social Science Fiction of Isaac Asimov," places "The Machine That Won the War" among a number of Asimov's works that deal with "man and his battle with advancing technology."

A watershed in the criticism of Asimov, and of science fiction in general, occurred with the

In 1950, Ray Bradbury published a short story called "There Will Come Soft Rains." The story describes an automated house. This very impractical idea is an icon of the twentieth-century myth of progress. In this house, everything normally done by human beings, such as vacuuming, raising and lowering blinds, cooking, mowing the lawn, and even reading poetry, is instead done either by automated systems in the house or by robots controlled by the house. A display predicting that such houses would become universal among middle-class Americans was sponsored the Westinghouse company at the 1934 and 1939 World's Fairs. The same idea was taken up in a 1939 article by George Bucher in *Popular Mechanics*. It was immortalized on the screen by Chuck Jones in his 1939 cartoon *Dog Gone Modern*, in which two dogs wreak havoc in an automated house. Bradbury chose the automated house because it was

WHAT DO I READ NEXT?

- Art Spiegelman's 1986 graphic novel *Maus* presents the story of one species (cats) attempting to completely annihilate another (mice) as an allegory of the Holocaust.

- In the 1964 cold war, science fiction novel *Farnham's Freehold*, Robert A. Heinlein depicts the detonation of a Soviet nuclear bomb directly at the site of a fallout shelter of an American family that sends them into the future. They find the world dominated by a technologically advanced civilization descended from the survivors of a war in Central Africa.

- Asimov wrote a series of novels for a young-adult audience about the character Lucky Starr, of which the first, written in 1952, was *David Starr, Space Ranger*.

- Asimov's *Foundation Trilogy*, first published as a set in 1961, is the story of the death and rebirth of a galactic empire. It is generally considered his most important work.

- *I, Robot*, first collected in 1950, is a series of interconnected short stories that make up the heart of Asimov's well-known robot series, the source of the frequently quoted three laws of robotics.

- David Seed's 1999 *American Science Fiction and the Cold War* provides a history of the cultural reception of the cold war, especially as seen through and influenced by science fiction.

universally recognized in American popular culture as a symbol of progress and the unlimited promise of the future. However, Bradbury's house is strangely empty. It goes on carrying out its preprogrammed functions with no people in it to enjoy them. Bradbury describes each new operation of the house as it goes into action. Eventually the sprinklers come on in the garden:

> The water pelted window panes, running down the charred west side where the house had been burned evenly free of its white paint. The entire

> THE WAR WITH DENEB IS AT BEST A THIN VEIL FOR THE COLD WAR; THE STORY CONCERNS THE AFTERMATH OF AN OVERWHELMING AND LOPSIDED VICTORY FOR THE UNITED STATES OVER THE SOVIET UNION MADE POSSIBLE BY PROGRESS."

east face of the house was black, save for five places. Here the silhouette in paint of a man mowing a lawn. Here, as in a photograph, a woman bent to pick flowers. Still farther over, their images burned on wood in one titanic instant, a small boy, hands flung into the air; higher up the image of a thrown ball, and opposite him a girl, hands raised to catch a ball which never came down.

Bradbury's cold war audience, who had seen films of nuclear bomb tests in which the heat of the blast sets the paint on a house on fire, who had seen the bridge in Hiroshima, blackened except where a pedestrian had cast a shadow against the terrible light of the nuclear explosion for an instant before he was vaporized, would recognize what had happened. This typical American house of the future had been destroyed in a nuclear war. Later in the story, the family dog, shielded from the initial blast somehow, dies of radiation sickness. The house itself burns down in a thunderstorm, a miniature of the conflagration that had engulfed the world.

The house was programmed to read a poem to the housewife each day at 9:05 p.m. It reads Sarah Teasdale's *There Will Come Soft Rains*, a poem written in reaction to World War I (whose carnage had killed about twenty million people, instead of everyone in the world). It describes how the seasons and the life of plants and animals would go on undisturbed, even if mankind annihilated itself. Of course, in a nuclear war, the whole biosphere would be destroyed. Bradbury's point is to emphasize the unimaginable extent of the destruction, that there could be no possible reason or justification for carrying out such a war in which there would be no victory but only death for everyone. Progress is revealed as a false myth, since the goal it reaches is not paradise but the charnel house.

Philip K. Dick made a similar point in his story "The Defenders," published in the science fiction pulp magazine *Galaxy* in 1953. That story begins in a giant bomb shelter deep underground, like a few others in the United States and the Soviet Union, where the remnant of the world's people have been huddling for the last eight years, since the beginning of a nuclear war. In that time, the war has continued on the surface, fought by robots. Every square inch of the planet has been hit with hydrogen bombs and weapons even more terrible, so that nothing is left but craters and plains of fused glass. The main character is a senior scientist. He takes some sort of pleasure in seeing news reports that show the site where Moscow used to stand being blasted again and again with more nuclear bombs. He considers it a victory, something to celebrate. However, no human being has been back to the surface for eight years, and now it seems as if the robots that come down to make reports on the war are not as radioactive as expected. Therefore, a committee is sent to the surface to see what is going on. They discover that the robots have not been waging the war at all and that all the film footage of nuclear attacks was fabricated. The robots on both sides had immediately recognized that their orders to continue the war were irrational, so instead they set about to restore the Earth after the damage done in the initial war. The human beings do not rejoice in the miracle of salvation but immediately start to plot how it can be turned to their advantage to defeat the Soviets. The robots take the survey team captive; they seal off communication between the surface and the shelters and introduce the humans to a similar Soviet team. The robots tell them they will let the remaining human population back onto the surface after they have learned to live together in peace.

Turning to works marketed to a general, rather than a science fiction, audience, *Fail-Safe*, a 1962 novel by Eugene Burdick and Harvey Wheeler, showed how, with the armed forces of the two nuclear superpowers constantly alert to retaliate in the case of an attack, a nuclear war could start by accident, specifically through a mistake that occurs in the computer system that manages the forces involved. After the attack is put into motion, the efforts of both sides are unable to prevent the destruction of Moscow. The president of the United States must agree to destroy New York in turn to prevent a full nuclear exchange. The reader is left to

wonder whether the destruction of those two great cities—with a loss of life about equal to all of World War II—is preferable to a nuclear war, exactly why such careful and extensive preparation have been made to wage a nuclear war, and whether those very preparations actually make the war inevitable.

A similar theme is handled by the 1958 novel *Red Alert* by Peter George and especially its 1964 satirical film adaptation by Stanley Kubrick, *Dr. Strangelove, or: How I Learned to Stop Worrying and Love the Bomb*. In both the novel and film version of the story, the war is triggered by a U.S. Air Force general who is mentally ill and driven by his delusions to start a nuclear exchange. The audience cannot help but think that there is something insane about actually arming and planning to fight a nuclear war.

Each of these stories forces the reader to reconsider the myth of progress. Technology and industrialization had undoubtedly improved life for the middle classes and even the poor in Western countries. The expansion of wealth has made everyone better off, and the lengthening of life though modern medicine is another universal benefit. However, the same advances have also led to more and more terrible weapons, more and more destructive wars. As early as the 1950s, a general war would have meant something between hundreds of millions of people dead and the extinction of all life on Earth. Moreover, the myth of progress itself seemed to argue that such a war was inevitable, that there is an inescapable logic that if such weapons can be used, they will be used sooner or later, merely because they were a technological advance, another step forward in the relentless march of progress. The point of these science fiction authors is that this is *not* progress, that preparing for nuclear war is insane and that humanity must somehow find the ability to step back from the brink. Indeed, it is in part thanks to these stories and others like them that public awareness of the real risks involved in nuclear war was raised, which has helped to lessen the threat of a nuclear conflagration. The doomsday clock at the University of Chicago, run by the *Bulletin of the Atomic Scientists*, is a symbolic expression of how close the world is to nuclear war. It was set at two minutes to midnight in 1953, the year the United States and the Soviet Union both tested hydrogen bombs. In 1960, it was set back five minutes

According to Swift, they had won the war thanks to Multivac. (Serp | Shutterstock.com)

further from disaster because of increased public awareness of the insanity of nuclear war.

In "The Machine That Won the War," Asimov deals with precisely the same range of issues as the stories mentioned above, but he interprets them in a radically different manner. The war with Deneb is at best a thin veil for the cold war; the story concerns the aftermath of an overwhelming and lopsided victory for the United States over the Soviet Union made possible by progress. The United States has better weapons and better computers, so its further progress makes victory inevitable. And after the standoff of the cold war, the victory is progress to be celebrated:

> They're destroyed! They're destroyed! It's what I keep saying to myself over and over and I still can't believe it. We all talked so much, over so many years, about the menace hanging over Earth and all its worlds, over every human being, and all the time it was true, every word of it. And now we're alive and it's the Denebians who are shattered and destroyed. They'll be no menace now, ever again.

The threat is gone, and all mankind had to do was wipe out an entire civilization. Kill every

last one of them. It is a remarkable that a Jewish person writing only sixteen years after the end of the Holocaust can entertain such an idea as anything other than a tragedy. If the veil of allegory is pulled back, what Asimov is crowing so triumphantly over is killing three hundred million people in the Soviet Bloc, which is what total victory over the Soviet Union would have required. He is so blinded by the myth of progress, so convinced that advances in science and technology can only have good ends, that he is unable to see the reality of what he has written. If one function of allegory is to protect politically sensitive works from censorship, here it seems almost to be shielding Asimov from the censorship of his own conscience. Asimov does not provide one single fact about the Denebians precisely because he must avoid at all costs his audience thinking about them as real creatures. His story can work only if blotting them out of existence does not raise a moral qualm. No circumstance or event of the war is ever mentioned so that no suspicion or fault can fall on humanity. The reader must never think about the Denebians' art, their music, their loving families. The breathless pace of the story discourages the reader from thinking about the ethical dimension of an act of genocide. Everything must justify a war of total annihilation so that Asimov can make his point that human weakness and imperfection will prevent even computers, the new gods of progress, from achieving perfection. A whole race of sentient beings—or the entire population of Russia—is ruthlessly exterminated for the sake of the punch line that good old-fashioned human—or American—luck won out in the end. In Bradbury's story there is a tragic and melancholy sense of loss. In Dick's there is a miracle like the descent of the New Jerusalem from heaven. In both there is a transcendent feeling of some kind, and in neither one would it be possible for the reader to feel a sense of triumph over any destruction wrought. While Dick and Bradbury say that the cold war demonstrated that the myth of unlimited progress was false, Asimov clung fast to the myth and so arrived at an impossible and inhuman solution to the cold war.

Source: Rita M. Brown, Critical Essay on "The Machine That Won the War," in *Short Stories for Students*, Gale, Cengage Learning, 2011.

Donald M. Hassler

In the following excerpt, Hassler explores Asimov's use of Enlightenment philosophy in I, Robot.

One difficulty in describing the SF [Science Fiction] that Asimov continues to produce stems from his rational drive for coherence and unified generality. Like all "scientific" thinkers who have written after the methodological revolution of John Locke and the other reformers of the new science, Asimov can never leave his best ideas alone. He must continually elaborate and link new insights to old on the assumption that accumulating and interlocked knowledge is the only sort of valid knowledge. His continual moves toward the general, even the abstract, can be seen both in the long time schemes of his future history and in the conceptual ideas of his own, implicit (and left open-ended) throughout his writings. Moreover, Asimov, along with other "hard SF" writers, seems to question the absolute insights of intuitive or "inspired" art by affirming the Lockean methodology of gradual accumulation. This is not to say that the images (e.g. of robots and Empire) at the core of Asimov's fiction are totally logical, transparent, and systematically arranged for purposes of Lockean, open-ended accumulation. In spite of

> THE BELIEF IN NECESSITY OR IN THE OVERALL GENERAL AND BENEVOLENT OUTCOME FREES THE 'PLAYER,' IN FACT, TO MANIPULATE THE CALCULUS OF THE GAME."

himself, the clear and coherent rationalist contacts depths of meaning that are sometimes not on the surface. In other words, the resonance in both *I, Robot* and the *Foundation* trilogy seems to me significant; and that resonance or echoing is consistently from the 18th-century Enlightenment.

I will suggest here some ways in which Asimov's ideas on robotics and on history in these two early fictions, both of which are collections of shorter pieces written in the decade of the '40s for *Astounding*, remind us of key dilemmas stemming from our Enlightenment heritage. These dilemmas always balance "truth" against method, so that followers of the Enlightenment (and I believe Asimov is one of these) continually discover that the most effective methodology leads to the most "indeterminate" conclusions. I am not arguing that Asimov is a conscious scholar of his roots in this context, though any critic would have to think carefully before maintaining positively that Asimov is *not* consciously aware of some idea. Rather, I simply think it helps in understanding these remarkable and seminal longer fictions from the Campbell years to suggest their echoes from the Enlightenment. Also, though Asimov continues to make use of these ideas in much of his fiction written after these two works, to cover all the work through his most recent *Foundation and Earth* (1986) would be much too vast a topic for this essay.

One additional qualification needs to be stated at the outset—a qualification pointing to an entirely different essay that a critic of mine might write, or rather that several fine critics have been at work on for some time. I find that the resonances in Asimov echo more directly from the 18th-century Enlightenment with little benefit from the more organic, 19th-century reworkings of notions about history and about mechanism. Hence Asimov seems somewhat of an anachronism, even anathema, to more comprehensive inheritors of the Enlightenment tradition. Specifically, the images for cybernetics and robotics, along with the ideas which they imply, in the work of Stanislaw Lem and John Sladek as well as many other modernists, suggest more tonal and organic complexities and interfaces than Asimov allows for in his work. Similarly, historical determinism as understood by Marxist critics represents a quantum leap in complexity over Asimov and his 18th-century precursors. But Asimov is complex enough and interesting in his evasive anachronism. So it is the story of *his* ideas I am telling here rather than the total story of the ideas themselves. Certainly Asimov has been taken to task for being too simple; I intend to describe some of this "simpleness" more sympathetically than critics who are convinced that it is too narrow have been able to do. After all, one tenet of the 18th-century Enlightenment was clarity of vision; but this is not to say that the more complex shadows and "ghostlier demarcations" may not also be interesting. As unifying devices for *I, Robot*, Asimov employs both the character of Dr Susan Calvin and the Three Laws of Robotics. Both devices seem to me, also, imbued with resonance from the Enlightenment.

In his fine introduction to the whole canon of Asimovian SF up to but not including the recent outpouring of new Foundation and robot novels, James Gunn [in *Isaac Asimov: The Foundations of Science Fiction*, 1982] has worked out the "fixed-up" chronology for Calvin's life and spinster's career at US Robots and Mechanical Men, Inc. and how that scientific career as "robopsychologist" interacts with key product robots and other employees. There are other psychologists in the early short stories, even one or two "robopsychologists"; but Susan Calvin is special. She supplies not only the unity of *I, Robot* as a collection but also part of the Enlightenment resonance that makes this such an important book. Writing in an August 1952 "Foreword" to one of the early hardcover editions of the "novel," the anthologist Groff Conklin comments: "[Miss Calvin's] name may have been chosen by the author with a wry eye on the significance of . . . Calvinism." John Calvin, in fact, laid out a general framework, a time scheme and a theological set of assumptions, that did much to permit the gradualism of the secular Enlightenment and ultimately the technological and moral experimentation that Susan Calvin devotes her life to advancing. Calvin's move to posit an immensely long time scheme,

along with a built-in "uncertainty" about any one particular judgment or "election" that God might hand down, did much to liberate thinkers for the gradual experimentation necessary in modern science. A recent critic who makes suggestions similar to those I am making here writes that Calvin, more than Vico or Spengler, ought to be a "likely candidate" for influencing the vast temporal frameworks characteristic of both Enlightenment science and hard SF:

> Do we not catch a glimpse in these 'time charts' and thousand-year sagas of a return of the repressed Calvinistic background of the modern sciences? Without a doubt Calvin would be horrified, could he return from the grave, to see where his ideas have led, yet we could hardly underestimate the significance of his role in undermining the sacramental world picture which had prevailed throughout the [M]iddle [A]ges and thus laying the ground for a rational investigation of natural phenomena [David Clayton, "What Makes Hard Science Fiction, 'Hard,'" in *Hard Science Fiction*, edited by George E. Slusser & Eric S. Rakin, 1986].

I think this resonance fits Asimov perfectly although the theology itself, of course, is never his. He might prefer to invoke the immensely long and gradual history of the Israelites, which does, in fact, seem calculated to postpone indefinitely any absolute appearance of final truth. But the name Susan Calvin reminds us of the Puritan work ethic, and she does work long and hard—and has still not arrived at any absolute truth at the age of 82, when she dies. Asimov has commented in numerous places how he loves this character and has her say finally, "I will see no more. My life is over. You will see what comes next" (*I, Robot*). Verbs for seeing, I think, are no accident in the usage of an Enlightenment heroine.

Moreover, the adjectives used to describe this driven robopsychologist whose presence does so much for unifying *I, Robot* complement what Asimov correctly labels at the beginning of the book as her "cold enthusiasm"—"thin-lipped," "frosty pupils." Such ideological excitement as presumably she shares with the other workers at US Robots and, of course, with Asimov himself focusses on the virtues of control, pattern, predictability. The resonance I see here is not only with the great advocate of complete control, John Calvin, but also with that secular determinist of the end of the 18th century: William Godwin. Discarding all theological reference, Godwin simply "believed in" a coherence and order that governed all systems. Hence what he called "Necessity," which many critics have described in terms that resemble Calvinistic determinism rather than a strictly mechanistic determinism, seems to be echoed in Asimov's final story in *I, Robot*, which I will describe next, as well as in Asimov's world of the Foundations.

In "The Evitable Conflict," benevolent machines seem able to anticipate and control *all* events in a way that sounds much like the completeness of Necessity in Godwin; and at the same time Susan Calvin's "enthusiasm" is clear as she says finally:

> ... it means that the Machine is conducting our future for us not only simply in direct answer to our direct questions, but in general answer to the world situation and to human psychology as a whole... . Think, that for all time, all conflicts are finally evitable. Only the Machines, from now on, are inevitable.

Asimov's youthful wordplay over "evitable" and "inevitable" will grow into a more sophisticated wit in the later novels where robotics play important roles. But his celebration of large, general systems (along with the implicit realization of the dilemma in the need to keep systems open-ended and hence "indeterminate") seems clearly to be linked to the cool wordplay that he gives to Susan here.

In order to reach such high levels of reliable generality, Calvin and her US Robots colleagues had to devise the simple calculus of the Three Laws of Robotics and then continually try out the balancing and interaction of the laws in all their combinations and permutations. Those continual games of "if this, then the next" consume the stories in *I, Robot* and provide a further resonance with Godwinian Necessity. Not only is the general outcome of such a grand scheme as Necessity or the "Machines" completely reliable and determined, but also the continual adjustments and "calculus" of the relations within the scheme are continually fascinating. It is as though Susan Calvin, Asimov, and any other such generalist and determinist has both nothing at stake and, at the same time, must always be making adjustments to their system. The belief in Necessity or in the overall general and benevolent outcome frees the "player," in fact, to manipulate the calculus of the game.

Calvinistic theology as well as Godwinian Necessity and Asimovian Robotics all liberate a sort of freeplay of will due to the most general sort of overall system. Such a paradox of free will existing within and because of a rigid system has been agonized over most by the theologians in ways that are inappropriate for this discussion, but the echoes from Godwin in the Enlightenment Asimov should be listened to if we are to hear the real effects of the Susan Calvin narratives. Here is a key passage from Godwin writing about Necessity—both the overall determinism and the individual moves in the calculus—that resounds all through the cool, hard work of Susan Calvin in *I, Robot*:

> ... if the doctrine of necessity do not annihilate virtue, it tends to introduce a great change into our ideas respecting it... . The believer in free-will, can expostulate with, or correct, his pupil, with faint and uncertain hopes, conscious that the clearest exhibition of truth is impotent, when brought into contest with the unhearing and indisciplinable faculty of will; or in reality, if he were consistent, secure that it could produce no effect. The necessarian on the contrary employs real antecedents, and has a right to expect real effects.

Godwin's matter-of-fact dismissal of free will as just too absurdly random suggests Asimov's firm ending to *I, Robot*, with its notion that the machines control all reactions but disguise this total control because they know that a full realization of total control would cause mental anguish or "harm" to humans. Similarly, the three Laws themselves (or three "rules" of robotics as they are labelled in the first story where Asimov mentions them explicitly—"Runaround") seem hardly profound or a great invention of the imagination. They are "neutral," as one recent critic has noted [see Alessandro Portells, "The Three Laws of Robotics: Laws of the Text, Laws of Production, Laws of Society," *Science Fiction Studies*, Vol. 7, 1980, pp. 150–56]. Over the years they have gone on to have almost a life of their own as "ideas" outside of the fiction. Usually they are listed and worded with a sort of Godwinian flatness and their position and function in *I, Robot* is forgotten or confused. It was in the 1942 *Astounding* story, however, and in a fictional dialogue between Powell and Donovan, who are the key "right stuff" associates of Calvin, that the Three Laws first appear:

> 'And three, a robot must protect its own existence as long as such protection does not conflict with the First or Second Laws.'

> 'Right! Now where are we?'

Donovan and Powell could figure out exactly where they were and did solve their problem on Mercury, but it would take more robot stories and finally the book *I, Robot* itself for Asimov to know what a fine gimmick he had invented. Finally, of course, he doctored all the stories in the "novel" so that they would be consistent with the Three Laws.

Further, just as Godwin paradoxically insists (like Calvin before him), that the believer in Necessity will work even harder to make things happen in this world, so Asimov's roboticists (and the robots themselves in his most recent fictions) never tire of discussing and trying to manipulate some implication of these three simple statements in relation to one another. The paradox is simply that the apparent certainty *liberates* continual and near-infinite permutations. Though, as in "Runaround," this continual balancing act often "strikes an equilibrium [whereby] . . . Rule 3 drives him back and Rule 2 drives him forward," the permutations of all the robots seem infinite. And so the accomplishment lies not only with the general outcome of "control" but also with the tinkering; it is a wonderful example of Asimov's inventiveness how complex and variable the Three Laws become.

Godwinian inclinations toward such clarity of analysis and such control may seem inhuman, even monstrous, so that Robotics itself, even though the Laws are benevolent towards humans, takes on the effects of the very *Frankenstein* motif that Asimov was trying to avoid. It is the continual acknowledgment of what I would call the calculus of complexity, however, that keeps Asimov himself lively and benevolent and "human" in his writing, especially his writing on the robots. He always is trying to teach and to clarify, and the material itself contains layer upon layer of complexity . . . .

Source: Donald M. Hassler, "Some Asimov Resonances from the Enlightenment," in *Science Fiction Studies*, Vol. 15, No. 44, March 1998, pp. 36–47.

SOURCES

Asimov, Isaac, *In Joy Still Felt: The Autobiography of Isaac Asimov*, Doubleday, 1980.

———, "The Machine That Won the War," in *Nightfall and Other Stories*, Doubleday, 1969, pp. 319–27.

———, *Nemesis*, Bantam, 1990, p. ix.

Batchelor, John, *H. G. Wells*, Cambridge University Press, 1985, pp. 113–22.

Bradbury, Ray, "There Will Come Soft Rains," in *The Martian Chronicles*, Doubleday, 1958, pp. 205–11.

Bryant, Peter, *Red Alert*, Ace, 1958.

Bucher, George H., "The Electric Home of the Future," in *Popular Mechanics*, Vol. 72, No. 2, August 1939, pp. 161–65.

Burdick, Eugene, and Harvey Wheeler, *Fail-Safe*, McGraw-Hill, 1962.

Dick, Philip K., "The Defenders," in *The Collected Stories of Philip K. Dick*, Carol, 1990, pp. 67–85.

"Doomsday Clock Overview," in *Bulletin of the Atomic Scientists*, http://www.thebulletin.org/content/doomsday-clock/overview (accessed September 14, 2010).

Gunn, James, *Isaac Asimov: The Foundations of Science Fiction*, Rowman & Littlefield, 2005, pp. 59, 65.

Miller, Marjorie Mithoff, "The Social Science Fiction of Isaac Asimov," in *Isaac Asimov*, edited by Joseph D. Olander and Martin Harry Greenberg, Taplinger, 1977, pp. 13–31, 207.

Olander, Joseph D., and Martin Harry Greenberg, *Isaac Asimov*, Taplinger, 1977.

O'Reagan, Gerald, *A Brief History of Computing*, Springer, 1996.

Samuelson, David N., "The Legendary Dr. Asimov," in *Science Fiction Studies*, Vol. 5, No. 1, March 1978, pp. 81–83.

Walker, Martin, *The Cold War: A History*, Holt, 1995.

White, Michael, *Isaac Asimov: A Life of the Grand Master of Science Fiction*, Carroll & Graf, 2005.

FURTHER READING

Asimov, Isaac, *Asimov's New Guide to Science*, Basic Books, 1984.
    Updated several times between 1960 and its final edition in 1984, this book is typical of the kind of educational writing that Asimov turned to during the cold war to make up the gap in science education he perceived between the United States and the Soviet Union.

———, *I. Asimov*, Doubleday, 1994.
    This autobiographical volume, published posthumously, covers fifty years of Asimov's life.

———, ed., *Machines That Think*, Allen Lane, 1984.
    This is a collection of science fiction stories about computer science collected and introduced by Asimov.

Edwards, Paul N., *The Closed World: Computers and the Politics of Discourse in Cold War America*, MIT Press, 1996.
    Edwards presents a history of early computer technology from a social perspective. The book is a history of the human perception of computers as much as of the machines themselves.

Hassler, Donald M., *Isaac Asimov*, Starmont House, 1992.

> This study of Asimov tends to associate Asimov's writings with the methodologies of the Enlightenment.

Upgren, Arthur, *Many Skies: Alternative Histories of the Sun, Moon, Planets, and Stars*, Rutgers University Press, 2005.

> In this highly inventive book, Upgren imagines in each chapter one slight and entirely plausible alteration of the night sky. For instance, what if our sun had a companion star, or what if Deneb and Vega switched their locations (making Deneb the second brightest object in the night sky after the Moon)? Upgren explores how these scenarios might have changed the history of astronomy and science on Earth.

SUGGESTED SEARCH TERMS

Isaac Asimov

The Machine That Won the War

science fiction

cold war

science fiction AND cold war

Deneb

mutual assured destruction

first strike

hyperspace

punch card

stellar evolution

The Norwegian Rat

NAGUIB MAHFOUZ

1984

First published in Arabic in 1984, Naguib Mahfouz's "The Norwegian Rat" is a striking example of both social realism and magic realism. The short story, like most of Mahfouz's works, takes place in urban Cairo, Egypt, reflecting the author's own experiences in the city. It examines the lives of ordinary people in an apartment building, painting a picture of social realism, but the author adds elements of mysticism to create a political commentary on the government and bureaucracy. Denys Johnson-Davies translated "The Norwegian Rat" and other short stories by Mahfouz into English for the 1991 collection *The Time and the Place and Other Stories*.

AUTHOR BIOGRAPHY

Mahfouz was born on December 11, 1911, in Gamaleyya, a section of Cairo, Egypt. He was the youngest of seven children. Although he came from a large family, a large age gap separated Mahfouz from his four brothers and two sisters. He grew up in a traditional, middle-class Muslim family and enjoyed visiting museums with his mother, which prompted a love of history. The Egyptian Revolution of 1919 against the British had a profound impact on his life and view of the world. He supported Egyptian nationalism and later democracy, a fact that is apparent in many of his writings.

Naguib Mahfouz (AP Images)

He attended King Fouad I University, which would later become the University of Cairo, from 1930 to 1934 and graduated with a degree in philosophy. Mahfouz attended a graduate program for one year before quitting to become a writer. Although he wrote throughout his college career, his work was not published until 1939. Mahfouz also held several positions in civil service while writing, until he retired in 1972. He married late in life so he could focus on his writing, and he and his wife had two daughters.

Mahfouz adapted the Western novel and short story to Egyptian culture. Most of his early works were historical novels, and he gained popularity as a writer with the publication of his *Cairo Trilogy* in 1956. He held the attention of his readers by shifting to modern social realism and examining life in Egypt in the twentieth century. A few of his books were translated into English in the 1980s and 1990s, including *The Time and the Place and Other Stories*, the collection containing "The Norwegian Rat." Winning the Nobel Prize for Literature in 1988, however, brought him global recognition. He was the first Arabic writer to be awarded the prize, and he was surprised by the honor. In

fact, Mahfouz admitted in an interview with the *Paris Review* that he believed "the Nobel was a Western prize."

Despite his popularity as a writer, Mahfouz had detractors in Islamic fundamentalist circles. His novel *Children of Gebelawi* was banned in most countries in the Middle East, including Egypt. It was, however, published in Lebanon in 1967. Mahfouz was placed on a "kill list" for his political and religious views. In 1994, he was attacked by religious extremists and stabbed in the neck. He survived the murder attempt but spent the rest of his life with bodyguards. Mahfouz died in Cairo, after a fall, on August 30, 2006.

PLOT SUMMARY

Mahfouz's "The Norwegian Rat" is a tale of both domestic realism and magical realism. A nameless narrator tells the story, and only one character possesses a name. The narrator begins the story when he attends a tenants' meeting held by Mr. A. M., who is the senior householder of an apartment building. The few tenants are assembled to discuss the potential invasion of Norwegian rats into their city and building. The news and gossip describe the rats as dangerous. In fact, they are reported to attack both cats and humans. The group fears that the rats will destroy their homes.

To prevent the destruction, Mr. A. M. advises that the tenants proactively prepare for the invasion of Norwegian rats. He instructs all of the tenants to follow his instructions, which he promises are also the instructions of the Governor. Mr. A. M. admonishes them not to rely on him or the government completely. The tenants agree to follow his instructions, even though they will have to pay for the recommended traps, cats, and poison themselves. Mr. A. M. quotes from the Koran to encourage their cooperation.

The narrator describes the attitude of the tenants after the first meeting. They are grateful to Mr. A. M., but they are also obsessed with the rats and consider the causes of the potential infestation. The reasons people give for the rats range from empty towns, to the government, to the High Dam, to the wrath of God. The rats come to embody all of the tenants' problems, as the narrator explains that the rats "engross us as life's main difficulty."

At the second meeting at Mr. A. M.'s home, the tenants report that no Norwegian rats have been caught or seen in the traps. One tenant reports catching a local rat, and Mr. A. M. warns him that all rats are dangerous. He also justifies the cost of feeding the additional cats by saying that "this is of little importance when we think of our safety and security." He then introduces a new poison and tells the tenants to place it in the kitchen and other "vulnerable places." The poison is a risk, and Mr. A. M. acknowledges that there is a chance that children or animals could be killed by it.

Again, the tenants obey the directives of Mr. A. M. The responsibility for preventing an invasion of Norwegian rats falls directly on the tenants, and the tension mounts as they wait for the rats to come. On top of the tension and stress of everyday life, the new poison kills a few animals, specifically a cat and some chickens. Meanwhile, the narrator hears more rumors about the rats from a man at the bus stop. The man tells him that "the rats have annihilated an entire village." The man seems convinced that the news is true even though there is no news of it in the media. The man's demeanor and the news of the rats make the narrator consider the Norwegian rats to be the end of the world. The narrator again questions why God would allow the rats to come.

Things begin to unravel at the third meeting with Mr. A. M. As the tenants suffer from the stress of fighting an unseen enemy, the senior householder's mood is "cheerful." He explains that the Governor is happy with their work and reminds them that their losses are few as he admonishes them not to make the same mistakes with the poison that resulted in the animals dying. This is the first meeting in which a tenant blatantly complains about the job of preparing for the rats. His main complaint is about their nerves, but Mr. A. M. refuses to listen and accuses the tenant of trying to spoil their success. With the tenant silenced, Mr. A. M. gives the group their latest instructions.

The tenants are now required to keep the doors and windows closed at all times, regardless of the temperature, and to board up any space "through which a mere straw could pass." The only time the windows are to be opened is when they are cleaning, and a man is supposed to wait at the window with a stick to guard against rats.

Mr. A. M. reminds the tenants that they are at war with the rats when one tenant notes that living in closed-off spaces makes them virtual prisoners. Mr. A. M. also reminds the men that a rat infestation would lead to an epidemic of disease as well as destruction of property.

Following the meeting, the mental state of the tenants deteriorates even further. As they wait for the rats to appear, the tenants become depressed and bored. They begin to fight with each other and also with their families. The tenants obsess about news of Norwegian rats, and they live under constant fear of the rats' arrival.

At the final meeting with Mr. A. M., the tenants learn that experts from the bureaucracy are checking on the buildings to determine their risk for rat infestations. At first the tenants hope that the experts will help them with their work and alleviate the stress that is making them so miserable. The tenants do not see a bureaucrat immediately. They are informed, however, that a bureaucrat did come visit and was pleased with the number of cats at the building.

After a week, an expert from the bureaucracy, making his inspection of the building, visits the narrator. The narrator is amused by the bureaucrat's appearance because he reminds the narrator of a cat. The bureaucrat arrives before the narrator and his wife have had time to eat their lunch and is pleased overall with his inspection of their flat. His only order is to close a window that is screened with wire because "the Norwegian rat can gnaw through wire." The narrator invites the bureaucrat to lunch and tells the visitor that he and his wife have already eaten.

The bureaucrat agrees to eat lunch at their house, and he has a voracious appetite. The couple leave their guest to eat in privacy, but the narrator does check on the bureaucrat to offer him another helping of food. The narrator is startled by what he sees. The bureaucrat's face ceases to resemble a cat as he eats, and he takes on the features of a rat. The narrator leaves the bureaucrat and tells his wife to make their guest comfortable without informing her of what he saw. When his wife returns from checking on the bureaucrat, she looks pale and confirms the narrator's suspicions. The bureaucrat leaves and blesses their house. The last thing that the narrator sees is the bureaucrat's "Norwegian smile."

CHARACTERS

The Bureaucrat

The bureaucrat is an expert assigned to assess buildings for potential Norwegian rat infestations.

He appears late in the tale, and when he first arrives to inspect the narrator's home, he resembles a cat. It is important to note that he is the only character the narrator provides with a physical description. The narrator sees "a middle-aged, sturdily built man with a thick mustache, his square face with its short snub nose and glassy stare reminding me of a cat." At first, the bureaucrat's appearance amuses the narrator.

His inspection of the narrator's home coincides with lunch, and he sniffs the air to smell the food after noting one infraction. There is the possibility that the bureaucrat scheduled his inspection during lunch on purpose. The narrator asks the bureaucrat to stay and eat. The bureaucrat eats both helpings of the couple's lunch greedily. His features change with this act of excess, and the narrator and his wife both notice that he comes to resemble a rat. This metamorphosis is an example of magic realism because it is something fantastic that occurs in a realistic setting.

The Concierge

The concierge gives the residents news from the bureaucrat and informs the narrator and his wife when they have the honor of being inspected by the bureaucrat.

Mr. A. M.

Mr. A. M. is the senior householder who takes authority over the other tenants in the building when faced with the Norwegian rat crisis.

He is the only character in the short story that the narrator names. He is also older and wealthier than his peers in the building. Egyptian culture traditionally grants respect to older members of society, and Mr. A. M. is given a great deal of respect from the other tenants, who are willing to follow his instructions in the beginning. The narrator describes the gratitude that the tenants first feel toward Mr. A. M.'s willingness to guide them at the first meeting. As well as being the oldest and wealthiest man in the building, Mr. A. M. has connections to the local government. He is friends with the Governor, and he speaks with authority concerning the coming Norwegian rat invasion.

Mr. A. M. is a member of the upper middle class, and as the tenants emotionally break down under the pressure of waiting for the rats to invade, he remains focused and occasionally cheerful. He refuses to listen to tenants complain about the effect of the preparations on their nerves or how his instructions are limiting their freedom. He gives orders and expects his orders to be obeyed because they are in a war. The narrator is careful to distinguish Mr. A. M. from the other tenants. It would not be easy for most of Mahfouz's readers to identify with the controlled and attentive householder. Mr. A. M.'s reaction to the impending disaster distinguishes him from the crowd. His directions, however, cause the tenants to deteriorate emotionally. After the third meeting with Mr. A. M., the tenants are submissive, but the narrator no longer describes them as grateful. The tension of waiting for the rats to invade affects the every relationship, including the relationship between the tenants and their senior householder.

The Narrator

The narrator tells the story, but he never reveals his name and does not describe himself in any way.

The audience does not know the age or occupation of the narrator. He counts himself part of a collective with the other tenants in his building. The common enemy, the Norwegian rat, unites them all. The narrator uses the pronouns "we" and "us" in the narrative to explain the effects of preparing for the Norwegian rats. For example, "As time went on we became more and more tense and alert, and the suspense weighed heavily on us." The narrator represents everyman in the story. His questions about the causes of the rat infestation are everyone's questions. He mirrors the anxiety of his neighbors.

The narrator struggles with fear and with his faith. He questions the reasons why God would allow the plague of rats. The narrator describes quintessential human responses to adversity. Unlike the unfaltering Mr. A. M., the narrator reacts emotionally. By creating such a nondescript character, Mahfouz makes it easier for the audience to relate to the narrator.

Tradition dictates that the narrator and the other tenants have to follow the directions of Mr. A. M. The narrator finds it easy to play his role in the beginning of the story; however, this changes over time. As part of a collective, the nameless tenants who voice anxiety or frustration echo the narrator's own feelings. The narrator and other tenants become obsessed with news of Norwegian rats, and they wait for the invasion to come.

The narrator uses the pronoun "I" only twice. The first time is when he describes a conversation with a neighbor at a bus stop. The neighbor increases the narrator's anxiety about the rats by telling him about a village being destroyed by them. The second incident of the narrator using the first person is when he meets the bureaucrat. The narrator's observations of the bureaucrat are his own. No other tenants are there to witness the transformation of the bureaucrat. Only the narrator's wife is there to see what happens, and her confused response mirrors his own.

The Narrator's Wife

The narrator's wife serves as his witness to confirm the change in the bureaucrat.

The Neighbor

The narrator's neighbor tells him at a bus stop that the rats destroyed a neighboring village, and he is convinced that the news is true even though it is not confirmed.

The Tenants

The tenants are part of a collective, and the narrator refers to anyone who speaks with Mr. A. M. as "one of us."

THEMES

Fear

"The Norwegian Rat" examines the effect of fear on the lives of the people in the story. Fear is a common theme in the later works of Mahfouz. In this brief narrative, Mahfouz examines how the fear of the rats invading their city and their building takes its toll on the narrator and his fellow tenants. The Norwegian rats are the enemy, but they never make an appearance in the short story. It is the fear of the rats' coming rather than an actual attack that causes the tenants to panic. The fear of the unknown weighs on the tenants, and they begin to imagine the worst possible scenario.

As the tenants deteriorate mentally, one asks the crucial question: "When will the rats begin their attack?" The potential for Norwegian rats to invade and the attempts to prepare for their attack mirrors the fear and uncertainty associated with the ongoing Arab-Israeli conflicts. The tenants are not soldiers, and they are not trained to handle the threat of imminent danger.

Mahfouz leaves the episode with the bureaucrat open to the reader's interpretation. Either the bureaucrat literally transforms into the rat or the stress of the situation has caused the narrator and his wife to hallucinate the entire incident. Considering the emotional state of the tenants after waiting for the rats, it is not difficult to believe that living in a constant state of fear can reduce the narrator to a state of hysteria.

Egyptian Culture

Mahfouz describes Egyptian culture in all of his writings, and "The Norwegian Rat" is no exception. The multiple political changes throughout the author's life and their impact on Egyptian culture are apparent in his short stories. Even when facing a threat, there are some aspects of the culture that do not change. For example, Mr. A. M. is given the respect that both his age and position afford him. He leads the tenants, who work together. The narrator also illustrates traditional Egyptian culture by asking the bureaucrat to stay to lunch, even if it means that he and his wife go without theirs. This act of hospitality is not uncommon in the narrator's culture and is to be expected.

The tenants' culture, however, is threatened by outside elements. As the tenants prepare for the rat invasion, their convictions become vulnerable. The gratitude that the tenants feel toward their leader fades into simple submission as they begin to question their circumstances. They question the reason for the rats, when the rats will come, and who will help them. The loss of confidence in their leadership leaves them in a state of fear and confusion.

Bureaucracy

"The Norwegian Rat" explores the bureaucracy of Egypt in the 1970s. The leadership that the narrator encounters offers him little consolation in a time of stress. The Governor, through Mr. A. M., has cost the tenants money for the supplies needed to fight the Norwegian rats. Mr. A. M. advises the tenants not to expect too much support, but he still expects them to take orders. The Governor and Mr. A. M. do nothing to help

TOPICS FOR FURTHER STUDY

- Read *The Metamorphosis* by Franz Kafka. Compare its elements of magic realism with "The Norwegian Rat." Create a social network page (Facebook, Twitter, MySpace) for the bureaucrat and have him discuss their individual metamorphoses with Gregor on the message board.

- Read the book *Terror in the Name of God: Why Religious Militants Kill* by Jessica Stern, one of the Outstanding Books for the College Bound and Lifelong Learners in 2009. Compare the author's observations with Mahfouz's experiences. Write a scene for a play in which he and Stern meet. What would they say to each other? How are their views similar, and how are they different? Record or perform your scene for the class. Invite classmates to watch and review your scene on your blog site.

- Research the Arab-Israeli conflict that began when Israel became a nation in 1948. Create a multimedia presentation or video documentary covering the causes and effects of the conflict in Egypt between 1967 and 1980. Make sure that you include a time line of Mahfouz's work as part of the documentary.

- Research Norwegian rats using print and online sources. Write a paper that compares the information in the short story with your research. Insert into your paper several charts, graphs, and images to illustrate the information you are presenting.

- Read *Egyptian Tales and Short Stories of the 1970s and 1980s.* Edited by William M. Hutchins, this is a diverse collection of short stories, most suitable for young adult readers, written by many of Mahfouz's contemporaries. Choose a short story from the book to compare and contrast with "The Norwegian Rat." Write a review for both stories. Create a chart for each review that includes the date of the piece, relevant background information, themes, and writing styles found in the story. Post to your blog site and invite comments from classmates who have read the stories.

---

the tenants directly. In fact, the tenants face increasingly strict restrictions as the story progresses. The idea of a bureaucrat inspecting the building gives the narrator hope "that we would be able to relieve ourselves of some of the distress we had been suffering."

When the narrator finally meets with the actual bureaucrat, all of his hopes are destroyed. The bureaucrat only serves to point out an infraction, which further limits the freedom of the narrator and his wife. Rather than helping him fight the rats, the bureaucrat behaves like one and eats the narrator's food without regard for the narrator's needs or condition. By his act of greed, the bureaucrat literally transforms in front of the narrator. He now views the bureaucracy as a source of loss than a source of help, and he remarks on the bureaucrat's "Norwegian smile."

STYLE

Short Story

"The Norwegian Rat" is one of Mahfouz's many short stories. Short stories are one of the oldest forms of storytelling in literature and are defined as a concise fictional prose narrative that can be read in one sitting. "The Norwegian Rat" is a short-short story. This is the definition given to stories that are shorter than 12,000 words in length. Long-short stories are between 12,000 and 15,000 words.

By creating a short-short story that does not require his audience to wade though pages of back story, Mahfouz can easily keep the attention of his readers and elicit an emotional response. The short story shows how quickly life changes for the tenants, and the abbreviated length makes the mental collapse of his narrator

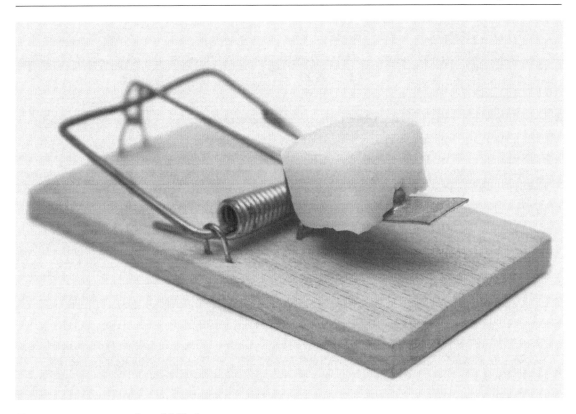

Traps were set to catch and kill the rats. (*Marc Dietrich | Shutterstock.com*)

especially dramatic. Rather than deteriorating over hundreds of pages, the narrator deteriorates in a few thousand words.

Social Realism

Mahfouz is known for incorporating social realism into his novels. "The Norwegian Rat" and other short stories also use social realism. Social realism in literature shows the reality of ordinary, working-class citizens. This literary form first became popular in the 1930s. It shows the flaws in society and human nature and is popular with writers who support ideas of socialism.

In the short story, Mahfouz describes the view of ordinary tenants as they prepare for rats to invade. The story is set in a typical middle-class building in Cairo. The narrator's story could happen to anyone. Social realism allows Mahfouz's audience to connect with and understand the characters. It also shows the familiar flaws in the bureaucracy and the effect of inflation and conflict on Egyptian society at the time.

Magical Realism

"The Norwegian Rat" is an example of magic realism. Magic realism employs realistic or mundane settings, but a supernatural, magical, or mystical element enters these settings. This occurs in "The Norwegian Rat" when the bureaucrat transforms before the narrator and his wife. By adding magic at the end of a realistic story, the author allows the reader to interpret whether or not the narrator imagined everything. Magic realism also creates a dramatic ending that is difficult to forget.

Among other critics, Ahmad Muhammad 'Atiyya notes in the essay "Naguib Mahfouz and the Short Story," published in *Critical Perspectives on Naguib Mahfouz*, that Mahfouz's short stories written after 1967 move "beyond the reality into surrealism." Salman Rushdie is a contemporary of Mahfouz whose works also display elements of magic realism.

HISTORICAL CONTEXT

1967 Arab-Israeli War

Roger Allen explains in his article "Contemporary Egyptian Literature," published in the *Middle East Journal*, that "political factors have regrettably to be added to that complex set of

COMPARE
&
CONTRAST

- **1970s:** Egypt is a founding member of the Arab League, created in 1945 to protect and promote the interests of Arab countries.

  1980s: Egypt is removed from the Arab League in 1979 in response to Egyptian President Anwar Sadat's negotiations with Israel.

  Today: Egypt is again part of the Arab League after rejoining in 1989. The Arab League's headquarters are located in Cairo.

- **1970s:** The hydroelectric aspects of the Aswan High Dam are still being constructed in the early 1970s. The dam is completed in 1976.

  1980s: The Aswan High Dam is complete and functioning.

  Today: The Aswan High Dam irrigates crops and provides hydroelectric power, but erosion and flooding are still problems along the Nile River.

- **1970s:** The Arab-Israeli conflict continues, and the Soviet Union funds the Egyptian military. The United States provides assistance to Israel.

  1980s: The Egyptian-Israeli Peace Treaty is signed in 1979.

  Today: There is still tension with Israel. America provides financial aid to both the Egyptian military and the Israeli military.

issues within which any assessment of post-1967 Egyptian literature has to be placed." After the Arab rejection of Israel once it became a nation in 1948, the tension between Israel and surrounding Arab nations led to many violent encounters. The 1967 Arab-Israeli War (also called the Third Arab-Israeli War or Six-Day War) officially began when Egyptian President Gamal Abdel Nasser posted a blockade on Israel's port at the Strait of Tiran. Jordan and Syria, Israel's neighbors, supported the Egyptian blockade. Israeli troops successfully removed all troops from their territory and actually increased the nation's borders after six official days of fighting. Israel captured the Sinai Peninsula from Egypt in the war, but the 1967 conflict did nothing to mend the strain between Egypt and Israel. In fact, after the fighting was finished, most Arab nations still refused to recognize the sovereignty of Israel.

Egyptian literature after 1967 reflected the feelings of insecurity and the threat of potential danger. Thousands of Egyptians lost their lives in battle, and the continuing hostility between the nations meant that the conflict was not officially over. Mahfouz explores the fear of an uncertain future in many of his later writings,

and several take on violent imagery. Written in 1984, "The Norwegian Rat" explores the fear of impending conflict.

1973 Arab-Israeli War

The 1973 Arab-Israeli War (also known as the Fourth Arab-Israeli War, Ramadan War, Yom Kippur War, or October War) was inevitable after the defeat of Egypt in 1967 and began on October 6, 1973. Syria and Egypt entered into the war with Israel, and the Soviet Union and America intervened. The Soviet Union sent weapons to Egypt, and America sent weapons to Israel. During the conflict, Egypt was able to cross the Suez Canal into the Sinai Peninsula. Egypt suffered heavy losses, but the ability to cross into the Sinai Peninsula was a source of pride to Egyptians, according to Ahmed S. Khalidi in his article "The War of Attrition" in the *Journal of Palestine Studies*. The war ended on October 25, 1973, when both the Soviet Union and the United States intervened to enforce the cease-fire ordered by the United Nations (UN).

Following the war, a stretch of the Sinai Peninsula became a UN buffer zone. Israel withdrew from some of its occupied land in the

We had cats in the stairwells, on the roofs, and by the front doors. *(Jiri Vaclavek | Shutterstock.com)*

peninsula in 1975 and 1976 after signing the Sinai II peace treaty, negotiated by U.S. Secretary of State Henry Kissinger, to improve relationships with the United States. This adjusted the buffer zone and added more land to the Egyptian zone.

Aswan High Dam

For centuries, the river Nile has been known for its seasonal floods and droughts. Since antiquity, people in Egypt have attempted to manage the river that is so important to the agriculture of the region. The first Aswan Dam was constructed in 1902 under British occupation and was raised twice, in 1912 and 1934. According to Richard Elliot Benedick in his article "The High Dam and the Transformation of the Nile," published in the *Middle East Journal*, early attempts to dam the Nile were not completely successful. The old Aswan Dam "was simply unable to contain the massive volumes of water and accompanying silt at the peak of the Nile flood," wrote Benedick.

The Egyptian population doubled between 1897 and World War II, development was

growing, and the water supply was uncertain. Building the new High Dam at Aswan kept the water it collected under the control of Egypt. The Soviet Union helped design and finance the project, which began in 1960 and was completed in the mid-1970s. While the country needed water to support its growing population, there were serious concerns over the environmental and cultural impact of building the dam. "The Norwegian Rat" reflects the concern people had over the spread of pests and diseases.

CRITICAL OVERVIEW

Mahfouz is primarily known for his novels, which are the focus of most of his critics. His body of work, however, also included short stories, plays, and screenplays. He wrote short stories throughout his career. Miriam Cooke, writing in the *Middle East Journal*, divides the author's work into four periods. The 1930s to the 1940s were devoted to short stories and historical novels, while the mid-1940s to the 1950s represented his social realism period. Stories written from the mid-1950s to 1967 showed the purpose of life, and stories written after 1967 examined the reality of Egyptian politics. Published in 1984, "The Norwegian Rat" falls into the last period.

His short stories illustrate life in Cairo during decades of change. *The Time and the Place and Other Stories* is a collection of twenty years of Mahfouz's work. The style and themes in this collection are easy for Western readers to understand and enjoy because they are familiar. John Haywood, a reviewer for *World Literature Today*, describes the dry humor of this collection as being "in the spirit of classical anecdotes" and observes that it "is widely represented in modern literature." Mahfouz experimented with style in his later stories, such as the "Norwegian Rat." 'Atiyya explains in "Naguib Mahfouz and the Short Story" that Mahfouz "has given up the traditional narrative tale and devoted himself to the extrasensory, to anxiety and to confused visions." The style for this story is easy for readers of Franz Kafka and James Joyce to understand regardless of their cultural background.

At the beginning of his career, Mahfouz gained popularity in Egypt and neighboring countries through his historical fiction and the *Cairo Trilogy*. Roger Allen explains in his article "Contemporary Egyptian Literature" that "Mahfouz's works have been widely read throughout the Arab world, and during this period he undoubtedly became the most famous literary figure in the region." Religious extremists criticized some of Mahfouz's work as offensive to Islam. In fact, his book *The Children of Gebelawi* was banned in Egypt. This did not prevent its publication in Lebanon, however, or seriously damage his reputation as a writer.

Mahfouz is credited with making the Egyptian novel popular and continued to have devoted readers in Egypt and neighboring countries throughout his career. His work has remained relevant by reflecting the continuing changes that Egypt has faced. Mahfouz won global recognition for his work when he was awarded the Nobel Prize for Literature in 1988, and many of his books and short stories were translated into different languages to supply the growing demand for his fiction.

CRITICISM

April Dawn Paris

Paris is a freelance writer with a bachelor's degree in classics and a minor in English. In the following essay, she argues that "The Norwegian Rat" explores the theme of freedom and what happens when freedom is lost.

Mahfouz sets his story in an ordinary building filled with nondescript, nameless individuals, yet he uses this venue to examine humanity. As Roger Allen explains in an article for *World Literature Today*, within this mundane setting, Mahfouz "shows a continuing and particular concern for such questions as the nature of madness, the alienation of modern man and his search for consolation, and the role of religion in contemporary societies." Within his observations of humankind's psyche, Mahfouz explores the theme of individual freedom and its impact on society.

When asked by Charlotte El Shabrawy, in her interview "Naguib Mahfouz, The Art of Fiction No. 129" for the *Paris Review*, what topic was the closest to his heart, Mahfouz answered, "Freedom." The idea of freedom resonates throughout Mahfouz's writing, and "The Norwegian Rat" is no exception. The political unrest in Egypt during the 1970s due to the Arab-Israeli wars is also echoed in the short story. As often happens in times of conflict, people give up their freedom to promote safety. In order to survive the coming invasion and preserve their homes, the narrator and other tenants willingly sacrifice their personal freedoms, but this sacrifice also costs them their emotional stability. They slowly lose their individual freedom as they wait and prepare for an enemy that never appears in the story.

The narrator and tenants of the building meet with their leader, Mr. A. M., throughout the narrative. Mr. A. M. and the tenants exercise two separate levels of authority. Mr. A. M. has greater authority because of his age and wealth, and he describes himself as someone speaking for the Governor. Still, he alternates between acting as part of the ruling class and identifying himself as one of the tenants. As the one of the tenants, he uses the pronoun "we" to encourage the men to action. For example, when the tenants first discuss the Norwegian rats, Mr. A. M. says, "we are not alone." Later in that same conversation, however, he identifies himself with the Governor and says, "We are with you, . . . but do not rely upon

WHAT DO I READ NEXT?

- *The Kite Runner*, a novel by Khaled Hosseini published in 2003 by Riverhead, explores the impact of political changes in Afghanistan on the lives of ordinary people. The book examines politics, culture, family, and religion.

- *Voices from the Other World* is another English collection of short stories by Mahfouz. Published in 2002 by American University in Cairo Press, its stories are examples of the historical fiction that dominated the author's early writing.

- George Orwell's *Animal Farm* was published in 1945 and is often read in high school literature courses. It is not realism but uses magical elements to make political observations about life in Communist Russia under the leadership of Joseph Stalin.

- *Naguib Mahfouz: His Life and Times* is a biography by Rasheed El-Enany, published in 2007 by the American University in Cairo Press. This biography outlines Mahfouz's life and body of work in light of the political and cultural environment in Egypt.

- *Homeland: The Illustrated History of the State of Israel* by Marv Wolfman, Mario Ruiz, and William J. Rubin is a Sydney Taylor Notable book and a National Jewish Book Award Winner. This nonfiction book was published in 2007 by Nachshon Press and examines the history, politics, and religion of Israel as well as the conflicts that they still spark.

- Anthony Gorman's 2010 book *Historians, State and Politics in Twentieth Century Egypt: Contesting the Nation* is a nonfiction book that examines the impact of Egyptian politics on academia, particularly in interpreting literature.

- *The Meaning of Consuelo* by Judith Ortiz Cofer, published by Farrar, Straus & Giroux, was the winner of the 2003 Américas Award. This is a fictional account of a girl who observes the impact of Operation Bootstrap on those around her. Set in Puerto Rico in the 1950s, the story presents her view of the social unrest in a manner similar to the narrator in "The Norwegian Rat."

---

us wholly." The stress of the situation takes a great toll on the tenants who are on the front line against the rats, while Mr. A. M. remains calm throughout the situation.

The tenants' loss of freedom does not occur immediately, and in the beginning, they are grateful to Mr. A. M. for leading them. Their first assignment is to employ traditional measures for preventing rats, specifically traps, poison, and cats. It is apparent, however, that the tenants do not have the authority to determine the course of action used to ward off the rat invasion. When one tenant points out that the Norwegian rats attack cats, Mr. A. M. dismisses his objection on the grounds that "cats are not without their use." The tenants do not seem pleased with the extra cats because of the extra money it costs to feed

them. But they do not have the freedom to refuse the cats, and the cost of their upkeep comes out of the tenants' finances, not the authorities.' They are told that the sacrifice must be made to protect their security.

The second meeting with Mr. A. M. adds one more aspect to the tenants' duties. He orders them to use a newer and more deadly poison. Using this poison is risky. Mr. A. M. admits that mistakes could cost the lives of children and animals, but he claims that the risk is worth it. The tenants do not even attempt to argue against using this type of poison, even when there is no sign of Norwegian rats near their home. At this point, they are still too frightened by the rats to argue. At this meeting, Mr. A. M. classifies Egyptian rats as dangerous, and finding one in the trap

> WITHIN HIS OBSERVATIONS OF
> HUMANKIND'S PSYCHE, MAHFOUZ EXPLORES
> THE THEME OF INDIVIDUAL FREEDOM AND ITS
> IMPACT ON SOCIETY."

justifies their extreme measures. The poison does cost the lives of some animals, and the stress gradually becomes too much for the tenants to handle.

Between the second and third meetings, the narrator and other people become so obsessed with the idea of Norwegian rats invading that they are willing to accept unsubstantiated information as proof of their impending doom. Unlike Mr. A. M., they are not pleased with their tedious efforts. The third meeting with the senior householder shows the emotional strain on the tenants as well as their disillusionment with their leader. The loss of personal freedom becomes apparent at the third meeting, and feelings of gratitude have faded.

Mr. A. M. dismisses the stress of the tenants as trivial when compared to their success. He is not able to give the tenants a direct answer about the position of the rats and believes that it does not matter as long as the residents are "prepared for the battle." At this meeting, the imagery of rats as military opponents is obvious. Mr. A. M. refuses to listen to the concerns of the tenants, and he imposes rules that further limit their personal freedoms and individual choices.

The tenants are now to keep the building sealed at all times, on top of their other responsibilities. Mr. A. M. orders that each "flat should be left like a firmly closed box, whatever the weather." This new condition means that the tenants will live under harsher conditions than prisoners do, as one tenant points out. Basically, entering their homes completely cuts the tenants off from the rest of the world. Even the simple act of opening a window is taken from them. Doing so would leave the entire building open to rats that they have yet to see. Interestingly, the tenants do nothing to fight the new rule. One person does break the silence by saying, "It's

impossible to go on like that." Nevertheless, Mr. A. M. continues to ignore their concerns.

The tenants submit to the new directive and silently do as they are ordered. Living under the fear of a rat invasion and the growing restrictions placed on them by their leader, the tenants deteriorate even more. They fall into a state of depression and anxiety. Their new living conditions make them irritable. The narrator describes a situation in which the men are short-tempered with their families and each other. The tenants suffer in silence, hoping that someone or something will come help them.

The fourth and final meeting brings some hope to the tenants. Here, Mr. A. M. informs them of the new experts coming to inspect the buildings. He is quick to point out that the experts from the bureaucracy are helping them "without any demand for additional rates." Again, the tenants are funding their own misery. The tenants believe that this will mean less work for them, but the bureaucrat assigned to their building does little to help them or restore any sense of normalcy. His first inspection is of the outer structures. His only comments following the inspection are to praise the cats on the premises and to order the concierge to contact him if they find a single rat, regardless of whether it is Egyptian or Norwegian. The new leader of their cause is just another person issuing orders.

The final scene, in which the bureaucrat inspects the narrator's home, is enlightening. It confirms that the narrator and tenants can expect no help from the bureaucracy.

After the third tenant's meeting, the narrator describes their collective vision of the Norwegian rat as having a "huge body, long whiskers, and alarming glassy look." When the narrator meets the bureaucrat, he compares the stranger to a cat. It is interesting to note that he first describes the bureaucrat in terms that mirror his description of a Norwegian rat: "I found myself standing before a middle-aged, sturdily built man with a thick mustache, his square face with its short snub nose and glassy stare reminding me of a cat."

The bureaucrat places more restrictions on the narrator's household. After inspecting all the doors and windows, the bureaucrat orders a window that is covered by a wire mesh to be closed. Covering a window with wire mesh is not against Mr. A. M.'s rules as long as the holes are smaller than a straw. The narrator's wife had been cooking lunch and opened the window to cool the

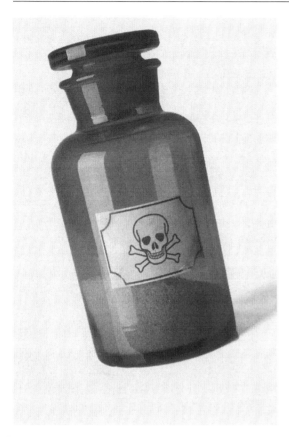

Poison was mixed with corn meal as a means of extermination. *(Jiri Hera | Shutterstock.com)*

Source: April Dawn Paris, Critical Essay on "The Norwegian Rat," in *Short Stories for Students*, Gale, Cengage Learning, 2011.

Matti Moosa

In the following essay, Moosa chronologically traces Mahfouz's contributions to Arabic literature.

Among the major figures in the development of modern Arabic fiction, none has received higher international acclaim than Naguib Mahfouz, who in 1988 became the first Arab writer to win the Nobel Prize for literature. Before then he was—like Tahn Husayn (d. 1973) and Tawfiq al-Hakim (d. 1987)—known in the West only to a very limited audience despite an output that includes over thirty novels and a number of short-story collections and plays. In fact, until the 1940's, Mahfouz was little known even in his native Egypt, where he began his literary career as an essayist. He gained some fame with the publication of three historical novels, but his undisputed literary renown came from a series of realistic contemporary novels in which he portrayed various aspects of life in Cairo. *Al-Thulathiyya (The Trilogy)*, published in 1956–57, was immediately seen as a major achievement and brought him wide recognition in literary circles outside Egypt.

Mahfouz was born into a middle-class family, the youngest of seven children. Though he seldom discusses his early life, it appears that he grew up in a solid family environment with happily married parents whom he loved and respected and who nurtured his intellectual interests, particularly in ancient history. He also took an interest in politics, soccer, and composing poetry in both traditional and free verse. He began reading Arabic translations of Western detective stories and historical novels, and then the works of prominent Egyptian writers. After completing his formal education, he concentrated on the masterpieces of Western literature.

Mahfouz began his literary career in high school, writing essays on various topics in philosophy and literature, along with an occasional short story. Initially viewing philosophy more important than literature, he eventually chose fiction only after he saw his short stories being readily accepted for publication. Even so, he spent the years from 1930 to 1945 largely in writing essays, and his first short-story collection, *Hams al-Junun (The Whisper of Madness)*, did not appear until 1938.

kitchen. She attempts to protest but is cut off. Just like Mr. A. M., the bureaucrat expects his orders to be obeyed without question. He does, however, offer an explanation for his demand by insisting that Norwegian rats can eat through wire.

This final loss of personal freedom in his own home changes the narrator's point of view. The bureaucrat shows his true nature by planning his inspection during lunch. Custom dictates that the narrator should be hospitable to the bureaucrat and invite him to stay, which is what happens. When the bureaucrat takes advantage of the situation, he literally transforms before the narrator and his wife.

The bureaucrat flashes a "Norwegian smile" as he leaves, and the narrator sees that losing his individual freedom to protect himself from the unseen enemy leaves him vulnerable to a danger closer to home. He loses more to the dictates of Mr. A. M. and the bureaucrats than to the Norwegian rats.

His first philosophical essay, "Ihtidar Mu'taqadat wa Tawallud Mu'taqadat" ("The Death and Birth of Doctrines"), appeared in Salama Musa's periodic *al-Majalla al-Jadida* (*The New Periodical*) in October 1930. In it Mahfouz points out that life is subject to constant change and evolution, which man must accept as the inevitable result of civilization. Yet man is also by nature a believer who needs religious faith or an acceptable substitute to achieve tranquility and happiness.

Though imported Western doctrines like socialism and communism had been finding some acceptance among the intelligentsia, Mahfouz desired an egalitarian system which would benefit the majority while not offending Muslim believers, something between capitalism and communism. He settled on moderate socialism but recognized that, while it can fulfill some of man's material needs, it cannot bring him spiritual happiness. In the late 1960's, when an interviewer suggested that Mahfouz appeared to sympathize with Marxism, he expressed antipathy toward the materialistic tenets on which it is based and doubt about its workability. In his vision of society, individual freedom and happiness must prevail; everything depends on science, which ultimately leads to understanding of the highest truth and the acquisition of knowledge.

Mahfouz's early articles on philosophy reveal him as an intelligent young Muslim trying to reconcile various Western concepts with his traditional beliefs. Despite his respect for philosophy, he seems convinced that the modern age is dominated by science, technology, and pragmatism. Caught between the idea that the concept of God has always been inherent in the collective society and the mystics' view that God is a transcendental essence which man feels in the depths of his soul, Mahfouz grew more perplexed than ever. Years later, calling himself a Muslim believer, he declared that in his heart he had combined an aspiration for God, faith in science, and a predilection for socialism.

Mahfouz also wrote on psychology, music, and literature, and two of his articles on Arabic writers are especially significant. In one he calls Abbas Mahmud al-Aqqad the soul of the Arab literary *nahda* ("awakening"), Taha Husayn its intellect, and Salama Musa its will. In a 1945 article, however, he sharply disagrees with al-Aqqad, whose little book *Fi Bayti* (*At My House*) praises poetry at the expense of fiction, which he calls inferior. Art in any form, Mahfouz says, is an expression of life, and should not be scorned because it brings pleasure to many. He contends that story is more popular than poetry because its technique is simpler and its purposes is to entertain.

With encouragement and help from Salama Musa, Mahfouz published three historical novels before moving to other concerns. He called the first *Hikmat Khufu* (*The Wisdom of Cheops*), but Musa renamed it *Abath al-Aqdar* (*Ironies of Fate*) and printed it as a separate issue of his magazine in September 1939. Two others followed, *Radobis* (1943) and *Kifah Tiba* (1944). In writing these novels, Mahfouz was continuing the tradition of Salim al-Bustani and Jurji Zaydan, later carried to greater heights by Ibrahim Ramzi, Muhammad Said al-Uryan, and others. Several educated writers of his generation, eager to portray current social and political movements, sought parallels between Egypt's ancient and contemporary history, giving the historical novel a new nationalistic emphasis.

After writing this series of novels, however, Mahfouz abandoned historical themes to focus on contemporary life in his native Cairo. "To me," he says, "history had lost its charm. There was a time when I wanted to write more historical novels, but I could not." Between 1945 and 1951 he published five novels dealing with social themes drawn from city life. These include *al-Qahira al-Jadida* (*New Cairo*, 1945), which contrasts the city's upper- and lower-middle classes in the 1930's, confronting us with the stark, absolute dichotomy between them. The upper class had wealth, power, and prestige, but was morally bankrupt; the poor struggled to improve their lot but could succeed only by compromising their principles. The moral climate was change-able, and when the members of the lower class sought answers to society's problems, they were faced with diverse, often conflicting values.

Khan al-Khalili (1946), named for an old quarter of Cairo, focuses on the many Egyptians squeezed in between the upper-middle class, which controlled wealth and land, and the *falla-hin* (peasants). It depicts well the growing semi-literate segment of the population in the 1940's, people who dabbled in a variety of disciplines, mastering none and impressing only those less educated than themselves. Mahfouz also shows here the dramatic effect of World War II on the common people. Cairo has been turned upside down, with a new class of profiteers having risen to join the aristocracy, and thus having blurred the old class distinctions. Mahfouz vividly shows people's credulity and their vulnerability to propaganda from both sides.

In *Zuqaq al-Midaqq* (*Midaqq Alley*, 1947), the alley becomes the protagonist, defiant and changeless, while its inhabitants hate it, leave it, and return. A timeless relic of the Fatimid and Mamluk periods, it is a monument to antiquity; its people, showing little interest in the outside world, carry on its tradition. *Zuqaq al-Midaqq* has no formal plot and no dominant character. It is filled with common folk from the lower-mid-dle class, mostly semiliterate or uneducated. The action is set in the last years of World War II; the war directly affects only a few inhabitants, though the conflict between their traditional values and those imposed upon them by the war is clear.

Al-Sarab (*The Mirage*, 1948), is a continua-tion of Mahfouz's contemporary social novels with a different technique and emphasis. A careful reading shows that it explores male-female rela-tionships, family ties, and the social gap between the Turkish aristocracy and common Egyptians. Mahfouz experiments here with a first-person nar-rative, letting the protagonist describe his own actions without comment. Mahfouz's aim is not to write a psychological novel but to reveal Cairo life from the viewpoint of a Turko-Egyptian who happens to suffer from an Oedipus complex.

Bidaya wa Nihaya (*The Beginning and the End*, 1949) presents the hopes and fears of a lower middle-class family struggling against the hardships caused by the death of its head and sole breadwinner. It is set in the 1930's, when British imperialists controlled Egypt with the aid of subservient, self-seeking politicians.

Al-Thulathiyya (*The Trilogy*, 1956–57), is undoubtedly Mahfouz's most important work and one of his personal favorites. In studying the novel as a genre, he became interested in the "generations novel," which follows a single family over an extended period. Subsequently he composed *al-Thulathiyya*, the saga of three gen-erations of a Cairo family that offers a compre-hensive view of major social and political events from 1917 to 1944 from the perspective of the Egyptian middle class, then caught in the clash between traditional Islamic ideals and Western doctrines.

The first volume, *Bayn al-Qasrayn* (*Palace Walk*), examines the family's basic relationships and interactions, and reveals the hypocrisy of the patriarch Sayyid Ahmad Abd al-Jawad, who pretends to be a good Muslim but is actually a libertine. Kamal, only a young boy (a character many believe modeled after Mahfouz himself), fears his father and takes refuge in his mother and in Islam. In addition, we learn of the patri-arch's political apathy toward the Egyptian national leader Sa'd Zaghlul and his revolution-ary movement against the British authorities in 1919. Sadly, Abd al-Jawad's other son—Fahmi, a high school student who had a promising future—is killed while demonstrating against the British in the Revolution of 1919.

The second part of the trilogy, *Qasr al-Shawa* (*Palace of Desire*), covers from 1924 to Sa'd Zaghlul's death in August 1927. In it Mah-fouz depicts the deterioration of the national movement into petty squabbling between the politicians and the palace, and shows the clash of traditional values and concepts with those imported from the West. In essence, Kamal is a perplexed young man attempting to reconcile his faith and idealism with social reality. The novel also explores the social tension between the aris-tocracy and the middle class, as exemplified in the account of Kamal's love for the noble Aida, who ultimately spurns him. Kamal then becomes a skeptic and turns to science for the salvation of both himself and mankind, espousing Darwin-ism. As a result he is totally estranged from his own culture and society, which is still controlled by the British.

In the final book of the trilogy, *al-Sukkariyya* (*Sugar Street*), covering the period from 1935 to 1944, Mahfouz looks closely at political upheav-als, the conflict between Western ideologies and traditional Muslim beliefs, and the cultural and social changes wrought by modern civilization and World War II. Kamal's nephews—Ahmad (a Marxist) and Abd al-Munim (who joins the Muslim Brotherhood)—represent the opposing poles of this spectrum. Western ideas now enter more pervasively through radio. In the midst of all this change, Kamal becomes emotionally paralyzed, incapable of significant action for good or evil, while his nephews, as the embodiment of the new generation, suffer no such ambivalence. Although Mahfouz also pictures here the strong demarcation between the Muslims and the Coptic Christian community, his most significant concern remains the confusion of the middle class about their place and identity in society.

Shortly after Mahfouz finished his trilogy in 1952, a group of army officers overthrew King Farouk and proclaimed the dawning of a new day. For seven years Mahfouz waited for the revolution to yield the social changes he had envisioned. In 1959, disillusioned by the outcome of the revolution, he wrote the allegorical *Awlad Haratina* (literally "Children of Our Quarter," but translated as *Children of Gebelawi*) to comment specifically on the Egyptian situation within the general context of the human condition. Divided into five chapters, each named for its central figure, the book (like Shaw's *Back to Methuselah*) follows a loose chronological sequence. The first chapter retells the thinly disguised story of Adam and Eve; the next three parallel the lives of Moses, Jesus, and Muhammad; and the final chapter introduces Arafa, who symbolizes modern science. The characters dwell in the *hara* (alley) of history, which is dominated by the nearby house of the powerful, enigmatic Gebelawi; they experience history as an endless cycle of hope and despair, escaping tyranny only briefly. Mahfouz is interested here not in religious questions but in social and political issues and the role science plays in settling them.

Awlad Haratina reflects Mahfouz's doubt that any society can maintain justice for long. Religious figures come and go, but the people remain powerless and miserable. Science represents the last great hope for mankind, but whether it can overcome human tyranny is unclear. Mahfouz seems to think that religion, if freed from fanaticism, parochialism, and superstition, could lead men's rulers to use science for the good of all. At the same time, he appears to accept the contention of Ibn Rushd (Averroes, 1126–98) that there are two kinds of truth, philosophical and theological, and that a single phenomenon can be understood rationally in philosophy and allegorically in theology.

This theory, which has long aroused the wrath of Islamic theologians, led to attacks on *Awlad Haratina* and prompted the clerics of the Islamic University of as-Azhar to ban the publication of the novel. Although the Egyptian government itself neither condemned nor banned the book, the initial publication came in Lebanon in 1967, and the title remained unpublished in Egypt until relatively recently. Nevertheless, even after Mahfouz received the 1988 Nobel Prize the book was still troubling some people, and the blind Shaykh Umar Abd al-Rahman, a member of an extremist religious group, issued a *fatwa* (juristic opinion) condemning Mahfouz as a blasphemer. According to Islamic Sahri'a (law), Mahfouz should have then either repented or been killed.

Between 1961 and 1967 Mahfouz published six novels and two collections of short stories, an astonishing burst of literary productivity all the more remarkable became of his increasing distress at the direction Egypt was taking under President Nasser. In the last stage of his literary career, beginning with the publication of *Miramar* in 1967, Mahfouz appears to have synthesized the social realism of the contemporary novels and the trilogy with the allegory of *Awlad Haratina*. Since 1969 he has published several more novels and collections of short fiction, constantly experimenting with new forms and techniques as he moved further from conventional realism. Even after retiring from the Ministry of Culture in 1972, Mahfouz continued to write fiction in addition to working on film adaptations of several of his novels and producing a weekly column for the newspaper *al-Ahram*. He has, to be sure, been publicly criticized for some of his political and religious positions, but he has attracted many readers throughout the Arab world and is commonly viewed as the conscience of Egypt.

Events took an ominous turn in October 1994, however, when the Cairo evening newspaper *al-Masa* began to give many Egyptians their first look seventeen years after its initial publication outside of Egypt—at the controversial novel *Awlad Haratina*. Mahfouz had authorized neither that newspaper's daily serialization of the novel nor the almost immediate printing of 45,000 copies of the complete book by another newspaper, *al-Ahali*. But that was of little consequence to Muslim fundamentalists, who rekindled their attack on Mahfouz. On the evening of 14 October 1994, while Mahfouz was in a car waiting to be driven to a weekly literary meeting, he was stabbed twice in the neck by Muhammad Naji Mustafa, a Muslim militant who subsequently admitted that he had never read the novel but acted on the strength of the blind shykh's five-year-old *fatwa*.

Fortunately, Mahfouz, though he nearly bled to death, was moved to a nearby hospital and saved with blood transfusions. He has recovered and seems likely to continue his sharp criticism of both the current government and the Islamic movement that vies with that government for power. *Awlad Haratina* is not against religion, he insists; it has suffered from misinterpretation.

Though sometimes called the Dickens or the Balzac of Egypt, Mahfouz has by now surely earned a standing of his own. He is the Mahfouz of the Arab world, and it will benefit other cultures to read his work on its own merits. His realistic style, his interest in social issues, and indeed his whole ethos are non-Western, genuinely Egyptian. But his works reflect so many Arab and Islamic traditions—and do so with such unparalleled skill—that he deserves to be claimed by all Arabs.

Source: Matti Moosa, "Naguib Mahfouz: Life in the Alley of Arab History," in *Georgia Review*, Vol. 49, No. 1, Spring 1995, pp. 224–30.

Ahmad Muhammad 'Atiyya

In the following excerpt, 'Atiyya explains why Mahfouz returns to the short story genre from time to time.

Naguib Mahfouz is a novelist, yet his literary activity began with short story writing and this is a form to which he has since occasionally returned. I once asked him why he wrote short stories at the initial stage of his literary life, and enquired about that intellectual restiveness evident in his first collection entitled *The Whisper of Madness* (*Hams al-Junun*, 1938). He replied that he had been at that time in a state of confusion, undergoing a crisis of ideas and expression, having not yet settled into that stability of thought that, he told me, had been with him throughout the period he wrote novels, between *The Struggle for Thebes* (*Kifah Tiba*) and *Miramar*.

> THESE STORIES DO, HOWEVER, REVEAL TO US THE BEGINNINGS OF MAHFOUZ'S CONCERN FOR THE EGYPTIAN SOCIAL REALITY, AND ESPECIALLY FOR ITS DESPAIRING AND POVERTY-RIDDEN CLASSES."

He said, "Let me tell you a secret. I began writing short stories influenced by Mahmud Taymur and al-Mazini and the fiction translations done by Muhammad al-Siba'i. But when I later returned to the form, I was no longer influenced by any short story writer. I wrote my stories in the spirit of the novel, almost all my reading since having been in the novel. And so my latest stories are closest to the genre of the 'long short story,' ranging between fifty and eighty foolscap pages."

In that conversation, he stated that he would write no more novels and would restrict himself to the short story because it was a medium more appropriate to our current times. He has since published many volumes of short stories, giving proof of the great importance of that genre to him. Yet this range of his writing has not received comparable attention to that devoted to his novels. This essay seeks, then, to explicate Naguib Mahfouz as a writer of the short story.

The short story is the form that arouses the greatest dissension amongst writers. But however views differ, the short story is certainly the art of the partial, the individual and the simple, through which we are led to totalities and generalities. The short story is the art of concentration, and consequently its methods often parallel those of poetry.

Short stories are capable of transmitting directly, with speed and effectiveness. This results from the fact that they can be written quickly and published immediately in the newspapers because of their limited size. Therefore the short story is capable of expressing the changes and crises in society, and that is why the form flourishes in periods of anxiety and change. The novel, however, requires a somewhat static reality, it being the art of the 'deep breath,' of the concerns of groups of persons. And because novels require much time to write and are difficult to publish, they are not capable of accompanying a society or an individual during their rapid transformations.

Frank O'Connor's dictum, that the short story is the art of the oppressed and the obscure, accords completely with the short stories of Naguib Mahfouz.

Naguib Mahfouz has published short stories during important periods of Egypt's modern history. Those of his first collection, *Whisper of Madness* (*Hams al-Junun*, 1938), were written in a painful period that saw the success of the grand conspiracy in which the Egyptian bourgeoisie engaged by making peace with British imperialism and suppressing the Revolution of 1919. This all led to the signing of the 1936 pact through which the British gained a legal presence. The stories in *Whisper of Madness* were written during that period of angry unrest among the Egyptian people that ended with the outbreak of World War II but exploded again in 1946 after the war was over.

In the beginnings of the socialist transformation of the early sixties, Mahfouz returned to the short story with his second collection entitled *God's World* (*Dunya Allah*, 1962). This appeared during a period when the short story was in apparent crisis, since the majority of its exponents in the fifties had turned their efforts toward the novel, or were writing for the newly flourishing Egyptian theater. The newspapers almost stopped publishing stories. Since the new generation of writers was expressing their interest in the theater, the short story seemed in a state of abandonment; the older writers had stopped producing them and the younger ones had not begun. But it was soon evident that the crisis was one of birth, not of death, for short stories appeared thereafter in such profusion as to overwhelm the facilities for publication, both public and private, a fact that constitutes a very interesting phenomenon.

For a period following the 1967 war (between Israel and the Arabs), Naguib Mahfouz devoted himself totally to writing the short story.

In his book *The Short Story in Egypt* (*al-Qissat al-Qasira fi Misr*), Dr. Shukri 'Ayyad relates that in the early years of this century the Egyptian short story was looked upon with derision, and that after some splendid new beginnings

in the early twenties, it declined to a state of near bankruptcy in the late thirties.

It is well known that the Egyptian short story came to maturity after World War I and the Revolution of 1919. This followed a period of the translation and open imitation of French short stories. However, the 'New School,' consisting of Mahmud Tahir Lashin, Husain Fawzi, Ibrahim al-Misri and others (see Yaha Haqqi's *The Dawn of Egyptian Fiction* [*Fajr al-Qissat al-Misriyya*]), was influenced by the Russian story. These writers also opened their minds to international fiction in general through translation of major writers, and they set about creating a genuine Egyptian short story. But this 'school' was essentially bankrupt by the late thirties, as Dr. 'Ayyad has observed.

It was during this period that Mahfouz began writing short stories. This fact perhaps explains why his works were initially so lacking in sophistication, both artistically and intellectually, for all their faithfulness to the Egyptian social reality and their intent to create stories truly Egyptian in flesh and blood.

The lack of sophistication of Mahfouz's first collection is evident from the stories' dearth of ideas and weakness of artistic structure. Whisper of Madness, the story from which the collection takes its title, is a simple moralistic tale that tells directly of the activities of a madman who steals food, is violent to others, assaults girls and tears his clothing. Its long introduction about madness exceeds the needs of the short story, which demands concentration and economy. The story then proceeds to external description of characters, these characterizations being superficial and lacking in artistry.

These stories do, however, reveal to us the beginnings of Mahfouz's concern for the Egyptian social reality, and especially for its despairing and poverty-ridden classes. Whisper of Madness features people wallowing in luxury and fine food while all around them young people are starving. The madman takes revenge on the rich by stealing a chicken from them and giving it to the poor.

This unsophisticated expression of the social reality is clearly revealed in stories like Falseness (al-Zayf), which tells of the competition between two bourgeois women over possession of a poet. It ends unconvincingly with the surprise discovery of their mistake in confusing the poet with someone who had assumed his identity. This too is a story devoid of philosophical, social or psychological content, other perhaps than exposing the triviality and decadence of the Egyptian bourgeoisie. It relies upon artless surprises and coincidences.

Similar is the story Delirium (al-Hudhyan), which relates how a husband, discovering the infidelity of his wife when delirious on her death bed, is so shocked that he commits suicide. And then there are stories like Female Wiles (Kayduhunna), Pleasure Gardens (Ruwad al-Faraj) and Letters (Rasa 'il). This last depicts through an exchange of letters the infidelity of a girl towards her lover, and how his discovery of this leads him to break off his relationship with her. This story clearly condemns the closed society of upper Egypt, which the story's two main characters deride by establishing a love relationship in denial of its taboos.

Mahfouz often filled the stories of his first collection with direct sermonizing and moral platitudes. Also, the stories' frameworks often extend to include a great number of extraneous events from the characters' childhood. Sex for its own sake is similarly a dominant theme. In the story Whisper of Madness, the madman fondles the breasts of a woman in the street, following the author's lengthy and erotic description of them. Falseness revolves around a night of sex and violence. The protagonist, as well as the central figure of The Vagrant Woman (al-Sharida) admits that he craves all women and therefore has no self-control when with any woman, regardless of her attractiveness. Here sex is called 'sinful love,' and it is rejected with exhortation and advice. All this reveals a misunderstanding of the role of art, which clearly should exclude making speeches and sermonizing. These early works of Mahfouz make that plain, since they evidence every beginner's error.

In Whisper of Madness, his first treatment of the tormented, Mahfouz states directly: "This human world of ours is intently grim." In the story Memoirs of a Young Man (Mudhakkarat Shabb), he condemns society by demonstrating that to gain a position, what is needed is not ability or success in school, but marriage, contacts and influence. These are the very means employed by Mahjub 'Abd al-Da'im, hero of the novel *New Cairo (al-Qahira al-Jadida)*. He ends this novel with an eloquent sermon, the gist of which is that " ... the truly happy person is one who contents himself with reality, someone who attains the means to contentment and satisfaction wherever he may be." It is this acceptance of reality that leads the hero of this story to a position he does not deserve, and to participation in a mission abroad, and so on.

Source: Ahmad Muhammad 'At iyya, "Naguib Mahfouz and the Short Story," in *Critical Perspectives on Naguib Mahfouz*, edited by Trevor Le Gassick, Three Continents Press, 1991, pp. 9–26.

Roger Allen

In the following essay, Allen argues the merits of awarding the Nobel Prize to an author of Arabic literature.

The reception of Arabic literature in the West has ... always been set within a complicated array of cultural attitudes. The intricate questions of "influence" and cultural exchange between the two remain the subject of much controversy. While research on the implications of the presence of Arabic lyric poetry and picaresque narrative in ninth-century al-Andalus (as Spain was termed) continues to tantalize some scholars and antagonize others, the influence of Sir William Jones's translations of Eastern poetry and of Galland's translation of *The Thousand and One Nights* on the history of European literature is scarcely open to debate. More recently, and particularly following the colonization of many countries in the Arab world by Europe in the nineteenth century, the process has been predominantly unidirectional. The genres of the novel and drama were to a large degree transplanted into modern Arabic literature direct from the Western tradition, rapidly superseding any attempts at reviving older genres. It was in the realm of poetry, the most vigorous of the classical genres, that the neoclassical tendency persisted longest, but it too came under the influence of Western "schools" of poetry.

It is within the context of this confusing set of influences and attitudes that modern Arabic literature and the West confront each other. That there should be misunderstanding and "anxiety" on both sides is hardly surprising. It would also seem unreasonable to expect that any exercise in transcultural evaluation such as that essayed by the Nobel Prize Committee should not be a reflection of the general situation. With that in mind, I will address some of the issues raised within the framework of the prize and its selection committee under three headings: access to Arabic literature in the West; the Nobel Prize criteria; and finally, a short segment concerning

> "NAJIB MAHFUZ IS ACKNOWLEDGED
> THROUGHOUT THE ENTIRE ARAB WORLD AS THE
> GREAT PIONEER IN THE MATURE ARABIC NOVEL,
> AND HE HAS ACHIEVED THAT DISTINCTION BY
> DINT OF SHEER HARD WORK, TENACITY, PATIENCE
> IN ADVERSITY (BOTH POLITICAL AND MEDICAL),
> AND A DISARMING HUMILITY."

those Arab authors whose candidacy seems plausible within the current terms of reference.

Many Western readers are exposed to a monument of Arabic literature at a relatively early age in the form of *The Thousand and One Nights*, a work which has for a long time provided a rich source of entertainment for children. I myself can vividly remember being taken to see pantomime versions of both Aladdin and Ali Baba as a child. Ironically, this huge collection of tales was never regarded as literature by the Arabs themselves, and current scholarly interest is largely the result of Western attention, initially to the sources and, more recently, to narrative structure and techniques. The popularity and exoticism of these tales within Western culture seems to have produced two major results. In the first place, it fostered a fantastic view of Middle Eastern culture, something which has been documented by a large number of sources and which finds what is perhaps its extreme representation in such media as the cinema (from the Sinbad films of Douglas Fairbanks Sr. to more recent examples such as *The Jewel of the Nile*). Second, the almost automatic selection of tales from this collection for anthologies of world literature succeeded to a large degree in blocking any further interest in searching for other examples of literature written in Arabic. The wealth of classical Arabic poetry remained essentially a closed book except to a few scholars, and even they were not of any great assistance: the German scholar-poet Noldeke gave his opinion (in the introduction to a collection of Arabic poetry) that the esthetic pleasure gained from a reading

of the poems hardly justified the pain involved. Thus, the general Western readership, endeavoring to evaluate examples of literature produced in today's Arab world, may perhaps be considered to be at a double disadvantage: not only are they presented with works which seem to show a strong reliance on Western models with which they are already familiar; but also the history of the Arabic literary tradition, available to them through their own general education and the more direct avenue of translation of the classics, is incomplete and distorted. There is thus an unsettling lack of context.

If we turn now to a consideration of the criteria under which the Swedish Academy's Nobel Committee operates, some of the issues which need to be raised in connection with the above survey become clear. One of the members of the jury itself, the Swedish physician-novelist Lars Gyllensten, readily acknowledges a point which has already been made: Literary works are more or less bound to the literary environment in which they are created, and the farther away from it one is, the harder it is to do them justice. I might observe that, on the basis of my comments above, the epithet *far* in this instance needs to be interpreted within the context of cultural attitudes rather than pure geographic distance. The same writer then goes on to make what is, for the purposes of Arabic literature, a statement of major importance.

> The task of awarding the Nobel Prize in Literature involves the obligation of trying to find methods for keeping oneself *au fait* with what is happening in literature all over the world and for appraising it, either on one's own or with the aid of specialists. Finally, the prize awarders must try to familiarize themselves with the works of most value, directly or via translations, and to make a careful assessment of their quality with all the viewpoints conceivably necessary for a reasonable evaluation.

Two issues emerge here: first, the question of evaluation; and second, that of translation. On the matter of translation, one has to state fairly bluntly that, as far as English is concerned, modern Arab *litterateurs* have not been particularly well served by translation (although the situation seems at least marginally better in French).

The second issue raised by Gyllensten's statement involves evaluation, and most particularly the phrase *with the aid of specialists*. If we assume the phrase Arabic literature to incorporate literary works written in the Arabic language throughout the Arabic-speaking world, then we have to acknowledge that the Nobel Committee is presented with an enormous and probably impossible task; for few indeed are the critics and scholars, whether Arab or non-Arab, whose knowledge of the field is sufficiently broad to encompass the entire region and the variety of genres involved and to present the committee with a list of nominees which will transcend political, religious, and cultural boundaries. Here we must refer to the documentation regarding the nomination procedure itself.

> The right to nominate candidates for the Prize in Literature is granted to members of the Swedish Academy; and of the French Academies which are similar to it in character and objectives; to members of the humanistic sections of other academies, as well as to members of the humanistic institutions and societies as enjoy the same rank as academies and to university professors of aesthetics, literature and history.

In view of the extremely small number of specialists in Arabic literature to whom the members of the Nobel Committee might have access and indeed of the relatively few contacts between Western scholars in the field and Arab *litterateurs* and literary critics, it is hardly surprising that this nominating procedure has not worked in favor of nominations from the field of Arabic literature.

Another feature of the criteria for nominations which has been much debated concerns the stipulation in Alfred Nobel's will that the prize honor someone whose writings have been of an ideal tendency, a phrase which is interpreted by Gyllensten to mean a striving for the good of mankind, for humaneness, common sense, progress and happiness... literary achievements with constructive aims. While this rubric has been liberally interpreted, several critics have suggested dropping it altogether. Those who have any familiarity with the history of the Arab world during the course of this century, and most particularly in the decades since World War II, will perhaps realize that common sense, progress and happiness have not been attributes which have provided the driving force for the majority of Arab authors. Alienation, rebellion, confrontation, rejection, revolution, self-sacrifice, struggle—these have been far more characteristic of the literature of the last several decades.

All this said, it will perhaps not be a surprise if I eschew the opportunity to compare recent prizewinners with potential nominees from the Arab world. No Arab has as yet won the prize; whether one will (or can) under the current criteria seems open to doubt. That is not to say, of course, that there are not Arab *litterateurs* who are worthy of nomination. I would like to devote just a few lines to a consideration of my own short list: Najib Mahfuz (sometimes written as Naguib Mahfouz) of Egypt and Adunis (or Adonis) of Lebanon. Both manage to combine two considerations: in the first place, they are preeminently great writers; second, translations of many of their works are available in at least English and French. However, this availability in English translation itself presents us with a problem. In the case of Mahfuz, the novels which are now available in translation are, in the main, part of a series being published by the American University in Cairo Press. Because of the order in which the translations were completed, the novels have appeared in essentially random sequence; most especially, Mahfuz's major monument and contribution to modern literature as a whole, *Al-Thulathiyya* (*The Trilogy*; 1956–57), has yet to appear. The slightly earlier *Al-Bidaya wa-al-Nihaya* (1951; Eng. *The Beginning and the End*) is now available, along with *Zuqaq al-Midaqq* (1947; Eng. *Midaq Alley*), but the bulk of the published translations are from novels which were written in the 1960s; though all are of extreme interest within the perspective of the recent history of Egyptian society, they are of varying literary quality in both the original and in translation. (pp. 202–03)

Najib Mahfuz is acknowledged throughout the entire Arab world as the great pioneer in the mature Arabic novel, and he has achieved that distinction by dint of sheer hard work, tenacity, patience in adversity (both political and medical), and a disarming humility. He is recognized as the Arab world's leading writer of fiction because he has not only produced a whole stream of excellent novels over a period of four decades, but also turned the novel, as a means of societal comment and criticism, into an accessible and accomplished medium. His is a nomination which, the normalities of Arab politics aside, would be welcomed throughout the Arab world.

Source: Roger Allen, "Arabic Literature and the Nobel Prize," in *World Literature Today*, Vol. 62, No. 2, Spring 1988, pp. 201–03.

SOURCES

Allen, Roger, "Contemporary Egyptian Literature," in *Middle East Journal*, Vol. 35, No. 1, Winter 1981, pp. 25–39.

———, "Najib Mahfuz: Nobel Laureate in Literature, 1988," in *World Literature Today*, Vol. 63, No. 1, Winter 1989, pp. 5–9.

'Atiyya, Ahmad Muhammad, "Naguib Mahfouz and the Short Story," in *Critical Perspectives on Naguib Mahfouz*, edited by Trevor Le Gassick, Three Continents Press, 1991, pp. 9–25.

Benedick, Richard Elliot, "The High Dam and the Transformation of the Nile," in *Middle East Journal*, Vol. 33, No. 2, Spring 1979, pp. 119–44.

Cooke, Miriam, "Book Reviews: Naguib Mahfouz," in *Middle East Journal*, Vol. 43, No. 3, Summer 1989, pp. 507–11.

El Shabrawy, Charlotte, "Naguib Mahfouz, The Art of Fiction No. 129," in *Paris Review*, No. 123, Summer 1992, http://www.theparisreview.org/interviews/2062/the-art-of-fiction-no-129-naguib-mahfouz (accessed September 15, 2010).

Haywood, John, Review of *The Time and the Place and Other Stories*, in *World Literature Today*, Vol. 67, No. 1, Winter 1993, pp. 226.

Khalidi, Ahmed S., "The War of Attrition," in *Journal of Palestine Studies*, Vol. 3, No. 1, Autumn 1973, pp. 60–87.

Mahfouz, Naguib, "The Norwegian Rat," in *The Time and the Place and Other Stories*, translated by Denys Johnson-Davies, Doubleday, 1991, pp. 127–33.

FURTHER READING

Ahmed, Moustafa, *Egypt in the 20th Century: Chronology of Major Events*, MegaZette Press, 2003.
    Ahmed explores the changing political climate of Egypt in the twentieth century, providing a valuable tool to understanding the setting of Mahfouz's fiction.

Al-Ghitani, Gamal, *The Cairo of Naguib Mahfouz*, photographs by Britta Le Va, American University in Cairo Press, 2000.
    As a lifelong resident of Cairo, Mahfouz set most of his work in his hometown. Photographs by Britta Le Va show readers the actual locations in which Mahfouz's fiction is set. Each picture is accompanied by a passage from one of Mahfouz's stories.

Mahfouz, Naguib, *Echoes of an Autobiography*, Doubleday, 1997.
    This is a collection of brief personal passages in which Mahfouz reflects on the different events and situations of his life. Beginning with his childhood memories and working through the late 1990s, this rare piece of nonfiction provides insight into the author's personal experiences and point of view.

Somekh, Sasson, *The Changing Rhythm*, Brill Academic Publishers, 1973.
    This research-based publication provides an in-depth look at Mahfouz's early work, life, and social setting. Written before Mahfouz won the Nobel Prize, it is ideal for studying his historical novels.

SUGGESTED SEARCH TERMS

Naguib Mahfouz AND short stories

Arab-Israeli War

Nobel Prize AND 1988

Egyptian novel

Naguib Mahfouz AND Cairo

Modern Egyptian literature

Aswan High Dam

Egyptian short stories

Egyptian Revolution

Naguib Mahfouz AND Egypt

Sonata for Harp and Bicycle

JOAN AIKEN

1976

Joan Aiken is an English writer of short stories, novels, plays, and poetry in all of the fantastic literary genres: fantasy, horror, mystery thrillers, fairy tales, and ghost stories. Though known primarily as a children's author, she has a long list of adult fiction as well; readers, she says, are not readily segregated into groups and like to read across age lines. Her most famous children's book, *The Wolves of Willoughby Chase*, for instance, is read by children and adults and has been made into a film. This novel made her famous in the 1960s for inventing a new genre that mixes details of history with fantasy in a way that changes history. Aiken's wild and inventive imagination has delighted generations of children with fantasy series such as the "Arabel and Mortimer" books, about a young girl and a talking raven. However, although Aiken has been appreciated, she is perhaps underrated as being merely a popular author.

A few critics have noted that her best contribution is in her short stories, both thrillers and lovely original fairy tales, such as "Over the Cloudy Mountain" from *The Winter Sleepwalker*. Aiken loved the classic fantasy authors and learned from George MacDonald, Charles Dickens, and E. Nesbit. Without preaching, Aiken creates a moral universe with courageous and inventive characters unafraid of confronting evil. She believes stories should leave the reader feeling wonder and hope. This is evident in her Christmas ghost story, "Sonata for Harp

He snuck back into the building through the fire escape in the alley. (Ken Schulze / Shutterstock.com)

and Bicycle" (1976), in which a pair of lovers lay London ghosts to rest on Christmas Eve. The story is contained in the 1978 Penguin collection *A Bundle of Nerves*.

AUTHOR BIOGRAPHY

Aiken was born on September 4, 1924, in Rye, East Sussex, England, to American Pulitzer Prize–winning poet Conrad Aiken and his Canadian-born wife, Jessie MacDonald. Her mother had a master's degree from Radcliffe and taught Joan at home until she was twelve. Aiken's parents divorced, and her mother remarried Martin Armstrong, a British novelist. Joan had an older brother, John, and sister, Jane Aiken Hodge, who also became writers. From 1936 to 1940, Aiken attended Wychwood School in Oxford, England. Since childhood, she had been writing stories and telling them to her younger stepbrother.

Aiken did not attend college. During World War II, she was employed by the British Broadcasting Corporation (BBC) (1942–1943) and the United Nations Information Office (1943–1949). She married journalist Ronald Brown in 1945 and had two children with him. When Brown died of cancer in 1955, Aiken joined the staff of *Argosy* magazine from 1955 to 1960 as an editor to support her children. She was also an advertising copywriter for J. Walter Thompson in London from 1960 to 1961.

At the age of sixteen, Aiken had her stories produced by the BBC for *The Children's Hour*. Her first short story was published when she was eighteen. Her first short-story collections include *All You've Ever Wanted and Other Stories* (1953) and *More Than You Bargained For* (1955). Aiken wrote fairy stories in *A Necklace of Raindrops* (1968), folk tales in *The Kingdom under the Sea* (1971), and horror stories in *A Bundle of Nerves* (1976).

Finally, with *The Wolves of Willoughby Chase* in 1962, later extended to a series of a dozen novels, she gained fame and could write full time. This fantasy was an alternate history of England in which the Stuart kings were never deposed, leading to adventures for several young characters, such as Dido Twite, a Cockney waif. The book won the 1965 Lewis Carroll Shelf Award and was made into a successful film in 1989.

Aiken married New York painter Julius Goldstein in 1976. Although she is known primarily as a children's author, she wrote more than a hundred books for children and adults, including novels, plays, poems, and short stories. The ghost story was a specialty, and *The Haunting of Lamb House* (1991) is an adult novel based on a real haunted house in her birthplace of Rye, where Henry James wrote "The Turn of the Screw." Other popular books include the "Arabel and Mortimer" series (starting with *Arabel's Raven*, 1972) and sequels to the novels of Jane Austen, such as *Mansfield Revisited* (1985).

Her awards include the Carnegie Medal, 1968; the *Guardian* Award for children's literature, 1969; Mystery Writers of America Edgar Allan Poe Award, 1972; *New York Times* outstanding book, 1974; and Member of the Order of the British Empire for services to children's literature. Aiken died at her home in Petworth, West Sussex, England, of natural causes on January 4, 2004, at the age of 79.

PLOT SUMMARY

Mr. Manaby explains, as he shows his new assistant into his office, that no one is allowed to stay in the Grimes office building after five p.m. When questioned why this is so, Manaby says it is a company policy. The intercom system begins to instruct the employees to put away their work and wash their hands at four forty-five. The staff of Moreton Wold and Company rush to put on their hats and coats and leave the building. As the bells of St. Paul's Cathedral ring the five o'clock hour in the cold, dark air, the crowd hurriedly vacates the premises. The new advertising copywriter, Jason Ashgrove, asks his secretary, as they are finishing their work, why they have to leave in such a hurry. Berenice Golden says that Jason will find out when he becomes a permanent staff member. He wants to know now, though, and asks whether she knows the reason. She says that she does, but they must focus to finish the Oat Crisp job before a quarter to five.

Jason is not satisfied and thinks up sarcastic slogans about Oat Crisps to goad his secretary. He suddenly asks her what she wants for Christmas. She replies in the same witty tone that she wants to finish the Oat Crisp job. The narrator says that what Miss Golden really wants is Jason Ashgrove, but he has not yet discovered it. Jason threatens to do something desperate if she will not tell him what is revealed when an employee is permanently hired, and she looks frightened. He offers to take her to dinner, and they exit the building with the others at five. As they hurry out, she gives him a few hints about why they must leave so promptly: it has to do with the fire escape, a bicycle and a harp. When they reach the street, it is a cold and dark winter twilight. She refuses to tell any more of the secret and gets on her bus, while he stands on the curb, trying to think what to do next.

He knows there is a back entrance to the building. Jason enters a narrow alley behind the building until he finds the fire escape. He climbs the ladder up the dark and deserted building and finally opens the door on the ninth floor. The Grimes complex is triangular in shape, and the fire escape is at the point of the triangle. Two corridors come towards him and meet at the point where he stands. There is no night watchman because no burglar would dare enter the eerie building.

He notices the sound of a bell, a ringing that does not sound like a telephone. The rings get louder and more insistent. In fear, Jason runs up a flight of stairs to the tenth floor, where he hears musical notes that keep fading before him as he moves towards them. Now he hears the bell again, and knowing it to be a bicycle bell, he feels it bearing down on him. He jumps out of the way with a beating heart, seeing two eyes in the dark and feeling hands holding him. A voice asks whether this is Daisy come to give her answer. Jason replies it is not Daisy and asks who is there. Jason feels he is being pushed, and then the fire door opens automatically and he is out on the platform. A whisper advises him to jump—does he have anything to live for? He thinks of Berenice Golden, his secretary. He suddenly understands she would miss him, so he shakes himself free and climbs down the fire escape.

The next morning, Miss Golden comes into their office in Room 92 and is shocked to find that Jason's hair has turned silver overnight. She asks how it happened, but she knows that he must have been in the Grimes Buildings after dark. He asks her who Daisy is. She asks whether he saw William Heron, the Wailing Watchman, and cries out that if he has, he is doomed! Over coffee, she tells him the story of the ghosts in the building. Fifty years ago, Heron was the night watchman of the building and rode his bicycle up and down the hallways. He fell in love with Daisy Bell, who taught harp lessons in the very room they are in now, room 92. Daisy began to stay late and share a picnic supper with William Heron every night at eleven o'clock.

Heron decided to propose to Daisy on Christmas Eve. The day before, he told her that he had a very important question, so she would be prepared. He bought a bouquet of roses and a bottle of wine, but she did not come that night. It was her habit to sleep from seven till ten every night in her music room, so she could stay up with him. She asked her father, a relative of Alexander Graham Bell, to install a sort of telephone device in her room so he could awaken her at ten o'clock. She did not tell her lover she did this. On Christmas Eve, the device did not work, and Daisy slept on past the time of their appointment. Heron waited, and when she did not come, he assumed she did not want to marry him. He jumped to his death from the tenth floor holding the roses and wine. Daisy died soon after him, and their ghosts now haunt the building. Heron searches the hallways on his bicycle for her, and she plays her harp, but they never meet. Anyone who sees the ghost of Heron will die within five days by jumping from the fire escape.

Jason jumps up to kiss Berenice Golden and tells her they cannot waste any time. He will not let these clumsy ghosts spoil his life, for he has no intention of following Heron to his death. He tells her to meet him in the switchboard room at ten that evening. She will be safe from the ghost in there. That evening Jason comes into Grimes Buildings with two bottles of wine, two bunches of roses, and a backpack. He tells Berenice to ring the extension in their room, 92. She says no one will answer, but he believes that Daisy will answer. And true, the phone is answered by a sleepy voice. Berenice tells the ghostly Daisy that this is her ten o'clock call. Then she plugs in the intercom and announces that the night watchman should go to Room 92 on urgent business.

Jason and Berenice race up the stairs to room 92. They hear harp music. Jason opens the door and leaves one of the bunches of roses and one bottle of wine there. The lovers hold hands and wait. Suddenly, the door flies open, and they both have the impression of a bicycle passing them with a harp, a bottle of wine, and the roses on the saddle, going down the hallway. Jason and Berenice then go to the fire escape. He puts the other bottle of wine in his jacket and tells her to hold the roses. He grabs Berenice and jumps off the fire escape as he pulls the rip cord of a parachute, kissing her while rose petals shower around their descent.

CHARACTERS

Jason Ashgrove

Jason Ashgrove is the hero of the story. He gets a job as an advertising copywriter at Moreton Wold and Company in the Grimes Buildings of London, but he is not like the other employees, who do what they are told. One thousand employees meekly pack up and get out quickly by dark every night to avoid the danger of meeting the ghosts. Ashgrove has a lot of curiosity, individuality, and courage. He wants to investigate the situation for himself. It is obvious he does not accept orders without considering them. He is annoyed that no one will tell him the secret of the building, and he does not let the prohibition stand in his way. Once he confronts the ghost for himself, he does experience fear and horror, so much so that his hair turns silver overnight. However, Ashgrove has an inherent strength, for the thought of Miss Golden is enough to fortify him to resist the suggestion of the ghost to jump to his death. When he finds out about the curse, he is not daunted but springs into

action. For him, the situation, no matter how life-threatening, is a creative challenge, like finding an advertising slogan. He makes his plan and carries it out, including a parachute jump off the fire scape to fulfill the curse but thwart it at the same time. His romantic nature is revealed by his plan to not only find happiness for himself with Miss Golden but also get the ghosts together so the building will be free of their tragedy.

Daisy Bell

Daisy Bell is the music teacher who taught harp lessons fifty years earlier in room 92 of the Grimes Buildings, where Jason Ashgrove and Berenice Golden now work. Daisy was in love with the night watchman, William Heron. After giving music lessons all day, she would take a nap in her room until 10 p.m. each night, when she would have a picnic supper with Heron. Her modesty about staying in the building and taking a nap becomes the trigger for the misunderstanding. When she does not wake up in time to meet Heron, he assumes she has rejected him. After Heron commits suicide, she wastes away and becomes a ghost with him in the building, where her harp music is still heard. It is implied that she finally meets up with her ghost lover at the end, riding off with him on his bicycle through the corridors.

Berenice Golden

Miss Berenice Golden is the secretary in Jason Ashgrove's office, who helps him write ads for clients. She has been there longer than Jason has and knows the secret of the haunted building, but she will not disclose it when Ashgrove asks about it. He teases her, and though she remains professional in her behavior, she is secretly in love with Ashgrove. After he kisses her and declares his love, she is ready to risk her life to help save him from the curse. She gets her Christmas wish (Ashgrove) as she jumps off the fire escape in his arms and parachutes to the ground on Christmas Eve.

William Heron

William Heron is the rash former night watchman of the Grimes Buildings. Fifty years before the start of the story, he performed his duties while bicycling up and down the corridors. He was in love with Daisy Bell, the music teacher who also worked in the building at the time. The night before Christmas Eve, he warns her he will ask her an important question the next night. He brings wine and roses to work planning to

TOPICS FOR FURTHER STUDY

- Read *Lafcadio Hearn's Japanese Ghost Stories*, rewritten by Sean Michael Wilson and illustrated by Haruka Miyabi as manga, or Japanese comics (Demented Dragon Press, 2007). Compare and contrast these Japanese ghost stories with Aiken's story or some other favorite ghost story. Are ghost stories basically the same in different cultures, or do they have unique traits in the details of plot, character, and theme? Write a short paper that provides examples of your conclusions.

- Give a group presentation on the relationship of the goth subculture to gothic stories, using visual media and music lyrics. What similarities are there in theme, philosophy, mood, and lifestyle in gothic tales such as Bram Stoker's *Dracula* or Poe's "The Fall of the House of Usher" and goth music, poetry, and dress? End by evaluating whether gothic stories and the goth subculture are a creative expression or harmful to the individual and society. Supplement your oral presentation with pictures, music, video clips, and excerpts from works of literature.

- Create a multimedia presentation on burial practices from various ancient and modern cultures with slides and/or documentaries. Do cultures try in their burial practices to ensure that ghosts will not return from the dead to the living, or are there some societies that welcome visits from the dead?

- Collaborate in a digital forum with several others to write a ghost story, adding visuals. Distribute the story to the class and collect feedback. In a discussion, bring out the creative challenges of creating suspense, atmosphere, and plot sequence. Revise and submit to an online magazine for horror stories.

- Give an individual or group presentation on horror films, using clips to show various ways that ghosts have been portrayed on film. Have the audience rate the most frightening scenes and discuss the emotions they evoke. Why do people attend movies that frighten them? Answer this question in a written film review of a favorite horror film that is posted on the teacher Web log.

- Read the young-adult ghost novel *The Woman in Black* by Susan Hill (1983). Compare this ghost story to Aiken's "Sonata for Harp and Bicycle." What message about life and society does each story present the reader? Write a short summary and analysis, giving examples from the stories.

propose to her, but she does not show up. He believes she has rejected him and commits suicide by jumping off the fire escape with the wine and roses. Although in life he seemed to be rather gentle and romantic, in death, he is frightening and dangerous. Heron seems pacified at the end of the story, riding past the live characters with Daisy, her harp, and the gifts from the living people, the wine and roses, on his bicycle.

Mr. Manaby

Mr. Manaby is the supervisor of Jason Ashgrove in the Moreton Wold and Company offices at the Grimes Buildings. He shows Jason into his office and explains the rule about getting out of the building promptly at five o'clock.

THEMES

Fate

The feeling of a fated doom is conveyed through both sets of lovers, William and Daisy from fifty years before and Jason and Berenice in the present. Unlike other tragic lovers who can meet as ghosts after death (such as Heathcliff and Cathy in *Wuthering Heights*), William and Daisy are, it

The sound of the bicycle bells chased him through the empty building. *(Jan Schuler / Shutterstock.com)*

seems, fated never to meet in the building, even after death, thus repeating their tragedy for eternity. This feeling of fate and futility recalls the pitiful ghost of Jacob Marley in "A Christmas Carol," who repeats his tragedy by never being able to help the humans he shunned in life. Usually, ghost stories involving a curse have the curse continue to be played out by someone in the story. The reader, through identification with the characters, experiences the relentless quality of a fate that cannot be changed. The characters and reader feel a helpless terror as the doom descends, despite all efforts to avoid it. Ashgrove sees Heron's ghostly eyes and feels his hands around his throat. He is magically escorted to the fire escape, where the door opens by itself. This expectation of continuing tragedy is thwarted by Aiken's providing a surprise ending for the modern lovers, who figure out how to avoid their fate.

Imagination

Aiken had a strong belief in the power of imagination and hoped to stimulate this faculty in her readers. One way she does this is by showing characters using their imaginations to solve problems. Her heroes and heroines are strong individuals who run up against tough situations in life, including evil and the supernatural, yet they find creative solutions. Jason Ashgrove does not meekly meet his fate or try to hide from it as cowardly characters often do in ghost stories. Ashgrove is contrasted to the other employees in the building, who move like "lemmings" to the exit as they are told over the loudspeaker to wash their hands, tidy their desks, and leave the building. His courage saves himself, the ghosts, and the company.

Love

Although Heron's ghost would like the modern lovers to repeat the tragedy of unrequited love, Ashgrove finds a way for all lovers to be satisfied, thus making this tale into a Christmas story of love and reconciliation. It takes the ghost to give him a push towards Miss Golden, but he quickly gets the point and does not waste any time declaring his love to her. Aiken has chosen to write against the grain of the usual tragic or horrible ending of ghost stories. She implies that love is more powerful than fate.

STYLE

Short Story

The modern short story gained popularity in the nineteenth century, with the stories of Nathaniel Hawthorne, Edgar Allan Poe, Nikolai Gogol, and Guy de Maupassant. They gave the short narrative its modern form as a compressed story with a unified plot striving for a single effect. Though the modern short story generally concerns the everyday world of realistic events and settings, it can also use complex symbols and mysterious atmosphere to suggest deeper meanings or to explore the human psyche. Contemporary short-story writers explore developed characters but often leave the story open-ended, such as John Steinbeck's "Chrysanthemums." Joan Aiken published many volumes of short stories, which typically begin in the recognizable everyday world, showing the characters facing ordinary challenges, as Jason Ashgrove does on his first day at a new job. Soon, though, the narratives turn into mysteries, fantasies, or horror stories. *A Bundle of Nerves*, which contains "Sonata for Harp and Bicycle," is a collection of nineteen very short narratives with surprise turns. The characters are not developed, though they are sketched out enough to be interesting and unique. Aiken's short stories have an undercurrent of realism but never stay put in the realm of the normal because she is primarily a fantasist.

Speculative Fiction

Fiction writers who use the novel or short story to explore alternate realities fall into the broad category of speculative fiction writers. This includes science fiction, superhero fiction, fantasy, gothic and horror stories, mystery, utopian and dystopian fiction, alternate history, and apocalyptic fiction. These narrative genres often overlap and may use realism to a certain degree but are free to explore imagined worlds, the future, or the supernatural. Speculative fiction asks, What if? The author begins with a hypothesis and then imagines the implications. The story "Sonata for Harp and Bicycle" makes the assumption that ghosts exist and can affect the living. Well-known examples of speculative fiction include J. R. R. Tolkien's fantasy series *The Lord of the Rings* (1954-1955), Isaac Asimov's science fiction novel *Foundation* (1951), Ursula Le Guin's *The Dispossessed: An Ambiguous Utopia* (1974), Bram Stoker's gothic horror

Dracula (1897), and the adventure story *Tarzan* by Edgar Rice Burroughs (1914).

Gothic Fantasy

The gothic fantasy is a supernatural mystery story evoking fear and awe. The foundation of the genre was Horace Walpole's *The Castle of Otranto* (1764). The gothic story takes its name from the spooky Gothic mansions and cathedrals of its settings. Originating in eighteenth- and nineteenth-century Europe, this particular form of romance has been adapted to other genres, such as the short story and film. The style may include old buildings with a tragic history, a confrontation with evil, threats of violence, grotesque characters or situations, death or a murder mystery, decay, an appeal to the supernatural, a haunting past with family secrets, omens and prophesies, and a spiritual or moral dimension. The ghost story is one particular type of gothic story, focusing on the haunting of the living by the dead, as in "Sonata for Harp and Bicycle."

HISTORICAL CONTEXT

Nineteenth-Century London

Aiken sets the plot not in traditional gothic architecture, such as a ruined church or chateau, but in the heart of London in a dilapidated office building. The events that gave rise to the ghosts happened at least fifty years earlier than the present time in the story (mid-twentieth century), which would date William Heron's suicide to around the turn of the century. The building is old and dark with a crumbling exterior, probably built in Victorian times as a monument to progress. The Grimes Buildings in name and description are similar to settings and names used by Charles Dickens (1812-1870), and Aiken admits she was influenced by Dickens as a writer. Many of her stories have Victorian settings. Dickens criticized progress at the cost of human suffering in stories such as "A Christmas Carol," which is an important background for this Christmas ghost story. In that famous story, Scrooge, like Ashgrove, learns a Christmas lesson from a ghost. In the nineteenth century, London was the most advanced industrial city in the world. The architect of the Grimes Buildings in "Sonata for Harp and Bicycle" is proud of the huge office complex, boasting that every office gets a "crumb of light," but the light

COMPARE & CONTRAST

- **Late nineteenth century:** When William Heron and Daisy Bell are courting, women are still largely in the home. Daisy has one of few professions open to women, as music teacher, but doing so in an office building is somewhat unusual.

  Mid-twentieth century: When Jason Ashgrove and Berenice Golden are courting, women are in the public workplace alongside men but still in subordinate positions. For instance, Berenice is only a secretary, though she has been in the company longer than Jason has.

  Today: Miss Golden might well be an advertising agent or executive with a staff under her.

- **Late nineteenth century:** Advertising is a new and growing field, with agencies largely brokering ads for newspapers at first, and then later beginning to write the ads themselves.

  Mid-twentieth century: Advertising agencies like Moreton Wold and Company employ thousands of people to produce advertisements for diverse clients in the mass media markets, including radio, television, and print.

  Today: Advertising is all-pervasive, done by professionals and amateurs alike, using a wide array of communication technologies for mass marketing, including social media, Web sites and pop-up ads, telephone, radio, television, film, film spin-offs, video, print, T-shirts, mugs, posters, and other memorabilia.

- **Late nineteenth century:** Ghost stories are often sentimental, with a moral emphasis.

  Mid-twentieth century: Ghost stories are well-structured and ambiguous, and they often aim for an effect of psychological terror.

  Today: Ghost stories often emphasize pure terror with sensational gore.

---

is minimal, and the office workers are packed in like animals in pens. Heron and Daisy Bell carry on their courtship in the deserted office building at night in the dark corridors. They are dwarfed by the building's size, suggested by Heron's having to use a bicycle to patrol the corridors of the ten-story building as night watchman.

The diminishing of human importance is also suggested in the story by the older historical layers of London. The twentieth-century characters hear the London church bells ring out as they leave work. St. Paul's Cathedral is a major landmark of London, built by Christopher Wren in the seventeenth century and designed to make a human feel small in the presence of God. The Grimes Buildings are built to make humans feel small in the presence of the company.

Aiken describes the Grimes Buildings as "gaunt and sooty" and "lurch[ing]" up the hill towards Clerkenwell. The tendency to personify buildings and objects is characteristic of Dickens's style. Here the building seems alive, like a ghost itself, in the heart of London. Clerkenwell has a rich history, beginning in the Middle Ages, when churches and monasteries stood there and mystery plays were performed. In the seventeenth century, it was a resort area for the rich. That gave way to prisons and commercial ventures such as breweries, and finally it became an area for immigrants. This image of change and decay for both the city and the building creates a suitable atmosphere for a modern ghost story.

Aiken's sense of humor is evident in the name of Daisy Bell for the harp teacher. Daisy Bell is the girl's name in a popular song of that era, "A Bicycle Built for Two." The young man in the song wants his girl Daisy to ride on a tandem bike with him as a metaphor for marriage, and at the end of this story, we imagine the two ghosts riding off together on Heron's bicycle.

The office building was very dimly lit. *(Kokhanchikov/*
Shutterstock.com)

Twentieth-Century London

In mid-twentieth-century London, commuters went to work in the inner city, the business district, far from their homes in the suburbs. Berenice Golden has to take a bus after work to get home. Instead of courting secretly, as Heron and Daisy had to, young couples go out on dates together, as when Ashgrove tries to take Miss Golden to dinner. The lifestyle of the employees suggests a scene from a science fiction story, with the impersonal and mechanical movement of people. Joan Aiken draws on her own experience as an advertising writer for the large J. Walter Thompson agency in London, 1960–1961.

The modern era is also signaled in the story by a somewhat irreverent attitude towards ghosts. Ashgrove decides that no ghost is going to dictate his life for him, and it would have been a pleasure for this story's original audience to see the ghost outwitted by modern gadgets. Instead of a faulty telephone alarm that fails, the modern characters use a telephone switchboard and intercom system

to get the ghosts together. Ashgrove may not be Superman, but he knows how to jump off a building without dying. Although parachutes had been used since the eighteenth century, the type of modern knapsack parachute that Ashgrove uses was invented in the twentieth century. It became part of military paraphernalia in World War I. Ashcroft borrows it from a friend who is a member of the Royal Air Force. Aiken thus uses the past, as ghost story writers frequently do, but she sets the story in the present to provide a surprise twist.

CRITICAL OVERVIEW

Aiken published more than one hundred books from 1952 to 2004. They received varying degrees of notice and review when they appeared. The famous "Wolves of Willoughby Chase" series, the Jane Austen novels, and the "Arabel and Mortimer" series received multiple reviews of every new installment. Other books by Aiken, particularly the collections of short stories such as *A Bundle of Nerves*, containing "Sonata for Harp and Bicycle" (1976), were largely ignored. Nevertheless, Aiken's total body of work has scored consistently high marks with critics and educators since the publication of her most famous novel, *The Wolves of Willoughby Chase* (1962). Her reputation as a children's fantasy author and writer of thrillers is secure.

In 1971, John Rowe Townsend published *A Sense of Story: Essays on Contemporary Writers for Children*. In it he considers Aiken in the same group with Madeleine L'Engle and Andre Norton. Townsend notes Aiken's originality, wild plots, and humor. He calls her a "caricaturist and a mimic" with "high Dickensian colour." He considers her essentially "a lightweight writer," but he does not intend this label as a slur. In 1979, the reference book *Fantasy Literature: A Core Collection and Reference Guide*, by Marshall B. Tymn, Kenneth J. Zahorski, and Robert H. Boyer, recommends Aiken's books as suitable fantasy for all ages, citing her "consummate craftsmanship," polished prose, and fast-paced narrative. In *A Teacher's Guide to the Novels of Joan Aiken* (1982), Charles F. Reasoner prepares a guide for teachers who wish to focus on the "Willoughby Chase" series, noting that the beauty of her work is "that which lies beneath the surface."

In an overview of Aiken's work for *Language Arts* (1989), Anne Rose samples reviews over the years, noting that critics agree on Aiken's fertile imagination, but some readers have criticized her lack of original plots and use of formulaic writing. In terms of scary short stories, Chris Sherman in *Booklist* describes *A Fit of Shivers* as being satisfyingly creepy rather than depicting shocking horror. The stories in *A Creepy Company* are reviewed by Jo Goodman in *Magpies* (1994), who praises them as intelligent and well-written ghost stories. Sarah V. Clere's evaluation in *British Children's Writers since 1960* (1996) notes that it is the vast number of Aiken's books that has kept her from being appreciated as a serious writer. She praises the horror stories that are full of real danger and evil but always promote humane values.

Aiken's reputation for fantasy was still strong in the 1990s. Amanda Craig, in her essay "World of Wonders" in the *New Statesman* (1999), compares Aiken to A. S. Byatt in terms of being able to write new fairy tales. John Clute, in *Supernatural Fiction Writers: Contemporary Fantasy and Horror* (2003), appreciates the total body of Aiken's work, especially her lesser-known short stories, as containing a "central liberating sense that escapes can be made." The cumulative excellence of Aiken's contribution to children's literature was recognized in 1999 with her award as a member of the Order of the British Empire.

CRITICISM

Susan K. Andersen

Andersen is a writer with a Ph.D. in literature. In the following essay, she considers Aiken's conscious use of imagination in "Sonata for Harp and Bicycle" as both a theme in the story and as a strategy for writing and reading.

Aiken believes the imagination is a muscle to be stretched and exercised. This is as true for her characters as for readers and writers. The problem, she says in her essay "On Imagination," is that "we have turned over our imaginations to the professionals," including our computers. Imagination is the faculty of problem-solving, but it is also the faculty of hope, of making alternate realities in contrast to the current one. "Imagination is a leap into new ground," she concludes. In her ghost story "Sonata for Harp and Bicycle," Aiken shows the hero, Jason Ashgrove, imaginatively

> THE CONFRONTATION WITH THE GHOST TRIGGERS JASON ASHGROVE'S IMAGINATION IN MORE THAN ONE WAY. HERON'S GHOST IS A CATALYST FOR JASON'S OWN ROMANTIC AWAKENING."

creating his way out of the curse of Heron's ghost by leaping off a ten-story building with a parachute, holding his girlfriend in his arms.

Until the curious Jason shows up at Moreton Wold and Company advertising agency in London, the Grimes Buildings have been dominated by the will of a ghost who has been terrorizing the building for fifty years. The employers have accepted the haunting as something fixed and permanent. They count on the employees being obedient and unquestioning when they give orders over the loudspeaker to vacate the building.

Jason's independence and originality are shown to benefit himself and the company in unexpected ways. Since he is an advertising agent, he obviously needs his imagination in his job, but imagination is not something to use merely nine to five. Aiken says in "On Imagination" that the imagination has "life-and-death importance." The confrontation with the ghost triggers Jason Ashgrove's imagination in more than one way. Heron's ghost is a catalyst for Jason's own romantic awakening.

Aiken has created two sets of lovers in the story, one at the end of the nineteenth century and one in the mid-twentieth century, occupying the same space in the same building. The Heron-Bell romance from an earlier time is like many old legends of lovers tragically separated from one another by circumstance. Legendary lovers tend to be somewhat passive or lack power within their world, subject to the restrictions of their elders or culture. Aiken's humor is seen in the circumstances for this tragedy, however. There are no villains forbidding Heron's marriage. The heroine simply falls asleep, and the technology of the telephone wake-up call fails. They have, essentially, a communication problem.

WHAT DO I READ NEXT?

- Aiken's most famous series of fantasy chronicles for young adults begins with *The Wolves of Willoughby Chase* (1962; Yearling reprint, 1987), an alternate history of Britain in the fictitious reign of James III during the nineteenth century. Two young girls are attacked by wolves and an evil governess. The story was made into a film in 1989 (Atlantic Releasing Corporation), starring Stephanie Beacham.

- Gavin Baddeley's *Goth Chic: A Connoisseur's Guide to Dark Culture* (Plexus, 2006) explains the goth subculture with its music, fashion, horror comic books, and vampire movies. The book is richly illustrated and explains the goth aesthetic.

- *The Oxford Book of English Ghost Stories*, edited by Michael Cox (2008), contains classic stories from the early nineteenth century to the 1960s, including those of Sir Walter Scott, H. G. Wells, Walter de la Mare, Henry James, and others. M. R. James's "Oh, Whistle, and I'll Come to You, My Lad," which Aiken and others have declared the scariest ghost story ever written, is included.

- Richard Davenport-Hines shows the gothic in its many faces through the centuries in *Gothic: 400 Years of Excess, Horror, Evil and Ruin* (1996; North Point Press, 2000), bringing together such diverse figures as Mary Shelley and American filmmaker David Lynch in their fascination with the dark side. He argues that the gothic urge is a nonconformist and irrational trend underlying Western civilization.

- Elizabeth Gaskell's *Gothic Tales* (Penguin, 2001) includes the classic "The Old Nurse's Story," first published as one of Dickens's Christmas ghost stories in his magazine *Household Words* in 1852. The story deals with the social issue of Victorian cruelty towards women and children.

- *Haunting Christmas Tales: An Anthology* (Scholastic, 1993) boasts nine holiday ghost tales for young adults, including stories by Joan Aiken, Garry Kilworth, and others.

- *The Dark Thirty: Southern Tales of the Supernatural* by Patricia C. McKissack is a Knopf Book for Young Readers (1996) with ghost stories based on African American history and culture, including tales of slavery and the civil rights movement. The book won the 1993 Coretta Scott King Award for its handling of racism and is illustrated by Brian Pinkney.

Jason also seems to have a communication problem with Berenice, though he is unaware of it. He asks her what she wants for Christmas and asks her out to dinner, but he seems to be viewing her as a secretary who can give him information, rather than as a love interest. She does not respond, though the narrator tells us that what she wants for Christmas is him. It is only at the point of death, when the ghost asks Jason if he has any reason to live, that he realizes he is in love with Berenice. Thus, he makes a bid to avoid Heron's lonely fate by living through the ordeal and passionately embracing Berenice Golden the next day.

In her foreword to *The Collected Ghost Stories of E. F. Benson*, Aiken tells us that "what frightens us most of all, is the doppelganger, the obverse side of our own selves." The doppelganger or double is a technique in many ghost and horror stories. For instance, Frankenstein's monster represents Frankenstein's own worst self, and Marley's ghost is an image of Scrooge. Heron can thus be seen as another aspect of Jason's character, warning him not to let love slip away. The two couples also mirror each other. Jason and Berenice re-create the last scene of the ghost lovers' story to correct the drama, in a way, so that both couples are happily united. Just as Aiken leads us to imagine Heron and Daisy finally together on a bicycle built for two, so Jason and Berenice make a tandem jump by parachute with their wine and roses. We assume the ghosts will no longer haunt the building in their futile attempt to find one another.

Aiken creates a visual symbol for Jason's imaginative act in the shape of the building itself. It is triangular. He stands at the point of the triangle staring down two long passages that come towards him. Berenice tells Jason that despite the fact both ghosts are in the building, "*they never meet.*" Jason is the one who joins the separate paths of Daisy and Heron. Jason and Berenice have a mystical perception of the ghosts leaving together with harp, wine, and roses on the saddle of a bicycle. They do not actually see this happen but are left with a radiant memory of this image. The impression is "as bright as the picture on a Salvador Dali calendar." The surreal image engulfs both of them and the reader at the same time, without being concrete.

Aiken does not explain mystery. She simply leaves clues, expecting the reader's imagination to fill in the gaps. In her book *The Way to Write for Children*, Aiken asserts that the ending of a story has to be satisfying but not explained. In *Mystery in Children's Literature: From the Rational to the Supernatural*, Adrienne E. Gavin and Christopher Routledge state, "A key difference between fantasy and mystery is that mystery has a question mark in it." Some of Aiken's fiction can be very dark, but it must not be too dark, she cautions. The young need to get an accurate sense that there is evil in the world, but they also need to be reassured, as in fairy tales, that good ultimately triumphs. In the introduction to the collection *Dread and Delight: A Century of Children's Ghost Stories*, which includes a ghost story by Joan Aiken, Philippa Pearce speaks of the child's pleasure in "safe fear." Aiken provides safe fear: her fiction is full of enterprising characters, both children and adults, like Jason, who do not give in to evil.

The happy ending of this ghost story can also be explained in terms of Charles Dickens's "A Christmas Carol." Pearce explains how Dickens exploited the old oral tradition connecting Christmastime with the telling of ghost stories, and Aiken picks up this motif. "Sonata for Harp and Bicycle" is set in London at Christmas. Jason and Berenice bravely parachute off Grimes Building on Christmas Eve to bring peace by canceling a

curse. Aiken leaves off the moralizing so common to Victorian fiction, though she implies that this act is one of love and charity. She shows but does not tell Jason's lesson from the ghost. Was Aiken possibly thinking, when she chose the title of her story, of George MacDonald's essay "The Fantastic Imagination," in which he declares that fantastic tales do not need to mean something specific but merely suggest, like a sonata?

H. G. Wells popularized the idea of the fantastic story as a game that writer and reader play together. The writer has to trick the reader into buying an initial assumption for the moment, as in this story we temporarily accept the existence of ghosts. Though a ghost story should not be overexplained, it must be carefully structured to deliver its fear and surprise. In *Elegant Nightmares: The English Ghost Story from Le Fanu to Blackwood*, Jack Sullivan mentions that stories must lead up gradually to their secret; "the best chills are evoked with care and control." Peter Penzoldt details the structures that successful horror writers use in *The Supernatural in Fiction*. The climax is the moment of shock, when the apparition finally appears or the secret for its appearance is known. Penzoldt quotes M. R. James, one of Aiken's favorite ghost-story writers, as using the principle of the crescendo; that is, the writer shows ordinary reality in the beginning and then unobtrusively introduces the marvelous more and more, building to the climax.

The idea of crescendo, a musical term meaning a gradual increase in intensity, works nicely for "Sonata for Harp and Bicycle," a highly structured short story, like the sonata itself. A sonata is a musical arrangement in three or four movements that develops a theme and keeps restating it, finally resolving it in a different key. It is often composed for solo instruments, and here, Aiken suggests that her sonata is for harp and bicycle, the instruments of the two ghost lovers. The story falls into four parts. The first part is the exposition, building suspense, as Jason Ashgrove, the new employee, discovers an oddity in his workplace. The second part is Jason's solo encounter with the ghost that turns his hair silver. The third part is Berenice's explanation of the ghosts and the danger that the curse represents to Jason. The fourth part is the suspenseful resolution, with the modern lovers risking their lives to foil the curse.

Another structural principle Aiken uses in writing is brought out in her introduction to

He asked if she could work the switchboard to place a call. (*2009fotofriends | Shutterstock.com*)

Moonshine and Shadows, where she mentions that a short story needs to have two narrative strands, a "basic thread," and a "fertilizing agent." A creative idea by itself does not lead anywhere. In "Sonata for Harp and Bicycle," the basic thread of the story is the modern advertising company in London haunted by a Victorian night watchman. The fertilizing agent is the Christmas love story between Jason and Berenice.

Aiken states in *The Way to Write for Children* that stories are "instruments of healing, of teaching." By saying that stories teach, Aiken is not falling into the nineteenth-century trap of obvious moralizing, but neither does she fit into the opposite camp of pure horror for its own sake, set by the standards of the famous horror writer H. P. Lovecraft. Jack Sullivan in *Elegant Nightmares* concludes that the trends of modern horror stories are not towards any catharsis (the releasing of emotions through literature) but rather "move us toward an ever-darkening vision of chaos in a hostile universe." Aiken, on the contrary, feels a responsibility towards her readers, both to provide thrills and to inspire. "The world," she writes, "is an infinitely rich, strange, confusing,

wonderful, cruel, mysterious, beautiful, inexplicable riddle."

Source: Susan K. Andersen, Critical Essay on "Sonata on Harp and Bicycle," in *Short Stories for Students*, Gale, Cengage Learning, 2011.

Michael Dirda

In the following review, Dirda proclaims Shadows & Moonshine *very suitable for bedtime reading.*

Sometimes it's hard to decide whether the tsunami-like success of J.K. Rowling has been good or bad for children's literature, and for fantasy in particular. On the plus side, the Harry Potter books have certainly encouraged kids—and many grown-ups—to read . . . Harry Potter books. But, and this is the more tentative minus side, do they read anything else? More than popular, more than fashionable, the young bespectacled wizard-in-training inspires rabid cultishness. To find an apt comparison, one thinks of Pet Rocks, Cabbage Patch dolls and Beanie Babies, or, to go back even further in time, Dutch tulipmania and the similar crazes chronicled in Charles MacKay's *Extraordinary Popular Delusions* and the *Madness of Crowds*.

None of this should be construed as knocking Rowling's work: Who doesn't admire her story-telling magic? But I do wish young readers might go on and rediscover some of the other, equally wonderful children's fantasies: the Oz books, above all, but also the classic English adventures of E. Nesbit (*Five Children and It*) and her American counterpart Edward Eager (*Half Magic*); Alan Garner's folkloric *The Weirdstone of Brisingamen*, William Mayne's poetic and disturbing *A Game of Dark*, the works of Daniel Pinkwater, Diana Wynne-Jones, Susan Cooper, Robert Westall, John Bellairs, Natalie Babbitt and Richard Kennedy (try the sinister novella "Inside My Boots" from his *Collected Stories*), those twin masterpieces Russell Hoban's *The Mouse and His Child* and Philippa Pearce's *Tom's Midnight Garden*, John Masefield's insufficiently known Christmas classic, *The Box of Delights*, and, not least, the amazing oeuvre of Joan Aiken.

Now in her seventies, Joan Aiken has probably turned out a book for every year of her life. Maybe more. These have ranged from romantic suspense for adults to a translation of a children's novel by the Comtesse de Segur. She's written mysteries, ghost stories and comic tales about a raven named Mortimer. She once set a spooky literary thriller in Lamb House, the home of Henry James and E. F. Benson (of "Lucia" fame). Not least, Aiken sternly but justly remarked that if you weren't prepared to read aloud to your kids for an hour a day, you shouldn't have any.

Still, for all her astonishing fertility and variousness, Aiken is best known for her mini-Victorian sensation novel *The Wolves of Willoughby Chase* and the wonderful adventure series, set in the same 19th-century England, about Dido Twite. Dido is a resourceful street urchin—a female Tom Sawyer—who first appears in *Black Hearts in Battersea*, when she helps thwart a scheme to blow up the houses of Parliament. Later she undergoes misadventures in Puritan America (where she helps a 9-year-old girl named Dutiful Penitence and is eventually helped herself by a great pink whale) and South America, before returning to England, all the while foiling various dastardly plots to dethrone King James III. Two late books, *Is Underground* and *Cold Comfort Road*, focus on Dido's sister and, I think, may have influenced Philip Pullman's *The Golden Compass*, particularly when Is goes to the rescue of London children spirited off to a vast underground mine in the North.

Shadows & Moonshine, handsomely illustrated by Pamela Johnson, offers a selection of Aiken's short stories, mainly geared toward middle readers. Most are cast as fairy tales, a form that Aiken knows better than anyone else now living. Take the opening paragraph of "The Gift Pig":

"Once upon a time there was a king whose queen, having just presented him with a baby princess, unfortunately died. The king was very upset and grieved, but he had to go on with the arrangements for the christening just the same, as court etiquette was strict on this point. What with his grief and distraction, however, and the yells of the royal baby, who was extremely lively and loud-voiced, the invitations to the christening were sent out very carelessly, and by mistake the list included two elderly fairies who were known to loathe the very sight of one another, though when seen alone they were pleasant enough."

In her introduction to *Shadows & Moonshine*, Aiken likens writing short stories to a sleigh ride—"you get on course, and then some terrific power, like the power of gravity, takes command and whizzes you off to an unknown destination." In younger days, she tells us, she might actually write two stories in a single evening. Certainly such bountiful inventiveness can be a mixed blessing, as Joyce Carol Oates or Phyllis Reynolds Naylor can probably testify: Naive readers may dismiss the resulting work as facile, shallow or the product of automatic writing rather than painstaking craft.

In truth, Aiken's short stories occasionally suffer from rather wan endings, but her limpid style, flair for dialect, subdued (or slapstick) humor and, most of all, her comforting voice make up for this weakness. If weakness it is. Some endings are perforce dictated by the demands of the fairy tale genre: The pattern established at the beginning must be completed by the end. An opening of "Once upon a time" requires a concluding "and they all lived happily ever after."

But make no mistake: People die in these stories (though sometimes happily); some heroines are plain and unattractive and remain so; mermaids have their hearts broken. But any of these tales would be just right for bedtime reading aloud. You can certainly finish one or maybe two in an hour:

"At that very instant a black, magic cloud swept down on Griselda as she stood making a salad, and carried her into the middle of the desert where the dragon lived. She was rather annoyed, but put a good face on it, and at once began looking for an oasis."

Source: Michael Dirda, "*Shadows & Moonshine* Stories by...," in *Washington Post*, December 23, 2001, p. T15.

Amanda Craig

In the following review, Craig holds up The Youngest Miss Ward *as an example of Aiken's persona as author of suspenseful romantic fiction.*

Best known for her children's classic *The Wolves of Willoughby Chase*, Joan Aiken has another persona as author of accomplished and suspenseful romantic fiction. In recent years, the cod-history of her children's books has fertilised the adult ones in the form of novels inspired by minor characters and events in Jane Austen's fiction. The result may not please Janites but it is far, far better—and funnier—than anything by Georgette Heyer.

The Youngest Miss Ward follows the fortunes of Fanny Price's unmentionable Aunt Hattie who, not capturing either a Sir Thomas Bertram or a Mr Norris, has to make her way in the world far from Mansfield Park. Here we have a worm's-eye view of the disastrous marriage of Fanny's mother, of the future Mrs Norris's heartbreak over a gamekeeper and of the Portsmouth from which Fanny escapes to Mansfield Park.

Those who detest Fanny's meekness will derive considerable entertainment from her spirited aunt; like the best romantic heroines she combines sense and sensibility, and soon has not only her boorish cousin but the radical Lord Camber interested in her. Camber's attentions inspire the particular enmity of the bossy Lady Ursula but, before he embarks for America and the hope of a more equable society, he introduces Hattie to his house in the woods and his servant Godwit.

Aiken's tone is as briskly captivating as her protagonists: she shows how reason and fair-mindedness triumph over both snobbery and sex. This is far from being the inch of ivory on which Jane Austen famously painted; politics, feminism and even the French Revolution intrude onto the canvas. Confronted with Gothic horrors and the mentally handicapped, Hattie rolls up her sleeves and boldly routs ignorance, prejudice and greed. In doing so she finds true love and a career as a pseudonymous poet.

If this is romantic fiction, it is of a very particular and commendable kind. Aiken's language and tone go beyond pastiche. The independence of mind shown by her protagonists is very much that recently described in Amanda Vickery's striking study of Georgian women *The Gentleman's Daughter* (Yale).

Aiken's heroines, however, go further. They question received opinions; they are genuinely brave; they are aware of politics and a world beyond that of the good match. Romantics could do nothing better than to read her.

Source: Amanda Craig, "Jane Without the Pain," in *London Times*, August 1, 1998.

Danny Karlin

In the following review, Karlin finds Jane Fairfax *to be an unsuccessful attempt "to be both like Jane Austen (substitute for the real thing) and to revise Jane Austen (be the real thing)."*

Jane Austen's work seems, at first, hospitable to that literary parasite, pastiche: there isn't much of it, so ersatz continuations or alternative narratives must satisfy the hunger for more; at the same time, the passionate familiarity which many Jane Austen readers have with her novels (demonstrated in Kipling's wonderful story 'The Janeites') ensures a ready frame of reference for the imitator. But Jane Austen is, in fact, notoriously hard to 'do' convincingly. Joan Aiken (their names are horribly homophonic—could this have given her the idea?) is the author of *Mansfield Revisited*, which seems to have been successful enough to persuade her to try the market again. I have only ever read one such work, the continuation of *Sanditon* by 'a Lady' published some years ago; the bitter taste still lingers on, and I have a grudging sense that *Jane Fairfax* may not be quite as thin a dish of gruel as that. Instead it has an unappealing, mixed-up wrongness of flavour. It wants to be both *like* Jane Austen (to substitute for the real thing) and to *revise* Jane Austen (to be a real thing itself). Aiken disastrously fails to recognise that these are incompatible aims. She plunders Austen's novel (sometimes quoting it verbatim or paraphrasing it closely, though 'her' Miss Bates or Mr Woodhouse or Emma have embalming-fluid in their literary veins); other characters derive weakly from other Austen novels (a brutal fop from *Northanger Abbey*, a kind-hearted mother from *Sense and Sensibility*) and one has strayed in wearing Mrs Jellyby's clothes from *Bleak House*. At the same time, Aiken misreads *Emma* in crassly uninteresting ways. The plot turns on Emma's fantasies about sexual relationships being mistaken, yet Aiken makes her daft suspicion of a liaison between Jane and Mr Dixon, formed at Weymouth, turn out to be true after all. This makes absolute nonsense of Jane's relationship with Frank Churchill: the upright, pure-hearted, melancholy Jane is represented as choosing to enter into a clandestine engagement with a man she does not really love, and (even more ludicrously) is endowed with a romantic yearning for Mr Knightley worthy of Harriet Smith herself.

A line in feminist literary criticism takes Jane Fairfax, along with Marianne Dashwood from *Sense and Sensibility*, as an exemplary figure of the repressions and suppressions which Austen's art both questions and practises. But of this struggle Aiken's own wretchedly bad writing can say little. Jane Fairfax does indeed, I think, step into *Emma* out of the pages of Mary Wollstonecraft: but the protest which her presence in Highbury registers against the prevailing social order is defused by the fairy-tale plot which takes care to avert her grim social destiny as impoverished governess. She is clearly an intellectual where Emma is a dilettante; socially and economically trapped where Emma is at large; Romantic and self-thwarted in her emotional life where Emma is carefree and self-indulged. However pointed and suggestive this contrast may be, it does not imply equivalence. Jane is outshone by Emma (so is the other Jane, Jane Bennett, by Elizabeth in *Pride and Prejudice*: as though characters gifted with their creator's name were relegated to an ironic secondariness); Austen does not make the injustice of Jane's lot tell against Emma's privilege as such: rather, it shows up Emma's misuse of her resources. Those resources include the lion's share of the reader's attention, which is not given to Emma as a privilege but because she earns it. She is, in Austen's judgment, more interesting than Jane. It is this judgment which Aiken implicitly challenges: but in order to do so convincingly she would have to break free of precisely the aspect of pastiche which offers the reader a comfortably familiar tone and texture. The book's mock-Georgian front (disfigured occasionally by the stylistic equivalent of double-glazing: 'Solicitous to protect Jane, Emma's mother did not reflect that the boot might conceivably be on the other foot') is fatally at odds with its modern interior.

Source: Danny Karlin, "Mary Swann's Way," in *London Review of Books*, Vol. 12, No. 8, September 27, 1990, pp. 20–21.

SOURCES

Aiken, Joan, "Foreword," in *The Collected Ghost Stories of E. F. Benson*, edited by Richard Dalby, Carroll & Graf, 1992; reprint, 2001, p. xii.

———, "Introduction," in *Moonshine and Shadows: Stories by Joan Aiken*, David Godine, 2001, pp. vii–viii.

———, "On Imagination," in *Horn Book Magazine*, Vol. 60, No. 6, November/December 1984, pp. 735–37, 740–741.

———, "Sonata for Harp and Bicycle," in *A Bundle of Nerves*, Penguin, 1978, pp. 203–13.

———, *The Way to Write for Children*, St. Martin's Griffin, 1982, reprint, 1998, pp. 16, 17, 52, 53, 61, 78, 86, 94.

Clere, Sarah V., "Joan (Delano) Aiken," in *Dictionary of Literary Biography*, Vol. 161, *British Children's Writers since 1960: First Series*, edited by Caroline C. Hunt, Gale Research, 1996, pp. 3–11.

Clute, John, "Joan Aiken," in *Supernatural Fiction Writers: Contemporary Fantasy and Horror*, Vol. I, *Peter Ackroyd to Graham Joyce*, edited by Richard Bleiler, Charles Scribner's Sons, 2003, p. 21.

Craig, Amanda, "World of Wonders," in *New Statesman*, Vol. 128, May 31, 1999, p. 49.

Gavin, Adrienne E., and Christopher Routledge, "Introduction," in *Mystery in Children's Literature from the Rational to the Supernatural*, edited by Adrienne E. Gavin and Christopher Routledge, Palgrave, 2001, p. 3.

Goodman, Jo, Review of *A Creepy Company*, in *Magpies*, Vol. 9, No. 3, July 1994, p. 30.

Lovecraft, Howard Phillips, *Supernatural Horror in Literature*, Dover, 1973, pp. 12–16.

MacDonald, George, "The Fantastic Imagination," in *Fantasists on Fantasy: A Collection of Critical Reflections*, edited by Robert Boyer and Kenneth J. Zahorski, Avon Books, 1984, p. 18.

Pearce, Philippa, "Introduction," in *Dread and Delight: A Century of Children's Ghost Stories*, edited by Philippa Pearce, Oxford University Press, 1995, pp. ix–x.

Penzoldt, Peter, *The Supernatural in Fiction*, Humanities Press, 1965, p. 192.

Punter, David, *The Literature of Terror: A History of Gothic Fictions from 1765 to the Present Day*, Vol. 1, 2nd ed., Longman, 1996, pp. 188–92.

Reasoner, Charles, *A Teacher's Guide to the Novels of Joan Aiken*, Dell, 1982, p. 7.

Rose, Anne, "Profile: Joan Aiken," in *Language Arts*, Vol. 66, No. 7, November 1989, pp. 784–90.

Sherman, Chris, Review of *A Fit of Shivers*, in *Booklist*, Vol. 89, No. 1, September 1, 1992, p. 46.

Sullivan, Jack, *Elegant Nightmares: The English Ghost Story from Le Fanu to Blackwood*, Ohio University Press, 1978, pp. 8, 130.

————, "Golden Age of the Ghost Story," in *The Penguin Encyclopedia of Horror and the Supernatural*, Viking, 1986, pp. 174–76.

Townsend, John Rowe, *A Sense of Story: Essays on Contemporary Writers for Children*, J. B. Lippincott, 1971, pp. 19–21.

Tymn, Marshall B., Kenneth J. Zahorski, and Robert H. Boyer, eds., *Fantasy Literature: A Core Collection and Reference Guide*, R. R. Bowker, 1979, p. 39.

Wells, H. G., "Preface," in *The Complete Science Fiction of H. G. Wells*, Avenel Books, 1978.

FURTHER READING

Aiken, Joan, *The Haunting of Lamb House*, St. Martin's Press, 1993.

> This thriller blends fictional and historical characters in three interwoven ghost stories. Set in a real haunted house in Aiken's hometown of Rye, the first story is about a family tragedy in the eighteenth century. The second story adds author Henry James living in the same house haunted by the ghost, and the third is about horror writer E. F. Benson later living in the house and being aware of all its ghosts.

Bloom, Clive, *Gothic Horror: A Guide for Students and Readers*, Palgrave Macmillan, 2007.

> The revised edition collects historical criticism on gothic and horror stories from the eighteenth to the twenty-first centuries. It includes an introduction on the historical and social background of the gothic genre.

Cornwell, Neil, *Literary Fantastic from Gothic to Postmodernism*, Harvester Wheatsheaf, 1990.

> Surveying the fantastic in literature from the gothic novel in the eighteenth century through the romantic horror stories of the nineteenth century, such as *Frankenstein* and *Dracula*, the book traces the reappearance of the fantastic in postmodern fiction. The discussion includes modern authors such as Salman Rushdie and Toni Morrison.

Goodlad, Lauren M. E., and Michael Bibby, eds., *Goth: Undead Subculture*, Duke University Press, 2007.

> This multidisciplinary collection of essays includes ethnographic stories, cultural criticism, and historical analysis of the goth subculture. An in-depth discussion of a postmodern trend, it investigates the fashion, music, dance, literature, sexual behavior, aesthetics, and ideology of goth.

Heller, Terry, *The Delights of Terror: An Aesthetics of the Tale of Terror*, University of Illinois Press, 1987.

> Why do people enjoy being scared? The book looks at reader response from the theories of Sigmund Freud, Jacques Lacan, and Wolfgang Iser and applies it to close readings of tales of terror.

SUGGESTED SEARCH TERMS

supernatural fiction

horror fiction

Joan Aiken AND children's literature

Sonata for Harp and Bicycle

gothic fiction

speculative fiction

ghost story

fantasy short fiction

goth subculture

modern short story

War

LUIGI PIRANDELLO

1918

"War" is a short story by Italian writer Luigi Pirandello, one of the major figures in twentieth-century European literature. He is known primarily for his plays, but he also wrote hundreds of short stories as well as novels. Pirandello wrote "War" in 1918, during the last year of World War I. The story is set in a railroad carriage in Italy. Several travelers are journeying from Rome and are joined at dawn by a man and his wife. The couple are on their way to visit their son, who is going off to war. The mother is unhappy because she thinks no one understands how she feels. A discussion ensues among the men, several of whom have sons and other relatives fighting in the war. They discuss who suffers the most in such situations. One traveler claims that young men are happy to die for their country and so their deaths should not be mourned, but a strange remark by the woman leads him to reveal his true feelings involuntarily.

"War" was translated into English and appeared in a collection of Pirandello's short stories, *A Character in Distress*, published in England in 1938. The book was published in the United States the following year under the title *The Medals and Other Stories*. This book is no longer in print, and "War" has not been reprinted since in any English-language collection of Pirandello's short stories. However, it is currently available in at least two anthologies: *Literature: Reading Fiction, Poetry, and Drama* (2000), edited by Robert Di Yanni and published by McGraw-Hill, and

Luigi Pirandello (© *Pictorial Press | Alamy*)

From Idea to Essay: A Rhetoric, Reader, and Handbook, 12th edition (2009), edited by Jo Ray McCuen-Metherell and Anthony Winkler and published by Cengage Learning.

AUTHOR BIOGRAPHY

Renowned Italian playwright, novelist, and short-story writer Pirandello was born on June 28, 1867, in Girgenti, on the island of Sicily, a region of Italy. He was the son of Stefano and Caterina Ricci-Gramitto. His father was a prosperous businessman and expected his son to follow the same line of work, but Pirandello soon revealed a talent for academic study rather than business.

Pirandello began his studies at the University of Rome in 1887 and transferred to the University of Bonn, in Germany, where he received his doctorate in linguistics in 1891.

Pirandello wrote his first short story when he was sixteen, and in 1889 he published his first volume of poetry, *Mal giocondo* (*Joyful Pain*). In 1894 his first collection of short stories was published.

In the mid-1890s Pirandello lived in Rome and married Antonietta Portulano, with whom he would later have three children. The marriage was arranged by his father; Antonietta was the daughter of his business partner, and Pirandello barely knew her. The marriage was not a happy one. Antonietta became mentally ill; Pirandello endured her hostility to him and the children for many years until finally, in 1919, she was placed in a sanatorium.

Beginning in 1897, Pirandello taught Italian literature for twenty-five years at a women's teaching college. In the first decade of the twentieth century, his creative life centered on writing fiction. From 1901 to 1912 he published five novels and six volumes of short stories, and during the 1910s he also emerged as a successful playwright. His plays from this period include *Liolà*, *Right You Are (If You Think So)*, and *The Pleasure of Honesty*. In 1918, affected by the enlistment of his two sons in World War I, he wrote the short story "War," which was originally titled "Quando si comprende" ("When Will They Learn?").

In 1921, Pirandello's masterpiece, the play *Six Characters in Search of an Author*, premiered in Rome, and within two years was produced in London, Paris, and New York. In 1922, *Henry IV*, another of Pirandello's highly successful plays, was produced for the first time.

By 1924, Pirandello was internationally famous. During the remainder of the decade, he dedicated himself to work for the theater, writing more plays and becoming the artistic director, from 1925 to 1928, of his own repertory company, Teatro D'Arte di Roma. While based in Berlin or Paris, he also traveled extensively.

Pirandello joined the Italian Fascist Party in the 1920s and was a strong supporter of the Fascist dictator Benito Mussolini (1883–1945), who ruled Italy from 1926 to 1943.

In 1934, Pirandello was awarded the Nobel Prize for Literature for his work in drama.

After becoming ill in November 1936, he died on December 10, at the age of sixty-nine. The cause of death was not specified. Against his wishes, he received a state funeral.

PLOT SUMMARY

"War" is set in Italy during World War I. At dawn, several passengers who have traveled from Rome on the night train board another train at Fabriano in order to continue their journey.

An old woman and her husband step into the second-class carriage. The other passengers make some room for them. The woman is wearing mourning clothes, and her husband explains to the other passengers that her only son, who is twenty years old, is being called up to the front in three days' time; his parents are going to see him, to bid him farewell.

The woman is uncomfortable. She does not expect to receive any sympathy from the other passengers because she assumes that they are all in similar positions.

One passenger tells her that she is fortunate. He says that his son has been at the front since the war began, has been wounded twice, and has been sent back to the front.

Another passenger says that he has two sons and three nephews at the front, to which the husband replies that it is their only son who is being sent off to war. The passenger replies that this does not make any difference since a father loves all his sons equally, with all his love.

The husband replies that even though that may be true, if two sons go to war and one is killed, the father still has one left. This reply irritates the other man. He says that if one son survives, the father is obliged to go on living, whereas if an only son dies, the father can choose to end his own life and so put an end to his distress. The man argues that it is he who is in the worst position.

Their conversation is interrupted by another passenger, a fat, red-faced man who is panting. He asks the question, "Do we give life to our children for our own benefit?"

The other passengers are surprised by his comment. The one whose son has been at the front since the beginning of the war agrees with him. He says that children belong not to their parents, but to their country.

But the fat man disagrees. He says that sons do not belong to their parents; on the contrary, it is the parents who belong to the sons. He admits that love of country is strong in sons as well as in parents, but he thinks that a father's love for his son is greater. He says that all fathers would take their sons' place in war if they could.

There is silence, and the other passengers nod their agreement.

The fat man goes on to say that at the age of twenty, young men put their love of country before their love of their parents, and this is natural. It is natural for them to want to defend their country. If it happens that they die fighting for their country, they are happy to do so. The man sees nothing to grieve about in such an eventuality. He then speaks of his own son. Before he was killed in the war, he sent his father a message saying that should he be killed, he could not imagine a better way to die. This is why, the man now says, that he is not dressed in mourning attire.

He ends with a laugh, but he is also close to crying. The other passengers indicate their agreement with what he has said.

The woman who is about to visit her son has been listening to this conversation. For months she has been trying to find something to console her for the fact that her son is being put in harm's way. Nothing anyone has said during this period has helped her, and she feels that no one understands her feelings.

However, she is now deeply affected by the fat man's words. She realizes that there is something lacking in her that makes her unable to resign herself to the possibility of her son's death in the war. She had never thought that such an attitude as that displayed by the fat man could be possible, and she enjoys listening to the other passengers express their appreciation of him.

She turns to the man and asks him bluntly, "Then...is your son really dead?" Everyone turns to look at her. The fat man tries to answer but is unable to get any words out. He looks as if he has only then suddenly realized that his son is indeed dead and will never return. He starts to sob uncontrollably.

CHARACTERS

The Fat Man

This man is described as a "fat, red-faced man with bloodshot eyes of the palest gray." He is also described as old. Two of his front teeth are missing. He has a different attitude from that of the other passengers, and he speaks only after he has heard what they have to say. He thinks that nothing is stronger than a parent's love for his or her child and says that fathers would be willing to take the place of their sons at the front if they could. But he also thinks that young men are so patriotic that they are happy to die for their country; they think it is the best thing they can do. He then confesses that his own son has been killed in the war, but he does not grieve because he knows his son was happy to meet this fate. Everyone congratulates him on possessing such an enlightened attitude, but his stoicism collapses when the woman asks him if his son is really dead. For some reason this brings home to him the reality of the situation, that he will never see his son again. He cannot hold his emotions in, and he begins to sob uncontrollably.

First Passenger

The first passenger is a man who listens attentively to the husband's explanation of why his wife is in mourning clothes. He comments that the couple should be grateful that their son is only leaving now for the front. His own son has been at the front for years and has been wounded twice. Each time he got sent back to the front. He believes that children belong not to their parents but to their country.

The Husband

The husband of the woman in mourning clothes is described as much smaller than his wife: "a tiny man, thin and weakly, his face death-white, his eyes small and bright and looking shy and uneasy." He gives the impression of having suffered a lot and of being rather world-weary. "Nasty world," he utters at one point. He has been devastated by the news that his only son is about to be sent to the front. He feels compelled to explain to his fellow travelers the situation he and his wife are in since it is obvious that his wife is very unhappy. He tells them how devoted he and his wife are to their son. They had even uprooted themselves from their home to go with him to Rome when he became a student there. They had also given him permission to volunteer for the army. Like his wife, the man is naturally worried about the danger his son is in. He tries to convince the second passenger that because he has only one son, he is in a worse situation than the other man, who has two sons at the front. But he seems embarrassed by the arguments the other two passengers bring to the discussion, and he does not defend his own opinion with much force.

Second Passenger

The second passenger enters into a conversation with the husband of the woman. He notes that the husband and wife have only one son, and he comments that in contrast, he has two sons and three nephews at the front. In spite of what the husband, worried about losing his only son, says, this man thinks that he himself is in a worse position. He loves both his sons with all his love, so losing one would be just as much of a loss as if he had only one son. In addition, he says, he would still have to go on living for the sake of the surviving son, whereas the father of an only son can simply choose to die and so end his grief.

The Wife

The wife is the only female character in the story. She is dressed in mourning clothes because she is going to visit her son who is about to depart for the front. She says nothing at first, not even replying when her husband asks her, just after they have sat down in the railway carriage, whether she is all right. She is obviously suffering silently because she fears that her son may be killed in the war. When her husband explains her situation to the other passengers, she is physically uncomfortable because she cannot believe that anyone would be sympathetic to her plight. She thinks everyone else must be in the same position. For three months people have been trying to help her find some peace and stop worrying about her son's possible fate, but nothing has given her any peace of mind. However, she is moved by what the fat man says, which is so far beyond any attitude that she could have imagined regarding the death of a son. She admires the man for adopting such a stoic attitude to his loss.

THEMES

Patriotism

All the characters in the story uphold the virtue of patriotism. No one questions it. No one speaks out against the war, not even the mother, who does not question the fat man's contention that his son died "as a hero, for his King and his Country." The initial question debated is simply about which parent suffers more when a son is killed in battle. Patriotism is presented as a natural emotion, the sort of thing that everyone

TOPICS FOR FURTHER STUDY

- Read "Old Man Travelling," a poem by William Wordsworth that was first published in 1798 in his *Lyrical Ballads*. It features a man who has just lost his son in war. Write a short essay in which you compare the state of mind of this man to that of the fat man in "War." In what ways are they similar? How do they differ? The poem can be found at the Web site maintained by Cyber Studios (http://wordsworth.underthesun.cc/Lyrical-Ballads/LyricalBallads27.html).

- Working with another student, research trench warfare during World War I and give a class presentation on it. Why was trench warfare developed? How were battles fought? Why were casualties so high? To make the presentation more interesting, go to http://www.firstworldwar.com/diaries/trenchesatvimyridge.htm and read the personal account of trench warfare by Private Harold Saunders, a British soldier. Incorporate some of his account in your presentation.

- Write a poem in which a man bids farewell to his son who is going off to war. For inspiration, you may consult *Peace and War: A Collection of Poems,* an anthology designed with young adults in mind. The anthology is edited by Michael Harrison and Christopher Stuart-Clark and features a number of World War I poets. Post your poem to the teacher's Web page and invite classmates to review it.

- Go to http://www.firstworldwar.com/posters/index.htm and click on "propaganda posters," which allows you to see hundreds of posters designed by the United States, Britain, and other countries to recruit soldiers for the war or to promote some other aspect of the war effort. Imagine that you are a recruiter for the U.S. Army. Go to glogster.com and create a poster that would encourage young people to enlist in the U.S. armed forces either during World War I or today.

feels, especially the young. For example, the fat man says, "Isn't it natural that at their age they should consider the love for their Country ... even greater than the love for us?" He says this is true "of decent boys"; he means those respectable young men who feel all the emotions that society approves of, including the kind of patriotism that allows a man to go off to war and get killed defending his country. The young will volunteer for war duty even if their parents say no, so in this sense, according to the fat man, patriotism is more important, at least for the young, than family. Older men, too, he says, have the same feelings, but there is a difference. They feel patriotism, but they love their sons more than they love their country, because they would go to war themselves, instead of sending their sons, if they were able to. The theme of patriotism is strongly linked to concepts of honor and loyalty, but the question raised for the reader to consider is loyalty to what, and to whom? To family or to country?

Sacrifice

Everyone in the story is making a sacrifice and refers to others who are making even greater sacrifices. The story is about who endures the most pain and grief from his or her sacrifice. All the actions and sentiments expressed are noble: young men are wounded or die bravely in battle, and their parents, albeit with a heavy heart, accept their loss or the possibility of loss. But the physical descriptions of the characters tend to undermine the nobility and stoical nature of the words they speak. Their humanity has been cruelly warped by what they have been compelled to endure. The woman, for example, is nearly broken by the sorrow of sending her beloved only son off to war. She is described as a "shapeless bundle" and has to be helped into her seat by others. She cannot sit still, "at times growling like a wild animal." She feels isolated in her pain. Her husband has a "death-white face"; it is as if he is in shock from what is happening to his family. Every word used to describe him suggests a stunted, fearful life. These are people who are close to cracking under unendurable strain. As with the theme of patriotism, the notion of sacrifice seems to invite the reader to question whether the sacrifice in question is ugly and dehumanizing rather than noble. Seen in this light, the discussion about who suffers most—the father with one son in harm's way or the father with two—begins to look rather absurd. It is as if people are taking refuge in mental games instead of tackling the question whether such sacrifices are really necessary.

Honesty

The theme of honesty concerns emotional honesty. It shows the importance of being true to what one is really feeling rather than trying to convince oneself that one feels a certain way by constructing an intellectual argument. The theme is conveyed unwittingly by the words and actions of the fat man. He is a man at war with himself, harboring enormous grief for his dead son but unwilling to face up to it. The struggle he is involved in is clear from the description of him when he is first introduced: "From his bulging eyes seemed to spurt inner violence of an uncontrolled vitality which his weakened body could hardly contain." There is something inside this man that is struggling to get out, but he manages to disguise this fact as he launches into a monologue—the longest speech in the entire story. He constructs a careful argument that young men are happy to die for their country, because they love their country more than anything else. He tries to persuade his listeners that there is even something advantageous about dying young in battle. Such young men are spared "the ugly sides of life," which are only realized as a man gets older: "the boredom of it, the pettiness, the bitterness of disillusion." He includes instructions for others, based on his elaborate reasoning: "Everyone should stop crying, everyone should laugh as I do." By this time the reader is perhaps becoming a little suspicious since the man's argument is an extreme one and goes against the innate human instinct to mourn the dead, especially one's own offspring. The fat man has even tried to make his outer appearance conform to the philosophy he claims to live by ("I do not even wear mourning . . . .") But the precariousness of his state of mind is again hinted at by the narrator as the man stops speaking: "his livid lip over his missing teeth was trembling, his eyes were watery and motionless, and soon after he ended with a shrill laugh which might well have been a sob." It only needs the woman to ask him a direct question about the death of his son—strangely put though the question may be—for his carefully constructed argument to collapse. He can no longer deny the reality of his loss as overwhelming grief wells up inside him. Raw emotion finally finds an outlet as he weeps uncontrollably. He cuts a pathetic figure, but at least he is finally being honest with himself.

They talked of their soldier children as they rode the train. (Ronald Sumners / Shutterstock.com)

STYLE

Irony

One aspect of irony occurs when the meaning of something is different, either opposite or unexpected, from what it might appear on the surface. The final section of the story, after the fat man has finished speaking, contains a subtle example of irony. Up to this point in the story, the unhappiness of the woman has been compounded by her belief that no one understands how she feels regarding the fact that her son is about to go off to war. When the fat man speaks, it seems as if his words will only add to her distress, since he claims to believe that for a young man to die in war is no tragedy because such individuals are happy to die for their country. Ironically, though, his words have the opposite effect on her; she is inspired by what he says and thinks she has been the one at fault, unable to "rise up to the same height of those fathers and mothers willing to resign themselves, without crying, not only to the departure of their sons but even to their death." The irony is that after seeking someone who understands her feelings, she is now inspired by someone who appears not to. However, there is another irony embedded in this situation: the man is speaking inauthentically, although he covers up the fact, even to himself. Impressed by him, and not realizing that he is covering up, the woman tries to embrace this inauthentic position, one that is not true to her real feelings. Then she asks him the strange question, as if she has not heard what he has been saying, "Then . . . is your son really dead?" which produces the emotional response from the man. This brings out another aspect of the multiple ironies contained here: the irony lies in the fact that he did understand her feelings from the beginning, but he had erected an intellectual smoke screen that hid his feelings from others and from himself. Yet another irony is that the truth of the man's feelings is brought out not by a process of argument and exchange of views that has formed the bulk of the story but by a question that is so odd and incongruous (since the man has already said his son is dead) that it bypasses all his defenses and brings his real feelings to the surface.

Setting

The story is set in a railway carriage. This suits the author's purpose since he wants to tell a story in which a group of strangers are placed together. The railway carriage is described as "stuffy"; it is also small and crowded, since the other passengers have to make room for the woman when she boards. Stuffy means there is a lack of air in the carriage; this suggests metaphorically that the characters are being stifled by the difficult circumstances they share because their sons are involved in a war. The carriage is a "second-class" one. This makes it clear that these are ordinary folk, not wealthy or aristocratic, a point further brought home by the fact that no character is given an individual name. They are representative of all the people who are caught up in the war.

HISTORICAL CONTEXT

World War I

Pirandello wrote "War" in 1918, the year World War I ended. The war began in 1914 and would eventually involve almost all the major world powers, resulting in the deaths of over fifteen million people.

The immediate cause of the war was the assassination in Sarajevo of Archduke Franz Ferdinand, the heir to the throne of Austria-Hungary. However, the rivalries that would lead to war had been developing for many years among the imperialistic European powers. When the war began, it pitted what were known as the Central Powers or Triple Alliance (Germany, Austria-Hungary, and the Ottoman Empire) against the Triple Entente (sometimes referred to simply as the Allies) of Great Britain, France, and Russia, as well as Serbia, Belgium, and, later, Italy.

The war began with the successful German invasion of Belgium followed by an invasion of France. The Germans came to within fifteen miles of Paris, the French capital, before being checked at the First Battle of the Marne. The German failure to reach Paris and end the war quickly ensured that a long struggle would follow. Both sides along the 400-mile western front consolidated their defensive positions, and the result was trench warfare, which, over the next few years, yielded little in terms of territory gained but much in terms of casualties.

On the eastern front, the Russian invasion of Germany that began in 1914 failed, and the Russians were forced to retreat. However, the Russians had more success in an offensive against the Austrians, who had invaded Poland. The Austrians failed in an invasion of Serbia.

The seas were controlled primarily by Britain, which kept its trade routes open and blockaded the coasts of Germany and its navy.

The year 1915 was disastrous for the Allied powers. Britain and France failed to break through German lines in the west, and on the eastern front, Austria and Germany inflicted an ignominious defeat on Russia, which lost the territory it had gained the previous year. Britain and France failed in the Gallipoli campaign (on a peninsula in Turkey) to link up with Russia, their isolated ally. It was during this year that Italy entered the war, on the side of the Allies.

In 1916, the Germans launched a furious assault on Verdun, a fort in northeast France, but failed to capture it. A quarter of a million men died in the battle. Verdun was saved by a counter-offensive launched by Britain and France that resulted in the Battle of the Somme in France, one of the most deadly conflicts in the history of war. In a battle that lasted four and a half months, casualties on all sides amounted to

COMPARE
&
CONTRAST

- **1918:** Pirandello is part of the modernist movement in literature. Other modernist writers of the period include the novelists Virginia Woolf, James Joyce, Franz Kafka, Marcel Proust, and the poet T. S. Eliot. Modernist writers live in a world in which traditional beliefs and institutions are breaking down, and individuals are increasingly isolated in a chaotic world that appears to lack meaning.

   Today: The dominant literary movement is postmodernism. Postmodernist writers include the novelists Kurt Vonnegut, John Barth, Thomas Pynchon, and Paul Auster. Postmodernists often deny the possibility of objective truth, viewing all reality as socially and culturally determined.

- **1918:** World War I ends in November. In the Treaty of Versailles signed in 1919, the victorious Allies impose harsh settlement terms on the defeated Germans. Germany has to accept responsibility for the war, disarm, and pay reparations. In separate treaties, the other defeated powers also face harsh terms. Austria loses much territory and is itself reduced in size, as is Hungary. Turkey loses many of its possessions in the Middle East.

   Today: Europe is at peace. It is impossible to imagine the European powers that fought on opposite sides in World War I engaging in military confrontation with one another. As allies, almost all of them are bound tightly together economically through their membership in the European Union. The European Union consists of twenty-seven nations, including most of the countries that were on opposite sides in World War I: Britain, France, Italy, Greece, and Portugal, on the one hand, and Germany, Austria, Hungary, and Bulgaria on the other. As of 2010, Turkey has applied for membership, and Serbia is likely to follow soon. The same countries, in this case including Turkey, are also members of NATO (the North Atlantic Treaty Organization), a mutual defense organization.

- **1918:** As World War I ends, plans to form the League of Nations are drawn up, with U.S. President Woodrow Wilson playing a leading role. The League of Nations comes into being in 1919 as part of the Treaty of Versailles. The League attempts to usher in a new era in international relations in which war is prevented by collective security arrangements, disarmament, and negotiation.

   Today: The United Nations, the successor to the League of Nations, has 192 member states. The United Nations conducts peacekeeping missions around the world as well as humanitarian assistance of various kinds.

---

more than a million men. When it was over, the Allies had advanced a mere six miles.

The tide of the war was turning against Germany and its allies, and at the end of 1916 there was talk of peace negotiations. However, there was no common ground in what each side was prepared to agree to, and the war would last another two years. During this time, Greece and Portugal entered the war on the Allied side.

In 1917, Germany announced that it would step up its submarine warfare and that all ships in the war zone, whether enemy or neutral, would be sunk on sight. The Allies lost hundreds of ships within a few months. The escalating submarine warfare, which threatened neutral U.S. ships, brought relations between Germany and the United States to a low point, and in April 1917, the United States declared war on Germany. Other nations, including many in Central and South America as well as China, also declared war on the Germany. The U.S. entry into the war was a huge boost to the Allied cause and

One father argued it was worse to lose an only child. (*Sergey Kamshylin | Shutterstock.com*)

guaranteed eventual victory. However, during 1917, there were more bloody battles. In Belgium, the third battle of Ypres (also known as the battle of Passchendaele) was fought between July and November. It produced about half a million casualties on all sides.

In the spring of 1918, Germany launched a series of offensives in the west but gradually, especially with the arrival of the first U.S. forces, the Allies recovered and themselves went on the offensive. Germany's allies were faring poorly. In September, Bulgaria surrendered, followed by Turkey in October and Austria-Hungary in early November. This left Germany alone, facing defeat. On November 9 Germany's Kaiser Wilhelm II abdicated, and an armistice was signed between Germany and the Allies two days later, on November 11, thus bringing World War I to an end.

Italy in World War I

Italy entered the conflict on May 23, 1915, declaring war against Austria and mobilizing about 870,000 men. Italy attacked Austria along the border of northern Italy, which had been heavily fortified by the Austrians. From May to November 1915 the Italians attacked four times in the area near the Isonzo River. They gained little and suffered 161,000 casualties; Austrian losses were on a similar scale. Italy continued the struggle on the Isonzo front during 1916, launching five more attacks from March to November, again with heavy casualties and little to show for their efforts. Italy also had to counter an Austrian offensive in Trentino, known as the Asiago offensive. This also went badly for the Italians, who sustained, at the minimum, 147,000 casualties. The Italian government collapsed.

Between May 1915 and August 1917, the Italians launched a total of eleven assaults on the Isonzo front. However, in the German-Austrian Caporetto offensive in October 1917, Italy lost all of the small amount of territory it had won in those eleven battles. The Italians retreated, and 280,000 Italian soldiers were taken prisoner by the Germans. This was a catastrophe for Italy that brought down the government.

In 1918, however, Italy recovered and got the better of the Austrians at the Battle of the Piave River in June and July. An Italian offensive in October, supported by British and French troops, was successful: the Battle of Vittorio Veneto resulted in a defeat for Austria-Hungary. On November 3, 1918, the Austrians asked Italy for an armistice.

CRITICAL OVERVIEW

According to Fiora A. Bassanese in *Understanding Luigi Pirandello*, Pirandello wrote over fifteen volumes of short stories between 1880s and the 1920s. In considering these stories, Bassanese makes some comments that are relevant for "War," although she does not mention the story directly. She states that the characters in Pirandello's short stories are "often depicted during a single critical episode" (In "War," the action covers only a few minutes in the lives of the characters), and that the stories frequently feature "irony and paradox." Irony is a marked feature of "War." Bassanese also notes that "characters fall prey to chance as the unexpected intrudes upon them, all attempts at controlling life being futile." This might be applied to the attempts of the fat man in "War" who attempts to exert a rigid control over his beliefs and his emotional life until his chance encounter with the woman on the train shatters his best efforts. Death is a frequent theme in the stories, states Bassanese, with characters displaying a variety of attitudes to it, including "resignation, bitterness, isolation, and surrender."

In his essay "Luigi Pirandello as Writer of Short Fiction and Novels," Douglas Radcliff-Umstead notes that Pirandello wrote a total of 233 short stories. Radcliff-Umstead observes, "Quite often the scene takes place in a train compartment, usually second class, or a railroad station restaurant where the restless reach out in vain to each other." Radcliff-Umstead also comments that in Pirandello's stories there is "an entire language of silence made up of nonverbal communication through gestures and expressions of the eyes as well as represented voice inflections." A good example of what Radcliff-Umstead is referring to occurs in "War," in the description of the fat man, from whose eyes "seemed to spurt inner violence of an uncontrolled vitality"—a clue to his real state of mind, beyond the actual words he utters. Another example occurs when the fat man, as he speaks, tries to cover his mouth with his hand in an attempt to hide his two missing front teeth—a nonverbal clue that there is something

duplicitous or inauthentic in his words, even though he seems to be expressing fine and noble sentiments. Radcliff-Umstead concludes that such techniques "contribute to creating a language of deception, to oneself and others, that Pirandello's humoristic art unmasks."

CRITICISM

Bryan Aubrey
Aubrey holds a Ph.D. in English. In the following essay, he discusses "War" in the context of the difficulties and dilemmas that Pirandello experienced in his own life during World War I that led him to write the story in the way he did.

Hovering like a giant dark cloud over the conversation that takes place in the railroad carriage in Pirandello's story "War" is World War I. Every character is affected by it; the death or the possibility of the death of a son overshadows them all. They have good cause to worry. World War I claimed lives in staggeringly huge numbers. In a conflict that lasted four years and three months, about sixteen million people were killed and twenty-one million wounded. Estimates of casualties for individual nations vary, but historian John Keegan, in *An Illustrated History of the First World War*, writes that the French lost 1,700,000 dead, as did the Russians, while Austria-Hungary lost 1,500,000 men. The British Empire lost one million dead. Italy suffered terribly, too. Although it did not enter the war until nine months after it started, and fought mainly along its own borders, Italy nonetheless lost 460,000 dead. The high number of casualties on all sides was partly the result of trench warfare, in which each side dug deep trenches to set up very effective defensive positions; in order to gain even small amounts of ground, the enemy infantry would have to go "over the top" of the trenches, exposing themselves to devastating artillery fire. Just to give one example, on July 1, 1916, on the first day of the Battle of the Somme, the British Army sustained over 57,000 casualties, including over 19,000 dead.

Also lying behind "War" is Pirandello's own personal story, which goes a long way toward explaining not only why he wrote "War" but why it took the form it did. The story of Pirandello's life during this period is told by Gaspare Giudice in his book *Pirandello: A Biography*.

WHAT DO I READ NEXT?

- *Six Characters in Search of an Author*, the play for which Pirandello is best known, was originally staged in Rome in 1921. It aroused great controversy at the time but soon became an established theatrical classic. It is about a number of fictional characters who have not been completed by their author. They arrive at a rehearsal of another play by Pirandello and demand that the director and cast enact their story. The director at first thinks they are insane but eventually agrees to their request over the objections of the actors. The play is available in a Signet Classics edition published in 1998.

- *All Quiet on the Western Front* is a famous novel by the German author Erich Maria Remarque. First published in 1929, it tells the story of some young German soldiers during World War I. It does not focus on heroic exploits but on the day-to-day realities of being a soldier in this war, including boredom and the search for food in addition to the dangers of battle. The main character, Paul, becomes so accustomed to army life that he finds it difficult to adjust to civilian life when home on leave or as the war nears its end. An illustrated edition of the novel was published by Little, Brown in 1996.

- *Journey's End* is a play by R. C. Sherriff. First performed in England in 1928, it is now regarded as a classic example of the antiwar sentiment produced by the carnage of World War I. The play takes place over a four-day period in March 1918 and centers around a group of British army officers on the front line, in the trenches in France. An eighteen-year-old English officer joins them and discovers that one of the men, a friend to whom he looks up, has been greatly changed by his experiences in the war. An edition of the play is available in the Penguin Classics series, published in 2000. From 2004 to 2005, the play was revived in London, and it had a successful Broadway run in 2007.

- *The War to End All Wars: World War I* (2010), by Russell Freedman, is a history of World War I for young adults. Freedman concisely explains the many causes of the war and the course it took, including the trench warfare that cost so many lives in the battles of the Somme, Verdun, and many others. Freedman also explains the Treaty of Versailles, which ended the war and the legacy the war left, including an end to American isolation, the Russian revolution, and the rise of Nazi Germany.

- Wilfred Owen (1893–1918) was one of the great poets of World War I. He fought in the British army in 1916 and suffered from shell shock. He returned to the war in 1918 and was killed in action one week before the war ended. His poetry reveals the horror of the war that lay behind the patriotic slogans. *The Poems of Wilfred Owen* (1986), edited by Jon Stallworthy, contains 103 poems by Owen.

- *A Teenager in the Chad Civil War: A Memoir of Survival, 1982–1986* (2006), by Esaie Toingar, is a memoir of a teenager caught up in a civil war in Chad. Chad is a central African country that endured a long civil war, beginning in 1965 and continuing until the 1980s. Toingar was driven from his home during the early 1980s and joined the rebels. He witnessed many atrocities before managing to escape from the carnage. He later immigrated to the United States.

Pirandello was an Italian patriot; he had grown up in a patriotic household and never for a moment questioned it. For him, in Giudice's words, patriotism was a "romantic and idealistic term," fueled by stories he must have heard as a boy about the activities of the Risorgimento, the movement in the 1850s and 1860s that brought about Italian unification. Pirandello's father,

> WHAT A DILEMMA THIS PRESENTED FOR PIRANDELLO, HIS LOVE FOR HIS SON PITTED AGAINST HIS LOVE FOR HIS COUNTRY: IF HE FREES HIS SON, ITALY MAY PAY A PRICE; IF HE FAVORS HIS COUNTRY, HIS SICK SON MAY LANGUISH FOR YEARS AS A PRISONER OF WAR."

Stefano, had fought with the Risorgimento in several battles in the 1860s and on one occasion had been rescued during a street battle by the great Garibaldi himself—this was Giuseppe Garibaldi [1807–1882], one of the principal architects of Italian unification.

Given this patriotic background, it is not surprising that when war broke out, Pirandello supported Italian entry into the conflict. At forty-seven, he was probably too old for the rigors of combat, but this did not stop him from entertaining thoughts of signing up for some kind of military service. In the end he did not, but the topic remained on his mind, as can be seen from the two stories he wrote around this time, titled "Berecche and the War" and "An Episode in the Life of Marco Leccio and His War on Paper." Both feature older men who are so upset at their sons' departure for war that they do manage to enlist themselves—with comic results. The idea of fathers enlisting for military service also found its way into "War," when the fat man says, "Is there any one of us here who wouldn't gladly take his son's place at the front if he could?" and all the travelers nod in agreement.

But if Pirandello was too old for military service, his two sons were not. The devotion of father to son that is a theme in "War" was something that manifested strongly in Pirandello's own life. His older son, Stefano, was twenty years old in 1915, and his younger son, Fausto, was sixteen. Pirandello, by all accounts, was an excellent father who was devoted to his sons (just as the characters in "War" are devoted to theirs). Trapped in an unhappy marriage, he found in his sons an outlet for his deepest and best emotions.

Like his father, Stefano was a patriot. When war broke out in August 1914, he was studying at the university in Rome. By January the following year, he had enrolled in an officer's training college, and when Italy declared war on Austria in May 1915, Stefano volunteered for duty. He was sent to the front in July. (Stefano's history roughly corresponds to that of the son of the husband and wife in "War.") Pirandello did not oppose Stefano's decision to fight in the war but it was a wrenching blow for him to be parted from his son and to contemplate the fact that Stefano was in mortal danger on the battlefield. He worried about it all the time. Giudice quotes from Pirandello's writings at the time:

> While I tortured myself helplessly and was obliged to wait and to satisfy all the little material needs of life, he was risking his life up there; and every moment that elapsed could be his last, and I would have had to go on living this terrible life.

Fortunately, Pirandello did not also have to worry about Fausto. Fausto was called up for military duty as soon as he was old enough but he was in poor health and was later found to have tuberculosis, so he did not serve in the army.

As for Stefano, he fought heroically. Wounded in the chest during an attack by the Austrians in November 1915, he refused to remain at the first-aid station where he was receiving medical attention. Instead, he insisted on returning to the battle. Eventually, he and his men were surrounded and left with no alternative but to surrender. He was taken to a prison camp.

Naturally enough, Pirandello was deeply concerned about his son's welfare. Becoming a prisoner of war did not necessarily mean that there would be adequate provision for the essentials of life. He wrote letters to his son, covering up his own distress and telling his son to be patient.

In 1917, after the heavy Italian defeat at Caporetto, conditions for Italian prisoners of war deteriorated, largely because there were so many of them, and there was a food shortage. When Stefano contracted tuberculosis, his father decided he would do everything he could to get him released. He enlisted the help of the Italian government, and eventually a deal was proposed to the Austrians: owing to his ill health, Stefano would be released in exchange for one Austrian prisoner. However, the Austrians said that because Stefano was the son of an important man in Italian culture, they would only release him in exchange for three Austrian prisoners,

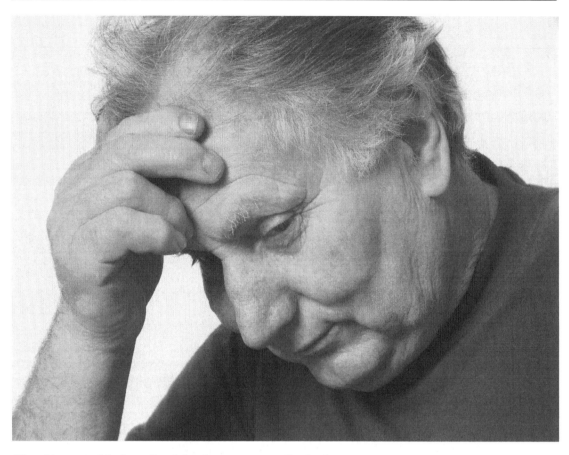

The old man suddenly realized that his son was really dead. *(Kruchankova Maya | Shutterstock.com)*

and they named the three officers they had in mind. Pirandello met with the Italian prime minister, Vittorio Emanuele Orlando, who informed him that the three prisoners the Austrians were willing to release were naval officers who could be expected to rejoin the conflict and cause trouble for the Italians. But Orlando allowed Pirandello to make the decision about whether the prisoner exchange should go ahead.

What a dilemma this presented for Pirandello, his love for his son pitted against his love for his country: If he frees his son, Italy may pay a price; if he favors his country, his sick son may languish for years as a prisoner of war. Pirandello left no memoir of his feelings at this moment, but his dilemma must have been acute. He gave the prime minister his answer: no, he could not allow the deal to go through. He could not act in a way that might harm his country, just for the private satisfaction of having his son come home. As a consequence, Stefano was to remain a prisoner until the end of the

war. Pirandello's biographer believes that in the later years of this terribly destructive war, Pirandello's patriotism was on the wane, but nonetheless, he could not bring himself to favor family interest over patriotic duty.

So here in Pirandello's life from 1915 to 1918 are all the ingredients of "War" that give the story its emotional force. Two loves collide: the love of country, strong in all but especially so in the young, and filial love, the love of fathers and mothers for their sons. All the characters feel this conflict and deal with it in their own way. Both types of love are rooted so deeply in them that they cannot be questioned. When Pirandello first published the story in 1918, he seemed to make it clear in the title which side should be favored in this cruel dilemma. He titled it "Quando si comprende," which means "When Will They Learn?" The antiwar implication is clear: When will people learn the futility of sacrificing their sons in this way? However, perhaps deciding that the title was too explicit and made the theme of the story too plain from the beginning, rather than encouraging readers to feel it out for themselves as they read, he altered it to the more neutral "War."

In teasing out the delicate balance between the competing calls of country and filial love, Pirandello put most care into his portrait of the fat man. It is as if he was trying to dramatize in the story his own complex feelings as a father with a son in danger. The fat man seems to be trying to pull off a balancing act. He says that for the young, love of country is all-consuming and takes precedence over whatever parents might say. But he also pinpoints what he sees as a generational difference. He says, "Now at our age, the love of our Country is still great, of course, but stronger than it is the love for our children." Nonetheless, in spite of saying this, the fat man tries to reconcile himself to his loss by adopting what he thinks is the young person's view, and which he claims his son put to him before he was killed: dying for your country, when you can conceive no higher destiny, is not a thing to be mourned. Rather, one should either "laugh as I do . . . or at least thank God." Readers of the story know, however, that the position the fat man tries to uphold is false to his deeper feelings. The loss of his son is in fact causing him great grief. The moving final sentence of the story surely tilts the balance against the call of country that demands so much sacrifice from so many fathers and mothers, and one can surely also read in that sentence the author Pirandello imaginatively entering into the grief that would have been his had his son perished along with the hundreds of thousands of Italy's brave sons: "His face contracted, became horribly distorted, then he snatched in haste a handkerchief from his pocket and, to the amazement of everyone, broke into harrowing, heart-rending, uncontrollable sobs."

Source: Bryan Aubrey, Critical Essay on "War," in *Short Stories for Students*, Gale, Cengage Learning, 2011.

Olga Ragusa

In the following excerpt, Ragusa explicates Pirandello's ghost story "Granella's House" as a commentary on the limits of reason and science.

Richard Kelly's recent "The Haunted House of Bulwer-Lytton" (*Studies in Short Fiction*, Vol. 8) calls to mind Pirandello's "La casa del Granella," a story first published in 1905 and which later became part of Pirandello's short story *summa*, *Novelle per un anno*. It appears to

> NO DOUBT ONE OF THE REASONS, IF NOT *THE* REASON, WHY PIRANDELLO WAS ATTRACTED TO THE AREA OF THE OCCULT WAS THE TENSION SET UP IN ITS THEORETICAL FOUNDATIONS AND IN THE EXPERIENCE OF ITS PRACTITIONERS BETWEEN FACT AND FICTION."

have been translated into English twice, once with the title of "Granella's House" and the second time as "The Haunted House." Aside from inclusion in collections of Pirandello stories published in the United States and England, it also found its way into *Strange to Tell*, an anthology subtitled "Stories of the Marvelous and Mysterious," edited by Marjorie Fischer and Rolfe Humphries.

As the second English title reveals, "La casa del Granella" is a ghost or mystery story with at least some of the conventional ingredients of the genre. But early as it came in his career, it already bears the peculiar Pirandellian stamp, and it is therefore a ghost story with a difference. Like Bulwer-Lytton's "The Haunted and the Haunters" it shows its author to have been conversant with the spiritualist movement of the mid- and late nineteenth century, but in contrast to Bulwer-Lytton's rationalist examination of the supernatural with the consequent dissolution of the mystery and the actual and figurative laying of the ghost, it proclaims the defeat of science and recognizes the irreducible presence in life and in the experience of life, of the unexplainable and the mysterious.

The story begins with a metaphorical direction sign that alerts the reader to the presence of a meaning beneath the surface of plot and characterization. To the actions of a mouse who has fallen into a trap and unaware of the finality of its plight is desperately trying to get out, is contrasted the behavior of men who have recourse to the law, know that they are stepping into a trap and are yet able to present an impassive face to the world, while all the time inside them their feelings go scurrying about madly, worse than the mouse.

The setting of the scene that follows is a lawyer's reception room in a small town in Sicily, specifically Agrigento, Pirandello's birthplace, as we come to learn later. It is hot, the room is crowded; and every time the door opens, lawyer Zummo's prospective clients surge forward, then disappointedly sink back, as the chosen one is admitted while the rest must return to their extenuating wait in the shadow of dusty bookcases overloaded with "old litigations and proceedings, the wrack and ruin of so many once happy families." To make things worse, Zummo's ten-year old son has on this particular morning invaded the room and is busy harassing those who are waiting with needling questions and impertinent remarks.

Three individuals stand out from the rest: they show no sign of impatience, and to their neighbors' surprise and discomfiture three times already they have permitted newcomers to take their turn. The husband, gloomy, almost funereal in appearance, is wearing an old frock-coat just out of moth balls. The wife, "stout, thriving, with a full bust and a whiskered red face," flashes looks of "defiant, self-satisfied stupidity" about her. While the daughter, pale, emaciated, squinting like her father, sits hunched forward and distraught like him, both of them looking ready to keel over were it not for the mother's amplitude between them holding them up. Three early Pirandello grotesques, reminiscent, for instance, of his portrayal of Batta Malagna or of the *vedova* Pescatore in *Il fu Mattia Pascal* (*The Late Mattia Pascal*). "What disaster could have befallen them?" asks the impersonal narrator. "What persecution were they subjected to? What violent death was crying to be avenged? Or was financial ruin staring them in the face?" The answer to the last question at least is negative, for the mother is generously bejewelled.

Around these three figures Pirandello has created the space that sets them off as within a magic circle. Later in his work that same space will isolate Signor Ponza and Signora Frola from the chorus of small-town gossips around them, and will encircle the Six Characters, keeping their life-in-art inviolate. In Zummo's waiting room the other clients try to push the pestering boy in the direction of the three, but he is unwilling to get close to them, repulsed by their mournful gloom and perhaps even by something else—but if there is a something else, it lies at this point tightly encapsulated within the normal suspense of story telling that Pirandello has so far created.

The tempo of the story changes abruptly as the three are admitted to the office, and dialogue replaces the narrative voice. The second part of the story is almost exclusively dramatic encounter, and Zummo shows himself at once to belong to that group of hyper-active, emotionally volatile intellectually alert, restless and irascible men that are part and parcel of Pirandello's portrayal of the Sicilian world. Mention of only one other such instance will have to suffice here: the unforgettable *don* Lollò Zirafa in "La giara" ("The Jar").

The case the three are bringing to the lawyer concerns the summons for breach of contract and defamation with which the landlord Granella has served them because they moved out of a house they had rented and paid for when they discovered that it was inhabited by ghosts. "By what?" Zummo interrupts incredulously. "By ghosts, yes sir!" the wife repeats defiantly, waving her hands in the air. Zummo's indignation knows no bounds: people who believe in ghosts belong in insane asylums and not in a lawyer's office. Suddenly he remembers that it is after his lunch hour, that he is tired and hungry. But the three won't let him go. They surround him and force him to listen to the details of the persecution to which they have been subjected: chairs moving about the room of their own accord, objects hurled through the house as though by invisible hands, cupboards moaning and straining, mocking laughter issuing from dark corners. "Playful ghosts," Zummo muses, showing that for all his scepticism he knows something of the subdivisions of the species. "Playful!" the wife retorts indignantly. "Not playful at all! Infernal!" The upshot is that at the end of an hour's arguing, Zummo capitulates. Contrary to what the Author does when he sends the Six Characters packing, Zummo agrees to become the Piccirillis' spokesman. Attracted by the novelty and the speciousness of the case, as he himself describes it, he will take up the Piccirillis' defense: "You understand, of course, that I cannot accept your story of the ghosts. Hallucinations, old wives tales. But I'm considering the legal side of the question . . . ."

The legal side of the question takes Zummo further than it takes Judge D'Andrea, for instance, who in "La patente" ("The License") is faced by quite as disconcerting a case, this one involving a form of primitive magic: the evil eye. In spite of the pressures that are brought to bear on him, Judge D'Andrea remains on the side of reason, interpreting the phenomena he witnesses as the results of superstition and psychological coercion and aberration, not of the supernatural. Zummo's mind, instead, wanders immediately to childhood memories, to the irrational: ghost stories he had been told as a child and that had frightened him. But to believe in ghosts, he now reasons with himself, one must first believe in the immortality of the soul. And does he or doesn't he believe in it? When, as a matter of fact, has he ever given these problems serious thought? No more than anyone else does he have time to think about death: "Even science stops at the threshold of death, as though death did not exist and one should not worry about it. Science says: 'You're still here; concern yourselves with being alive. The lawyer should worry about being a lawyer, the engineer about being an engineer . . . .'" And rebelling at what we recognize as a general emphasis on role to the exclusion of self, it is with relief that Zummo welcomes the possibility of the existence of ghosts: how narrow his life in that provincial town had become! How wasted are his energies among the petty concerns of his fellow-citizens! And so the ghosts that are now knocking at his office door fill him not with apprehension but with glee. Through them he is beginning to understand things that his colleagues don't even know exist! The ghosts whisper to him insinuatingly:

> We're here, too, you know. You, men of reason, materialists who believe only in what you can touch, you don't want to bother with us, do you? You don't want to worry about death? But here we come, gaily, from the kingdom of the dead, knocking at the doors of those who are still alive, making fun of you, making chairs and tables dance around the room, frightening your clients, laughing at them from the depths of some old wardrobe, puzzling you today, my learned lawyer, and puzzling tomorrow a body of equally learned judges who will have to try a most novel case . . . .

In preparing his case, Zummo spends more time on the literature of the occult than on his law books. The latter have quickly convinced him that he will have to prove the actual existence of the ghosts, that only if the landlord can be considered responsible for having rented a house unfit for human habitation can the Piccirillis win their case. He applies himself with boundless zeal. He first reads "a history of spiritualism from the origins of mythology to the present," and then a work on the wonders wrought by fakirs. After that there follows, pell mell, the whole international roster of writers on the supernatural, all of whom Pirandello mentions by name: Crookes, the British physicist who in the '70's and '80's estranged the scientific community by his research into mediumship; Aksakov, the Russian statesman who translated Swedenborg and conducted experimental seances with his friends; the professors of chemistry and zoology at the University of St. Petersburg (Pirandello names the latter of the two: Wagner); Zoellner, professor of astrophysics at Leipzig and enthusiastic exponent of spiritualism; Janet, professor of philosophy at the Sorbonne, follower of Victor Cousin, anti-positivist and anti-materialist; Rochas, ex-army officer and administrator at the Ecole Polytechnique, who conducted experiments on psychical phenomena and wrote extensively of parapsychological subjects; Richet, professor of physiology at the Medical School of the Sorbonne, founder of the *Annales des Sciences Psychiques*, coiner of the term "metapsychique" (the French equivalent of parapsychology), and later winner of a Nobel Prize in physiology; Morselli, anthropologist, neurologist and psychiatrist, author among other works of the 1906 *Psicologia e spiritismo*; and Lombroso, the famous criminologist and psychiatrist, author of the controversial *Genio e follia* (1864), whom Pirandello had already had occasion to cite in his 1893 essay, "Arte e coscienza d'oggi."

What amazes Zummo and fires him with uncontrollable enthusiasm is that what he had been in the habit of dismissing as old wives tales he now finds supported, defended, and rationally explained by reputable scientists, educated as he has been in accordance with the tenets of Positivism. But what is characteristic for him—as well as for Pirandello—in the attraction he feels for the new field of knowledge he has just discovered, is the total absence of frivolity. He is in deadly earnest, convinced that he has found a clue to the ultimate mystery, death, that he has found an answer to what he calls Hamlet's "terrible question," *to be or not to be.* Thus of what might be considered the three components of the science of the occult—spiritualism, theosophy, and the study of psychic or psychological phenomena— it is the first, spiritualism or, to be more precise, spiritism, that has the strongest appeal for him. This is borne out by two details in the story: Zummo's initial rejection of the "biological explanation" for psychic phenomena in favor of the "metaphysical hypothesis"; and his invoking of Allen Kardech as the new messiah [in a footnote, the critic adds: "Allen Kardech was the name taken by Denizard Rivail (1804–1869) after his conversion to spiritualism. In his *Livre des esprits* (1857) he laid the foundations of his doctrine, further exemplified in the pages of the long-lived *La Revue spirite*."] in the course of his impassioned peroration in court, which loses him the case but wins him the great moral victory to which he aspires:

> He spoke of Allan Kardech as of a new messiah. He defined spiritism as the new religion of humanity. He said that science with its solid but cold instruments, with its too rigorous formalism had overwhelmed nature; that the tree of life nourished artificially by science had lost its leaves and grown sterile, or else was bearing small and wrinkled fruits that shrivelled up, tasting of ashes and poison because no warmth of faith matured them. But now, behold, the mystery was beginning to unclose its dark gates: tomorrow they would stand wide open! Meanwhile through this first narrow slit uncertain and fearful shadows were appearing to reveal to mankind in its dismay and anguished longing the world beyond: strange lights, strange signs . . . .

But before this *dénouement* is reached—reminiscent in its spectacular *coup de scène* of the court scene in *Il turno* (*The Merry-Go-Round of Love*)—Pirandello has had occasion to weave yet another cultural and ideological clarification into the texture of his fiction. Zummo's proud rejection of the "biological explanation" had been followed by his unsettling discovery that *signorina* Piccirilli was a "portentous" medium. Therefore the appearance of the ghosts in the house was not Granella's fault but the Piccirillis'. Undismayed, however, Zummo turns this defeat into an advantage for his passion: he is now in a position to witness the phenomena he had so far only read about. With merciless single-mindedness he forces the Piccirillis to engage in experiment after experiment, subjecting them to the very persecution from which they had tried to escape. Pirandello underlines the irony of the situation: while Zummo exults at having discovered proof of the immortality of the soul, the Piccirillis, *terre à terre* in their faith, having never doubted the immortality of "their tormented, paltry little souls," are overcome with guilt at what to them is "commerce with demons." The established religions, in other words, looked upon this growth of interlocking para-scientific endeavors and beliefs with even greater suspicion and revulsion than science itself.

With the trial scene the story that had begun in the lawyer's waiting room comes to an end. The Piccirillis have served their function and can now move back into their anonymity. But Granella, technically the winner, is left standing center-stage. He has been rewarded by the law but humiliated by that public opinion that Zummo, lawyer turned magician, bearer of charisma, has succeeded in convincing of the existence of "something beyond." The *coda* to the story generalizes the experience and asks the Pirandellian epistemological question, "Fiction? Reality?"

As in all good ghost stories the reader is now taken into the haunted house itself. To hearsay and report will be added direct, personal experience. The agent of the experience is Granella. He has won his case, but the reputation of his house has been effectively ruined. Not even the old servant who has been with him all her life has the courage to return to it. It is up to him to show that the house is *not* haunted, and he challenges the ghosts derisively: just let them show their faces! Contrary to what is often the case with haunted houses, this house is in an urban and not a country setting, and though it gives the impression of being solitary, situated as it is in an open space with an abandoned shed opposite, it is actually but a few steps from one of the town's most populous districts. The location is determined on one level of Pirandello's creative strategy by the exigencies of the plot whose thrust is towards a direct encounter between Granella and Zummo in which the roles of winner and loser will be inverted. And on a different level, by his recurrent concern with the problem of "conscience"—a particularly difficult concept to translate but which we could perhaps for the sake of clarity subdivide into its dual aspects of soul and consciousness.

. . . The ghost question remains unsolved. Are there or aren't there ghosts? Was Granella frightened by an actual apparition, as Zummo's question would seem to imply? Or was it auto-suggestion that affected him, as a rehearsal of the phenomena Pirandello describes for his first night in the haunted house would indicate? And is there really any difference between the two? In the post-Kantian universe is what we imagine any less real than what we "know"?

No doubt one of the reasons, if not *the* reason, why Pirandello was attracted to the area of the occult was the tension set up in its theoretical foundations and in the experience of its practitioners between fact and fiction. If Bulwer-Lytton sought, as Richard Kelly concludes, "to rationalize that indefinable something," to bring "the supernatural within the boundaries of the believable," then Pirandello sought instead to undermine the solidity of the rational and to enlarge the boundaries of the believable so that it could include the supernatural without it having to be reduced to anything else. In the course of the story, the image of the mouse falling into the trap has been extended to the Piccirillis falling into the trap of legal disputation, to Zummo falling into a trap of his own making, and to Granella falling into the trap that awaits every man, the awareness to the existence of "that indefinable something" that scientific probing has not yet been able to dispel.

Source: Olga Ragusa, "Pirandello's Haunted House," in *Studies in Short Fiction*, Vol. 10, No. 3, Summer 1973, pp. 235–42.

Irving Howe

In the following review, Howe relates Pirandello's 1959 collection Short Stories *to nineteenth-century realism.*

About half a year ago, when a collection of Pirandello's stories appeared in English, I began to read them casually and with small expectations. Like other people, I had once looked into a few of his plays and been left cold; had accepted the stock judgment that he was clever theatrically but lacking in literary range and depth; and had disliked him because of his friendliness to Italian Fascism.

Two or three stories were enough to convince me that here, beyond doubt, was the work of a master. Not all the stories in [*Short Stories by Pirandello*] are first-rate; some show the marks of haste or fatigue, others are finger-exercises in which Pirandello plays with his main themes yet does not fully release them. But even in the slightest of these twenty-two stories—only one had previously been translated into English—there is that uniqueness and assurance of voice which is the first sign of a major writer. And in the best of them there is writing which can bear comparison with the masters of the short story, Chekhov and Joyce.

Now this is not an estimate for which modern criticism has prepared us. Outside of Italy, there is little Pirandello criticism; the books about him in English range from Italianate rhapsody to American academic, but none provides

> WRITERS, LIKE THE REST OF US, DO NOT CHOOSE THEIR MOMENT OF BIRTH, AND IT WOULD BE ABSURD TO RELATE PIRANDELLO TOO CLOSELY WITH THE DEPRESSING QUALITIES OF HIS STORIES."

enough material or adequate criticism. A good but too brief essay by Eric Bentley helps one find direction in the labyrinth of Pirandello's vast production, and equally helpful are some incisive reviews by Stark Young, written in the twenties for the *New Republic* and reprinted in his *Immortal Shadows*. But for the most part, in America Pirandello is a name, not a force. He has seldom been welcomed to the pantheon of modernism, and those of us raised on modernist taste have suffered a loss.

Nor is this true in regard to Pirandello alone. Taste can be a tyrant, even the best or most advanced taste. Literary people who reached maturity two or three decades ago often felt zealous in behalf of writers like Eliot, Stevens and Joyce, for they, in Harold Rosenberg's phrase, had established the "tradition of the new new" and it was this tradition which roused one's excitement and loyalties. Soon, however, the tradition of the new was being shadowed by a provincialism of the new.

The *avant garde* impulse was the most vital in the literary life of our century, but by now we might as well admit that it also exacted a price in narrowness of interest, some times in smugness of feeling. Because its spokesmen told us so forcibly which poets and novelists were relevant to an age of terror and war, we assumed a little too quickly that other writers could be left to molder in darkness. Now, by way of penance, middle-aged writers regularly—and if they have any humor about themselves, ruefully—announce literary "discoveries" based on reading with pleasure the writers whom they had felt free to dismiss in their youth.

So here are some notes—inexpert, rueful—on Luigi Pirandello.

Pirandello's stories are in the main tradition of 19th Century European realism. Except for those set in Sicily, which have a distinctive regional flavor, they often seem close in manner and spirit to the writings of the French realists and naturalists. Ordinary social life forms their main setting. The frustrations of the city, the sourings of domesticity, the weariness of petty-bourgeois routines, provide their characteristic subjects. Like Flaubert, though with less fanatic insistence, Pirandello cuts himself out of his picture. His prose is neither elevated nor familiar; it is a middle style, denotative, austere and transparent, the style of an observer who achieves sympathy through distance rather than demonstration.

Far more than we have come to expect in the modern short story, the impact of Pirandello's stories depends upon their action, which sometimes contains enough incident to warrant a good deal of expansion. There are rarely Joycean epiphanies of insight or Chekhovian revelations through a massing of atmosphere. The function of Pirandello's style is to serve as a glass with a minimum of refraction or distortion; and whatever we may conclude as to his purpose or bias must come not from a fussing with details of metaphor but from a weighing of the totality of the action. In this respect, Pirandello the story writer is not quite a "modern" writer.

He is not quite "modern" in still another way. Though Pirandello in his plays would break with the psychology and epistemology of 19th Century realism, abandoning the premises of both a fixed individual character and the knowability of human relationships, his stories were still accessible to educated people of his generation who had been brought up on rationalist assumptions. Such readers may have found them excessively bleak—one does not leave Pirandello in a mood to embrace the universe—but they had no difficulty in grasping them, as later they might with his plays.

The stories deal with human problems, but do not threaten the reader with a vision of human lot as beyond comprehension or as open to so many meanings that there follows a paralysis of relativism. Pirandello has a sharp eye for absurdities, but this is still far from the view that life is inherently absurd. One can find anticipations of existentialism in these stories, as one can find them in many writers of Pirandello's day who were oppressed by the collapse of 19th Century certainties; but precisely those writers, like Pirandello, who seem to have anticipated the existentialist posture of an affirmed insecurity are the ones, in the end, who resist its full display. They

stopped short, often at a depressed stoicism, a sense of life as weariness. And this, in turn, has some relation to their having been raised in a more or less Christian culture: for if they no longer had a radiant or sustaining faith they preserved from it a feeling for duties, burdens, limits.

Fantasy, playfulness, sexual pleasure, religious emotion, any sort of imaginative abandon or transcendence—these seldom break through in Pirandello's stories, though some of them can at times be heard pulsing quietly beneath the surface. A full tragic release is rare. Much more characteristic are stories in which the final sadness arises from the realization of characters that they will have to live on, without joy or hope. In a five-page masterpiece, "The Soft Touch of Grass," a bereaved, aging man is mistakenly suspected by a girl of having lewd intentions; overcome by a sense of the hopeless entanglements of life, he returns to his lonely room and "turned his face to the wall."

In "Such Is Life," a masterpiece that would do honor to Chekhov, a hopeless marriage, long broken, is hopelessly resumed. This story, written with a repressed austerity and unrelieved by a rebellious gesture or tragic resolution, stays terribly close to life; in a sense, its power depends upon Pirandello's scrupulous decision not to allow either his emotions or imagination to interfere with what he sees. At the end, the central figure is left with "an ever-present torment... for all things, all earthly creatures as she saw them in the infinite anguish of her love and pity, in that constant painful awareness—assuaged only by fleeting peaceful moments which brought relief and consolation—of the futility of living like this...."

There are humorous stories too, such as "The Examination," in which a good-tempered glutton studying for a state examination is regularly deflected from his work by friends tempting him to share their pleasures. One smiles at the end, for Pirandello manages it with suavity and tact. But it is a humor of sadness, a twist upon the idea of incongruity as the very heart of life, and it brings little gaiety or relief. Of the pleasure that can come from simply being alive Pirandello's stories have little to say, certainly nothing to compare with his one marvelously lighthearted play *Liola*, in which youthful energies bubble without restraint or theory.

Stark Young, in a review of the play *Henry IV*, has described the Pirandello theme as

... the dualism between Life on one hand and Form on the other; on the one hand Life pouring in a stream, unknowable, obscure and unceasing; on the other hand forms, ideas, crystallizations, in which we try to embody and express this ceaseless stream of life. Upon everything lies the burden of its form, which alone separates it from dust, but which also interferes with the unceasing flood of Life in it.

This description, partly drawn from Pirandello himself, is an excellent one, though some amendment is required in regard to the stories, for there the stream of Life is much weaker than the barrier of Form. In Young's version, the Pirandello theme is concerned with constants that apply to any moment in history, and there is plenty of evidence in both the stories and plays that Pirandello sees it this way. But I think that a sharper focus can be had upon the stories if one also regards the Life-Form theme as closely related to the stresses and tensions of late 19th- and early 20th-century life in Europe.

To all of this, one group of Pirandello stories is something of an exception. Those set in Sicily are comparatively buoyant and combative, not because Pirandello, himself a Sicilian, glosses over the misery of his homeland or indulges in peasant romanticism, but simply because here the human drama plays itself out with quick violence. Men rise, men fall; but they do not know the dribbling monotonies of an overly-rationalized mode of existence, as do so many characters in Pirandello's urban stories. In "Fumes," the best of the Sicilian group, a decent hardworking farmer, to frustrate the local money-lender, agrees to sell his land to a sulphur-mining company, appalled though he is at the thought of the fumes that will now blight the whole region. The spectacle of a man being pressed beyond endurance is a familiar one in Pirandello's stories; but the farmer, while hardly a Promethean figure, does cry out at the end, "Neither he nor I!"

Behind Pirandello stands his master in fiction, the Sicilian Giovanni Verga, from whom he learned to disdain rhetoric and grandeur. Reading Verga's stories one feels they are not so much "made-up" fictions as communal fables, the record of a people born to catastrophe. Reading Pirandello's stories, one feels they have been wrought by a man increasingly estranged from a world he knows intimately. Pirandello does not achieve the virile spareness of Verga; no one does. In Verga everything is subordinated to the decisiveness of the event; in Pirandello one

must always be aware of his psychological motives, even if these seldom appear on the surface of the story, and then mainly as a film of melancholy. Verga's happenings are much more terrible than Pirandello's, yet are easier to take, since in Verga men scream and howl as they suffer. Only a few decades separate the two writers, but the distance between them reflects a deep change in the spiritual temper of European life, a certain loss of zest and will.

Writers, like the rest of us, do not choose their moment of birth, and it would be absurd to relate Pirandello too closely with the depressing qualities of his stories. So quick an intelligence must have been aware of the difference in the literary possibilities open to Verga and himself, and realized that most of the advantage did not lie with him. But no serious writer chooses his subject; he can only choose whether to face it. And that Pirandello did with exemplary courage and honesty.

Source: Irving Howe, "Some Words for a Master," in *New Republic*, Vol. 141, No. 2341, September 28, 1959, pp. 21–24.

SOURCES

Baldwin, Hanson W., *World War I: An Outline History*, Harper & Row, 1962, pp. 62–64.

Bassanese, Fiora A., *Understanding Luigi Pirandello*, University of South Carolina Press, 1997, p. 139.

Giudice, Gaspare, *Pirandello: A Biography*, translated by Alastair Hamilton, Oxford University Press, 1975, p. 93.

Keegan, John, *An Illustrated History of the First World War*, Knopf, 2001, p. 407.

Ketelbey, C. D. M., *A History of Modern Times*, 4th ed., George G. Harrap, 1966, pp. 409–44.

Pirandello, Luigi, "War," in *Literature: Reading Fiction, Poetry and Drama*, compact ed., edited by Roberet Di Yanni, McGraw-Hill, 2000, pp. 249–52.

Radcliff-Umstead, Douglas, "Luigi Pirandello as Writer of Short Fiction and Novels," in *A Companion to Pirandello Studies*, edited by John Louis DiGaetani, Greenwood Press, 1991, p. 345.

FURTHER READING

Arthur, Max, *The Faces of World War 1: The Great War in Words and Pictures*, Cassell Illustrated, 2007.
    This illustrated history of the war, by one of Britain's leading historians of the period,

contains over 200 images from the collection of the Imperial War Museum in London.

Mayer, G. J., *A World Undone: The Story of the Great War, 1914 to 1918*, Delacorte Press, 2006.
This is a clearly written account of World War I, its causes and the course it took.

Radcliff-Umstead, Douglas, *The Mirror of Our Anguish: A Study of Luigi Pirandello's Narrative Writings*, Associated University Presses, 1978.
This is the most detailed study in English of Pirandello's novels and short stories.

Thomson, Mark, *The White War: Life and Death on the Italian Front, 1915–1919*, Basic Books, 2009.
This book tells the entire story of the Italian front during World War I, when Italy and Austria fought a succession of battles over disputed territory. The gripping narrative includes interviews with survivors.

SUGGESTED SEARCH TERMS

Luigi Pirandello

Italy AND World War I

Italian Front

Battle of Caporetto

Battle of Isonzo

modernism

Italy AND World War I

trench warfare

Pirandello AND World War I

Pirandello AND modernism

Pirandello AND fascism

A Way of Talking

PATRICIA GRACE

1975

Patricia Grace, a Maori (indigenous to New Zealand) writer, explores issues of race, cultural identity, and personal identity in her short story "A Way of Talking." The work was first published in 1975 in the collection *Waiariki*, which was awarded a PEN/Hubert Church Prose Award in 1976. "A Way of Talking" is like many of Grace's works in that it highlights the cultural differences between the Maori people and whites, referred to by the Maori as Pakehas. In "A Way of Talking," two Maori sisters visit a white dressmaker in order to be fitted for dresses for the older sister's wedding. Hera fears her younger sister Rose, who has always been more outspoken and is home visiting from university, will embarrass her by being brash or confrontational. When the dressmaker makes a remark that both girls take to be negative in tone and exemplary of the attitude of whites toward Maoris, Rose does not let the matter drop but politely confronts the dressmaker. Hera's reaction to her sister's approach is mixed; her initial anger is tempered by a new understanding of her sister's pain. The girls return home, joking about the matter, and then join their family for a meal. By focusing on Hera, her relationship with her sister, and her place within the family, Grace situates her theme of family within the larger contextual theme of community. In the course of the story, Hera re-envisions not only her own place within her family and community, but her sister's as well.

Patricia Grace (Getty Images)

Grace's "A Way of Talking" was published in 1975 by Longman Paul in the collection *Waiariki and Other Stories*.

AUTHOR BIOGRAPHY

Grace was born on August 17, 1937, in Wellington, New Zealand. The daughter of Edward and Joyce Gunson, Grace attended St. Anne's School as a youth. She went on to study at St. Mary's College, as well as Wellington Teachers' College. She received a diploma from Victoria University in teaching of English as a second language. When she was around twenty-five years old, Grace began writing. At this time she was also teaching in North Auckland, New Zealand. She published short pieces in various journals while raising a family that grew to include seven children. Eventually Grace settled in Plimmerton, a small town near Wellington. She published her first book, the

collection of short fiction titled *Waiariki* in 1975. Not only was this work the first short-story collection published by a Maori woman writer, the collection also won the PEN/Hubert Church Award for Best First Book of Fiction. After continuing to both write and teach for a number of years, in 1985 Grace was awarded the Victoria University writing fellowship and subsequently quit teaching to write full time. The following year, Grace published her second novel, *Potiki*, which became one of her most popular works and which also won the New Zealand Book Award for Fiction. Another novel and two short-story collections followed, including the 1994 collection *The Sky People*, which focuses heavily on characters who are wounded, depressed, or lost. Grace won several other prominent awards for her fiction, including the Prime Minister's Award for Literary Achievement in 2006. In 2008, she was selected as the 2008 Laureate of the Neustadt International Prize for Literature. Her 2010 nonfiction work *Ned and Katrina* tells the story of a Maori World War II veteran and his Greek bride.

PLOT SUMMARY

"A Way of Talking" opens with the first-person Maori narrator announcing the return of her sister Rose. As the narrator's recollection progresses, the reader infers that Rose has returned from college. The family stays up most of the night catching up with her. In the morning, the narrator, whom the reader later learns is named Hera, takes her younger sister Rose to the dressmaker's shop for a fitting. Rose expresses reluctance, but Hera insists. She cautions Rose against speaking her mind if displeased and thinks to herself that Jane Frazer, the dressmaker, "often says the wrong thing without knowing." Rose is getting fitted for her bridesmaid's dress for Hera's upcoming wedding. Despite Hera's worries, Rose gets along well with Jane and entertains Jane's children. Hera is amazed to discover that Jane, who has "a lovely house and clothes and everything she needed to make life good for her," seems to envy Rose's life as a college student. As the young women talk, Hera becomes increasingly proud of her sister and her amiable nature. After Jane has measured Rose and sent the children out to play, the women settle in for a cup of coffee. At this point, a truck is heard at the bottom of the driveway. Jane explains that it is her husband, returning after "getting the Maoris for scrub cutting." Her comment marks a turning point in the story.

Hera flushes at the remark, growing angry at Jane's casual reference to the Maori people who have been hired for work by Jane and her husband. Fearful that Rose will not be able to contain her indignation, Hera attempts to think of something to say, to smooth the matter over or to change the subject, but feels frozen. Rose remains calm, pausing before speaking and smoking her cigarette. She finally asks Jane if these Maori have names. Jane, now realizing that she has offended Rose and Hera, begins to blush but acts as if she does not know about whom Rose is speaking. Rose explains, "The people from down the road whom your husband is employing to cut scrub." Hera is annoyed with her sister, particularly with the way she is speaking, "all Pakehafied," that is, like a white person. As Rose continues to question Jane, Jane hesitatingly admits that she does not know the names of the workers, although they know hers. Rose presses on, wondering aloud at the fact that Jane has not ever taken it upon herself to learn the names of those Maori workers whom her husband has hired. Jane finds it difficult to respond, and after a long silence, Rose stands, tells Hera to come with her, and leaves.

Fuming silently at what she perceives to be her sister's rudeness, Hera can think of nothing to say. Recalling something a teacher once told her about the way Hera sulked when she did not know how to speak her mind, Hera is ashamed to admit that she was old enough to be married but had not "learned yet how to get the words out." After Hera admits to Rose that she has embarrassed her, Rose tells her older sister not to worry about it. However, the way Rose phrases her response, calling Hera "Honey," suddenly triggers in Hera a new understanding about Rose. Hera realizes that Rose not only seems older and wiser, having used that expression, but also that Rose was hurt. The new way of speaking that Rose uses with Hera generates in Hera a sorrow for herself and for her sister, as Hera realizes how lonely Rose must have felt to always have been the one standing up to insults and prejudice. Hera now sees that she has always allowed Rose to fight the family's battles. At the same time, Hera wonders at her own culpability, when she and her family speak in a disparaging

way about the Pakehas, but Rose makes it clear that the family is always careful to only speak that way amongst themselves and that it is really only the older generation who continues to do so. Rose then goes on to explain to Hera how "fashionable" it is for whites to have Maori friends and that Jane will not hold this incident against either one of them. The sisters then giggle over Rose's impersonation of Jane and how she would brag about her Maori friends to her white friends. As they return to the house, the family is just sitting down to share a meal together, and Rose, Hera, their brothers, and their parents joke warmly with one another. The story ends with Hera insisting that she will try to make Rose understand that she is not alone.

CHARACTERS

Alan Frazer
Alan Frazer is mentioned in the story but does not appear. He is Jane's husband. The women hear his truck approach, prompting Jane to comment about Alan's recent whereabouts. According to Jane, Alan has been hiring Maori workers to help cut scrub (unwanted vegetation, such as grasses and weeds) from the Frazer's land.

Jane Frazer
Jane Frazer is the dressmaker Hera has hired to sew her wedding dress and the bridesmaid dresses for her upcoming wedding. Hera informs the reader that Jane "often says the wrong thing without knowing." Jane appears to be amiable and seems to get along well with Hera's sister Rose. However, she soon makes a comment that offends Rose and Hera, when she observes that her husband has "been down the road getting the Maoris for scrub cutting." This is just the type of slip that Hera feared Jane would make in front of Rose. Jane awkwardly answers Rose's inquiries about the Maori workers, admitting that while they know her name she has not made an effort to learn theirs. Her comments and her silence suggest that Jane is embarrassed to have offended Hera and Rose but also indicate that Jane is perhaps unclear about precisely why her comment has been perceived as prejudiced or disrespectful. Jane later becomes the object of Rose's and Hera's joke, when Rose tells Hera that having Maori friends is in vogue for whites. Rose then

mimics Jane telling her white friends about Rose and Hera.

Heke

Heke is one of Hera's brothers. He appears at the end of the story as the family sits down to share a meal.

Hera

Hera is the protagonist of the story and the story's first-person narrator. Hera is older than her sister Rose, but as the story progresses, she reveals herself to be more insecure than her younger sister. In preparation for her wedding, Hera takes Rose to get fitted for her bridesmaid dress. Knowing Rose to be friendly but often outspoken, Hera cautions Rose, telling her she should not "get smart" while they were at Jane's. Once the two are at Jane's, Hera observes her sister, and her pride is evident. Jane is clearly interested in Rose and her life at school in Auckland. Hera even perceives with some surprise that Jane seems a little jealous of Rose. After Jane makes an offhand comment about the Maori workers her husband has hired, however, Hera senses the tone of their visit shifting. She is angered by the comment but worried about how her sister will respond. Hera contrasts her own blustery, tongue-tied, flushed outrage with her sister's calm demeanor. Hera says nothing while Rose questions Jane, shaming her. After they leave, Hera is consumed with frustration with her sister because Rose was unable to just let Jane's comment go. Hera finds it difficult to accuse Rose of anything more than embarrassing her; rather, she resorts to name-calling as the only way to express her conflicted emotions, calling Rose a "stink thing" for what she had done. While she confesses to Rose that Rose has embarrassed her, Hera's own angry response to Jane's comment indicates that her feelings run deeper than embarrassment regarding Rose's perceived lapse in social courtesy. Her frustration and her own admission to herself that when she sulks it is because she cannot speak her mind both signify that Hera is ashamed of herself for not speaking to Jane about the insensitive comment. When Rose calls Hera "Honey," Hera suddenly feels that Rose's experiences have made her seem as though she is the older sister. As Hera reflects upon her childhood, she sees that Rose took it upon herself to speak for the family. Rose did all the "objecting" for Hera, and for the whole family, whenever anyone was

"too scared to make known when we had been hurt or slighted." Significantly, Hera realizes that by not speaking her mind when she felt wounded by a comment like Jane's, she missed an opportunity to educate people about how seemingly benign comments can have a negative impact. She wonders "How can Jane know us?" if they always pretend "all is well." These understandings generate a shift in Hera's feelings about Rose. She feels sorry that Rose has carried this weight on her own for so long. At the end of the story, Hera insists that her sister Rose "won't have to be alone again."

Hera's Mother

Hera's mother appears only briefly in the story. Before Hera and Rose leave for the dressmaker's, they joke with their mother about making Maori bread. At the end of the story, she suspects that something happened with Hera and Rose but does not press the matter.

Hera's Father

Hera's father jokes with his family at the end of the story during the meal. He is referred to earlier in the story as being present and staying up late with the family, something that is unusual for him, when Rose arrives home.

Matiu

Matiu is one of Hera's brothers. At the end of the story he shares a meal with his family.

Nanny

Nanny is Hera's grandmother. She appears at the beginning and end of the story. After Rose returns home from college, the family members all stay up late getting caught up with her. It is Nanny who urges everyone to go to bed, employing a unique turn of phrase to do so. Hera comments on how beautiful Nanny's way of talking is, when she uses Maori concepts or speech patterns, but speaks in English, as when she says, "Time for sleeping. The mouths steal the time of the eyes." Nanny also appears at the end of the story for the family meal.

Rose

Rose is Hera's younger sister. Referred to affectionally as "Rohe" by her family, she has been away at college and has returned home to visit her family. Hera describes her sister as a "hard-case," as well as "the kamakama one" of the family and "the one with the brains." ("Kamakama" is a Maori term that, according to V. Lakshmi Pathy in an article for the *Journal of the Polynesian Society*, means "joyous.") Repeatedly, Hera refers to the way Rose makes the whole family laugh. Rose also inspires both pride and anger in her sister. Hera is frustrated because Rose refuses to back down from conflict. At the same time, this quality also makes the more insecure Hera both proud and jealous. Rose does not back away from confronting Jane about an insensitive comment, and when Jane's response is unsatisfactory, Rose commands Hera to leave with her. Later, Rose attempts to soothe Hera's fears and insists that the way their own family refers to and talks about whites is different than the way Jane spoke about the Maori workers in front of them. Rose's argument hinges on "not so much what is said, but when and where and in whose presence." As Rose continues to explain her point of view to her sister, she jokes about Jane's perceptions of them and is able to tease her worried sister into laughter.

THEMES

Family

In "A Way of Talking," the notion of family is treated with reverence. Grace posits the family unit at the heart of the larger community in her story, depicting with tenderness the relationships Hera most values. Rose is treated as a returning hero on her visit home from college. The family members stay up late catching up with her, "even Dad and Nanny who usually go to bed after tea." Before Hera and Rose leave for the dressmaker's, they finish chores around the house. Hera mentions this in passing, but the fact that the sisters aid their mother in taking care of the home and make this act a priority before their departure is indicative of their respect for their family and their family's home. Hera also notes that despite her mother's joking, her Mum always makes "a big Maori bread" when a family member returns home. Such a detail underscores the significance of tradition in Hera's family. As in many cultures, food plays a major role in family ritual in Hera's family. At the close of the story, this notion is repeated, as the family gathers to enjoy a meal. Hera's brothers joke about having grown and tended the corn the family is now enjoying, drawing attention to their role in helping to sustain and nourish the family. The easy, teasing, joking manner the family members have with one another creates

a sense of warmth and affection. At the same time, Hera becomes aware earlier in the story that her family is far from perfect. After Rose chastises Jane for the inappropriateness of her remark, Hera reflects on the family's collective past, acknowledging with a sense of shame that the whole family has relied on Rose to speak up for them. While everyone else has avoided conflict, Rose has always objected to the comments people have made that have resulted in her family feeling "hurt or slighted." This understanding draws Hera closer to her sister, inspiring in Hera feelings of protectiveness for Rose. Hera vows to be more like her sister, so that Rose will not have to feel alone. This deepening of the bond between the sisters further highlight's Grace's efforts to portray a family that, however flawed, is united and loving.

Community

The community in Grace's story is one comprised of both a white and a Maori population. A major component of the story is the conflict between Rose and Jane in the dressmaker's shop. The issue is a subtle one, and the way the characters in the story handle the conflict is indicative of both the depth of the rift between the two sub-sectors of the community, as well as their good intentions to begin to mend the breach. Grace depicts a Maori family in a way that is respectful of the Maori people and that also demonstrates that Hera's family is a family like any other, with its own way of handling problems and its own way of interacting. When Jane's insensitive comment sparks a strong and immediate response in Hera and her sister, the tone of the story subtly changes, and the existence of a rift between the white and Maori communities is suddenly illuminated for the reader. Rose attempts to point out to Jane that referring to the Maori workers in this way, as an unindividuated mass of laborers, is offensive. Rose suggests to Jane that there is something wrong with the fact that the various Maori people hired to cut scrub know her name, but that she knows none of them individually. Jane is clearly surprised that what she has said could be taken as insulting. She flushes, indicating her embarrassment and discomfort, and stammers responses to Rose's questions.

As Hera and Rose discuss the matter once they have left Jane's shop, Hera wonders if her family is as guilty of racial ignorance as Jane is, for they often, she points out to Rose, refer to whites as Pakehas or talk about Pakeha ways in a

TOPICS FOR FURTHER STUDY

- Many of Grace's writings deal in some way with the Maori people and culture. Using print and online sources, research the history of the Maori people or modern Maori culture. Create a presentation about the Maori that includes such items as a map of New Zealand with Maori names for various regions, information about Maori traditions, music, and food, and a timeline of Maori history. Your presentation may be created as a Web page, in PowerPoint, or as a combination of display board and written or oral report.

- In her depiction of a Maori family in "A Way of Talking," Grace explores the tensions within the family while at the same time portraying the family as a supportive unit. With a small group, watch the 2002 movie *Whale Rider*, a film based on the 1987 young-adult novel by Maori writer Witi Ihimaera. How are the Maori family relationships portrayed in the film? How would you characterize the relationship between the young female protagonist and her community? Are there similarities between the portrayals of Maori families and communities in the film and Grace's story? Create a blog on which members of your group can discuss the film and any connections between the film and Grace's story. Alternatively, prepare a report to share with the class.

- *Skins: Contemporary Indigenous Writing* is a collection of short fiction compiled by Kateri Akiwezie-Damm and Josie Douglas and published by Jukurrpa Books in 2000. The collection contains work by Maori authors, by Aboriginal Australian authors, and by Native American authors. All of the authors, despite their differences in racial backgrounds, share the bond of belonging to an indigenous culture that was nearly eradicated by white settlers during a colonial past. Read a selection of the stories. What themes are common among the writers of various backgrounds? What are the most significant differences in the stories? Consider the way the authors use the English language. Do they incorporate words, rhythms, or images from their particular cultures? Write an analytical essay in which you compare several of these stories.

- In "A Way of Talking," Grace makes several references to the land, the clearing of scrub, the growing of crops. Research the agricultural economy of New Zealand. What types of crops are grown? How many people are employed in this industry? How has agriculture changed in New Zealand since the 1970s? Have environmental concerns changed agricultural practices? Create a report in which you summarize your findings that contains charts and graphs to illustrate changes and statistics. Be sure to cite all of your sources.

---

negative manner. Rose insists that because they only do this in the presence of one another rather than in the presence of whites, it is different, as it offends no one. What Rose fails to acknowledge is that what she objected to in Jane's comment—the generalizations implied about the Maori as a group—is what is sometimes being done to whites when the Maori use the term Pakeha. Hera senses the inequity here. When a term is used to make generalizations about an ethnic group, whether or not there are members of that group around to hear it, there is an effect made upon the individuals making the generalization. To speak of Maoris or Pakehas as a group with a typical set of behaviors, characteristics, or tendencies ignores the fact that each group is made up of individuals, people with names, as Rose would point out, who, while affiliated with a group, cannot be

The family was there to pick Rose up at the bus station. (s_oleg | Shutterstock.com)

dismissed simply as the Maori hired to cut the scrub, for example, or the Pakehas who think it is fashionable to have Maori friends. Grace uses Rose's humor to diffuse the tension between the ethnic sectors of the community. She concludes her story with a focus on Hera's family rather than on the conflict between Rose and Jane, a conflict Rose had forgotten about "At the sight of Mum's bread."

STYLE

First-Person Narration

Grace uses Hera as a first-person narrator in "A Way of Talking." A first-person narrator refers to himself or herself as "I" throughout the story. Typically, if a first-person narrator is used, he or she is the story's protagonist, although this is not always the case. By telling the story through one person's point of view and by using the first-person voice to do so, an author has unrestricted access to the protagonist's thoughts. However, the first-person voice can be seen as a limiting method of narration because the author can only describe other characters through the filter of the narrating character. As a reader, one must determine whether the narrator is a reliable one, whether the narrator's state of mind, experiences, or personality, for example, biases his or her view of the other characters. In "A Way of Talking," Hera appears to be a relatively reliable narrator. Her personal insecurities do not seem to interfere with the way she views the people around her. While she is frustrated with her sister Rose's way of speaking candidly, Hera nevertheless praises her sister on many counts, thereby attesting to her own attempt to be objective. Hera further demonstrates this desire to be fair and objective when she and Rose discuss Jane's comment. Hera recognizes that although her family has been hurt by the careless comments whites make about Maori people, her own family has used the Maori term for white people, Pakeha, in an negative manner as well.

Interior Monologue

By employing a first-person narrator in "A Way of Talking," Grace conveys Hera's thoughts through the use of interior monologue. Interior monologue is a prose technique through which an author conveys the thoughts of a character. While this technique may sometimes take the form of a stream of consciousness passage, in which the author attempts to capture the organic, unfiltered flow of a characters thoughts, it may also take the form of more structured prose in which the author relates the content of the character's thoughts. There are several passages in Grace's story in which Hera is reflecting on the distant past, on something that has just occurred, or on something that is bothering her rather than simply relating events. Grace uses this technique when Hera is thinking about Rose's way of speaking her mind. She recalls her mother telling Rose that while Rose had "the brains," she should rely on Hera "for the sense." While Rose and Jane converse, Hera observes and shares her thoughts with the reader. She notes how friendly Rose is, how jealous Jane seems. Perhaps the longest and most significant use of interior monologue in the story occurs when Hera realizes that because the family has always relied on Rose to "do the objecting" when they were not treated fairly, Rose must consequently feel very hurt and alone. Through the course of Hera's interior monologue, the reader is witness to Hera's growing desire to become more like her sister, to speak up for herself, and in doing so, to protect Rose from the hurt of having to do all the speaking up on her own.

HISTORICAL CONTEXT

Maori Culture in the 1970s
The early and mid-1970s saw a dramatic shift in the way Maoris were treated in New Zealand. After years of discrimination, which led to losses of native lands, language, and cultural identity, legislative changes, inspired by a renewed spirit of activism, empowered the Maori people. The Maori Affairs Amendment Act, passed in 1974, simplified the designation of Maori status to anyone with Maori ancestry. Land protest movements were on the rise as well, with advocates demanding Maori control and retention of ancestral lands. Additionally, the educational system was examined during this time, in light of the academic struggles and cultural isolation faced by Maori students. As Jeffery Sissons explains in a 1993

essay for the journal *Oceania*, the "social alienation" experienced by some of the Maori population was thought to be a contributing factor to "lower school achievement." Maori leaders, along with various government agencies were tasked with "enhancing Maori cultural pride and increasing the understanding and appreciation of Maori culture among the wider population." Increasingly, the necessity of preserving Maori cultural identity became a priority. One important step along this path was the introduction of the Maori language into the educational system. In a process begun in 1973, great strides were made over the course of the decade to educate teachers and to certify fluent Maori speakers to teach the language in school. During the 1970s, the Department of Maori Affairs worked not only on this language initiative but also on encouraging the introduction of other elements of Maori culture into the school systems as well.

New Zealand Literature in the 1970s
As the political and social culture shifted, generating a more inclusive and welcoming atmosphere for Maori people in New Zealand society, the literature of this time period experienced its own transformation. The literature of New Zealand up to this point had been dominated by the work of white New Zealanders, the descendants of European settlers. As observed by Nicholas Birns in the 2001 *Encyclopedia of Postcolonial Studies*, in the early to mid-twentieth century, some New Zealand authors attempted to craft a uniquely New Zealand form of literature and rebelled against the more Victorian themes and styles of writers who had come before them. By the 1970s feminist authors such as Janet Frame had also begun to emerge. At the same time, Maori writing in English, which had begun to develop in the 1960s, took hold in the 1970s, with the work of poet Hone Tuwhare and the fiction of Grace and Witi Ihimaera, according to Birns. Maori culture and society began to take center stage in the work of these authors, changing the landscape of New Zealand fiction. The work of Maori authors during this time both illuminates cultural differences and explores political and social issues. At the same time, the descendants of the colonizers, of the settlers, in the tide of postcolonial literary developments, were forced to examine their own issues of cultural identity, explains Sara Dugdale in an article on Pakeha identity in *Race, Colour and Identity in Australia and New Zealand*. Dugdale focuses her

COMPARE
&
CONTRAST

- **1970s:** Because of expansions in the industrial sector in the 1950s and 1960s, an increasing number of Maori are employed in urban occupations by the mid-1970s. This development leads in part to Maori activism, which is initially focused on labor union activity, but soon the spirit of activism spreads to other areas as well.

  Today: Since the 1970s, organizations designed to facilitate Maori educational and economic advancement, such as the Department of Maori Affairs, have been established and subsequently abolished. Other governmental departments, such as the Ministry of Maori Development, and private groups have formed and continue to seek to improve the quality of life among the Maori people throughout New Zealand.

- **1970s:** Maori and non-indigenous New Zealand authors explore themes of personal, cultural, and national identity in New Zealand literature. Such writers include Witi Ihimaera, Grace, and Maurice Gee.

  Today: Many writers who were publishing in the 1970s remain popular today, and they focus on twenty-first-century approaches to themes of identity, which remain salient in New Zealand culture. In addition to Ihimaera, Grace, and Gee, other popular New Zealand writers include Bernard Beckett, Alice Tawhai, and James George.

- **1970s:** Robert Muldoon becomes Zealand's prime minister in 1975. The government, led by Muldoon, becomes engaged in a dispute over land claimed by both the New Zealand government and by the Maori. Muldoon is sometimes regarded as anti-Maori in his policies.

  Today: Maori candidates run for public office, affiliating themselves with an emerging political party, the Maori Party, and seeking greater control over their governance. The current prime minister of New Zealand is John Key, elected in 2008. In May of 2010, Prime Minister Key made a comment linking Maori tribes with cannibalism, generating much controversy and making himself very unpopular among Maori populations. He later apologized for the comment.

---

study of the negotiation of a postcolonial non-indigenous New Zealand identity on the work of New Zealand author Maurice Gee, who began writing in the 1960s and published a number of novels in the turbulent period of the 1970s. Dugdale maintains that, as Gee's work shows, the non-indigenous New Zealanders' anxiety about their identity is manifested in "an endemic culture of evasion."

CRITICAL OVERVIEW

"A Way of Talking" is often examined in terms of its mediation between Maori and white cultures in New Zealand. Otto Heim, in *Writing along Broken Lines: Violence and Ethnicity in Contemporary Maori Fiction*, states that in "A Way of Talking," Grace employs "various tones of irony" to suggest "that her characters establish communication and a sense of community in the space between the lines of what is written down." Heim goes on to compare the character of Rose to a character in another one of Grace's works, noting that both characters are able to recognize "the pretense of patronising Pakeha attitudes toward Maori." Other critics focus on the volume of stories *Waiariki* as a whole. In the 1998 essay on Grace in *The Oxford Companion to New Zealand Literature*, reprinted in part on the New Zealand Book Council Web site, the

Rose made a good impression with the dressmaker while she took measurements for the dress. *(Picsfive /*
Shutterstock.com)

critic views the stories as a progression toward cultural identity, a journey in which the Maori find their own "way of talking." Because "A Way of Talking" is the first in the collection, Hera is regarded by the critic as a starting point; she is viewed as possessing "almost autistic inarticulateness." By the end of the collection, the critic maintains, the Maori harmoniously embrace their own voice. Taking another approach, Ulla Ratheiser, in a 2008 essay for *Bodies and Voices: The Force-Field of Representation and Discourse in Colonial and Postcolonial Studies*, examines the role language plays in individual and group identity. Ratheiser states that Rose establishes a sense of individuality predicated on her own sense of self as an individual Maori, rather than on a sense of self crafted through the Pakeha perceptions of the Maori as a social group. From Rose, Hera learns that "language can and must be used to defend this individuality," Ratheiser insists. Phillip Mann, prior to discussing the plot and characterization of "A Way of Talking" for a 1999 essay in *English Literature and the Other Languages*, praises Grace's short stories as "remarkable both for the delicacy with

which she explores relations between people, especially the complexity of race relations, and the authenticity of her language."

CRITICISM

Catherine Dominic

Dominic is a novelist and a freelance writer and editor. In the following essay, she explores the significance of the title in "A Way of Talking," demonstrating the way in which the author uses the notions of communication and modes of expression to highlight the story's themes of family connection and community conflict.

"A Way of Talking" offers a portrait of a close-knit Maori family and at the same time explores tensions in the community between Maori and white cultures. As the story progresses, Grace examines Hera's family, revealing a web of conflict within the family and illuminating aspects of the Maori culture. This is partly achieved through Grace's reiteration of the story's title within a number of different contexts.

WHAT DO I READ NEXT?

- Grace's *Dogside Story*, published by Penguin in 2001, is a family drama set within a coastal Maori community. Grace offers an exploration of the intertwining notions of family and community.

- Grace's work of historical fiction *Tu* is centered on Maori soldiers stationed in Italy in an all-Maori battalion during World War II. The novel was published in 2005 by the University of Hawaii Press.

- Maori writer Alice Tawhai's collection of short stories for young adults *Luminous* was published by Huia Publishers in 2007. The stories focus on Maori characters, often in their teens, and explore the complexities of identity and relationships.

- *This is the World* is a collection of short fiction by Native American writer W. W. Penn, published by Michigan State University Press in 2000. Penn's work examines the conflict and tensions present in the negotiation between Native American and American cultures. Like Grace's fiction, Penn's collection is written from the perspective of people from an indigenous culture struggling to maintain their identity in a nation no longer their own.

- *Tikanga Whakaaro: Key Concepts in Maori Culture*, by Cleve Barlow, was published by Oxford University Press in 1991. The work provides an overview of Maori terms and concepts, discussing their cultural meaning and significance.

- *Going Public: The Changing Face of New Zealand History*, edited by Bronwyn Dalley and Jock Phillips, is a collection of essays on new approaches to New Zealand history. The essays included in the volume focus on historical study through new media, museums, and treaty analysis, among other methods. The book was published in 2001 by Auckland University Press.

> GRACE'S FOCUS ON COMMUNICATION—
> SUCCESSFUL AND FAILED—POINTS THE READER
> TOWARD A DEEPER UNDERSTANDING OF THE
> STORY'S THEMATIC SUBTEXTS."

In addition to the use of this phrase, "way of talking," and variations of it, Grace refers to verbal expression repeatedly in the story, emphasizing the notions of speaking out and speaking one's mind as well as drawing attention to thwarted efforts of expression, that is, not being able to say what one means or saying something other than what one actually means. Grace's focus on communication—successful and failed—points the reader toward a deeper understanding of the story's thematic subtexts.

As the story opens, Hera thinks about her sister's manner of expression. Rose, she states, "Talks all the time flat out and makes us laugh with her way of talking." Recounting the way Hera's family stays up laughing, talking, and catching up with Rose, Grace here emphasizes the power of communication as a means of cementing family bonds. This is underscored when Hera states that she and Rose stayed up longer, just the two of them, talking. The sisterly bond, one aspect of the larger family bond, is reinforced through communication. Hera's focus on speech is once again brought to the reader's attention when she shares an expression used by her grandmother, who says, "The mouths steal the time of the eyes." Grace accomplishes much in this portion of the story. Firstly, Nanny's expression is *about* talking, as she suggests that a person's desire to sleep is subverted by his or her desire to talk. Secondly, they *way* she expresses herself is admired by Hera, who reflects fondly on Nanny's "lovely way" of talking, "when she speaks in English." Here, Grace draws the reader's attention to the fact that Nanny's mode of expression is endearing to Hera because Nanny uses English to express herself. This suggests that Nanny does not always speak in English, and the unique phrasing Nanny employs further underscores the difference between the Maori language and English. In Hera's observations and comments about

Nanny, then, Grace suggests that for Hera, language, or verbal communication, may serve as a bridge between the Maori and Pakeha cultures. Additionally, after hearing Nanny speak this way, Hera's thoughts are warm and loving toward her grandmother, further reminding the reader that for Hera, communication is a means of solidifying family bonds.

For Hera, though, words, or at least the right words, do not come easily. In others she admires the ease with which they communicate, as with Rose, or the way in which they express themselves, as with Nanny. As for herself, Hera seems to perpetually be searching for the right words. Trying to describe Jane to Rose, Hera "looked for words," finally offering the very general summary, "She's nice." Repeatedly Hera notes that Rose "speaks out when something doesn't please her." Hera is therefore fearful of what Rose will say to Jane who is known, according to Hera, for often saying "the wrong thing without knowing." With the introduction of Jane, then, Grace ushers in a new kind of speaker into the story. While Hera is reluctant to speak at all, Jane simply does a poor job of expressing herself. Increasingly the reader is made aware that communication is an exchange between the speaker and the listener. Its efficacy is rooted in both how and what one says as in how a particular speech is received, or perceived, by the listener. Rose and Jane converse with ease until Jane does what Hera feared she would do: she says the wrong thing without knowing that what she said was wrong. Now, the three young women each assume their respective roles as different kinds of speakers. Jane has spoken poorly. In response, Hera is too overcome with emotion to speak and remains silent, asserting her position as a non-speaker. In the void, Rose speaks her mind, with ease. The comment Jane has offered has angered those who have received her words; she never takes an opportunity to clarify her meaning, and so the exchange has failed.

Significantly, Hera observes that her sister is "talking all Pakehafied." Unlike Nanny, who uses English to express a Maori sentiment, Rose uses English like a Pakeha, like a white person. At the same time, she is, in effect, using English as a bridge. Rose employs English the way, in Hera's opinion, a white person would. Rose's speech is cold and intellectual and lacks the colorful way of speaking Nanny possesses.

Rose attempts to draw Jane's attention to her arguably unintentional insensitivity toward Maoris. Spoken language, particularly English, once again serve as a cultural bridge, just as it bridged the gap for Hera when Nanny spoke English, but in a Maori way. Hera does not see the bridge in the exchange between Rose and Jane. As Rose, a Maori, uses English like a Pakeha to speak to a Pakeha, Hera sees only Maori and Pakeha, not the possibility of bridges between the cultures.

The incident additionally draws Hera's attention self-consciously to her own inability to speak up. Not only did she not respond to Jane's comment, which clearly angered her, but she also does not know how to approach Rose, whose ability and willingness to address Jane's comment frustrates Hera. Unsure of what to say or how to say it, Hera sinks into a "big sulk," which, she explains, is her habit. Hera admits to sulking when she is unable to say what is on her mind. She finally manages to weakly scold Rose for embarrassing her, a scolding Rose nonchalantly brushes off. In doing so, by dismissing Hera's reaction and by calling her "Honey," Rose triggers in Hera a revelation. Surprised by being thus addressed, Hera now begins to feel "very sad because it's not our way of talking to one another." Now Rose seems more worldly, older, "tougher" and "very hurt." Rose's "new way" of speaking to Hera sparks in Hera an understanding of Rose's isolation. Admitting that she "had been sitting back and letting [Rose] do the objecting," Hera realizes that her whole family had been doing the same thing. Rose's "new way" of speaking to Hera, then, may be regarded as a more adult way of interacting that the sisters will now explore. Communication has been achieved through a new mode of expression and has yielded a more fruitful exchange between the sisters.

Hera attempts to put her new realizations about her sister to use in broadening her understanding of the tension between Maori and Pakeha. She wonders, "how can the likes of Jane know when we go round pretending all is well. How can Jane know us?" Hera begins to comprehend that her silence, her inability to communicate and her family's similar failing have contributed to the misunderstandings between the Maori people and the white people in the community. She tries to explain this to Rose, but Rose does not see things in the same way. Before Hera can object or respond to Rose's argument that the Maori use

The ride home in the station wagon was much different than the ride there. *(efiplus / Shutterstock.com)*

the term Pakeha differently than the Pakeha use the term Maori, Rose turns the incident into a way to distract Hera from her worries, to amuse her. Insisting that Pakeha women like Jane are proud to show off their Maori friends, Rose imitates Jane, imagining what Jane might say about Rose and Hera to her white friends. Rose returns to her characteristic way of talking. This is the Rose to whom the reader was introduced at the beginning of the story, the Rose who "talks all the time flat out and makes us laugh with her way of talking."

Although Hera repeatedly has difficulty expressing herself throughout the story and admits to having always been this way, by the story's end she claims she will speak out, like Rose and for Rose. She insists that she will find a way to let Rose know she is not alone, acknowledging that "it will be difficult for me because I'm not clever the way she is. I can't say things the same and I've never learned to stick up for myself." However, Hera is determined to express to Rose that she is not alone anymore. While she has not quite found her own way of talking, her love for her sister inspires Hera to seek a way to communicate

effectively. However, the exchanges between Maori and Pakeha are left, for now, as failed attempts at communication.

Source: Catherine Dominic, Critical Essay on "A Way of Talking," in *Short Stories for Students*, Gale, Cengage Learning, 2011.

Briar Wood

In the following excerpt, Wood defines the theme of mana wahine used in Grace's fictional texts.

This paper will carry out a reading of Patricia Grace's novel *Cousins* in terms of mana wāhine, a movement supported by a framework of Matauranga Maori (Maori knowledge) that works towards further recognition of Maori women's rights and responsibilities. This reading will approach the text through a consideration of Maori centered ways of understanding the world, Indigenous rights, mana wāhine, and the innovations to Anglophone literary traditions developed by writers like Patricia Grace.

Cousins was published in 1992. It tells the story of three cousins Mata, also called May, Makareta and Missy, and their families, and is

COUSINS EXEMPLIFIES MANY OF THE VALUES OF MANA WĀHINE; IT IS FEMALE AUTHORED AND IT FOCUSES CLOSELY ON THE IMPORTANCE OF MAORI WOMEN, AND RELATIONSHIPS BETWEEN THEM, IN THEIR OWN TERMS."

set mostly after World War Two, at a time when Maori movement to the cities increased at a rapid rate. A story of both continuity of traditions and of change in a rapidly modernising world, the novel describes a period when Maori women had, in some ways, an increasing freedom of choice which brought with it responsibility both to uphold ongoing traditions and to thrive in the changing conditions of mid-twentieth century Aotearoa New Zealand.

Themes of Mana Wahine

Patricia Grace's fictional texts develop syncretically in terms of genre, theme and language. They combine Maori oral storytelling traditions in which, like the marae environment (now reproduced in media such as television and radio) so central to Maori community life, there are multiple points of view, with family history and mythical narratives. Grace approaches this fusion of genres from specifically female perspectives. Courtney Bates' thesis 'Taki Toru: Theme, Myth and Symbol in Patricia Grace's *Cousins*' reads the novel as an exemplary text of Indigenous women's writing in its particular mixture of autobiography and realism, and she identifies a number of repeated Maori centered tropes and patterns in the writing.

The structure of *Cousins* (is) like a tukutuku panel's complex web of interwoven threads that echoes the criss-crossing of relationships. There is also an association with tutaki, to meet; to shut; to join together, which in turn is related to taki toru, meaning to gather in groups of three.

She notes a number of significant triple patterns and pinpoints the various ways in which they are signified through characterization: the three kete of knowledge—kete—uruuru—matua—peace, goodness and love, kete uruuru-rangi, karakia and ritual, and kete-uruuru-tau,

warfare, agriculture and crafts, also described as Ritual, Occult and Secular knowledge, three orders of reality—Te Taha Tinana (the physical plane), Te Taha Hinengara (the psychic plane) and Te Taha Wairua (the spiritual plane), the three tiers of the universe—Te Korekore, the potential world, Te Po, the world of becoming and Te Ao Marama, the world of Being—and these tiers as indicative of time—past, present and future. At times Bates associates particular elements of the pattern of three with a specific character, yet it is a vital aspect of the novel that the portrayal recognizes some interchangeability between the characters, as well as between the dead and the living—the signification of character is represented in terms of specific aspects of time and place, represented in Maori terms.

Like Grace's novel *Potiki* set a generation later than *Cousins*, the 1992 novel does not refer to European markers of time; events are indicated principally in a Maori framework of time marked by arrivals, births, departures, deaths, returns and marriages at the intersection of mythological i.e. ancestral and linear historical time. Both ancestral and linear historical time are marked by signifiers in nature, yet 'natural' signs also take on mythical qualities and become less fixed as they function in narratives about ancestry. Missy for example, sees herself as 'skinny and toothy and scarry-legged with multi-coloured hair' but in the eyes of the families whom she brings together in accepting an arranged marriage (taumou) she becomes 'Tall like the tipuna, with eyes like Ava Gardner, they said ancestress and actress.' Missy's identity is both inherited and performed anew in accordance with the rights she is given as a representative of the community to help her with the responsibilities the position entails. The influence of movies and a female star system in imagining an ideal self converges with the authority of the kaumatua (elders) who were 'like the teko-teko coming dancing off the boards of the house with their spread fingers, sharp elbows, their paua eyes coming to life with brand new whites showing and centres glinting, faces stretched and mouths turned down. Making it real.'

Short poems included at the beginning of some chapters in the section narrated by the spirit of Missy's twin (Pirgos or Platanius 161) refer to stories about goddesses and ancestresses, a reminder of the Maori language chants and genealogies that gesture towards founding female figures such as Hine-titama, Papatüänuku, and Mahuika.

This trio, and variations on it, is sometimes understood as having similarities to models of the triple goddess found in many cultures. They can be imagined as mythological representatives of youthful, maternal and mature women. The short poems or fragments are a link to oral narratives, both stories and chants, that connect contemporaries to the goddess/ancestress figures; sparking off comparisons, parallels and departures. The passage (Ch. 31) that tells of the birth of Missy, who is named Maleme, begins with a reference to Hine-nui-te-po, goddess of night and dreams, and it describes how her father Bobby is inspired to fight for his life in the midst of World War Two by the image of her birth. It's a retelling of the myth in which Maui, the trickster and bringer of fire, enters Hinenui-te-po 'who crushed Maui between her legs,' bringing death to humans, in a reversal through which her spirit twin, Maui-like, narrates her story, brings her story to life. Chapter 38 begins with the phrase 'Titama, Titama,' indicating Missy's entry into sexuality and adolescence by comparing her to Hine-titama, the Dawn Maid, as she goes to her end of school concert to perform poi songs, enacting her connection to whakapapa and the waka (canoe) of genealogy. Her father's relaxed singing and dancing, often of Maori language songs, at home, has encouraged her and he is there to support her entry into the performance of public life: a kindly father figure and not the incestuous father of the myth. Like the constantly shifting focalization of the narration, the changing poetic headings direct the reader towards a wide variety of mythological stories, their teachings and varied perspectives.

In concentrating on the relationship between cousins, Grace situates her study of Maori women's rights and responsibilities between nuclear families with biological connections and the wider community of extended families and social networks. This is crucial since Maori values are closely based on whanau and whakapapa (extended family and genealogical ties), which this novel foregrounds, and yet it also recognizes the extensions of these values into a wider community and the degree to which, for some people, they can become lost. The subject matter, although fictionalized is, as Courtney Bates demonstrates, closely based on historical events (as well as on family letters and stories) and therefore accurately represents the struggles of Maori women from the 1930s and earlier, through to the present, to access Indigenous rights such as land and home ownership, cultural equality and recognition, adequate representation in national institutions such as those responsible for child care, hospitals and schools, and for equal rights and pay in the work place. Reading in terms of mana wahine—that is, the recognition of Maori women's ongoing social influence and cultural authority—*Cousins* is very much a novel about how Maori women's lives constituted an on-going struggle, both at a national level and in terms of individualized experience. Mana wahine differs from feminism in being Maori centred, but it was often developed in a relationship to feminism, both internationally and at a local New Zealand level; Patricia Grace's novel *Potiki*, for example, is published by the U.K. based Women's Press.

Cousins exemplifies many of the values of mana wāhine; it is female authored and it focuses closely on the importance of Maori women, and relationships between them, in their own terms. Of all Grace's texts it is the one that does this in greatest detail and it may be no coincidence that to this point it is one of the least studied and appreciated of her novels. Unlike the sensational and controversial *Once Were Warriors*, this novel is focused on domestic lives that don't feature extreme and dramatic events such as suicide, rape, incest, pub brawling and wife beating, although it is clearly registered in Makareta's narrative that Maori communities did and do experience these problems. The most extreme form of violence in the novel is associated with World War Two, which happens overseas, and for the most part the main characters experience its lasting effects indirectly. Relationships between a sisterhood of women are presented in more positive and romantic aspects than were perhaps usual, but this does not diminish a realistic reading of the novel nor its contribution to a portrait of the successful performance of Maoritanga (Maori culture).

Portraits of Maori people as both traditional and contemporary (cultural) warriors are popular; *Cousins* is related to this way of thinking since it examines the war years very closely, yet as Irihapeti Ramsden asked in her contribution to Toi Wahine 'Own the Past and Create the Future' when she called for Maori people to reclaim their own histories and to refuse romantic mythology about colonial settlement: 'What does warrior imagery achieve for us? It does validate the colonial takeover and sustains it. It also reinforces the symbolism of Maori as an aggressive people, randomly violent and savage, and fulfils the expectation of those behaviours in television programmes such as *Crimewatch* .... A book entitled *Once Were Gardeners* would just not have had much of a ring to it.' Such a critique of warrior culture is not endorsed by all the characters of the novel or the implied narrator: Polly, for example, loves and honours her soldier husband and has to come to terms with his absence fighting in World War Two and then with his death; Makareta's life, too, is profoundly affected by these events, as is the life of Ada, who befriends and mothers Mata in the city factory in which she works. The novel also includes a description of male comradeship during war, of Rere (Makareta's father) saving Bobby's (Missy's father) life. Bobby, as a returned soldier, suffers nightly trauma which Gloria, his partner, tries to ease. Children in the novel are named after places in World War Two where Maori soldiers were involved—Egypt, Maleme, Alamein—The acts of naming register historical events in terms of both women's time and mana wāhine—the children, signifiers of the future in postcolonial literatures—emerge from both the ancestral lineage of whakapapa and the impact of contemporary world events and places ....

Source: Briar Wood, "Freedom and Responsibility: Narrating Maori Women's Lives in Patricia Grace's *Cousins*," in *Hecate*, Vol. 34, No. 1, 2008, p. 72.

Janet Wilson

In the following excerpt, Wilson finds that Tu *continues the themes Grace developed in* Cousins.

... In Patricia Grace's novel *Tu* (2004), about the Maori fighting in World War Two, the Tainui Maori leader Te Puea Herangi makes a brief appearance to articulate a view which was unfashionable for those times: the incongruity of Maori fighting a war of Empire on soil not their own, of participating in the colonisers' battle. Defying the expectation that her people should 'go away to fight for God, King and Country' Te Puea asks: 'Why would they want to fight for the people who had stolen their country?' Yet the prospect of fighting was a serious temptation to young men seeking new horizons overseas and keen for adventure, and colonial troops like the ANZACs made a massive contribution in both wars although they also suffered serious losses. The Maori troops in World War One gained renown for their courage in Gallipoli where they fought with the ANZAC soldiers, while the Maori 28th Battalion of the 2nd New Zealand Expeditionary Force (2NZEF) in World War Two performed deeds

> THE NOVEL'S DUAL SETTINGS AND PLOT STRUCTURE, IN WHICH THE FAMILY SCENES IN WELLINGTON PROVIDE THE BACKGROUND AND 'EXPLANATION' FOR THE NOVEL'S CLIMAX WHICH OCCURS IN THE WAR SCENES IN ITALY, YIELDS CERTAIN PARALLELS."

of heroism in the Mediterranean and North African campaigns, being rivalled in bravery only by the Ghurkas.

Tu develops a direction hinted at in Grace's earlier novel *Cousins* (1992), which tells of the lives of three women living in Wellington during and after World War Two, whose loved ones return home traumatised, in that it locates much of its action in the exclusively masculine domain of the battlefields overseas which in *Cousins* is only talked about. The novel was inspired, as Grace says in the Author's Notes, by her father's active service with the Maori Battalion in the Italian Campaigns from 1944 (283). Along with other texts published early in the new millennium, notably Witi Ihimaera's *The Uncle's Story* (2000), which studies masculinity and Maori identity in relation to the Vietnam War, and Alistair Campbell's volume of poetry, *Maori Battalion* (2001), dedicated to his brother Stuart who joined the infantry company, Division D of the Maori Battalion, it marks out the twentieth-century wars of empire as a subject for Maori fiction for the first time. Although Otto Heim has noted the previous neglect of this topic with surprise, given the central place of violence in Maori Renaissance writing, such neglect may be due to the orientation of these wars to the cause of empire and the fact that local sacrifices were made in the name of this monolithic geo-political ideology during an era of assimilation at home. This may have been considered less urgently in need of fictionalising in the early decades of the Maori Renaissance which focussed on the politics of Maori sovereignty and survival through cultural recuperation and revival.

The current recreations of the Maori presence in the international world of war can be described as transnational and, in their consideration of issues of home and belonging which arise when fighting on foreign soil, can also, more speculatively, be described as diasporic, a point which this paper will address later. The theme of war inspires what Elizabeth Deloughrey calls the 'transnational geographical imagination,' but the authors approach their subject through detailed research. Grace reconstructs the Maori Battalion's part within the New Zealand Division in the battles for Cassino in 1944, and their capture of the railway station round house and attack on the Hotel Continental, a centre of German resistance, drawing upon J. F. Cody's official army history, *28th (Maori) Battalion* (1956), Wira Gardiner's *Te Mura a Te Ahi* [*The Blazing of the Fire*], *The Story of the Maori Battalion* (1992), and accounts of the Cassino campaign such as those by Fred Magdalany (*Cassino, Portrait of a Battle* (1957) and *The Monastery* (1945)); for her personal tragedy of three brothers fighting in the Maori 28th Battalion, she turned to family memoirs, memorial programmes, oral accounts, photos and tape recordings (284–86).

The recent fictions about Maori fighting in foreign wars of the twentieth century have also had to accommodate to new legends of valour the cultural heritage of warriorhood, the fighting codes of traditional Maori society, which was reinforced by the customary codes of mana ('prestige, power, authority'), tapu ('sacredness') and the obligations of leadership. Grace's narrative focuses on one of the most relentless and unrewarding ventures in which the New Zealand Division was involved: the battle for Cassino, a town with the crucial Highway 6 running through it, seen as the key to the capture of Rome and hence the liberation of central Italy. The intense neighbourhood fighting with Germans in their fortified dugouts and cellars which developed in the second offensive (March 1944), involving Brigades 5 and 6 of the New Zealand Division, including the Maori 28th Battalion, gave Cassino the reputation of being 'a First World War battle fought with Second World War weapons.' This thwarted initiative, culminating in the destruction of the great Benedictine Abbey that overlooked Cassino town, also appears in *The Uncle's Story*, having now acquired legendary status as a new benchmark of

heroism. Grace represents the modern fighting spirit and techniques as overlapping with the ancient Maori warrior codes, showing them as different but persistent types of power relations. Keown points out that the traditional method of fighting with the taiaha which Tu had learnt from his uncle gives him skill with the bayonet, while on one occasion two chiefs, fellow soldiers, 'draw olden-day patterns of chiefly moko on each other's skins,' and then terrify a Spandau gunner with haka-like movements, leaping into the air and protruding their tongues. Tu himself, who enlists without his family's knowledge or consent, and before the official age, is a consummate fighter as his full name, Tumatauenga ('God of War') implies: his bravery and lack of fear of death are powerfully imaged in the first-person representations of his thought processes and in his affectless responses to danger.

Tu's commitment to war as a way of life brings him into direct conflict with family expectations and the value that Maoridom places on the collectivities of the whanau ('family') and the community; the moral issue of sending more than one son to war (in the case of Tu's family three brothers go) was one faced by all families caught up in the war effort on both sides, and it critically raises the question of survival of the whanau for a minority Indigenous group which had been demoralised and marginalised due to illness, disease, infant mortality and other ills of colonisation. But the values invoked by his brothers when they decide to maim Tu on the battlefield to prevent him from being killed or wounded are closer to those of the archaic codes than of the modern fighting spirit, and the dramatising of this surprise attack from Tu's point of view implies on the narrative level that the strategy is flawed and counter-productive. This ambivalent attitude towards the Maori heritage is later reinforced by the representation of family anomalies as secrets which cover up an allegedly shameful past: Tu wonders why the truth about the paternity of his niece Rimini has been concealed after the deaths of his brothers and the disappearance of her mother; like the present-day narrator, Michael, in *The Uncle's Story* his role is to reveal the truth about the past. The growth of Tu's self-agency and the convergence in the novel between his contrasting roles as victim and agent as he comes to voice Grate's political sub-text about the state of Maoridom in post-war Aotearoa/ New Zealand, urges the reader to revalue the questionable morality of the brothers' act and the meaning of strategic victimhood.

In this paper I suggest that Tu dramatises the fracture within the warrior cult, due to the moral complexity that war throws up, showing it as turning against itself in order to inaugurate a critique of Pakeha hegemony through a Maori counter-discourse. Tu, the victim of this flawed heritage, upon returning to New Zealand discovers his new identity as a writer and moral commentator and, in so doing, defines a new direction for his culture, the values and autonomy of which have been tested by war. I also suggest that the novel's shifting locations, diverse concepts of migration, home and belonging, and Tu's search for identity, demonstrate affinities with diasporic fiction which in a broad sense is about cultural minorities trying to establish a cultural identity; it also problematises 'the sacred unity of the national state,' and emphasises 'the fluid and constructed notion of identity.' The novel's critique of mid-twentieth-century society, both Maori and Pakeha, therefore, points to new constructions of masculinity and cultural identity, rearticulations of Indigenous rights and citizenship in the modern world and stresses the need for revised representations of race relations. The Uncle-from-Parliament's comment, that 'Maybe fighting will make the brown man equal to the white man,' for example, anticipates Tu's monologue on rights and true citizenship at the novel's end, voicing a widespread grievance that was felt in the decades after the war, especially among Maori leaders: that the motivation on the part of the Maori people—'that this was the opportunity to demonstrate pride of race. The pride, the hopes of the people were pinned on this Battalion of volunteers'—had not only been undermined by the waste and devastation making 'the price [. . .] too high,' but also by the lack of recognition in peacetime of the Maori desire for increased responsibility and participation in governance. Grace therefore re-examines local Indigenous issues concerning equal rights, freedom and citizenship in relation to World War Two, and marks out the limits of the victory in terms of Maori hopes for improved civil rights. As Tu concludes: 'We took full part in a war, but haven't yet been able to take full part in peace.'

Grace projects the political issues through the dislocation and relocation associated with Tu's suffering. The novel has a doubled plot structure, a third person omniscient narrator (telling the story of Pita, Tu's older brother) and first person narrators (Tu's voice projected through his journals and brother Rangi's telling of his story to Tu at the hypodiegetic level of narrative); while flashback and prolepsis effect transitions between the rural and urban locales of New Zealand/Aotearoa (in the domestic narrative) and between New Zealand/Aotearoa and Italy (in the war narrative). Reinforcing the novel's diasporic dimension is Grace's distinctive handling of Indigenous migration in ways which synthesise dominant themes of early Maori short stories which were published in the journal *Te Ao Hou* in the 1950s: the urban migration of Tu's family from Taranaki to Wellington recalls the narratives of archetypal migration away from the rural Maori community such as Arapera Blank's 'Yielding to the New' and Mason H. Durie's 'Dreamer's Return'; Tu's return from Italy to New Zealand is a global reworking of the later narratives of archetypal return to the marae such as J.H. Moffatt's 'The Homecoming.' In the novel, anticipation on the battlefield of returning home (or not), makes the motif of the return a conceptual site where tensions explode, demanding solutions.

Tu's actual return, as physically and psychologically maimed, can also be interpreted in terms of the politics of agency and disability, a recent model for reading Maori fiction which Clare Barker has established: this is evinced in Grace's earlier work through the function of the disabled but visionary child, Toko in *Potiki* (1986), as well as through the deeply wounded Simon in Keri Hulme's the bone people. Unlike these protagonists who exist within the structures of whanau and community, Tu misogynistically locates himself outside society upon his return; but through writing to his nephew and niece and so discovering a form of agency, he constructs new meaning from the past which has been fragmented by dislocation, disability and death: the deaths of his father, his brothers, Johnny (the fiance of Tu's sister, Sophie), the Uncle who had helped the family upon their arrival in Wellington, Pita's wife, Ani Rose. In planning yet another return, this time to Italy, after a gap of some twenty years, he aims to reconnect with the places and people of this land, and to heal the wounds of the past for the benefit of the next generation. The novel, therefore, representing strategies of disability in a progressive way, and hence arguing in favour of disabled social self-determination, cultural agency and survival, maps these strategies onto new symbolic space which is situated outside the community and beyond the borders of the nation.

Strategic Survival: The Individual versus Society

Alistair Fox's analysis of masculinity in Maori society, referring to Ihimaera's work, that the 'pressure [for young men] to identify with the elders, to conform to certain values and expectations of traditional Maori culture does entail too great a sacrifice of personal impulse, leaving them with insufficient room for the expression of individual identity' (153), can usefully be applied to women in Grace's novels. Missy in *Cousins* takes the place of Makareta, and marries someone she has never met for dynastic reasons: to join two families whose land is adjacent. In this sacrificial act she resembles Mata, whose mother died of tuberculosis and who, neglected by her English father, was raised in a 'Christian' Home: as Paloma Fresno Calleja points out, Missy and Mata 'share the same discursive position of being unable to articulate their needs.'

Grace represents such intergenerational issues and inequalities less dramatically than Maori male writers who dwell on the violence of the Maori warrior code and its destructive effects on the younger generation, exposing the codes of conduct as anachronistic and dysfunctional: for example, Man Duffs account in *Once Were Warriors* (1990) of the downfall of Jake Heke, the man who lives by his fists, and Ihimaera's use of the traditional trope of the individual at odds with the codes of the tribe in *The Uncle's Story, Bulibasha* (1994) and *The Whale Rider* (1987) where, in a gender switch, the granddaughter challenges her grandfather's paternalistic view of leadership. Rather than dramatising violent encounters between members of the whanau in an intergenerational clash, Grace ironises this conflict and exposes the delusions and contradictions that such codes give rise to. In her writing the same conflict between the individual and their immediate community is informed by a political consciousness; empathy for so-called victims of the status quo is balanced by the presence of empowering role models such as Makareta in *Cousins* who rejects a prearranged marriage, and becomes an activist in Maori politics in Wellington, and Tangimoana, the politically engaged, university-educated daughter in *Potiki*. Tu combines both positions in that his sacrificial victimhood becomes a condition of his later self-empowerment. In running away to war at age fifteen, and willing to risk his life, he threatens to destroy the hopes of his family by deviating from the path which his school uniform symbolises:

> My school uniform was more than just a uniform. It was part of a pathway, part of my mother's dream, part of the Uncle's wish, part of my brothers' and sisters' work and money, part of our family's hopes. It was the pride of everyone, including the backhome grandmothers, grandfathers, uncles and aunts and cousins.

Tu's victimisation, therefore, occurs as a consequence of his family's expectations and his brothers' determination that he should survive in order to fulfill them; it takes place at the hands of his brother Rangi who in an attempt to save him from possible death in the last minutes before a decisive battle at Cassino, mutilates him by cutting and deforming his arm and breaking his bones. If *Tu* is read as a realistic novel the fact that this horrific deed can ultimately be seen as catalysing family renewal in the post-war era is a supreme irony; if read 'allegorically' as a coded statement of Grace's political agenda, then this volte face, arguing for strategic survival, is the key to its realisation.

The novel's dual settings and plot structure, in which the family scenes in Wellington provide the background and 'explanation' for the novel's climax which occurs in the war scenes in Italy, yields certain parallels. The deliberate wounding of Tu can be seen as a legacy of sacrifices already made by the previous generation in the name of King, God and Country. Tu's name is also associated with Te Hokowhitu-a-Tu, the name given to the Pioneer Battalion of Maori volunteers during World War One, and it links him to his father who had been gassed in the Great War: an invalid and subject to fits of violence, their father is visible to his children as a whole, normal human being only from pre-war photographs. After he returns to New Zealand in his maimed and deracinated state Tu, as his name suggests, comes to resemble his father.

Crucial also is the move of Tu's struggling, impoverished family from their run-down farm at the foot of Mount Taranaki to Wellington, after the children's father's slow, agonising decline and death at the early age of 37. The domestic narrative which concerns this migration from the countryside to the city is echoed in the longer journey of the three brothers—Rangi, Pita and Tu—from New Zealand to Italy in the war narrative. The tension between urban and rural lifestyles and values manifested in the family's initial disorientation in the city and gradual relocation, helps explain the perversion of the warrior ideal when it is turned against Tu on the battlefield . . . .

Source: Janet Wilson, "The Maori at War and Strategic Survival: *Tu* by Patricia Grace," in *Hecate*, Vol. 34, No. 1, May 2008, pp. 89–104.

Simone Oettli

In the following review, Oettli calls Grace a consummate storyteller who uses an omniscient narrator to give Dogside Story *cultural breadth and psychological depth.*

Once upon a time two sisters, Maraenohonoho and Ngarua, quarreled to the point of splitting up a Maori tribe living on the north bank of an estuary. As their names suggest, Maraenohonoho stayed at home and Ngarua, accompanied by her followers, rode the waves to the south bank. This produced two new communities, humorously called the Godsiders and the Dogsiders. The former was characterized by conservatism and a certain affluence, whereas the latter saw itself as adventurous: as the "movers, changers, seekers."

Against this background of Maori legend, Patricia Grace sets the tale of a one-legged young man, Te Rua Tapaerangi, and his life in the Dogside community at the turn of the twentieth century. Initially, Rua comes to terms with the loss of his leg by asserting his independence and living on the edge of the settlement, opting for a "physical life," as he puts it. He is depicted as most at ease in the sea, and his role is to provide the community with fresh fish and cray. The physical context of land and ocean, and their healing power, are beautifully evoked by Grace as we witness the agility with which Rua has adapted to his handicap and moves through bush and water.

Rua means "fish," and his function and integral place within the community is emphasized by his name, which is contained within the name of his ancestress Ngarua. He soon finds himself drawn back into closer involvement with his extended family as he takes responsibility for Kid, or Kiri, a ten-year-old girl who is neglected and mistreated by her two aunts. As a result Rua finds himself involved in a quarrel caused by another pair of sisters, who, in parallel to their forebears, also risk splitting up the community.

Grace uses the story of Rua in a very subtle and unostentatious manner to evoke the difficulties that confront a contemporary Maori community living in accordance with the traditional values of its whanau (tribal group). Problems such as incest, child neglect custody, drinking, drugs, loss of land, poaching, socially determined environmental damage, a cyclone, financial survival, and even the potential disintegration of the whanau itself—as the younger generations are either forced to move to the city in search of work or leave because of internal strife—are all handled discreetly and naturally. Consequently, Grace's political stance in favor of Maori tribal values is not only unobtrusively conveyed but also totally persuasive. She effectively demonstrates that problem-solving is most efficiently and humanely achieved by traditional means and by ignoring the white legal system.

The traditional means consist primarily of telling stories, and *Dogside Story* is, above all, about the power and importance of storytelling. At the center of these stories lie several secrets that create suspense: How does Rua lose his leg? Who are Kid's parents? Why don't the sisters hand over the custody of Kid to her father? The need for secrets to be revealed in order to ensure the wholesome development of both the individual and the community is emphasized by Kid's reiterated request, "Tell me," while their enigmatic quality is intensified by the complexity of the narrative discourse. Grace moves smoothly and effortlessly back and forth in time, in place, and in perspective. The problems are eventually solved at a hui or communal meeting called for that purpose, where the secrets are revealed and the stories told in chronological order. It is through this oral tradition that solutions are found, as different members of the community tell their version of the narrative events and mutual understanding is reached.

This oral tradition is also reflected in Grace's representation of numerous and diverse individual voices. They express themselves in the lively, direct, and imaginative idiom of Maori English, which is blended harmoniously with the auditory imagery used in evocations of the environment. The novel is full of talk, ranging from dialogue to free indirect thought and investing the narrative discourse with an immense vitality. This is reinforced by the activities of the Maori community, whether working, dancing and singing, or helping each other out and dealing with recalcitrant family members. However, Grace does not sentimentalize or idealize her own people; her characters run the normal human gamut between good and evil.

This life-affirming novel reveals once again that Patricia Grace, who emerged in the seventies as the first Maori woman writing in English, is a consummate storyteller. The skillful shifting in perspective provided by the use of an omniscient narrator who presents events either "objectively," in the third person, or subjectively as they pass through Rua's head, which simultaneously places them in a historical context and gives the novel both cultural breadth and psychological depth. Moreover, the novel is a sheer delight in its exuberance and in its nonjudgmental understanding of both the destructive and the productive aspects of human interaction.

Source: Simone Oettli, Review of *Dogside Story*, in *World Literature Today*, Vol. 76, No. 3–4, Summer 2002, p. 90.

SOURCES

"Biography Award for Patricia Grace," in *Radio New Zealand*, http://www.radionz.co.nz/news/regional/54508/biography-award-for-patricia-grace (accessed September 8, 2010).

Birns, Nicholas, "New Zealand/Maori Literature," in *Encyclopedia of Postcolonial Studies*, edited by John C. Hawley, Greenwood Press, 2001, pp. 330–35.

Dugdale, Sarah, "Chronicles of Evasion: Negotiating Pakeha New Zealand Identity," in *Race, Colour and Identity in Australia and New Zealand*, edited by John Docker and Gerhard Fischer, University of New South Wales Press, 2000, pp. 190–202.

Grace, Patricia, "A Way of Talking," in *Waiariki and Other Stories*, Longman Paul, 1975, pp. 1–6.

Gustafson, Barry, "Turbulent Times: SIS, Abortion, the Moyle Affair, and the Governor-General," in *His Way: A Biography of Robert Muldoon*, Auckland University Press, 2000, pp. 192–213.

Heim, Otto, "Articulating Disjointed Lives: Short Stories," in *Writing along Broken Lines: Violence and Ethnicity in Contemporary Maori Fiction*, 1998, pp. 151–70.

Mann, Phillip, "Cross-Cultures: Tensions within the New Zealand English of Present-Day Prose Writers," in *English Literature and the Other Languages*, edited by Ton Hoenselaars and Marius Buning, Rodopi, 1999, pp. 293–306.

Meikle, James, "New Zealand's Prime Minister Apologizes for Cannibalism Joke," in *Guardian* (London, England), May 13, 2010, http://www.guardian.co.uk/world/2010/may/13/john-key-apologises-cannibalism-joke (accessed September 8, 2010).

"Ministry of Maori Development Act of 1991," in *New Zealand Legislation: Acts*, http://www.legislation.govt.nz/act/public/1991/0145/latest/DLM257770.html (accessed September 8, 2010).

"New Zealand Country Profile," in *BBC News*, http://news.bbc.co.uk/2/hi/asia-pacific/country_profiles/1136253.stm (accessed September 8, 2010).

Pathy, V. Lakshmi, "Are There Linguistic Affinities between Maori and Kannada? Some Reflections," in *Journal of the Polynesian Society*, Vol. 63, No. 1, 1954, pp. 35–42.

"Patricia Grace," in *The Arts Foundation*, http://www.thearts.co.nz/artist_page.php&aid = 9&type = bio (accessed September 8, 2010).

"Patricia Grace," in *The Oxford Companion to New Zealand Literature*, reprint, *New Zealand Book Council*, http://www.bookcouncil.org.nz/writers/gracep.html (accessed September 8, 2010).

Ratheiser, Ulla, "A Voice of One's Own: Language as Central Element of Resistance, Reintegration and Reconstruction of Identity in the Fiction of Patricia Grace," in *Bodies and Voices: The Force-Field of Representation and Discourse in Colonial and Postcolonial Studies*, Rodopi, 2008, pp. 251–66.

Sissons, Jeffrey, "The Systematisation of Tradition: Maori Culture as a Strategic Resource," in *Oceania*, Vol. 64, No. 2, 1993, p. 97–117.

"Update: Election Result: 2005," in *Maori Party*, http://twm.co.nz/Maori_Party.html (accessed September 8, 2010).

Walker, Simon, "Obituary: Sir Robert Muldoon," in *Independent* (London, England), August 6, 1992, http://www.independent.co.uk/news/people/obituary-sir-robert-muldoon-1538341.html (accessed September 8, 2010).

FURTHER READING

Allen, Chadwick, *Blood Narrative: Indigenous Identity in American Indian and Maori Literary and Activist Texts*, Duke University Press, 2002.
> Allen offers a literary and cultural comparison of the literary responses to the experiences of Native Americans and Maori writers and activists since World War II. Allen focuses in particular on the radical changes in the writings of these two groups in the late 1960s and early 1970s.

Ihimaera, Witi, *The Rope of Man*, Reed Books, 2005.
> Ihimaera is the Maori author of the young-adult novel *The Whale Rider*. In The *Rope of Man*, Ihimaera explores the notion of Maori identity in a new context, telling his story from the unique perspective of a Maori man who has lived in England much of his life.

Orbell, Margaret, *The Illustrated Encyclopedia of Maori Myth and Legend*, Canterbury University Press, 1995.

Orbell provides a detailed description of Maori myths, beliefs, legends, folklore, history, and customs in this illustrated volume, illuminating the Maori culture and its complexities.

Vaggioli, Felice, *The History of New Zealand and Its Inhabitants*, University of Otago Press, 1999.
Vaggioli was an Italian monk living in New Zealand at the end of the nineteenth century. His history is based on first-hand accounts of the negotiations between European settlers and indigenous inhabitants. This early history, originally published in 1896, was translated from the Italian by John C. Crockett.

SUGGESTED SEARCH TERMS

Patricia Grace AND Waiariki

Patricia Grace AND Way of Talking

Patricia Grace AND Maori writers

Patricia Grace AND New Zealand

Patricia Grace AND cultural identity

Patricia Grace AND politics

Patricia Grace AND Maori culture

Patricia Grace AND feminism

Patricia Grace AND biography

Yours

MARY ROBISON

1982

Originally published on November 1, 1982, in the *New Yorker* magazine, Mary Robison's short story "Yours" was published as part of a compilation in 1983's *An Amateur's Guide to the Night*. More recently, it was included in the collection *Tell Me: 30 Stories* (2002).

"Yours," like all of Robison's other works, focuses on the seemingly insignificant moments of life, those moments that, when removed from their context, are nothing more than just that: moments. However, when taken as part of the bigger picture, such moments are laden with meaning both personal and universal. In the case of "Yours," Robison touches on themes of love and marriage as well as human dignity as she allows her characters to show—rather than tell—the reader what those concepts mean.

Robison's story is written in what critics refer to as a minimalist style in that every word counts. With a final count of just under 750 words, Robison tells a powerful story, one that takes place over the course of an evening, with brevity and yet a great deal of detail. It is in that detail that the observant reader comes to understand the message Robison is attempting to convey.

AUTHOR BIOGRAPHY

The third of eight children and the eldest girl of the family, Robison was born Mary Reiss on

They sat together on the glider and looked at the orange faces they had carved. *(3drenderings / Shutterstock.com)*

January 14, 1949, in Washington, D.C. She spent her formative years in Ohio and eventually graduated from Ohio State University. While there, she met her first husband, Robert Watson. The couple had two daughters before divorcing while still in their early twenties. Several years later, Robison married fellow writer James Robison, but that marriage was dissolved in 1996.

After graduating from Ohio State, Robison attended Johns Hopkins University in Baltimore, Maryland, and earned her master's degree in 1977. Two years later, her first collection of short stories, *Days*, was published and was followed after another two years by her first novel, *Oh!* Her best-known collection of stories, *An Amateur's Guide to the Night: Stories*, was published in 1983 and includes one of her most widely anthologized stories, "Yours." Robison continued to write throughout the 1980s, both in book form and in the popular literary magazine the *New Yorker*. She is considered by many critics a key factor in the resurgence of the popularity of short stories in the literary scene of that decade.

While writing and publishing in the 1980s, Robison held several positions—from visiting lecturer to assistant professor—at a number of reputable colleges across the country, including Ohio State University, University of North Carolina at Greensboro, and Harvard University. In 1994, the author moved to Mississippi to teach creative writing at the University of Southern Mississippi, a position she held for ten years.

For Robison, the first decade of the new century was busy. In 2001, she published her fifth work, the novel *Why Did I Ever*, and followed that two years later with *Tell Me: 30 Stories*, a collection of stories previously published but never all in one book. Robison left Mississippi in 2004 to teach in the English department at the University of Florida. Her 2009 novel *One D.O.A., One on the Way* is unique in its style: it is divided into two hundred and twenty-five chapters despite the fact that it is not quite two hundred pages in length.

In addition to publishing in the *New Yorker*, Robison has enjoyed bylines in *Esquire*, *Paris Review*, *GQ*, and other upscale periodicals. Since she earned her master's degree, Robison's writing has been recognized with various awards and honors, including the Authors Guild and PEN awards (1979), a fellowship from the Guggenheim Foundation (1980), the *Los Angeles Times* Award for fiction (2001), and the Rea Award for the short story (2010), which is an annual prize that recognizes only the most significant contributors to the short-story form. Winners also receive $30,000. Robison joined such renowned authors as John Updike and Joyce Carol Oates when she received the award.

PLOT SUMMARY

"Yours" opens as thirty-five-year-old Allison struggles to carry eight pumpkins from her Renault to the back porch of her house. Her husband of four months, seventy-eight-year-old Clark, is waiting for her on the porch. He is sitting on the glider, wearing a wool shawl to keep away the chill of the autumnal evening air. Clark and Allison are both tall and even look somewhat alike, though Allison wears a blonde wig and is dressed in clothes that can withstand work; she volunteers at a day-care center each weekday afternoon.

After delivering the pumpkins to the porch, Allison quickly sorts through the mail she finds on the hallway table. Nestled amidst the junk mail and bills is an opened birthday letter from Clark's daughter. In it, she warns Clark that

Allison is only with him for what she can get from him. The letter included a check for Clark, but it was just a joke because it was signed "Jesus H. Christ." It is clear that Clark is well off. The desk in the hallway is a Hepplewhite, carved by the famous eighteenth-century furniture maker George Hepplewhite and worth a small fortune. In addition, Clark was once an internist and probably earned a decent living and so lives comfortably in retirement, comfortable enough to be able to afford a maid.

Allison says nothing to Clark about the letter, which he has obviously read. Instead, the couple carves jack-o'-lanterns into the wee hours of the morning. Clark's creations are artsy, with great attention paid to detail. A weekend painter in his younger days, he has an eye for detail. Allison's four pumpkins are more simple, relying on general shapes for mouths, noses, and eyes. Clark relaxes on the porch, enjoying the darkness of the Virginia night, while Allison cleans up the pumpkin guts and mess.

As she cleans, Clark tells his wife he thinks her jack-o'-lanterns are better than his. Allison rebuffs his remark, and he tells her to look him in the eye, which she does, while he reiterates his belief in the superiority of her pumpkin-carving skills. Allison tells him again that he is wrong and that he will realize it once the jack-o'-lanterns are lit by candlelight. It takes her quite some time to get each tiny candle lit and placed just so inside each pumpkin and then to set the pumpkins in a row on the porch railing. Together, husband and wife relax and admire their handiwork until Allison announces it is time for bed. She lets the candles burn, telling Clark she will replace them tomorrow.

That night, however, Allison's body gives in to the cancer that has been ravaging it. Doctors had predicted she would have more time, but she knows what is happening. She tells Clark not to look at her if her wig falls off.

Clark gets on the telephone to call for help, but all he can think about is how he wishes he had more time with his beloved wife. He wants to share with her his wisdom, the kind gained only by living a long time. He would tell her that she never should have felt somehow less than, that to have a modicum of talent was worse, in some ways, than having none at all because it left its possessor always wanting more and feeling not quite good enough. He wants her to

know, without doubt, that she missed nothing by being who she was.

As he speaks into the phone, Clark stares at the jack-o'-lantern faces, and they seem to return his gaze.

<h1>CHARACTERS</h1>

Allison

Allison is the much younger wife of Clark. She is the more active of the two and yet the more fragile as well. Allison knows what Clark's family thinks of her: that she married him just to take advantage of him. She lets that assumption roll off her, perhaps because there is nothing she can do to change it, or maybe because she is secure in knowing the truth. Allison is dying, presumably of cancer, since she wears a wig. She does not let her diagnosis slow her down, as she is the one to haul pumpkins here and there, clean up after she and Clark are done carving them, and volunteer every afternoon at a local day-care center in her Virginia town.

Allison does not seem to have high self-esteem but considers her husband her superior. He was once an internist, after all, which requires dexterity and skill as well as intelligence. Couple that with his hobby of painting, and he becomes, in her eyes, a creative man whose talent is over-shadowed only by his intelligence. In comparison, she feels she falls short.

Clark

Clark is Allison's seventy-eight-year-old husband. Although not feeble by any means, his age makes him slower than her, less able-bodied. In his heyday, Clark was a doctor as well as a weekend painter of watercolors. This tells us he is both intelligent and creative. His creativity unfolds as he carves his jack-o'-lanterns, giving them expressive faces well suited to their shape and size.

Clark loves his younger wife and wants her to realize her own worth. That is why his last thoughts of her as she is dying revolve around wanting to assure her that her life was not lacking anything simply because she did not have what she considered a special talent.

TOPICS FOR FURTHER STUDY

- Re-read the story, paying particular attention to the role of the pumpkins. What happens to them as the story progresses? How do they change? How are the pumpkins involved with the themes of the story? Write a response paper, using evidence from the story to support your viewpoint.

- Using available graphic or drawing software, illustrate a scene from the story that you feel is important to the success of the short story. Be prepared to share your illustration and explanation.

- Read Flannery O'Connor's short story "Good Country People," widely anthologized in high school literature textbooks. Compare the author's use of irony to that used in "Yours." Using a program such as Inspiration or Mindomo.com, map the similarities and differences.

- Either by hand or using graphics software, transform this short story into a comic strip, complete with the author's dialogue as well as some that you invent. Each frame should be its own slide. Synchronize your slide show to music, paying attention to the tone set by Robison. Present your project to the class.

- The marriage portrayed in "Yours" is not traditional simply because Allison is decades younger than Clark. Read any one of the eleven stories in Chitra Banerjee Divakaruni's collection *Arranged Marriage: Stories.* Gleaning details from both stories, determine the ways in which the two traditions differ. Make a list, and provide evidence from each story to support your idea.

- Consider your own assumptions about marriage. List them. Then research the tradition of American marriage. Are your assumptions based on what you've heard or seen from your own parents or caregivers? Has media influenced your attitude toward marriage? If so, how? Have your attitude or assumptions changed from what they once were, and if so, how? Write a one- or two-page paper answering these questions and exploring how society and culture have informed your assumptions about marriage.

THEMES

Death

Although the reader does not realize it until the end of the story, death is one of the primary themes of "Yours." This particular theme is bolstered by the setting—autumn in general, a time when nature's cycles enter dormancy or die completely, and Halloween in particular, a traditional celebration of the dead—as well as some of the finer details such as word choice. Robison writes in a minimalist style, which means that every word must count for something. She chooses words like "twilight," "innards," "reeked," and "struggled" to set the tone. These are not ambivalent words; each has a distinct, intense meaning in this context.

Attitudes toward death are examined as Clark and Allison carve their pumpkins. Allison's own carvings are primitive. She uses basic shapes for the eyes, noses, and mouths. It is as if she is merely going through the motions of what is expected. It is Halloween and so she is carving jack-o'-lanterns for the children. Has she resigned herself to her fate? Her carving could not have taken much time or effort. Does she feel nothing is quite worth her attention since her life is almost over?

Clark, conversely, carves four expressive pumpkins. He takes into consideration the size and shape of each pumpkin and gives it a suitable face. Perhaps the pumpkins reflect his own grieving process as he learned of Allison's condition and diagnosis. Two of the pumpkins are angry, their mouths sharp. The next wears an

Clark was much older, seventy-eight to Allison's thirty-five. (Dana E. Fry | Shutterstock.com)

expression of surprise, as if life took an unexpected turn. The last pumpkin is smiling, the picture of peace. Clark knows Allison is going to die soon; it is possible that he wants to milk every last moment with her of as much happiness and comfort as he can.

Love

Robison explores several aspects of love in "Yours." Her first treatment of the theme considers cultural assumptions. She counts on the reader applying his own assumption about Clark's relationship with Allison when she pointedly indicates that he is forty-three years older than his wife. In American society, it is often believed that a much younger woman marries an older man solely for his wealth and the security he provides. Robison devotes an entire paragraph to this topic as she describes the nasty letter from Clark's daughter, in which Clark is chastised for being a fool to fall for one of the oldest tricks of all time.

Robison continues to explore the theme of love as she describes the death scene. In the throes of death, Allison's love for her husband is still foremost in her mind. She wants him to remember her as pretty, and so she instructs him

not to look at her should her wig fall off. Even as the pain becomes unbearable, Clark's safety is her main concern, as she reminds him to check that the garage is locked.

Clark's love for Allison is rooted in tenderness. He knew what his family thought of his choice to marry Allison, but there is nothing to indicate that he ever informed them that he would most definitely outlive his young bride. He let them think what they wanted to think and instead focused his attention on taking care of his wife. Part of loving her includes reassuring her. Robison makes clear that Clark is an intelligent man and talented artist. By comparison, Allison is less skilled. Clark knows she feels as if she falls short and that his life must have been more rewarding because it was more enriched.

However Clark's final thoughts in the story are of how he would like Allison to know that he does not really have that much talent, and "to own only a little talent, like his, was an awful, plaguing thing." More than anything, he wants Allison to know that she missed nothing in her brief life, that having her love him gave him more satisfaction than anything else he experienced.

STYLE

Minimalism

Minimalism is a style that is concise and in which very few adverbs are used. Minimalist writers prefer to convey meaning through context instead. For "Yours," this style supports the tone and main event of Allison's death. The spare style, with few details, manages to convey a bleak yet loving atmosphere. Rather than explain to the reader either through description or dialogue that Allison has cancer, she includes one brief mention of a wig. It is so brief that its meaning may be lost on the reader upon the first read-through. After the pumpkins have been carved and the couple is getting ready for bed, Robison does not go into detail about Allison's condition and her sudden downward spiral. The author indicates, rather simply, that "she began to die." The lack of description makes this a startling, high-impact statement.

Third-person narrative

A third-person narrator is one whose voice does not belong to any character in the story. This narrator is simply the storyteller, trying to convey the facts as an outsider would watch the story unfold. A story told in third-person uses the pronouns "he" and "she" in all their variant forms rather than "I."

By telling "Yours" from the third-person point of view, Robison allows the reader to make inferences and assumptions about the characters that may or may not be accurate. For example, when Allison finds the nasty letter to Clark from his daughter, she conveys no feeling, not so much as a facial expression. The reader cannot know for certain how Allison feels about the letter. Interpretation lies solely with the reader and his or her own experiences or knowledge.

With third-person narration, the reader is not swayed or influenced by any character's own feelings or bias. The result is an interpretation that is more objective. Ironically, "Yours" is more emotional because emotions are left out of its creation. Robison trusts the reader to soak in all the facts and come to his own conclusion.

Irony

Robison employs irony throughout "Yours." Although Allison is by far the younger of the two characters, it is she who lays dying at the end of the story, though Clark's daughter was certain she was just hanging around him until he died so that she could take everything he had. Robison specifically points out this particular piece of irony by calling the "extremely unkind letter" the "worst thing, the funniest." The daughter insisted her father was being "cruelly deceived." It is not until further along in the story that the reader recognizes this instance of irony, yet Robison plainly states it.

It is ironic, too, that Allison dresses in durable, brightly colored clothing, an image that implies long-lasting exuberance, when in truth she is ill and will not live much longer. It is she who does all of the physical work in the story: carrying pumpkins, cleaning up the mess left from carving, lighting the candles, and lifting the jack-o'-lanterns one by one onto the porch railing. She also volunteers at a day-care center, a job that requires physical stamina. She behaves like a healthy person, yet within hours, Allison is dying, and Clark is not.

The last scene, in which Clark is speaking into the phone yet thinking about what he would like to be able to explain to Allison, is ironic. As he gazes out over the jack-o'-lanterns, they seem to stare back at him. Carving those pumpkins was the last enjoyable activity he and Allison shared, and now they accompany him in his loneliness as he makes what is probably the most difficult phone call of his life.

As Allison lies in bed tossing and turning and trying to shed death like a blanket, her mind is concerned with seemingly insignificant details. After instructing Clark not to look at her if her wig falls off, her thoughts turn to an even more mundane topic: "She said something to Clark about the garage being locked." Allison is literally dying, yet all she can focus on is whether or not the garage is locked.

Foreshadowing

Foreshadowing is a technique authors use to give readers hints about something integral to the story, usually an event. Robison uses foreshadowing to clue the reader in to Allison's death, although she does so subtly. Set around the time of Halloween—literally, the day of the dead—the story opens with a scene in which Allison is struggling, limping. She finds her husband in the twilight, a word used to describe a particular time of day but also to refer to one's decline.

Allison wears a wig, though the reader is never told why, and because it is simply listed

COMPARE & CONTRAST

- **1980s:** After years of being overshadowed by the novel form, the short story returns to the literary spotlight. The renaissance is led by minimalist writers such as Raymond Carver, Ann Beattie, and Mary Robison who, according to *BOMB* reporter Maureen Murray, "upended the short story and made us question what a story is and how one could be told."

  Today: The genre of the short story is enjoying a revival of sorts. According to *Citizen-Times.com* reporter Rob Neufeld, "The short story is showing some muscle.... Publishers are giving short story writers a lot of slots in their hardcover catalogs." Trend experts cite the debut of e-readers as partially responsible for the upward trend. Just as listeners can now purchase music one song at a time for use on MP3 players, so readers are buying stories one at a time from Web sites such as Google Books or Amazon.com for use on e-readers.

- **1980s:** Throughout the decade, lung and bronchus cancer kills more women than any other form of the disease.

  Today: In 2010, breast cancer is the most common type of the disease suffered by women, but the number-one killer remains lung and bronchus cancer.

- **1980s:** Renault automobiles are a sign of prestige. The Alliance wins Motor Trend's "Domestic Car of the Year Award" in 1983. Made by a European car manufacturer, the Renault is a symbol of wealth—and consequently, good fortune—in the United States.

  Today: French-owned Renault joins with Japanese automaker Nissan in 1999 to form the Renault-Nissan alliance. It is the first industrial and commercial partnership of its kind involving France and Japan. The alliance ranks as the third-largest automobile manufacturer in the world.

---

along with the rest of what she is wearing, it is easy to overlook or assume she wears a wig just because she likes the way it looks.

Robison uses foreshadowing even in the kind of candles she has her characters use. Vigil candles are those used when people are gathering together to protest or honor something. In the Roman Catholic Church, a vigil is held the eve before a funeral. Vigils are often associated with death.

The moment in which Clark has "a clear view out back and down to the porch" is another example of foreshadowing. He sees clearly the carved pumpkins, their blank faces staring back at him. That pumpkin-carving was the last shared moments of serenity he shared with his dying wife; in that simple phrase, the reader sees Clark's impending loneliness.

HISTORICAL CONTEXT

Revival of the Short Story

Robison is largely acknowledged as a major writer in the revival of public and literary interest in the short-story genre in the 1980s. She, along with Raymond Carver and Ann Beattie, is credited with using her style to breathe life into a form of writing that had largely fallen out of favor. Short stories achieved great popularity at the end of the nineteenth century, as magazines published them. This trend continued into the first half of the twentieth century, and as demand for quality short stories increased, so did the pay offered to prolific writers. Novelists like F. Scott Fitzgerald relied on the sale of their short stories to bring in a steady income.

As the 1950s ushered in the Beat movement and popular writers experimented with both form and content, the short story gave way to novellas (longer than short stories but shorter than novels) and full-length novels, with writers like Jack Kerouac, Allen Ginsberg, and William S. Burroughs at the helm. In the 1960s, social and cultural identity became popular short-story topics with the advent of the counterculture movement and the civil rights movement. The 1970s saw a surge in the publication of novels and nonfiction with a wider variety of themes, including freedom and independence (in conjunction with the birth of the second wave of feminism). Self-help books became popular as this generation of readers turned its focus inward and self-actualization and analysis became topics of interest.

The short-story form got an additional boost in the 1980s in part because of the horror and suspense genres. Horror fiction writer Stephen King topped best-seller lists in the 1970s, and his success remained steady throughout the 1980s. In addition to novels, King published collections of short stories.

Marriage

Mainstream Americans in the 1980s fought to hold onto their idea of traditional marriage being the true and only legitimate form of marriage. Marriage as an institution had been questioned by feminists in the 1970s. The idea that women did not need to get married to have a fulfilling life suddenly became fodder for water cooler discussions, and the media—both print and electronic—covered and lamented the demise of this institution, the very foundation upon which the American way of life was founded.

Traditional marriage devotees felt threatened by advocates of same-sex marriage as well, who were publicly active as early as 1971. Cohabitation without marriage increased in the 1980s, and the country was divided according to what individuals considered morally correct. Robison incorporated this concept of inappropriate marriage into her story and very pointedly let the reader know that Clark and Allison's marriage was sometimes judged wrong simply because of the age difference.

According to Hilda Rodriguez of the Center for Law and Social Policy, cohabitation before marriage spiked in the 1980s. Whereas only 11 percent of marriages between 1965 and 1974 were precluded by cohabitation, that figure jumped to 44 percent from 1980 to 1984. Experts estimate

Most leaves had been blown away already, and the trees stood unbothered. *(Lane V. Erickson / Shutterstock.com)*

that half of all marriages taking place after 1985 included at least one spouse who had previously lived with a partner outside of marriage.

CRITICAL OVERVIEW

"Mary Robison's role as a so-called minimalist over the past 25 years of so has been consistently under sung, if not overlooked entirely," says Alan Cheuse, book commentator for National Public Radio and contributor to the *Chicago Tribune*. Cheuse praises Robison's collection *Tell Me: 30 Stories* as a "quirky, pleasurable experience" and cites "Yours" as a personal favorite he admired enough to include in an essay he wrote on the contemporary short story.

In general, critics agree with Cheuse's analysis. *Booklist*'s Donna Seaman calls Robison "a writer who extracts a maximum of meaning and feeling from a minimum of words." Seaman compares Robison's stories to a skittering "leaf in the wind until, suddenly, everything begins to make quirky but gratifying sense."

Rarely has a review been printed or an interview conducted that some form of the word "minimalist" was not mentioned. Murray, in the *BOMB* interview with Robison in 2001, brings up the fact that most critics consider the author as one of the originators of minimalism. Asked how she feels about being considered as responsible for establishing the genre, Robison replies, "That's hooey. Raymond Carver was a master of the short story and the master of a kind of short story. There was no one else." Robison mentions other writers who have been "convicted" as minimalists, a clear indication of how she felt when first she had been labeled. "I detested it . . . . Minimalists sounded like we had tiny vocabularies and few ways to use the few words we knew." Robison prefers the term subtractionist because it at implies an intentional effort to use vocabulary in a minimalist way, not just a lack of words.

Of the *Tell Me: 30 Stories* collection, a *Kirkus Review* contributor praises Robison's realism for its irony but criticized some of the stories as relying too much on the emotional upheaval of death. "Still," the contributor reports, it is "good to see an important voice back in print."

CRITICISM

Rebecca Valentine

Valentine is a writer with an extensive background in literary theory and analysis. In the following essay, Valentine argues that Mary Robison's short story "Yours" is best suited to be interpreted through a literary lens of formalism.

"Yours" is a short story generally agreed upon to be written in Robison's typical minimalist style. Minimalist literature typically includes a starkness of vocabulary, which is not to say word choice is limited in any way, but that each word is of the utmost importance and must work with other words to convey meaning not by telling, but by creating a message culled from the work as a whole. In this sense, Mary Robison's "Yours" can most effectively be read using formalist theory, which was once called new criticism.

The purpose of literary criticism is to enable us to form judgments about a particular work. In order to understand why formalism is the best analytical theory to apply to "Yours," it is

> BECAUSE OF A RELIANCE ON THE INTERCONNECTEDNESS OF FORM AND TECHNIQUE, FORMALISM IS THE BEST LITERARY LENS THROUGH WHICH TO INTERPRET AND ANALYZE THIS SHORT STORY."

helpful to explore other critical theories and eliminate them from the mix. Feminist theory does not help us in analyzing Robison's story because gender plays no role in understanding its meaning or plot. Likewise, the psychoanalytic approach does little to enable readers to objectively assess the text since there is no indication that the story's real content is masked by its obvious content: Robison is not saying one thing with her story but meaning another.

Reader response criticism considers the reader's role in determining the meaning of a text. On the spectrum of literary criticism, this theory is the most opposite that of formalism. Reader response posits that literature has no meaning outside that which a reader gives it. The words alone mean nothing. According to this theory, there can be no such concept as universal meaning because each reader has a unique and individual interpretation. Given that "Yours" has been written in a style in which word choice is paramount to creating a particular meaning that can be interpreted with little or no description from the author, using a reader response lens is not a logical choice.

Structuralism is a theory based on the idea that all literature is regulated by a system of organizational codes or signs. Meaning is derived not by individual words or phrases, but in how the words relate to other elements within the system. This literary theory relies heavily on the identification of patterns within texts. Deconstruction is similar to structuralism in that its effectiveness relies on language alone rather than an author's intended meaning. Deconstructionists believe language has nearly limitless meanings and inherent instability, but that readers repress that instability in their quest for absolute truth and certainty.

WHAT
DO I READ
NEXT?

- *Distortions* (1991) is fellow minimalist Ann Beattie's debut short-story collection. Beattie captures the longing that typifies the 1980s with humor and insight.

- Mary Robison's 2002 novel *Why Did I Ever* is divided into 527 segments of various lengths, a format reflective of narrator Mary Breton's attention-deficit disorder. Although the themes and plot are tragic, Robison presents the story with humor that does not detract from the powerful message of the story.

- *American Eyes: New Asian-American Short Stories for Young Adults* (1995) is editor Lori Carlson's intriguing collection of ten stories that provides readers insight into the difficulties faced by Asian American teens. No theme is off limits to these writers. The collection is brief, making it accessible to readers of nearly every level.

- Editors Sandra Lee Kleppe and Robert Miltner have put together a fascinating reference work on the life and works of Raymond Carver. *New Paths to Raymond Carver: Critical Essays on his Life, Fiction, and Poetry* (2008) includes pieces written by Carver

scholars as well as personal friends and colleagues. This compendium provides an in-depth overview of the writer and his life as well as valuable analysis and interpretations of his work.

- Cynthia Whitney Hallett tackles three of the most highly respected minimalist writers of contemporary literature in *Minimalism and the Short Story: Raymond Carver, Amy Hempel, and Mary Robison* (2000). Hallett suggests that literary minimalism is a by-product of the short-story genre and provides general assessments and analyses of works by all three authors. The focus here is more on the history of minimalism and the style itself rather than the writers Professor Hallett analyzes.

- *The Collected Stories of Amy Hempel* (2007) received starred reviews from *Booklist* and *Publishers Weekly* and was selected as One of the Ten Best Books of the Year by the *New York Times Book Review*. This volume brings together the masterful short-story writer's entire oeuvre: four short collections of slice-of-life stories revolving around unforgettable characters.

The mimetic approach seeks to find meaning of a text in terms of how well it works within and reflects the real world. While this theory may be applied to the story, it would provide only a partial and not entirely accurate interpretation because it fails to take into consideration style and form. Robison employs irony and symbolism as well as foreshadowing in "Yours," and those elements must be taken into consideration.

New historicism looks to connect a work and its meaning to the time in which it was written. Students of this school of thought believe the meaning of the text relies upon the cultural and political movements of the time the author lived and wrote, examining how the text fits in with

other texts from the same time period and whether the meaning of the story has changed with the passage of time because the meaning of words in the text have changed. Robison's story is not set in any determined time or period; its meaning is fixed.

Not one of the preceding theories can easily be applied like a template to the story; each has at least one aspect that cannot be adapted to analysis of "Yours." Formalism, however, analyzes each literary work as a freestanding text, beyond the influence of its environment, the time period in which it was written, and even author intention. Meaning is inherent in the text itself, derived from literary technique and style as well

They carved jack-o-lanterns for the children. (V. J. Matthew / Shutterstock.com)

as how the words work together to create that meaning. Formalists ask, how are the parts of the text interconnected? How does each piece work to unify as a whole? How do symbolism, irony, and paradox work together to create continuity? Because of a reliance on the interconnectedness of form and technique, formalism is the best literary lens through which to interpret and analyze this short story.

Using formalism, a reader can recognize that the meaning of "Yours" remains static, regardless of the time in which it was written or read. Robison did not make meaning dependent upon any prejudices or meanings her readers might bring to the piece. Instead, she relies heavily upon particular techniques to impart the meaning of this brief story. For example, irony is rampant throughout the story: it is ironic that Allison is by far the younger of the couple, yet she is the one who is dying. Robison uses words like "durable" to describe Allison's clothes and gives her a volunteer position in a job that requires great stamina—despite the fact that Allison suffers from cancer and is operating in a body that has betrayed itself.

Clark's daughter ironically chastises her father for his foolishness in marrying a younger woman she is sure is out to take his money; she does not realize that death is indeed right around the corner, but it will claim the vibrant Allison before the withered and wise Clark. Irony is also seen in Allison dying suddenly, without awareness that the time has come, and worrying about locking the garage door.

Symbolism is another technique used effectively by Robison. The jack-o'-lanterns can be interpreted to symbolize Clark's and Allison's attitudes toward her illness. As she listlessly cuts crude shapes into her four pumpkins—slits and triangles form rudimentary mouths, eyes, and noses—the reader senses that Allison has become resigned to her fate. It is neither here nor there, good or bad. It just is what it is. Meanwhile, Clark uses his artistic talent to carve four exquisite, detailed faces, each thoughtfully placed on a pumpkin of appropriate size and shape. With expressions ranging from ferocious to surprised to serene, one can interpret that Clark has come to terms with the death of his young wife; he has started his journey through grief and has reached a level of acceptance.

Robison includes few adverbs or adjectives. She does not tell the reader how to feel about the story that is unfolding but allows the concise form to speak for itself and provide clues to the astute reader. We are never explicitly told that Allison is dying, although clues to death in general at some point in the story are certainly provided. Set during Halloween the (day of the dead) and autumn, the story finds the elderly Clark in the twilight, a word used to refer to one's later years.

Finally, the very form of the story supports the ultimate ironic twist of the story, that Allison is dying. There is very little dialogue; she and Clark do not say much to one another. Sentences are clipped as readers are specifically not told Allison has cancer. Even as she is going to bed that night after carving pumpkins, Allison does not die, but begins to die, a phrase that suggests the process may take some time. It is significant that Robison chose to say that her protagonist had begun to die. The difference between "dying" and "began to die" is not great, but the meaning is explicit; it will take a while before Allison and Clark, as he watches on, are out of their misery.

In thinking about the form of "Yours" and what it says about the work, one might safely assume that Robison knew exactly what she was doing as she wrote with brevity, sparingly, and without obvious pathos. Without giving the reader any hint of her protagonists' emotional states, the author conveyed their feelings and attitudes. Rather than rely on the reader to bring to her story a particular set of assumptions or abilities based on the cultural and political climate of America in the 1980s, Robison created a short story, the form of which completely conveys and supports the grim and heart-rending reality of the death of a beloved young wife.

Source: Rebecca Valentine, Critical Essay on "Yours," in *Short Stories for Students*, Gale, Cengage Learning, 2011.

Donna Seaman

In the following review, Seaman remarks that the stories in Tell Me *are precision-built.*

Thirty precision-built short stories old and new by a writer who extracts a maximum of meaning and feeling from a minimum of words make for a thrilling collection. Robison's stories, many of which were first published in the *New Yorker*, come at the reader from oblique angles, skittering like a leaf in the wind until, suddenly, everything begins to make quirky but gratifying sense. A deft conjurer of place, Robison is most intrigued with the telegraphic dialogue with which annoyed but loving family members communicate with each other and with the oddball configurations the concept of family can yield. Here are funky, three-generational households, mothers of young children left without husbands, a 35-year-old mother passing as her teenage daughter's sister, and a college football coach trying anxiously to please his skeptical daughter and artist-wanna-be wife. Like Ann Beattie, Robison neatly exposes the pathos beneath the placid veneer of middle-class life, the seeds of chaos in seemingly orderly existences, and finds sweet humor and bemused hope in our stubborn quest for security, even happiness.

Source: Donna Seaman, Review of *Tell Me: 30 Stories*, in *Booklist*, Vol. 99, No. 6, November 15, 2002, pp. 569–70.

Publishers Weekly

In the following review, a Publishers Weekly *contributor describes the sharply delineated stories in* Tell Me.

Thirty brief, sharply delineated short stories written over three decades by Robison (*Days*) chronicle emotional dislocation with witty dispassion. Robison's characters, usually members of middle-class families, are often pictured grappling with the redefinition of roles, such as the teenaged star-gazing narrator of "An Amateur's Guide to the Night" and her pill-popping single mother who pass for sisters and go on double-dates together. Or the newly idle Helen of "Independence Day," recently returned to her father's grand lakeside house in Ohio, who halfheartedly resists the pressure of her estranged husband, Terry, to get on with her life. Epiphanies are of less interest to Robison than rendering the shimmering immediacy of situation: "I could be getting married soon. The fellow is no Adonis," establishes straightaway the art teacher of "In Jewel," whose engagement means a way out of the dead-end eponymous miner town she's always lived in. Robison locates her fairly comfortable characters anywhere from Beverly Hills ("Smoke") to Ophelia, Ohio ("While Home"), to Washington, D.C. ("Smart"); they are waiting for rides in the rain or for babies to be born or for life, simply, to go on. And in every story her characters make valiant, hit-or-miss attempts to connect with one another. The brevity of these tales sometimes leaves the reader hanging, especially since their author delights in oblique details and non sequiturs. Yet nothing is superfluous, and in the spare sadness of Robison's prose entire lives are presented. As the fiancée of "In Jewel" concludes, "All that I've ever owned or had is right out here for you to examine."

Forecast: Readers who've enjoyed Robison's stories in the *New Yorker* will find this a handy compendium. And those fans of realist short fiction who have yet to sample Robison may be profitably steered toward this collection.

Source: Review of *Tell Me: 30 Stories*, in *Publishers Weekly*, Vol. 249, No. 43, October 28, 2002, p. 48.

Kirkus Reviews

In the following excerpted review, a Kirkus Reviews *contributor reflects on Robison being back in print with a new collection called* Tell Me.

... Robison's stories always have the rare intimacy of confession, as though after each subtle, blunt detail she expects to be assigned a reasonable penance. Four new pieces accompany 26 tales from the previous volumes: *Days* (1979), *Believe Them* (1988), and *An Amateur's Guide to the Night* (1990). The award-winners here include "Coach," about a small-town football coach who staggers through an afternoon of domestic inebriation; "I Get By," about a woman who's lost her husband to a somewhat mysterious flying accident but takes solace in the impression made by his replacement at the local high school; "Pretty Ice," in which the visit of a fiancée after a period of separation in may be too much for a woman forced to bring her mother along to meet the potential new man of the family; and the odd "Happy Boy, Allen," about a young man visiting a drunk and probably disturbed aunt to discuss the matter of his widower father taking a new wife—and leaving the question of who's more disturbed, the aunt or the nephew. Robison is realism in the form of narrative non sequitur, but what is gained by strategic anti-reliance on plot is, in the lesser efforts, lost to an over-reliance on the emotional pyrotechnics of death, either random or self-inflicted.

Still, good to see an important voice back in print.

Source: Review of *Tell Me: 30 Stories*, in *Kirkus Reviews*, Vol. 70, No. 8, September 15, 2002, p. 1349.

Richard Eder

In the following review, Eder considers the hidden messages in the stories from Believe Them, *concluding that the stories are "boundless in their emotion."*

Mary Robison's characters need to grieve and lament but they can't. They can only smile, be kind, be recklessly witty, and push enlightened self-mockery to suicidal extremes.

Sorrow and pain are underground messages in these finely made stories [in *Believe Them*]. They are hidden pictures, as in the children's books where, if you look hard—but not too hard or it won't work—you see a giant concealed in a peaceable barnyard.

Behind Robison's intelligent and decent faces—with ruefulness and irony as the limits of expression—there is a face of anguish.

Why should the message be hidden? Why must pain take an Aesopian form; like dissent under a dictatorship, where fables are quietly slipped into a film or a play under the eyes of the State? Does our state—lower-case—make unfeasible, as situation comedies do, a howl of despair? And how sick does this render our buoyancy?

These are the kinds of questions that Robison points to, without ever quite pointing. The minimalist authors do not separate their voices from those of their characters; they do not point. Only once does Robison, who is a minimalist in some respects though not in others, wave to us directly.

In "Your Errant Mom," a woman who has left home for an older and richer man is trying to hold on to her old life even while abandoning it. At the end, after realizing that she has lost her involvement with her husband's and daughter's affairs, and perhaps her own identity as well, she says:

"I would sleep on my stomach now, without a pillow, and with no sustained thoughts. I wanted what I wanted. Before bed, I had read stories with I-narrators who could've been me."

They *are* "her," of course; the stories are by Robison. The author's wave is jaunty and cramped. Waving *and* drowning.

All of the stories in *Believe Them* are written with a mastery of the surface. Whether the narrative voice is calm and matter-of-fact, cheerful, or mildly overwrought, we are presented with a world where matters are proceeding, perhaps not terribly well, but at least under some kind of reasonable control. What makes the difference between the merely well-written and the genuinely moving is the quality of the hidden picture that emerges.

In "While Home," the exchanges among a father, an adult son who is having trouble getting his life started, and a younger son who is still at home are affectionate and marked by evident good will. Underneath is something rawer: the older son's shock at finding that the world is not easy, and the father's fear for a child he can no longer help. The contrast does not really come off, though; the tones are too subdued.

"Adore Her" is about a young man who has settled for a decently paying job, a comfortable apartment and a pretty girlfriend. Finding a stranger's wallet that contains a small chamber of horrors—pictures of 15 different women and an address that identifies the owner as a settled, middle-class householder—the young man realizes he has settled too easily. His apartment is tacky; he hates his job; his girlfriend uses him as a convenience. Again, the hidden picture is almost as flat as the one on the surface.

"For Real" is much stronger. The narrator is a young woman who presents an afternoon B-movie show on a small TV station. Her commentary is derisive and comical, and she wears a clown's outfit to deliver it.

Between camera sessions, she thinks of the man she's been living with. He is a German; she had intended to marry him to help him get resident status, even though she doesn't love him. But he has just told her that he may not need her help and won't marry her because she might fall in love with someone "for real."

All this while, she is adjusting her floppy shoes, her purple gloves, her clown's wig. They mock her thoughts. It is as if Hamlet delivered his soliloquies standing on his head. What is "for real" to someone who faces the world in disguise? Perhaps she does love the German; perhaps she has no way of distinguishing.

The picture emerges, painful and moving. So it does in "Trying," one of the best stories in the collection. The narrator is Bridey, a knowing, irrepressible teen-ager. She is the bright eccentric in her convent school—arguing with her teachers, making speeches when called on instead of answering questions, sneaking out of class, giving agit-prop lectures on nuclear disarmament in the locker room, and eternally in detention.

It is amiable detention. The nuns are exasperated but loving. Her parents are unconventional and loving. Bridey bursts with charm, originality, promise. And Robison suggests her

peril. She may literally burst. She is at the naked, unarmed hinge of growing up. The grown-ups are all too understanding; she has nothing to butt her head against or to contain her flights.

Another of the best stories is "Seizing Control." Five children spend a night alone at home. Their father is at the hospital where their mother is giving birth. The neighbors are available, if necessary; it is perfectly safe.

It *is* safe, in fact, and nothing terrible happens; only a few minor mishaps and disorders. The children play in the snow rather too long. They do forbidden things: Terrence, who is 17, has a glass of wine; the others split a bottle of beer; they make coffee. They put Sarah, the baby, in bed with Hazel, who is the oldest but feeble-minded. In her sleep, Hazel punches Sarah, making her nose bleed. Terrence drives them slowly through the snow to the hospital. It's nothing serious, and afterwards, they stop for pancakes. "We'd been through an emergency," the narrator explains solemnly.

It is true: Nothing serious, but everything has slipped a little. With the parents away, the walls are gone; the world's wind—a tiny breeze, really—has blown through. The ending is brilliant and heartrending. Next day, when the parents ask what has gone on, Hazel tries to answer. All she can get out are the phrases she's been taught; the phrases of parental protection:

> Don't pet strange animals.... It is never all right to hit.... We have Eastern Standard Time.... Put baking soda on your bee stings .... Whatever Mother and Father tell you, believe them....

The most powerful stories in *Believe Them* tend to touch upon children and adolescents. Robison uses a minimalist discipline and barely ruffled surfaces, but her hidden pictures of childhood and other states of vulnerability can be boundless in their emotion.

Source: Richard Eder, "Hidden Pictures of Sorrow and Pain," in *Los Angeles Times Book Review*, June 19, 1988, pp. 3, 12.

SOURCES

American Cancer Society, "Age-Adjusted Cancer Death Rates, Females by Site, US, 1930–2006," in *Surveillance and Health Policy Research*, 2010, http://www.cancer. org/acs/groups/content/@epidemiologysurveilance/documents/document/acsp c-026209.pdf (accessed September 17, 2010).

Cheuse, Alan, "Mary Robison's Quirky, Pleasurable Stories," in *ChicagoTribune.com*, December 15, 2002, http://articles.chicagotribune.com/2002-12-15/entertainment/0212150013_1_mary-robison-contemporary-short-story-collections (accessed September 18, 2010).

"Formalism (1930s–Present)," in *Purdue Online Writing Lab*, http://owl.english.purdue.edu/owl/resource/722/03/ (accessed September 20, 2010).

Gibson, Bridget, "Mary Robison: A Biography," in *Mississippi Writers & Musicians*, http://www.mswritersandmusicians.com/writers/mary-robison.html (accessed September 15, 2010).

"Minimalist Writer Robison Wins $30K Prize," in *Canadian Broadcasting Corporation*, May 11, 2010, http://www.cbc.ca/arts/books/story/2010/05/11/robison-rea-award.html (accessed December 28, 2010).

Murray, Maureen, "Mary Robison," in *BOMB*, Vol. 77, Fall 2001, http://bombsite.com/issues/77/articles/2438 (accessed September 18, 2010).

Neufeld, Rob, "Novels Are Intense, but Short Stories Are Turning Heads," in *The Read on WNC*, July 25, 2010, http://thereadonwnc.ning.com/forum/topics/local-and-international-short (accessed September 17, 2010).

Review of *Tell Me: 30 Stories*, in *Kirkus Reviews*, September 15, 2002, p. 1349.

Robison, Mary, "Yours," in *Tell Me: 30 Stories*, Counterpoint, 2002, pp. 275–77.

Rodriguez, Hilda, "Cohabitation: A Snapshot," in *Policy Archive*, http://www.policyarchive.org/handle/10207/bitstreams/13773.pdf (accessed September 28, 2010).

Seaman, Donna, Review of *Tell Me: 30 Stories*, in *Booklist*, November 15, 2002, p. 569–70.

"2010 Estimated US Cancer Deaths," in *American Cancer Society*, 2010.

FURTHER READING

Ehrlich, Amy, *When I Was Your Age, Volume Two: Original Stories about Growing Up*, Candlewick, 2002.
Ten contemporary young-adult authors from various cultures offer memoirs of their own childhoods and adolescent years. With humor and grace, the well-known writers share with teens their experiences with anxiety, stress, and the more poignant moments that, in hindsight, make up the significant milestones of growing up.

Fletcher, Ralph, *Boy Writers: Reclaiming Their Voices*, Stenhouse Publishers, 2006.
Father of four and children's author Fletcher spent years in teacher staff development. His experience as well as his interviews with teachers across the globe led him to the conclusion that classrooms are not boy friendly in terms of writing. In this book, he provides suggestions on how to pull boys into the realm of writing so that they can find and share their unique voices. With a focus on helping teachers help male students, *Boy Writers* offers a practical section on how teachers can draw out the interests of their male students with simple, easy-to-implement ideas and strategies.

Gardner, John, *The Art of Fiction: Notes on Craft for Young Writers*, Vintage, 1991.
Known for his generosity to young writers, master craftsman Gardner covers literary theory and style for beginning writers as he talks about the creative process of writing and errors common to novice authors. This book is useful in writing classes of all levels as Gardner provides examples and exercises for anyone who wants to improve his writing skills.

Murakami, Haruki, *Blind Willow, Sleeping Woman*, Vintage, 2007.
Originally published in the author's native Japanese, this collection of short stories has been translated into English. The stories are primarily set in Japan but explore universal themes from the perspectives of both men and women. Murakami writes with a unique style laden with symbolism and metaphor, so this collection will surely stretch the young reader's analysis skills.

Rochman, Hazel, and Darlene Z. McCampbell, eds., *Who Do You Think You Are? Stories of Friends and Enemies*, Little, Brown Books for Young Readers, 1997.
Recommended for grades seven and up, this collection of stories provides a perspective on adolescent friendship from a variety of cultures and voices. Selections have been culled from works written by some of America's most widely read and respected modern authors, including Joyce Carol Oates, John Updike, Carson McCullers, and Maya Angelou.

Yolen, Jane, *Twelve Impossible Things before Breakfast*, Sandpiper, 2001.
Yolen has written a collection of twelve short stories in the fantasy genre, each with its own ironic twist or screwy plot. Several of the stories are reworked versions of traditional fantasy tales like *Alice in Wonderland* and *Peter Pan*. Although categorized for a middle-school reading audience, these stories would be great read-alouds in the classroom and are written entertainingly enough to keep older students engaged.

SUGGESTED SEARCH TERMS

Yours AND short story

Yours AND Mary Robison

Mary Robison

Minimalism AND Mary Robison

Mary Robison AND short story

minimalism AND short story

irony AND Mary Robison

Mary Robison AND Raymond Carver

minimalism AND 1980s

short stories AND 1980s

Glossary of Literary Terms

A

Aestheticism: A literary and artistic movement of the nineteenth century. Followers of the movement believed that art should not be mixed with social, political, or moral teaching. The statement "art for art's sake" is a good summary of aestheticism. The movement had its roots in France, but it gained widespread importance in England in the last half of the nineteenth century, where it helped change the Victorian practice of including moral lessons in literature. Oscar Wilde and Edgar Allan Poe are two of the best-known "aesthetes" of the late nineteenth century.

Allegory: A narrative technique in which characters representing things or abstract ideas are used to convey a message or teach a lesson. Allegory is typically used to teach moral, ethical, or religious lessons but is sometimes used for satiric or political purposes. Many fairy tales are allegories.

Allusion: A reference to a familiar literary or historical person or event, used to make an idea more easily understood. Joyce Carol Oates's story "Where Are You Going, Where Have You Been?" exhibits several allusions to popular music.

Analogy: A comparison of two things made to explain something unfamiliar through its similarities to something familiar, or to prove one point based on the acceptance of another. Similes and metaphors are types of analogies.

Antagonist: The major character in a narrative or drama who works against the hero or protagonist. The Misfit in Flannery O'Connor's story "A Good Man Is Hard to Find" serves as the antagonist for the Grandmother.

Anthology: A collection of similar works of literature, art, or music. Zora Neale Hurston's "The Eatonville Anthology" is a collection of stories that take place in the same town.

Anthropomorphism: The presentation of animals or objects in human shape or with human characteristics. The term is derived from the Greek word for "human form." The fur necklet in Katherine Mansfield's story "Miss Brill" has anthropomorphic characteristics.

Anti-hero: A central character in a work of literature who lacks traditional heroic qualities such as courage, physical prowess, and fortitude. Anti-heroes typically distrust conventional values and are unable to commit themselves to any ideals. They generally feel helpless in a world over which they have no control. Anti-heroes usually accept, and often celebrate, their positions as social outcasts. A well-known anti-hero is Walter Mitty in James Thurber's story "The Secret Life of Walter Mitty."

Archetype: The word archetype is commonly used to describe an original pattern or model from which all other things of the same kind are made. Archetypes are the literary images that grow out of the "collective unconscious," a theory proposed by psychologist Carl Jung. They appear in literature as incidents and plots that repeat basic patterns of life. They may also appear as stereotyped characters. The "schlemiel" of Yiddish literature is an archetype.

Autobiography: A narrative in which an individual tells his or her life story. Examples include Benjamin Franklin's *Autobiography* and Amy Hempel's story "In the Cemetery Where Al Jolson Is Buried," which has autobiographical characteristics even though it is a work of fiction.

Avant-garde: A literary term that describes new writing that rejects traditional approaches to literature in favor of innovations in style or content. Twentieth-century examples of the literary avant-garde include the modernists and the minimalists.

B

Belles-lettres: A French term meaning "fine letters" or" beautiful writing." It is often used as a synonym for literature, typically referring to imaginative and artistic rather than scientific or expository writing. Current usage sometimes restricts the meaning to light or humorous writing and appreciative essays about literature. Lewis Carroll's *Alice in Wonderland* epitomizes the realm of belles-lettres.

Bildungsroman: A German word meaning "novel of development." The *bildungsroman* is a study of the maturation of a youthful character, typically brought about through a series of social or sexual encounters that lead to self-awareness. J. D. Salinger's *Catcher in the Rye* is a *bildungsroman*, and Doris Lessing's story "Through the Tunnel" exhibits characteristics of a *bildungsroman* as well.

Black Aesthetic Movement: A period of artistic and literary development among African Americans in the 1960s and early 1970s. This was the first major African-American artistic movement since the Harlem Renaissance and was closely paralleled by the civil rights and black power movements. The black aesthetic writers attempted to produce works of art that would be meaningful to the black masses. Key figures in black aesthetics included one of its founders, poet and playwright Amiri Baraka, formerly known as Le Roi Jones; poet and essayist Haki R. Madhubuti, formerly Don L. Lee; poet and playwright Sonia Sanchez; and dramatist Ed Bullins. Works representative of the Black Aesthetic Movement include Amiri Baraka's play *Dutchman*, a 1964 Obie award-winner.

Black Humor: Writing that places grotesque elements side by side with humorous ones in an attempt to shock the reader, forcing him or her to laugh at the horrifying reality of a disordered world. "Lamb to the Slaughter," by Roald Dahl, in which a placid housewife murders her husband and serves the murder weapon to the investigating policemen, is an example of black humor.

C

Catharsis: The release or purging of unwanted emotions—specifically fear and pity—brought about by exposure to art. The term was first used by the Greek philosopher Aristotle in his *Poetics* to refer to the desired effect of tragedy on spectators.

Character: Broadly speaking, a person in a literary work. The actions of characters are what constitute the plot of a story, novel, or poem. There are numerous types of characters, ranging from simple, stereotypical figures to intricate, multifaceted ones. "Characterization" is the process by which an author creates vivid, believable characters in a work of art. This may be done in a variety of ways, including (1) direct description of the character by the narrator; (2) the direct presentation of the speech, thoughts, or actions of the character; and (3) the responses of other characters to the character. The term "character" also refers to a form originated by the ancient Greek writer Theophrastus that later became popular in the seventeenth and eighteenth centuries. It is a short essay or sketch of a person who prominently displays a specific attribute or quality, such as miserliness or ambition. "Miss Brill," a story by Katherine Mansfield, is an example of a character sketch.

Classical: In its strictest definition in literary criticism, classicism refers to works of ancient Greek or Roman literature. The term may also be used to describe a literary work of recognized importance (a "classic") from any time period or literature that exhibits the traits of classicism. Examples of later works and authors now described as classical include French literature of the seventeenth century, Western novels of the nineteenth century, and American fiction of the mid-nineteenth century such as that written by James Fenimore Cooper and Mark Twain.

Climax: The turning point in a narrative, the moment when the conflict is at its most intense. Typically, the structure of stories, novels, and plays is one of rising action, in which tension builds to the climax, followed by falling action, in which tension lessens as the story moves to its conclusion.

Comedy: One of two major types of drama, the other being tragedy. Its aim is to amuse, and it typically ends happily. Comedy assumes many forms, such as farce and burlesque, and uses a variety of techniques, from parody to satire. In a restricted sense the term comedy refers only to dramatic presentations, but in general usage it is commonly applied to nondramatic works as well.

Comic Relief: The use of humor to lighten the mood of a serious or tragic story, especially in plays. The technique is very common in Elizabethan works, and can be an integral part of the plot or simply a brief event designed to break the tension of the scene.

Conflict: The conflict in a work of fiction is the issue to be resolved in the story. It usually occurs between two characters, the protagonist and the antagonist, or between the protagonist and society or the protagonist and himself or herself. The conflict in Washington Irving's story "The Devil and Tom Walker" is that the Devil wants Tom Walker's soul but Tom does not want to go to hell.

Criticism: The systematic study and evaluation of literary works, usually based on a specific method or set of principles. An important part of literary studies since ancient times, the practice of criticism has given rise to numerous theories, methods, and "schools," sometimes producing conflicting, even contradictory, interpretations of literature in general as well as of individual works. Even such basic issues as what constitutes a poem or a novel have been the subject of much criticism over the centuries. Seminal texts of literary criticism include Plato's *Republic,*

Aristotle's *Poetics,* Sir Philip Sidney's *The Defence of Poesie,* and John Dryden's *Of Dramatic Poesie.* Contemporary schools of criticism include deconstruction, feminist, psychoanalytic, poststructuralist, new historicist, postcolonialist, and reader-response.

D

Deconstruction: A method of literary criticism characterized by multiple conflicting interpretations of a given work. Deconstructionists consider the impact of the language of a work and suggest that the true meaning of the work is not necessarily the meaning that the author intended.

Deduction: The process of reaching a conclusion through reasoning from general premises to a specific premise. Arthur Conan Doyle's character Sherlock Holmes often used deductive reasoning to solve mysteries.

Denotation: The definition of a word, apart from the impressions or feelings it creates in the reader. The word "apartheid" denotes a political and economic policy of segregation by race, but its connotations—oppression, slavery, inequality—are numerous.

Denouement: A French word meaning "the unknotting." In literature, it denotes the resolution of conflict in fiction or drama. The *denouement* follows the climax and provides an outcome to the primary plot situation as well as an explanation of secondary plot complications. A well-known example of *denouement* is the last scene of the play *As You Like It* by William Shakespeare, in which couples are married, an evildoer repents, the identities of two disguised characters are revealed, and a ruler is restored to power. Also known as "falling action."

Detective Story: A narrative about the solution of a mystery or the identification of a criminal. The conventions of the detective story include the detective's scrupulous use of logic in solving the mystery; incompetent or ineffectual police; a suspect who appears guilty at first but is later proved innocent; and the detective's friend or confidant—often the narrator—whose slowness in interpreting clues emphasizes by contrast the detective's brilliance. Edgar Allan Poe's "Murders in the Rue Morgue" is commonly regarded as the earliest example of this type of story. Other practitioners are Arthur Conan Doyle, Dashiell Hammett, and Agatha Christie.

Dialogue: Dialogue is conversation between people in a literary work. In its most restricted sense, it refers specifically to the speech of characters in a drama. As a specific literary genre, a "dialogue" is a composition in which characters debate an issue or idea.

Didactic: A term used to describe works of literature that aim to teach a moral, religious, political, or practical lesson. Although didactic elements are often found inartistically pleasing works, the term "didactic" usually refers to literature in which the message is more important than the form. The term may also be used to criticize a work that the critic finds "overly didactic," that is, heavy-handed in its delivery of a lesson. An example of didactic literature is John Bunyan's *Pilgrim's Progress*.

Dramatic Irony: Occurs when the reader of a work of literature knows something that a character in the work itself does not know. The irony is in the contrast between the intended meaning of the statements or actions of a character and the additional information understood by the audience.

Dystopia: An imaginary place in a work of fiction where the characters lead dehumanized, fearful lives. George Orwell's *Nineteen Eighty-four*, and Margaret Atwood's *Handmaid's Tale* portray versions of dystopia.

E

Edwardian: Describes cultural conventions identified with the period of the reign of Edward VII of England (1901–1910). Writers of the Edwardian Age typically displayed a strong reaction against the propriety and conservatism of the Victorian Age. Their work often exhibits distrust of authority in religion, politics, and art and expresses strong doubts about the soundness of conventional values. Writers of this era include E. M. Forster, H. G. Wells, and Joseph Conrad.

Empathy: A sense of shared experience, including emotional and physical feelings, with someone or something other than oneself. Empathy is often used to describe the response of a reader to a literary character.

Epilogue: A concluding statement or section of a literary work. In dramas, particularly those of the seventeenth and eighteenth centuries, the epilogue is a closing speech, often in verse, delivered by an actor at the end of a play and spoken directly to the audience.

Epiphany: A sudden revelation of truth inspired by a seemingly trivial incident. The term was widely used by James Joyce in his critical writings, and the stories in Joyce's *Dubliners* are commonly called "epiphanies."

Epistolary Novel: A novel in the form of letters. The form was particularly popular in the eighteenth century. The form can also be applied to short stories, as in Edwidge Danticat's "Children of the Sea."

Epithet: A word or phrase, often disparaging or abusive, that expresses a character trait of someone or something. "The Napoleon of crime" is an epithet applied to Professor Moriarty, arch-rival of Sherlock Holmes in Arthur Conan Doyle's series of detective stories.

Existentialism: A predominantly twentieth-century philosophy concerned with the nature and perception of human existence. There are two major strains of existentialist thought: atheistic and Christian. Followers of atheistic existentialism believe that the individual is alone in a godless universe and that the basic human condition is one of suffering and loneliness. Nevertheless, because there are no fixed values, individuals can create their own characters—indeed, they can shape themselves—through the exercise of free will. The atheistic strain culminates in and is popularly associated with the works of Jean-Paul Sartre. The Christian existentialists, on the other hand, believe that only in God may people find freedom from life's anguish. The two strains hold certain beliefs in common: that existence cannot be fully understood or described through empirical effort; that anguish is a universal element of life; that individuals must bear responsibility for their actions; and that there is no common standard of behavior or perception for religious and ethical matters. Existentialist thought figures prominently in the works of such authors as Franz Kafka, Fyodor Dostoyevsky, and Albert Camus.

Expatriatism: The practice of leaving one's country to live for an extended period in another country. Literary expatriates include Irish author James Joyce who moved to Italy and France, American writers James Baldwin, Ernest Hemingway, Gertrude Stein, and F. Scott Fitzgerald who lived and wrote in Paris, and Polish novelist Joseph Conrad in England.

Exposition: Writing intended to explain the nature of an idea, thing, or theme. Expository writing is often combined with description, narration, or argument.

Expressionism: An indistinct literary term, originally used to describe an early twentieth-century school of German painting. The term applies to almost any mode of unconventional, highly subjective writing that distorts reality in some way. Advocates of Expressionism include Federico Garcia Lorca, Eugene O'Neill, Franz Kafka, and James Joyce.

F

Fable: A prose or verse narrative intended to convey amoral. Animals or inanimate objects with human characteristics often serve as characters in fables. A famous fable is Aesop's "The Tortoise and the Hare."

Fantasy: A literary form related to mythology and folklore. Fantasy literature is typically set in non-existent realms and features supernatural beings. Notable examples of literature with elements of fantasy are Gabriel García Márquez's story "The Handsomest Drowned Man in the World" and Ursula K. Le Guin's "The Ones Who Walk Away from Omelas."

Farce: A type of comedy characterized by broad humor, outlandish incidents, and often vulgar subject matter. Much of the comedy in film and television could more accurately be described as farce.

Fiction: Any story that is the product of imagination rather than a documentation of fact. Characters and events in such narratives may be based in real life but their ultimate form and configuration is a creation of the author.

Figurative Language: A technique in which an author uses figures of speech such as hyperbole, irony, metaphor, or simile for a particular effect. Figurative language is the opposite of literal language, in which every word is truthful, accurate, and free of exaggeration or embellishment.

Flashback: A device used in literature to present action that occurred before the beginning of the story. Flashbacks are often introduced as the dreams or recollections of one or more characters.

Foil: A character in a work of literature whose physical or psychological qualities contrast strongly with, and therefore highlight, the corresponding qualities of another character. In his Sherlock Holmes stories, Arthur Conan Doyle portrayed Dr. Watson as a man of normal habits and intelligence, making him a foil for the eccentric and unusually perceptive Sherlock Holmes.

Folklore: Traditions and myths preserved in a culture or group of people. Typically, these are passed on by word of mouth in various forms—such as legends, songs, and proverbs—or preserved in customs and ceremonies. Washington Irving, in "The Devil and Tom Walker" and many of his other stories, incorporates many elements of the folklore of New England and Germany.

Folktale: A story originating in oral tradition. Folk tales fall into a variety of categories, including legends, ghost stories, fairy tales, fables, and anecdotes based on historical figures and events.

Foreshadowing: A device used in literature to create expectation or to set up an explanation of later developments. Edgar Allan Poe uses foreshadowing to create suspense in "The Fall of the House of Usher" when the narrator comments on the crumbling state of disrepair in which he finds the house.

G

Genre: A category of literary work. Genre may refer to both the content of a given work—tragedy, comedy, horror, science fiction—and to its form, such as poetry, novel, or drama.

Gilded Age: A period in American history during the 1870s and after characterized by political corruption and materialism. A number of important novels of social and political criticism were written during this time. Henry James and Kate Chopin are two writers who were prominent during the Gilded Age.

Gothicism: In literature, works characterized by a taste for medieval or morbid characters and situations. A gothic novel prominently features elements of horror, the supernatural, gloom, and violence: clanking chains, terror, ghosts, medieval castles, and unexplained phenomena. The term "gothic novel" is also applied to novels that lack elements of the traditional Gothic setting but that create a similar atmosphere of terror or dread. The term can also be applied to stories, plays, and poems. Mary Shelley's *Frankenstein* and Joyce Carol Oates's *Bellefleur* are both gothic novels.

Grotesque: In literature, a work that is characterized by exaggeration, deformity, freakishness, and disorder. The grotesque often includes an element of comic absurdity. Examples of the grotesque can be found in the works of Edgar Allan Poe, Flannery O'Connor, Joseph Heller, and Shirley Jackson.

H

Harlem Renaissance: The Harlem Renaissance of the 1920s is generally considered the first significant movement of black writers and artists in the United States. During this period, new and established black writers, many of whom lived in the region of New York City known as Harlem, published more fiction and poetry than ever before, the first influential black literary journals were established, and black authors and artists received their first widespread recognition and serious critical appraisal. Among the major writers associated with this period are Countee Cullen, Langston Hughes, Arna Bontemps, and Zora Neale Hurston.

Hero/Heroine: The principal sympathetic character in a literary work. Heroes and heroines typically exhibit admirable traits: idealism, courage, and integrity, for example. Famous heroes and heroines of literature include Charles Dickens's Oliver Twist, Margaret Mitchell's Scarlett O'Hara, and the anonymous narrator in Ralph Ellison's *Invisible Man.*

Hyperbole: Deliberate exaggeration used to achieve an effect. In William Shakespeare's *Macbeth,* Lady Macbeth hyperbolizes when she says, "All the perfumes of Arabia could not sweeten this little hand."

I

Image: A concrete representation of an object or sensory experience. Typically, such a representation helps evoke the feelings associated with the object or experience itself. Images are either "literal" or "figurative." Literal images are especially concrete and involve little or no extension of the obvious meaning of the words used to express them. Figurative images do not follow the literal meaning of the words exactly. Images in literature are usually visual, but the term "image" can also refer to the representation of any sensory experience.

Imagery: The array of images in a literary work. Also used to convey the author's overall use of figurative language in a work.

In medias res: A Latin term meaning "in the middle of things." It refers to the technique of beginning a story at its midpoint and then using various flashback devices to reveal previous action. This technique originated in such epics as Virgil's *Aeneid.*

Interior Monologue: A narrative technique in which characters' thoughts are revealed in a way that appears to be uncontrolled by the author. The interior monologue typically aims to reveal the inner self of a character. It portrays emotional experiences as they occur at both a conscious and unconscious level. One of the best-known interior monologues in English is the Molly Bloom section at the close of James Joyce's *Ulysses.* Katherine Anne Porter's "The Jilting of Granny Weatherall" is also told in the form of an interior monologue.

Irony: In literary criticism, the effect of language in which the intended meaning is the opposite of what is stated. The title of Jonathan Swift's "A Modest Proposal" is ironic because what Swift proposes in this essay is cannibalism—hardly "modest."

J

Jargon: Language that is used or understood only by a select group of people. Jargon may refer to terminology used in a certain profession, such as computer jargon, or it may refer to any nonsensical language that is not understood by most people. Anthony Burgess's *A Clockwork Orange* and James Thurber's "The Secret Life of Walter Mitty" both use jargon.

K

Knickerbocker Group: An indistinct group of New York writers of the first half of the nineteenth century. Members of the group were linked only by location and a common theme: New York life. Two famous members of the Knickerbocker Group were Washington Irving and William Cullen Bryant. The group's name derives from Irving's *Knickerbocker's History of New York*.

L

Literal Language: An author uses literal language when he or she writes without exaggerating or embellishing the subject matter and without any tools of figurative language. To say "He ran very quickly down the street" is to use literal language, whereas to say "He ran like a hare down the street" would be using figurative language.

Literature: Literature is broadly defined as any written or spoken material, but the term most often refers to creative works. Literature includes poetry, drama, fiction, and many kinds of nonfiction writing, as well as oral, dramatic, and broadcast compositions not necessarily preserved in a written format, such as films and television programs.

Lost Generation: A term first used by Gertrude Stein to describe the post-World War I generation of American writers: men and women haunted by a sense of betrayal and emptiness brought about by the destructiveness of the war. The term is commonly applied to Hart Crane, Ernest Hemingway, F. Scott Fitzgerald, and others.

M

Magic Realism: A form of literature that incorporates fantasy elements or supernatural occurrences into the narrative and accepts them as truth. Gabriel Gárcia Márquez and Laura Esquivel are two writers known for their works of magic realism.

Metaphor: A figure of speech that expresses an idea through the image of another object. Metaphors suggest the essence of the first object by identifying it with certain qualities of the second object. An example is "But soft, what light through yonder window breaks? / It is the east, and Juliet is the sun" in William Shakespeare's *Romeo and Juliet*. Here, Juliet, the first object, is identified with qualities of the second object, the sun.

Minimalism: A literary style characterized by spare, simple prose with few elaborations. In minimalism, the main theme of the work is often never discussed directly. Amy Hempel and Ernest Hemingway are two writers known for their works of minimalism.

Modernism: Modern literary practices. Also, the principles of a literary school that lasted from roughly the beginning of the twentieth century until the end of World War II. Modernism is defined by its rejection of the literary conventions of the nineteenth century and by its opposition to conventional morality, taste, traditions, and economic values. Many writers are associated with the concepts of modernism, including Albert Camus, D. H. Lawrence, Ernest Hemingway, William Faulkner, Eugene O'Neill, and James Joyce.

Monologue: A composition, written or oral, by a single individual. More specifically, a speech given by a single individual in a drama or other public entertainment. It has no set length, although it is usually several or more lines long. "I Stand Here Ironing" by Tillie Olsen is an example of a story written in the form of a monologue.

Mood: The prevailing emotions of a work or of the author in his or her creation of the work. The mood of a work is not always what might be expected based on its subject matter.

Motif: A theme, character type, image, metaphor, or other verbal element that recurs throughout a single work of literature or occurs in a number of different works over a period of time. For example, the color white in Herman Melville's *Moby Dick* is a "specific" motif, while the trials of star-crossed lovers is a "conventional" motif from the literature of all periods.

N

Narration: The telling of a series of events, real or invented. A narration may be either a simple narrative, in which the events are recounted chronologically, or a narrative with a plot, in which the account is given in a style reflecting the author's artistic concept of the story. Narration is sometimes used as a synonym for "storyline."

Narrative: A verse or prose accounting of an event or sequence of events, real or invented. The term is also used as an adjective in the sense "method of narration." For example, in literary criticism, the expression "narrative technique" usually refers to the way the author structures and presents his or her story. Different narrative forms include diaries, travelogues, novels, ballads, epics, short stories, and other fictional forms.

Narrator: The teller of a story. The narrator may be the author or a character in the story through whom the author speaks. Huckleberry Finn is the narrator of Mark Twain's *The Adventures of Huckleberry Finn.*

Novella: An Italian term meaning "story." This term has been especially used to describe fourteenth-century Italian tales, but it also refers to modern short novels. Modern novellas include Leo Tolstoy's *The Death of Ivan Ilich,* Fyodor Dostoyevsky's *Notes from the Underground,* and Joseph Conrad's *Heart of Darkness.*

O

Oedipus Complex: A son's romantic obsession with his mother. The phrase is derived from the story of the ancient Theban hero Oedipus, who unknowingly killed his father and married his mother, and was popularized by Sigmund Freud's theory of psychoanalysis. Literary occurrences of the Oedipus complex include Sophocles' *Oedipus Rex* and D. H. Lawrence's "The Rocking-Horse Winner."

Onomatopoeia: The use of words whose sounds express or suggest their meaning. In its simplest sense, onomatopoeia may be represented by words that mimic the sounds they denote such as "hiss" or "meow." At a more subtle level, the pattern and rhythm of sounds and rhymes of a line or poem may be onomatopoeic.

Oral Tradition: A process by which songs, ballads, folklore, and other material are transmitted by word of mouth. The tradition of oral transmission predates the written record systems of literate society. Oral transmission preserves material sometimes over generations, although often with variations. Memory plays a large part in the recitation and preservation of orally transmitted material. Native American myths and legends, and African folktales told by plantation slaves are examples of orally transmitted literature.

P

Parable: A story intended to teach a moral lesson or answer an ethical question. Examples of parables are the stories told by Jesus Christ in the New Testament, notably "The Prodigal Son," but parables also are used in Sufism, rabbinic literature, Hasidism, and Zen Buddhism. Isaac Bashevis Singer's story "Gimpel the Fool" exhibits characteristics of a parable.

Paradox: A statement that appears illogical or contradictory at first, but may actually point to an underlying truth. A literary example of a paradox is George Orwell's statement "All animals are equal, but some animals are more equal than others" in *Animal Farm.*

Parody: In literature, this term refers to an imitation of a serious literary work or the signature style of a particular author in a ridiculous manner. A typical parody adopts the style of the original and applies it to an inappropriate subject for humorous effect. Parody is a form of satire and could be considered the literary equivalent of a caricature or cartoon. Henry Fielding's *Shamela* is a parody of Samuel Richardson's *Pamela.*

Persona: A Latin term meaning "mask." Personae are the characters in a fictional work of literature. The persona generally functions as a mask through which the author tells a story in a voice other than his or her own. A persona is usually either a character in a story who acts as a narrator or an "implied author," a voice created by the author to act as the narrator for himself or herself. The persona in Charlotte Perkins Gilman's story "The Yellow Wallpaper" is the unnamed young mother experiencing a mental breakdown.

Personification: A figure of speech that gives human qualities to abstract ideas, animals, and inanimate objects. To say that "the sun is smiling" is to personify the sun.

Plot: The pattern of events in a narrative or drama. In its simplest sense, the plot guides the author in composing the work and helps the reader follow the work. Typically, plots exhibit causality and unity and have a beginning, a middle, and an end. Sometimes, however, a plot may consist of a series of disconnected events, in which case it is known as an "episodic plot."

Poetic Justice: An outcome in a literary work, not necessarily a poem, in which the good are rewarded and the evil are punished, especially in ways that particularly fit their virtues or crimes. For example, a murderer may himself be murdered, or a thief will find himself penniless.

Poetic License: Distortions of fact and literary convention made by a writer—not always a poet—for the sake of the effect gained. Poetic license is closely related to the concept of "artistic freedom." An author exercises poetic license by saying that a pile of money "reaches as high as a mountain" when the pile is actually only a foot or two high.

Point of View: The narrative perspective from which a literary work is presented to the reader. There are four traditional points of view. The "third person omniscient" gives the reader a "godlike" perspective, unrestricted by time or place, from which to see actions and look into the minds of characters. This allows the author to comment openly on characters and events in the work. The "third person" point of view presents the events of the story from outside of any single character's perception, much like the omniscient point of view, but the reader must understand the action as it takes place and without any special insight into characters' minds or motivations. The "first person" or "personal" point of view relates events as they are perceived by a single character. The main character "tells" the story and may offer opinions about the action and characters which differ from those of the author. Much less common than omniscient, third person, and first person is the "second person" point of view, wherein the author tells the story as if it is happening to the reader. James Thurber employs the omniscient point of view in his short story "The Secret Life of Walter Mitty." Ernest Hemingway's "A Clean, Well-Lighted Place" is a short story told from the third person point of view. Mark Twain's novel *Huckleberry Finn* is presented from the first person viewpoint. Jay McInerney's *Bright Lights, Big City* is an example of a novel which uses the second person point of view.

Pornography: Writing intended to provoke feelings of lust in the reader. Such works are often condemned by critics and teachers, but those which can be shown to have literary value are viewed less harshly. Literary works that have been described as pornographic include D. H. Lawrence's *Lady Chatterley's Lover* and James Joyce's *Ulysses*.

Post-Aesthetic Movement: An artistic response made by African Americans to the black aesthetic movement of the 1960s and early 1970s. Writers since that time have adopted a somewhat different tone in their work, with less emphasis placed on the disparity between black and white in the United States. In the words of post-aesthetic authors such as Toni Morrison, John Edgar Wideman, and Kristin Hunter, African Americans are portrayed as looking inward for answers to their own questions, rather than always looking to the outside world. Two well-known examples of works produced as part of the post-aesthetic movement are the Pulitzer Prize–winning novels *The Color Purple* by Alice Walker and *Beloved* by Toni Morrison.

Postmodernism: Writing from the 1960s forward characterized by experimentation and application of modernist elements, which include existentialism and alienation. Postmodernists have gone a step further in the rejection of tradition begun with the modernists by also rejecting traditional forms, preferring the anti-novel over the novel and the anti-hero over the hero. Postmodern writers include Thomas Pynchon, Margaret Drabble, and Gabriel Gárcia Márquez.

Prologue: An introductory section of a literary work. It often contains information establishing the situation of the characters or presents information about the setting, time period, or action. In drama, the prologue is spoken by a chorus or by one of the principal characters.

Prose: A literary medium that attempts to mirror the language of everyday speech. It is distinguished from poetry by its use of unmetered, unrhymed language consisting of logically related sentences. Prose is usually grouped into paragraphs that form a cohesive whole such as an essay or a novel. The term is sometimes used to mean an author's general writing.

Protagonist: The central character of a story who serves as a focus for its themes and incidents and as the principal rationale for its development. The protagonist is sometimes referred to in discussions of modern literature as the hero or anti-hero. Well-known protagonists are Hamlet in William Shakespeare's *Hamlet* and Jay Gatsby in F. Scott Fitzgerald's *The Great Gatsby*.

R

Realism: A nineteenth-century European literary movement that sought to portray familiar characters, situations, and settings in a realistic manner. This was done primarily by using an objective narrative point of view and through the buildup of accurate detail. The standard for success of any realistic work depends on how faithfully it transfers common experience into fictional forms. The realistic method may be altered or extended, as in stream of consciousness writing, to record highly subjective experience. Contemporary authors who often write in a realistic way include Nadine Gordimer and Grace Paley.

Resolution: The portion of a story following the climax, in which the conflict is resolved. The resolution of Jane Austen's *Northanger Abbey* is neatly summed up in the following sentence: "Henry and Catherine were married, the bells rang and every body smiled."

Rising Action: The part of a drama where the plot becomes increasingly complicated. Rising action leads up to the climax, or turning point, of a drama. The final "chase scene" of an action film is generally the rising action which culminates in the film's climax.

Roman a clef: A French phrase meaning "novel with a key." It refers to a narrative in which real persons are portrayed under fictitious names. Jack Kerouac, for example, portrayed various friends under fictitious names in the novel *On the Road*. D. H. Lawrence based "The Rocking-Horse Winner" on a family he knew.

Romanticism: This term has two widely accepted meanings. In historical criticism, it refers to a European intellectual and artistic movement of the late eighteenth and early nineteenth centuries that sought greater freedom of personal expression than that allowed by the strict rules of literary form and logic of the eighteenth-century neoclassicists. The Romantics preferred emotional and imaginative expression to rational analysis. They considered the individual to be at the center of all experience and so placed him or her at the center of their art. The Romantics believed that the creative imagination reveals nobler truths—unique feelings and attitudes—than those that could be discovered by logic or by scientific examination. "Romanticism" is also used as a general term to refer to a type of sensibility found in all periods of literary history and usually considered to be in opposition to the principles of classicism. In this sense, Romanticism signifies any work or philosophy in which the exotic or dreamlike figure strongly, or that is devoted to individualistic expression, self-analysis, or a pursuit of a higher realm of knowledge than can be discovered by human reason. Prominent Romantics include Jean-Jacques Rousseau, William Wordsworth, John Keats, Lord Byron, and Johann Wolfgang von Goethe.

S

Satire: A work that uses ridicule, humor, and wit to criticize and provoke change in human nature and institutions. Voltaire's novella *Candide* and Jonathan Swift's essay "A Modest Proposal" are both satires. Flannery O'Connor's portrayal of the family in "A Good Man Is Hard to Find" is a satire of a modern, Southern, American family.

Science Fiction: A type of narrative based upon real or imagined scientific theories and technology. Science fiction is often peopled with alien creatures and set on other planets or in different dimensions. Popular writers of science fiction are Isaac Asimov, Karel Capek, Ray Bradbury, and Ursula K. Le Guin.

Setting: The time, place, and culture in which the action of a narrative takes place. The elements of setting may include geographic location, characters's physical and mental environments, prevailing cultural attitudes, or the historical time in which the action takes place.

Short Story: A fictional prose narrative shorter and more focused than a novella. The short story usually deals with a single episode and often a single character. The "tone," the author's attitude toward his or her subject and audience, is uniform throughout. The short story frequently also lacks *denouement*, ending instead at its climax.

Signifying Monkey: A popular trickster figure in black folklore, with hundreds of tales about this character documented since the 19th century. Henry Louis Gates Jr. examines the history of the signifying monkey in *The Signifying Monkey: Towards a Theory of Afro-American Literary Criticism,* published in 1988.

Simile: A comparison, usually using "like" or "as," of two essentially dissimilar things, as in "coffee as cold as ice" or "He sounded like a broken record." The title of Ernest Hemingway's "Hills Like White Elephants" contains a simile.

Socialist Realism: The Socialist Realism school of literary theory was proposed by Maxim Gorky and established as a dogma by the first Soviet Congress of Writers. It demanded adherence to a communist worldview in works of literature. Its doctrines required an objective viewpoint comprehensible to the working classes and themes of social struggle featuring strong proletarian heroes. Gabriel Gárcia Márquez's stories exhibit some characteristics of Socialist Realism.

Stereotype: A stereotype was originally the name for a duplication made during the printing process; this led to its modern definition as a person or thing that is (or is assumed to be) the same as all others of its type. Common stereotypical characters include the absent-minded professor, the nagging wife, the troublemaking teenager, and the kindhearted grandmother.

Stream of Consciousness: A narrative technique for rendering the inward experience of a character. This technique is designed to give the impression of an ever-changing series of thoughts, emotions, images, and memories in the spontaneous and seemingly illogical order that they occur in life. The textbook example of stream of consciousness is the last section of James Joyce's *Ulysses.*

Structure: The form taken by a piece of literature. The structure may be made obvious for ease of understanding, as in nonfiction works, or may obscured for artistic purposes, as in some poetry or seemingly "unstructured" prose.

Style: A writer's distinctive manner of arranging words to suit his or her ideas and purpose in writing. The unique imprint of the author's personality upon his or her writing, style is the product of an author's way of arranging ideas and his or her use of diction, different sentence structures, rhythm, figures of speech, rhetorical principles, and other elements of composition.

Suspense: A literary device in which the author maintains the audience's attention through the buildup of events, the outcome of which will soon be revealed. Suspense in William Shakespeare's *Hamlet* is sustained throughout by the question of whether or not the Prince will achieve what he has been instructed to do and of what he intends to do.

Symbol: Something that suggests or stands for something else without losing its original identity. In literature, symbols combine their literal meaning with the suggestion of an abstract concept. Literary symbols are of two types: those that carry complex associations of meaning no matter what their contexts, and those that derive their suggestive meaning from their functions in specific literary works. Examples of symbols are sunshine suggesting happiness, rain suggesting sorrow, and storm clouds suggesting despair.

T

Tale: A story told by a narrator with a simple plot and little character development. Tales are usually relatively short and often carry a simple message. Examples of tales can be found in the works of Saki, Anton Chekhov, Guy de Maupassant, and O. Henry.

Tall Tale: A humorous tale told in a straightforward, credible tone but relating absolutely impossible events or feats of the characters. Such tales were commonly told of frontier adventures during the settlement of the west in the United States. Literary use of tall tales can be found in Washington Irving's *History of New York,* Mark Twain's *Life on the Mississippi,* and in the German R. F. Raspe's *Baron Munchausen's Narratives of His Marvellous Travels and Campaigns in Russia.*

Theme: The main point of a work of literature. The term is used interchangeably with thesis. Many works have multiple themes. One of the themes of Nathaniel Hawthorne's "Young Goodman Brown" is loss of faith.

Tone: The author's attitude toward his or her audience maybe deduced from the tone of the work. A formal tone may create distance or convey politeness, while an informal tone may encourage a friendly, intimate, or intrusive feeling in the reader. The author's attitude toward his or her subject matter may also be deduced from the tone of the words he or she uses in discussing it. The tone of

John F. Kennedy's speech which included the appeal to "ask not what your country can do for you" was intended to instill feelings of camaraderie and national pride in listeners.

Tragedy: A drama in prose or poetry about a noble, courageous hero of excellent character who, because of some tragic character flaw, brings ruin upon him- or herself. Tragedy treats its subjects in a dignified and serious manner, using poetic language to help evoke pity and fear and bring about catharsis, a purging of these emotions. The tragic form was practiced extensively by the ancient Greeks. The classical form of tragedy was revived in the sixteenth century; it flourished especially on the Elizabethan stage. In modern times, dramatists have attempted to adapt the form to the needs of modern society by drawing their heroes from the ranks of ordinary men and women and defining the nobility of these heroes in terms of spirit rather than exalted social standing. Some contemporary works that are thought of as tragedies include *The Great Gatsby* by F. Scott Fitzgerald, and *The Sound and the Fury* by William Faulkner.

Tragic Flaw: In a tragedy, the quality within the hero or heroine which leads to his or her downfall. Examples of the tragic flaw include Othello's jealousy and Hamlet's indecisiveness, although most great tragedies defy such simple interpretation.

U

Utopia: A fictional perfect place, such as "paradise" or "heaven." An early literary utopia was described in Plato's *Republic,* and in modern literature, Ursula K. Le Guin depicts a utopia in "The Ones Who Walk Away from Omelas."

V

Victorian: Refers broadly to the reign of Queen Victoria of England (1837-1901) and to anything with qualities typical of that era. For example, the qualities of smug narrow-mindedness, bourgeois materialism, faith in social progress, and priggish morality are often considered Victorian. In literature, the Victorian Period was the great age of the English novel, and the latter part of the era saw the rise of movements such as decadence and symbolism.

Cumulative
Author/Title Index

Cumulative
Nationality/Ethnicity Index

Subject/Theme Index

U

Uncertainty
  Father and I: 116, 126, 127
Understanding
  A Way of Talking: 251
Unhappiness
  War: 228, 231
Universality
  The Bet: 20
Unknown
  Father and I: 107, 108, 110

V

Vanity
  The Bet: 5

Verisimilitude
  The Bet: 19
Violence
  The Distant Past: 90, 92, 93, 97–98
Vulnerability
  A Country Doctor: 71
  Father and I: 116

W

Wars
  The Machine That Won the War:
    171, 174–176
  War: 228, 230, 234–237
Wealth
  The Distant Past: 100

Western culture
  The Norwegian Rat: 203–204
Western United States
  The Californian's Tale: 50
Wonder
  Sonata for Harp and Bicycle:
    211
World War I, 1914-1918
  War: 228, 230, 234–240

Y

Youth
  Broken Chain: 26
  Father and I: 114